**FOURTH
CANADIAN
EDITION**

MANAGING
HUMAN RESOURCES

MONICA BELCOURT

PROFESSOR OF ADMINISTRATIVE STUDIES, YORK UNIVERSITY

GEORGE BOHLANDER

PROFESSOR OF MANAGEMENT, ARIZONA STATE UNIVERSITY

SCOTT SNELL

PROFESSOR OF HUMAN RESOURCE STUDIES, CORNELL UNIVERSITY

THOMSON

NELSON

Australia   Canada   Mexico   Singapore   Spain   United Kingdom   United States

Managing Human Resources
Fourth Canadian Edition

by Monica Belcourt, George Bohlander, and Scott Snell

Editorial Director and Publisher:
Evelyn Veitch

Acquisitions Editor:
Anthony Rezek

Marketing Manager:
Don Thompson

Senior Developmental Editor:
Karina Hope

Permissions Coordinator:
Karen Becker

Production Editor:
Wendy Yano

Copy Editor/Proofreader:
Wendy Thomas

Indexer:
Elizabeth Bell

Production Coordinator:
Renate McCloy

Creative Director:
Angela Cluer

Interior Design:
Brenda Grannan

Cover Design:
Concrete Design
Communications Inc.

Cover Image:
Veer Incorporated

Compositor:
Rachel Sloat

Printer:
Transcontinental

**National Library of Canada
Cataloguing in Publication Data**

Main entry under title:

Belcourt, Monica, 1946–
    Managing human resources /
Monica Belcourt, George
Bohlander, Scott Snell.—
4th Canadian ed.

First-3rd Canadian eds. written by
Monica Belcourt ... [et al.].
Includes bibliographical references
and index.
ISBN 0-17-622456-4

1. Personnel management—
Textbooks. I. Bohlander, George
W. II. Snell, Scott, 1958– III. Title.

HF5549.B333 2004   658.3
C2003-907349-1

To my son Brooker for his intelligent and insightful observations on the complexities of human behaviour

To my wife, Ronnie Bohlander, and to our children, Ryan and Kathryn

To my wife, Marybeth Snell, and to our children, Sara, Jack, and Emily

CONTENTS in Brief

EXCALIBUR CASES 677

Contents

Chapter 2

Equity and Diversity in Human Resources Management 49

CONTENTS

PART 2

Chapter 3

MEETING HUMAN RESOURCES REQUIREMENTS

Job Analysis, Employee Involvement, and Flexible Work Schedules   89

CONTENTS

Chapter 4

Human Resources Planning   129

CONTENTS

PART 3

Chapter 6

DEVELOPING EFFECTIVENESS IN HUMAN RESOURCES

Training and Development 231

CONTENTS

CONTENTS

Chapter 7   Career Development   283

(**Chapter 8**)   **Appraising and Improving Performance 329**

PART
4

Chapter 9

IMPLEMENTING COMPENSATION AND SECURITY

CONTENTS

(Chapter 10)   Pay-for-Performance: Incentive Rewards   421

Chapter 12

Chapter 13

Employee Rights and Discipline   537

CONTENTS

Chapter 14

The Dynamics of Labour Relations   583

PART 5

EXPANDING HORIZONS IN HUMAN RESOURCES MANAGEMENT

Chapter 15

International Human Resources Management   625

CONTENTS

Chapter 16
Chapter 16 is available on the *Managing Human Resources* website (www.belcourt4e.nelson.com).

Preface

The fourth Canadian edition of *Managing Human Resources* will place your students at the forefront in understanding how organizations can gain sustainable competitive advantage through people. The role of HR managers is no longer limited to service functions such as recruiting and selecting employees. Today, HR managers assume an active role in the strategic planning and decision making at their organizations. Meeting challenges head-on and using human resources effectively are critical to the success of any work organization.

In the first chapter, we begin by explaining the key challenges to HRM in developing the flexible and skilled workforce needed to compete effectively. Side by side with the competitive challenges, HRM must also address important employee concerns such as managing a diverse workforce, recognizing employee rights, and adjusting to new work attitudes. The chapter also discusses the important partnership with line managers and the competencies required of HR management. Then the textbook continues with the introduction, explanation, and discussion of the individual practices and policies that make up HRM. We recognize the manager's changing role and emphasize current issues and real-world problems and the policies and practices of HRM used to meet them.

Although we focus on the HR role of managers, we do not exclude the impact and importance of the HR department's strategic role in developing, coordinating, and enforcing policies and procedures relating to HR functions. Whether the reader becomes a manager, a supervisor, or an HR specialist, or is employed in other areas of the organization, *Managing Human Resources* provides a functional and practical understanding of HR programs to enable readers to see how HR affects all employees, the organization, the community, and the larger society.

Organizations in today's competitive world are discovering that it is how the individual HR functions are combined that makes all the difference. Managers typically don't focus on HR issues such as staffing, training, and compensation in isolation from one another. Each of these HR practices is combined into an overall system to enhance employee involvement and productivity. *Managing Human Resources* ends with a final online chapter that focuses on development of high-performance work systems. We outline the various components of the system, including work-flow design, HR practices, management processes, and supporting technologies. We also discuss the strategic processes used to implement high-performance work systems and the outcomes that benefit both the employee and the organization as a whole.

WHAT'S NEW IN THE FOURTH EDITION

Many new features and much new information are provided in this revision. We introduce overall text improvements that more accurately reflect HRM in today's business world and help the reader understand HRM issues more effectively.

▶ The fourth Canadian edition reflects the body of knowledge required by students to pass the new national knowledge exam, given by the Canadian Council of Human Resource Associations, as one of the steps toward the granting of the HR designation, the CHRP (Certified Human Resources Professional). The lead author, Professor Monica Belcourt, participated in the development of the standards for the new national certification process. This text covers more than 90 percent of the material being tested on the national knowledge exam. As a CHRP herself, Professor Belcourt is very familiar with the competencies required for the profession and has written the text with these required professional competencies (RPCs) as the foundation for learning about HR.

▶ Structure: The organization of the text has been changed to accommodate the wise suggestions of our reviewers. Recruitment is now with selection in Chapter 5, exactly where it belongs, allowing expanded coverage of the all-important HR planning in Chapter 4. The two chapters on labour relations and collective bargaining have been revised and the most important content is now contained in one new chapter, "The Dynamics of Labour Relations."

▶ Developing Managerial Skills: Each chapter contains a new experiential exercise to explore significant issues in HRM. These skill-building exercises will help students gain practical experience when dealing with employee/management concerns such as pay-for-performance; effective training; employee benefits; reducing employee stress; balancing competitive challenges and employee concerns; customizing HR for different types of human capital; designing selection criteria and methods; and assessing the strategic fit of High Performance Work Systems. Students can work through these new exercises on either an individual or a team basis.

▶ Human Resources Information Systems: Throughout the text, we have specifically highlighted the use of HRIS to facilitate the managing of employees and the efficient performance of HR functions. For example, the impact of information technology on HR and the role of HRIS in such areas as compensation, recruitment and selection, training, job analysis, and safety are discussed.

▶ Diversity: Because we believe that diversity issues are an integral part of every HRM activity, updated and expanded coverage is included throughout the text.

▶ HRM Strategy: The increasingly important role HRM plays in strategic planning is covered in discussion of the role of human capital and Six Sigma in Chapter 1; HR benchmarking in Chapter 4; balanced scorecard and performance diagnosis in Chapter 8; global HR strategy in Chapter 15; as well as Chapter 16's coverage of strategic alignment and implementing high-performance work systems.

▶ A complete update of all laws, regulations, and court decisions governing HRM includes such recent developments as interest-based bargaining and ergonomics; added emphasis on arbitration to resolve employee discipline and discharge; genetic testing; e-mail and voice-mail privacy; privacy legislation and other employee rights issues. In Chapter 13, we have added a new section on resolving employee complaints through employment mediation.

▶ Comprehensive Cases: Four new comprehensive cases will be found at the end of the book. This exciting new development features real cases used in Excalibur, the Canadian University Tournament in Human Resources, in which university students from across Canada are asked to demonstrate their knowledge of HR to a jury. After students have developed solutions to the problems faced by dynamic companies such as Cirque du Soleil and Labatt Breweries, the instructor can compare their responses to the one generated by the winning university team, and the answer prepared by an HR professor.

▶ The Business Case is a new feature on the business or financial implications of the adoption of HR practices in every chapter. This feature was included to address the concerns that employers have with the inability of HR professionals to make the business case for recommended HR practices. We analyze, for example, the financial benefits of interest-based bargaining over traditional bargaining.

▶ We have readdressed the important role of compensation in HRM by heightening our discussion of pay-for-performance, health care cost savings, strategic pension planning, and effective employee awards.

▶ Expanded discussions cover major issues, including

balanced scorecard	performance diagnosis
child and elder care	person-organization fit
competency assessment for training	role of human capital
conflict resolution techniques	strategic compensation planning
cumulative trauma disorders	safety issues for youth
interest-based bargaining	violence and terrorism in the workplace
privacy legislation	

▶ Many new Highlights in HRM boxes and new Reality Checks present the reader with up-to-date real-world examples, such as SARS, from a variety of large and small Canadian organizations across the country. Monica Belcourt, as president of the Human Resources Professionals Association of Ontario, is very involved in the HR profession, with access to some of the leaders in HR in Canada. The Reality Checks and Highlights reflect this access.

▶ Ethics in HRM: After the Enron scandal and scandals closer to home, Canadians are preoccupied with the ethics of those working in organizations. The popular Ethics in HRM provides new examples of the ethical dilemmas faced by HR practitioners.

▶ Internet: The ever-growing role of the Internet in HR activities is evident throughout the text. A few examples include online recruiting and online staffing in Chapter 5; web-based training and e-learning in Chapter 6; and online 360-degree performance appraisal in Chapter 8.

▶ Each chapter has at least one new end-of-chapter case study highlighting chapter content.

▶ Ancillaries: There are online ancillaries for instructors and students. A completely revised test bank plays a strategic role in the Integrated Learning System.

▶ A new set of PowerPoint presentation slides makes teaching and preparation easier and more convenient.

FEATURES OF THE BOOK

Use of the Integrated Learning System is featured for the fourth edition and ancillaries. This integrated structure creates a comprehensive teaching and testing system. Designed to facilitate understanding and retention of the material presented, each chapter contains the following pedagogical features:

▶ **Learning objectives** listed at the beginning of each chapter provide the basis for the Integrated Learning System. Icons that identify the learning objectives appear throughout the text and all ancillaries.

▶ **Highlights in HRM** provides real-world examples of how organizations perform HR functions. These popular boxed features are introduced in the text discussion and include topics such as small businesses and international issues.

▶ **Reality Check** presents an interview with a Canadian expert in the field, illustrating how the material in the chapter is used in the real world.

▶ **Ethics in HRM** provokes debate and discussion among students, as they struggle with the often grey areas of Human Resources Management, such as drug testing of employees and electronic surveillance of employees at work.

▶ **The Business Case** features the business or financial implications of the adoption of HR practices The Business Case will help students build the skills necessary to recommend HR practices and projects, based on the projected costs and benefits, to senior management.

▶ **Career Counsel** on the *Managing Human Resources* website (www.belcourt4e. nelson.com) provides a dynamic link to the Internet, enabling students to relate chapter content to job searching and career development. The Career Counsel exercises allow students to develop a career plan.

▶ **The Internet** is referenced in all chapters, with new government, research, and business Internet links and addresses.

▶ **Key terms** appear in boldface and are defined in margin notes next to the text discussion. The key terms are also listed at the end of the chapter and appear in the glossary at the end of the text.

▶ **Figures**, with an abundance of graphic materials and flowcharts, provide a visual, dynamic presentation of concepts and HR activities. All figures are systematically referenced in the text discussion.

▶ **Summary** includes a paragraph or two for each learning objective, providing a brief and focused review of the chapter.

▶ **Discussion questions** following the chapter summary offer an opportunity to focus on each of the learning objectives in the chapter and to stimulate critical thinking. Many of these questions allow for group analysis and class discussion.

▶ **Developing Managerial Skills,** a new experiential activity (described earlier), is included in each chapter.

▶ **Two or more case studies** per chapter present current HRM issues in real-life settings that allow for student consideration and critical analysis.

▶ **Chapter 16, Creating High-Performance Work Systems,** and the chapter feature Career Counsel, appear on the Internet at the *Managing Human Resources* website (www.belcourt4e.nelson.com). The Career Counsel sections help students with job search strategies and value assessment and salary negotiation tactics.

ANCILLARY TEACHING AND LEARNING MATERIALS

For Students

▶ **Online Study Guide to Accompany Managing Human Resources.** In partnership with Captus Press, Nelson is pleased to offer a free online study guide prepared by Monica Belcourt (to access, visit www.belcourt4e.nelson.com). Complete with chapter summaries, multiple-choice questions, short-answer questions, and progress checks, this supplement will enhance your learning experience. Equally important, the study guide provides the opportunity to practise taking multiple-choice tests in preparation for the National Knowledge Examination, given by the Canadian Council of Human Resource Associations (CCHRA), a first step in becoming a CHRP (Certified Human Resource Professional).

▶ **Internet Course.** For students seeking extra help, a full online HRM course is available from Captus Press. Supplement classroom teaching by accessing the Internet server and listening to lectures given by Monica Belcourt. You can then scroll to areas of interest and access necessary information. Please contact Captus Press directly for information on the cost of these options (www.captus.com).

▶ **InfoTrac® College Edition.** With InfoTrac, students can receive anytime, anywhere online access to a database of full-text articles from hundreds of popular and scholarly periodicals, such as *Canadian Business, Canadian Business Review, Business Week, Canadian Labour, HR Magazine,* and *HR Professional,* among others. Students can use its fast and easy search tools to find relevant news and analytical information among the tens of thousands of articles in the database—updated daily and going back as far as four years—all at a single website. InfoTrac is a great way to expose students to online research techniques, with the security that the content is academically based and reliable. An InfoTrac College Edition subscription card is packaged free with all new copies of *Managing Human Resources.*

▶ **Website.** A comprehensive website includes practice quizzes, chapter web links, study tips, and information on degrees and careers in human resource management (www.belcourt4e.nelson.com).

▶ **New Feature.** The Canadian Council of Human Resources Associations (CCHRA) offers an online preparation course for the National Knowledge Exam, the first exam leading to the designation of CHRP (Certified Human Resource Professional). The course includes a diagnostic test that assesses knowledge of the Required Professional Capabilities (RPCs) and links to appropriate content in this text and others. There are also three practice exams, online multimedia lectures, and quizzes. For more information, contact your provincial HR association, the CCHRA website (www.cchra-ccarh.ca), or Captus Press (http://webclients.captus.com/cchra/).

For Instructors

The following instructor support materials are available to adopters from your sales representative.

▶ **Instructor's Manual.** For each chapter in the textbook, the *Instructor's Manual* contains a chapter synopsis and learning objectives, a very detailed lecture outline, and answers to the end-of-chapter discussion questions.

▶ **Test Bank.** The new test bank provides more than 100 questions for each text chapter and includes a matrix table that classifies each question according to type and learning objective. There are true/false, multiple-choice, and essay items for each chapter, arranged by learning objective. Page references from the text are included. Each objective question is coded to indicate whether it covers knowledge of key terms, understanding of concepts and principles, or application of principles.

▶ **Computerized Test Bank.** The computerized testing software contains all the questions from the test bank and allows the instructor to edit, add, delete, or randomly mix questions for customized tests.

▶ **PowerPoint™ Presentation Slides.** Created specifically for the new edition by Monica Belcourt, these presentation slides will add colour and interest to lectures.

▶ **Instructor's Resource CD. (0-17-641492-4)** The Instructor's Manual, Test Bank, Computerized Test Bank, and PowerPoint slides are provided on a single CD-ROM.

▶ **CBC Videos. (0-17-641491-6)** Video segments from CBC news programming, featuring real companies and business situations, accompany the text and were selected to help you integrate the videos with the text material. Use them to introduce a topic, cover lecture material, or stimulate discussion.

▶ **CNN Today: Managing Human Resources. (0-324-18412-3)** Video segments taken from real companies as well as business features shown on CNN—the cable business news network—were chosen to accompany the text chapters. Use them to introduce a topic, highlight lecture material, or stimulate discussion.

▶ **Website.** A comprehensive website includes practice quizzes, chapter web links, study tips, and information on degrees and careers in human resource management. We have also included a link for instructors that contains downloadable ancillaries and supplementary cases and solutions. The website can be found at www.belcourt4e.nelson.com.

▶ **Nelson ePacks.** Online content in WebCT and Blackboard is available for this title. Visit the Instructor's Resource area at www.belcourt4e.nelson.com for details.

ACKNOWLEDGMENTS FOR THE FOURTH CANADIAN EDITION

In preparing the manuscript for this edition, we have drawn not only on the current literature but also on the current practices of organizations that furnished information relating to their HR programs. We are indebted to the leaders in the field who have influenced us through their writings and personal associations. We have also been aided by our present and former students, by our colleagues at the Human Resources Professionals Association of Ontario with whom we have been associated, by HR managers, and by our academic colleagues. We would like to express our appreciation to the following reviewers who have helped shape the text:

Gordon Barnard, Durham College

Stéphane Brutus, Concordia University

Tim DeGroot, McMaster University

Robert Isaac, University of Calgary

Don MacCormac, University of PEI

Colleen Marshall, Confederation College

Jessica Nicholson, McMaster University

Robert Oppenheimer, Concordia University

Carolin Rekar, Durham College

Maria Rotundo, University of Toronto

Sudhir Saha, Memorial University

Pat Sniderman, Ryerson Polytechnic University

Diane White, Seneca College

Deborah Zinni, Brock University

Additionally, we would like to thank the HR students who provided research assistance in the preparation of the fourth edition:

Alfred Adjetey, Jr., Nancy Bogojeski, Nancy Camilli, Jacqueline Cheah, Lois Coholan, Aymen Dewji, Irene Fuda, Gagan Ghuman, Amanda Leaman, Hatel Pandya, Jennifer Peleikis, Laura Polsinelli, Lien Thich, Josef Winter, Zoya Zayer

We appreciate the efforts of the team at Nelson Thomson who helped to develop and produce this text. They include Anthony Rezek, Acquisitions Editor; Karina Hope, Senior Developmental Editor; and Don Thompson, Marketing Manager; as well as the wonderful sales representatives who have enthusiastically supported the book.

Our greatest indebtedness is to our spouses—Michael Belcourt, Ronnie Bohlander, and Marybeth Snell—who have contributed in so many ways to this book. They are always sources of invaluable guidance and assistance. Furthermore, by their continued enthusiasm and support, they have made the process a more pleasant and rewarding experience. We are most grateful to them for their many contributions to this publication, to our lives, and to our families.

Monica Belcourt

Monica Belcourt is a full Professor, Human Resources Management, and Director of the Graduate Program in HRM at the Atkinson Faculty of Liberal and Professional Studies, York University. She has an extensive and varied background in human resources management. After receiving a B.A. in psychology from the University of Manitoba, she joined the Public Service Commission as a recruitment and selection specialist. During her tenure with the federal government, she worked in training, HRM research, job analysis, and HR planning.

Dr. Belcourt alternated working in HRM with graduate school, obtaining an M.A. in psychology from York University, an M.Ed. in adult education from the University of Ottawa, and a Ph.D. in management from York University. She also holds the designation of Certified Human Resource Professional (CHRP). Her research is grounded in the experience she gained as Director of Personnel for the 63 000 employees at CP Rail; Director of Employee Development, National Film Board; and as a functional HR specialist for the federal government. She has taught HRM at Concordia University, Université du Québec à Montréal, McGill University, and York University, where she founded and managed the largest undergraduate program in HRM in Canada. She created Canada's first degrees in human resources management: B.HRM, B.HRM (honours), and a Master's in HRM. A full description of these degrees can be found at www.atkinson.yorku.ca/mhrm/.

Dr. Belcourt is Director of the International Alliance for HR Research (IAHRR), which is a catalyst for the discovery, dissemination, and application of new knowledge about HRM. The IAHRR programs are described at www.yorku.ca/hrresall. Her research interests focus on strategic HRM, and she has published more than 100 articles, several of which received best paper awards. Her most recent publication is *Making Government the Best Place to Work: Building Commitment,* published by the Institute of Public Administration of Canada; it can be downloaded and ordered at IPAC's website, www.ipac-iapc.ca.

Dr. Belcourt is Series Editor for the Nelson Series in Human Resources Management: *Performance Management through Training and Development; Occupational Health and Safety; Human Resources Management Systems; Recruitment and Selection in Canada; Compensation in Canada; Strategic Human Resources Planning; Research, Measurement and Evaluation in HRM;* and *The Canadian Labour Market.*

Active in many professional associations and not-for-profit organizations, Dr. Belcourt is currently the President of the Human Resources Professionals Association of Ontario, serves on the national committee for HR certification, and is a past board member of CIBC Insurance and the Toronto French School. She is a frequent commentator on HRM issues for CTV, *Canada AM,* CBC, *The Globe and Mail, The Canadian HR Reporter,* and other media.

George Bohlander

George Bohlander is Professor of Management at Arizona State University. He received his M.B.A. from the University of Southern California and his Ph.D. from the University of California at Los Angeles. His areas of expertise include employment law, training and development, work teams, public policy, and labour relations. He has received the Outstanding Undergraduate Teaching Excellence Award presented by the College of Business at ASU and also received the prestigious ASU Parents Association Professorship for his contributions to students and teaching.

Dr. Bohlander is an active researcher and author. He has published over 50 articles and monographs in professional and practitioner journals such as *National Productivity Review, HR Magazine, Labor Law Journal, The Journal of Collective Bargaining in the Public Sector,* and others. Dr. Bohlander continues to be a consultant to public and private organizations including the U.S. Postal Service, American Productivity & Quality Center, BFGoodrich, McDonnell Douglas, Rural/Metro Corporation, and Del Webb. He is also an active labour arbitrator.

Scott Snell

Scott Snell is Professor of Human Resource Studies and Director of Executive Education in the School of Industrial and Labor Relations at Cornell University. He received a B.A. in Psychology from Miami University as well as M.B.A. and Ph.D. degrees in Business Administration from Michigan State University. Prior to joining the faculty at Cornell, Dr. Snell was on the faculty of business at Penn State University. During his career, he has taught courses in human resource management and strategic management to undergraduates, graduates, and executives.

Professor Snell has worked with companies such as AT&T, GE, IBM, Merck, and Shell to address the alignment of human resource systems with strategic initiatives such as globalization, technological change, and knowledge management. His research and teaching interests focus on the development and deployment of intellectual capital as a foundation of an organization's core competencies. He has published a number of articles in professional journals and is the author of two textbooks. In addition, Dr. Snell has served on the editorial boards of *Journal of Managerial Issues, Digest of Management Research, Human Resource Management Review, Human Resource Planning,* and *Academy of Management Journal.*

The Challenge of Human Resources Management

After studying this chapter, you should be able to

objective
Identify how firms gain sustainable competitive advantage through people.

objective
Explain how globalization is influencing human resources management.

objective
Describe the impact of information technology on managing people.

objective
Identify the importance of change management.

objective
State HR's role in developing intellectual capital.

objective
Differentiate how TQM and reengineering influence HR systems.

objective
Discuss the impact of cost pressures on HR policies.

objective
Discuss the primary demographic and employee concerns pertaining to HRM.

objective
Provide examples of the roles and competencies of today's HR managers.

T here's an old joke that goes ...

The organization of the future will be so technologically advanced that it will be run by just one person and a dog. The person will be there to feed the dog, and the dog will be there to make sure that the person doesn't touch anything.

In the past, observers feared that machines might one day eliminate the need for people at work. In reality, just the opposite has been occurring. People are more important in today's organizations than ever before. As Ed Gubman, author of *The Talent Solution*, points out, "In many fast-growing economies, it may be easier to access money and technology than good people. Competitive advantage belongs to companies that know how to attract, select, deploy, and develop talent."[1]

We use a lot of words to describe the importance of people to organizations. The term *human resources* implies that people have capabilities that drive organizational performance (along with other resources such as money, materials, and information). Other terms such as *human capital* and *intellectual assets* all have in common the idea that people make the difference in how an organization performs. Successful organizations are particularly adept at bringing together different kinds of people to achieve a common purpose. This is the essence of human resources management (HRM). **Human Resources Management** is a set of inter-related policies, practices, and programs whose goal is to attract, socialize, motivate, maintain, and retain an organization's employees.

Human Resources Management
a set of inter-related policies, practices, and programs whose goal is to attract, socialize, motivate, maintain, and retain an organization's employees

Why Study Human Resources Management?

objective

As you embark on this course, you may be wondering how the topic of human resources management relates to your interests and career aspirations. The answer to the question "Why study HRM?" is pretty much the same regardless of whether you plan on working in an HR department or not. Staffing the organization, designing jobs and teams, developing skilful employees, identifying approaches for improving their performance, and rewarding employee successes—all typically labelled HRM issues—are as relevant to line managers as they are to managers in the HR department.

To work with people effectively, we have to understand human behaviour, and we have to be knowledgeable about the various systems and practices available to help us build a skilled and motivated workforce. At the same time, we have to be aware of economic, technological, social, and legal issues that either facilitate or constrain our efforts to achieve organizational goals.

Competitive Advantage through People

While people have always been central to organizations, today they have taken on an even more central role in building a firm's competitive advantage. Particularly in knowledge-based industries such as software and information services, success increasingly depends on "people-embodied know-how." This includes the knowledge, skills, and abilities imbedded in an organization's members.[2] In fact, a growing number of experts now argue that the key to a firm's success is based on establishing a set of **core competencies**—integrated knowledge sets within an organization that distinguish it from its competitors and deliver value to customers. McDonald's, for example, has developed core competencies in management efficiency and training. Federal Express has core competencies in package routing, delivery, and employee relations. Canon Corporation has core competencies in precision mechanics, fine optics, and microelectronics. British Petroleum has core competencies in oil exploration.[3] Core competencies tend to be limited in number, but they provide a long-term basis for technology innovation, product development, and service delivery.

Core competencies
Integrated knowledge sets within an organization that distinguish it from its competitors and deliver value to customers

Organizations can achieve sustained competitive advantage through people if they are able to meet the following criteria:[4]

1. *The resources must be of value.* People are a source of competitive advantage when they improve the efficiency or effectiveness of the company. Value is increased when employees find ways to decrease costs, provide something unique to customers, or some combination of the two. Empowerment programs, total-quality initiatives, and continuous improvement efforts at companies such as CIBC and MDS Nordian are intentionally designed to increase the value that employees represent on the bottom line.

2. *The resources must be rare.* People are a source of competitive advantage when their skills, knowledge, and abilities are not equally available to competitors. Companies such as Microsoft, McKinsey, and Four Seasons Hotels invest a great deal to hire and train the best and the brightest employees in order to gain advantage over their competitors.

3. *The resources must be difficult to imitate.* People are a source of competitive advantage when employee capabilities and contributions cannot be copied by others. Disney, CREO, and Intuit are each known for creating unique cultures that get the most from employees (through teamwork) and are difficult to imitate.

4. *The resources must be organized.* People are a source of competitive advantage when their talents can be combined and deployed to work on new assignments at a moment's notice. Companies such as AT&T Canada have invested in information technology to help allocate and track employee assignments to temporary projects. Teamwork and cooperation are two other pervasive methods for ensuring an organized workforce.

These four criteria highlight the importance of people and show the closeness of HRM to strategic management. As the CEO of TELUS, one of the largest communications companies in Canada with 26 000 employees, says, "Within our industry, there is a lot of talk about technology, but truth be known, people have never been more important to the success of our organization than they are right now." In a recent survey, nearly 80 percent of corporate executives said the importance of HRM in their firms has grown substantially over the past ten years, and two-thirds said that HR expenditures are now viewed as a strategic investment rather than simply a cost to be minimized.[5] There are clear and tangible benefits to be gained for investing in HRM practices and policies as described in the Business Case. Because employee skills, knowledge, and abilities are among the most distinctive and renewable resources

The Business Case

THE CONTRIBUTION OF HR TO ORGANIZATIONAL PERFORMANCE

Survival: HR strategies account for about 22 percent of the probability of survival of a new venture

Market value: effective human resources practices can raise company market value by as much as 47 percent

Profits: about 15 percent of firm profits can be traced to HR strategies

Sales per employee: studies have shown that sophisticated HR practices increase average sales per employee by about $27 000 (US)

Turnover: HR programs can decrease turnover among employees by about 7 percent

More detailed benefits are described in Chapter 16 of this text, to be found on the Nelson website: www.belcourt4e.nelson.com.

Source: M. Belcourt & K. McBey, *Strategic Human Resources Planning,* 2nd ed., Nelson, Toronto, 2003; David Brown, "Profit Driven by Good HR," *Canadian HR Reporter* 14, no. 20: 3.

upon which a company can draw, their strategic management is more important than ever. As Thomas J. Watson, founder of IBM, said, "You can get capital and erect buildings, but it takes people to build a business."[6]

While "competing through people" may be a theme for human resources management, the idea remains only a framework for action. On a day-to-day basis, managers focus on specific challenges and issues that pertain to human resources. Figure 1.1

Figure 1.1 | Overall Framework for Human Resources Management

COMPETITIVE CHALLENGES
- Globalization
- Technology
- Managing change
- Human capital
- Responsiveness
- Cost containment

HUMAN RESOURCES
- Planning
- Recruitment
- Staffing
- Job design
- Training/development
- Appraisal
- Communications
- Compensation
- Benefits
- Labour relations

EMPLOYEE CONCERNS
- Background diversity
- Age distribution
- Gender issues
- Educational levels
- Employee rights
- Privacy issues
- Work attitudes
- Family concerns

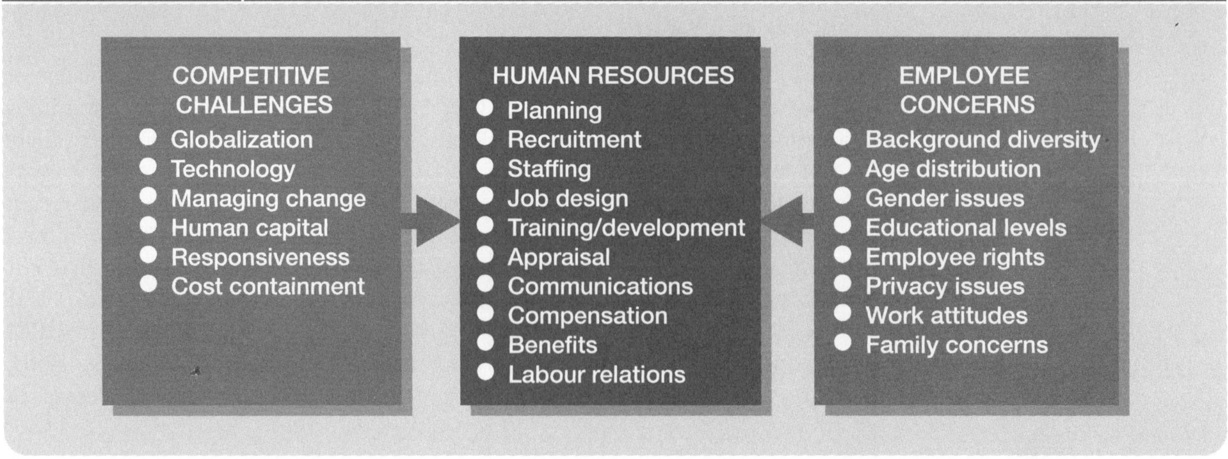

Organizations can achieve competitive advantage through people.

PHOTODISC

provides an overall framework for human resources management. From this figure, we can see that HRM has to help blend many aspects of management; at this point we will simply classify them as either "competitive challenges" or "employee concerns." By balancing sometimes competing demands, HRM plays an important role in getting the most from employees and providing a work environment that meets their short-term and long-term needs. We will use this framework as a basis for our discussion throughout the rest of this chapter.

COMPETITIVE CHALLENGES AND HUMAN RESOURCES MANAGEMENT

Organizations such as the Conference Board of Canada, the Society for Human Resource Management (SHRM), and the Human Resource Planning Society (HRPS) conduct ongoing studies of the most pressing competitive issues facing firms. By seeking the input of chief executives and HR managers, these organizations keep a finger on the pulse of major trends. For the past decade or so, there has been a constant theme on the following issues:

▶   Going global
▶   Embracing technology
▶   Managing change
▶   Developing human capital
▶   Responding to the market
▶   Containing costs

These trends extend beyond "people issues" per se, but they all focus on the need to develop a skilled and flexible workforce in order to compete in the twenty-first century.

Challenge 1: Going Global

In order to grow and prosper, many companies are seeking business opportunities in global markets. Competition—and cooperation—with foreign companies has become an important focal point for business. Indeed, exporting accounts for a large portion of the Canadian economy. Canadian exports are expected to account for about $500 billion a year by 2004.[7]

Impact of Globalization

Globalization
Trend toward opening up foreign markets to international trade and investment

By partnering with firms in other regions of the world and using information technologies to coordinate distant parts of their businesses, companies such as Bombardier, General Electric, and Toyota have shown that their vision for the future is to offer customers "anything, anytime, anywhere" around the world. But **globalization** is not just something of interest to large firms. Though estimates vary widely, it is believed that 70 to 85 percent of the Canadian economy is affected by the international economy. Finning International, one of the world's largest dealers in Caterpillar heavy equipment and based in Vancouver, British Columbia, generates about 60 percent, more than $3 billion, in annual revenue from its worldwide markets. Meanwhile, international companies are looking to Canada to expand, as it has been rated by the *Economist* magazine as the best country in the world to do business.[8]

Efforts to lower trade barriers and open up global markets to the free flow of goods, services, and capital among nations have created three zones of economic activity. Within North America, the North American Free Trade Agreement (NAFTA) was created to facilitate commerce between Mexico, Canada, and the United States. Although some Canadian opponents of NAFTA have feared the loss of jobs to the United States and Mexico, where wages are lower, proponents of NAFTA argue that the agreement is helping to remove impediments to trade and investment, thereby creating jobs. NAFTA may soon be replaced by a broader set of economic agreements called the Free Trade Area of the Americas (FTAA). FTAA will encompass the entire Western hemisphere and extend from the tip of Alaska to the bottom of Argentina. Similarly, the European Union (EU) focuses on the integration of European markets, while the Asia Pacific Economic Cooperation (APEC) has helped establish freer trade among Pacific Rim countries. The impact of these trade agreements has been impressive. For example, the EU Commission calculates that there are somewhere in the range of 300 000 to 900 000 more jobs than there would be without the union.[9]

Today, these markets are merging on a global scale. The World Trade Organization (WTO), headquartered in Lausanne, Switzerland, has more than 140 member countries, accounting for more than 97 percent of world trade. The WTO uses the General Agreement on Tariffs and Trade (GATT) to establish rules and guidelines for global commerce. While the economic impact of such agreements is immense, some people raise concerns about the economic welfare of developing countries as well as the human rights issues of individuals (particularly the poor) affected by the trade.[10]

USING THE INTERNET

Learn more about NAFTA by checking out NAFTAnet, sponsored by the North American Forum.

www.nafta-sec-alena.org

Effect of Globalization on HRM

For all of the opportunities afforded by international business, when managers talk about "going global," they have to balance a complicated set of issues related to different geographies, cultures, laws, and business practices. Human resources issues underlie each of these concerns and include such things as identifying capable *expatriate managers* who live and work overseas; designing training programs and development opportunities to enhance the managers' understanding of foreign cultures and work practices; and adjusting compensation plans to ensure that pay schemes are fair and equitable across individuals in different regions with different costs of living.

So, while managing across borders provides new and broader opportunities for organizations, it also represents a quantum leap in the complexity of human resources management. In fact, the international arena for HRM is so involved that we have devoted an entire chapter (Chapter 15) to discussing its competitive, cultural, and practical implications.

Challenge 2: Embracing New Technology

objective 3

Advancements in information technology have enabled organizations to take advantage of the information explosion. With computer networks, unlimited amounts of data can be stored, retrieved, and used in a wide variety of ways, from simple record keeping to controlling complex equipment. The effect is so dramatic that at a broader level, organizations are changing the way they do business. Use of the Internet to transact business has become so pervasive for both large and small companies that *e-commerce* is rapidly becoming the organizational challenge of the new millennium. Even following the "dot-com bust," in which many promising new Internet companies failed rapidly, the Web is transforming the way traditional brick-and-mortar companies do business. Organizations are connected via computer-mediated relationships, and they are giving rise to a new generation of "virtual" workers who work from home, hotels, their cars, or wherever their work takes them. The implications for HRM are at times mind-boggling.

From Touch Labour to Knowledge Workers

Knowledge workers
Workers whose responsibilities extend beyond the physical execution of work to include planning, decision making, and problem solving

The introduction of advanced technology tends to reduce the number of jobs that require little skill and to increase the number of jobs that require considerable skill. In general, this transformation is referred to as a shift from "touch labour" to **"knowledge workers,"** where employee responsibilities expand to include a richer array of activities such as planning, decision making, and problem solving.[11] In many cases, current employees are being retrained to assume new roles and responsibilities. Even in cases where employees are displaced, they also require retraining. We thus experience the paradox of having pages of newspaper advertisements for applicants with technical or scientific training while job seekers without such training register for work with employment agencies.

Technology training makes up a growing portion of all formal training provided by employers. Today, fully one-third of all courses are devoted to computer skills training (compared with 25 percent in 1996). Manpower Inc., the largest employment agency in the world, offers free information technology training through its Manpower Global Learning Center, an online university for its two million employees. The learning centre

For more information about Manpower Inc. go to www.manpowernet.com.

Human resources information system (HRIS)
Computerized system that provides current and accurate data for purposes of control and decision making

enables employees to access material at their leisure on a variety of technical subjects. In fact, Manpower is so focused on developing technical skills in potential employees that it has set up the system so that some training and career planning information is available to those who simply send the company a resumé.[12]

Influence of Technology in HRM

Information technology has, of course, changed the face of HRM in Canada and abroad. Perhaps the most central use of technology in HRM is an organization's **human resources information system (HRIS)**. An HRIS provides current and accurate data for purposes of control and decision making; in this sense it moves beyond simply storing and retrieving information to include broader applications such as producing reports, forecasting HR needs, strategic planning, career and promotion planning, and evaluating HR policies and practices.

The impact of information technology (IT) within HR has been both pervasive and profound. IT allows firms to store and retrieve large amounts of information quickly and inexpensively. It also enables them to rapidly and accurately combine and reconfigure data to create new information. Further, because it allows organizations to store and quickly use the judgment and decision models developed in the minds of experts, IT systems help to institutionalize organizational knowledge. With IT networks, managers can communicate more easily and selectively with others in remote parts of the world, thereby allowing for even better use of the information at their disposal. In that regard, IT can be a potent weapon for lowering administrative costs, increasing productivity, speeding response times, improving decision making, and enhancing service. It may also be vital for coordinating activities with parties external to the firm. Ultimately, IT can provide a data and communications platform that helps HR link and leverage the firm's human capital to achieve competitive advantage.

The operational impact. IT influences HRM in three basic ways. The first is its operational impact; that is, automating routine activities, alleviating the administrative burden, reducing costs, and improving productivity internal to the HR function itself. The most frequent uses of IT in HRM include automating payroll processing, maintaining employee records, and administering benefits programs (see Highlights in HRM 1.1). At Merck and Company, Inc. there is a major initiative under way to create a global HR data warehouse that provides a uniform architecture for HR reporting (such as payroll, benefits enrolment, address changes, and retirement). To ensure consistency across databases in various locations—a condition necessary for analysis and decision making on a global scale—IT and HR managers are working together to develop standardized data definitions and coding structures for all transactions. The goal of this project is to establish one comprehensive repository for employee data while simultaneously making the reporting process more timely and accurate.[13]

The relational impact. While the operational impact of IT emphasizes efficiency and productivity improvements within HR, IT also enhances service by providing line managers and employees with remote access to HR databases, supporting their HR-related decisions, and increasing their ability to connect with other parts of the corporation. At Merck, several HR practices have been redesigned to enable line

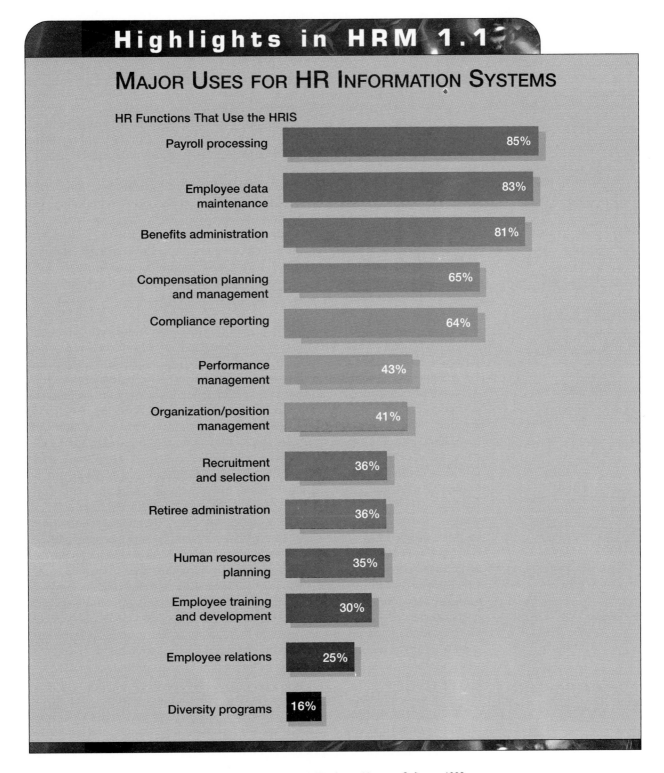

Highlights in HRM 1.1

MAJOR USES FOR HR INFORMATION SYSTEMS

HR Functions That Use the HRIS

- Payroll processing — 85%
- Employee data maintenance — 83%
- Benefits administration — 81%
- Compensation planning and management — 65%
- Compliance reporting — 64%
- Performance management — 43%
- Organization/position management — 41%
- Recruitment and selection — 36%
- Retiree administration — 36%
- Human resources planning — 35%
- Employee training and development — 30%
- Employee relations — 25%
- Diversity programs — 16%

Source: HR and Technology Survey, Deloitte & Touche and Lawson Software, 1998.

managers and employees to enter, retrieve, and edit data (by themselves) from remote locations in order to make better decisions. Perhaps the best example is in the area of staffing. Merck's staffing management system supports the hiring process by tracking application information, scanning resumés, and making the information immediately accessible to line managers so they can search for skills systematically. The system allows Merck managers to search online for internal and external talent by posting jobs, reviewing resumés, or running searches of candidates who have been categorized by skill set. An outside vendor who specializes in web-based recruiting administers the system and acts as a conduit between Merck and broader databases such as Monster.com and Hotjobs.com.[14]

A growing number of organizations such as Canada Post and Mercer are using company-specific "intranets" to establish home pages and employee portals that provide up-to-date information. In addition to company information, the technology allows them to take advantage of online services designed especially for HR departments. As technology allows for distributed communication and exchange, HR functions can "run faster and jump higher." Particularly in multinational firms trying to coordinate activities worldwide, IT can dramatically expand HR's reach while providing better integration.

The transformational impact. While IT can improve operational efficiency and enhance relational connections, the transformational impact of IT refers to expanding the scope and function of the HR department. That is, instead of just changing how HR activities are undertaken, IT also redefines the activities HR undertakes.

A specific example of HR transformation at Merck can be seen in the evolution of education and training. Rather than relying solely on traditional approaches to learning, Merck is developing a "blended" approach to learning. In combination with traditional classroom experiences, Merck is creating web-based e-learning opportunities as well. For example, in association with Forum Corporation, Merck piloted the use of an online 360-degree diagnostic tool called *Performance Compass* for its Leadership Development Program. The tool helps managers assess their developmental needs and then connects them to a wide array of external training and educational resources. Similarly, Merck worked with Developmental Dimensions International (DDI) to implement the *On-line Performance and Learning (OPAL)* system, which provides coaching tips and learning tools and resources for employees and managers. Systems such as these transform the learning process by enabling individuals to search through a virtual sea of information and customize their own learning. This dramatically reduces employee research time, not to mention the cost savings associated with producing and distributing typical hard-copy reference material. But more important, systems such as these facilitate just-in-time skill development by bringing the training to the employees, rather than vice versa.

Examples such as these show that technology is changing the face of HRM—altering the methods used to manage employee information, speeding up the processing of data, and improving the process of communication. However, despite the enormous promise of technology, a recent survey conducted by Deloitte & Touche found that only 37 percent of HR managers believe their organizations are innovative in the use of technology. Surprisingly, only 21 percent said their enterprises use the best available HR technology on the market, and only 19 percent thought their companies have the technology required to rapidly provide human resources information for business planning purposes.[15]

As organizations think about making investments in IT, HR and line managers should jointly plan for its implementation. In small companies, in particular, managers should consider the following factors in their needs assessment for IT investments:

- ▶ Initial costs and annual maintenance costs
- ▶ Fit of software packages to the employee base
- ▶ Ability to upgrade
- ▶ Increased efficiency and time savings
- ▶ Compatibility with current systems
- ▶ User-friendliness
- ▶ Availability of technical support
- ▶ Needs for customizing
- ▶ Time required to implement
- ▶ Training time required for HR and payroll[16]

On the front end, HR and line managers can identify methods for introducing new technology that minimize disruption. Communication with employees clearly plays a crucial role, as management must demonstrate a real commitment to supporting change through staffing, training, job redesign, and reward systems. Specifically, HR managers can provide guidance to line managers to ensure that the right technological skills are identified and sought in new employees, as well as in developing technology-literacy training programs. HR can also identify and evaluate the changes in organizational relationships brought about by new technology. In this regard, privacy issues are becoming more of a concern. Finally, HR should work with line managers to develop new structures that use technology to improve service, increase productivity, and reduce costs.[17]

Challenge 3: Managing Change

objective

Technology and globalization are only two of the forces driving change in organizations and HRM. As John Kotter, leadership guru, noted, "Efforts to transform organizations have increased dramatically. These changes are being driven by powerful forces associated with technology, the globalization of competition and markets, and workforce demographics."[18]

Organizations can rarely stand still for long. In highly competitive environments, where competition is global and innovation is continuous, change has become a core competency of organizations.

Reactive change
Change that occurs after external forces have already affected performance

Proactive change
Change initiated to take advantage of targeted opportunities

Types of Changes

Programs focused on total quality, continuous improvement, downsizing, reengineering, outsourcing, and the like are all examples of the means organizations are using to modify the way they operate in order to be more successful. Some of these changes are **reactive,** resulting when external forces have already affected an organization's performance. Other changes are more **proactive,** being initiated by managers to

All managers play an important role in managing change. Home Depot has been a leader in involving employees in its change programs.

DICK HEMINGWAY

take advantage of targeted opportunities, particularly in fast-changing industries where followers are not successful. Bob Nardelli, for example, recognized the need for change when he took over as CEO of Home Depot. Even though the company was the leader in the home improvement industry, Nardelli realized the unrealized potential of the company and its capacity for growth. In the first year of his term, Nardelli and Dennis Donovan, executive vice-president of HR, utilized their experience at GE (working under Jack Welch) to initiate organization-wide transformation of the company. The main thrust of the change-management program was to involve employees in instituting continuous innovation and excellent customer service. These types of change initiatives are not designed to fix problems that have arisen in the organization so much as they are designed to help renew everyone's focus on key success factors.[19]

Managing Change through HR

In one survey, 84 percent of executives polled said that they have at least one change initiative going on in their organizations. Yet surprisingly, in contrast to the Home Depot experience, only about two-thirds said that their companies have any sort of formal change-management program to support these initiatives![20] This is unfortunate, because successful change rarely occurs naturally or easily. Most of the major reasons why change efforts can fail come down to HR issues. Some of the top reasons are as follows:[21]

1. Not establishing a sense of urgency
2. Not creating a powerful coalition to guide the effort
3. Lacking leaders who have a vision

4. Lacking leaders who communicate the vision
5. Not removing obstacles to the new vision
6. Not systematically planning for and creating short-term "wins"
7. Declaring victory too soon
8. Not anchoring changes in the corporate culture

Most employees—regardless of occupation—understand that the way things were done five or ten years ago is very different from how they are done today (or will be done five or ten years from now). Responsibilities change, job assignments change, work processes change. And this change is continuous—a part of the job—rather than temporary. Nevertheless, people often resist change because it requires them to modify or abandon ways of working that have been successful or at least familiar to them. As Dr. Marilyn Buckner, president of National Training Systems, put it: "Nontechnical, unattended human factors are, in fact, most often the problem in failed change projects." To manage change, executives and managers have to envision the future, communicate this vision to employees, set clear expectations for performance, and develop the capability to execute by reorganizing people and reallocating assets. Of course, this is easier said than done. Therefore all managers, including those in HR, have an important role in facilitating change processes, particularly in helping communicate business needs to employees and in listening to employee concerns.[22]

Challenge 4: Developing Human Capital

objective

Human capital
The knowledge, skills, and capabilities of individuals that have economic value to an organization

The idea that organizations "compete through people" highlights the fact that success increasingly depends on an organization's ability to manage **human capital**. The term *human capital* describes the economic value of knowledge, skills, and capabilities. Although the value of these assets may not show up directly on a company's balance sheet, it nevertheless has tremendous impact on an organization's performance. The following quotations from notable CEOs illustrate this point:[23]

▶   "If you look at our semiconductors and melt them down for silicon, that's a tiny fraction of the costs. The rest is intellect and mistakes." (Gordon Moore, Intel)

▶   "An organization's ability to learn, and translate that learning into action rapidly, is the ultimate competitive business advantage." (Jack Welch, General Electric)

▶   "Successful companies of the 21st century will be those who do the best jobs of capturing, storing and leveraging what their employees know." (Lew Platt, Hewlett-Packard)

Human Capital and HRM

Human capital is intangible and elusive and cannot be managed the way organizations manage jobs, products, and technologies. One of the reasons for this is that the employees, *not* the organization, own their own human capital. If valued employees leave a company, they take their human capital with them, and any investment the company has made in training and developing those people is lost.

To build human capital in organizations, managers must continue to develop superior knowledge, skills, and experience within their workforce. Staffing programs focus on identifying, recruiting, and hiring the best and the brightest talent available. Training programs complement these staffing practices to provide skill enhancement, particularly in areas that cannot be transferred to another company if an employee should leave.[24] In addition, employees need opportunities for development on the job. The most highly valued intelligence tends to be associated with competencies and capabilities that are learned from experience and are not easily taught.[25] Consequently, managers have to do a good job of providing developmental assignments to employees and making certain that job duties and requirements are flexible enough to allow for growth and learning.

Beyond the need to invest in employee development, organizations have to find ways of using the knowledge that currently exists. Too often, employees have skills that go unused. As Robert Buckman, CEO of Buckman Laboratories, noted, "If the greatest database in the company is housed in the individual minds of the associates of the organization, then that is where the power of the organization resides. These individual knowledge bases are continually changing and adapting to the real world in front of them. We have to connect these individual knowledge bases together so that they do whatever they do best in the shortest possible time."[26] Bruncor, the parent company of NB Tel (New Brunswick's telecommunications company), has created the Living Lab, a think tank that produces, applies, and sells knowledge. Efforts to empower employees and encourage their participation and involvement more fully utilize the human capital available. (Employee empowerment is discussed fully in Chapter 3.)

In companies such as Bell Canada and Toys "R" Us, managers are evaluated on their progress toward meeting developmental goals. These goals focus on skill development and gaining new competencies and capabilities. In a growing number of instances, pay is attached to this knowledge and skill acquisition. Skill-based pay, for example, rewards employees for each new class of jobs they are capable of performing. We will discuss skill-based pay (or pay-for-knowledge) more in Chapter 9.

Developmental assignments, particularly those involving teamwork, can also be a valuable way of facilitating knowledge exchange and mutual learning. Effective communications (whether face to face or through information technology) are instrumental in sharing knowledge and making it widely available throughout the organization. As Dave Ulrich, professor of business at the University of Michigan, noted: "Learning capability is *g* times *g*—a business's ability to *generate* new ideas multiplied by its adeptness at *generalizing* them throughout the company."[27]

HR programs and assignments are often the conduit through which knowledge is transferred among employees. A recent survey by the Human Resource Planning Society revealed that 65 percent of responding companies believed that their HR group plays a key role in developing human capital. Boeing Satellite Systems, for example, has created a "lessons learned architecture" on the Internet where all areas of the company can store the knowledge they have learned. As information and intellectual capital are posted to the company's electronic newsgroups, it can be analyzed and consolidated by editorial teams. Employees can access and use this new codified knowledge directly from the Internet. Executives at Boeing estimate that this form of intellectual capital has reduced the cost of developing a satellite by as much as $25 million.[28]

HR managers and line managers each play an important role in creating an organization that understands the value of knowledge, documents the skills and capabilities available to the organization, and identifies ways of utilizing that knowledge to benefit the firm. We will address these issues throughout the text, but particularly in Chapters 6 and 7 on training and career development.

objective

Challenge 5: Responding to the Market

Meeting customer expectations is essential for any organization. In addition to focusing on internal management issues, managers must also meet customer requirements of quality, innovation, variety, and responsiveness. These standards often separate the winners from the losers in today's competitive world. How well does a company understand its customers' needs? How fast can it develop and get a new product to market? How effectively has it responded to special concerns? *"Better, faster, cheaper ... "* These standards require organizations to constantly align their processes with customer needs. Management innovations such as total quality management (TQM) and process reengineering are but two of the comprehensive approaches to responding to customers. Each has direct implications for HR.

Total Quality Management, Six Sigma, and HRM

Total quality management (TQM) is a set of principles and practices whose core ideas include understanding customer needs, doing things right the first time, and striving for continuous improvement. The TQM revolution began in the mid-1980s, pioneered by companies such as Motorola, Xerox, and Ford. But since that time, criteria spelled out in the Malcolm Baldrige National Quality Award have provided the impetus for both large and small companies to rethink their approach to HRM.[29]

Unfortunately, early TQM programs were no panacea for responding to customer needs and improving productivity. In many cases, managers viewed quality as a quick fix and became disillusioned when results did not come easily. When TQM initiatives do work, it is usually because managers have made major changes in their philosophies and HR programs. More recently, companies such as Motorola, GE, and Home Depot have adopted a more systematic approach to quality, called **Six Sigma,** which includes major changes in management philosophy and HR programs. Six Sigma is a statistical method of translating a customer's needs into separate tasks and defining the best way to perform each task in concert with the others. By examining the optimal process, Six Sigma can have a powerful effect on the quality of products, the performance of customer services, and the professional development of employees. The use of Six Sigma at a Goodyear tire plant in Medicine Hat, Alberta, is described in Highlights in HRM 1.2. What makes Six Sigma different from other quality efforts is that it catches mistakes before they happen. In a true Six Sigma environment, variation from standard is reduced to only 3.4 defects per million.[30] John Deere Limited Canada won an award for quality improvement from the National Quality Institute, which found that about one-third of the payroll costs in Canadian small and medium-sized businesses was spent on quality issues.

The importance of HR to Six Sigma begins with the formation of teams and extends to training, performance management, communications, culture, and even rewards. As individuals progress through Six Sigma training, they can move up from "green belt" to eventually achieve "black belt" status. If this all sounds a bit hokey, take note of the successful companies that have made cultural—and performance—transformation as a result.[31] The most important quality-improvement techniques stress employee motivation, change in corporate culture, and employee education. Organizations known for product and service quality strongly believe that employees are the key to that quality.

Total quality management (TQM)
A set of principles and practices whose core ideas include understanding customer needs, doing things right the first time, and striving for continuous improvement

Six Sigma
A process used to translate customer needs into a set of optimal tasks that are performed in concert with one another

One of the reasons that HR programs are so essential to programs such as Six Sigma is that they help balance two opposing forces. According to Laurie Broedling, senior vice-president of HR and quality at McDonnell Douglas, "One set

Highlights in HRM 1.2

SIX SIGMA

Nine months after conducting a pilot class for Six Sigma Black Belts in October 2002, Goodyear Canada is in the midst of a major business transformation. Already there are nineteen Black Belts (full-time project leaders) and seven Green Belts (part-time project leaders, working in offices, warehouses, and the eight Canadian tire and rubber products manufacturing plants). Projects currently under way are projected to yield $10 million in waste reduction, capital equipment purchase avoidance, and increased sales through elimination of production bottlenecks.

Goodyear's tire manufacturing facility in Medicine Hat, Alberta, needed to produce more rubber from its Banbury rubber mixer in order to meet its daily quota and lessen its dependence on rubber produced by outside sources. In buying material, the factory was paying freight charges to get the rubber to the factory. By optimizing the Banbury uptime and increasing the Banbury output, the factory could reduce the amount of rubber it needed to purchase. Using the tools of Six Sigma, the factory determined that it could stagger shift rotations so that an operator was always available to keep the Banbury mixer running. They also were able to increase the batch weight sizes of some of the compounds by 4 percent to 11 percent. In addition, staging batches at the top of the conveyor and reducing the gate delay realized gains of two to three seconds per batch. Although three seconds does not sound like a great amount, over the course of a week, it adds about 150 minutes of productivity. After six months, the factory has increased its Banbury mixer output by more than 5 percent, generating savings of over $110 000. The Medicine Hat plant estimates that it can save $250 000 to $400 000 annually by implementing the new procedures.

Gary Blake, Goodyear Canada Six Sigma champion, and a Black Belt, says that it is a problem-solving model that applies rigorous statistical thinking to reduce defects, improve cycle time, and increase customer satisfaction. The methodology is being applied not only to traditional manufacturing processes, but also to transactional processes—supply chain, purchasing, invoicing, sales, and marketing. A Six Sigma team follows five major steps known as DMAIC to clearly Define the scope of the project, Measure customer requirements and process outputs, Analyze the current situation and set clear goals, Improve the process through planned experimentation, and finally Control to validate and lock in the improvement—then sustaining it so that there is no backslide. The model moves the organization to whatever goals are required by the customer. Six Sigma derives its name from the Greek letter, *sigma*, which is sometimes used to denote variation from a standard, and the statistical concept that if you measure the defects in a process, you can figure out how to get rid of them and get ever closer to perfection. A Six Sigma company cannot produce more than 3.4 defects per million opportunities. For a process with only one specification limit, this results in six process standard deviations between the mean of the process and customer's specification limit.

of forces (the need for order and control) pulls every business toward stagnation, while another set of forces (the need for growth and creativity) drives it toward disintegration."[32] Six Sigma's focus on continuous improvement drives the system toward disequilibria, while Six Sigma's focus on customers, management systems, and the like provide the restraining forces that keep the system together. HR practices help managers balance these two forces.

Reengineering and HRM

Reengineering
Fundamental rethinking and radical redesign of business processes to achieve dramatic improvements in cost, quality, service, and speed

In addition to TQM and Six Sigma programs, some companies take a more radical approach to process redesign called reengineering. **Reengineering** has been described as "the fundamental rethinking and radical redesign of business processes to achieve dramatic improvements in cost, quality, service and speed."[33] Reengineering often requires that managers start over from scratch in rethinking how work should be done, how technology and people should interact, and how entire organizations should be structured. HR issues are central to these decisions. First, reengineering requires that managers create an environment for change and, as we mentioned previously, HR issues drive change. Second, reengineering efforts depend on effective leadership and communication processes, two other areas related to HRM. Third, reengineering requires that administrative systems be reviewed and modified. Selection, job descriptions, training, career planning, performance appraisal, compensation, and labour relations are all candidates for change to complement and support reengineering efforts. We will return to these issues, and discuss more directly the organizational development tools necessary for reengineering, in Chapter 7.

Challenge 6: Containing Costs

Investments in reengineering, TQM, human capital, technology, globalization, and the like are all very important for organizational competitiveness. Yet, at the same time, there are increasing pressures on companies to lower costs and improve productivity to maximize efficiency. Labour costs are one of the largest expenditures of any organization, particularly in service and knowledge-intensive companies. Organizations have tried a number of approaches to lower costs, particularly labour costs. These include downsizing, outsourcing and employee leasing, and productivity enhancements, each of which has a direct impact on HR policies and practices.

Downsizing

Downsizing
The planned elimination of jobs

Downsizing is the planned elimination of jobs. For example, when L.L. Bean saw that sales had fallen, the company undertook a number of efforts to identify what it called "smart cost reductions." Bean's TQM activities helped the company target quality problems and saved an estimated $30 million. But the cuts were not enough, and ultimately the company realized it needed to eliminate some jobs. Instead of simply laying off people, however, the company started early retirement and "sweetened" voluntary separation programs. Then the company offered employee sabbaticals for continuing education.[34]

The pain of downsizing has been widespread throughout the Canada. About 50 percent of Canadian employers have engaged in some type of downsizing and have reduced their workforces by an average of 13 percent.[35]

Figure 1.2 shows the results of the American Management Association survey of nearly 1200 major companies. What's most surprising from this study is not the number of firms that are eliminating workers, or even the ones that are adding workers. What's surprising is the growing proportion that is doing both—eliminating jobs and then adding them back in. Fully 72 percent of those eliminating jobs during the previous twelve months said they had also created new positions. This suggests two possibilities. Either poor planning is resulting in cyclical hiring, or—also likely—the changes represent a shift in the kinds of skills and employees the companies are looking for.

Whatever the reason, while some firms improve efficiency (and lower costs) from layoffs, many others do not obtain such benefits. These kinds of trade-offs have led some firms to establish a policy of "no layoffs." For example, in an industry that has seen layoffs in the tens of thousands, Southwest Airlines hasn't laid off a single employee. In fact, the company hasn't had layoffs in thirty years. These practices are admittedly an exception, but some firms are taking such an approach because of downsizing's toll on retention and recruitment. A study by Watson Wyatt of 750 companies showed that companies with excellent recruiting and retention policies provide a return to shareholders nearly 8 percent higher than those that don't. Those with a strong commitment to job security earned an additional 1.4 percent for shareholders.

Advocates of a no-layoff policy often note that layoffs may backfire after taking into account such hidden costs as these:

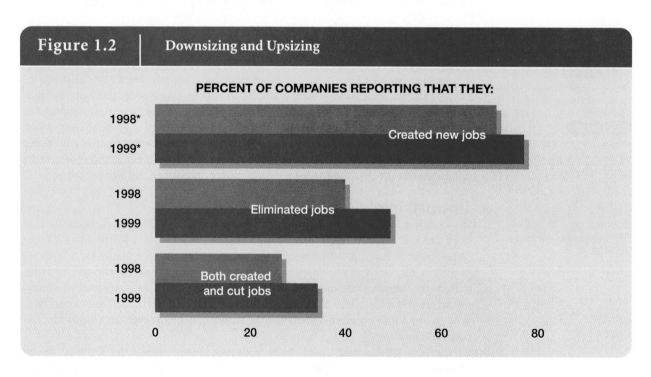

Figure 1.2 | Downsizing and Upsizing

Source: From "Hire Math: Fire 3, Add 5," by Gene Koretz in March 13, 2000, online issue of *Business Week*, © 2000. Reprinted by permission of *Business Week*.

▶ Severance and rehiring costs

▶ Accrued vacation and sick day payouts

▶ Pension and benefit payoffs

▶ Potential lawsuits from aggrieved workers

▶ Loss of institutional memory and trust in management

▶ Lack of staffers when the economy rebounds

▶ Survivors who are risk-averse, paranoid, and political

In contrast, companies that avoid downsizing say they get some important benefits from such policies:

▶ A fiercely loyal, more productive workforce

▶ Higher customer satisfaction

▶ Readiness to snap back with the economy

▶ A recruiting edge

▶ Workers who aren't afraid to innovate, knowing their jobs are safe[36]

More than one executive has come to the conclusion that you don't get dedicated and productive employees if at the first sign of trouble you show them you think they are expendable.

To approach downsizing more intelligently, companies have made special efforts to reassign and retrain employees for new positions when their jobs are eliminated. This is consistent with a philosophy of employees as assets, as intellectual capital.

Outsourcing and Employee Leasing

Outsourcing simply means hiring someone outside the company to perform tasks that could be done internally. Companies often hire the services of accounting firms, for example, to take care of financial services. They may hire advertising firms to handle promotions, software firms to develop data-processing systems, or law firms to handle legal issues. Interest in outsourcing has been spurred by executives who want to focus their organization's activities on what they do best—their core competencies. Increasingly, activities such as maintenance, security, catering, and payroll are being outsourced in order to increase the organization's flexibility, lower its overhead costs, and gain access to expertise that others may have.

There are several HR concerns with regard to outsourcing, not the least of which is that if employees are likely to lose their jobs when the work is outsourced, morale and productivity can drop rapidly. To minimize problems, line and HR managers have to work together to define and communicate transition plans, minimize the number of unknowns, and help employees identify their employment options.[37]

Increasingly, outsourcing is changing the way HR departments operate as well. In a recent survey, about 93 percent of all HR departments reported outsourcing at least some of their work. Technology enables companies to try to find ways of reducing their administrative overhead—and cost pressures mandate it. Companies such as CIBC have outsourced payroll and benefits, information systems, training, and other activities. Like other trends, the results have been mixed. While some organizations have achieved cost savings, others have found that the outsourcing efforts resulted in fragmented service to employees and managers. Worse, outsourcing of important activities can erode the key competencies of the HR function.[38]

Outsourcing
Contracting outside the organization to have work done that formerly was done by internal employees

Employee leasing
Process of dismissing employees who are then hired by a leasing company (which handles all HR-related activities) and contracting with that company to lease back the employees

As an alternative to layoffs and outsourcing, some companies are exploring the idea of **employee leasing.** The Bank of Montreal outsourced its human resources processing services (payroll and benefits administration, HR call centres, and employee records) to Exult, a company specializing in outsourcing, in a contract that saw the transfer of 100 BMO employees to Exult.

The value of employee leasing lies in the fact that an organization can essentially maintain its working relationships but shift the administrative costs to the PEO (Professional Employer Association). Depending on their size, PEOs offer a variety of services. All provide the basics: payroll processing, payroll tax payments, and health insurance. Most offer retirement plans, worker's compensation insurance, risk management, and regulatory-compliance monitoring.[39]

Productivity Enhancements

Pure cost-cutting efforts such as downsizing, outsourcing, and leasing may prove to be disappointing interventions if managers use them as simple solutions to complex performance problems. Overemphasis on labour costs perhaps misses the broader issue of productivity enhancement.

Since productivity can be defined as the "output gained from a fixed amount of inputs," organizations can increase productivity either by reducing the inputs (the cost approach) or by increasing the amount that employees produce.

$$\text{Productivity} = \frac{\text{Output (goods and services)}}{\text{Inputs (people, capital, materials, energy)}}$$

It is quite possible for managers to cut costs only to find that productivity falls at even a more rapid rate. Conversely, managers may find that increasing investment in employees (raising labour costs) may lead to even greater returns in enhanced productivity. This in turn may lead to increased profits, and better pay, benefits, and working conditions for employees. Except in extremely cash-poor organizations, managers may find that looking for additional ways to boost productivity may be the best way to increase the value of their organizations.

Canada trails other leading industrial economies in manufacturing productivity, defined as output per worker. From 1991 to 2001, manufacturing productivity in Canada rose only 22 percent, compared to 90 percent for Sweden, 51 percent for France and Japan, and 45 percent for the United States. This gap may continue as Canadian companies invest in machinery and equipment at rates lower than the United States.[40]

Employee productivity is the result of a combination of employee abilities, motivation, and work environment. When productivity falls off—or more positively, when productivity improves—the change is usually traceable to enhanced skill, motivation, or a work environment conducive to high performance. In general, this can be summarized in the following equation:

$$\text{Performance} = f \text{ (ability, motivation, environment)}$$

If any of these three dimensions is low, productivity is likely to suffer. Figure 1.3 shows some of the topics that we cover in this textbook that help managers increase productivity in their organizations.

| Figure 1.3 | Productivity Enhancements |

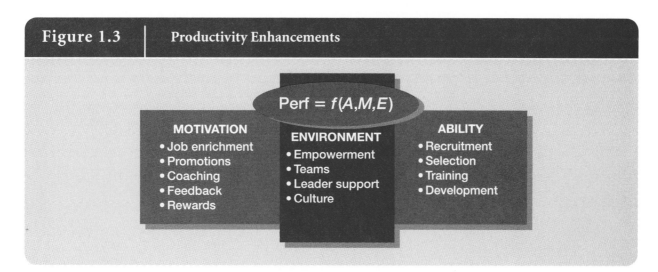

$$Perf = f(A, M, E)$$

MOTIVATION
- Job enrichment
- Promotions
- Coaching
- Feedback
- Rewards

ENVIRONMENT
- Empowerment
- Teams
- Leader support
- Culture

ABILITY
- Recruitment
- Selection
- Training
- Development

DEMOGRAPHIC AND EMPLOYEE CONCERNS

objective 8

In addition to the competitive challenges facing organizations, managers in general—and HR managers in particular—need to be concerned about changes in the makeup and the expectations of their employees. As we noted at the beginning of this chapter, HRM involves being an advocate for employees, being aware of their concerns, and making sure that the exchange between the organization and its employees is *mutually* beneficial. Highlights in HRM 1.3 shows a summary of social concerns in HRM. We will discuss some of these issues here and address all these issues in greater detail throughout the book.

Demographic Changes

Among the most significant challenges to managers are the demographic changes occurring in Canada. Because they affect the workforce of an employer, these changes—in employee background, age, gender, and education—are important topics for discussion.

The Diversity Challenge

Of course, Canadian workers continue to be a diverse group. As will be demonstrated in Chapter 2, in the year 2010 minorities will make up an even larger share of the Canadian labour force than they do today. According to the 2001 census, immigrants represent almost 70 percent of labour force growth and now constitute one-fifth of the workforce. Although Caucasians will still constitute the largest percentage of the labour force, visible minorities will increase and will account for one-fifth of the Canadian population by 2016.[41] In cities such as Toronto and Vancouver, visible minorities represent a significant portion of the population. Toronto is the most ethnically diverse city in North American, with 44 percent of its citizens born in other countries. The majority of immigrants coming to Canada are from China, India, the Philippines, and Hong Kong. Aboriginals make up 3.3 percent of the population, and more than half are under twenty-five years of age.

Highlights in HRM 1.3

SOCIAL ISSUES IN HRM

Changing Demographics: The coming decades will bring a more diverse and aging workforce. This has major implications for all aspects of HRM as it alters traditional experience and expectations regarding the labour pool. Among the issues in this area are

▶ Shrinking pool of entry-level workers
▶ Individual differences
▶ Skills development

▶ Productivity
▶ Retirement benefits
▶ Use of temporary employees

Employer/Employee Rights: This area reflects the shift toward organizations and individuals attempting to define rights, obligations, and responsibilities. Among the issues here are

▶ Job as an entitlement
▶ Contagious diseases
▶ Concern for privacy

▶ Right to work
▶ Equal pay for work of equal value
▶ Mandated benefits

Attitudes toward Work and Family: Because of the increase of working women as well as employee mobility and a growing concern about family issues, there is demand for recognizing and supporting family-related concerns. Among the issues are

▶ Day care
▶ Job sharing
▶ Elder care
▶ Parental leave

▶ Flextime
▶ Alternative work schedules
▶ Job rotation
▶ Telecommuting

Unfortunately, nearly one-third of immigrants older than fifteen did not speak either English or French. Learning one of Canada's official languages increases the integration of immigrants into the workforce. Bilingual (French and English) Canadians make more money than unilingual Canadians.[42]

Age Distribution of Employees

In the next decade, Canada's labour force is expected to change dramatically as the workforce is aging and issues such as retirement and retention of older workers will force changes in HR practices, as outlined in Highlights in HRM 1.4. The number of older workers (age fifty-five to eighty) is beginning to rise as baby boomers approach retirement age and is projected to reach 40 percent by 2026. Over the next ten years, the number of workers aged fifty-five to sixty-four is expected to double. Only 24 percent of the workforce will be under thirty-five by 2026, placing a strain on businesses looking for employees just entering the job market.[43]

Imbalance in the age distribution of the labour force has significant implications for employers. Companies such as Inco and sectors such as education are finding that large portions of their workforces are nearing retirement. Beyond the sheer number

Highlights in HRM 1.4

OLD, BUT NOT OUT

The number of Canadians fifty-five and older is about 27 percent of the workforce, compared to 29 percent under thirty-five, and 44 percent between thirty-five and fifty-five. The average age of retirement is declining, from sixty-five in the early 70s to about sixty-one in 2003. Those who are laid off just before retirement are often unable to find work again. The numbers who are unemployed more than fifty-two weeks rose from 4 percent in 1976 to 17 percent in 1998. Most of these workers are concentrated in traditional sectors, such as manufacturing, which have seen no growth. The combination of low literacy and education rates, coupled with high salary expectations and their unwillingness to move to where the jobs are located, makes this group fairly unemployable.

However, after 2010, older workers will have higher education levels, more training, and more transferable skills, all of which will make them more employable. Many older workers want to continue to work after they retire, mostly because they enjoy work. Their ability to learn and adapt to new technologies does not differ from those of younger workers. However, they do want flexible arrangements such as reduced hours, special assignments, temporary work, job sharing, telecommuting, and consulting work.

As employers face labour shortages in specific occupations such as health care workers, there will be more attempts to provide innovative HR programs to retain older workers. For example, the average age of retirement for a registered nurse is fifty-seven, so in an attempt to retain these experienced nurses, the Province of New Brunswick is introducing a phased-in retirement program. Nurses can reduce their work hours by about 50 percent and access their pension plans to supplement their incomes. The Older Worker Pilot Project of Human Resources Development Canada seeks to test innovative approaches to help older workers remain employed. This collaborative project between the federal government and the provinces and territories attempts to reintegrate displaced older workers into the labour market.

Sources: Adapted from Jennifer Thomas and Marianne Chilco, "Coming of Age," *Benefits Canada* 25, no. 3, March 2001: 36–38; Nicole Wassink, "Your Workforce Is Ageing…Are You Ready?" The Conference Board of Canada, May 2001; "Retention Strategies for Older Nurses Could Ease Shortages," *Canadian HR Reporter*, August 1, 2003: 1.

of employees they will have to replace, managers are concerned that the expertise of these employees is likely to be drained too rapidly from the company. As a stopgap measure, employers are making positive efforts to attract older workers, especially those who have taken early retirement. "We're looking to recruit additional senior workers," says Lynn Taylor, director of research at staffing firm Robert Half International. "They have a vast amount of experience that is invaluable and irreplaceable—and our clients are thrilled to tap that expertise." Older workers, for example, have significantly lower accident rates and absenteeism than younger workers. Further, they tend to report higher job satisfaction scores. And while some motor skills and cognitive abilities may start to decline (starting around age twenty-five), most individuals find ways to compensate for this fact so that there is no discernible impact on their performance.[44]

There is an old cliché: "You can't teach an old dog new tricks." Probably we should revise this to say, "You can't teach an old dog the same way you teach a puppy." Sun Life Assurance Company of Canada found no differences in the abilities of old and young worker to adapt to new technologies. However, to address the fact that seniors learn in different ways, McDonald's, a heavy recruiter of older workers, has developed its McMasters program in which newly hired seniors work alongside experienced employees so that in a matter of four weeks they can be turned loose to work on their own. The training program is designed to help seniors "unlearn" old behaviours while acquiring new skills. More programs like these will be discussed throughout the book.

The other problem that accompanies age imbalances in the workforce might be referred to as the "echo boom" effect. Similar to the trends with baby boomers, those who constitute the new population bulge are experiencing greater competition for advancement from others of approximately the same age. This situation challenges the ingenuity of managers to develop career patterns for employees to smooth out gaps in the numbers and kinds of workers.[45]

Gender Distribution of the Workforce

Statistics Canada reports that women will continue to join the Canadian labour force and are expected to account for about 48 percent of workers by 2006. However, there is some evidence that a glass ceiling exists—women continue to face barriers to top-paying jobs. About 11 percent of women, compared to 29 percent of men, are among the top 20 percent income earners. Only 21 percent of senior managers are women.[46] Employers are under constant pressure to ensure equality for women with respect to employment, advancement opportunities, and compensation. They also need to accommodate working mothers and fathers through parental leaves, part-time employment, flexible work schedules, job sharing, telecommuting, and child care assistance. In addition, because more women are working, employers are more sensitive to the growing need for policies and procedures to eliminate sexual harassment in the workplace. Some organizations have special orientation programs to acquaint all personnel with the problem and to warn potential offenders of the consequences. Many employers are demanding that managers and supervisors enforce their sexual harassment policy vigorously. (The basic components of such policies will be presented in Chapter 2.)

Rising Levels of Education

In recent years the educational attainment of the Canadian labour force has risen dramatically. Not coincidentally, the most secure and fastest-growing sectors of employment over the past few decades have been in areas requiring higher levels of education. Those occupations requiring a university degree rose by 32.9 percent over the last decade, compared to a growth rate of 9.5 percent for all occupations and 5.4 percent for occupations requiring high school education. Women accounted for the majority of degrees, diplomas, and certificates awarded by universities, receiving 59 percent of the total. The Conference Board of Canada estimates that about half a million Canadians are unemployed or under-employed because the educational qualifications of immigrants are not recognized by Canadian employers, and yet most of these immigrants possess the skills needed in critical areas of labour shortages.[47] Figure 1.4 shows the average payoff in annual earnings from education.

It is important to observe that while the educational level of the workforce has continued to rise, there is a widening gap between the educated and noneducated. At the lower end of the educational spectrum, many employers must cope with individuals who are functionally illiterate—unable to read, write, calculate, or solve problems at a level that enables them to perform even the simplest technical tasks. More than 40 percent of our adult population have inadequate levels of literacy—defined as the ability to use printed and written information to function in society. Employees with inadequate literacy skills make it difficult for employers to adopt new technology or new work methods.[48]

HR managers are interested in these job trends because of their effects on all the HRM functions. For example, given that minorities and women are increasing their share of the labour force, HR managers frequently analyze how each group is represented in both fast-growing and slow-growing occupations. Women, for example, are

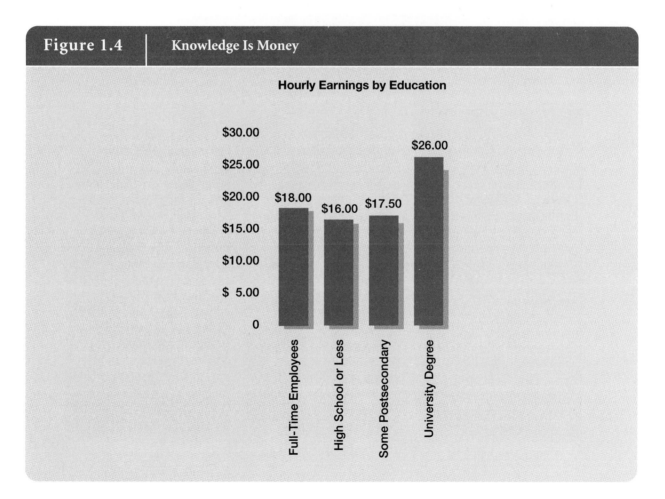

Figure 1.4 | **Knowledge Is Money**

Hourly Earnings by Education

Source: Statistics Canada.

fairly well represented in fast-growing occupations such as health services but are also represented in some slow-growth occupations such as secretarial, computer processing, and financial records processing. Given these data, a number of efforts have been undertaken to encourage recruitment, selection, and training of those in designated groups, such as women, aboriginals, persons with disabilities, and visible minorities.

But these are only the initial efforts to provide an overall environment that values and utilizes a diverse workforce. **Managing diversity** means being acutely aware of characteristics *common* to employees, while also managing these employees as *individuals*. It means not just tolerating or accommodating all sorts of differences but supporting, nurturing, and utilizing these differences to the organization's advantage.[49] Figure 1.5 summarizes a model for developing a diversity strategy in organizations.

Managing diversity
Being aware of characteristics common to employees, while also managing employees as individuals

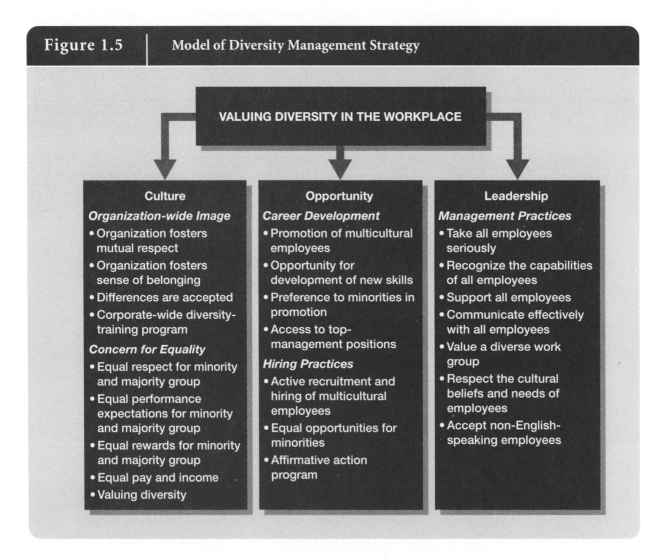

| Figure 1.5 | Model of Diversity Management Strategy |

VALUING DIVERSITY IN THE WORKPLACE

Culture

Organization-wide Image
- Organization fosters mutual respect
- Organization fosters sense of belonging
- Differences are accepted
- Corporate-wide diversity-training program

Concern for Equality
- Equal respect for minority and majority group
- Equal performance expectations for minority and majority group
- Equal rewards for minority and majority group
- Equal pay and income
- Valuing diversity

Opportunity

Career Development
- Promotion of multicultural employees
- Opportunity for development of new skills
- Preference to minorities in promotion
- Access to top-management positions

Hiring Practices
- Active recruitment and hiring of multicultural employees
- Equal opportunities for minorities
- Affirmative action program

Leadership

Management Practices
- Take all employees seriously
- Recognize the capabilities of all employees
- Support all employees
- Communicate effectively with all employees
- Value a diverse work group
- Respect the cultural beliefs and needs of employees
- Accept non-English-speaking employees

Source: From "Managing for Effective Workforce Diversity" by Kathleen Iverson from *The Cornell Hotel and Restaurant Administration Quarterly* 41, no. 2 (April 2000): 31–38. Reproduced by permission of the *Cornell Hotel and Restaurant Administration Quarterly*.

While there are important social reasons for including a broader spectrum of workers, there are some essential business reasons as well. Highlights in HRM 1.5 shows the primary business reasons for diversity management.

The Changing Nature of the Job

The era of the full-time permanent job seems to have disappeared. Nearly half of all the jobs created in the last two decades have been nonstandard—that is, part-time, temporary, or contract work. As job security erodes, so do pension plans and health care benefits, especially for part-timers. Nonstandard jobs represent about 30 percent of all employment now. The number of Canadians who are self-employed has also risen, from 10 percent in 1976 to 18 percent in 1998. As shown in Ethics in HRM, labour force participants have become increasingly polarized into haves and have-nots. We return to the subject of changing employment options in Chapter 4.

Cultural Changes

The attitudes, beliefs, values, and customs of people in a society are an integral part of their culture. Naturally, their culture affects their behaviour on the job and the environment within the organization, influencing their reactions to work assignments,

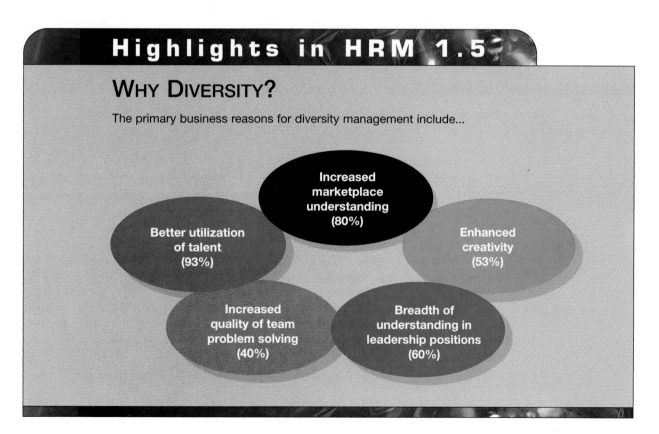

Highlights in HRM 1.5

WHY DIVERSITY?

The primary business reasons for diversity management include...

- Increased marketplace understanding (80%)
- Better utilization of talent (93%)
- Enhanced creativity (53%)
- Increased quality of team problem solving (40%)
- Breadth of understanding in leadership positions (60%)

Source: Survey data from Gail Robinson and Kathleen Dechant, "Building a Business Case for Diversity," *Academy of Management Executive* 11, no. 3 (August 1997): 21–31; permission conveyed through the Copyright Clearance Center.

Ethics in HRM

SKYWALKERS AND GROUNDWORKERS

Canadian workers can be divided into two classes: skywalkers and groundworkers. Skywalkers, those working in white-collar jobs in highrise buildings, are well educated and well trained and earn good incomes. Their jobs are secure and they receive full benefits. For these knowledge workers, the employment prospects in computer programming, financial analysis, insurance, business services, and real estate are bright. Those working in the highrises on Bay Street, Howe Street, and rue St-Jacques earned a weekly average of $1469 in 1996—a 62 percent increase from 1990. (A Canadian worker earned, on average, about $679 per week in 2002.)

Below the highrise buildings toil the groundworkers. Those with little education and outdated skills are suffering massive unemployment. Groundworkers suffer further from job insecurity and lack of benefit programs. Look for these workers in restaurants, hotels, and shops. The "McJobs" they hold in the accommodation, food, and beverage industries paid a mere $240 per week in 1996—a 0.005 percent increase since 1990. Those working part-time—a growing segment of the Canadian economy—fare even worse. Companies have discovered cost savings by replacing full-time employees with part-time workers, thereby eliminating benefits and increasing staffing flexibility. This restructuring of the job market has produced winners and losers, but many would argue that all Canadians lose when the unemployment rate is high and citizens feel insecure about their futures.

Source: Statistics Canada, *Statistics Canada Measures of Weekly Earnings*, Cat. No. 72-0002-XPB, 1997, 2002.

leadership styles, and reward systems. Like the external and internal environments of which it is a part, culture is undergoing continual change. HR policies and procedures therefore must be adjusted to cope with this change.

Employee Rights

Over the past few decades, federal legislation has changed the rules for management of employees by granting them many specific rights. Among these are laws granting the right to equal employment opportunity (Chapter 2), union representation and collective bargaining (Chapter 14), a safe and healthful work environment (Chapter 12), a pension plan that is fiscally sound (Chapter 11), equal pay for men and women performing essentially the same job (Chapter 9), and privacy in the workplace (Chapter 13). An expanded discussion of the specific areas in which rights and responsibilities are of concern to employers and employees will be presented in Chapter 13.

Concern for Privacy

HR managers and their staffs, as well as line managers in positions of responsibility, generally recognize the importance of discretion in handling all types of information about employees. The Personal Information Protection and Electronic Documents Act (PIPEDA) is a federal law that deals with the collection, use, and disclosure of personal information (note that Quebec is the only province with similar laws, although Ontario and others have draft legislation in place). This law requires federally regulated organizations holding personal information on customers or employees to obtain their consent before it uses, collects, or discloses this information. Employer responses to the issue of information privacy vary widely. IBM was one of the first companies to show concern for how personal information about employees was handled. It began restricting the release of information as early as 1965 and in 1971 developed a comprehensive privacy policy. The Royal Bank, the Hudson's Bay Company, and Zero Knowledge Systems in Montreal are among other employers that have developed privacy programs.[50] We will discuss the content of such programs and present some recommended privacy guidelines in Chapter 13.

Changing Attitudes toward Work

Employees today are less likely to define their personal success only in terms of financial gains. This trend has been evolving for some time, but observers have noted that it has peaked since the terrorist attacks of September 11, 2001. Personal fulfilment and self-expression—as well as a balance between work and family—are key factors in a complex array of job attitudes. Many people view life satisfaction as more likely to result from balancing the challenges and rewards of work with those in their personal lives. Though most people still enjoy work and want to excel at it,

USING THE INTERNET

The Canadian Policy Research Network is a great site for information on workplace trends and job issues:

www.jobquality.ca

they tend to be focused on finding interesting work and may pursue several careers rather than being satisfied with just "having a job." People also appear to be seeking ways of living that are less complicated but more meaningful. These new lifestyles cannot help having an impact on the way employees must be motivated and managed. Consequently, HRM has become more complex than it was when employees were concerned primarily with economic survival. Research conducted by the Canadian Policy Research Network outlines the types of job attributes desired by employees, as shown in Figure 1.6. What matters most to Canadians is the soft stuff—relationships with others and the intrinsic aspects of a job.

Balancing Work and Family

Work and the family are connected in many subtle and not-so-subtle social, economic, and psychological ways. Because of the new forms that the family has taken—such as the two-wage-earner and the single-parent family—work organizations find it necessary to provide employees with more family-friendly options. "Family friendly" is a broad term that may include unconventional hours, day care, part-time work, job sharing, pregnancy leave, parental leave, executive transfers, spousal involvement in

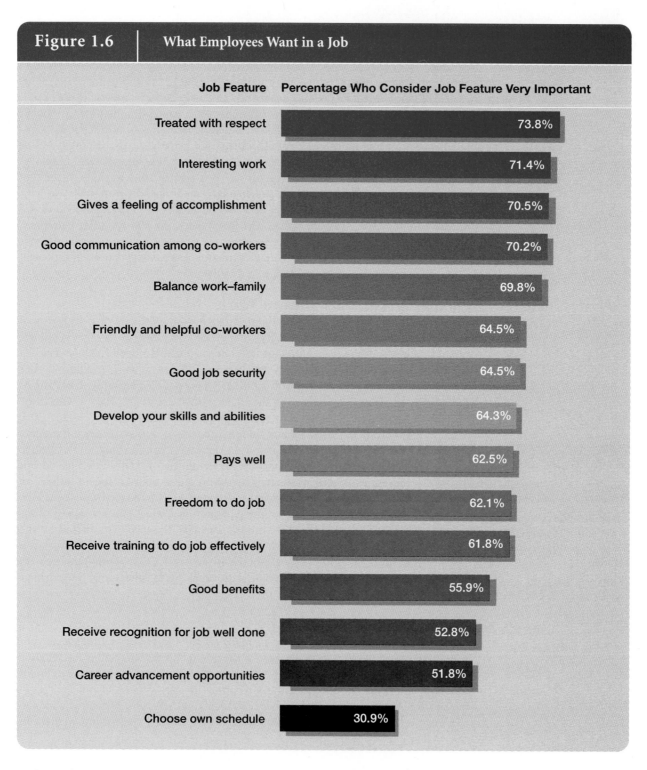

Figure 1.6 | **What Employees Want in a Job**

Source: Graham S. Lowe and Grant Schellenberg, "Employee Basic Value Proposition: Strong HR Strategies Must Address Work Values," *Canadian HR Reporter* 15, no. 12: 18; www.jobquality.ca. Reprinted with permission.

career planning, assistance with family problems, and telecommuting. These issues have become important considerations for all managers and are more fully discussed in Chapter 11. Figure 1.7 shows some of the top concerns managers have about balancing work and home. Nora Spinks, an expert in work life harmony, speaks about these issues in Highlights in HRM 1.6.

Still, there are acknowledged costs. In professional firms such as law, career paths and promotions are programmed in a lockstep manner. Time away from work can slow down—and in some cases derail—an individual's career advancement. Health Canada estimates the annual financial loss from the challenge of employees balancing work and family obligations at $2.7 billion due to lost time relating to stress, medical leaves, dealing with dependants, and other family responsibilities.[51]

Further, family-friendly companies may risk alienating those who cannot capitalize on the benefits. Only a small minority of employees can actually take advantage of such policies. A recent Conference Board survey of companies with family-friendly programs found that 56 percent of the companies acknowledge that childless employees harbour resentment against those with children.[52]

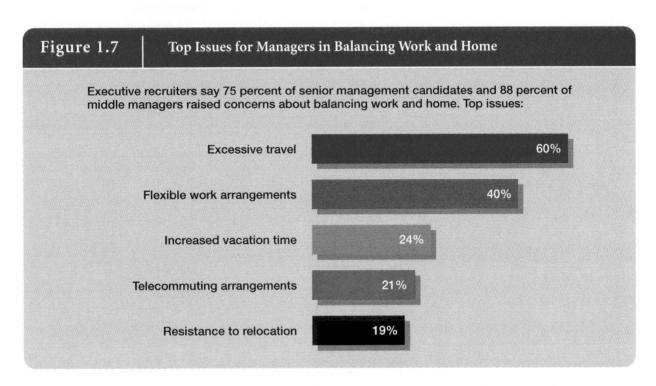

Figure 1.7 | **Top Issues for Managers in Balancing Work and Home**

Executive recruiters say 75 percent of senior management candidates and 88 percent of middle managers raised concerns about balancing work and home. Top issues:

Excessive travel — 60%
Flexible work arrangements — 40%
Increased vacation time — 24%
Telecommuting arrangements — 21%
Resistance to relocation — 19%

Source: Association of Executive Search Consultants (member survey).

As more and more employees strive to balance the demands of their jobs with the needs of their families, employers are responding by offering greater flexibility, such as telecommuting and flex time.

PHOTODISC

Highlights in HRM 1.6

WORK-LIFE HARMONY

Nora Spinks, president and CEO of Work-Life Harmony, a consulting company specializing in work-life balance issues, comments on the demographic issues affecting employee behaviour: "Women are in the workplace to stay; they have fewer and shorter career breaks and have more opportunities to make or influence organizational decisions. There is a high proportion of the aging 'boomer' workforce that are asking, 'What is my legacy?' They are rethinking priorities and lifestyles and reducing the number of hours they are working. At the same time, the nexus generation [i.e., the generation born in the 1980s] is entering the workforce and managerial positions with a fresh perspective and different outlook on the work experience. They see work as a means to having a life, not as life in and of itself. The boomers tend to live to work, the nexus generation work to live. Growing up, they witnessed people give up a life for the sake of a job, only to see them ultimately lose employment in periods of downsizing and restructuring. They don't want the same experience.

"A recent international study of students found that young people about to enter the workforce wanted to have a challenging career with plenty of opportunity to grow personally and professionally, and they wanted to be able to take advantage of those opportunities while achieving work-life balance. It is up to organizations, executives, and managers to create the kinds of environments to make that possible. It is the only way for them to meet increasing customer/client demands, meet the challenges of global competition, and reach their organizational objectives."

THE PARTNERSHIP OF LINE MANAGERS AND HR DEPARTMENTS

We have taken a good deal of time up front in this book to outline today's competitive and social challenges to reinforce the idea that managing people is not something that occurs in a back room called the HR department. Managing people is every manager's business, and successful organizations combine the experience of line managers with the expertise of HR specialists to develop and utilize the talents of employees to their greatest potential. Addressing HR issues is rarely the exclusive responsibility of HR departments acting alone. Instead, HR managers work side by side with line managers to address people-related issues of the organization. And while this relationship has not always achieved its ideal, the situation is rapidly improving. HR managers are assuming a greater role in top-management planning and decision making, a trend that reflects the growing awareness among executives that HRM can make important contributions to the success of an organization.

Responsibilities of the Human Resources Manager

Although line managers and HR managers need to work together, their responsibilities are different, as are their competencies and expertise. The major activities for which an HR manager is typically responsible are as follows:

1. *Advice and counsel.* The HR manager often serves as an in-house consultant to supervisors, managers, and executives. Given their knowledge of internal employment issues (policies, collective agreements, past practices, and the needs of employees) as well as their awareness of external trends (economic and employment data, legal issues, and the like), HR managers can be an invaluable resource for making decisions. As in-house consultants, HR managers should be concerned with the operating goals of the managers and supervisors. In turn, these managers must be convinced that the HR staff is there to assist them in increasing their productivity rather than to impose obstacles to their goals. This requires not only the ability on the part of the HR executive to consider problems from the viewpoint of line managers and supervisors but also skill in communicating with the managers and supervisors.[53]

2. *Service.* HR managers also engage in a host of service activities such as recruiting, selecting, testing, planning and conducting training programs, and hearing employee concerns and complaints. Technical expertise in these areas is essential for HR managers and forms the basis of HR program design and implementation.

3. *Policy formulation and implementation.* HR managers generally propose and draft new policies or policy revisions to cover recurring problems or to prevent anticipated problems. Ordinarily, these are proposed to the senior executives of the organization, who actually issue the policies. HR managers may monitor performance of line departments and other staff departments to ensure conformity with established HR policies, procedures, and practice. Perhaps more important, they are a resource to whom managers can turn for policy interpretation.

4.　*Employee advocacy.* One of the enduring roles of HR managers is to serve as an employee advocate—listening to the employees' concerns and representing their needs to managers. Effective employee relations provide a support structure when disruptive changes interfere with normal daily activities.

In the process of managing human resources, increasing attention is being given to the personal needs of the participants. Thus throughout this book we will not only emphasize the importance of the contributions that HRM makes to the organization but also give serious consideration to its effects on the individual and on society.

Increasingly, employees and the public at large are demanding that employers demonstrate greater social responsibility in managing their human resources. Complaints that some jobs are devitalizing the lives and injuring the health of employees are not uncommon. Charges of discrimination against women, minorities, the physically and mentally disabled, and the elderly with respect to hiring, training, advancement, and compensation are being levelled against some employers. Issues such as comparable pay for comparable work, the high cost of health benefits, day care for children of employees, and alternative work schedules are concerns that many employers must address as the workforce grows more diverse. All employers are finding that privacy and confidentiality of information about employees are serious matters and deserve the greatest protection that can be provided.

Top management generally recognizes the contributions that the HR program can make to the organization and thus expects HR managers to assume a broader role in the overall organizational strategy.

STRATEGIC HUMAN RESOURCES MANAGEMENT

Strategy

The formulation of an organization's missions, goals, and objectives as well as the action plans to execute the strategy

Strategy is the formulation of an organization's missions, goals, and objectives as well as the action plans to execute the strategy. Think of strategy as a flight plan. The flight plan is to go from Vancouver to Hong Kong. The number of passengers determines the size of the aircraft, which in turn influences the type of pilot and the number of crew. However, while en route, weather conditions may alter the flight plan, or a sick passenger may even force an emergency landing. Except in extreme situations such as the events of September 11, 2001, where planes never did arrive at their destinations, almost all flight plans are executed as planned. Organizational strategies are like these flight plans—an intent to achieve a goal, with some minor adaptations as conditions change.

It is important to recognize the distinction between *corporate strategies* and *business strategies*. Corporate strategy deals with questions such as these: Should we be in business? What business should we be in? Corporate strategies are company-wide and focus on overall objectives such as long-term survival and growth. There are two main types of corporate strategies. The first is a restructuring strategy, to ensure long-term survival, and under this option, we can find turn-around situations (Loewen Group Inc.), divestitures (Air Canada getting rid of its regional airline Jazz), liquidation (Eatons), and bankruptcy (Confederation Life). Reality Check outlines the strategic thinking of the vice-president of Human Resources at Inco.

Under the growth strategy, organizations can grow incrementally (by adding new products or new distribution networks). For example, Procter & Gamble added skin care lotion and hair conditioners for babies and began to distribute to drugstores as

Reality Check

STRATEGY AT INCO

Inco is a Canadian-based global company with operations and an extensive marketing network in over forty countries and overall sales of about $2.5 billion (U.S.). Inco is one of the world's premier mining and metals companies and the world's second largest producer of nickel.

For over half of its first century of existence, Inco Limited had a quasi-monopoly in the nickel market, and by the early 1950s it was supplying about 85 percent of the western world's nickel. However, in the late 70s nickel went on the London Metal Exchange. The world, not Inco, began to set prices. Over the next twenty-five years, Inco continued to produce about the same amount of nickel in a growing market, experiencing a significant drop in its market share. Realizing that the company would probably not survive in such a state—too big to be a niche player, and too small to fend off predators—the board and senior management developed a new growth strategy for its core mining and metals business. The growth strategy included developing new low-cost ore bodies in New Caledonia and Labrador, as well as innovative new products and increased market presence and sales in Asia.

There was a need for a strong leadership team to execute the new strategies. Inco had been downsizing for twenty-five years, however (going from 50 000 employees in 1975 to 10 000 in 2002), and did not have all the managerial talent it required. Increased effort needed to be put into developmental programs to identify and develop high-potential employees, not only in Canada, but wherever Inco operated. Mark J. Daniel, vice-president of Human Resources at INCO, explains, "Our goal is to have leadership be a competitive advantage. We started in the future and worked back. What will the industry look like in twenty years? What part do we want to play in that? How will we get there and what talent will be required?"

The company's view of the future revealed that it needed international managers with technical and engineering training. In addition to all the usual issues associated with developing people with global experience, Inco also faced the reality that some developing countries, such as Indonesia (as well as many developed countries), want to maximize the employment of their own nationals. At the same time, Inco was losing some promising Indonesian engineers because of the lack of developmental opportunities at the management level. These engineers were using Inco as a training ground and then moving on to other companies to become managers. Inco's approach to solving this problem was to develop an arrangement with the Indonesian government whereby additional Canadians could be sent to Indonesia for development and Indonesians would be sent for developmental assignments in Canada.

All these efforts are part of a comprehensive HR strategy to support the Inco business strategies.

well as grocery stores. Organizations can gain new customers by expanding internationally as Finning International Ltd. accomplished when it started selling Caterpillar equipment to the United Kingdom and Chile. Growth can also be achieved through mergers and acquisitions. TELUS was created through the merger of BC Tel and Alberta-based Telus.

Business strategy focuses on one line of business and is concerned with the question "How should we compete?" Porter has developed a classification system that helps us understand five ways in which a business unit can compete.[54] Let us illustrate his model by analyzing how hamburgers are sold. Restaurants can compete by being a low-cost provider (McDonalds); by trying to differentiate its products in a way that will still attract a large number of buyers (e.g., Burger King introduces the Whopper); by being a best-cost provider through giving more value for the money (e.g., East Side Mario's sells hamburgers, but on a plate in an attractive environment); by focusing on a niche market based on lower cost to a select group of customers (e. g., offering fish burgers or vegetarian burgers); or by offering a niche product or service customized to the tastes of a very narrow market segment (Bymark restaurant in downtown Toronto sells a hamburger, with a specialty cheese, for $35).

Strategic HRM
A set of interrelated practices, policies, and philosophies whose goal is to enable the achievement of the corporate or business strategy

Strategic HRM is a set of interrelated practices, policies, and philosophies whose goal is to enable the achievement of the corporate or business strategy. For example, if the organization has a corporate strategy of growth, HR must develop programs to rapidly recruit and train new employees. HR strategy must also support business strategies. The recruitment training and compensation policies and practices for employees at McDonalds Restaurants are very different than those at the Bymark restaurant. If the business strategy is to develop a niche market for luxury items, employees must be hired and given extensive training in meeting the high demands of this customer base. HR leaders spend about 30 percent of their time on these strategic issues.[55]

However only about two-thirds of organizations have a documented HR strategy, and few are tracking the success of their strategies. The most common measures include turnover, revenue per employee, employee performance evaluations, and employee feedback surveys.[56] HR managers must remember the bottom line if they are to fulfil their role and must be evaluated like every other function. A prescription for this is outlined in Highlights in HRM 1.7.

THE ORGANIZATION OF THE HR FUNCTION

The responsibility for HR in small organizations usually resides with the owner-manager, or with the administrator. However, once an organization employs about one hundred people, a full-time HR professional usually is hired. The job, at this stage, consists mainly of payroll administration, with some recruitment, training, and employee relations. However, as organizations grow, more HR professionals are hired, and various HR functions are added to deal with more complex functions such as labour relations and training. How many HR professionals should organizations employ? In Canada, the average tends to be 1.4 HR professionals for every 100 employees, although the range might be as low as 1 to 400. The HR department in a large organization (more than 1000 employees) might look like that found in Figure 1.8.

Highlights in HRM 1.7

THE FIVE C MODEL FOR ASSESSING HR

Executives, employees, and clients of the human resources department judge the effectiveness of this function in five ways:

1. *Compliance.* The HR department is responsible for ensuring that the organization complies with the laws that govern employee–employer relations (employment equity, health and safety, labour law, employment standards, etc). When it does this, savings are achieved in legal costs, fines, and damaging publicity.
2. *Client satisfaction.* Those external and internal clients who interact with the HR professional can be assessed on their satisfaction with services, in the same way that customers of other organizational services are measured.
3. *Culture management.* Highly effective organizations create and monitor the culture of their organizations, by surveying employee attitudes and developing programs (such as empowerment) to create the kinds of employee attitudes that result in increased motivation and productivity.
4. *Cost control.* In organizations where employees are viewed as an expense, the role of the HR department is to cut costs by reducing the labour component. Other cost control strategies include reducing turnover, absenteeism, smoking and other employee behaviours that are costly to the organization.
5. *Contribution.* Research has established that certain high-performance HR practices can have a positive effect on employee performance, by increasing knowledge, skills, and abilities; improving motivation; reducing shirking; and increasing retention of competent employees. These in turn affect organizational effectiveness.

Figure 1.8 | A Typical Organizational Chart

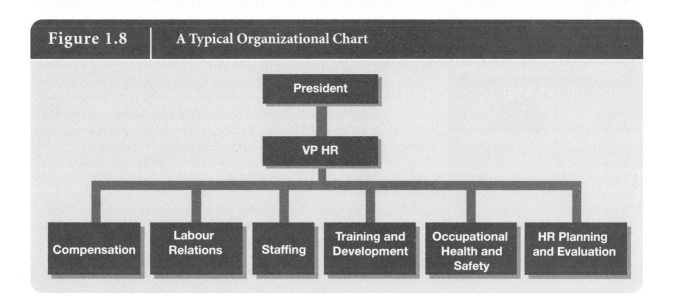

Competencies of the Human Resources Manager

As top executives expect HR managers to assume a broader role in overall organizational strategy, many of these managers will need to acquire a complementary set of competencies.[57]

1. *Business mastery.* HR professionals need to know the business of their organization thoroughly. This requires an understanding of its economic and financial capabilities so that they can "join the team" of business managers. It also requires that HR professionals develop skills at external relations focused on their customers.

2. *HR mastery.* HR professionals are the organization's behavioural science experts. In areas such as staffing, development, appraisal, rewards, team building, and communication, HR professionals should develop competencies that keep them abreast of changes.

3. *Change mastery.* HR professionals have to be able to manage change processes so that HR activities are effectively merged with the business needs of the organization. This involves interpersonal and problem-solving skills, as well as innovativeness and creativity.

4. *Personal credibility.* HR professionals must establish personal credibility in the eyes of their internal and external customers. Credibility and trust are earned by developing personal relationships with customers, by demonstrating the values of the firm, by standing up for one's own beliefs, and by being fair-minded in dealing with others.

The ability to integrate business, HR, and change competencies is essential. By helping their organizations build a sustained competitive advantage and by learning to manage many activities well, HR professionals are becoming full business partners. The competencies required for obtaining the HR professional designation (CHRP—Certified Human Resource Professional) are outlined in Figure 1.9. Those working in HR positions who hold a CHRP are compensated at better rates than those without a CHRP.[58] In 2003, about 14 000 people held the CHRP designation. In this field, which has been growing at about 10 percent a year, the employment rate is higher than the national average.[59]

At lower levels in the organization, a rapidly growing number of companies such as Air Canada assign HR representatives to business teams to make certain that HR issues are addressed on the job and that HR representatives, in turn, are knowledgeable about business issues rather than simply focusing on the administrative function.

Role of the Line Manager

As much as we might say about the role of the HR department, in the final analysis, managing people depends upon effective supervisors and line managers. As one executive at Merck put it, "Human resources are far too important to be left to the personnel department." Although HR managers have the responsibility for coordinating programs and policies pertaining

USING THE INTERNET

Compensation rates and the job outlook for those working in HR can be found on the HRDC website:

www.jobfutures.ca

USING THE INTERNET

CHRP, Certified Human Resource Professional, is the professional designation in HR. To read about becoming a CHRP go to their website and click on PARC (Professional Assessment Resource Centre):

www.cchra-ccarh.ca

Figure 1.9	Human Resource Competency Model

The Canadian Council of Human Resource Associations (www.cchra-ccarh.ca) has delineated the body of knowledge that a Certified Human Resources Professional (CHRP) in Canada must acquire. The Required Professional Competencies (RPCs) were grouped into the following eight functions:

Function	*Example*
Professional Practice in HR	Understands and adheres to the HR association code of ethics
	Stays current in professional development
Organizational Effectiveness	Maintains an inventory of talent for the use of the organization
	Gathers and analyzes employee feedback to assist decision making
Staffing	Identifies potential sources of qualified applicants
	Evaluates recruitment effectiveness
Employee and labour relations	Interprets the collective agreement
	Collects and develops information required for decision making in bargaining
Total compensation	Ensures compliance with legally required programs
	Monitors the competitiveness of the compensation program relative to comparable organizations
Organizational learning and development	Conducts an evaluation of the program
	Monitors, documents, and reports on career development activities
Workplace health and safety	Responds to any refusals to perform work that is considered to be unsafe
	Establishes effective programs for accident prevention, incident investigation, inspections, fire and emergency response, and required training
Human Resources information management	Assesses requests for HR information in light of corporate policy, freedom of information legislation, evidentiary privileges, and contractual or other releases
	Contributes to the development of information security measures.

All RPCs are listed and described on the CCHRA website, www.cchra-ccrarh.ca, and then go to PARC (Professional Assessment Resource Centre). Information about becoming a CHRP is also provided on this site.

to people-related issues, managers and employees themselves are ultimately responsible for performing these functions.

We understand that most readers of this book will be line managers and supervisors, rather than HR specialists. The text is, therefore, oriented to *helping people manage people more effectively,* whether they become first-line supervisors or chief executive officers. Students now preparing for careers in organizations will find that the study of HRM provides a background that will be valuable in managerial and supervisory positions. Discussions concerning the role of the HR department can serve to provide a better understanding of the functions performed by this department. A familiarity with the role of HR should help to facilitate closer cooperation with the department's staff and to utilize more fully the assistance and services available from this resource.

SUMMARY

People have always been central to organizations, but their strategic importance is growing in today's knowledge-based industries. An organization's success increasingly depends on the knowledge, skills, and abilities of employees, particularly as they help establish a set of core competencies that distinguish an organization from its competitors. When employees' talents are valuable, rare, difficult to imitate, and organized, an organization can achieve a sustained competitive advantage through people.

Globalization influences approximately 70 to 85 percent of the Canadian economy and affects the free flow of trade among countries. This influences the number and kinds of jobs that are available and requires that organizations balance a complicated set of issues related to managing people in different geographies, cultures, legal environments, and business conditions. HR functions such as staffing, training, compensation, and the like have to be adjusted to take into account the differences in global management.

Advanced technology has tended to reduce the number of jobs that require little skill and to increase the number of jobs that require considerable skill, a shift we refer to as moving from touch labour to knowledge work. This displaces some employees and requires that others be retrained. In addition, information technology has influenced HRM through human resources information systems (HRIS) that streamline the processing of data and make employee information more readily available to managers.

Both proactive and reactive change initiatives require HR managers to work with line managers and executives to create a vision for the future, establish an architecture that enables change, and communicate with employees about the processes of change.

In order to "compete through people," organizations have to do a good job of managing human capital: the knowledge, skills, and capabilities that have value to organizations. Managers must develop strategies for identifying, recruiting, and hiring the best talent available; for developing these employees in ways that are firm-specific; for helping them to generate new ideas and generalize them through the company; for encouraging information sharing; and for rewarding collaboration and teamwork.

In order to respond to customer needs better, faster, and more cheaply, organizations have instituted total quality management (TQM) and reengineering programs. Each of these programs requires that HR be involved in changing work processes, training, job design, compensation, and the like. HR issues also arise when communicating with employees about the new work systems, just as with any change initiative.

In order to contain costs, organizations have been downsizing, outsourcing and leasing employees, and enhancing productivity. HR's role is to maintain the relationship between a company and its employees, while implementing the changes.

The workforce is becoming increasingly diverse, and organizations are doing more to address employee concerns and to maximize the benefit of different kinds of employees. Demographic changes, social and cultural differences, and changing attitudes toward work can provide a rich source of variety for organizations. But to benefit from diversity, managers need to recognize the potential concerns of employees and make certain that the exchange between the organization and employees is mutually beneficial.

 In working with line managers to address the organization's challenges, HR managers play a number of important roles; they are called on for advice and counsel, for various service activities, for policy formulation and implementation, and for employee advocacy. Increasingly, HR managers are aligning HR policies and practices with the strategic orientation of their companies. To perform these roles effectively, HR managers must contribute business competencies, state-of-the-art HR competencies, and change-management competencies. Ultimately, managing people is rarely the exclusive responsibility of the HR function. Every manager's job is managing people, and successful companies are those that combine the expertise of HR specialists with the experience of line managers to develop and utilize the talents of employees to their greatest potential.

KEY TERMS

core competencies 3
downsizing 17
employee leasing 20
globalization 6
human capital 13
human resources information
   system (HRIS) 8

human resources management 2
knowledge workers 7
managing diversity 26
outsourcing 19
proactive change 11
reactive change 11
reengineering 17

Six Sigma 15
strategic HRM 36
strategy 34
total quality management
   (TQM) 15

DISCUSSION QUESTIONS

 1. Are people always an organization's most valuable asset? Why or why not?

 2. Suppose you were asked by your boss to summarize the major people-related concerns in opening up an office in Tokyo. What issues would be on your list?

3. Will technology eliminate the need for human resources managers?

4. What are the pros and cons of change? Does it help or hurt organizational performance? Do you like change? Why or why not?

 5. Can you think of a situation where, if a particular person left an organization, the organization's expertise would drop rapidly?

 6. In groups, prepare to debate this issue: Employees are an expense and their numbers should be reduced.

 7. Do pressures on cost containment work against effective management of people? Why or why not?

 8. What are the pros and cons of having a more diverse workforce? Is Canada in a better position to compete globally because of its diverse population?

 9. Visit three HR departments. Determine the roles they play (advisor, service, etc.). Is there any evidence that these HR departments are strategic partners and are directly responsible for organizational outcomes?

Developing Managerial Skills

BALANCING COMPETITIVE CHALLENGES AND EMPLOYEE CONCERNS

Today, human resources management is not just the responsibility of the personnel department. If people are a competitive resource, then line managers play an increasingly important role in managing the workforce. But this is not an either/or situation. Rather than seeing line managers take over responsibility from HR managers, we see both groups working together to handle workforce issues. But how do they work together?

Assignment

1. Working in teams of four to six individuals, identify what role the HR department would play and what role line managers would play in the following activities. Where would overlaps occur, and would there be any likely problems?
   a. Recruiting and selection
   b. Training and development
   c. Compensation
   d. Performance evaluation
   e. Labour relations
2. How would potential problems be resolved?
3. Write the groups' findings on flip charts and post for all to see. One member from each team should explain the team's findings to all class members.
4. Point out the similarities and differences across the teams. Save these points and revisit them—possibly revising them—as you study subsequent chapters in this textbook.

Case Study 1

Outsourcing HR at BMO

In 2003, the Bank of Montreal outsourced all the HR processing work to Exult Inc., a human resources outsourcer. Exult will take over BMO's HR systems and administrative functions in a deal worth $75 million over ten years. Exult will handle all payroll, HR call centre management and information systems and support, employee data, staffing, and records management for BMO's 34 000 employees. BMO is Exult's first Canadian client. Rose Patten, executive vice-president of HR for BMO, sees the arrangement as a partnership, not a hand-off. According to Ms. Patten, the outsourcing arrangement will allow BMO to concentrate its HR strategy on four key areas: "talent management, performance alignment and compensation, equity and employment, and learning and development."

Exult chairman and CEO Jim Madden is very pleased with the 100 BMO employees who have accepted offers to manage the HR outsourced functions and to expand the number of Canadian clients. A BMO former manager of Information Management, says, "The one thing that is exciting is being able to see outside the box that we are in today, being able to see different businesses." The majority of the 250 employees affected by the outsourcing arrangement have been offered positions with Exult or other BMO departments.

More companies are turning to self-service applications by which clients or employees can do such things as change their home address online as a way to empower customers and employees and cut down on administrative costs. If Exult performs as promised, BMO will save 20 percent over what it would cost to do the same functions in-house. "It's no surprise that companies are outsourcing functions as a way to save money and focus on core business," says David Rhodes, a principal at management-consulting firm Towers Perrin. He says businesses are "buying expertise and the ability to work very effectively" when they decide to outsource.

Sources: George Tischelle and Elisabeth Goodridge, "Prudential Financial Expects Savings by Outsourcing HR," *InformationWeek* (January 28, 2002): 873–81; Virginia Galt, "Take Our Business; Take Our People," *The Globe and Mail,* May 19, 2003: B1.

QUESTIONS

1. What are the pros and cons of outsourcing the HR function?
2. What do you think BMO should worry about most?
3. How can Exult make certain that BMO is happy with its service?

Case Study 2

Organizational Change at Honeywell

Honeywell Limited is Canada's leading heating control company. It offers technology that enhances comfort, saves energy, protects the environment, and increases security and safety. Honeywell, which has operated in Canada since 1930, currently employs 2800 people at more than fifty locations across the country. Its annual sales are $500 million.

In 1991 the main Honeywell Canada operation in Scarborough, Ontario, faced a tough challenge: it was no longer competitive, and if it did not change how it did business, every employee's job would be at risk. The traditional manufacturing operations were to be set aside and replaced by empowered teams of skilled and motivated workers. This did not look easy at the time. The average unionized employee was forty-eight years old and had worked at his routine factory job for eighteen years. Among the plant's workers, more than fifty ethnic groups were represented.

Relations with the union were strained. However, both the Canadian Auto Workers (CAW) and management had one goal in common: to improve worker skills. This could be done by implementing work teams, which could also result in saving jobs.

Throughout the change process, the union was treated as a partner. It collaborated with management in establishing a Learning for Life program that encouraged workers to take courses in computer technology, total quality management, English as a second language, and diversity management. Today, more than 70 percent of the company's employees are taking courses. As their chairman stated: "At Honeywell, learning isn't an option; it's required. Everyone is expected to complete at least forty hours of learning each year." There is a $10-million state-of-the-art learning centre that each year provides an average of 31 000 student days of learning and more than 1400 classes.

The Honeywell plant is now organized into forty-three teams, which produce six types of heating control products. The empowered and trained workers order their own supplies, set up the machines according to established production schedules, and are responsible for quality. Employees rotate between positions and learn all aspects of production. Barriers between managers and employees have been eliminated—in other words, there are no suits, ties, or reserved parking spaces.

The results to date? Cycle times have been reduced to 1.2 hours from 80 hours; inventory has been decreased from $13.5 million to $3 million; and factory throughput per person has been increased from $85 000 to $155 000. The rotating of jobs has meant a reduction in repetitive strain injuries. Because their jobs have become more technologically advanced and require more skills, the workers are earning higher wages. The Scarborough factory now employs 400 people and is a Honeywell Centre of Excellence for producing valves and actuators, which are exported all over the globe.

Source: Adapted from K. Dorrell, "Breaking Down the Barriers," *Plant* 56, no. 17 (Nov. 24, 1997), 12–13. honeywell.ca. Reprinted by permission.

QUESTIONS

1. Identify the trends affecting the management of people that Honeywell Canada faced in 1991.
2. Discuss what role the HR department played, and how its results should be measured.

CAREER COUNSEL

Most students are legitimately worried about jobs and career prospects. Career Counsel is a feature at the end of each chapter designed to help students manage their working lives and to prepare for a career. The assessment exercises are designed to encourage introspection and self-discovery. We encourage you to complete these exercises on the *Managing Human Resources* website and compile them into a separate career planning workbook. Start by accessing www.belcourt4e.nelson.com.

NOTES AND REFERENCES

1. Edward L. Gubman, *The Talent Solution: Aligning Strategy and People to Achieve Extraordinary Results* (New York: McGraw-Hill Professional Publishing, 1998).

2. C. K. Prahalad and G. Hamel, "The Core Competence of the Corporation," *Harvard Business Review* 68, no. 3 (1990): 79–91; Christopher A. Bartlett and Sumantra Ghoshal, "Building Competitive Advantage through People," *MIT Sloan Management Review* 43, no. 2 (Winter 2002): 34–41.

3. For more information on methods to identify a firm's core competencies, see the following: Khalid Hafeez, YanBing Zhang, and Naila Malak, "Core Competence for Sustainable Competitive Advantage: A Structured Methodology for Identifying Core Competence," *IEEE Transactions on Engineering Management* 49, no. 1 (February 2002): 28–35. See also Geert Duysters and John Hagedoorn, "Core Competences and Company Performance in the World-Wide Computer Industry," *Journal of High Technology Management Research* 11, no. 1 (Spring 2000): 75–91; G. Hamel and C. K. Prahalad, *Competing for the Future* (Boston: Harvard Business School Press, 1994); J. B. Quinn, "The Intelligent Enterprise: A New Paradigm," *Academy of Management Executive* no. 4 (1992): 48–63.

4. Scott A. Snell, Mark Shadur, and Patrick M. Wright, "Human Resources Strategy: The Era of Our Ways," in M. A. Hitt, R. E. Freeman, and J. S. Harrison (eds.), *Handbook of Strategic Management* (Oxford: Blackwell Publishing, 2002): 627–49; Patrick M. Wright, Benjamin Dunford, and Scott A. Snell, "Human Resources and the Resource-Based View of the Firm," *Journal of Management* 27, no. 6 (2002): 701–21.

5. "The Importance of HR," *HRFocus* 73, no. 3 (March 1996): 14. For data from a similar survey conducted in Canada, see David Brown, "HR's Role in Business Strategy: Still a Lot of Work to Be Done," *Canadian HR Reporter* 14, no. 19 (November 5, 2001): 1–20. "CEO's Talk," *Canadian HR Reporter* 14, no. 5, March 12, 2001: 17.

6. T. J. Watson, Jr., *A Business and Its Beliefs: The Ideas That Helped Build IBM* (New York: McGraw-Hill, 1963).

7. Bruce Little, "We're Less Dependent but More Entangled," *The Globe and Mail*, May 15, 2000: A-2.

8. Gordon Pitts, "Finning CEO Paves the Way for British, Chilean Expansion," *The Globe and Mail*, July 29, 2002: B7; Simon Tuck, "Canada Will Be No. 1 Spot for Business, Study Says," *The Globe and Mail*, July 17, 2003: B3.

9. Charles Whalen, Paul Magnusson, and Geri Smith, "NAFTA's Scorecard: So Far, So Good," *Business Week*, no. 3740 (July 2001): 54; "FTAA Progress Report," *The New American* 18, no. 12 (June 17, 2002): 7. For more information, see the web page for the World Trade Organization at www.wto.org/english/thewto_e/whatis_e/10ben_e/10b07_e.htm.

10. Padideh Ala'i, "A Human Rights Critique of the WTO: Some Preliminary Observations," *George Washington International Law Review* 33, no. 3 (2001): 537–54.

11. Peter F. Drucker, "Knowledge-Worker Productivity: The Biggest Challenge," *California Management Review* 41, no. 2 (Winter 1999): 79–94; A. D. Amar, *Managing Knowledge Workers* (Westport, CT: Quorum, 2002); Cynthia C. Froggat, *Work Naked: Eight Essential Principles for Peak Performance in the Virtual Workplace* (New York: John Wiley and Sons, 2002); Mary Ann Roe, "Cultivating the Gold-Collar Worker," *Harvard Business Review* 79, no. 5 (May 2001): 32–33. See also D. P. Lepak and S. A. Snell, "The Human Resource Architecture: Toward a Theory of Human Capital Development and Allocation," *Academy of Management Review* 24, no. 1 (1999): 31–48.

12. "Industry Report 1998: Information-Technology Training," *Training* 35, no. 10 (October 1998): 63–68; Barb Cole-Gomolski, "Recruiters Lure Temps with Free IT Training," *Computerworld* 33, no. 31 (August 2, 1999): 10; Ben Worthen, "Measuring the ROI of Training," *CIO* 14, no. 9 (February 15, 2001): 128–36.

13. Scott A. Snell, Donna Stueber, and David P. Lepak, "Virtual HR Departments: Getting Out of the Middle," in R. L. Heneman and D. B. Greenberger (eds.), *Human Resource Management in Virtual Organizations* (Columbus, OH: Information Age Publishing, forthcoming); Samuel Greengard, "How to Fulfill Technology's Promise," *Workforce* (February 1999): HR Software Insights supplement, 10–18.

14. Snell, Stueber, and Lepak, "Virtual HR Departments: Getting Out of the Middle."

15. Greengard, "How to Fulfill Technology's Promise," 10–18.

16. Ruth E. Thaler-Carter, "The HRIS in Small Companies: Tips for Weighing the Options," *HRMagazine* 43, no. 8 (July 1998): 30–37; Andrew Stargowski and Satish Deshpande, "The Utility and Selection of an HRIS," *Advances in Competitiveness Research* 9, no. 1 (2001): 42–56.

17. Erik R. Eddy, Dianna L. Stone, and Eugene F. Stone-Romero, "The Effects of Information Management Policies on Reactions to Human Resource Information Systems: An Integration of Privacy and Procedural Justice Perspectives," *Personnel Psychology* 52, no. 2 (Summer 1999): 335–58; Joan C. Hubbard, Karen A. Forcht, and Daphyne S. Thomas, "Human Resource Information Systems: An Overview of Current Ethical and Legal Issues," *Journal of Business Ethics* 17, no. 12 (September 1998): 1319–23; Bill Roberts, "Who's in Charge of HRIS?" *HRMagazine* 44, no. 6 (June 1999): 130–40.

18. John P. Kotter, "Ten Observations," *Executive Excellence* 16, no. 8 (1999): 15–16.

19. Chad Terhune, "Home Depot's Home Improvement—Retail Giant Aims to Spur Sales with Less-Cluttered Stores, Increased Customer Service," *The Wall Street Journal*, March 8, 2001, B1.

20. Jennifer J. Laabs, "Change," *Personnel Journal* (July 1996): 54–63.

21. John P. Kotter, "Leading Change: Why Transformation Efforts Fail," *Harvard Business Review* (March–April 1995): 59–67; Kotter, "Ten Observations," 15–16.

22. Lee G. Bolman and Terry E. Deal, "Four Steps to Keeping Change Efforts Heading in the Right Direction," *Journal of Quality and Participation* 22, no. 3 (May/June 1999): 6–11; "Coaching Employees through the Six Stages of Change," *HRFocus* 79, no. 5 (May 2002): 9.

23. For information on a company that does measure its intellectual capital, see the Skandia AFS website and look at the company's Business Navigator at www.skandia.com/en/index.

24. Thomas A. Stewart, "Intellectual Capital," *Fortune* (October 3, 1994): 68–74. David Lepak and Scott Snell, "Knowledge Management and the HR Architecture," in S. Jackson, M. Hitt, and A. DeNisi (eds.), *Managing Knowledge for Sustained Competitive Advantage: Designing Strategies for Effective Human Resource Management* (SIOP Scientific Frontiers Series, forthcoming); David Lepak and Scott Snell, "Examining the Human Resource Architecture: The Relationship among Human Capital, Employment, and Human Resource Configurations," *Journal of Management*, forthcoming; Steve Bates, "Study Links HR Practices with the Bottom Line," *HRMagazine* 46, no. 12 (December 2001): 14.

25. Gary S. Becker, *Human Capital* (New York: Columbia University Press, 1964); Charles A. O'Reilly III and Jeffrey Pfeffer, "Cisco Systems: Acquiring and Retaining Talent in Hypercompetitive Markets," *Human Resource Planning* 23, no. 3 (2000): 38–52.

26. For more on Buckman Labs and its approach to managing human capital, visit its website at www.buckman.com/. The company is also well-known for its knowledge management initiatives, called Knowledge Nurture, as well as its knowledge management system, called K'Netix; see www.knowledge-nurture.com/; Nick Bontis, "There's a Price on Your Head: Managing Intellectual Capital Strategically," *Business Quarterly*, Summer 1996, 41–47.

27. Dave Ulrich, Steve Kerr, and Ron Ashkenas, *The GE Work-Out: How to Implement GE's Revolutionary Method for Busting Bureaucracy & Attacking Organizational Problems* (New York: McGraw-Hill Professional Publishing, 2002).

28. Joseph E. McCann, *Managing Intellectual Capital: Setting the Agenda for Human Resource Professionals* (New York: Human Resource Planning Society, 1999); Benoit Guay, "Knowledge Management Is a Team Sport," *Computing Canada* 27, no. 3 (July 13, 2001): 23; Pimm Fox, "Making Support Pay," *Computerworld* 36, no. 11 (March 11, 2002): 28.

29. C. W. Russ Russo, "Ten Steps to a Baldrige Award Application," *Quality Progress* 34, no. 8 (August 2001): 49–56.

30. The term Six Sigma is a registered trademark of Motorola. It is based on the Greek letter sigma, used as a symbol of variation in a process (the standard deviation). For more information see Peter S. Pande, Robert P. Neuman, and Roland R. Cavanagh, *The Six Sigma Way: How GE, Motorola, and Other Top Companies Are Honing Their Performance* (New York: McGraw-Hill, 2000).

31. Joseph A. Defeo, "Six Sigma: Road Map for Survival," *HRFocus* 76, no. 7 (July 1999): 11–12; Michele V. Gee and Paul C. Nystrom, "Strategic Fit between Skills Training and Levels of Quality Management: An Empirical Study of American Manufacturing Plants," *Human Resource Planning* 22, no. 2 (1999): 12–23.

32. Laurie A. Broedling, "The Business of Business Is People," speech delivered to the Quality Conference, Washington Deming Study Group, George Washington University, Washington, DC, April 8, 1996.

33. M. Hammer and J. Champy, *Reengineering the Corporation* (New York: HarperCollins, 1994). See also Michael Hammer, *Beyond Reengineering: How the Process-Centered Organization Is Changing Our Work and Our Lives* (New York: Harper Business, 1996).

34. "Up to Speed: L. L. Bean Moves Employees as Workloads Shift," *Chief Executive* (July–August 1996), 15; Darrell Rigby, "Look before You Lay Off," *Harvard Business Review* 80, no. 4 (April 2002): 20–21.

35. Charles R. Greer, Stuart A. Youngblood, and David A. Gray, "Human Resource Management Outsourcing: The Make or Buy Decision," *Academy of Management Executive* 13, no. 3 (August 1999): 85–96; T. Wagar, "The Death of Downsizing—Not Yet!" *Research Forum, HR Professional* 16, no. 1 (February–March 1999): 41–43.

36. Stephanie Armour, "Some Companies Choose No-Layoff Policy," *USA Today*, December 17, 2001, B-1; Gene Koretz, "Hire Math: Fire 3, Add 5," *Business Week Online* (March 13, 2000); Michelle Conlin, "Where Layoffs Are a Last Resort," *Business Week Online* (October 8, 2001).

37. James Brian Quinn, "Strategic Outsourcing: Leveraging Knowledge Capabilities," *Sloan Management Review* (Summer 1999): 9–21; William C. Byham and Sheryl Riddle, "Outsourcing: A Strategic Tool for a More Strategic HR," *Employment Relations Today* 26, no. 1 (Spring 1999): 37–55; Grover N. Wray, "The Role of Human Resources in Successful Outsourcing," *Employment Relations Today* 23, no. 1 (Spring 1996): 17–23.

38. Thomas W. Gainey, Brian S. Klaas, and Darla Moore, "Outsourcing the Training Function: Results from the Field," *Human Resource Planning* 25, no. 1 (2002): 16–23; Helen G. Drinan, "Outsourcing: Opportunity or Threat?" *HRMagazine* 47, no. 2 (February 2002): 8–9; George Tischelle and Elisabeth Goodridge, "Prudential Financial Expects Savings by Outsourcing HR," *InformationWeek* (January 28, 2002): 873, 81; Denise Pelham, "Is It Time to Outsource HR?" *Training* 39, no. 4 (April 2002): 50–52.

39. Elliot Spagat, "Procter & Gamble to Outsource about 80% of Back-Office Work," *The Wall Street Journal Online* (June 14, 2002); "Outsourcing HR," *Industry Week* 249, no. 10 (May 15, 2000): 71; Carolyn Hirschman, "For PEOs, Business Is Booming," *HRMagazine* 45, no. 2 (February 2000): 42–47; Brian Klaas, "Trust and the Role of Professional Employer Organizations: Managing HR in Small and Medium Enterprises," *Journal of Managerial Issues* 14, no. 1 (Spring 2002): 31–49.

40. David Brown, "Manufacturers Pressed to Improve Productivity," *Canadian HR Reporter* 16, no. 3 (July 14, 2003): 1 and 13; Jim Balsillie and Roger Martin, "We're Number 8: So What?" *Toronto Star*, August 5, 2003.

41. www.statscan.ca/english/labor/CANSIM Table 179-002.

42. Jack Auby, "It Pays to be Bilingual," *The Globe and Mail*, July 10, 2003: A1; *Performance and Potential 2002–2003*, The Conference Board of Canada, 133.

43. "Challenges of an Aging Workforce," Human Resources Development Canada, May 2002; Jennifer Thomas and Marianne Chilco, "Coming of Age: The Aging Population Is Forcing Employers to Rethink Benefits and Human Resources Strategies," *Benefits Canada* 25, no. 3 (March 2001): 36–38.

44. Shelley Donald Coolidge, "Retired. And Ready to Work. Selling Slow-Built Wisdom in a Churn-It-Out World, Senior Workers Get a Handle on the Hot Job Market," *Christian Science Monitor* (October 25, 1999): 11.

45. Peter Francese, "My, You've Grown: The Teen Economy Is Like Totally Awesome," *The Wall Street Journal*, June 28, 2000: S3.

46. Statistics Canada, "Labour Participation Rates by Gender," www.statcan.ca/english/Pgdb/labor07b.htm. CANSIM II Table 282-0002, August 3, 2003; Karen Hadley, "And We Still Ain't Satisfied: Gender Inequality in Canada: A Status Report for 2001," National Action Committee on the Status of Women, 2001.

47. Eric Anderson, "People Deficit Gives Workers Upper Hand," *The Globe and Mail*, February 12, 2002; www.statisticscanada.com/education.

48. Organization for Economic Co-operation and Development, Statistics Canada, *Literacy in the Information Age: Final Report of the International Adult Literacy Survey*.

49. Kathleen Iverson, "Managing for Effective Workforce Diversity," *Cornell Hotel and Restaurant Administration Quarterly* 41, no. 2 (April 2000): 31–38.

50. Chris Conrath, "Complying with PIPEDA," *Computer World Canada* 18, no. 1, January 11, 2002.

51. Todd Raphael, "The Drive to Downshifting," *Workforce* 80, no. 10 (October 2001): 23; Wendy Creelman and Jane Boyd, "What Do Employees Want and Need? Work/Life Balance," *Canadian HR Reporter* 13, no. 21, December 4, 2000: G4.

52. Dan Seligman, "Who Needs Family-Friendly Companies?" *Forbes* 163, no. 1 (January 11, 1999): 72–76.

53. Helen G. Drinan, "Partnering with Business," *HRMagazine* 47, no. 1 (January 2002): 8–16; Wayne Brockbank, "If HR Were Really Strategically Proactive: Present and Future Directions in HR's Contribution to Competitive Advantage," *Human Resource Management* 38, no. 4 (Winter 1999): 337–57.

54. Michael Porter, *Competitive Advantage* (New York: Free Press, 1985).

55. David Brown, "HR's Role in Business Strategy: Still a Lot of Work to Be Done," *Canadian HR Reporter* 14, no. 19, November 5, 2001: 1, 20.

56. David Brown, "The Measure of a Function," *Canadian HR Reporter* 14, no. 20 (November 19, 2001): 1.

57. Michael R. Losey, "Mastering the Competencies of HR Management," *Human Resource Management* 38, no. 2 (Summer 1999): 99–102; Wayne Brockbank, Dave Ulrich, and Richard W. Beatty, "HR Professional Development: Creating the Future Creators at the University of Michigan Business School," *Human Resource Management* 38, no. 2 (Summer 1999): 111–17; Dave Ulrich, "The Future Calls for Change," *Workforce* 77, no. 1 (January 1998): 87–91; David Ulrich, Wayne Brockbank, Arthur Yeung, and Dale G. Lake, "Human

Resource Competencies: An Empirical Assessment," *Human Resource Management* 34, no. 4 (Winter 1995): 473–95.

58. Monica Belcourt and Andrew Templer, "The CHRP Edge: Part 2," *HR Professional*, December 2002/January 2003: 36–39.

59. Canadian Council of Human Resources Associations, "How to Certify," www.cchra-ccarh.ca, August 6, 2003.

2

Equity and Diversity in Human Resources Management

After studying this chapter, you should be able to

Explain the reasons for employment equity legislation.

Identify and describe the major laws affecting employment equity, and explain how they are enforced.

Describe pay equity and strategies for implementing it.

Discuss the Employment Equity Act with respect to its origins, its purpose, and its continued enforcement.

Describe how employment equity is implemented in organizations.

Discuss sexual harassment as an employment equity issue.

Explain and give examples of diversity management.

anada is one of the most diverse countries in the world—a kaleidoscope of cultures, languages, and nationalities consisting of more
than 200 different ethnic groups. Nearly 20 percent of our citizens
were born outside Canada, with more than nine out of ten of these
immigrants making their homes in urban centres. By 2016, about one in every
five citizens will be a visible minority. The workplace must not only reflect this
reality but accommodate this diversity. In the field of HRM, perhaps no topic
has received more attention in recent decades than employment equity.
Employment equity, or the treatment of employed individuals in a fair and
nonbiased manner, has attracted the attention of the media, the courts, practitioners, and legislators. Employment equity legislation affects all aspects of
the employment relationship. When managers ignore the legal aspects of
HRM, they risk incurring costly and time-consuming litigation, negative public
attitudes, and damage to organization morale.

Employment equity
The employment of indi-
viduals in a fair and nonbiased manner

Employment equity is not only a legal topic; it is also an emotional issue. It concerns
all individuals regardless of their sex, religion, age, national origin, colour, or position
in an organization. Supervisors should be aware of their personal biases and how these
attitudes can influence their dealings with subordinates. It should be emphasized that
covert as well as blatantly intentional discrimination in employment is illegal.

In this chapter we emphasize the legislation governing employment equity, and
describe the organizational response to this legislation. Today, compliance with
employment equity involves managing diversity with the goal of utilizing fully the
organization's human capital.

EMPLOYMENT EQUITY

Central to Canada's economic growth and prosperity in a highly competitive global
marketplace will be a barrier-free environment in which all Canadians can fully
explore and develop their career potential. Labour force statistics (see Chapter 1) indicated changing patterns of immigration, rising labour force participation rates for
women, and an aging population with a proportionally higher incidence of disabilities. Women, visible minorities, and people with disabilities make up over 60 percent
of Canada's labour force, and their numbers continue to rise.[1] Members of designated
groups entering Canada's labour pool constitute a vital resource, and their full participation in the workplace will be fundamental to an organization's ability to understand and respond to the needs of a rapidly changing marketplace. As a society, we
have moved beyond principle to imperative in ensuring equal access to employment
opportunities.

By definition, equity means fairness and impartiality. In a legal sense, it means justice based on the concepts of ethics and fairness and a system of jurisprudence administered by courts and designed mainly to mitigate the rigours of common law. The
implementation of employment equity—or "affirmative action," as it is termed in the
United States—has involved establishing policies and practices designed to ensure

Designated groups
Women, visible minorities, aboriginal peoples, and persons with disabilities who have been disadvantaged in employment

equitable representation in the workforce and to redress past discriminations. There are four **designated groups** in Canada that have not received equitable treatment in employment.

Status of Designated Groups

Women, aboriginal peoples, visible minorities, and people with disabilities face significant (albeit different) disadvantages in employment, even though they make up about 60 percent of Canada's workforce. Some of these disadvantages include high unemployment, occupational segregation, pay inequities, and limited opportunities for career progress.

Women tend to be concentrated in occupations that are accorded lower status and pay. In 2001, women constituted 44.8 percent of the total workforce but were not equally represented in all occupations. Women are under-represented as semi-professionals and technicians; as supervisors in crafts and trades; in skilled crafts and trades; and as other sales and service personnel.[2] Women are also under-represented in management positions and as members of boards. Women cite the top barriers to women's advancement in Highlights in HRM 2.1.

First Nations people constitute roughly 3.3 percent of the population, but in western Canada they will account for a substantial portion of labour market growth. However, many aboriginal people face major barriers to employment, which are often compounded by low educational achievement and lack of job experience, as well as by language and cultural barriers. In urban centres, many aboriginal workers are concentrated in low-paying, unstable employment. Economic self-sufficiency and participation in the economy are seen as essential to aboriginal development. Interestingly, Native values such as cooperation and consensus decision making have become more closely aligned with management approaches.[3] Highlights in HRM 2.2 describes how Manitoba Hydro reaches out to the aboriginal population.

Highlights in HRM 2.1

BARRIERS TO THE ADVANCEMENT OF WOMEN

1. Commitment to personal and family responsibilities
2. Lack of mentoring opportunities
3. Lack of female role models
4. Stereotyping and preconceptions of women's roles and abilities
5. Exclusion from informal networks of communication
6. Failure of senior leaders to assume accountability for women's advancement

Source: A. Tomlinson, "Wall Street Rougher than Bay Street," *Canadian HR Reporter* 15, no. 5 (March 11, 2002): 1 and 14.

Highlights in HRM 2.2

EMPLOYMENT EQUITY VISION AWARD

Human Resources Development Canada awarded Manitoba Hydro the Vision award for creativity and innovation in its employment equity programs. Currently, aboriginal people make up 8.3 percent of Manitoba Hydro's workforce. In northern Manitoba, where there is a greater concentration of aboriginal people, 27.4 percent of the corporation's workforce is aboriginal. The goal is to get the overall corporate representation of aboriginal people up to 10 percent by 2005, and up to 33 percent in the north. The creative ways in which these goals are being reached include the following:

▶ A zero tolerance policy of workplace harassment and discrimination.
▶ An outreach and partnership program with aboriginal organizations to provide information about employment and training opportunities.
▶ Partnerships with postsecondary institutions to provide educational programs and career information and to brand Manitoba Hydro as an employer of choice.
▶ A review of training programs to ensure that there are no systemic barriers.
▶ Systematic recruitment efforts to introduce aboriginals by means of internships, co-op placements, summer employment, and part-time work.

The most successful program is the pre-employment training designed to facilitate the entry of aboriginals into Manitoba Hydro's training programs, which are more like apprenticeship programs. The pre-employment training provides academic upgrading, a rotation through three trades to familiarize candidates with these jobs, and workshops to deal with the concerns and issues about being away from home.

Source: Cheryl Petten, "Manitoba Hydro Recognized for Employment Equity Efforts," *Windspeaker* 20, no. 4 (August 2002): 31.

The unemployment rate for employable people with disabilities is much higher than the national unemployment rate, which was 7.5 percent in 2003. People with disabilities face attitudinal barriers, physical demands that are unrelated to actual job requirements, and inadequate access to the technical and human support systems that would make productive employment possible. Employers seek to redress attitudinal barriers by focusing on abilities, not disabilities.

The visible minority population in Canada experienced a growth rate of 25 percent since the 1996 census, compared to an overall population growth of 4 percent. Visible minority groups vary in their labour force profiles and in their regional distributions. Studies have shown that Latin Americans and Southeast Asians experience lower-than-average incomes, higher rates of unemployment, and reduced access to job interviews, even when they have the same qualifications as other candidates. Systemic barriers that

When looking for employees, employers need to assess abilities.

negatively affect employment for visible minorities include culturally biased aptitude tests, lack of recognition of foreign credentials,
and excessively high language requirements. Recent statistics indicate that although visible minorities—73 percent of whom are
immigrants—tend to be better educated, they also have the
highest unemployment rates.[4] The unemployment rate of recent
immigrants (12.1 percent) was still nearly twice that of the
Canadian-born population (6.4 percent).[5] As such, there are targeted efforts to recruit them to ensure representation.

Figure 2.1 shows the workforce representation of the designated groups in the Canadian labour force. Ethics in HRM
describes some of the issues in employment equity.

Benefits of Employment Equity

Employment equity makes good business sense. It contributes to
the bottom line by broadening the base of qualified individuals
for employment, training, and promotions, and by helping
employers avoid costly human rights complaints. Employment
equity enhances an organization's ability to attract and keep the
best-qualified employees, which results in greater access to a
broader base of skills. It also enhances employee morale by
offering special measures such as flexible work schedules and
work sharing. Finally, it improves the organization's image in the
community.[6]

The Charter of Rights and Freedoms, the federal Canadian
Human Rights Act, and pay equity and employment equity acts
are the governing pieces of legislation dealing with employment
equity.

Figure 2.1	Representation of Designated Groups in the Labour Force	
	REPRESENTATION IN THE CANADIAN POPULATION	**REPRESENTATION IN THE WORKFORCE**
Women	50.85%	44.8%
Aboriginal people	3.3	1.6
People with disabilities	12.4	2.3
Members of visible minorities	13.4	11.7

Source: Statistics Canada website: http://www.statcan.ca/english/Pgdb/labor20a.htm, table 282-0002.

Ethics in HRM

ETHICS: EQUALITY OR EQUITY

The federal Department of Fisheries ran an ad on the government's website that stated explicitly that those who can apply are "persons working or residing in Canada and Canadian citizens living abroad, who are members of the visible minority groups." The Employment Equity Act defines visible minorities as being persons, other than aboriginal peoples, who are non-Caucasian in race or non-white in colour. The decision to restrict applicants to visible minorities is part of the government's efforts to have its employees look more like the Canadian population. About 14 percent of Canadians identify themselves as visible minorities, and they represent about 9 percent of the labour market. However, only 7 percent work in the public service. Therefore, the government decreed that about 3 percent of job postings would be restricted to visible minorities. Unlike the Americans, quotas are not in place. But words such as benchmarks, targets, and quotas have the same impact. Critics argue that candidates should be judged on merit, not colour. Other programs to increase minority candidates would be better: provide more education and training for minorities or create an office culture that values diversity. The public service has a good track record in increasing the number of francophones and women, and restricted competitions may not be the best route. But the commissioner of the public service counters that treating all people the same way does not always lead to equitable results, and special measures are necessary.

Sources: E. Greenspon, "Don't Apply," *The Globe and Mail*, May 30, 2003: A16; M. Wente, "Whites Need Not Apply," *The Globe and Mail*, May 29, 2003: A21.

THE LEGAL FRAMEWORK

The Charter of Rights and Freedoms

The Constitution Act of 1982, which contains the Canadian Charter of Rights and Freedoms, is the cornerstone of equity legislation. The Charter guarantees some fundamental rights to every Canadian, including these:

- Fundamental freedoms (s. 2) that comprise the standard rights of freedom of speech, press, assembly, association, and religion.
- Democratic rights (ss. 3 to 5), covering franchise rights.
- Mobility rights (s. 6), concerning the right to move freely from province to province for the purposes of residence and/or employment.
- Legal rights (ss. 7 to 14), conferring standard procedural rights in criminal proceedings.

▶ Equality rights (s. 15), guaranteeing no discrimination by law on grounds of race, ethnic origin, colour, religion, sex, age, or mental and physical ability.

▶ Language rights (ss. 16 to 23).[7]

Although the Charter has offered many Canadians opportunities with regard to their own individual rights and responsibilities, it has also been a source of disappointment. The enactment of the Charter created high expectations on the part of various groups, especially unions, which believed that under Section 2 all employees would have a fundamental right to associate, to bargain collectively, and to strike. However, in 1987 the Supreme Court of Canada, in ruling on a challenge to federal public-sector laws relating to compulsory arbitration, back-to-work legislation, and wage restraint legislation, declared that Section 2 of the Charter does not include the right to bargain collectively and to strike. In the Court's view, these were not fundamental freedoms, but rather statutory rights created and regulated by legislation. As a result of this ruling, governments can weaken the collective bargaining process by limiting salary increases, legislating strikers back to work, and imposing compulsory arbitration.

Canadian Human Rights Act (CHRA)

The Canadian Human Rights Act was passed by Parliament on July 14, 1977, and became effective in March 1978. This act proclaims that

> every individual should have an equal opportunity with other individuals to make for himself or herself the life that he or she is able and wishes to have, consistent with his or her duties and obligations as a member of society, without being hindered in or prevented from doing so by discriminatory practices based on race, national or ethnic origin, colour, religion, age, sex or marital status, or convictions for an offence for which a pardon has been granted or by discriminatory employment practices based on physical handicap.[8]

The act applies to all federal government departments and agencies, to Crown corporations, and to other businesses and industries under federal jurisdiction, such as banks, airlines, railway companies, and insurance and communications companies.

For those areas not under federal jurisdiction, protection is available under provincial human rights laws. Provincial laws, although very similar to federal ones, do differ from province to province. Every province and territory has a human rights act (or code), and each has jurisdiction prohibiting discrimination in the workplace.

The prohibited grounds of discrimination in employment include race, religion, sex, age, national or ethnic origin, physical handicap, and marital status (see Figure 2.2 for a complete listing). Employers are permitted to discriminate if employment preferences are based on a **bona fide occupational qualification (BFOQ)** or BFOR (bona fide occupational requirement). A BFOQ is justified if the employer can establish necessity for business operations. In other words, differential treatment is not discrimination if there is a justifiable reason. For example, adherence to the tenets of the Roman Catholic Church was deemed a BFOQ for employment as a teacher in a Roman Catholic school.[9] Business necessity also relates to the safe and efficient operation of an organization. There is an ongoing debate as to whether male guards should be allowed to work in women's prisons.

Bona fide occupational qualification (BFOQ)
A justifiable reason for discrimination based on business reasons of safety or effectiveness

Figure 2.2 | Prohibited Grounds of Discrimination in Employment by Jurisdiction

	Federal	BC	AB	SK	MB	ON	QC	NB	PE	NS	NL	NT	YK
Race or colour	•	•	•	•	•	•	•	•	•	•	•	•	•
Religion	•	•	•	•	•	•	•	•	•	•	•	•	•
Age	•	•	•	•	•	•	•	•	•	•	•	•	•
Sex	•	•	•	•	•	•	•	•	•	•	•	•	•
Marital status	•	•	•	•	•	•	•	•	•	•	•	•	•
Physical/mental disability	•	•	•	•	•	•	•	•	•	•	•	•	•
Sexual orientation	•	•		•	•	•	•	•	•	•	•		•
National or ethnic origin*	•			•	•	•	•	•	•	•	•	•	•
Family status	•	•		•	•	•	•		•	•	•	•	•
Dependence on alcohol or drugs	•	•	•	•	•	•	•	•	•	•			
Ancestry or place of origin		•	•	•	•	•		•				•	•
Political belief		•			•		•		•	•	•		•
Based on association					•	•		•	•	•			•
Pardoned conviction	•	•				•	•					•	
Record of criminal conviction		•					•		•				•
Source of income			•	•	•		•		•	•			
Assignment, attachment, or seizure of pay											•		
Social condition/origin							•				•		
Language						•	•						•

Source: Copyright © The Canadian Human Rights Commission, "Prohibited Grounds of Employment Discrimination in Jurisdictions Across Canada," 1993. Reproduced with the permission of the Minister of Public Works and Government Services Canada, 2003.

Enforcement of the Canadian Human Rights Act

The Canadian Human Rights Commission (CHRC) deals with complaints concerning discriminatory practices covered by the Canadian Human Rights Act. The

CHRC may choose to act on its own if it feels that sufficient grounds exist for a finding of discrimination. It also has the power to issue guidelines interpreting the act.

Individuals have a right to file a complaint if they feel they have been discriminated against. (The CHRC may refuse to accept a complaint if it has not been filed within a prescribed period of time, if it is deemed trivial, or if it was filed in bad faith.) The complainant must first complete a written report describing the discriminatory action. A CHRC representative reviews the facts and determines whether the claim is legitimate. Once a complaint has been accepted by the CHRC, an investigator is assigned the task of gathering more facts from both the complainant and the accused. The investigator then submits a report to the CHRC recommending a finding of either substantiation or nonsubstantiation of the allegation. If the allegation is substantiated, a settlement may be arranged in the course of the investigation. If the parties are unable to reach agreement, a human rights tribunal consisting of up to three members may be appointed to further investigate the complaint. If the tribunal finds that a discriminatory practice did take place, or that the victim's feelings or self-respect have suffered as a result of the practice, it may order the person or organization responsible to compensate the victim. Former employees of Majestic Electronics received $300 000 in compensation because they were harassed after they refused to obey the racist and sexist orders of the company president.[10]

Any person who obstructs an investigation or a tribunal, or who fails to comply with the terms of a settlement, can be found guilty of an offence, which may be punishable by a fine and/or jail sentence. If the guilty party is an employer or an employee organization, the fine can be as high as $50 000 (up to $5000 for individuals).[11]

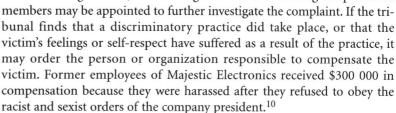

The Canadian Human Rights Commission (www.chrc-ccdp.ca) deals with complaints concerning discriminatory practices covered by legislation. This site includes a summary of the duty to accommodate:

www.chrc-ccdp.ca/ee/bfe-eso.asp

The Enforcement of Provincial Human Rights Laws

Provincial human rights laws are enforced in a manner very similar to that of the federal system. At the provincial level, the employers tend to be small and medium-sized businesses, many of which lack an HR professional who is knowledgeable about human rights legislation. Employers and employees alike may have little experience in matters of discrimination.

The majority of cases are resolved at the investigation stage. If no agreement can be reached, the case is presented to the province's human rights commission. The members of the commission study the evidence and then submit a report to the minister in charge of administering human rights legislation. The minister may appoint an independent board of inquiry, which has powers similar to those of a tribunal at the federal level. Failure to comply with the remedies prescribed by the board of inquiry may result in prosecution in provincial court. Individuals may be fined between $500 and $1000, and organizations or groups between $1000 and $10 000. These levies vary from province to province.

PAY EQUITY

objective **3**

As a result of a 1978 amendment to the Canadian Human Rights Act, pay equity became enacted as law. Pay equity law makes it illegal for employers to discriminate against individuals on the basis of job content. The goal of pay equity is to eliminate the historical wage gap between men and women and to ensure that salary ranges reflect the value of the work performed. In 2002, women aged fifteen and over who had employment income made 79.3 cents for every $1 earned by their male counterparts (the gap was smaller for younger women).[12]

By definition, pay equity means equal pay for work of equal value. It is based on two principles. The *first* is equal pay for equal work.[13] Male and female workers must be paid the same wage rate for doing identical work. The *second* is equal pay for similar or substantially similar work (equal pay for work of comparable worth). This means that male and female workers must be paid the same wage rate for jobs of a similar nature that may have different titles (e.g., "nurse's aide" and "orderly").

Implementation of pay equity is based on comparing the work of female-dominated job classes to the value of work performed by males. Comparisons require the use of a gender-neutral, unbiased comparison system to evaluate the jobs in an establishment.[14] Comparisons must be based on the amount and type of skill, effort, and responsibility needed to perform the job and on the working conditions where it is performed. The comparison must be done in such a way that the characteristics of "male" jobs, such as heavy lifting and "dirty" working conditions, are valued fairly in comparison to the characteristics of "female" jobs, such as manual dexterity and caring for others.[15]

The federal pay equity legislation applies to that section of the workforce under its jurisdiction and covers all organizations regardless of number of employees. The federal pay equity system is complaint-based, meaning that complaints can be raised by an employee, a group of employees, or a bargaining agent.[16] A more comprehensive review of pay equity is provided in Chapter 9.

AN ACT RESPECTING EMPLOYMENT EQUITY (FEDERALLY REGULATED COMPANIES)

objective **4**

The Royal Commission on Equality in Employment (Abella Commission), chaired by then Ontario judge Rosalie Silberman Abella, reviewed the employment practices of federal Crown and government-owned corporations.[17] Its report, tabled in 1984, made recommendations on how four traditionally disadvantaged groups—women, aboriginal peoples, members of visible minorities, and people with disabilities—could be brought into the mainstream of Canada's labour force. The report recommended that legislation be enacted to cover all federally regulated employers and urged provincial governments to consider developing compatible legislation. To reach employees who did not fall under federal jurisdiction, the report further recommended that a contract compliance program be included for organizations that did business with the federal government.

The Abella Commission also stressed that data collection and reporting should be an important component of compliance, since the success of an employment equity program would be measured by results. Data were to be collected on new hires, promotions, terminations, layoffs, part-time work, and other conditions of employment. Also recommended were enforceable requirements and the creation of an independent, well-resourced overseer.

In response to the findings of the Abella Commission, the federal government introduced the Employment Equity Act in 1986. It was updated in 1995.

The Employment Equity Act (1995)

Employers and Crown corporations that have 100 employees or more and that are regulated under the Canada Labour Code must implement employment equity and report on their results. Under the act, the employer is required to

▶ provide its employees with a questionnaire that allows them to indicate whether they belong to one of the four designated groups;

▶ identify jobs in which the percentage of members of designated groups falls below their availability in the labour market;

▶ communicate information on employment equity to its employees, and consult and collaborate with employee representatives;

▶ identify possible barriers in existing employment systems that may be limiting the employment opportunities of members of designated groups;

▶ develop an employment equity plan aimed at promoting an equitable workplace;

▶ make all reasonable efforts to implement its plan;

▶ monitor, review, and revise its plan from time to time; *and*

▶ prepare an annual report on its employment equity data and activities.[18]

The concept of employment equity is rooted in the wording of federal and provincial employment standards legislation, human rights codes, and the Canadian Charter of Rights and Freedoms. Employment equity involves identifying and removing systemic barriers to employment opportunities that adversely affect women, visible minorities, aboriginal peoples, and people with disabilities. Employment equity also involves implementing special measures and making reasonable accommodation. The purpose of the act is further defined under Section 2:

> To achieve equality in the workplace so that no person shall be denied employment opportunities or benefits for reasons unrelated to ability and in the fulfilment of that goal, to correct the conditions of disadvantage in employment experienced by women, Aboriginal peoples, persons with disabilities and visible minorities by giving effect to the principle that employment equity means more than treating persons in the same way but also requires special measures and the accommodation of differences.[19]

Under the Federal Contractors Program (FCP), contractors who bid for goods and services contracts with the federal government valued at $200 000 or more, and who employ 100 persons or more, are required to implement an employment equity program. (For a list of this program's implementation criteria, see Highlights in HRM 2.3.) To assist in the process, the federal government provides professional consulting services to employers throughout Canada regarding how to implement employment equity. Federally regulated employers must conduct a workforce analysis

Highlights in HRM 2.3

IMPLEMENTATION CRITERIA FOR FEDERAL CONTRACTORS PROGRAM

1. Communication by the organization's CEO to employees, unions, and/or employee associations of the commitment to achieve equality in employment through the design and implementation of an employment equity plan.

2. Assignment of senior personnel with responsibility for employment equity.

3. Collection and maintenance of information on the employment status of designated-group employees by occupation and salary levels and with regard to hiring, promotion, and termination in relation to all other employees.

4. Analysis of designated-group representation within the organization in relation to their representation in the supply of qualified workers from which the contractor may reasonably be expected to recruit employees.

5. Elimination or modification of those human resource policies, practices, and systems, whether formal or informal, shown to have or likely to have an unfavourable effect on the employment status of designated-group employees.

6. Establishment of goals for the hiring, training, and promotion of designated-group employees. Such goals will consider projections for hiring, promotions, terminations, lay-offs, recalls, retirements, and, where possible, the projected availability of qualified designated-group members.

7. Establishment of a work plan for reaching each of the goals in 6 above.

8. Adoption of special measures where necessary to ensure that goals are achieved, including the provision of reasonable accommodation as required.

9. Establishment of a climate favourable to the successful integration of designated-group members within the organization.

10. Adoption of procedures to monitor the progress and results achieved in implementing employment equity.

11. Authorization to allow representatives of the CHRC access to the business premises and to the records noted in 3 above in order to conduct on-site compliance reviews for the purpose of measuring the progress achieved in implementing employment equity.

Source: Reproduced with the permission of the Minister of Public Works and the Government Services Canada, 2003.

to identify under-representation of members of designated groups; review their employment systems, policies, and practices to identify employment barriers; and prepare a plan outlining the steps they will take to remove any identified barriers. Most provinces have similar legislation governing employment equity.

Winners of merit awards for initiatives in employment equity include the Bank of Nova Scotia, for increasing the number of visible minorities in its workforce to

19 percent, and the Saskatchewan Wheat Pool, for its partnerships with the aboriginal community—particularly its investment in an MBA program in Aboriginal Business. In the face of threats to employment equity legislation, employers are showing willingness to keep the practice alive. As Robert Rochon, director of employment equity for National Grocer Co., puts it: "Regardless of any legislative requirement, [employment equity] is a good business decision for us. When you consider the changing face of Canada, it just makes good business sense to reflect the customers that you serve."[20]

Administration and Enforcement of the Employment Equity Act

Human Resources Development Canada is responsible for administering the Federal Contractors Program. The Canadian Human Rights Commission is mandated under the Canadian Human Rights Act[21] to prohibit discrimination in the establishments of federally regulated businesses.[22]

The CHRC is authorized to conduct on-site compliance reviews. Failure to comply may result in fines ranging from $10 000 for first offenders to $50 000 for repeat offenders.

THE IMPLEMENTATION OF EMPLOYMENT EQUITY IN ORGANIZATIONS

The implementation of employment equity in an organization follows the precepts of any change management program. Thus, successful implementation must employ strategic planning, which must be incorporated into an overall business strategy. The Federal Contractors Program outlined in Highlights in HRM 2.3 provides a good overview of what a plan should incorporate. The process involves six main steps: senior management commitment; data collection and analysis; employment systems review; establishment of a work plan; implementation; and a follow-up process that includes evaluation, monitoring, and revision.

Step 1: Senior Management Commitment

Commitment to an employment equity plan necessitates a top-down strategy. A more supportive culture is created when the CEO or owner–operator publicly introduces written policy describing the organization's commitment to employment equity. This policy must be strategically posted throughout the organization and sent to each employee.

An employment equity policy statement may raise many questions, so it is important to be thorough in this process in order to keep concerns to a minimum. The policy statement should be supplemented with a communiqué explaining what employment equity is, the rationale for the program, and its implications for current and future employees. Assurances must be given at this time that all information provided will be treated confidentially and will not be used to identify individuals other than for the purpose of employment equity program activities. The communiqué should also list the names of persons responsible for administering the program and outline any planned activities the employer may deem necessary to establish the program (e.g., analysis of the workforce or of policies and procedures).

This commitment to employees and candidates for employment applies to all aspects of the employment relationship, including recruitment, work assignment, training opportunities, compensation, promotions, transfers, and terminations.

Communication tools may include periodic information sessions, workplace posters, departmental or small-group meetings conducted by line management, orientation and training programs, newsletters, and vehicles such as videos, brochures, employee handbooks, and memos from the union. An innovative approach to communications was taken at the Centre de recherche industrielle du Québec (CRIQ), where employees decided to create a video to demonstrate that seemingly harmless comments and attitudes can have devastating consequences for members of designated groups. Their goal was to sensitize people without lecturing or pointing fingers. The employees acted in the video, selected its music, and directed and produced it. Its title was *Moi ... des préjugés?* (*Me ... prejudiced?*). The video depicts the experiences of a Black man, a person who is deaf, and a woman, all of whom are seeking employment with a company, and who are confronted with opinions and attitudes that have everything to do with prejudice and nothing to do with the requirements of the job.[23]

Assignment of Accountable Senior Staff

Senior management must place the responsibility for employment equity in the hands of a senior manager, a joint labour–management committee, and an employment equity advisory committee with mechanisms for union consultation (or, in nonunionized settings, for consultation with designated employee representatives). They must designate line management responsibility and accountability. Anyone given responsibility for employment equity must be knowledgeable about the problems and concerns of designated groups; have the status and ability needed to gain the cooperation of employees at all levels in the organization; have access to financial and human resources required to conduct planning and implementation functions; have sufficient time to devote to employment equity issues; monitor and be in a position to report to the CEO on the results of employment equity measures; and be prepared to serve as the employment equity contact person with federal and provincial government agencies.

Among the employment areas committee members may be required to review are employment practices, advertising and recruitment policies, company-sponsored training, the organization of work schedules and facilities, and systems for promotion to management positions. While committees are usually given responsibility for making recommendations and reporting on issues, ultimate authority generally rests with senior management.

Employers covered by the Employment Equity Act are legally obligated to consult with designated employee representatives or, in unionized settings, with bargaining agents. Consultation means that the employer must supply sufficient information and opportunity to employee representatives or bargaining agents to enable them to ask questions and submit advice on the implementation of employment equity.

The labour movement in Canada generally supports the concept of employment equity, so long as unions are fully informed and involved from the beginning with respect to an employer's planning process. This makes sense considering that unions are the legitimate representatives of employee interests in unionized settings. Supportive mechanisms for achieving employment equity have been reported by Human Resources Development Canada.[24] Many employers and unions have successfully negotiated family-friendly policies such as parental leave, child care provisions, and flexible hours.

Step 2: Data Collection and Analysis

The development of an internal workforce profile is an important tool in employment equity planning. Without this information an organization would not be able to determine where it stands relative to the internal and external workforce. Profiles must be based on both stock data and flow data. **Stock data** provide a snapshot of the organization. They show where members of designated groups are employed in the organization, at what salaries and status, and in what occupations on a particular date. **Flow data** refer to the distribution of designated groups in applications, interviews, hiring decisions, training and promotion opportunities, and terminations. They provide information on the movement of employees into and through the organization. Computerized reporting systems and tracking software are available from Human Resources Development Canada to assist employers in gathering, reporting, and analyzing their internal workforce data.

Most of the information necessary for equity planning (e.g., salary, sex, access to benefits, seniority status, occupational and career history within the organization) is contained in existing personnel files. Information pertaining to the distribution of members of designated groups in the employer's organization must be accumulated by the employer through a self-identification process. Under the Employment Equity Act, employers may gather data on members of designated groups as long as employees voluntarily agree to be identified or identify themselves as members of designated groups, and as long as the data are used only for employment equity planning or reporting purposes.

Stock data
Data showing the status of designated groups in occupational categories and compensation level

Flow data
Data that provide a profile of the employment decisions affecting designated groups

First Nations University is a unique university in Canada that caters to the advanced education needs of Aboriginals.

COURTESY OF FIRST NATIONS UNIVERSITY OF CANADA

Creating a climate of trust in the management of the program is a major challenge. Employers can encourage participation and confidence in the program by providing focused employment equity training to managers and by providing opportunities for managers to be recognized for their contributions to the development and administration of effective employment equity strategies. Companies such as Pratt & Whitney have introduced equity and diversity training for their supervisors. Cameco Corporation in northern Saskatchewan has committed to improving the job prospects of aboriginals as part of its long-term employment strategy, based on economics, not just a keen sense of social responsibility. Mentoring, basic training, educational support, and family assistance programs mean a lot to those employees who may be the first in their families to have full-time paid employment.[25]

If an employer administers a self-identification questionnaire, confidentiality and a clear commitment at senior levels to the concept of employment equity should be communicated. Having employees self-identify is crucial to the success of the program, but problems may arise with self-identification. Under some provincial employment equity acts, terms such as "aboriginal" and "racial minority" are not defined. Some employees, who have "hidden" disabilities such as epilepsy or partial deafness, may not wish to label themselves for fear of future discriminatory treatment. Some minorities, such as aboriginals, have never disclosed their ethnic origins for similar reasons.

If too many employees with nonvisible disabilities do not identify themselves as disabled, the program could end up being designed to recruit more employees with disabilities, leaving another segment of the employee population under-represented. Thus, because inaccurate data were accumulated on one group, the other group will not benefit from the employment equity efforts. An additional concern is that individuals with disabilities may need some form of accommodation to help them perform their jobs better. If they do not self-identify, they have denied themselves certain basic rights. Highlights in HRM 2.4 outlines words and actions which are appropriate in dealing with persons with disabilities.

A self-identification form should contain the following:

▶ An explanation of the employer's employment equity policy, the purpose of the employment equity program, and the need for the information requested.
▶ An indication that the information supplied will be confidential and will be used only for employment equity purposes by those persons identified as responsible for the program.
▶ The categories for self-identification, with brief explanations and examples.
▶ An indication that the form has been reviewed by the relevant human rights agency.
▶ Space for comments and suggestions.
▶ The name of the contact person for information and suggestions.[26]

Once the personal information forms have been completed, all occupations within the organization must be cross-referenced to the National Occupational Classification (NOC)—formerly the Standard Occupational Classification (SOC). This manual was created by Statistics Canada for use in statistical surveys and for other purposes. Personal data are organized under the four-digit NOC classifications. When building a workforce profile, employers should first refer to the four-digit unit groups and then determine which one each job belongs in. For example, secretaries and stenographers

Highlights in HRM 2.4

SUGGESTIONS FOR INCLUSION

Person who is blind, or person with a visual impairment
Identify yourself and anyone with you; if you have met before, explain the context of the meeting; speak in a normal tone of voice and indicate to whom you are speaking if in a group; remove obstacles; describe the surroundings ("There is a door on your right"); if offering to guide, ask the person to take your arm above the elbow and walk about a half-step ahead; plan ahead to obtain material in audio cassettes or Braille.

Person with a physical disability or person with a mobility impairment
Re-arrange furniture or objects to accommodate a wheelchair or other mobility aids; avoid leaning on a mobility aid; push someone in a wheelchair only when asked; give directions that include distance and physical objects such as curbs.

Person who is deaf, deafened, or person with a hearing impairment
Speak clearly and at a pace that allows the sign language interpreter to interpret and to allow for questions; write notes or use gestures for one-on-one discussions; face the person to facilitate lip-reading; speak clearly, slowly, and directly to the person, not the interpreter; reduce or eliminate background noise.

Person who is unable to speak, or person with a speech impairment; person with a learning, developmental or psychiatric disability
When needed, offer assistance and provide guidance, repeat information when necessary, speak directly to the person and listen actively.

Sources: Treasury Board of Canada Secretariat, *Creating a Welcoming Workplace for Employees with Disabilities*; David Brown, "Focus on Ability not Disability," *Canadian HR Reporter* 13, no. 22 (December 18, 2000): 12.

Underutilization
Term applied to designated groups that are not utilized or represented in the employer's workforce proportional to their numbers in the labour market

Concentration
Term applied to designated groups whose numbers in a particular occupation or level are high relative to their numbers in the labour market

are classified in unit group 4111, which in turn can be assigned to the "clerical workers" group.

A full workforce analysis can be generated once all the information has been loaded and the reports are complete. This utilization analysis will include a distribution of members of designated groups according to occupations and salary levels throughout the organization. Comparisons will show which designated groups exhibit **underutilization** and which groups exhibit **concentration** in specific occupations or levels, in proportion to their numbers in the labour market.[27]

Step 3: Employment Systems Review

"Employment systems" or "employment practices" are the means by which employers carry out such personnel activities as recruitment, hiring, training and development, promotion, job classification, discipline, and termination. Some of these practices are found in personnel manuals and collective agreements, while others remain more informal and based on traditional practices.

An important legal principle is that employers are accountable even when discrimination is the unintended result of employment systems that block the progress of particular groups of employees or potential employees for reasons unrelated to qualifications, merit, or business requirements. This unintentional discrimination is referred to as systemic discrimination.

Systemic Barriers in Employment Practices

Systemic discrimination refers to the exclusion of members of certain groups through the application of employment policies or practices based on criteria that are neither job-related nor required for the safe and efficient operation of the business. Systemic discrimination can create legal concerns for an organization. Many employment barriers are hidden, unintentionally, in the rules and the procedures and even the facilities that employers provide to manage their human resources. (See Figure 2.3 for examples of systemic barriers, along with possible solutions.) Inequity can result if these barriers encourage or discourage individuals based on their membership in certain groups rather than on their ability to do a job that the employer needs done. In one case, the Supreme Court of Canada ruled that a physical fitness test discriminated against women and required the employer to re-instate the woman as a firefighter.[28]

Another example of systemic discrimination occurs when an employer's workforce represents one group in our society and the company recruits new employees by

Systemic discrimination
The exclusion of members of certain groups through the application of employment policies or practices based on criteria that are not job-related

Figure 2.3	Employment Practices

Examples of Systemic Barriers

1. Recruitment practices that limit applications from designated groups, e.g., word of mouth, internal hiring policies.

2. Physical access that restricts those who are mobility impaired, e.g., no ramps, heavy doors, narrow passageways.

3. Job descriptions and job evaluation systems that undervalue the work of positions traditionally held by women.

4. A workplace environment that does not expressly discourage sexual or racial harassment.

Examples of Possible Solutions

1. Word of mouth could be supplemented by calls to community organizations representing designated groups or to the local Canada Employment Centre.

2. Facility upgrading.

3. Rewrite job descriptions, rationalize evaluation systems, provide special training for supervisors.

4. Issue a company policy against these practices, with guidelines and follow-up through appraisal and discipline procedures, and develop complaint and problem-solving mechanisms for an employee to use.

Source: *Employment Equity: A Guide for Employers,* Employment and Immigration Canada, Cat. No. 143-5-91, May 1991, p. 19. Reproduced with permission from the Minister of Supply and Services, 1995.

posting job vacancies within the company or by word of mouth among the employees. This recruitment strategy is likely to generate candidates similar to those in the current workforce, thereby unintentionally discriminating against other groups of workers in the labour market. A better approach might be to vary recruitment methods by contacting outside agencies and organizations. The Toronto Police Force has established an eight-member recruitment task force to boost its community representation, in part by educating visible minority groups about career opportunities in the force.[29]

The following employment practices and issues may need to be reviewed: job classifications and descriptions, recruitment processes, training and development, performance evaluation systems, promotions and upward mobility, levels of compensation, access to benefits, termination processes, discipline procedures, facilities (i.e., building design, barrier-free access), and access to assistance.

The usual test for identifying systemic barriers involves using the following criteria to assess the policy:

▶ Is it job-related?
▶ Is it valid? (i.e., does it, or the required qualification, have a direct relationship to job performance?)
▶ Is it consistently applied?
▶ Does it have an adverse impact? (i.e., does it affect members of designated groups more than those of dominant groups?)
▶ Is it a business necessity?
▶ Does it conform to human rights and employment standards legislation?[30]

If the employee profiles indicate that certain types of people are under-represented, then special measures may be undertaken to correct this imbalance.

Special Measures and Reasonable Accommodation

Special measures are initiatives designed to accelerate the entry, development, and promotion of members of designated groups from among the interested and qualified workforce. For example, some special measures may include targeted recruitment or special training initiatives aimed mainly at correcting, over a specified period of time, employment inequities stemming from past discrimination. These measures are intended to hasten the achievement of fair representation of the four designated groups in an employer's workforce. Highlights in HRM 2.5 describes the special measures used by the federal government.

Reasonable accommodation involves adjusting employment policies and practices so that no individual is denied benefits, disadvantaged with respect to employment opportunities, or blocked from carrying out the essential components of a job because of race, colour, sex, or disability. Human rights tribunals across Canada have placed employers under a duty to demonstrate a degree of flexibility in meeting the reasonable needs of employees. It is no longer acceptable for employers to simply assume that all employees will "fit in" no matter what their special needs. Employers must find the means to alter systems to meet the needs of their employees as long as this does not cause "undue hardship to the employer." Reasonable accommodation may include redesigning job duties, adjusting work schedules, providing technical, financial, and human support services, and upgrading facilities. The City of Toronto developed

Reasonable accommodation
Attempt by employers to adjust the working conditions or schedules of employees with disabilities or religious preference

Highlights in HRM 2.5

PARTICIPATION IN THE FEDERAL PUBLIC SERVICE

The goals of the Employment Equity program in the federal government are to

▶ establish a workforce of qualified employees that reflects the diversity of the Canadian population which they serve,

▶ ensure equal access to job opportunities,

▶ correct conditions that have historically impeded the full participation of designated groups.

Discussions with Aloma Lawrence, Chief Employment Equity Advisor of the Public Service Commission, indicated that although visible minorities represented 8.7 percent of the labour force, they represented only 6.8 percent of the federal employee population in 2002. To accomplish the EE goals, the Public Service Commission has established a number of special measures, which include the following:

▶ Outreach: The recruiting teams of the federal government have established a visible presence within the visible minority communities. Through contacts with visible minority associations, such as the Association of Black Law Enforcers, recruiters make presentations and hold information sessions about the recruitment processes used by the federal government to fill jobs. Recruiters talk about the structured interviews and tests, procedures that may be unfamiliar to visible minority candidates.

▶ Creation of specific tools: The brochure "So You're Thinking of Working for the Federal Government" was developed specifically for the visible minority communities. Workshops that explain the types of tests used, such as the managerial in-basket or the written communications test, are held within these communities. The Public Service Commission has also introduced tools for use by managers and human resources professionals in developing and implementing employment equity strategies and approaches. New tools include "Improving Employment Equity Representation: Tips and Tools," "Guidelines for Assessing Persons with Disabilities," and "Guidelines for Fair Assessment in a Diverse Workplace."

▶ Composition of recruitment teams: An effort was made to place visible minorities on the recruitment teams, particularly because selection decisions could be made on perceptions of "fit," and culture plays a large role in this. In 2002, the PSC established an inventory of 100 visible minorities, trained in interviewing processes, who were invited by managers to sit on selection boards. The federal government, like other public sector employers, has been finding it difficult to recruit visible minorities in areas of law enforcement, such as correctional officers. However, building relationships with visible minority communities is beginning to result in greater interest in federal government jobs.

Is the process working? Yes; the number of visible minorities working in the federal public service has increased from 5.9 percent in 2001 to 6.8 percent in 2002. Career development is vital to the retention of good employees, and in 2001 the PSC launched a career assignment program for visible minorities. Because visible minorities represent only 4.1 percent of the executive group, for example, the Career Assignment Program develops participants for executive level positions. The ultimate goal is to match participation rates in the labour market. However, with the special measures adopted by the PSC, progress is slow but certain.

award-winning facilities in its Barrier Free Access program, which was designed to allow people with disabilities accessible passage throughout city facilities. The Canadian military has adopted a policy that allows Native service men to wear their hair in traditional braids.

Highlights in HRM 2.6 recounts several court cases on accommodation.

Reasonable accommodation benefits all employees. When a company provides compensation for child care expenses for employees taking company-sponsored courses it does more than remove a barrier to women; it also assists any employee with sole-parenting responsibilities. The flexible work schedules adopted by some companies in northern Canada benefit aboriginal employees, who are prepared to work

Highlights in HRM 2.6

THE DUTY TO ACCOMMODATE

▶ Two employees of the Ford Motor Company of Oakville, Ontario, became members of a religious group that observed its Sabbath from Friday sunset to Saturday sunset. Both employees were required to work two Friday nights out of four, which they refused to do. They tried, but failed, to make alternative arrangements with other workers. They were disciplined and ultimately terminated for unauthorized absenteeism. After a seventy-one-day hearing, the Human Rights Commission decided it would constitute undue hardship on Ford to accommodate the religious absences of these employees.

▶ The Ontario Human Rights Commission found that the City of Ancaster, Ontario, had discriminated against a part-time firefighter when they turned him down for a full-time job because he had partial vision in one eye. As such he was unable to obtain a class F driver's licence, a job requirement for driving ambulances that are driven by firefighters. The tribunal felt that the city should have accommodated him by assigning him to firefighter duties exclusively.

Sources: D. Brown, "Law Takes Tough Stand on Accommodation," *Canadian HR Reporter* 14, no. 4 (February 26, 2001): 1 and 5; P. Israel, "How Far Does an Employer Have to Go to Accommodate Religious Beliefs?" *Canadian HR Reporter* 15, no. 22 (December 16, 2002): 5.

atypical hours in exchange for significant breaks away from the work site to take part in traditional hunting and fishing activities. Many other employees also benefit from these flexible work schedules.

Special arrangements should be made to accommodate people who are visually impaired, illiterate, or unfamiliar with the English language by using tools such as Braille forms, confidential interviews, or translation. Suggestions for an accessible workplace are found in Figure 2.4.

Step 4: Establishment of a Workplan

The workforce analysis and the review of employment systems will provide the employer with a useful base from which to develop a workplan with realistic goals and timetables. A narrative statement or summary of the conclusions drawn from the examination of the workforce analysis forms part of the employment equity workplan.

Figure 2.4	Suggestions for an Accessible Workplace

- Install easy-to-reach switches.
- Provide sloping sidewalks and entrances.
- Install wheelchair ramps.
- Reposition shelves so materials are easy to reach.
- Rearrange tables, chairs, vending machines, dispensers, and other furniture and fixtures.
- Widen doors and hallways.
- Add raised markings on control buttons.
- Provide designated accessible parking spaces.
- Install hand controls or manipulation devices.
- Provide flashing alarm lights.
- Remove turnstiles and revolving doors or provide alternative accessible paths.
- Install holding bars in toilet areas.
- Redesign toilet partitions to increase access space.
- Add paper cup dispensers at water fountains.
- Replace high-pile, low-density carpeting.
- Reposition telephones, water fountains, and other needed equipment.
- Add raised toilet seats.
- Provide a full-length bathroom mirror.

Source: Statistics Canada website: http://www.statcan.ca/english/Pgdb/labor20a.htm, table 282-0002.

The summary should include any restrictions faced in hiring due to collective agreements, staff movements, or the need for specialized skills in a particular profession. The identification of restrictions helps form an overall employment equity strategy.

The plan should be considered a working tool designed to achieve results. It is a document that describes how proposed actions are to be achieved. The plan should be an integral part of the organization's overall operational plans, and must include

- numerical goals with time frames (numerical goals can be expressed in numbers—for example, 42 percent of our personnel should be women);
- explanations about the proposed improvement in the hiring, training, and promotion of the four designated groups to increase their representation and improve their distribution throughout the organization;
- descriptions of specific activities to achieve the numerical goals; and
- an outline of monitoring and evaluation procedures to follow program implementation.

Numerical goals must be realistic numbers related to the workforce analysis. The goals must catalogue opportunities for hiring, training, and promotion, and must demonstrate a valid effort to correct under-representation or concentration of all designated groups in specific occupations or occupational categories. Non-numerical goals include activities such as implementation of barrier-free design, targeted recruitment and advertising, modification of employment policies or practices, and provision of developmental training.

The overall goal for an organization is to achieve a representative workforce. An organization's workforce is representative when it reflects the demographic composition of the external workforce. A nonrepresentative workforce is an indicator of the need for evaluation and action to remove the barriers that block or discourage certain groups from employment and advancement. Workplan initiatives in conjunction with special measures and reasonable accommodation should contribute to the overall success of this goal.

Step 5: Implementation

The implementation of employment equity is idiosyncratic in that no two plans will be the same. Each strategy should be designed to meet the needs of the particular organization. The success of plan implementation depends on senior management's commitment to the process, how the roles and responsibilities are defined, what resources are available, the effectiveness of the communications strategy, the acceptance of plan initiatives and objectives, and the availability of training. The plan, in essence a living document, will be affected by the changes in the internal and external environment throughout the implementation period. Therefore, its strategies may be modified or eliminated when results are not achieved or if resource restraints or economic conditions necessitate a different strategy. The implementation is guided and monitored by those responsible and accountable for its outcome.

Step 6: Evaluation, Monitoring, and Revision

By monitoring progress, the employer will be able to evaluate the overall success of the equity initiatives used to achieve a representative workforce, as well as respond to organizational and environmental changes. Annual progress reports provided to all employees communicate initiatives and achievements. Interim reports on special projects heighten program visibility and acceptance; they also promote management commitment and accountability. Research suggests that the wage gaps between white men and the designated groups are closing more rapidly in organizations with formal employment equity programs than in organizations without such programs.[31]

The monitoring activity is an essential component in the planning cycle. Only through monitoring can an employer determine whether goals are being attained and problems resolved, whether new programs are succeeding, and whether strategies have been effective. If the employer finds, upon review of the program, that there are negative results, alterations to the existing plan will have to be made with new goals. In this regard, the planning process is evolutionary, in that the achievement of employment equity involves organizational changes and builds on experience.

SEXUAL HARASSMENT

objective

Sexual harassment
Unwelcome advances, requests for sexual favours, and other verbal or physical conduct of a sexual nature in the working environment

Sexual situations in the work environment are not new to organizational life. Sexual feelings are a part of group dynamics, and people who work together may come to develop these kinds of feelings for one another. Unfortunately, however, often these encounters are unpleasant and unwelcome, as witnessed by the many reported instances of sexual harassment.[32]

According to one study, only four of every ten Canadian women who suffer **sexual harassment** at work take any formal action, and only one out of every two women believes that a complaint would be taken seriously in her workplace.[33] This belief is reinforced by cases such as the one involving a female Sears employee who was shot to death by her manager. Fifteen months earlier, she had complained to her employer that she was being sexually harassed by her manager. The company maintained that his behaviour did not constitute sexual harassment and that he was merely a "persistent pursuer." In keeping with this position, they made no effort to stop the manager's behaviour.[34] Sexual harassment costs, as Highlights in HRM 2.7 shows.

Many organizations are developing policies to deal with sexual harassment in the workplace. Such policies are intended as preventive measures not only against damage to reputation and employee morale, but also against the kind of litigation that Magna International faced when it was sued on the grounds that Magna employees had attempted to win contracts from purchasing officers for the Big Three automakers by wooing them with gifts and entertainment, including trips to topless bars.[35] Some organizations have put policies in place to attempt to deal with the issue. For example, the sexual harassment policy at BC Hydro focuses on avoidance and resolution rather than punishment after the fact. In another organization, the Canadian Armed Forces, 90 000 members have been trained to recognize and avoid harassment of all kinds.

Highlights in HRM 2.8 provides a sample of questions that can be used during a sexual harassment audit. An instrument like this one, which is essentially a test, is a valuable tool for determining what employees know and do not know about sexual harassment.

Highlights in HRM 2.7

THE COST OF SEXUAL HARASSMENT

In 2002, sexual harassment complaints topped the list of complaints heard by provincial human rights commissions; 64 percent of working women say they have experienced some form of sexual harassment throughout their careers (up from 48 percent in the previous year). Harassment affects productivity, retention, morale, turnover, and absenteeism rates. It also affects an employee's self-esteem, home life, and stress levels. Some 48 percent of women executives say they left a job because of inhospitable organizational culture and harassment.

An employee at the Victoria Tea Company in Ontario was found guilty of sexual harassment and ordered to pay the victim $50 600. A supervisor at SkyCable in Brandon, Manitoba, was ordered to pay $100 000 in damages for creating a poisoned work atmosphere. The four women employees testified that the supervisor had made inappropriate remarks, sexual advances, and derogatory comments on an ongoing basis. The poisoned work environment generated by his conduct took a toll on their psychological and physical health and caused them significant pain and suffering. The supervisor's remarks were clearly persistent, repetitious, and serious enough to create a hostile work environment for all the complainants. The Canadian Human Rights Tribunal ruled that the supervisor must compensate four women for lost wages, hurt feelings, and legal costs. But what exactly is sexual harassment? According to Canadian legal cases, the following behaviours define sexual harassment:

▶ Sexually degrading words or remarks used to describe an individual or group;
▶ Inquiries or comments about an individual's sex life;
▶ Sexual flirtations, advances, and propositions;
▶ Demands for sexual favours;
▶ Verbal threats or abuse;
▶ Leering;
▶ Unwanted gestures;
▶ Display of sexually offensive material; and
▶ Sexual assault.

Sources: "Sexual Harassment Endangered Health," *Tribunal OH & S Canada* 18, no. 6 (September 2002): 10; Laura Cassiani, "Sexual Harassment Persists Despite Workplace Fallout," *Canadian HR Reporter* 14, no. 7 (April 9, 2001): 1.

The Ontario Human Rights Code identifies three kinds of sexual harassment:

1. When someone says or does things to you of a sexual nature and you do not want or welcome it. This includes behaviour that a person should know you do not want or welcome. For example, your supervisor makes you feel uncomfortable by talking about sex all the time. The Human Rights Code says that when you show that you do not welcome or want the remarks or actions, the person must stop doing those things right away.

Highlights in HRM 2.8

QUESTIONS ASKED IN AUDITING SEXUAL HARASSMENT

Activity	Is This Sexual Harassment?		Are You Aware of This Behaviour in the Organization?		
▶ Employees post cartoons on bulletin boards containing sexually related material.	Yes	No	Uncertain	Yes	No
▶ A male employee says to a female employee that she has beautiful eyes and hair.	Yes	No	Uncertain	Yes	No
▶ A male manager habitually calls all female employees "sweetie" or "darling."	Yes	No	Uncertain	Yes	No
▶ A manager fails to promote a female employee when she will not grant sexual favours.	Yes	No	Uncertain	Yes	No
▶ Male employees use vulgar language and tell sexual jokes that are overheard by, but not directed at, female employees.	Yes	No	Uncertain	Yes	No
▶ A male employee leans and peers over the back of a female employee when she wears a low-cut dress.	Yes	No	Uncertain	Yes	No
▶ A supervisor gives a female (male) subordinate a nice gift on her (his) birthday.	Yes	No	Uncertain	Yes	No
▶ Two male employees share a sexually explicit magazine while observed by a female employee.	Yes	No	Uncertain	Yes	No

2. A person who has authority or power to deny you something such as a promotion or a raise makes sexual suggestions or requests that you do not want or welcome. For example, your teacher says you must have sex with him or her or you will not pass the course. Even if you do not complain about a sexual suggestion or request, it can still be sexual harassment unless it is clear that you welcome or want it.

3. A person with authority or the power to deny you something important punishes you or threatens to do something to you for refusing a sexual request. For example, your employer fires you, or threatens to fire you, because you refuse to go on a date.

York University has developed a comprehensive program to deal with sexual harassment issues. To augment its program, it has published a booklet titled *Sexual Assault and Harassment on Campus*, which is intended for students and employees. This booklet provides safety tips for women and men as well as definitions of sexual harassment and other forms of harassment.[36] A pamphlet titled *Sexual Harassment and You: What Every Student Should Know* is made available to any interested person. York's policy states:

> York University strives to provide an environment wherein all students, faculty and staff are able to learn, study, teach and work, free from sexual harassment. Sexual harassment is:
>
> 1. Unwanted sexual attention of a persistent or abusive nature, made by a person who knows or ought reasonably to know that such attention is unwanted;
> 2. The making of an implied or express promise of reward for complying with a sexually oriented request;
> 3. The making of an implied or express threat or reprisal, in the form of actual reprisal or in the denial of opportunity, for refusal to comply with a sexually oriented request;
> 4. Sexually oriented remarks and behaviour which may reasonably be perceived to create a negative psychological and emotional environment [sometimes labelled a hostile environment] for work and study.
>
> Incidents of sexual harassment shall be investigated and dealt with by the University in accordance with guidelines and procedures put in place for that purpose from time to time.
>
> Students, faculty and staff who, it is determined, have sexually harassed another member(s) of the University community will be subject to discipline and sanctions as are appropriate in the circumstances, including but not limited to discipline and sanctions provided for in Presidential Regulations (in the case of students), and relevant collective agreements.[37]

For sexual harassment policies to succeed, confidentiality is necessary, and so is a method for filing complaints. Without organizational commitment to zero tolerance with respect to harassment, any such policy will be meaningless. Highlights in HRM 2.9 presents some suggestions for an effective sexual harassment policy.[38]

The concepts of harassment in the workplace are being broadened to include psychological harassment, such as bullying. A new law in Quebec bans psychological harassment, which is defined as any repeated, hostile or unwanted conduct, verbal comments, actions, or gestures that affect an employee's dignity or psychological or physical integrity. This protection, the first of its kind in Canada, requires employers to create policies to prevent this type of harassment. [39]

Highlights in HRM 2.9

BASIC COMPONENTS OF AN EFFECTIVE SEXUAL HARASSMENT POLICY

1. Develop a comprehensive organization-wide policy on sexual harassment and present it to all current and new employees. Stress that sexual harassment will not be tolerated under any circumstances. Emphasis is best achieved when the policy is publicized and supported by top management.
2. Hold training sessions with supervisors to explain their role in providing an environment free of sexual harassment, and proper investigative procedures when charges occur.
3. Establish a formal complaint procedure whereby employees can discuss problems without fear of retaliation. The complaint procedure should spell out how charges will be investigated and resolved.
4. Act immediately when employees complain of sexual harassment. Communicate widely that investigations will be conducted objectively and with appreciation for the sensitivity of the issue.
5. When an investigation supports employee charges, discipline the offender at once. For extremely serious offences, discipline should include penalties up to and including discharge. Discipline should be applied consistently across similar cases and among managers and hourly employees alike.
6. Follow up on all cases to ensure a satisfactory resolution of the problem.

MANAGING DIVERSITY

objective

Diversity management
The optimization of an organization's multicultural workforce in order to reach business objectives

Managing diversity goes beyond Canadian employment equity legislation's four designated groups in addressing the need to create a fair work environment. The terms "diversity management" and "employment equity" are often used interchangeably, but there are differences. **Diversity management** is voluntary; employment equity is not. Managing diversity is a broader, more inclusive concept encompassing such factors as religion, personality, lifestyle, and education. By managing diversity, organizations hope to gain a strategic and competitive advantage by helping all employees perform to their full potential.[40]

The City of Toronto led by example when it recognized "non-Christian City of Toronto staff" by giving them two days of paid time off for religious holidays if they agreed to work Christmas Day and Good Friday (Christian holidays) at straight time.[41] Also, McDonald's Restaurants of Canada used multi-age teams and found the diversity of ages led to a remarkable synergy.[42]

Organizations such as CN, the Bank of Montreal, and Warner-Lambert are pioneers in the diversity movement. According to Marie Tellier, Canadian National's assistant vice-president of employment equity, the hiring and development and good

Chung Kwong Cheung, winner of a contest sponsored by the National Movement for Harmony in Canada to promote racial understanding, was able to capture the essence of the new face of Canada.[45]

COURTESY OF HARMONY MOVEMENT

management of a diverse workforce whose values and expectations are different from their managers is no longer an option—it is an economic necessity. In the context of an increasingly diverse labour force, diversity management is not only a legal obligation, but also a necessity imposed by market laws, by competition, and by the need to be the best to survive.[43]

Statistics show that the ethnocultural profile of Canada has been changing since the 1960s and will continue to change dramatically over the next twenty years. European immigrants who led the first wave of immigrants in the early years of the twentieth century have been surpassed by immigrants from Asia, including the Middle East.[44]

According to the 2001 census, the number of Canadians who were born outside of Canada reached its highest level in seventy years, representing 18.4 percent of the population. The flow of immigrants to Canada has averaged about 1 percent of the population for decades, except during the 1990s when it averaged 0.6 percent to 0.9 percent. Of the 1.8 million immigrants who came to Canada between 1991 and 2001, 58 percent came from Asia, including the Middle East; 20 percent from Europe; 11 percent from the Caribbean and Central and South American; 8 percent from Africa; and 3 percent from the United States.[46] The goal of diversity management is to have the workforce at all levels resemble the population. Interestingly, the first television program celebrating diversity was *Star Trek*, where Lieutenant Uhura (played by African American Nichelle Nichols), Captain Chekov (Russian, played by Walter Konig), and Khan (played by Ricardo Montalban, a Hispanic American) took their places along with the aliens. However, the captain, chief engineer, and chief medical officer were all Caucasians, so even *Star Trek* needed a diversity management program.

CEOs in Canada recognize that ethnic groups possess expertise such as language skills, knowledge of foreign cultures and business practices, and natural trade links with overseas markets that can be used to capture market share in emerging economies and new Canadian markets.[47] Ebco, a manufacturing company in

The Business Case

THE ECONOMIC VALUES OF DIVERSITY

Although employment equity and its partner, employment diversity, were launched on moral grounds, increasingly, these initiatives are sustained on business grounds. The first principle to understand is that members of the designated groups are consumers, and not just potential employees. For example, the purchasing power of persons with disabilities is estimated to be $120 billion. Racial minorities control more than $300 billion of combined purchasing power. Women control 80 percent of the consumer dollars spent in North America.

The second business fundamental is that employees who are members of the designated groups represent an organizational resource that facilitates the understanding and linkages to these markets by helping various departments to understand the lifestyles, consumption needs and wants, purchasing preferences, media usage habits, and brand loyalty of these groups.

Source: B. Siu, "Beyond Quotas: The Business Case for Employment Equity," *Canadian HR Reporter*, June 4, 2001.

Richmond, British Columbia, which has won awards for excellence in race relations, is doing business in Germany and Taiwan because it was able to tap the networks and skills of its employees, who trace their origins to forty-eight different countries. The spending power of these groups is another motivating factor to incorporate them into all levels of the workforce.[48] According to Edgar Ware, ethnocultural business manager at Digital Equipment of Canada, "We have an obligation to the cultural fabric. We want to look like the people we sell to."[49] Digital's goal is to balance a diversity strategy with the organization's business plan.

Besides the moral issues surrounding diversity, there is a critical economic need for Canada to increase its share of world trade and expand its trade portfolio. Our export market is dominated by the United States, Japan, and the United Kingdom. If Canadian business continues to rely heavily on these markets, our export growth and standard of living may not keep pace with other international markets.[50] Third World countries in emerging markets are going to require new investments in infrastructure, public systems, and productive capital. Given the multicultural background of many of its workers, Canada is in an excellent position to provide these services.[51] Canadian companies such as Nortel and SNC-Lavalin have already begun to tap the potential of these emerging markets.

CREATING AN ENVIRONMENT FOR SUCCESS

Transforming an organizational culture into a culture that embraces diversity can be a complex and lengthy process. Diversity initiatives should be taken slowly so that everyone can understand that this change is an evolutionary process and that expec-

tations should be realistic. Individuals must fully understand the time, effort, commitment, and risk involved and the need for a systematic approach.[52]

Leadership is one of the most important variables in an organization's ability to successfully incorporate diversity into its business strategy. In a recent Conference Board of Canada survey, 86 percent of respondents indicated that responsibility rested with human resources.[53] The initiative should not be perceived as a human resources program or policy, but rather as a business imperative. In the words of Prem Benimadhu, vice-president of human resources research for the Conference Board, "Building a racially and culturally diverse workforce has been perceived as a human resources issue. But as long as it is, it's not going to be in the mission statement of organizations."[54] Only 6 percent of firms surveyed by the Conference Board study mentioned ethnic and cultural diversity in their mission statements.

Diversity initiatives should be linked directly to the business objectives and goals of the most senior levels of management. (See Figure 2.5.) Reality Check demonstrates how the BMO Financial Group has woven its program into its organizational fabric.

Organizations seeking to incorporate the value of diversity into their corporate philosophy must make use of appropriate internally and externally focused communications. For example, the National Bank of Canada participates annually in Montreal's La semaine des communautés culturelles, a week dedicated to the celebration of Montreal's multiculturalism. The bank believes that its visible demonstrations of commitment to ethnocultural diversity in the community it serves help raise the bank's profile.[55]

Cross-functional teams established to promote the diversity initiative are used successfully as communication vehicles by many leading-edge organizations. Toronto's Sunnybrook Health Sciences Centre has implemented the Patient Diversity Task Force to examine and report on the barriers faced by its patients, residents, and families.[56] Other organizations seek to raise the awareness of ethnocultural diversity.

Training is essential to the success of diversity implementation. A number of companies, including Imperial Oil and Connaught Laboratories, have incorporated diversity training. Cultural etiquette is an important aspect of diversity training that aims to explain the differences, or diversity, in people.

The Department of National Defence includes diversity training in its basic officer training course.[57] A consortium of European and North American businesses is attempting to develop a global diversity standard, by which companies will be able to use software to rate the success of their diversity programs.[58]

Of even greater importance than training is the need to incorporate elements of diversity into all core training programs and to tailor those elements to meet the needs of specific business units or groups of employees.[59]

An added advantage of implementing a diversity initiative relates to its impact on employee retention. Retention of well-qualified and skilled employees is an important goal, considering the amount of resources—in both time and money—spent on recruiting and hiring new employees. Canadian organizations spend an average of twenty-eight hours recruiting a new management or professional employee,

Figure 2.5 | Managing Diversity—A Strategic Approach

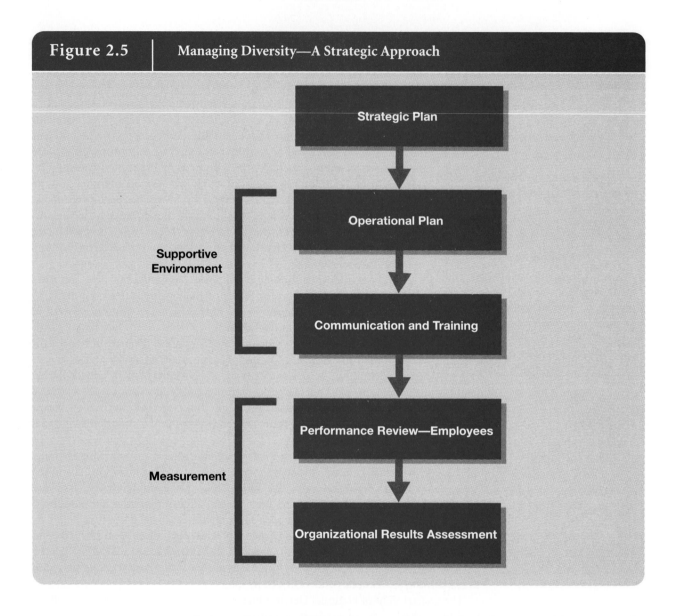

forty-two hours recruiting a new executive, and twenty hours recruiting a new technical/supervisory employee.[60] Maintaining a balanced and diversified workforce during periods of downsizing continues to be a major challenge.

Much the same as is required under employment equity, an overall review of policies and employment practices must be considered. In this regard, the use of an employee attitude survey may prove beneficial in finding areas of systemic or perceived discrimination. The evaluation criteria used most often by Canadian organizations are staff attitudes, increases in promotions for minority employees, reduction in turnover of minority employees, reduction in number of harassment suits, recruitment statistics for minorities, and improvements in productivity.[61]

Reality Check

BMO FINANCIAL GROUP

BMO Financial Group, well known throughout the Canadian marketplace as an exemplary leader in diversity and workplace equity issues, won the Catalyst Award for promoting women's careers. It was the first time a Canadian organization had won the award. (Catalyst recognizes organizations in North America for outstanding achievements in employment equity.) In 2002 and 2003, BMO was the only major Canadian bank to be cited by *Maclean's* magazine as one of Canada's top 100 employers and has twice won the Vision Award from Human Resources Development Canada. Rose M. Patten, senior executive vice-president, Human Resources, and head of Office of Strategic Management, oversees the equity campaign from her Toronto office.

"One of BMO's keys to success is the ability to integrate our programs into the fabric of the organization. At BMO Financial Group, our commitment to fostering a diverse and equitable workplace is reflected not only in our corporate values and part of our cultural fabric; it is how we do business. We don't just talk about values; we live them. BMO's people strategies focus on the importance of talented, engaged, and high-performing employees. An important element of this is maintaining an equitable and supportive workplace, which reflects the diversity of the communities in which we do business. These objectives are explicitly aligned with strategic initiatives from the top, and, subsequently, are carefully measured and connected to performance. As part of this, diversity is seen as a strategic imperative at BMO.

"In 1992, BMO put its commitment into action by establishing a National Advisory Council on the Equitable Workplace to oversee enterprise wide implementation of all workplace equality initiatives. Chaired by Tony Comper, then president of BMO, and comprised of the bank's most senior business line and corporate executives, the council set the strategic direction for quantitative and qualitative diversity goals, and measured performance against those goals on a quarterly basis. Today, the council is known as the Chairman's Council on the Equitable Workplace, and is still chaired by Tony Comper, now chairman and chief executive officer of BMO Financial Group.

"More recently, the council produced a unique diversity model linking diversity and workplace equity to the enterprise's strategic objectives. In the model, diversity and workplace equity are placed at the centre of six key business initiatives: corporate values and strategies, competition for talent acquisition and retention of people, managerial competency, customer and community business interface, corporate image and brand equity, and legislative compliance. Corporations in Canada, the U.S., and Europe have since adopted this framework to understand diversity's influence on business strategy—breaking traditional paradigms.

"When our efforts toward advancement of women began in 1990, we only had 6 percent of women in executive positions; today we have 35 percent. This was achieved in part as a result of a task force on the advancement of women sponsored by our then president, Tony Comper,

(continued on following page)

in 1990. Discussions with employees revealed several widely held beliefs about why women were so under-represented at senior levels at the company. To study whether these beliefs were supported by facts, the task force developed a statistical profile study on men and women at BMO. The results told a compelling story, and the company resolved to address the situation.

"In addition, BMO's Annual Employee Survey was re-designed to include a comprehensive Diversity Index, a compilation of questions enabling BMO to measure how well employees think their employer is doing in living up to its commitment to creating a diverse workforce and an equitable workplace. The index enables BMO to use fact-based information about our employee base in prioritizing diversity action plans and strategies. The most recent survey indicated that, more than ever, employees believe that men and women have an equal opportunity for promotion.

"Today, BMO's commitment to diversity and workplace equity continues to be supported by a comprehensive system of goal setting, monitoring and evaluation processes using clear metrics and benchmarks. As our progress towards the goal of a diverse workforce and an equitable and supportive workplace continues to be recognized, we at BMO will continue to be trailblazers pushing ourselves to new heights."

A final element in achieving success is monitoring progress and providing qualitative and quantitative evidence of change. For example, during their performance appraisals, all salaried employees at Levi Strauss & Co. (Canada) are evaluated on their ability to meet both business and aspirational goals. Aspirational goals are based on the company's core values, which include valuing diversity, following ethical management practices, and encouraging new behaviours, recognition, communications, and empowerment. These aspirations are the shared values and behaviours that will drive the company toward its mission of "sustained responsible commercial success."[62] When management measures performance as a function of diversity initiatives, values are instilled in the minds of all employees, and it is demonstrated that change and diversity are part of day-to-day business. To achieve success in diversity, it is vital to set an example and to create an atmosphere that respects and values differences. Canadian organizations have recognized the competitive advantage of embracing diversity in their business strategies.

SUMMARY

 Employment equity refers to the employment of individuals in a fair and nonbiased manner. Four groups in Canada—women, visible minorities, aboriginals, and persons with disabilities—tend to be concentrated in a few occupations that are accorded lower status and pay.

 The Canadian Human Rights Act applies to all federally governed departments and agencies, and all organizations incorporated under federal jurisdiction. The act prohibits discrimination on the basis of grounds such as race, religion, sex, age, national or ethnic origin, physical handicap, and marital status. The Canadian Human Rights Commission enforces the act through a formal complaint procedure.

 Pay equity is an amendment to the Canadian Human Rights Act that makes it illegal for employers to discriminate against individuals on the basis of job content. By definition, pay equity means equal pay for work of equal value.

 The Employment Equity Act requires all federally regulated employers to prepare an employment equity plan. The Canadian Human Rights Commission is mandated under the Canadian Human Rights Act to prohibit discrimination in the establishments of federally regulated businesses.

 The implementation of employment equity involves six steps: senior management support, data collection and analysis, an employment system review, establishment of a workplan, implementation, strategy, and a follow-up process that includes monitoring, reviewing, and revision.

 Sexual harassment is an employment equity issues undergoing continued debate.

 Managing diversity does more than incorporate employment equity. The goal of diversity management is to optimize the utilization of an organization's multicultural workforce with the goal of realizing strategic advantage.

KEY TERMS

bona fide occupational qualification (BFOQ) 55
concentration 65
designated groups 51

diversity management 76
employment equity 50
flow data 63
reasonable accommodation 67

sexual harassment 72
stock data 63
systemic discrimination 66
underutilization 65

DISCUSSION QUESTIONS

 1. Here are some myths about employment equity:
- It leads to hiring unqualified workers.
- It causes an overnight change in the workforce make-up.

- It's a plan that would make Calgary's workforce look like Toronto's.
- This program lays off white males to make room for designated group members.
- It's a program mainly for racial minorities.

▶ Employers who implement the plan can destroy hard-won seniority provisions that protect all workers.

▶ It's the end of hiring for white males.

In groups, determine if group members share these beliefs. As human resource professionals, how would you work with employees who held these beliefs?

Go to the website of the Alliance for Employment Equity (www.web.net/~allforee/empeqity.htm), and compare your answers.

 2. Identify the major federal laws that relate to employment equity, and discuss how they are enforced.

 4. Describe the purpose of the Employment Equity Act, and discuss some of its provisions.

 5. "Discrimination against older persons does not generate the same degree of moral outrage as other forms of discrimination." Do you agree? If you find this quote offensive, read the full text of the Human Rights Commission's discussion paper on human rights for the aging (www.ohrc.on.ca).

3. Define pay equity, and discuss strategies for implementing it.

 6. After receiving several complaints of sexual harassment, the HR department of a city library decides to establish a sexual harassment policy. What should be included in the policy? How should it be implemented?

7. Describe how an organization can make best use of a multicultural workforce.

Developing Managerial Skills

PREVENTING SEXUAL HARASSMENT

Over the past decade the problem of sexual harassment has captured the attention of all managers and employees. While it is widely known that sexual harassment is both unethical and illegal, the incidents of sexual harassment continue to plague business. Unfortunately, when these cases arise, they cause morale problems among employees, embarrassment to the organization, and costly legal damages. Consequently, all managers and supervisors play a central role in preventing sexual harassment complaints. It is important that managers understand the definition of sexual harassment, who is covered by sexual harassment guidelines, and how to prevent its occurrence. This skill-building exercise will provide you knowledge in each of these areas.

Assignment

1. Working in teams of five or six members, develop an outline for a sexual harassment training program. Assume that the organization has 1500 employees who work with both internal and external customers.
2. As a minimum your training outline should consider (1) who should attend the training sessions, (2) the content outline for the training program (the list of materials your team wants to teach), (3) specific examples to illustrate the training materials, and (4) how to investigate sexual harassment complaints.
3. This chapter will assist you with this assignment. Additional materials can be obtained from various HR magazines.
4. Be prepared to present your training outline to other class members.

Case Study 1

Hiring People with Disabilities: Determining Attitudes

In Canada, 40.3 percent of people with disabilities of working age have jobs. To accommodate 75 percent of these individuals would cost organizations less than $1000 each. A pool of talented and motivated people is available, and the accommodation costs are reasonable. Why won't more organizations hire them?

Norma Daggett, HR director for Denton Plastics, would like to introduce more diversity into the company's workforce by hiring qualified people with disabilities. Before proceeding to the hiring phase, she would like to get a sense of how the current workforce will respond to her diversity plan. To that end, she has developed the following test consisting of true/false statements that will help her determine employee attitudes toward people with disabilities.

1. Most people with disabilities do not require special work arrangements.
2. The real problem for the people with disabilities is holding a job, not getting one.
3. Employees with disabilities tend to have more accidents than other employees.
4. These employees are less likely to have a record of absenteeism.
5. People with the most severe impairments are likely to be at the top in job performance.
6. Turnover tends to be higher among employees with disabilities than among other employees.
7. Other employees tend to respond negatively when accommodations (e.g., wheelchair ramps) are made for employees with disabilities.

The Canadian Council on Rehabilitation and Work shares knowledge and attempts to influence attitudes for equitable employment for people with disabilities; visit their website at www.ccrw.org.

QUESTIONS

1. Give a true or false response to each of the above statements.
2. Refer to the correct answers (based on statistical evidence) given at the end of the chapter. For each item you answered incorrectly, ask yourself, "Where did I get that idea?" See if you can detect any personal bias toward people with disabilities.
3. Why are people with disabilities still underemployed?

Case Study 2

Fighting Fires

In British Columbia, the competition for firefighting jobs is fierce, with more than 1600 people applying for about sixty jobs. At one time, the provincial Ministry of Forests required all job applicants to pass this physical fitness test:

▶ Lift a twenty-three-kilogram bar in an upright rowing motion eighteen times.

▶ Carry pumps and hoses, weighting as much as fifty kilograms, over a timed distance.

▶ Perform a shuttle run, which involves darting back and forth at an increasingly faster pace between cones situated twenty metres apart.

The B.C. Government and Service Employees Union argued that the average man, with training, could easily pass the test, whereas the average woman, even with training, could not. Only 35 percent of women who applied for the firefighter's job passed the test; about 70 percent of the men did.

The University of Victoria scientists who designed the tests argued that most women could reach the standard, although they would have to work harder than most men to do so. Female firefighters said they had to train year round to pass the test, but they took this as a personal responsibility and as the cost of qualifying for the job. Their safety, as well as that of their colleagues and the public, depends on their strength and endurance. The B.C. Ministry of Forests spokeswoman suggested that lowering the standards would be a mistake: "Already male firefighters are asking if blazes will be designated as 'guy' fires and 'girl' fires. We want the fittest people."

QUESTIONS

1. Did the standards result in safer and more effective firefighting crews, or were they inadvertently keeping women out of a traditionally male job?

2. Was this a BFOQ? The ministry was challenged on the basis of sex discrimination. What did the Supreme Court rule, and what was its reasoning?

3. Female applicants had the chance to train and try the test at B.C. university campuses. Was this special preparation discriminatory?

4. Did the changes made fix the underlying problems? Explain.

5. What other advice would you give their managers?

CAREER COUNSEL

Find out how to handle prohibited questions during a job interview by visiting the *Managing Human Resources* website (www.belcourt4e.nelson.com).

NOTES AND REFERENCES

1. Human Resources Development Canada, "Annual Report, Analysis of Employers' Reports," www.hrdc-drhc.gc.ca/LEEP/Annual _Reports/03.

2. Human Resources Development Canada, *Annual Report, Employment Equity Act, 2003*, Labour Standards and Workplace Equity, Cat. No. MP31-5/2002; Human Resources Development Canada, "Workplace Equity," http://info.load-otea.hrdc-drhc.gc.ca/workplace_equity/leep/annual/2002/.

3. L. Redpath and M.O. Nielsen. "A Comparison of Native Culture, Non-Native Culture and New Management Ideology," *Canadian Journal of Administrative Studies* 14, no. 3 (1996): 327–39.

4. Statistics Canada website, "Designated Minority Representation," http://www.statcan.ca/english/IPS/Data/96F0030XIE2001008.htm.

5. Human Resources Development Canada, "Workplace Equity," http://www.statcan.ca/Daily/English/030311/d030311a.htm; http://info.load-otea.hrdc-drhc.gc.ca/workplace_equity/leep/annual/2002/2002annualrep08.shtml.

6. *Employment Equity: A Guide for Employers*, Employment and Immigration Canada, Cat. No. LM-143-5-91, May 1991: 9.

7. Victor S. Mackinnon, "The Canadian Charter of Rights and Freedoms," *Public Administration: Canadian Materials* (North York: Captus Press, 1993): 179–80.

8. Canadian Human Rights Act, Canadian Human Rights Commission, 1978, Paragraph 2, Subsection (a).

9. A.P. Aggarwal, *Sex Discrimination: Employment Law and Practices* (Toronto: Butterworths Canada, 1994).

10. "Firm Pays $300,000 in Racial Harassment Settlements," *Human Resources Management in Canada*, Report Bulletin No. 72 (February 1989) (Scarborough, ON: Prentice-Hall Canada): 1–2.

11. Canadian Human Rights Act, Paragraph 46, Section 2(a), (b).

12. Human Resources Development Canada, *Annual Report, Employment Equity Act, 2001*, Labour Standards and Workplace Equity, Cat. No. LT-020-12-01.

13. Russel J.G. Juriansz, *Equal Pay Legislation and Ontario's New Pay Equity Act* (Toronto: Blake, Cassels & Graydon, 1995): 3–5.

14. Susan Riggs, "Comparing Apples and Oranges: Job Evaluations," *Worklife* 8, no. 1 (1991): 7–10.

15. "Achieving Pay Equity First Goal, But through Co-operation: Commissioner," *Pay Equity Commission Report* 1, no. 1 (March 1988): 6.

16. Morley Gunderson and Roberta Edgecombe Robb, "Equal Pay for Work of Equal Value: Canada's Experience," *Advances in Industrial and Labour Relations* 5 (1991): 151–68. See also John G. Kelly, *Pay Equity Management* (Toronto: CCH Canadian, 1988): 45–54.

17. Mme. Justice Rosalie Silberman Abella, Commissioner, *Equality in Employment: A Royal Commission Report* (Ottawa: Supply and Services Canada, 1984): 9.

18. *Introduction to Employment Equity* (Ottawa: Human Resources Development Canada, 1996).

19. http://laws.justice.gc.ca/en/E-5.401/48928.html.

20. Kelly Toughill, "Firms Back Equity: To Some It's 'Good Business' Despite Harris's Vow to Scrap It," *Toronto Star*, June 21, 1995: A2.

21. Canadian Human Rights Act, S.C. 1976–77, c. as amended.

22. R.G.L. Fairweather, Canadian Human Rights Commission, *The Standing Committee on Legal and Constitutional Affairs*, May 29, 1986: 10.

23. *Towards Equity: 1993 Merit Awards*, Employment Equity Branch, Human Resources Development Canada, June 1994: 17–18.

24. *Workplace Innovations Overview—1996*, Bureau of Labour Information, Human Resources Development Canada: 1–84.

25. *Towards Equity: 1993 Merit Awards*: 11–12; Laura Cassiani, "Canada's Quiet Labour Crisis," *Canadian HR Reporter* 14, no. 3 (February 12, 2001): 1 and 8.

26. L. Young, "Employers Need to Scrutinize All Job Testing for Human Rights Violations, Supreme Court Rules," *Canadian HR Reporter*, October 4, 1999: 3.

27. Ibid., 18.

28. Aggarwal, *Sex Discrimination*.

29. Nicholas Keung, "Police Recruit Ethnic Officers to Boost Force," *Toronto Star*, July 25, 1997: A7.

30. *Employment Equity: A Guide for Employers*: 19.

31. Joanne Leck, Sylvie St. Onge, and Isabelle La Lancettee, "Wage Gap Changes among Organizations Subject to the Employment Equity Act," *Canadian Public Policy* 21, no. 44 (December 1995): 387–400.

32. Seymour Moskowitz, "Adolescent Workers and Sexual Harassment," *Labor Law Journal* 51, no. 3 (Fall 2000): 78–84. For an excellent reference guide on sexual harassment, see William Petrocelli and Barbara Kate Repa, *Sexual Harassment on the Job: What It Is and How to Stop It* (Berkeley, CA: Nolo Press, 1998).

33. "Sexual Harassment," *CACSW Fact Sheet*, Canadian Advisory Council on the Status of Women, March 1993.

34. "Inquest Probes Murder-Suicide Involving Harassment Victim," *Sexual Harassment, Workplace Diversity Update* 5, no. 3 (March 1997): 4.

35. Malcolm McKillop, "A Manager's Guide to Sexual Impropriety," *The Globe and Mail*, October 7, 1997: B23.

36. Dale Hall and Siobhan McEwan, *Sexual Assault and Harassment on Campus*, York University Sexual Harassment Education and Complaint Centre, York University, 1995.

37. *Sexual Harassment and You: What Every Student Should Know*, Sexual Harassment Education and Complaint Centre, York University, 1986.

38. For a good review of sexual harassment policy, see Dana S. Connell, "Effective Sexual Harassment Policies: Unexpected Lessons from Jacksonville Shipyards," *Employee Relations Law Journal* 17, no. 2 (Autumn 1991): 191–205.

39. Katherine Harding, "Taking Aim at Bullies," *The Globe and Mail*, March 19, 2003: C1.

40. Christine L. Taylor, "Dimensions of Diversity in Canadian Business: Building a Business Case for Valuing Ethnocultural Diversity," *Conference Board of Canada Report 143-95*, April 1995: 1.

41. Paul Moloney, "Toronto Okays Non-Christian Holidays for Staffers," *Toronto Star*, May 17, 1995: A6.

42. S. Hood, "Generational Diversity," *HR Professional*, June–July 2000: 19.

43. Jennie Constantinides, "Diversity Management: At CN, the 'Token' Will Be Broken," *Human Resources Professional* 7, no. 4 (April 1991): 29–30.

44. Statistics Canada, *Canada's Ethnocultural Portrait: The Changing Mosiac*, Cat. no. 96F0030XIE 2001008, Analysis Series, 2001; Erin Anderson, "Immigration Shifts Population Kaleidoscope," *The Globe and Mail*, January 22, 2003: A 6.

45. Lindsay Scotton, "We Are the World: The Many Faces of Canada Come Together on Winning Images in a Contest to Depict Racial Harmony," May 19, 1995: B3. See also "Logo & Poster Design Exhibition," *Voices of Harmony* 1, no. 1 (Summer 1995): 1–7.

46. Statistics Canada, *Canada's Ethnocultural Portrait*; Anderson, "Immigration Shifts Population Kaleidoscope."

47. Ibid.

48. Jana Schilder, "The Rainbow Connection: Employers Who Promote Diversity May Discover a Pot of Gold," *Human Resources Professional* 11, no. 3 (April 1994): 13–15.

49. Ibid.

50. Doug Nevison, "Profiting in the Pacific Rim: Can Canada Capture Its Share?" *Conference Board of Canada Report*, 1994: 117-94.

51. World Bank, 1993.

52. R. Roosevelt Thomas, Jr., "Beyond Race and Gender," *AMACOM*, 1991: 34.

53. Taylor, "Dimensions of Diversity in Canadian Business": 13.

54. John Spears, "The Many Colours of Money: Diversity Boosts Profit, Firms Told," *Toronto Star*, May 9, 1995.

55. Taylor, "Dimensions of Diversity in Canadian Business": 15.

56. *Continuing In-Patient Focused Care Excellence*, Sunnybrook Community and Public Affairs, Sunnybrook Health Science Centre, Toronto, April 1995.

57. P. Lungen, "Military Addresses Racism Issue," *Canadian Jewish News* 30, no. 7 (February 17, 2000): 6.

58. L. Young, "Global Diversity Standard in Works," *Canadian HR Reporter*, April 5, 1999: 1.

59. Claudine Kapel, "Variation Is the Theme: Organizations That Value Diversity Glimpse Profits in Improved Productivity," *Human Resources Professional* 1, no. 3 (April 1994): 9–12.

60. *Compensation Planning Outlook*, Conference Board of Canada, 1992.

61. Taylor, "Dimensions of Diversity in Canadian Business."

62. Ibid., 18.

ANSWERS TO CASE STUDY 1

1. T　　2. F　　3. F　　4. T
5. T　　6. F　　7. F

Job Analysis, Employee Involvement, and Flexible Work Schedules

After studying this chapter, you should be able to

objective 1

Discuss the relationship between job requirements and the performance of HRM functions.

objective 2

Indicate the methods by which job analysis typically is completed.

objective 3

Identify and explain the various sections of job descriptions.

objective 4

Provide examples illustrating the various factors that must be taken into account in designing a job.

objective 5

Discuss the various job characteristics that motivate employees.

objective 6

Describe the different group techniques used to maximize employee contributions.

objective 7

Differentiate and explain the different adjustments in work schedules.

O rganizations are "reengineering" themselves in an attempt to become more effective. Some, such as Ducks Unlimited Canada and Sunnybrook and Women's College Health Sciences Centre, are breaking into smaller units and getting flatter. There is emphasis on smaller scale, less hierarchy, fewer layers, and more decentralized work units. As organizational reshaping takes place, managers want employees to operate more independently and flexibly to meet customer demands. This requires that decisions be made by the people who are closest to the information and who are directly involved in the product or service delivered. The objective is to develop jobs and basic work units that are adaptable enough to thrive in a world of high-velocity change.

In this chapter, we discuss how jobs can be designed so as to best contribute to the objectives of the organization and at the same time satisfy the needs of the employees who are to perform them. Clearly, the duties and responsibilities present in jobs greatly influence employee productivity, job satisfaction, as well as employee retention.[1] Therefore, the value of job analysis, which defines clearly and precisely the requirements of each job, will be stressed. We will emphasize that these job requirements provide the foundation for making objective and legally defensible decisions in managing human resources. The chapter concludes by reviewing several innovative job design and employee contribution techniques that increase job satisfaction while improving organizational performance.

RELATIONSHIP OF JOB REQUIREMENTS AND HRM FUNCTIONS

objective

Job
A group of related activities and duties

Position
The different duties and responsibilities performed by more than one employee

Job family
A group of individual jobs with similar characteristics

A **job** consists of a group of related activities and duties. Ideally, the duties of a job should consist of natural units of work that are similar and related. They should be clear and distinct from those of other jobs to minimize misunderstanding and conflict among employees and to enable employees to recognize what is expected of them. For some jobs, several employees may be required, each of whom will occupy a separate position. A **position** consists of the duties and responsibilities performed by more than one employee. In a city library, for example, four employees (four positions) may be involved in reference work, but all of them have only one job (reference librarian). When different jobs have similar duties and responsibilities, they may be grouped into a **job family** for purposes of recruitment, training, compensation, or advancement opportunities.

Recruitment

Before they can find capable employees for an organization, recruiters need to know the job specifications for the positions they are to fill. A **job specification** is a statement of the knowledge, skills, and abilities required of the person performing the job.

Job specification
Statement of the knowledge, skills, and abilities required of the person who is to perform the job

In the HR department for the City of Calgary, Alberta, the job specification for a senior personnel analyst includes the following:

1. Appropriate university degree, preferably at the master's level.
2. Four to five years of corporate management experience.
3. Working knowledge of employment equity, human rights legislation, statistical analysis, investigative procedures, and organizational development.[2]

Because job specifications establish the qualifications required of applicants for a job opening, they serve an essential role in the recruiting function. These qualifications typically are contained in the notices of job openings. Whether posted on organization bulletin boards or HRIS Internet sites or included in help-wanted advertisements or employment agency listings, job specifications provide a basis for attracting qualified applicants and discouraging unqualified ones.

Selection

Job description
Statement of the tasks, duties, and responsibilities of a job to be performed

In addition to job specifications, managers and supervisors will use job descriptions to select and orient employees to jobs. A **job description** is a statement of the tasks, duties, and responsibilities of a job.

In the past, job specifications used as a basis for selection sometimes bore little relation to the duties to be performed under the job description. Examples of such non–job-related specifications abounded. Applicants for the job of labourer were required to have a high school diploma. Firefighters were required to be at least six feet tall. And applicants for the job of truck driver were required to be male. These kinds of job specifications discriminated against members of certain designated groups, many of whom were excluded from these jobs.

Employers must be able to show that the job specifications used in selecting employees for a particular job relate specifically to the duties of that job. In 1984, charges of discrimination were brought against the Vancouver Fire Department because it required that candidates for a firefighter's job be at least five feet nine. The Human Rights Board that heard the case could not find any correlation between the height of a firefighter and injuries or efficiencies or capacity to perform the job. The Vancouver Fire Department was found in violation of the Human Rights Act.[3] Job specifications should list the knowledge, skills, and abilities required to perform the job successfully, and should not be based on stereotypes or managerial preferences.

Training and Development

Any discrepancies between the knowledge, skills, and abilities (often referred to as KSAs) demonstrated by a job holder and the requirements contained in the description and specification for that job provide clues to training needs. Also, career development as a part of the training function is concerned with preparing employees for advancement to jobs where their capacities can be utilized to the fullest extent possible. The formal qualification requirements set forth in high-level jobs serve to indicate how much more training and development are needed for employees to advance to those jobs.

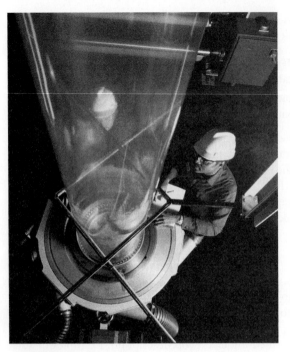

Job analysis can be used to design training programs.

Performance Appraisal

The requirements contained in the description of a job provide the criteria for evaluating the performance of the holder of that job. The results of performance appraisal may reveal, however, that certain requirements established for a job are not completely valid. As we have already stressed, these criteria must be specific and job-related. If the criteria used to evaluate employee performance are vague and not job-related, employers may find themselves being charged with unfair discrimination.

Compensation Management

In determining the rate to be paid for performing a job, the relative worth of the job is one of the most important factors. This worth is based on what the job demands of an employee in skill, effort, and responsibility, as well as the conditions and hazards under which the work is performed. The systems of job evaluation by which this worth may be measured are discussed in Chapter 9. As The Business Case outlines, job analysis has financial implications and could cause workplace problems if handled poorly.

The Business Case

FLYING FOR LOVE OR MONEY

The two unions representing pilots who fly for Air Canada and its regional airline, Air Canada Jazz, fought over pay scale. Pilots for both carriers must meet the same job requirements. However, those who fly for the mainline service earn about $140 000 to $200 000 annually while those who fly for the regional airline earn on average $75 000 to $100 000. The 3100 Air Canada pilots feel that the pay differential is justified because they fly bigger planes (carrying 150 to 250 passengers) at long distances (fourteen hours) with the latest technology. The 1400 Air Canada Jazz pilots do carry smaller passenger loads over shorter distances (sixty to ninety minutes). However this entails many more takeoffs and landings, which are considered the most difficult and stressful part of the flight. Air Canada pilots dispute this, saying compensation is not determined by the number of takeoffs and landings; if it was, then bush pilots would be making the most money of all.

Accurate job descriptions would help resolve this contentious and costly debate.

Source: John Partridge, "Air Canada, the Pilots and All That Jazz." *The Globe and Mail*, June 14, 2003: B1, B4.

JOB ANALYSIS

objective

Job analysis
Process of obtaining information about jobs by determining what the duties, tasks, or activities associated with those jobs are

Job analysis is sometimes called the cornerstone of HRM because the information it collects serves so many HRM functions. **Job analysis** is the process of obtaining information about jobs by determining what the duties, tasks, or activities of those jobs are. The procedure involves systematically investigating jobs and then following a number of predetermined steps specified in advance of the study.[4] When completed, job analysis results in a written report summarizing the information obtained from the analysis of twenty or thirty individual job tasks or activities.[5] HR managers use these data to develop job descriptions and job specifications. These documents, in turn, are used to perform and enhance various HR functions such as developing performance appraisal criteria and designing the content of training classes. The ultimate purpose of job analysis is to improve organizational performance and productivity. Figure 3.1 illustrates how job analysis is carried out, and shows the functions for which it is used.

As contrasted with job design, which reflects subjective opinions about the ideal requirements of a job, job analysis is concerned with objective and verifiable information about the actual requirements of a job. The job descriptions and job specifications developed through job analysis should be as accurate as possible if they are to be of value to those who make HRM decisions. These decisions may involve any of the HR functions, from recruitment to termination of employees.

Gathering Job Information

Job data can be gathered in several ways. The common methods of analyzing jobs are interviews, questionnaires, observation, and diaries.[6]

▶ *Interviews.* The job analyst questions individual employees and managers about the job under review.

▶ *Questionnaires.* The job analyst circulates carefully prepared questionnaires to be filled out by job holders and managers individually. These forms will be used to obtain data in the areas of job duties and tasks performed, purpose of the job, physical setting, requirements for performing the job (skill, education, experience, physical and mental demands), equipment and materials used, and special health and safety concerns.

▶ *Observation.* The job analyst may learn about the jobs by observing and recording on a standardized form the activities of those who hold it. Videotaping jobs for later study is an approach used by some organizations.

▶ *Diaries.* Job holders themselves may be asked to keep a diary of their work activities during an entire work cycle. Diaries are usually filled out at specific times during the work shift (e.g., every half-hour or hour) over a two- to four-week period.

Although HR specialists, called job analysts, are the personnel primarily responsible for the job analysis program, they usually enlist the cooperation of the employees and managers in the departments where jobs are being analyzed. It is these managers and employees who are the sources of much of the information about the jobs, and they may be asked to prepare rough drafts of the job descriptions and specifications the job analysts need.

Figure 3.1 | The Process of Job Analysis

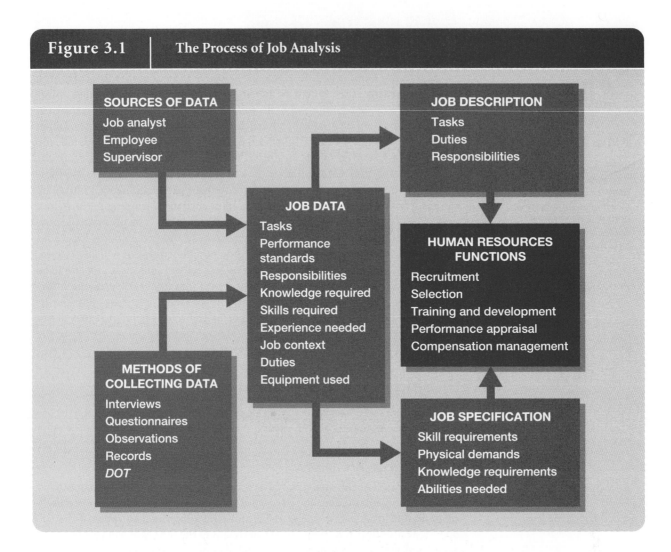

Controlling the Accuracy of Job Information

If job analysis is to accomplish its intended purpose, the job data collected must be accurate. Care must be taken to ensure that all important facts are included. A job analyst should be alert for employees who tend to exaggerate the difficulty of their jobs in order to inflate their egos and their paycheques. Ethics in HRM highlights such a case. When interviewing employees or reviewing their questionnaires, the job analyst must look for any responses that do not agree with other facts or impressions the analyst has received. Furthermore, when job information is collected from employees, a representative group of individuals should be surveyed. For example, the results of one study indicated that the information obtained from job analysis was related to race. In another study, the experience level of job incumbents influenced job analysis outcomes.

USING THE INTERNET

For a general information site on job analysis consult HR Guide.Com:

www.hr-guide.com/jobanalysis.htm

Ethics in HRM

INFLATION

At some point in your working life, you will be asked to describe your job, perhaps when being interviewed by a job analyst or by answering questions on a form. Most employees have a reasonable expectation that their answers will affect their lives in significant ways. The information obtained may be used to reclassify the job to either a higher or lower pay level. Most employees believe that standards of performance may change—and the employer will expect them to work faster or to do more—although that is not the goal of job analysis.

As a result of these beliefs and expectations, employees have a vested interest in "inflating" their job descriptions, by making the job sound very important and very difficult. Thus night clerks in hotels become auditors and receptionists become administrators. Making a job sound more important than it is may reflect an employee's sincere belief in the significance of his or her contribution, or an attempt to lobby for higher pay.

Whenever a job analyst doubts the accuracy of the information provided by employees, he or she should obtain additional information from them, from their managers, or from other individuals who are familiar with or perform the same job. It is common practice to have the descriptions for each job reviewed by the job holders and their managers. The job description summaries contained in the *National Occupational Classification* can also serve as a basis for the job analyst's review.

The NOC and Job Analysis

Commonly referred to as the *NOC*, the *National Occupational Classification* is compiled by the federal government. The purpose of the *NOC* is to compile, analyze, and communicate information about occupations. This information can be used for employment equity, human resource planning, and occupational supply and demand forecasts and analyses.

The *NOC* is a composite of the Canadian labour market and has helped bring about a greater degree of uniformity in the job titles and descriptions used by employers in different parts of the country. This uniformity has facilitated the movement of workers from regions that may be experiencing widespread unemployment to areas where employment opportunities are greater. Also, the *NOC* code numbers facilitate the exchange of statistical information about jobs and are useful in reporting research in the HR area, in vocational counselling, and in charting career paths through job transfers and/or advancements.[7] Some professional associations provide a job classification system that is intended to be more current than the *NOC*.

USING THE INTERNET

The *NOC* contains standardized and comprehensive descriptions of about 25 000 occupational titles:

www23.hrdc-drhc.gc.ca/2001/e/groups/index.shtml

USING THE INTERNET

The Canadian Technology Human Resources Board has established a comprehensive evaluation system that describes the major applied science and engineering technology disciplines. Visit its website:

www.cthrb.ca

Approaches to Job Analysis

The systematic and quantitative definition of job content that job analysis provides is the foundation of many HRM practices. Specifically, job analysis serves to justify job descriptions and other HRM selection procedures. Several different job analysis approaches are used, each with specific advantages and disadvantages. Four of the more popular methods are functional job analysis, the position analysis questionnaire system, the critical incident method, and computerized job analysis.

Functional Job Analysis (FJA)

The **functional job analysis (FJA)** approach utilizes an inventory of the various types of functions or work activities that can constitute any job. FJA thus assumes that each job involves performing certain functions. Specifically, there are three broad worker functions that form the basis of this system: (1) data, (2) people, and (3) things. These three categories are subdivided to form a hierarchy of worker-function scales, as shown in Figure 3.2. The job analyst, when studying the job under review, indicates the functional level for each of the three categories (for example, "copying" under Data) and then reflects the relative involvement of the worker in the function by assigning a percentage figure to each function (e.g., 50 percent to "copying"). This is done for each of the three areas, and the three functional levels must equal 100 percent. The end result is a quantitatively evaluated job. FJA can easily be used to describe the content of jobs and to assist in writing job descriptions and specifications; it is used as a basis for the *Dictionary of Occupational Titles (DOT)* code, the American equivalent of *NOC*.

Functional job analysis (FJA)
Quantitative approach to job analysis that utilizes a compiled inventory of the various functions or work activities that can make up any job and that assumes that each job involves three broad worker functions: (1) data, (2) people, and (3) things

Figure 3.2 | Difficulty Levels of Worker Functions

DATA (4TH DIGIT)	PEOPLE (5TH DIGIT)	THINGS (6TH DIGIT)
0 Synthesizing	0 Mentoring	0 Setting up
1 Coordinating	1 Negotiating	1 Precision working
2 Analyzing	2 Instructing	2 Operating-controlling*
3 Compiling	3 Supervising	3 Driving-operating
4 Computing	4 Diverting	4 Manipulating
5 Copying	5 Persuading	5 Tending
6 Comparing	6 Speaking-signalling*	6 Feeding-offbearing*
	7 Serving	7 Handling
	8 Taking instructions—helping*	

* Hyphenated factors are single factors.

Source: U.S. Department of Labor, Employment and Training Administration, *Revised Handbook for Analyzing Jobs* (Washington, DC: U.S. Government Printing Office, 1991): 5.

The Position Analysis Questionnaire System

The **position analysis questionnaire (PAQ)** is a quantifiable data collection method covering 194 different worker-oriented tasks. Using a five-point scale, the PAQ seeks to determine the degree, if any, to which the different tasks or job elements are involved in performing a particular job.

A sample page from the PAQ covering eleven elements of the Information Input Division is shown in Figure 3.3. The person conducting an analysis using this questionnaire rates each of the elements using the five-point scale shown in the upper right-hand corner of the sample page. The results obtained with the PAQ are quantitative and can be subjected to statistical analysis. The PAQ also permits dimensions of behaviour to be compared across a number of jobs and permits jobs to be grouped on the basis of common characteristics.

The Critical Incident Method

The objective of the **critical incident method** is to identify critical job tasks. Critical job tasks are those important duties and job responsibilities performed by the job holder that lead to job success. Information about critical job tasks can be collected through interviews with employees or managers or through self-report statements written by employees.

Suppose, for example, that the job analyst is studying the job of reference librarian. The interviewer will ask the employee to describe the job on the basis of what is done, how the job is performed, and what tools and equipment are used. The reference librarian may describe the job as follows:

> I assist patrons by answering their questions related to finding books, periodicals, or other library materials. I also give them directions to help them find materials within the building. To perform my job I may have to look up materials myself or refer patrons to someone who can directly assist them. Some individuals may need training in how to use reference materials or special library facilities. I also give library tours to new patrons. I use computers and a variety of reference books to carry out my job.

After the job data are collected, the analyst will write separate task statements that represent important job activities. For the reference librarian, one task statement might be "Listens to patrons and answers their questions related to locating library materials." Typically, the job analyst will write five to ten important task statements for each job under study. The final product will be written task statements that are clear, complete, and easily understood by those unfamiliar with the job. The critical incident method is an important job analysis method since it teaches the analyst to focus on employee behaviours critical to job success.

HRIS and Job Analysis

Human resource information systems have greatly facilitated the job analysis process. Available today are various software programs designed specifically to analyze jobs and to write job descriptions and job specifications based on those analyses. Typically, these programs contain generalized task statements that can apply to many different jobs. Managers and employees select those statements that best describe the job under review,

Position analysis questionnaire (PAQ)
Quantitative approach to job analysis that utilizes a compiled inventory of the various functions or work activities that can make up any job

Critical incident method
Job analysis method by which important job tasks are identified for job success

NEL

97

Figure 3.3 | A Sample Page from the Position Analysis Questionnaire

Information Input

1   INFORMATION INPUT

1.1   Sources of Job Information

Rate each of the following items in terms of the extent to which it is used by the worker as a source of information in performing his job.

1.1.1   Visual Sources of Job Information

	Extent of Use (U)
NA	Does not apply
1	Nominal / very infrequent
2	Occasional
3	Moderate
4	Considerable
5	Very substantial

01 U   Written materials (books, reports, office notes, articles, job instructions, signs, etc.)

02 U   Quantitative materials (materials which deal with quantities or amounts, such as graphs, accounts, specifications, tables of numbers, etc.)

03 U   Pictorial materials (pictures or picture like materials used as sources of information, for example, drawings, blueprints, diagrams, maps, tracings, photographic films, x-ray films, TV pictures, etc.)

04 U   Patterns/related devices (templates, stencils, patterns, etc., used as sources of information when observed during use; do not include here materials described in item 3 above)

05 U   Visual displays (dials, gauges, signal lights, radar scopes, speedometers, clocks, etc.)

06 U   Measuring devices (rulers, calipers, tire pressure gauges, scales, thickness gauges, pipettes, thermometers, protractors, etc., used to obtain visual information about physical measurements; do not include here devices described in item 5 above)

07 U   Mechanical devices (tools, equipment, machinery, and other mechanical devices which are sources of information when observed during use or operation)

08 U   Materials in process (parts, materials, objects, etc., which are sources of information when being modified, worked on, or otherwise processed, such as bread dough being mixed, workpiece being turned in a lathe, fabric being cut, shoe being resoled, etc.)

09 U   Materials not in process (parts, materials, objects, etc., not in the process of being changed or modified, which are sources of information when being inspected, handled, packaged, distributed, or selected, etc., such as items or materials in inventory, storage, or distribution channels, items being inspected, etc.)

10 U   Features of nature (landscapes, fields, geological samples, vegetation, cloud formations, and other features of nature which are observed or inspected to provide information)

11 U   Man-made features of environment (structures, buildings, dams, highways, bridges, docks, railroads, and other "man-made" or altered aspects of the indoor or outdoor environment which are observed or inspected to provide job information; do not consider equipment, machines, etc., that an individual uses in his work, as covered by item 7).

Source: *Position Analysis Questionnaire*, copyright 1969, 1989 by Purdue Research Foundation, West Lafayette, Indiana 47907.

USING THE INTERNET

For information about the Position
Analysis Questionnaire, consult

www.paq.com/.

indicating the importance of the task to the total job where appropriate. Advanced computer applications of job analysis combine job analysis with job evaluation (Chapter 9) and the pricing of organizational jobs. Computerized job analysis systems can be expensive to initiate, but where the organization has many jobs, the cost per job may be low. HR publications such as the *Canadian HR Reporter* contain advertisements from software companies that offer HRIS job analysis packages.

Job Analysis in a Changing Environment

The traditional approach to job analysis assumes a static job environment in which jobs remain relatively stable apart from the incumbents who hold these jobs. Here, jobs can be meaningfully defined by tasks, duties, processes, and behaviours necessary for job success. This assumption, unfortunately, discounts technological advances that are often so accelerated that jobs, as they are defined today, may be obsolete tomorrow. The following statement by two HR professionals highlights this concern: "Typically, job analysis looks at how a job is currently done. But the ever-changing business market makes it difficult to keep a job analysis up-to-date. Also, companies are asking employees to do more, so there is a question of whether 'jobs' as we know them are obsolete. This means we must do an analysis of work as quickly as possible, leading to more emphasis on technology related options, such as web-based job analysis."[8]

Furthermore, downsizing, the adoption of teams, the demands of small organizations, and the need to respond to global change can alter the nature of jobs and their requirements. In a dynamic environment where job demands change rapidly, outdated job analysis information can hinder an organization's ability to adapt to change.

Where organizations operate in a fast-moving environment, several novel approaches to job analysis may accommodate needed change. First, managers can adopt a future-oriented approach to job analysis. This "strategic" analysis of jobs requires that managers have a clear view of how jobs should be restructured with regard to duties and tasks in order to meet future organizational requirements. Second, organizations can adopt a competency-based approach to job analysis in which emphasis is placed on characteristics of successful performers rather than on standard job duties and tasks. These competencies would match the organization's culture and strategy and might include such things as interpersonal communication skills, decision-making ability, conflict resolution skills, adaptability, and self-motivation.[9] This technique of job analysis serves to enhance a culture of TQM and continuous improvement since organizational improvement is the stable concern. Either of these two approaches is not without its problems: managers must be able to predict future job needs accurately, job analyses must comply with employment equity legislation, and ways must be found to avoid the role ambiguity created by generically written job descriptions.

Although many would like to be able to broadly define work as any tasks that need to be completed, the provision of accurate and valid job descriptions is still necessary.

Job Descriptions

As previously noted, a job description is a written description of a job and the types of duties it includes. Since there is no standard format for job descriptions, they tend to vary in appearance and content from one organization to another. However, most job descriptions contain at least three parts: the job title, a job identification section, and a job duties section. If the job specifications are not prepared as a separate document, they are usually stated in the concluding section of the job description. Highlights in HRM 3.1 shows a job description for an HR employment assistant. This sample job description includes both job duties and job specifications and should satisfy most of the job information needs of managers who must recruit, interview, and orient new employees.

Job descriptions are of value to both the employees and the employer. From the employees' standpoint, job descriptions can be used to help them learn their job duties and to remind them of the results they are expected to achieve. From the employer's standpoint, written job descriptions can serve as a basis for minimizing the misunderstandings that arise between managers and their subordinates concerning job requirements. They also establish management's right to take corrective action when the duties covered by the job description are not performed as required.

Job Title

Selection of a job title is important for several reasons. *First*, the job title is of psychological importance, providing status on the employee.[10] For instance, "sanitation expert" is a more appealing title than "garbage collector." *Second*, if possible, the title should provide some indication of what the duties of the job entail. Titles such as "meat inspector," "electronics assembler," "salesperson," and "engineer" obviously hint at the nature of the duties of these jobs. The job title also should indicate the relative level occupied by its holder in the organizational hierarchy. For example, the title "junior engineer" implies that this job occupies a lower level than that of "senior engineer." Other titles that indicate the relative level in the organizational hierarchy are "welder's helper" and "laboratory assistant."

Job Identification Section

The job identification section of a job description usually follows the job title. It includes such items as the departmental location of the job, the person to whom the job holder reports, and the date on which the job description was last revised. Sometimes it also contains a payroll or code number, the number of employees performing the job, the number of employees in the department where the job is located, and the *NOC* code number. "Statement of the Job" usually appears at the bottom of this section and serves to distinguish the job from other jobs—something the job title may fail to do.

Job Duties Section

Statements covering job duties are typically arranged in order of importance. These statements should indicate the weight, or value, of each duty. Usually, but not always, the weight of a duty can be gauged by the percentage of time devoted to it. The statements should stress the responsibilities all the duties entail and the results they are to

Highlights in HRM 3.1

JOB DESCRIPTION FOR AN EMPLOYMENT ASSISTANT

Job Title: Employment Assistant
Division: Western Region   **Department:** Human Resources Management
Job Analyst: Virginia Sasaki   **Date Analyzed:** 12/3/04
Wage Category: Professional   **Report to:** HR Manager
Job Code: 11-17   **Date Verified:** 12/17/04

Job Statement — Summary

Performs professional human resources work in the areas of employee recruitment and selection, testing, orientation, transfers, and maintenance of employee human resources files. May handle special assignments and projects in Employment Equity, employee grievances, training, or classification and compensation. Works under general supervision. Incumbent exercises initiative and independent judgment in the performance of assigned tasks.

Essential Functions — specific duties

1. Prepares recruitment literature and job advertisements for applicant placement.
2. Schedules and conducts personal interviews to determine applicant suitability for employment. Includes reviewing mailed applications and résumés for qualified personnel.
3. Supervises administration of testing program. Responsible for developing or improving testing instruments and procedures.
4. Presents orientation program to all new employees. Reviews and develops all materials and procedures for orientation program.
5. Coordinates division job posting and transfer program. Establishes job posting procedures. Responsible for reviewing transfer applications, arranging transfer interviews, and determining effective transfer dates.
6. Maintains a daily working relationship with division managers on human resource matters, including recruitment concerns, retention or release of probationary employees, and discipline or discharge of permanent employees.
7. Distributes new or revised human resources policies and procedures to all employees and managers through bulletins, meetings, memorandums, and/or personal contact.
8. Performs related duties as assigned by the human resource manager.

Job Specifications — skills, knowledge, abilities needed. (core competencies)

1. University degree or college diploma with major course work in human resources management, business administration, or industrial psychology; OR a combination of experience, education, and training equivalent to a degree or diploma in human resources management.
2. Considerable knowledge of principles of employee selection and assignment of personnel.
3. Ability to express ideas clearly in both written and oral communications.
4. Ability to plan and organize one's own activities independently.
5. Knowledge of human resource computer applications desirable.

accomplish. It is also general practice to indicate the tools and equipment used by the employee in performing the job. Remember, the job duties section must comply with the law by listing only the essential functions of the job to be performed.

Job Specifications Section

As stated earlier, the personal qualifications an individual must possess in order to perform the duties and responsibilities contained in a job description are compiled in the job specification. Typically the job specification covers two areas: (1) the skill required to perform the job, and (2) the physical demands the job places on the employee performing it.

Job specifications should also include interpersonal skills or specific behaviour attributes necessary for job success. For example, behaviours might include the ability to make decisions using incomplete information, or the ability to handle multiple tasks. Skills relevant to a job include education or experience, specialized training, personal traits or abilities, and manual dexterities. The physical demands of a job refer to how much walking, standing, reaching, lifting, or talking must be done on the job. The condition of the physical work environment and the hazards employees may encounter are also among the physical demands of a job.

Problems with Job Descriptions

Managers consider job descriptions a valuable tool for carrying out HRM functions. Nevertheless, several problems are often associated with these documents, including the following:

1. If they are poorly written, using vague rather than specific terms, they provide little guidance to the job holder.
2. They are sometimes not updated as job duties or specifications change.[11]
3. They may violate the law by containing specifications not related to job success.
4. They can limit the scope of activities of the job holder.

Some of these problems are being addressed by new approaches to job analysis (see Reality Check).

Writing Clear and Specific Job Descriptions

When writing a job description, it is essential to use statements that are terse, direct, and simply worded. Unnecessary words or phrases should be eliminated. Typically, the sentences that describe job duties begin with a present-tense verb (an action verb), with the implied subject of the sentence being the employee performing the job. The term "occasionally" is used to describe those duties that are performed once in a while. The term "may" is used in connection with those duties that are performed only by some workers on the job.

Even when set forth in writing, job descriptions and specifications can still be vague. To the consternation of many employers, today's legal environment has created what might be called an "age of specifics." Human rights legislation requires that the specific performance requirements of a job be based on valid job-related criteria. Personnel decisions that involve either job applicants or employees and are based on

Reality Check

JOB ANALYSIS AT HAY MCBER

The nature of job analysis is changing, as competency-based models are gaining strength in Canadian workplaces. As we focus on people, the development of job descriptions, which consider the abilities, knowledge, and skill of our "job contributors," is predominating. A job used to be a piece of paper outlining what was expected of job holders—nothing less, nothing more. Today we are seeing that piece of paper change to address the needs of a changing workforce and workplace expectations.

Dr. Charles Bethell-Fox, vice-president of Hay McBer's Human Resources Planning and Development practice in New York and Toronto, works closely with organizations to help them manage change through the development of effective work processes and competencies aligned with strategic business needs.

Dr. Bethell-Fox says: "When we look at what is changing in the workplace, we see that the traditional job and the nature of work are not what they used to be. People who work for organizations increasingly find themselves performing work that may not be covered in a job description. People are working in teams, and the demands in terms of skills and knowledge change as the project changes. Functional silos are breaking down and cross-functional teams are becoming the norm. We have also seen a delayering in organizations where a part of the hierarchy—particularly middle management—is being taken away. What that means for people and jobs is that they don't fit into tidy slots within the organization.[12]

"When we try to capture what people do in their jobs it is important to look at what they bring to the work situation. Knowing what they are able to do determines what they can get involved with, what strengths they bring to the team, how they can contribute. For example, look at the technical support worker who knows about a content area such as information systems. He or she is asked to work on project teams to supply a particular type of skill the team requires. Then he or she may also be asked to work on a different team with different groups of people and contribute other types of knowledge."

In addition, organizations are becoming increasingly focused on customers as a means of gaining a competitive advantage. "If you want competitive advantage, you need to leverage all internal resources to the greatest degree," states Bethell-Fox. As a job holder, if you have a particular strength you don't want to be positioned in the organization in such a way that the organization cannot gain maximum competitive advantage from your strength. The old hierarchical structures used to foster people working within functional silos, but today you want people working together. When you combine the skills of Person A with those of Person B, the two together may meet customer or market needs that could not have been achieved had you not built on the combined strengths of your people. "If people are working this way, based on what they can contribute, how can we talk about a job as if it fits into one part of the organization?" asks Bethell-Fox.

(continued on following page)

Looking at what people bring to their roles—their abilities, knowledge, and skills—is important because it helps you understand what they can contribute to the team. Bethell-Fox goes on to state, "If the measures of what an individual brings to an organization are accurate and reliable, you are in a better position to assess people and can better put them on teams where they will be able to maximize their contributions."

Clearly, job descriptions must still contain a clear description of accountabilities. But we also need to capture what competencies are expected in the job and how the person needs to do the job. For example, when we say that the individual must have five years of management experience, this tells us little about what is expected. If instead we state that the individual must be able to generate a high level of teamwork and achievement, the expectations become clearer—we can almost visualize what is expected.

Bethell-Fox further states: "If people are to maximize their contribution to the organization we need to have a clear understanding of the competencies that will deliver superior results. To deal with that we have devised what are called 'Just Noticeable Difference' (JND) competency measurement scales. On these scales, different behavioural indicators of any one competency are organized into an ascending scale where behaviours known to deliver progressively higher levels of job output and performance appear at progressively higher levels on each scale."

Once the right competencies have been identified for a job or job family, the scales can be used to specify the level of behaviour required to deliver superior performance. Then current job holders and job applicants can be assessed against the scales to measure how well their demonstrated levels of competency match the requirements for superior performance. For those who do not meet the right competencies, training can be provided.

Different levels of competency lead to different job holders doing the same job in different ways and, in effect, thereby doing different jobs. For example, one job holder might be a willing participant in the team, doing his or her share of the work. Another person in the same job, however, might demonstrate more proactive team behaviours, such as actively soliciting input from other team members or taking action to calm down conflicts among other team members. Effectively, these two people are doing two different jobs because of the competencies they demonstrate. In this way, competencies define what a job means.

In closing, one of the advantages of looking at things from a competency-based point of view is that if you have a clear understanding of the competencies that drive superior performance in a role then you can integrate a whole range of human resource applications around the competency framework. In other words, selection, training and development, performance management, and even pay systems can all be built around the competency framework. This adds significant value by ensuring that you now have multiple HR programs all pointed in the same direction and closely aligned with the business strategy.

criteria that are vague or not job-related are increasingly being challenged successfully. Managers of small businesses, where employees may perform many different job tasks, must be especially concerned about writing specific job descriptions.

When preparing job descriptions, managers must be aware of human rights legislation. Written job descriptions must match the requirements of the job. Position descriptions may need to be altered to meet "reasonable accommodation." Reasonable accommodation is used most often in relation to religious or disability needs. The 1992 case *Renaud v. British Columbia School Board* made it clear that reasonable accommodation for religious reasons is valid.[13] Job descriptions written to match the needs for reasonable accommodation reduce the risk of discrimination. The goal is to match and accommodate human capabilities to job requirements. For example, if the job requires the job holder to read extremely fine print, to climb ladders, or to memorize stock codes, these physical and mental requirements should be stated in the job description.

Managers may find that writing job descriptions is a tedious process that distracts from other supervisory responsibilities. Fortunately, software packages are available to simplify this time-consuming yet necessary task. In one program, the user is provided an initial library of more than 2500 prewritten job descriptions. Since the program works much like a word processor, text can be easily deleted, inserted, or modified to accommodate user demands.

JOB DESIGN

objective

Job design
Outgrowth of job analysis that improves jobs through technological and human considerations in order to enhance organization efficiency and employee job satisfaction

It is not uncommon for managers to confuse the processes of job analysis and job design. Job analysis is the study of jobs as currently performed by employees. It identifies job duties and requirements needed to perform the work successfully.

Job design, which is an outgrowth of job analysis, is concerned with structuring jobs in order to improve organization efficiency and employee job satisfaction. Job design is concerned with changing, modifying, and enriching jobs in order to capture the talents of employees while improving organization performance. For example, organizations engaged in continuous improvement or process re-engineering may revamp their jobs to eliminate unnecessary job tasks or find better ways of performing work. Job design should facilitate the achievement of organizational objectives. At the same time, the design should recognize the capabilities and needs of those who are to perform the job.

As Figure 3.4 illustrates, job design is a combination of four basic considerations: (1) the organizational objectives the job was created to fulfil; (2) industrial engineering considerations, including ways to make the job technologically efficient; (3) ergonomic concerns, including workers' physical and mental capabilities; and (4) employee contributions. Employee contributions are reflected in the participation of employees in making job improvements or enhancing operational decisions.

Behavioural Concerns

There are two job design methods that seek to incorporate the behavioural needs of employees as they perform their individual jobs. Both methods strive to satisfy the intrinsic needs of employees. The job enrichment model and the job characteristics model have long been popular with researchers and practitioners as ways to increase the job satisfaction of employees.

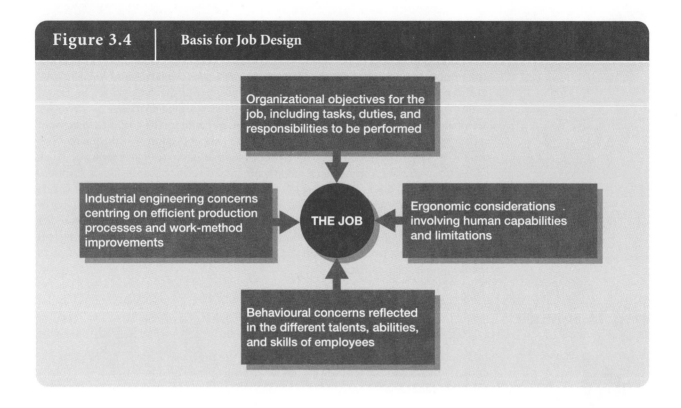

Figure 3.4 | **Basis for Job Design**

Organizational objectives for the job, including tasks, duties, and responsibilities to be performed

Industrial engineering concerns centring on efficient production processes and work-method improvements

THE JOB

Ergonomic considerations involving human capabilities and limitations

Behavioural concerns reflected in the different talents, abilities, and skills of employees

Job Enrichment

Any effort to make work more rewarding or satisfying by adding more meaningful tasks to an employee's job is called **job enrichment**. Originally popularized by Frederick Herzberg, job enrichment is touted as a means to fulfil the motivational needs of employees, such as for self-fulfilment and self-esteem, and as leading to long-term job satisfaction and the achievement of performance goals.[14] Job enrichment, or the vertical expansion of jobs, can be accomplished by increasing the autonomy and responsibility of employees. Herzberg discusses five factors involved in enriching jobs and thereby motivating employees: achievement, recognition, growth, responsibility, and performance of the whole job versus only parts of the job. For example, managers can enrich the jobs of employees by

Job enrichment
Enhancing a job by adding more meaningful tasks and duties to make the work more rewarding or satisfying

▶ increasing the level of difficulty and responsibility of the job;

▶ allowing employees to retain more authority and control over work outcomes;

▶ providing unit or individual job performance reports directly to employees;

▶ adding new tasks to the job that require training and growth; and

▶ assigning individuals specific tasks, thereby enabling them to become experts.

These factors allow employees to assume a greater role in the decision-making process and become more involved in planning, organizing, directing, and controlling their own work. Vertical job enrichment can also be accomplished by organizing workers into teams and giving these teams greater authority for self-management.

In spite of the benefits to be achieved through job enrichment, it must not be considered a panacea for overcoming production problems and employee discontent. Job enrichment programs are more likely to succeed in some jobs and work situations than in others. They are not the solution to such problems as dissatisfaction with pay, with employee benefits, or with employment security. Moreover, not all employees object to the mechanical pacing of an assembly line, nor do all employees seek additional responsibility or challenge. Some prefer routine jobs because they can let their minds wander while performing their work.

Job Characteristics

Job design studies explored a new field when behavioural scientists focused on various job dimensions that would improve simultaneously the efficiency of organizations and the job satisfaction of employees. Perhaps the theory that best exemplifies this research is the one advanced by Richard Hackman and Greg Oldham.[15] Their **job characteristics model** proposes that three psychological states of a job holder result in improved work performance, internal motivation, and lower absenteeism and turnover. The motivated, satisfied, and productive employee is one who (1) experiences meaningfulness of the work performed, (2) experiences responsibility for work outcomes, and (3) has knowledge of the results of the work performed. When these three psychological states are achieved, the employee is more strongly motivated to continue doing the job well.

Hackman and Oldham believe that five core job dimensions produce the three psychological states. The five job characteristics are as follows:

1. *Skill variety*. The degree to which a job entails a variety of different activities, which demand the use of a number of different skills and talents by the job holder.

2. *Task identity*. The degree to which the job requires completion of a whole and identifiable piece of work—that is, doing a job from beginning to end with a visible outcome.

3. *Task significance*. The degree to which the job has a substantial impact on the lives or work of other people, whether in the immediate organization or in the external environment.

4. *Autonomy*. The degree to which the job provides substantial freedom, independence, and discretion to the individual in scheduling the work and in determining the procedures to be used in carrying it out.

5. *Feedback*. The degree to which carrying out the work activities required by the job results in the individual being given direct and clear information about the effectiveness of his or her performance.

The job characteristics model seems to work best when certain conditions are met. One of these conditions is that employees must have the psychological desire for the autonomy, variety, responsibility, and challenge of enriched jobs. When this personal characteristic is absent, employees may resist the job redesign effort. Also, job redesign efforts almost always fail when employees lack the physical or mental skills, abilities, or education needed to perform the job. Forcing enriched jobs on individuals who lack these traits can result in frustrated employees.

objective

Job characteristics model
Job design that purports that three factors (meaningful work, responsibility for work outcomes, and knowledge of the results of the work performed) result in improved work performance, increased internal motivation, and lower absenteeism and turnover

Employee Empowerment

Job enrichment and job characteristics are specific programs that managers or supervisors can follow to formally change the jobs of employees. A less structured method is to allow employees to initiate their own job changes through the concept of empowerment. **Employee empowerment** is a technique for involving employees in their work through a process of inclusion. Empowerment encourages employees to become innovators and managers of their own work, and involves them in their jobs in ways that give them more control (see Highlights in HRM 3.2). Empowerment has been defined as "pushing down decision-making responsibility to those close to internal and external customers."

Employee empowerment
A technique of involving employees in their work through a process of inclusion

---

Highlights in HRM 3.2

ORGANIZATIONS EMPOWER THEIR EMPLOYEES

In today's highly competitive and dynamic business environment, employers as diverse as Home Depot, Wal-Mart, Cigna Health Care, Costco, Auto Zone, Disney, and Applebee's have turned to their employees to improve organizational performance. Empowered employees have made improvements in product or service quality, have reduced costs, and have modified or, in some cases, designed products.

▶ At Kraft Foods, employees at the company's food plant participated in work-redesign changes and team building that increased productivity, reduced overhead, and cut assembly time.

▶ Avon Products empowered its minority managers to improve sales and service in inner-city markets. Grounded in the belief that minority managers better understand the culture of inner-city residents, Avon turned an unprofitable market into a highly productive sales area.

▶ At Ford's factory, one group of employees made a suggestion saving $115 000 a year on the purchase of gloves used to protect workers who handle sheet metal and glass. The group figured out how to have the gloves washed so they could be used more than once.

▶ Home Depot's Special Project Support Teams (SPST) work to improve the organization's business and information services. Employees with a wide range of backgrounds and skills collaborate to address a great variety of strategic and tactical business needs.

▶ Herman Miller, Inc., a manufacturer of office equipment, expects its employees to participate with managers in decisions involving product quality and service. Herman Miller prides itself on having a corporate culture regarded as highly egalitarian.

▶ At Zero Knowledge Systems, a Montreal company that produces privacy software for Internet users, employees choose their own job titles. A top developer chose the title International Man of Mystery.

While defining empowerment can become the first step to achieving it, in order for empowerment to grow and thrive, organizations must encourage these conditions:

▶ *Participation.* Employees must be encouraged to take control of their work tasks. Employees, in turn, must care about improving their work process and interpersonal work relationships.

▶ *Innovation.* The environment must be receptive to people with innovative ideas and must encourage people to explore new paths and to take reasonable risks at reasonable costs. An empowered environment is created when curiosity is as highly regarded as technical expertise.

▶ *Access to information.* Employees must have access to a wide range of information. Involved individuals make decisions about what kind of information they need for performing their jobs.

▶ *Accountability.* Empowerment does not involve being able to do whatever you want. Empowered employees should be held accountable for their behaviour toward others. They must produce agreed-upon results, achieve credibility, and operate with a positive approach.

Additionally, employee empowerment succeeds when the culture of the organization is open and receptive to change. An organization's culture is created largely through the philosophies of senior managers and their leadership traits and behaviours. In an empowered organization, effective leadership is exemplified by managers who are honest, caring, and receptive to new ideas, and who treat employees with dignity and respect and as partners in organizational success.

Industrial Engineering Considerations

Industrial engineering
A field of study concerned with analyzing work methods and establishing time standards

The study of work is an important contribution of the scientific management movement. **Industrial engineering**, which evolved with this movement, is concerned with analyzing work methods and establishing time standards. Specifically, it involves the study of work cycles to determine which, if any, elements can be modified, combined, rearranged, or eliminated to reduce the time needed to complete the cycle. Next, time standards are established by recording the time required to complete each element in the work cycle, using a stopwatch or work-sampling technique. By combining the times for each element, the total time required is determined. This time is subsequently adjusted to allow for the skill and effort demonstrated by the observed worker and for interruptions that may occur in performing the work. The adjusted time becomes the time standard for that particular work cycle. The new Autotrans automotive plant in Ingersoll, Ontario, uses a hand-controlled crane, ensuring that the operator need never bend or lift. GDX, a producer of automotive sealing systems in Welland, Ontario, made ergonomic changes in all departments, but particularly in those where employees were required to do heavy repetitive work for six to eight hours. As a result of the ergonomics program, injuries have declined markedly and productivity has improved.[16]

Industrial engineering constitutes a disciplined and objective approach to job design. Unfortunately, the concern of industrial engineering focuses for improving efficiency and simplifying work methods may cause the behavioural considerations in job design to be neglected. What sometimes may be improvement in job design and efficiency from an engineering standpoint can sometimes be psychologically unsound. For example, the assembly line with its simplified and repetitive tasks embodies solid principles of industrial engineering, but these tasks are often not psychologically rewarding for those who must perform them. Thus, to be effective, job design must also provide for the satisfaction of human needs.

Ergonomic Considerations

Ergonomics
An interdisciplinary approach to designing equipment and systems that can be easily and efficiently used by human beings

Ergonomics attempts to accommodate the human capabilities and deficiencies of those who are to perform a job. It is concerned with adapting the entire job system—the work, the work environment, the machines, the equipment, and the processes—to match human characteristics.[17] In short, it seeks to fit the job to the person rather than the person to the job. Ergonomics attempts to minimize the harmful effects of carelessness, negligence, and other human fallibilities that otherwise might cause product defects, damage to equipment, or even the injury or death of employees.

Equipment design must take into consideration the physical ability of operators to use the equipment and to react through vision, hearing, and touch to the information the equipment conveys. Designing equipment controls to be compatible with the physical characteristics and reaction capabilities of the people who must operate them, and

A comfortable workstation lends itself to productivity improvement and a reduction in job-related stresses and injuries.

PHOTODISC

with the environment they work in, is increasingly important. Ergonomics also considers the requirements of a diverse workforce, accommodating, for example, women who may lack the strength to operate equipment requiring intense physical force. At General Motors of Canada's newly designed transmission plant in Windsor, Ontario, mechanical assists have been installed to insulate the operators from force factors. These ergonomically designed assists use articulating arms to help operators ward off the potentially strain-causing force of the heavy parts they must lift, push, or pull.

Ergonomics contributes to productivity improvements and has been cost-effective at organizations such as Chrysler and the *Toronto Star*. The latter organization sought to minimize repetitive strain injuries (RSIs) among its employees by introducing ergonomically designed workstations and by training people in the proper use of keyboards and other office equipment.[18] Figure 3.5 provides a checklist of potential repetitive strain injuries for employees using computers.

Designing Work for Group Contributions

Although a variety of group techniques have been developed to involve employees more fully in their organizations, all these techniques have two characteristics in common—enhancing collaboration and increasing synergy. By increasing the degree of collaboration in the work environment, these techniques can improve work processes and organizational decision making. By increasing group synergy, they underline the adage that the contributions of two or more employees are greater than the sum of their individual efforts. Research has shown that working in a group setting strengthens employee commitment to an organization's goals, increases employee acceptance of decisions, and encourages a cooperative approach to workplace tasks. Two collaborative techniques are discussed here: employee involvement groups and employee teams.

Employee Involvement Groups

Employee involvement groups (EIs)

Groups of employees who meet to resolve problems or offer suggestions for organizational improvement

Groups of five to ten employees doing similar or related work who meet together regularly to identify, analyze, and suggest solutions to shared problems are often referred to as **employee involvement groups (EIs)**. Also widely known as *quality circles* (QCs), EIs are used mainly to involve employees in the larger goals of the organization through their suggestions for improving product or service quality and cutting costs.[19] Generally, EIs recommend their solutions to management, which decides whether to implement them.

The employee involvement group process, illustrated in Figure 3.6, begins with EI members brainstorming job-related problems or concerns and gathering data about these issues. The process continues through the generation of solutions and recommendations, which are then communicated to management. If the solutions are implemented, results are measured and the EI and its members are usually recognized for the contributions they have made. EIs typically meet four or more hours each month. The meetings are chaired by a leader chosen from the group. The leader does not hold an authority position but instead serves as a discussion facilitator.

EIs have become an important employee contribution system, but they are not without their problems and their critics. First, to achieve the results desired, those participating in EIs must receive comprehensive training in

USING THE INTERNET

For sources of information about employee involvement, check out the Employee Involvement Association:

www.eianet.org/main.cfm

| Figure 3.5 | Computer Workstation Ergonomics Checklist |

Use the following list to identify potential problem areas that should receive further investigation. Any "no" response may point to a problem.

1. Does the workstation ensure proper worker posture, such as
   ▶ thighs in the horizontal position?
   ▶ lower legs in the vertical position?
   ▶ feet flat on the floor or on a footrest?
   ▶ wrists straight and relaxed?

2. Does the chair
   ▶ adjust easily?
   ▶ have a padded seat with a rounded front?
   ▶ have an adjustable backrest?
   ▶ provide lumbar support?
   ▶ have casters?

3. Are the height and tilt of the work surface on which the keyboard is located adjustable?

4. Is the keyboard detachable?

5. Do keying actions require minimal force?

6. Is there an adjustable document holder?

7. Are armrests provided where needed?

8. Are glare and reflections minimized?

9. Does the monitor have brightness and contrast controls?

10. Is there sufficient space for knees and feet?

11. Can the workstation be used for either right- or left-handed activity?

Source: The National Institute for Occupational Safety and Health (NIOSH), *Elements of Ergonomics Programs: A Primer Based on Workplace Evaluations of Musculoskeletal Disorders* (Washington, DC: U.S. Government Printing Office, March 1997).

problem identification and problem analysis, and in the use of various decision-making tools such as statistical analysis and cause-and-effect diagrams. Comprehensive training for EIs is often cited as the most important factor leading to their success. Second, managers should recognize the group when a recommendation is made, regardless of whether the recommendation is adopted. This approach encourages the group to continue coming up with ideas even when they are not all implemented by management. Third, some organizations have found that EIs run out of ideas, at which point management must feed them ideas to keep the process going.

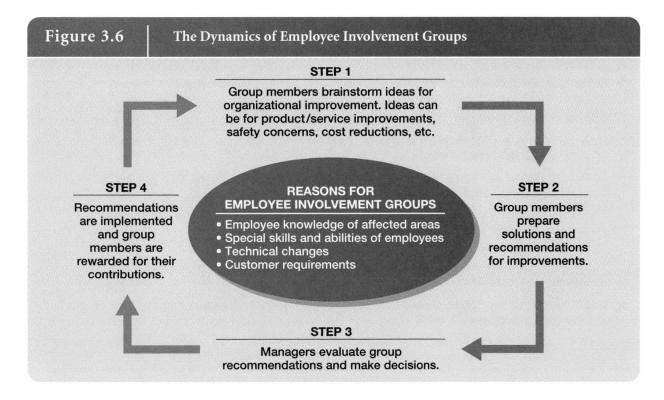

Figure 3.6 | The Dynamics of Employee Involvement Groups

STEP 1
Group members brainstorm ideas for organizational improvement. Ideas can be for product/service improvements, safety concerns, cost reductions, etc.

STEP 2
Group members prepare solutions and recommendations for improvements.

STEP 3
Managers evaluate group recommendations and make decisions.

STEP 4
Recommendations are implemented and group members are rewarded for their contributions.

REASONS FOR EMPLOYEE INVOLVEMENT GROUPS
- Employee knowledge of affected areas
- Special skills and abilities of employees
- Technical changes
- Customer requirements

Source: Adapted from materials prepared by The Family and Relationship Center, 7946 Ivanhoe Avenue, La Jolla, CA 92037.

Finally and most importantly, managers and supervisors must exhibit a participative/democratic leadership style where employees are encouraged to work collaboratively with management to improve organizational performance.

Employee Teams

During the past decade perhaps one of the more radical changes to how work is done is the introduction of employee teams. Employee teams are a logical outgrowth of employee involvement and of the philosophy of empowerment. While many definitions of teams exist, we define an **employee team** as a group of employees working together toward a common purpose, whose members have complementary skills, the work of the members is mutually dependent, and the group has discretion over tasks performed. Furthermore, teams seek to make members of the work group share responsibility for their group's performance. Inherent in the concept of employee teams is that employees, not managers, are in the best position to contribute to workplace improvements. With work teams, managers accept the notion that the group is the logical work unit, and then apply resources to resolve organizational problems and concerns.[20] Teamwork also embraces the concept of synergy. Synergy occurs when the interaction and outcome of team members is greater than the sum of their individual efforts. Unfortunately, synergy may not automatically happen, but rather, it must be nurtured within the team environment. Figure 3.7 lists the factors contributing to a synergistic team setting.

Employee teams
An employee contributions technique whereby work functions are structured for groups rather than for individuals and team members are given discretion in matters traditionally considered management prerogatives

| Figure 3.7 | Synergistic Team Characteristics |

Team synergy is heightened when team members engage in these positive behaviours.

▶ *Support.* The team exhibits an atmosphere of inclusion. All team members speak up and feel free to offer constructive comments.

▶ *Listen and Clarify.* Active listening is practised. Members honestly listen to others and seek clarification on discussion points. Team members summarize discussions held.

▶ *Disagree.* Disagreement is seen as natural and is expected. Member comments are nonjudgmental and focus on factual issues rather than personality conflicts.

▶ *Consensus.* Team members reach agreements through consensus decision making. Consensus decisions require finding a proposal that is acceptable to all team members, even if not the first choice of individual members. Common ground among ideas is sought.

▶ *Acceptance.* Team members are valued as individuals, recognizing that each person brings a valuable mix of skills and abilities to team operations.

▶ *Quality.* Each team member is committed to excellent performance. There is emphasis on continuous improvement and attention to detail.

For an excellent resource on creating team synergy, see *Kaizen Strategies for Improving Team Performance,* edited by Michael Colenso (London, England: Pearson Education, 2000).

Teams can operate in a variety of structures, each with different strategic purposes or functional activities. Figure 3.8 describes common team forms. One form, self-directed teams, is being adopted in many organizations. Self-directed teams, also called *autonomous work groups, self-managed teams,* or *high-performance teams,* are groups of employees who are accountable for a "whole" work process or segment that delivers a product or service to an internal or external customer. Team members acquire multiple skills that enable them to perform a variety of job tasks. To varying degrees, team members work together to improve their operations, handle day-to-day concerns, and plan and control their work. Typical team functions include setting work schedules, dealing directly with external customers, training team members, setting performance targets, budgeting, and purchasing equipment and services.[21]

Self-directed teams are designed to give the team "ownership" of a product or service. In manufacturing environments, a team might be responsible for a whole product or a clearly defined segment of the production process. At Eastman Kodak Company, teams are responsible for manufacturing entire "product lines," including processing, lab work, and packaging. Similarly, in a service environment a team usually has responsibility for entire groupings of products and services, often serving clients in a designated geographic area. Providing employees with this type of ownership usually requires broader job categories and the sharing of work assignments.

To compete in national and international markets, managers have formed **virtual teams**. Virtual teams use advanced computer and telecommunications technology to link team members who are geographically dispersed—often worldwide.[22] Management may form a cross-functional team (see Figure 3.8) to develop a new pharmaceutical drug and have the team operate in a virtual environment to achieve

Virtual teams
A team with widely dispersed members linked together through computer and telecommunications technology

Figure 3.8	Forms of Employee Teams

Cross-functional teams. A group staffed with a mix of specialists (e.g., marketing, production, engineering) and formed to accomplish a specific objective. Cross-functional teams are based on assigned rather than voluntary membership.

Project teams. A group formed specifically to design a new product or service. Members are assigned by management on the basis of their ability to contribute to success. The group usually disbands after task completion.

Self-directed teams. Groups of highly trained individuals performing a set of interdependent job tasks within a natural work unit. Team members use consensus decision making to perform work duties, solve problems, or deal with internal or external customers.

Task force teams. A task force is formed by management to immediately resolve a major problem. The group is responsible for developing a long-term plan for problem resolution that may include a charge for implementing the solution proposed.

Process-improvement teams. A group made up of experienced people from different departments or functions and charged with improving quality, decreasing waste, or enhancing productivity in processes that affect all departments or functions involved. Team members are normally appointed by management.

its goal. Virtual teams provide new opportunities for training, product development, and product market analysis. Importantly, virtual teams provide access to previously unavailable expertise and enhance cross-functional interactions. However, while the benefits of virtual teams are many, they are not without their problems, including language and cultural barriers and different goals and objectives across departments.[23]

Regardless of the structure or purpose of the team, the following characteristics have been identified with successful teams:

▶ Commitment to shared goals and objectives
▶ Consensus decision making
▶ Open and honest communication
▶ Shared leadership
▶ Climate of cooperation, collaboration, trust, and support
▶ Valuing of individuals for their diversity
▶ Recognition of conflict and its positive resolution[24]

Unfortunately, not all teams succeed or operate to their full potential. Therefore, in adopting the work team concept, organizations must address several issues that could present obstacles to effective team function, including overly high expectations, group compensation, training, career movement, and power.[25] For example, new team members must be retrained to work outside their primary functional areas, and compensation systems must be constructed to reward individuals for team accomplishments. Since team membership demands more general skills, and since it moves an employee out of the historical career path, new career paths to general management must be created from the team experience. Finally, as the team members become capable of carrying out functions, such as strategic planning, that were previously restricted to higher levels of management, managers must be prepared to utilize their newfound expertise.

Another difficulty with work teams is that they alter the traditional manager–employee relationship. Managers often find it hard to adapt to the role of leader rather than supervisor and sometimes feel threatened by the growing power of the team and the reduced power of management.[26] Furthermore, some employees may have difficulty adapting to a role that includes traditional supervisory responsibilities. Another difficulty with work teams is that they must be incorporated into the organization's strategic planning process. Therefore, from our experience in working with teams, extensive attention must be given to training team members as they go through the four stages of team development—forming, storming, norming, and performing.[27] Complete training would cover the importance of skills in team leadership, mission/goal setting, conduct of meetings, team decision making, conflict resolution, effective communication, and diversity awareness.[28]

Flexible Work Schedules

objective

Flexible work schedules are not a true part of job design, since job tasks and responsibilities are not changed. Nevertheless, we discuss adjustments in work schedules here because they alter the normal work week, in which all employees begin and end their workday at the same preset time (usually five eight-hour days). Employers may depart from the traditional workday or work week in an attempt to improve organizational productivity and morale by giving employees increased control over the hours they work. Flexible work schedules may be assigned by the organization or requested by individual employees; see Highlights in HRM 3.3. The more common alternative work schedules include the compressed work week, flextime, job sharing, and telecommuting.

Highlights in HRM 3.3

A SAMPLE FLEXTIME PROPOSAL FROM PRICEWATERHOUSECOOPERS

This proposal is an abbreviated version of PricewaterhouseCoopers' FWA [flexible work arrangement] policy. Employees interested in flexible scheduling must complete this form and have it approved by their superiors before they can activate flextime schedules.

The FWA proposal is designed to incorporate many of the issues that must be considered when designing a flexible work arrangement and must be completed by all PWC individuals on an FWA. Please complete the following proposal. Your mentor or others may assist you.

Part 1 Proposal

1. Benefits and barriers for the firm. What are the benefits of this flexible work arrangement for the firm? Identify potential barriers that a flexible work arrangement could raise with clients, partners, staff.

2. Flexibility and availability. Clarify your availability to travel or meet unexpected work needs on days or at times when you are not in the office or formally scheduled to work.
3. Communication. How will you maintain communication with the office? With clients? How will you let others know when you want to change your schedule?
4. Efficiency and coverage. How will you ensure that your new schedule won't be disruptive to work flow? Describe your backup plan when you are unavailable and someone—client, partner, staff—needs something fast.
5. Flexible Work Arrangement (check one):
    Reduced Hours
    Job Sharing
    Seasonal Employment
    Compressed Workweek
    Flextime
    Telecommuting

Part 2 Considerations
6. Reasons/benefits for yourself. What are the perceived benefits for you? Are you meeting your career and personal goals?
7. Describe current and proposed work schedules (include hours per week and per day if different from standard office hours).
8. Summarize your current workload and client responsibilities/relationships and proposed changes—transitioning clients to other staff, relinquishing main contact relationship, etc.

Using the completed proposal as a guide, discuss the proposed arrangement with your supervisor, coach, and local HR representative. The agreed-upon arrangement should be reviewed, evaluated, and discussed quarterly to ensure it is successful for the individual, the office, the clients, and staff.

Source: Sarah Fister Gale, "Formalized Flextime: The Perk That Brings Productivity," *Workforce* 80, no. 2 (February 2001).

The Compressed Work Week

Under a compressed work week, the number of days in the work week is shortened by lengthening the number of hours worked per day. This schedule is best illustrated by the four-day, forty-hour week, generally referred to as 4/10 or 4/40. Employees working a four-day work week might work ten hours a day, Monday through Thursday. Although the 4/10 schedule is probably the best known, other compressed arrangements include reducing weekly hours to thirty-eight or thirty-six hours, or scheduling eighty hours over nine days (9/80), taking one day off every other week.

Organizations that operate batch-processing systems (e.g., oil companies such as Shell Oil) use shorter work weeks to coordinate work schedules with production schedules. Used by about 15 percent of Canadian companies, compressed work weeks can assist with scheduling arrangements by improving plant and equipment utilization. The keying of work schedules to processing time for a specific operation rather than to a standard work week reduces startup and close-down time and often results in higher weekly output.

The major disadvantage of the compressed work week relates to employment standards legislation governing the payment of overtime to nonsupervisory employees who work more than a specified number of hours per week. This legislation, which varies from province to province, is discussed in greater depth in Chapter 9. Another disadvantage of the compressed work week is that it increases the amount of stress on managers and employees. Finally, long workdays can be exhausting.

Managers cite the following reasons for implementing compressed work week schedules:

▶ Recruitment and retention of employees
▶ Coordinating employee work schedules with production schedules
▶ Accommodating the leisure-time activities of employees while facilitating employee personal appointments
▶ Improvements in employee job satisfaction and morale.

Flextime

Flextime

Flexible working hours that permit employees the option of choosing daily starting and quitting times, provided that they work a set number of hours per day or week

Flextime, or flexible working hours, permits employees to choose their own daily starting and quitting times, provided that they work a certain number of hours per day or week. With flextime, employees are given considerable latitude in scheduling their work. However, there is a "core period" during the morning and afternoon when all employees are required to be on the job. Flexible working hours are most common in service-type organizations—financial institutions, government agencies, and other organizations with large clerical operations. Kraft Canada and Manulife Financial

An advantage of working flexible hours is the ability to commute during non-peak times.

PHOTODISC

have found that flextime provides many advantages for the company's employees. Royal Bank Financial Group found that about half of the nearly 4000 users choose flexible arrangements because of family responsibilities; the rest cite other reasons such as continuing education and community involvement. As shown in Highlights in HRM 3.4, Generation X values flextime, and most organizations offer this.

Used by about 20 percent of Canadian organizations, flextime provides employees and employers with several advantages. By allowing employees greater flexibility in work scheduling, employers reduce some of the traditional causes of tardiness and absenteeism. Also, employees can adjust their work to accommodate their particular lifestyles, and in doing so gain greater job satisfaction. Employees can also schedule their working hours for the time of day when they are most productive. Variations in

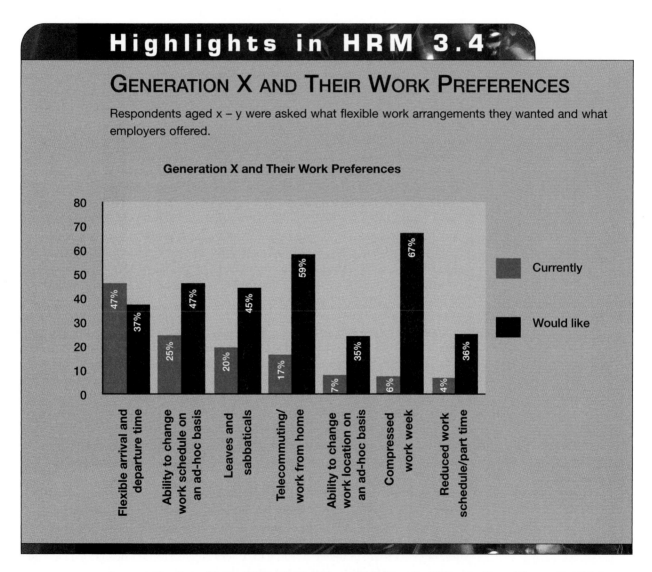

Highlights in HRM 3.4

GENERATION X AND THEIR WORK PREFERENCES

Respondents aged x – y were asked what flexible work arrangements they wanted and what employers offered.

Generation X and Their Work Preferences

Preference	Currently	Would like
Flexible arrival and departure time	47%	37%
Ability to change work schedule on an ad-hoc basis	25%	47%
Leaves and sabbaticals	20%	45%
Telecommuting/work from home	17%	59%
Ability to change work location on an ad-hoc basis	7%	35%
Compressed work week	6%	67%
Reduced work schedule/part time	4%	36%

Source: A. Thomlinson, "Younger Workers Not So Different after All," *Canadian HR Reporter* 15, no. 2 (January 28, 2002): 2.

arrival and departure times can help reduce traffic congestion at the peak commuting hours. In some situations, employees require less time to commute, and the pressures of meeting a rigid schedule are reduced.

From the employer's standpoint, flextime can be most helpful in recruiting and retaining personnel. It has proved invaluable to organizations that wish to improve service to customers or clients by extending operating hours. Bruncor, a telecommunications company, uses flextime to keep its business offices open for customers who cannot get there during the day. Research demonstrates that flextime can have a positive impact on reliability, quality, and quantity of employee work.

There are, of course, several disadvantages to flextime. First, it is not suited to some jobs. It is not feasible, for example, where specific workstations must be staffed at all times. Second, it can create problems for managers in communicating with and instructing employees. Also, flextime schedules may also force these managers to extend their work week if they are to exercise control over their subordinates.

Job Sharing

The arrangement whereby two part-time employees perform a job that otherwise would be held by one full-time employee is called "job sharing." Job sharers usually work three days a week, "creating an overlap day for extended face-to-face conferencing." Their pay is three-fifths of a regular salary; however, job sharers usually take on additional responsibilities beyond what the original job would require. Companies that use job sharing are primarily in the legal, advertising, and financial-services businesses. Canadian banks are well known for their job-sharing programs. Employers note that without job sharing two good employees might otherwise be lost.

Job sharing is suited to the needs of families in which one or both spouses desire to work only part-time.[29] It is also suited to the needs of older workers who want to phase into retirement by shortening their work week. For the employer, the work of part-time employees can be scheduled to conform to peaks in the daily workload. Job sharing can also limit layoffs in hard economic times. A final benefit is that employees engaged in job sharing have time off during the week to accommodate personal needs, so they are less likely to be absent.

Job sharing does have several problems, however. Employers may not want to employ two people to do the work of one, because the time required to orient and train a second employee constitutes an added burden. They may also want to avoid prorating employee benefits between two part-time employees. This problem can be addressed by permitting the employees to contribute the difference between the health insurance (or life insurance) premiums for a full-time employee and the pro rata amount the employer would otherwise contribute for a part-time employee. The key to making job sharing work is good communications between the partners, who will use a number of ways to stay in contact—phone calls, written updates, e-mail, and voice mail.

Telecommuting

Telecommuting
Use of personal computers, networks, and other communications technology to do work in the home that is traditionally done in the workplace

One of the more dynamic changes, and potentially the most far-reaching, is telecommuting. **Telecommuting** is the use of personal computers, networks, and other communications technology such as fax machines to do work in the home that is traditionally done in the workplace.[30] A variant of telecommuting is the *virtual office* where employees are in the field selling to or servicing customers or stationed at other remote locations working as if they were in the home office.

Telecommuting presents some limitations, including the loss of creativity as employees are not interacting with each other on a regular basis, the difficulty of developing appropriate performance standards and evaluation systems, and the need to formulate an appropriate technology strategy for allocation resources.

The advantages of telecommuting are

▶ increased flexibility for employees,

▶ ability to attract workers who might not otherwise be available,

▶ less time and money wasted on physical commuting,

▶ burden lessened on working parents,

▶ increased productivity, and

▶ reduced absenteeism.[31]

Perhaps the strongest economic reason in favour of telework is its power to retain valued employees. Retention is a top priority for employers largely because the costs of replacing employees are far higher than those involved in installing a telecommuting arrangement.[32] Figure 3.9 presents suggestions for establishing a successful telecommuting program.

These flexible job arrangements have significant advantages to employers and employees, as discussed in Highlights in HRM 3.5.

Figure 3.9	Keys for Successful Telecommuting

▶ *Identify jobs best suited to distance work.* Those involving sales, customer service, and auditing are logical choices.

▶ *Select responsible employees.* Employees who are self-starters, motivated, and trustworthy and who can work independently are ideal candidates. Establish employee feedback procedures and performance review methods for employee evaluation.

▶ *Establish formalized telecommuting procedures.* Telecommuting guidelines could cover hours of availability, office reporting periods, performance expectations, and weekly progress reports or e-mail updates.

▶ *Begin a formal training program.* Training for both telecommuters and managers should include the technical aspects of equipment usage and relationship factors such as how and when to contact the office or availability and location of support facilities.

▶ *Keep telecommuters informed.* Physical separation can make telecommuters feel isolated and invisible. Department and staff updates, inclusion of telecommuters on project teams, required attendance at meetings, and "chat room" discussions all serve to keep telecommuters "in the loop."

▶ *Recognize when telecommuting isn't working.* State in telecommunicating policies that the arrangement may be terminated when it no longer serves company needs or if the employee's performance declines.

Source: Adapted from "What Is the Future of Telework?" *HRFocus* 78, no. 3 (March 2001): 5–6.

Highlights in HRM 3.5

FLEXTIME AND WORK-LIFE BALANCE

Nora Spinks, president and CEO of Work-Life Harmony Enterprises, works with employers to create organizational cultures that enable employees to achieve work–life balance. The firm's goal is to develop successful work environments where individuals and organizations have the ability to reach their full potential and where employees have full and satisfying lives outside their work.

Spinks asserts that employers benefit from these family-friendly policies: "The most effective and productive employees are those who do work they enjoy, are challenged, have access to the necessary resources to meet that challenge, have control over how they work, receive recognition, rewards, and compensation based on the effort they put forth, and feel their life outside of work is respected and valued. These employees are highly resilient. In today's world of work, individual and organizational resiliency is critical for success. People in resilient, adaptable, responsive environments have the ability to change, the capacity to adapt to change, the energy to drive change and the flexibility to react positively to change, regardless of the intensity or the factors outside of their immediate control such as market forces, economic pressures and social or political circumstances."

Today's most popular employee support initiative is workplace flexibility: flextime with core hours and flexible start and end times, compressed work weeks (full workload completed in less than five days per week), and/or permanent part-time hours with equal status, pro-rated benefits, and the same development opportunities as full-time employees. Gaining in popularity are creative alternatives such as extended work weeks (full workload completed in six days) and self-funded or radical sabbaticals (setting aside a portion of pay for a period of time and taking an extended leave while collecting the banked salary—e.g., 2.5 years working at 85 percent pay and six months away from the workplace on a self-funded sabbatical).

Employees are using the time gained from workplace flexibility to fulfil family responsibilities, create a balanced lifestyle, continue their education, make a contribution to their community, or volunteer in developing countries.

Spinks argues strongly for these policies: "Establishing control over hours of work has very specific, well-documented results: reduction in illness, injury, absenteeism, presenteeism (physically present, but mentally and emotionally absent), turnover, conflict, and unhealthy lifestyles and behaviours such as smoking, drinking, and drugs.

"When you work too hard or too long, you tend to rely on substances such as nicotine, caffeine, or sugar boosters to get you through the day. When you are tired all the time, your ability to solve problems and resolve conflicts is decreased significantly. When you are run down, you become uninterested and disengaged. Employees who have control over their working hours have more energy, more time, and are more engaged at home, at work, and in the community. Employers, customers, and co-workers benefit during the day, and employees, their family, friends, and community benefit at the end of the day.

"When I started in this field many years ago, employers had no understanding of the issues. I received several letters from companies saying, 'Thank you for your interest, but all our charitable dollars have been allocated for this year.' So we began to build the business case for supportive work environments. In the eighties and nineties, progressive HR departments began to implement programs and policies to address the issues. Now in 2001, employers across all sectors, from all industries, are beginning to see the strategic advantages of a family-friendly, employee-supportive work environment. I now work with CEOs in boardrooms, integrating these concepts into corporate strategy.

"I think there are many reasons why employers are embracing these policies now: labour force demographics, tight labour markets, and an increasing body of evidence documenting the costs and benefits of supportive work environments and the high costs of work–life imbalance and stress in the workplace."

SUMMARY

 Job requirements reflect the different duties, tasks, and responsibilities contained in jobs. Job requirements, in turn, influence the HR function performed by managers, including recruitment, selection, training and development, performance appraisal, compensation, and various labour relations activities.

 Job analysis data can be gathered using one of several collection methods—interviews, questionnaires, observations, or diaries. Other more quantitative approaches include use of functional job analysis, the position analysis questionnaire system, and the critical incident method.

 The format of job descriptions varies widely, often reflecting the needs of the organization and the expertise of the writer. At a minimum, job descriptions should contain a job title, a job identification section, and an essential functions section. A job specification section can also be included. Job descriptions should be written in clear and specific terms, with consideration given to their legal implications.

 Job design is a combination of four basic considerations: organizational objectives; industrial engineering concerns (i.e., analyzing work methods and establishing time standards); ergonomic considerations, which accommodate human capabilities and limitations to job task; and employee contributions.

 In the job characteristics model, five job factors contribute to increased job performance and satisfaction: skill variety, task identity, task significance, autonomy, and feedback. All factors should be built into jobs, since each factor influences different employee psychological states. When jobs are enriched through the job characteristics model, employees experience more meaningfulness in their jobs, acquire more job responsibility, and receive direct feedback from the tasks they perform.

 To improve the internal processes of organizations and increase productivity, organizations are making greater efforts to involve groups of employees in work operations. Employee involvement groups are composed of employees in work units, who are charged with offering suggestions for improving product or service quality or fostering workplace effectiveness. Employee teams stress employee collaboration over individual accomplishment. Teams rely on the expertise and different abilities of their members to achieve specific objectives.

Changes in work schedules—which include the compressed work week, flextime, job sharing, and telecommuting—permit employees to adjust their work periods to accommodate their particular lifestyles. Employers can select from among these HR techniques to accommodate diverse employee needs while fostering organizational effectiveness.

KEY TERMS

critical incident method 97
employee empowerment 108
employee involvement groups
  (EIs) 111
employee teams 113
ergonomics 110
flextime 118
functional job analysis (FJA) 96

industrial engineering 109
job 90
job analysis 93
job characteristics model 107
job description 91
job design 105
job enrichment 106
job family 90

job specification 91
position 90
position analysis questionnaire
  (PAQ) 97
telecommuting 120
virtual teams 114

DISCUSSION QUESTIONS

1. Place yourself in the position of general manager of a service department. How could formally written job requirements help you manage your work unit?

2. Discuss the various methods for completing a job analysis. Compare and contrast these methods, noting the pros and cons of each.

3. Working with two or three other students, collect at least five different job descriptions from organizations in your area. Compare the descriptions, highlighting similarities and differences.

4. In small groups, write a job description for "student," with each group using a different technique. Compare and critique these job descriptions.

5. Figure 3.8 shows the different forms of employee teams. Provide an example of where each type of team can be used.

6. As a small business employer, explain how nontraditional work schedules might make it easier for you to recruit employees.

7. Flexible work arrangements at CIBC are labelled "Work and Lifestyle Options" and include flexible work hours, job sharing, part-time work, and telecommuting. Go to the HRDC website (http://labour-travail.hrdc-drhc.gc.ca/wip/casestudies/cibc-en.pdf) and search for the article "Family Friendly Policies at CIBC." Document the reasons why CIBC developed these work arrangements, and the benefits they hope to achieve. (Note that this site also contains other cases on employee empowerment and alternative work arrangements. Read about how MacMillan Bloedel used teams to achieve higher production levels and profitability, and how NB Tel redesigned work to increase organizational effectiveness.)

Developing Managerial Skills

IDENTIFYING THE CHARACTERISTICS OF SUCCESSFUL TEAMS

Professional trainers acknowledge that identifying the characteristics of successful teams is a cornerstone to any team training program. When trainees understand the key traits of successful teams, they can model (and, thus, internalize) the traits needed for effective team performance. Additionally, once identified, the characteristics of successful teams serve as a focal point for learning advanced team skills.

Organizations often begin their team training program by having trainees identify the characteristics of successful teams to which they have belonged (such as other work groups, sports teams, or a civic group). This exercise, called an "ice breaker" by organizational trainers, is easy to conduct and serves as an excellent way for trainees to become personally acquainted while learning valuable team knowledge.

Assignment

1. Working in teams of four to six individuals, identify what the group believes are successful characteristics of groups or teams. Strive to agree upon no more than eight to ten significant team characteristics.
2. Write the group's findings on flip charts and post for all to see. One member from each team should explain its findings to all class members.
3. Point out the similarities between team results. These points become your building blocks for successful team performance.

Case Study 1

Ducks Unlimited Canada

Ducks Unlimited Canada, a not-for-profit environmental agency, has as its goal the protection of wetland habitat in Canada. Relying on its 100 000 members, 7000 volunteers, and 330 employees, this charitable organization has saved more than 18 million acres in Canada. Ducks Unlimited has no problem attracting biologists, scientists, and accountants, because their recruits are committed to a conservation ethic and are dedicated to protecting the environment. It has also helped recruitment that Ducks Unlimited has reorganized itself to flatten its management structure. The goal was to empower the employees and facilitate decision making. People working in the field no longer have to go up and down the power ladder to obtain approvals at every step. Field employees feel more in control of what they are doing.

The human resources administrator cites many advantages to an empowered workforce: increased retention, increased motivation, and decreased absenteeism and sick days.

Source: Adapted from "Taking Care of the People," *Canadian Health Care Manager* 6, no. 3 (April–May 1999): 5–9.

QUESTIONS

1. What arguments could be advanced both for and against the use of employee empowerment?
2. Empowerment is mainly a motivational tool, but at Ducks Unlimited the employees arrive dedicated and committed to the environmental cause. Does Ducks Unlimited need to implement empowerment?
3. How might a manager at a traditional organization react to the implementation of empowerment?

Case Study 2

Flexible Work Arrangements

Empty Cubicles: How Would You Manage Vacancy?

In the July 2001 issue of *Training and Development Journal*, Darin E. Hartley explores many of the issues related to telecommuting. As a developer of new business ventures for the Advanced Society for Training and Development, Darin telecommutes about three-fourths of his working time. Here are some of the interesting and amusing comments he has heard about telecommuting:

"How can you stand being home with your husband/wife that much?"

"I couldn't work like that because I need to talk to people. I'm social."

"Do you wear your pajamas all day?"

"It must be a dream working at home. I wish I could do that."

"How can you get anything done? I need to be in the office."

"What happens when you have a computer problem?"

"Do you really work, or do you just watch daytime television?"

Misconceptions about telecommuting abound. In reality, telecommuting—when managed correctly—can provide important benefits to both the employee and the organization. Unfortunately, problems may also arise if managers ignore the possible negative aspects of telecommuting.

QUESTIONS

1. List all the positive benefits to a telecommuting program.
2. List all the concerns that both employees and managers could have about telecommuting.

3. What personal characteristics must employees possess to be successful telecommuters?

4. Write six to eight guidelines for a telecommuting procedural manual.

CAREER COUNSEL

Complete the exercise on the *Managing Human Resources* website to find your dream job (www.belcourt4e.nelson.com).

NOTES AND REFERENCES

1. Shari Caudron, "The Myth of Job Happiness," *Workforce* 80, no. 4 (April 2001): 32–36.

2. Personal correspondence with the city of Calgary Personnel Services Department.

3. L.E. Babillard, *Canadian Human Rights Reporter/ Canadien des Droits de la Personne* 6, 1985.

4. George T. Milkovech and Jerry M. Newman, *Compensation* 7th ed. (Boston, MA: McGraw-Hill Irwin, 2002).

5. Richard Henderson, *Compensation Management* 8th ed. (Englewood Cliffs, NJ: Prentice Hall 2000).

6. Monty Van Wart, "The Return to Simpler Strategies in Job Analysis," *Review of Public Personnel Management* 20, no. 3 (Summer 2000): 5–13.

7. Human Resources Development Canada, *National Occupational Classification*, Ottawa, 2002.

8. Helen Palmer and Will Valet, "Job Analysis: Targeting Needed Skills," *Employment Relations Today* 28, no. 3 (Autumn 2001): 85–92.

9. Van Wart, "The Return to Simpler Strategies in Job Analysis," 5–7.

10. Charlotte Garvey, "Getting a Grip on Titles," *HRMagazine* 45, no. 12 (December 2000): 112–17.

11. Carl A. Johnson, "Refocusing Jobs," *HRMagazine* 46, no. 1 (January 2001): 67–72.

12. Bob Cardy and Greg Dobbins, "Job Analysis in a Dynamic Environment," *Human Resources Development News* 16, no. 1 (Fall 1992). See also Benjamin Schneider and Andrea Marcus Konz, "Strategic Job Analysis," *Human Resource Management* 28, no. 1 (Spring 1989): 51–63.

13. Paul Wienberg, "Labour Law Overview," *Canadian Lawyer*, March 1995: 36–43.

14. For Herzberg's important article on job enrichment, see Frederick Herzberg, "One More Time: How Do You Motivate Employees?" *Harvard Business Review* 46, no. 2 (January/February 1968): 53–62.

15. For the original article on the job characteristics model, see J. Richard Hackman and Greg R. Oldham, "Motivation through the Design of Work: Test of a Theory," *Organizational Behaviour and Job Performance* 16, no. 2 (August 1976) 250–79.

16. Muriel Draaisma, "Auto Plant Finds Ergonomics Makes Good Business Sense," *Workplace News* 4, no. 2 (June 2001): 11.

17. Robert J. Grossman, "Make Ergonomics," *HR Magazine* 45, no. 4 (April 2000): 36–42.

18. "On the Front Lines: Taming RSI," *Benefits Canada* 21, no. 3 (March 1997): 32.

19. Christopher M. Avery, "Individual-Based Teamwork," *Training and Development* 56, no. 1 (January 2002): 47–49.

20. Debra J. Housel, *Team Dynamics* (Mason, OH: South-Western Publishing Co., 2002).

21. Bob Carroll, "Using Focus Activities to Drive a Self-Managed Team to High Performance," *National Productivity Review* 19, no. 2 (Spring 2000): 43–50. See also Kimball Fisher, *Leading Self-Directed Work Teams* (New York: McGraw-Hill, 2000).

22. Charlene Marmer Solomon, "Managing Virtual Teams," *Workforce* 80, no. 6 (June 2001): 60–66.

23. Interview with Paulette Tichenor, Arizona State University, Tempe, Arizona, January 18, 2002.

24. Mel Silberman, "Smells Like Team Spirit," *Training and Development* 55, no. 2 (February 2001): 66–67.

25. Paul F. Levy, "When Teams Go Wrong," *Harvard Business Review* 79, no. 3 (March 2001): 51–67.

26. Rudy M. Yandrick, "A Team Effort," *HR Magazine* 46, no. 6 (June 2001): 136–41. See also Nancy Nelson, "The HR Generalists Guide to Team Building," SHRM Information Centre at www.shrm.org.

27. Debbie D. Dufrene, *Building High Performance Teams* (Mason, OH: South-Western Publishing Co., 2002).

28. Arthur H. Bell and Dayle M. Smith, *Learning Team Skills* (Upper Saddle River, NJ: Prentice Hall, 2003).

29. Christopher Higgins, Linda Duxbury, and Karen Lea Johnson, "Part-Time Work for Women: Does It Really Help Balance Work and Family?" *Human Resource Management* 39, no. 1 (Spring 2000): 17–32.

30. Darin E. Hartley, "Observations of a Telecommuter," *Training and Development* 55, no. 7 (July 2001): 28–36.

31. Susan J. Wells, "Making Telecommuting Work," *HR Magazine* 46, no. 10 (October 2001): 34–45.

32. "What Is the Future of Telework?" *HR Focus* 78, no. 3 (March 2001): 5–6. See also Hartley, "Observations of a Telecommuter."

Human Resources Planning

After studying this chapter, you should be able to

objective

Identify the advantages of integrating human resources planning and strategic planning.

objective

Delineate strategies for dealing with employee surpluses.

objective

Describe quantitative and qualitative approaches to human resources planning.

objective

Outlines methods to deal with labour shortages.

objective

List methods of forecasting the supply of employees.

I n earlier chapters we stressed that the challenges of human resources management all centre on the idea that organizations increasingly compete on the basis of the talents and capabilities of their employees. It is therefore essential that managers do a careful job of recruiting, selecting, developing, and retaining valuable employees. In this chapter we focus on how organizations can meet these needs through effective human resources planning.

Essentially, we address two closely related processes: planning and recruitment. HR planning establishes a blueprint for staffing the organization. Virtually all of the available evidence suggests that employers have difficulty staffing jobs, ranging from the unskilled to the professional and highly technical; this condition is not likely to abate in the near future.[1]

HUMAN RESOURCES PLANNING

objective

Human resources planning (HRP)
  Process of anticipating and making provision for the movement of people into, within, and out of an organization

Human resources planning (HRP) is the process of anticipating and making provision for the movement of people into, within, and out of an organization. Its purpose is to deploy these resources as effectively as possible, where and when they are needed, in order to accomplish the organization's goals. Other, more specific purposes of HRP include anticipating labour shortages and surpluses; providing more employment opportunities for women, minorities, and the disabled; and mapping out employee training programs. HRP provides a launching point for almost all the activities that are subsumed under HRM.

Importance of Human Resources Planning

Consider these facts about the Canadian labour force:

▶ In 2002, about 17 million Canadians were in the labour force out of a population of about 32 million. The workforce is aging. About one-third of the workforce is over forty-five. By 2030, the last of the baby boomers will be sixty-five, and the elderly will account for one-quarter of the population.

▶ The fastest-growing segments of the workforce are women and Asian Canadians, the latter mainly as a result of immigration.

▶ Around 18 percent of Canadians were born in another country.

▶ Labour shortages are predicted in manufacturing industries, and employers will be forced to recruit overseas for engineers, tool and die makers, machinists, and other tradespeople.

▶ Today nearly one-third of workers are part-timers, temporary workers, or self-employed. Five percent of Canadians hold two or more jobs. The number of self-employed is around 18 percent of total employment.[2]

How do managers cope with all these changes? How do they make certain they have the right people at the right time doing the right things for their organizations? Dramatic shifts in the composition of the labour force require that managers become more involved in HRP, since such changes affect not only employee recruitment but also methods of employee selection, training, compensation, and motivation. Although planning has always been an essential process of management, increased emphasis on HRP becomes especially critical when organizations consider mergers, relocation of plants, downsizing, or the closing of operating facilities.

An organization can incur several intangible costs as a result of inadequate HRP— or, for that matter, no HRP. For example, inadequate HRP can lead to unfilled vacancies. The resulting loss in efficiency can be costly, especially when lead time is required to train replacements. Sometimes employees will be laid off in one department even while applicants are being hired for similar jobs in another department. This may cause overhiring and result in the need to lay off employees who were recently hired. Finally, lack of HRP makes it difficult for employees to plan their careers or personal development. As a result, some of the more competent and ambitious ones will look for work in other organizations, where their career prospects are better.[3]

HRP and Strategic Planning

As organizations plan for their future, HR managers must concern themselves with meshing HRP and strategic planning for the organization as a whole.[4] HRP and strategic planning are linked in three primary ways, discussed below.

Linking the Planning Processes

Through strategic planning, organizations set major objectives and develop comprehensive plans to achieve those objectives. Human resources planning relates to strategic planning at both the front end and the back end of this process. At the front end, human resources planning provides a set of inputs into the strategic *formulation* process with regard to what is possible—that is, whether the types and numbers of people are available to pursue a given strategy. On the back end, strategic planning and HRP are linked by *implementation* concerns. Once the strategy is set, executives must make primary resource allocation decisions, including those pertaining to structure, processes, and human resources.[5]

Figure 4.1 illustrates the basic outline of how companies have begun aligning HRP and strategic planning. Companies such as British Petroleum and Toys "R" Us have taken strides to combine these two aspects of management.[6] The integration of HRP and strategic planning tends to be most effective when there is a reciprocal relationship between the two processes. In this relationship, the top management team recognizes that strategic-planning decisions affect—and are affected by—HR concerns. As James Walker, noted HRP expert, has put it: "Today, virtually *all* business issues have people implications; *all* human resource issues have business implications."[7]

In the best of companies, such as Fairmont Hotels, BMO, and IBM, there is virtually no distinction between strategic planning and HRP; the planning cycles are the same and HR issues are seen as inherent in the management of the business. Lucent Canada, with 800 employees, links planning and HR and uses the acronym GROWS to summarize these behaviours: G for growth; R for results; O for the obsession with customers and competitors; W for a workplace that is open, supportive, and diverse; and S for speed to market.[8] HR managers are important facilitators of the planning process and are viewed as credible and important contributors to the process of creating the organization's future. This positive linkage is made when the HR manager

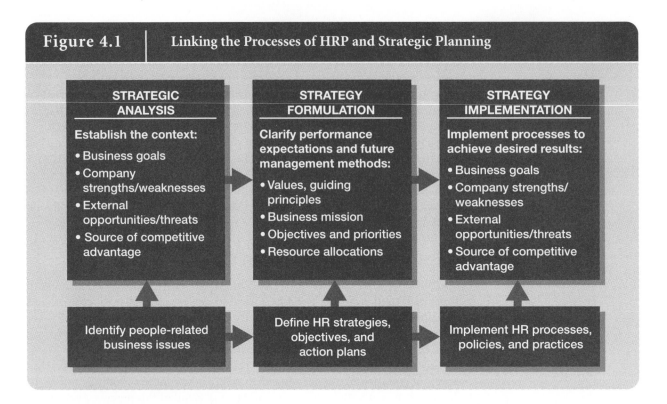

Figure 4.1 | Linking the Processes of HRP and Strategic Planning

STRATEGIC ANALYSIS	STRATEGY FORMULATION	STRATEGY IMPLEMENTATION
Establish the context:	**Clarify performance expectations and future management methods:**	**Implement processes to achieve desired results:**
• Business goals • Company strengths/weaknesses • External opportunities/threats • Source of competitive advantage	• Values, guiding principles • Business mission • Objectives and priorities • Resource allocations	• Business goals • Company strengths/weaknesses • External opportunities/threats • Source of competitive advantage
Identify people-related business issues	Define HR strategies, objectives, and action plans	Implement HR processes, policies, and practices

Source: Adapted from James A. Walker, "Integrating the Human Resource Function with the Business," *Human Resource Planning* 14, no. 2 (1996): 59–77. Copyright 1996 by The Human Resource Planning Society.

becomes a member of the organization's management steering committee or strategic planning group. Once this interactive and dynamic structure exists, HR managers are recognized as contributing strategic planners alongside other top managers.[9]

Mapping an Organization's Human Capital Architecture

In addition to aligning the planning processes themselves, the linkage between strategy and HR today also focuses on the development of core competencies. Companies such as Second Cup revolutionized their industries by developing skills— core competencies—that others didn't have. These competencies helped them gain an advantage over their competitors and leverage this advantage by learning faster than others in their industries.

Underlying a firm's core competencies is a portfolio of employee skills and human capital. Figure 4.2 shows that different skill groups in any given organization can be classified according to the degree to which they create strategic value and are unique to the organization. Employment relationships and HR practices for different employees vary according to which cell they occupy in this matrix.

USING THE INTERNET

For more information on HR planning, see The HRM Guide Network:
www.hrmguide.net/canada/

Figure 4.2	Linking the Processes of HRP and Strategic Planning

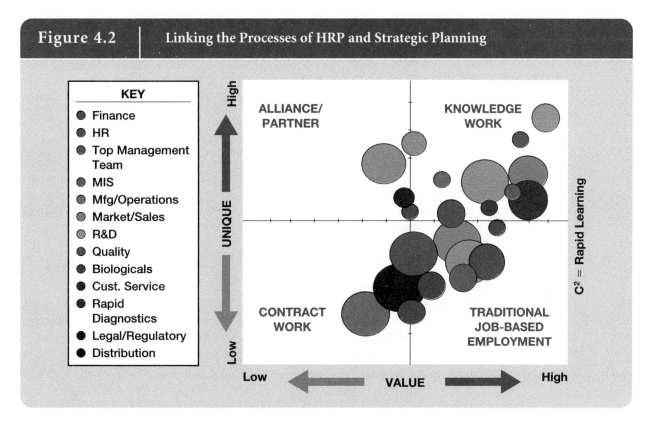

Source: Scott A. Snell, Cornell University.

▶ *Core knowledge workers.* These employees have firm-specific skills that are directly linked to the company's strategy (e.g., R&D scientists at a pharmaceutical company, computer scientists at a software development company). These employees typically are engaged in knowledge work that involves considerable autonomy and discretion. Companies tend to make long-term commitments to these employees, investing in their continuous training and development and perhaps giving them an equity stake in the organization.

▶ *Traditional job-based employees.* These employees have skills that are quite valuable to a company, but not unique (e.g., salespeople in a department store, truck drivers for a courier service). These employees are employed to perform a pre-defined job. As it is quite possible that they could leave to go to another firm, managers often make less investment in training and development and tend to focus more on paying for short-term performance achievements.

▶ *Contract labour.* These employees have skills that are of less strategic value and that are generally available to all firms (e.g., clerical workers, maintenance workers, accounting and human resources staff). More and more, individuals in these jobs are being hired from outside agencies on a contract basis. The scope of their duties tends to be limited. Employment relationships tend to be transactional, and focused on rules and procedures, with very little investment in development.

▶   *Alliance/partners.* These people have skills that are unique but are not directly related to a company's core strategy (e.g., lawyers, consultants, and research lab scientists). Although companies perhaps cannot justify employing them in-house, given their tangential link to strategy, they have skills that are both specialized and not readily available to all firms. As a consequence, companies tend to establish longer-term alliances and partnerships with them, and to nurture an ongoing relationship focused on mutual learning. Considerable investment is made in the exchange of information and knowledge.[10]

An increasingly vital element of strategic planning for organizations that compete on competencies is determining whether people are available, internally or externally, to execute an organization's strategy. Managers have to make tough decisions about whom to employ internally, whom to contract externally, and how to manage different types of employees with different skills who contribute in different ways to the organization. HRP plays an important role in helping managers weigh the costs and benefits of using one approach to employment versus another.

Ensuring Fit and Flexibility

The third main way that HRP and strategic planning are connected is in aligning the policies, programs, and practices in HR with the requirements of an organization's strategy. In this regard, HR policies and practices need to achieve two types of fit.[11]

External fit (or alignment) focuses on the connection between the business objectives and the major initiatives in HR. For example, if a company's strategy focuses on achieving low cost, HR policies and practices need to reinforce this idea by reinforcing efficient and reliable behaviour. On the other hand, if the organization competes through innovation, new product development, and the like, HR policies and practices would be more aligned with the notion of creating flexibility and creativity.

A research scientist has knowledge and firm-specific skills that are directly linked to a company's strategy. Companies tend to make long-term investments in such core knowledge workers.

PHOTODISC

134

This chapter deals mainly with the forecasting of supply and demand, and with managing labour surpluses and shortages. Readers interested in more strategic aspects of HR planning, such as mergers, should consult *Strategic Human Resource Planning*, by Belcourt and McBey (2004).

Internal fit (or alignment) means that HR practices are all aligned with one another in a mutually reinforcing configuration. For example, job design, staffing, training, performance appraisal, compensation, and the like would all focus on the same behavioural targets (such as efficiency and creativity). Unfortunately, it is all too often the case that (for example) training programs focus on teamwork and sharing, even while appraisal and compensation programs are reinforcing the ideas of individual achievement.

Apart from the need to establish a fit between HR and strategy, HRP is also focused on ensuring flexibility and agility when the environment changes. Ultimately, successful HRP helps increase **organizational capability**—the capacity of the organization to act and change in pursuit of sustainable competitive advantage.[12]

Organizational capability
The capacity to act and change in pursuit of sustainable competitive advantage

Flexibility can be achieved in two primary ways: coordination flexibility and resource flexibility. *Coordination flexibility* is achieved through rapid reallocation of resources to new or changing needs. Through HRP, managers can anticipate upcoming events, keep abreast of changes in legal regulations, forecast economic trends, recognize competitor moves, and the like. With advanced notice, managers can move people into and out of jobs, retrain them for new skill requirements, and modify the incentives they utilize. Use of a contingency workforce composed of part-timers, temporary employees, and external partners also helps to achieve coordination flexibility.[13]

Resource flexibility, on the other hand, results from having people who can do many different things in different ways. Cross-training, job rotations, team-based work modes, and the like are all focused on establishing a flexible workforce. We will discuss each of these issues at more length throughout the text. At this point, however, we want to emphasize that the process depends on a thorough understanding of the organization's environment. And this begins with environmental scanning.

HRP and Environmental Scanning

Changes in the external environment have a direct impact on how organizations are run and people are managed. *Environmental scanning* is the systematic monitoring of the major external forces influencing the organization.[14] Managers attend to a variety of external issues; however, the following six are monitored most frequently:

1. Economic factors, including general and regional conditions.
2. Competitive trends, including new processes, services, and innovations.
3. Technological changes, including robotics and office automation.
4. Political and legislative issues, including laws and administrative rulings.
5. Social concerns, including child care and educational priorities.
6. Demographic trends, including age, composition, and literacy.

By scanning the environment for changes that will likely affect the organization, managers can anticipate their impact and make adjustments early. In a rapidly changing environment, it is extremely dangerous to be caught off guard.

In Highlights in HRM 4.1, David Foot, a demographer at the University of Toronto, explains why HR professionals must become more aware of the need to scan.

Highlights in HRM 4.1

SPOTTING TRENDS IN THE GLOBAL ECONOMY

Every human resource professional recognizes that anticipating trends is an important part of the job. Furthermore, senior HR professionals want to influence strategy, not just respond to strategies determined by the "real players" at the boardroom table.

David Foot of the University of Toronto, a famous Canadian economist and demographer, says that HR professionals are often ill-equipped to contribute to their organization's strategy. He contends that HR people are experienced in dealing with micro issues, but often lack the big picture or macro perspective that is necessary to deal with corporate or strategic issues.

Having worked with executives and boards of directors, he is very familiar with the issues facing them and with the inability of HR managers to advance the HR view of the implications of strategic decisions. He offers this example: A company is thinking about going global—say, by expanding into Mexico. The HR person has very little knowledge about the labour market of that country (where there are many young people but relatively few seniors). Furthermore, he or she is likely to be preoccupied with important micro issues, such as how to hire employees and what the local health and safety rules are, when he ought to be considering, for example, Mexico's regional unemployment and education rates by region to determine plant location.

Other executives can think strategically when faced with changes in the environment. Foot asks: "How many HR professionals could answer the question 'How does the exchange rate impact HR planning?' Those with a macro perspective would immediately determine: 1. How much business is internal/external? 2. Have the financial people bought insurance against exchange rate fluctuations? 3. If the Canadian dollar depreciates, and there will be more demand for our products, what are the opportunities to access labour in external markets such as Poland or Mexico? How can we recruit these people faster than other companies? This mindset is crucial to being at the boardroom table.

"Let me give you another example of reactionary micro thinking. Low unemployment rates traditionally result in demands from business for higher immigration levels to ease labour shortages. But this traditional HR response will become increasingly inappropriate in the new millennium because more immigrants will only compete with the children of boomers who will be entering the labour force. A proactionary macro-thinking HR person will, therefore, be able to advise the CEO that this is likely to be a short-term, not a long-term labour shortage and to think internally rather than externally for new workers. This information could be crucial in influencing the company's strategic planning for the next five years."

The labour force trends listed earlier illustrate the importance of monitoring demographic changes as a part of HRP. Such changes can affect the composition and performance of an organization's workforce. These changes are important because employment equity plans must take into account the demographic composition of the population in the area where the organization is located. Furthermore, the Canadian workforce is maturing, and HRP must consider the many implications of this demographic fact on recruitment and replacement policies. Many other firms, including Tim Hortons, have made a stronger effort in recent years to hire older workers.[15] The Government of Canada, through Human Resources Development Canada, has committed $15 million to test innovative approaches to keep older workers employed.

In addition to scanning the external environment, organizations such as CIBC and Canadian Tire are careful to also scan their internal environments. Because these companies view their employee-oriented cultures as critical to success, they conduct cultural audits to examine the attitudes and activities of the workforce. Sears has found that positive employee attitudes on ten essential factors—including work load and treatment by bosses—are directly linked to customer satisfaction and revenue increases.[16]

Cultural audits essentially involve discussions among top-level managers of how the organization's culture reveals itself to employees and how it can be influenced or improved. The **cultural audit** may include such questions as these:

Cultural audits
Audits of the culture and quality of work life in an organization

▶   How do employees spend their time?

▶   How do they interact with one another?

▶   Are employees empowered?

▶   What is the predominant leadership style of managers?

▶   How do employees advance within the organization?

By conducting in-depth interviews and making observations over a period of time, managers are able to learn about the culture of their organization and the attitudes of its employees. With the increased diversity of the Canadian workplace, cultural audits can be used to determine whether there are different groups, or subcultures, within the organization that have distinctly different views about the nature of work, the quality of managers, and so on. Before any HR planning can take place, managers must gain a clear idea of how employees view their organization.

Because environmental scanning and HR planning are ultimately aimed at creating a competitive advantage, many firms benchmark their standing and progress against other firms. **Benchmarking** is the process of identifying "best practices" in a given area—say, training—and then comparing your practices to those of other companies. To accomplish this, a benchmarking team would collect information on its own company's operations and those of the other firm in order to determine gaps. The gaps help determine the causes of performance differences, and ultimately the team would map out a set of best practices that lead to world-class performance.

Benchmarking
Process of measuring one's own services and practices against the recognized leaders in order to identify areas for improvement

Interestingly, the target company for benchmarking does not need to be a competitor. For example, when Xerox wanted to learn about excellent customer service, it benchmarked L.L. Bean. By working with non-competing companies, Xerox was about to get access to information a competitor would not divulge. The Saratoga Institute publishes the annual *Human Capital Benchmarking Report,* which includes benchmarking information from almost 900 companies (see Highlights in HRM 4.2). Clients can use the information from studies of such areas as pay structure, return on investment per employee, turnover rates, and cost-per-hire and time-to-fill for key employees. This kind of detailed information clarifies potential bases of competitive advantage and reveals a path for developing HR strategies.[17]

USING THE INTERNET

For more information on HR benchmarking, check out InfoHRM's website. InfoHRM is a firm that does benchmarking for firms across a variety of industries.

www.infohrm.com

Highlights in HRM 4.2

THE MEASUREMENT OF HUMAN CAPITAL

The Office of the Auditor General of British Columbia recognized that human capital is critically important to the delivery of high-quality service to the province's citizens. So it set out to measure whether training and development (T&D) were being used to increase human capital in the B.C. public service. As a first step, it defined human capital as the collective brainpower in an organization. This brainpower consists of

▶ *facts* acquired through informal and formal education;
▶ *skills* gained through training and practice;
▶ *experience* gained through reflection on past successes and mistakes;
▶ *value judgments* based on individual perceptions; and
▶ *social networks* developed through relationships with co-workers, colleagues, and customers.

The audit took several measures, including a large-scale survey of a random sample of full-time employees and an in-depth audit of three ministries. Some of the data generated by this audit are the following:

▶ Thirty-six percent of government employees had received no formal training.
▶ The average B.C. government employee received 17 hours of training (compared to a Canadian benchmark of 29 hours).
▶ Less than 1 percent of payroll was spent on training (compared to the 4 percent that the best employers spend).
▶ Forty percent of employees had had their jobs redefined.
▶ Forty-three percent of senior managers would reach fifty-five in the next five years and be eligible to retire.
▶ Thirty-three percent of employees with less than one year of employment did not feel they had been trained properly to carry out their duties.

The audit revealed that most T&D decisions were based on requests made from individual employees, and that most programs they attended consisted of one- and two-day courses outside the organization. It had never been ascertained whether these courses increased employees' skills or helped the organization achieve its goals. There was no way knowing how effective this training was; nor was there any accounting for T&D expenditures.

Government employees generally believed that training was of great value to them and their organizations. Paradoxically, they also believed that they weren't being supported in their work; and only half thought they had the tools and resources they needed to do their jobs. (A full copy of the report is available at www.bcauditor.com/auditorgeneral.htm.)

Sources: Adapted from J. McCannel and L. McAdams, "The Learning Culture in the Public Service," *Public Sector Management* 11, no. 1 (2000); www.ipac-iapc.ca.

ELEMENTS OF EFFECTIVE HRP

objective 2

Managers follow a systematic process, or model, when undertaking HRP, as shown in Figure 4.3. The three key elements of the process are forecasting the demand for labour, performing a supply analysis, and balancing supply and demand considerations. Careful attention to each factor will help top managers and supervisors meet their staffing requirements.

Forecasting Demand for Employees

A key part of HRP is forecasting the number and type of people needed to meet organizational objectives. A variety of organizational factors, including competitive strategy, technology, structure, and productivity, can influence the demand for labour. For example, as noted in Chapter 1, utilization of advanced technology is generally accompanied by less demand for low-skilled workers and more demand for knowledge workers. External factors such as business cycles—economic and seasonal trends—can also play a role. For example, Canada Post and Statistics Canada rely heavily on temporary employees at their peak periods of business.

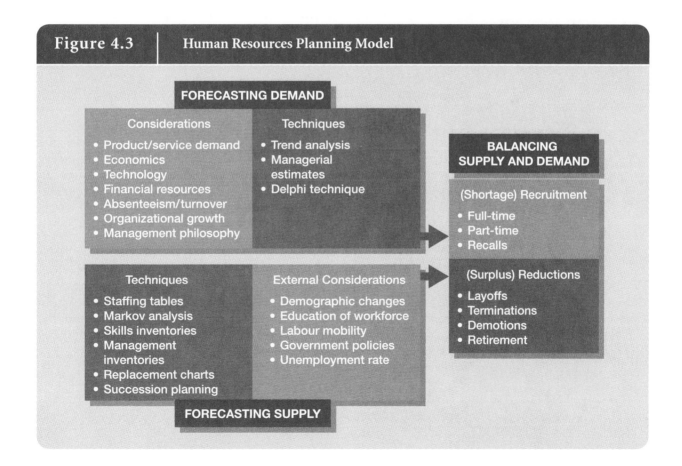

Figure 4.3 | **Human Resources Planning Model**

FORECASTING DEMAND

Considerations
- Product/service demand
- Economics
- Technology
- Financial resources
- Absenteeism/turnover
- Organizational growth
- Management philosophy

Techniques
- Trend analysis
- Managerial estimates
- Delphi technique

Techniques
- Staffing tables
- Markov analysis
- Skills inventories
- Management inventories
- Replacement charts
- Succession planning

External Considerations
- Demographic changes
- Education of workforce
- Labour mobility
- Government policies
- Unemployment rate

FORECASTING SUPPLY

BALANCING SUPPLY AND DEMAND

(Shortage) Recruitment
- Full-time
- Part-time
- Recalls

(Surplus) Reductions
- Layoffs
- Terminations
- Demotions
- Retirement

DICK HEMINGWAY

The ability to predict weather patterns, based on previous years, allows HR to plan for the needed labour supply.

Forecasting is often more an art than a science, in that it provides inexact approximations rather than absolute results. The ever-changing environment in which an organization operates contributes to this problem. For example, estimating changes in product or service demand is a basic forecasting concern, and so is anticipating changes in national or regional economics. A community hospital anticipating internal changes in technology, organization, or administration must consider these environmental factors in its forecasts of staffing needs. Also, the forecasted staffing needs must be in line with the organization's financial resources.

There are two approaches to HR forecasting: quantitative and qualitative. When the focus is on human resources needs, forecasting is mainly quantitative in nature and, in large organizations, is accomplished by highly trained specialists. Quantitative approaches to forecasting often employ sophisticated analytical models, although forecasting may be as informal as having one person who knows the organization anticipate future HR requirements. Ultimately, organizational demands will determine which technique is used. Regardless of the method, however, forecasting should not be neglected, even in relatively small organizations.

Quantitative Approaches

Quantitative approaches to forecasting involve the use of statistical or mathematical techniques; they are the approaches used by theoreticians and professional planners. One example is **trend analysis**, which forecasts employment requirements on the basis of some organizational index and is one of the most commonly used approaches for projecting HR demand.

Trend analysis
A quantitative approach to forecasting labour demand based on an organizational index such as sales

Trend analysis usually follows several steps.

First, select an appropriate business factor. This should be the best available predictor of human resources needs. Often, sales or value added (selling price less costs of materials and supplies) is used as a predictor in trend analysis. *Second*, plot a historical trend of the business factor in relation to the number of employees. The ratio of employees to the business factor will provide a labour productivity ratio (e.g., sales per employee). *Third*, compute the productivity ratio for at least the past five years. *Fourth*, calculate human resources demand by multiplying the business factor by the productivity ratio. *Finally*, project human resources demand out to the target year. This procedure is summarized in Figure 4.4 for a hypothetical building contractor.

Other, more sophisticated statistical planning methods include modelling or multiple predictive techniques. Whereas trend analysis relies on a single factor (e.g., sales) to predict employment needs, the more advanced methods combine several factors, such as interest rates, gross national product, disposable income, and sales, to predict employment levels. While the costs of developing these forecasting methods used to be quite high, advances in technology and computer software have made rather sophisticated forecasting tools affordable to even small businesses.

Qualitative Approaches

Management forecasts
The opinions (judgments) of supervisors, department managers, experts, and others knowledgeable about the organization's future employment needs

In contrast to quantitative approaches, qualitative approaches to forecasting are less statistical, attempting to reconcile the interests, abilities, and aspirations of individual employees with the current and future staffing needs of an organization. In both large and small organizations, HR planners may rely on experts who assist in preparing forecasts to anticipate staffing requirements. **Management forecasts** are the opinions (judgments) of supervisors, department managers, experts, and others who are knowledgeable about the organization's future employment needs. Various people

Figure 4.4	Human Resource Competency Model		
YEAR	BUSINESS FACTOR (SALES IN THOUSANDS) ÷	LABOUR PRODUCTIVITY (SALES /EMPLOYEE) =	HUMAN RESOURCES DEMAND (NUMBER OF EMPLOYEES)
1997	$2351	14.33	164
1998	2613	11.12	235
1999	2935	8.34	352
2000	3306	10.02	330
2001	3613	11.12	325
2002	3748	11.12	337
2003	3880	12.52	310
2004	4095	12.52	327
2005*	4283	12.52	342
2006*	4446	12.52	355

*Projected figures

scan conditions outside the organization for clues about what the future might hold, and then arrive at various scenarios, which the company can use in its planning. Shell Oil used management forecasts to anticipate the oil crisis in the 1970s.

Another qualitative forecasting method, the Delphi technique, attempts to decrease the subjectivity of forecasts by soliciting and summarizing the judgments of a preselected group of individuals. The final forecast thus represents a composite group judgment. The Delphi technique requires a great deal of coordination and cooperation to ensure satisfactory forecasts. This method works best in organizations where dynamic technological changes affect staffing levels.

Ideally, HRP should include the use of both quantitative and qualitative approaches. The two approaches complement each other, and when used together provide a more complete forecast by bringing together the contributions of both theoreticians and practitioners.

Forecasting Supply of Employees

Once an organization has forecast its future requirements for employees, it must determine whether it has enough employees, and the right employees, to staff anticipated openings. As with demand, this process involves both tracking current levels and making projections.

Internal Labour Supply

An internal supply analysis often begins with the preparation of staffing tables. **Staffing tables** are graphic representations of all organizational jobs, along with the numbers of employees currently occupying those jobs (and perhaps also future employment requirements derived from demand forecasts). Another technique, called **Markov analysis**, shows the percentage (and actual number) of employees who remain in each job from one year to the next, as well as the proportions of those who are promoted, demoted, or transferred, or who leave the organization. As shown in Figure 4.5, Markov analysis can be used to track the pattern of employee movements through various jobs and to develop a transition matrix for forecasting labour supply.

Forecasting the supply of human resources requires that managers have a good understanding of employee turnover and absenteeism. At the end of this chapter, we have included an appendix of formulas for computing turnover and absenteeism rates. The calculations are easily made and can be used by managers of both large and small organizations.

While staffing tables, Markov analysis, turnover rates, and the like tend to focus on the number of employees in particular jobs, other techniques are oriented more toward the types of employees and their skills, knowledge, and experience. **Skills inventories** can be prepared that list each employee's education, past work experience, vocational interests, specific abilities and skills, compensation history, and job tenure. Of course, confidentiality is a vital concern in setting up any such inventory. Nevertheless, well-prepared and up-to-date skill inventories allow an organization to quickly match forthcoming job openings with employee backgrounds. Organizations such as Hewlett-Packard and DuPont Canada use computers and special programs to perform this task. When data are gathered on managers, these inventories are called *management inventories*.

objective 3

Staffing tables
Graphic representations of all organizational jobs, along with the numbers of employees currently occupying those jobs and future (monthly or yearly) employment requirements

Markov analysis
Method for tracking the pattern of employee movements through various jobs

Skills inventories
Files of employee education, experience, interests, skills, etc., that allow managers to quickly match job openings with employee backgrounds

Figure 4.5 | Markov Analysis for a Hypothetical Retail Company

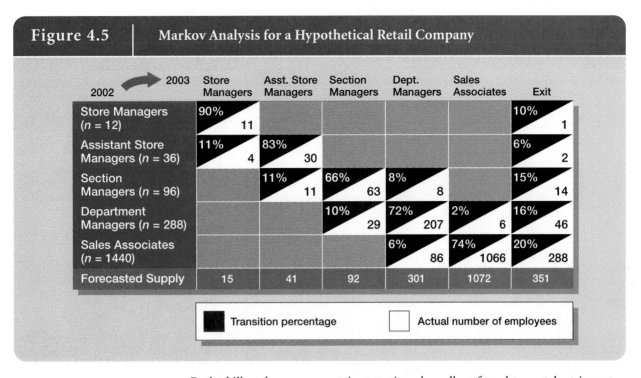

2002 → 2003	Store Managers	Asst. Store Managers	Section Managers	Dept. Managers	Sales Associates	Exit
Store Managers (n = 12)	90% / 11					10% / 1
Assistant Store Managers (n = 36)	11% / 4	83% / 30				6% / 2
Section Managers (n = 96)		11% / 11	66% / 63	8% / 8		15% / 14
Department Managers (n = 288)			10% / 29	72% / 207	2% / 6	16% / 46
Sales Associates (n = 1440)				6% / 86	74% / 1066	20% / 288
Forecasted Supply	15	41	92	301	1072	351

■ Transition percentage   □ Actual number of employees

Replacement charts
Listings of current job holders and persons who are potential replacements if an opening occurs

Succession planning
Process of identifying, developing, and tracking key individuals for executive positions

Both skill and management inventories—broadly referred to as talent inventories—can be used to develop employee replacement charts, which list current job holders and identify possible replacements should openings arise. Figure 4.6 shows how an organization can develop a **replacement chart** for the managers in one of its divisions. This chart provides information on the current job performance and promotability of possible replacements. As such, it can be used side by side with other pieces of information for **succession planning**, which is the process of identifying, developing, and tracking key individuals so that they may eventually assume top-level positions (see Reality Check).

In today's fast-moving environment, succession planning is often more important—and more difficult to conduct—than ever before. Canadian CEOs surveyed by William H. Mercer stated that attracting and retaining key talent was a major priority. Highlights in HRM 4.3 provides a checklist for succession planning.

USING THE INTERNET

Canadajobs links you to information about jobs in Canada, including government job databases, recruiters, and companies that are hiring.

www.canadajobs.com

External Labour Supply

When an organization lacks an internal supply of employees for promotions, or when it is staffing entry-level positions, managers must consider the external supply of labour. Labour supply is influenced by many factors, including demographic changes in the population, national and regional economics, the education level of the workforce, demand for specific employee skills, population mobility, and governmental policies. National and regional unemployment rates are often considered a general barometer of labour supply. Fortunately, labour market analysis is aided by published documents. Various government departments report unemployment rates, labour force projection rates, and population characteristics. Human

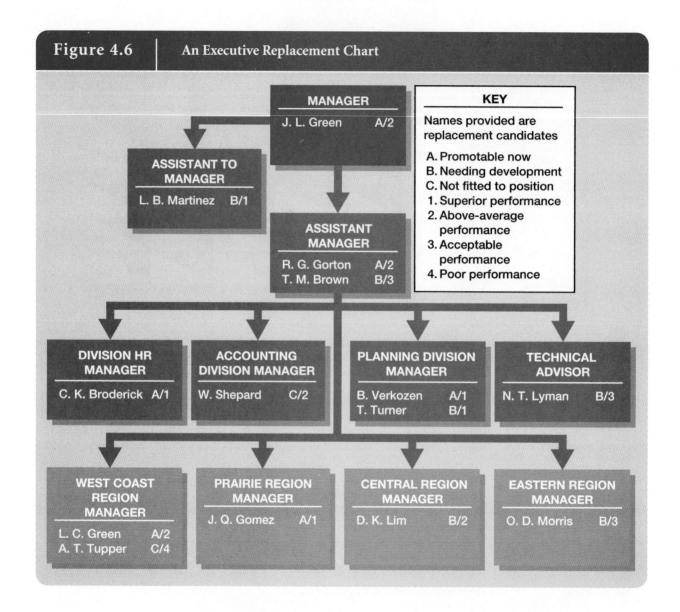

Figure 4.6 | An Executive Replacement Chart

MANAGER
J. L. Green   A/2

KEY
Names provided are replacement candidates

A. Promotable now
B. Needing development
C. Not fitted to position
1. Superior performance
2. Above-average performance
3. Acceptable performance
4. Poor performance

ASSISTANT TO MANAGER
L. B. Martinez   B/1

ASSISTANT MANAGER
R. G. Gorton   A/2
T. M. Brown   B/3

DIVISION HR MANAGER
C. K. Broderick A/1

ACCOUNTING DIVISION MANAGER
W. Shepard   C/2

PLANNING DIVISION MANAGER
B. Verkozen   A/1
T. Turner   B/1

TECHNICAL ADVISOR
N. T. Lyman   B/3

WEST COAST REGION MANAGER
L. C. Green   A/2
A. T. Tupper   C/4

PRAIRIE REGION MANAGER
J. Q. Gomez   A/1

CENTRAL REGION MANAGER
D. K. Lim   B/2

EASTERN REGION MANAGER
O. D. Morris   B/3

Resources Development Canada (HRDC) analyzes labour markets to determine the supply and demand for labour. The Canadian Occupational Projection System (COPS) analyzes labour supply and demand by occupation over a ten-year period. JobFutures 2002 is a group of publications that identify trends in the workplace and are available from HRDC. With access to information about occupational trends, entrants to the labour market can determine the prospects of finding employment in a specific occupation or field. HRDC also works with various sectors such as the biotechnology sector to forecast supply and demand for specific occupational areas. Chambers of Commerce and provincial development and planning agencies also may assist with labour market analysis. Highlights in HRM 4.4 describes how one Nova Scotia company dealt with a labour shortage.

Highlights in HRM 4.3

SUCCESSION PLANNING CHECKLIST

RATE THE SUCCESS OF YOUR SUCCESSION PLANNING

For each characteristic of a best-practice succession planning and management program appearing in the left column below, enter a number to the right to indicate how well you believe your organization manages that characteristic. Ask other decision makers in your organization to complete this form individually. Then compile the scores and compare notes.

Characteristics of a Best-Practice Succession Planning and Management Program Your organization has successfully...	How Would You Rate Your Organization's Succession Planning and Management Program on the Characteristic?				
	Very Poor (1)	Poor (2)	Neither Poor Nor Good (3)	Good (4)	Very Good (5)
1 Clarified the purpose and desired results of the succession planning and management program.					
2 Determined what performance is required now for all job categories in the organization by establishing competency models.					
3 Established a means to measure individual performance that is aligned with the competencies currently demonstrated by successful performers.					
4 Determined what performance is needed in the future by establishing future competency models for all job categories.					
5 Created an ongoing means by which to assess individual potential against future competency models.					
6 Established a means by which to narrow gaps through the use of individual development plans (IDPs).					
7 Created a means to follow up and hold people accountable.					
8 Created a means by which to document competence and find organizational talent quickly when needed.					
9 Created and sustained rewards for developing people.					
10 Established a means by which to evaluate the results of the succession planning and management program.					

Total (add up the scores for items 1–10 and place in the box on the right)

SCORES

50–40 Congratulations. The succession planning and management program in your organization conforms with best practices.

39–30 Pretty good. Your organization is on the way toward establishing a first-rate succession planning and management program.

29–20 Okay. While your organization could make improvements, you appear to have some of the major pieces in place for a succession planning and

19–10 Not good at all. Your organization is probably filling positions on an as-needed basis.

9–0 Give yourself a failing grade. You need to take steps immediately to improve the succession planning and management practices of your organization.

Source: William J. Rothwell, "Putting Success into Your Succession Planning," *Journal of Business Strategy* 23, no. 3 (May/June 2002): 32–37.

Reality Check

SUCCESSION PLANNING

Allianz Canada is the twelfth-largest insurance company in Canada, with sales of $850 million, and employs 850 direct employees, and another 550 in wholly owned subsidiaries. Allianz Canada is part of the Allianz Group, which is the world's twelfth-largest company by revenues with 500 member companies in the group, 180 000 employees and 60 million customers.

The parent company initiated a survey of the group companies in 2002, asking, "Given your expansion strategies and retention and turnover rates, what are your projected needs for senior management for the next five years?" The statistics were compiled. When the executives of the company regained consciousness, they realized there was a problem with meeting the HR needs of the organization. Paul Juniper, vice-president of HR, says, "The corporate objective is to have one person available to fill [replace] every senior job in the organization. There will simply not be enough internal people to fill the jobs expected at our current rates of development. With the anticipated demographic changes, it will become increasing difficult to recruit from outside to make up the shortfall."

The larger group members, including Allianz Canada, have been given a "quota" for leadership development. Juniper says, "We are expected not only to develop, grow, and recruit for our present and future needs but also to supply the needs of the group. In the first year, we expect to see development plans for at least one president and two senior vice-presidents. This means an increasing number of Canadians will be offered international postings within the organization and an increasing number of foreign nationals will rotate through positions within Allianz Canada."

To meet this need, Allianz Canada has initiated a succession planning and leadership development project. Completed first steps have included an overall inventory of management resources, including database information on education, background, special skills, development areas, languages spoken, and willingness to travel for all existing managers. The "tombstone data" (unchangeable information such as date of birth) provides a picture of the strengths and weaknesses of the internal labour supply, which then helps managers make decisions about development and helps to rank projects such as leadership development schools or stretch assignments.

The senior leadership of the organization has been asked to identify individuals who may be potential replacements for them. One priority is to prepare the development plans for those identified as successors for the senior executive committee, which includes an open discussion about their futures. Senior managers' bonuses contain a component for management development within their staff.

The next step is to push the program down two levels in the organization. Paul Juniper continues, "As Allianz Canada consists of a main company and a wholly owned subsidiary, HR is working to entrench a belief that we are managing one overall talent pool for the benefit of both companies and for the worldwide group. The parent company and the HR department ensure that the issue of succession planning is on the agenda."

Highlights in HRM 4.4

MANAGING LABOUR SHORTAGES

Dexter, a construction company based in Bedford, Nova Scotia, was facing a skills gap in its labour market. The demands in this sector have changed and there is less need for manual labourers and a greater demand for technicians with computer literacy skills. For example, a heavy equipment operator or surveyor used to operate by observing and pen and paper; now much of this work is dictated by GPS (Global Positioning Systems) and integrated software. Ron Hyson, director of HR for Dexter, decided to partner with the Nova Scotia Community College to recruit, select, and train employees in the required skills. About 350 candidates applied for the two-year training program, were tested, and then interviewed. A final group of thirty was selected to receive training in all fields of construction. They were cross-trained in surveying and heavy equipment operations and were given courses in management development, job costing, and safety. The training methods were varied. About 40 percent of the time, trainees were in the classroom. The remaining time was spent in the field in six to eight functional areas, such as surveying. Work terms of six months, consisting of rotations in each area for four weeks, were used to help the students determine their interests and abilities. At the end of the program, the trainees are guaranteed employment.

STRATEGIES TO DEAL WITH SURPLUSES OF LABOUR

objective

Through HRP, organizations strive for a proper balance between demand considerations and supply considerations. Demand considerations are based on forecasted trends in business activity. Supply considerations involve determining where and how candidates with the required qualifications are to be found to fill vacancies.

When HRP shows a surplus of job holders, organizations may restrict hiring, reduce work hours, institute work sharing, or consider layoffs, demotions, and/or terminations. Also, an organization may over time try to reduce its workforce by relying on attrition (a gradual reduction of employees through resignations, retirements, or deaths). Over the past decade, early retirements have become more and more common as a means for organizations to reduce their excess labour supply. Organizations as diverse as health care facilities, travel companies, and colleges and universities encourage employees to accept early retirement by offering "sweetened" retirement benefits (see Chapter 11).

Organizational Downsizing

As discussed in Chapter 1, organizations have taken the extremely painful task of downsizing and restructuring over the past decade to reduce "head count." Organizational restructuring is resulting in the laying off of tens of thousands of workers. In a survey of 1140 large Canadian organizations, over half reported engaging in permanent workforce reductions, with an average reduction of 15 percent.[18] **Restructuring** refers to any major change that occurs within an organization and can be the result of acquisitions, retrenchments, mergers, leveraged buyouts, divestiture, plant closures or relocations, or bankruptcies. Restructuring almost always results in cutbacks, downsizing, or consolidations.

Because of economic or competitive pressures, organizations have found themselves with too many employees or with employees who have the wrong kinds of skills. In an effort to reconcile supply and demand considerations, companies such as Nortel, Bombardier, and CN have eliminated literally thousands of jobs. Layoffs are not simply a result of a stagnant economy. In many cases, downsizing is part of a longer-term process of restructuring to take advantage of new technology, corporate partnerships, and cost minimization.

> **Restructuring**
> Any major change that occurs within an organization. It may be the result of acquisitions, retrenchments, mergers, leveraged buyouts, divestiture, plant closures or relocations, or bankruptcies.

Making Layoff Decisions

Decisions about employee layoffs are usually based on seniority and/or performance. In some organizations, especially those with collective agreements, seniority may be the main consideration. In other organizations, such factors as ability and fitness may take precedence over seniority in determining layoffs.

When economic conditions have brought about layoffs, employees who were let go while in good standing may be recalled to their jobs when the economic outlook brightens and job openings occur. However, these new jobs often require different sets of skills than the jobs they replace. Searching among previous employees or among current employees who can be transferred can identify individuals for these jobs, but often it requires searching externally in the broader labour market.[19]

There are several options available to employers when it comes to dealing with surplus employees: layoffs, attrition, and termination.

Layoff Strategies

Employee layoff decisions are usually based on seniority and/or ability. With unionized organizations, the criteria for determining an employee's eligibility for layoff are typically set forth in the collective agreement. As a rule, job seniority receives significant weight in determining which employees are laid off first. Similar provisions in the collective agreement provide for the right of employees to be recalled for jobs they are still qualified to perform. Organizational policy as well as provisions in the collective agreement should therefore establish and define clearly the employment rights of each individual and the basis on which layoff selections will be made and re-employment effected. The rights of employees during layoffs, the conditions concerning their eligibility for recall, and their obligations in accepting recall should also be clarified. It is common for collective agreements to preserve the re-employment rights of employees laid off for periods of up to two years, provided that they do not refuse to return to work if recalled sooner.

While it has become customary for employers to recognize seniority in unionized employees, nonunion employees are not always given the same consideration. Due to the demand for a technically skilled workforce, the ability of employees to change jobs and learn new skills, as well as their performance and competencies, is given a great deal of weight in layoff decisions. The most important reason for using seniority as a basis for layoffs is the objective nature of the decision: number of years of work, not perception of ability, is the basis for the decision. The system is fair, and employees themselves can calculate their own probability of being employed.

One of the major disadvantages of overemphasizing seniority is that less competent employees receive the same rewards and security as more competent ones. The seniority system ignores talent and effort. The payroll is also higher than under other systems, because more experienced workers tend to earn more money. Also, the practice of using seniority as the basis for deciding which workers to lay off may well have a disproportionate impact on women and minority workers, who often have less seniority than other groups.

Under the umbrella of layoff strategies are several work reduction options: reduced work week, reduced shifts, transfers to related companies, and so on. Under the reduced work week, employees work about twenty to thirty hours per week. This option allows the organization to retain a skilled workforce and lessens the financial and emotional impact of a full layoff, and at the same time reduces the costs of production. Some organizations have worked out arrangements so that employment insurance benefits make up most of the difference of the lost wages. However, it is sometimes difficult to predict how much work is available each week; also, overhead fixed costs such as rent and administration continue, independent of the number of hours worked.

Reduced shift work is based on a similar concept of reducing costs by reducing the number of hours worked. Some plants operate three shifts a day and may shut down the midnight to 8:00 a.m. shift to save money. General Motors of Canada eliminated the second shift at its assembly plant in Ste-Thérèse, Quebec, throwing 1400 employees out of work.[20] Another approach is to reduce the number of operators per shift.

In some rare cases, organizations can transfer laid-off employees to a sister company. For example, when Dylex closed its Town and Country stores, more than 500 of its 600 laid-off Ontario employees were placed in other Dylex chain stores.[21] Shell Canada has even been known to contact other organizations that are in the hiring mode. Under this scheme, Shell employees have been re-employed within days of being laid off. JDS Uniphase, in Victoria, B.C., produced a directory with the resumés of the 180 employees who were being laid off and mailed it to 400 employers.

Layoffs are the fastest way to achieve workforce reduction; attrition is the slowest.

Attrition Strategies

Attrition
A natural departure of employees from organizations through quits, retirements, and deaths

Some organizations have adopted a no-layoff policy. These firms view people as their most important asset and recognize that their competencies and attitudes are valuable and cannot be easily replaced. They prefer to reduce the workforce through attrition. **Attrition** refers to the "natural" departure of employees through quits, retirements, and deaths. The turnover rates of an organization vary greatly by industry and by occupation. For example, university professors rarely quit, while turnover among fast food workers can reach 300 percent a year. Most organizations can easily estimate how many people will leave the organization and so can slowly reduce the workforce through natural means. Since 1989 Dofasco Inc. has reduced its workforce from 12 200 to 7300 by using a number of job reduction strategies, including natural attrition, voluntary early retirement programs, and a voluntary severance program.

Attrition must be supplemented by other practices. Hiring freezes are usually implemented at the same time as the organization adopts a strategy of workforce

Hiring freeze
A practice whereby new workers are not hired as planned, or workers who have left the organization are not replaced

reduction through attrition. A **hiring freeze** means that organizations will not hire new workers as planned, or will hire only in areas critical to the success of the organization. Sometimes the practice is to not replace the worker who has left or been fired.

These practices have several advantages. Organizations can control and predict compensation expenses. But the savings go beyond the salaries and benefits redeemed from departing employees. Take, for example, the costs of employing a manager earning $60 000 a year. Her benefits probably cost another $20 000. However, the costs of replacing her would include recruitment costs ($5000), paperwork and time in hiring costs ($1000), orientation and training expenses ($7000), and office supplies and space ($10 000). Thus, the organization can save significantly by not replacing workers.

However, the disadvantages are significant. Current employees may be overburdened with the work of those who left; their skills may not match the skill sets of the departed workers; and, of course, no new skills or ideas are infiltrating the organization. The major disadvantage of reduction through attrition is that the organization cannot control who leaves and who stays. Valuable employees may be retiring, while less needed ones are still on the job. And the process takes a very long time compared to layoffs, which can be accomplished in days.

Some organizations attempt to accelerate attrition by offering incentives to employees to leave. These incentives include cash bonuses for people to leave during a specified time, accelerated or early retirement benefits, and free outplacement services. However, the buyout process must be carefully managed. Employees with valuable skills who can easily find another job may be the first to cash in. People in key positions should not be targeted for this program. Another disadvantage is that buyouts require a great deal of money up front, which may work against the goal of cost reduction. For example, Ontario Hydro paid out millions in buyouts for a few thousand employees. Employers must be cautious when extending offers of early retirements. An older worker was awarded $250 000 plus benefits in a wrongful dismissal suit, on the grounds that he had been forced to accept the "voluntary" early-retirement option.[22]

To sustain a no-layoffs policy, some organizations ask for volunteers to transfer into divisions where employee shortages are developing. This causes other problems. For example, highly competent employees who have years of experience, expertise, and contacts in one position may not be as productive in another division. Skill match is a recurrent problem. Mandatory transfers allow the employer to match employee skills with vacant positions more accurately. There may be associated morale problems as individuals move into jobs or divisions they do not like, or leave their team and its working style. In addition, union contracts may forbid or inhibit these types of transfers.

Another practice, which is extremely rare in Canada but emerging in the United States, is the worker loan-out program. Recognizing that the downsizing may be temporary, or that the policy of no layoffs is sacrosanct, organizations sometimes prefer to loan employees to other (noncompeting) organizations for temporary assignments. For example, IBM pays its employees for up to two years while they work in schools or charitable institutions. These loans, while apparently expensive, actually have some economic incentives. Because organizations keep their employees, there are no costs associated with severance pay, rehiring, and training. Employees return with new skills, ideas, and contacts. The good will generated in the community and among employees may result in free press and publicity.

If the surplus of employees is deemed to be permanent, terminations may be the only option.

Termination Strategies

Termination is a practice initiated by an employer to separate an employee from the organization permanently. Termination is different from firing, in which an employee is released for such causes as poor performance, high absenteeism, or unethical behaviour. The purpose of termination is to reduce the size of the workforce and thereby save money.

A termination strategy begins with the identification of employees who are in positions that are no longer considered useful or critical to the company's effectiveness. The managers of these employees are contacted about redeployment or termination options. Next the employee is told the news, with varying degrees of advance notice. CIBC gives three months' notice, allows the employee and the manager to prepare a redeployment plan, and allows up to six months for retraining and repositioning.[23] At CIBC, the emphasis is on retaining competent employees whose jobs have been eliminated; the title of the program, Employment Continuity, reflects this strategy. To assist the 500 employees it laid off, Dofasco established a transition centre that provided skills development, career counselling, and tuition assistance.

Employees should be concerned about their own marketability (i.e., employability). Some suggestions for surviving rightsizing are given in Highlights in HRM 4.5.

Employers cannot terminate without some form of compensation to the employee. **Severance pay**, a lump-sum payment given to terminated employees, is calculated on the basis of years of service and salary. Every province has legislation such as the Employment Standards Act, which establishes minimum standards for termination and severance pay. The legal minimum varies by province; for example, a clerk making $500 a week with eight years' service would receive about $4000 in severance pay. A typical severance package would include

- a lump sum severance payment,
- an extension of group benefits such as medical and dental plans for a predetermined period,
- an option for the employee to convert group life insurance to a private policy,
- some pension plan options.

These payments, if accepted by the employee, immediately discharge the employer from further obligations. Most employers now refer to "ballpark," "reasonable range," or "reasonable offer" court decisions. The ballpark approach offers some degree of certainty to both employers and employees, and thus helps minimize costly court battles.

Some organizations adopt "golden parachutes," a form of severance pay, to protect their employees (especially their executives) from the downsizing effects of mergers, acquisitions, and leveraged buyouts. Golden parachutes are guarantees by the employer that detail the compensation and benefits that employees will receive in termination situations. Golden parachutes encourage managers to work actively with the company during a restructuring, and reduce the possibility of legal challenges on termination. But they are costly.

Termination
Practice initiated by an employer to separate an employee from the organization permanently

Severance pay
A lump-sum payment given to terminated employees

Highlights in HRM 4.5

SURVIVAL IN THE NEW MILLENNIUM

Professionals and managers fear the 50/50 rule: If you are over fifty years old and make more than $50 000, your job is at risk. "We don't go out to lunch, we're afraid the doors will be blocked when we get back," says one anxious manager. About one-fifth of job losses occur at the management level. Loyalty is out; it is not reciprocated by the organization. In fact, companies may not want loyal (i.e., obedient and rule-minded) employees. They may actively prefer employees who are ready to push the boundaries of the organization, instead of being dominated and intimidated by those boundaries. Loyalty is to the profession, and it means developing different attitudes toward employment. Some suggestions:

▶ Develop portable skills. Invest in training in negotiation or general management skills.
▶ Build outside networks. Be a member of a professional association. Attend conferences. Keep abreast of trends in your industry by reading all trade magazines, business sections of newspapers, and company reports. Belong to volunteer organizations and other social networks. All these strategies will serve you well should you need to search for a job.
▶ Plan for transitions. Assume that you will not be employed by one organization for a long time. Save money for these transition periods. Identify industries where your portable skills could be useful. For example, if you have always worked in marketing, consider how these skills might be useful in the not-for-profit sector of social marketing, such as adult literacy efforts.

Sources: C. Heckcher, *White Collar Blues: Management Loyalties in an Age of Corporate Restructuring* (Toronto: HarperCollins, 1995); "Monkeys in the Middle," *The Globe and Mail*, May 9, 1995: B10.

Many organizations soften the blow of termination by offering *outplacement services*. Those services, most often offered by agencies outside the corporation, ease the impact of termination by providing terminated employees with stress counselling, financial advice, career counselling, and assistance in locating another job. The job search support often includes office space, telephones and secretarial support, vocational testing, resumé writing, and feedback on interviewing skills.[24]

Some suggestions for managing the termination process are presented in Highlights in HRM 4.6.

Evaluating Restructuring

There are hundreds of articles dealing with downsizing. However, very few even touch on its consequences. The following section considers the consequences of downsizing on finances, organization climate, and public image.

Highlights in HRM 4.6

EASING TERMINATION SHOCK

Any manager who has terminated an employee will describe it as one of the worst experiences in his or her working life. Some have reported sleepless nights, stomach pains, and inability to work. There is no way to mitigate the emotional distress for the supervisor who has to terminate an employee he or she knows well. However, some experts have suggested ways to ease tensions and reduce employee retaliation:

1. Plan the termination interview early in the week, so that the employee can start an action plan with the outplacement service during the week.

2. Make sure the date does not correspond with an important date (such as a birthday) for the employee. Recently, an employee was terminated on "Take Your Daughter to Work Day." The shock and bitterness he felt at being terminated in front of his daughter—she helped him carry out his box of belongings—resulted in a lawsuit.

3. Make the interview short (less than fifteen minutes). State the reasons clearly and firmly, establishing that the decision is final, and clearly communicate all aspects of the severance package (preferably in writing).

4. Tell the employee the next steps and, if possible, give him or her the name of the outplacement counsellor.

Source: Adapted from Phyllis Macklin and Lester Minsuk, "Ways to Ease Dismissal Dread," *HRMagazine* (November 1991).

Finances

A survey of hundreds of companies that laid off workers revealed that about one-half reported improved earnings, but only one-third reported that productivity or customer service improved. Two-thirds had to hire at the same time as the layoffs because they were losing skills they needed to keep.[25]

Investors generally react negatively to an announcement of layoffs or large-scale reductions in the workforce.[26] A large-scale study of organizations in Atlantic Canada concluded that downsizing fails to meet financial goals because workforce reduction results in considerable people costs, and because the remaining personnel are less productive.[27]

Climate

Study after study shows the following effects of downsizing: surviving employees become narrow-minded, self-absorbed, and risk averse; morale sinks; productivity drops; and survivors distrust management.[28] Internally, all forms of restructuring are likely to generate fear, anxiety, and hostility. Early retirement programs and other soft attrition strategies are likely to be interpreted with less resentment than mass terminations. The organization can assume that employees anxious about the next round of terminations will suffer many stress symptoms, including reduced performance, depression, and proneness to error. The Atlantic Canada study referred to above concluded that employee commitment and morale decreased while conflict increased. These attitudes are not limited just to those victims of restructuring. A 2002 study suggests that, after the Enron scandal, employees are losing trust in their leaders.[29]

These reactions underline the growing awareness of a problem associated with restructuring: survivor sickness. Survivor sickness encompasses a range of symptoms, which may include guilt, detachment, depression, and a sense of being violated and betrayed. An expert in corporate downsizing, speaking to managers at a Conference Board of Canada meeting, used a family metaphor to describe the emotional impact of downsizing: "Imagine a family that seems to be functioning and suddenly the parents tell the four kids that they can no longer afford to support two of them. The next day at breakfast, nobody talks about the ones who have left. The father talks about how 'this will make us closer-knit, but you will have to take on your brother's chores.'"[30]

Amdahl Canada is one organization that recognizes that survivor sickness is real. In a recent downsizing, Amdahl allocated 25 percent of its strategy to the "management of mourning"—that is, mitigating the inevitable pain by communicating with honesty, directness, and respect toward fired employees.[31] The remaining 75 percent of the strategy was targeted at revitalization.

Public Image

Terminations have the most adverse impact on public perceptions. While layoffs are seen as temporary and attrition as benevolent, terminations are interpreted as cold and unfeeling, especially if the terminations affect competent employees with long tenure. Baby boomers feel a loyalty to professions, not companies, after watching their loyal parents lose the security of lifelong employment. About two-thirds of those who have been laid off said that they would never work for the company again and would not recommend that others work for the company, and about half would not recommend that others purchase the company's products and services. Those who were laid off were especially bitter if their offices were locked, they were escorted to the door, and they were offered no other positions within the organization.[32]

However, a contrarian view suggests that the era of "entitlement" is over. The attitude that regular raises, scheduled promotions, and a secure job for life were the right of every worker has been replaced by the attitude that workers must take responsibility for their own employability by continually earning their jobs and by retraining.[33]

STRATEGIES TO DEAL WITH SHORTAGES OF LABOUR

According to demographic studies, Canada has neither the necessary population growth nor the right proportions of students entering technical and engineering schools to meet the predicted demand.[34] The result is going to be labour shortages in particular occupations, and this will affect strategic plans in certain industries. As we will discuss in Chapter 9, more and more organizations are using financial and other incentives in an effort to retain their existing staff.

One possible strategy will be to retain a small core of permanent employees, while maintaining a fluctuating number of less permanent, quasi-employment relationships.[35] Three of the above employment options—overtime, part-time employees, and temporary help agencies—are discussed later in this chapter.

Overtime

Asking employees to work extra hours is a strategy used by most firms during peak hours, or peak periods, such as the Christmas rush, or holiday weekends. Canadians work an average of five days per month on unpaid overtime. However, asking workers to expand their work days or weeks is not an effective long-term strategy. Workers become fatigued and report higher levels of stress, and there may be more accidents and higher scrap rates.[36]

Part-Time Employees

Part-time employment is growing rapidly as employers realize its benefits, such as increased flexibility in scheduling and reduced payroll costs. The proportion of people working part-time is at the highest level ever, 18.5 percent of the working population. Part-time employees usually cost less than full-time employees due to lower compensation rates and their ineligibility for a full range of company benefits. The ethical implications of employment contracts are addressed in Ethics in HRM.

Many employers use part-time or contract employees to cover for the absences of regular, full-time employees. The absenteeism rate for Canadian employees is rising and costing employers a great deal of money, as outlined in The Business Case. (Note that methods for calculating absenteeism and turnover are described in Appendix A.)

The advantages and disadvantages of part-time work for employees and organizations are detailed in Figure 4.7.

Temporary Staffing Agencies

The temporary services industry is one of the fastest-growing recruitment sources. The temp/contract job market is worth about $2 billion in Canada and accounts for about 10 percent of all jobs. Reflecting this, temporary services were among the strongest sectors through the 1990s and are certain to remain so.[37]

Employers often have difficulty finding employees with technical skills in the labour market.

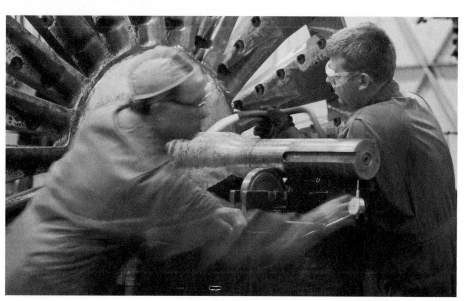

PHOTODISC

For more information about contract employees, see the website for the Professional Association for Contract Employees:

www.pacepros.com

It is estimated that nine out of ten Canadian companies—both large and small—make some use of temporary employees. "Temps" are typically used for short-term assignments or to help out when managers cannot justify hiring full-time employees, such as for vacation fill-ins, for peak work periods, or to cover an employee's pregnancy leave or sick leave. More and more often, temps are being employed to fill positions once staffed by permanent employees. This practice is growing because temps can be laid off quickly, and with less cost, when work slackens. Some companies use a just-in-time staffing approach: core employees are augmented by well-trained and highly skilled supplementary workers. The use of temps has become a viable way to maintain proper staffing levels. Temps often cost less than permanent employees because they don't receive benefits and can be dismissed without the need to file Employment Insurance claims. Although used mainly in office clerical positions, they are becoming more and more common in legal work, engineering, computer programming, and other jobs that require advanced professional training.[38] Agencies often specialize in specific occupational areas or professional fields. Figure 4.8 shows the results of a study that illustrates the occupations most represented by employment agencies.

Ethics in HRM

THE EMPLOYMENT CONTRACT

The number of organizations substituting part-time workers for full-time employees is growing. Employees—even those with excellent track records and many years of service—are considered expendable as organizations revise their strategies to become more competitive and more profitable. When yet another reorganization occurs, management reveals the new plan with excitement. However, while management thinks it is telling employees, "We will provide you with meaningful, challenging, and skill-building work that will be good for your resumé— you are responsible for your own employment," employees are hearing, "We will work you to the bone, pay you enough to prevent you from quitting, and fire you when we no longer need you. Oh, and by the way, you are our most valuable resource."

Some employment contracts are extremely one-sided, with employers determining when to hire and when to fire, without obligation or guilt. This kind of contract works when people need jobs more than organizations need employees. However, as some sectors continue to experience rapid growth, and as the labour market for certain skills becomes tighter, employees are making contractual demands that place them in the driver's seat. They are demanding signing bonuses, stock equity, retention bonuses, and sufficient notification with predetermined buyouts for termination. Furthermore, the courts are ruling that if an employee is retained for a series of uninterrupted contracts, then that contract worker is de facto an employee.

Sources: Barbara Moses, "Loss of Loyalty Cuts Both Ways," *The Globe and Mail*, November 6, 1997: B17. Also, R.S. Echlin, "Courts Apply Smell Test in Judging Contract Workers as Long Term Employees," *The Globe and Mail*, November 22, 1999: B1.

The Business Case

"My Right to Be Sick!"

Canadian employees are absent, on average, 6.9 days a year. The public sector rate of absenteeism is even higher at 8.1 days per month. These levels of short-term absenteeism are rising, due both to the increased stresses felt by the survivors of downsizing and to the sense of entitlement felt by many employees ("My contract says I can have 10 days of sick leave a year; therefore I will take 10 days"). The chart below illustrates the rising costs of absenteeism:

Factor	1997	2000	2003*
Average days absent	5.7	6.1	6.7
Direct cost per employee	$2843	$3550	$4100
Percentage of payroll	5.6%	7.1%	7.4%
Indirect costs (overtime/training)	5.8%	7.3%	7.6%

*projected

Most employers do not track absenteeism rates, and yet controlling absenteeism could alleviate labour shortages in certain sectors. Take, for example, the continuing shortage of health care workers. Canada's health care workers are absent 11.7 days a year compared to the average of 6.7. If the absenteeism rate in this sector was reduced to the national average, there would be 5500 fewer nursing jobs to fill.

Sources: David Brown, "Short Term Absences Double," *Canadian HR Reporter* 13, no. 18 (October 23, 2000): 1; Barbara Sibald, "Could Reducing Absenteeism Help Solve Health Care Worker Shortage?" *E-Canadian Medical Association Journal*, November 27, 2001.

Figure 4.7	The Advantages and Limitations of Part-Time Employment

Advantages for the Employer	Advantages for the Employee
Work scheduling flexibility	Control over personal time
Reduced compensation costs	More variety in jobs
Increased ability to add/reduce programs	Consultant tax advantages
Limitations for the Employer	**Limitations for the Employee**
No organizational loyalty	No job security
Costs of continuous replacement	Limited benefits
Costs of continual training	Stresses of continuous learning
Strategic competencies can quit	Lack of training and career progression

| Figure 4.8 | Occupational Breakdown of Staffing Agency Placement |

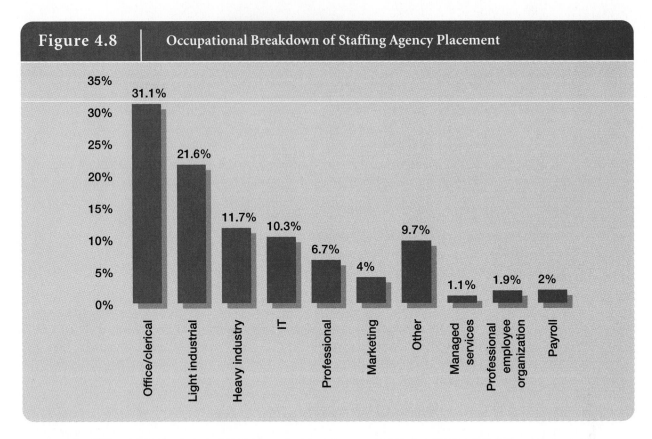

Source: Steve Jones, "You've Come a Long Way, Baby: What the Staffing Industry Offers Today," *Canadian HR Reporter* 14, no. 19 (November 5, 2001): 15.

SUMMARY

objective 1

As organizations plan for their future, top management and strategic planners must recognize that strategic planning decisions affect—and are affected by—HR functions. On the one hand, HRP plays a reactive role in making certain the right numbers and types of employees are available to implement a chosen business plan. On the other hand, HRP can proactively identify and initiate programs needed for developing organizational capabilities on which future strategies can be built.

objective 2

HRP is a systematic process that involves forecasting demand for labour, performing supply analysis, and balancing supply and demand considerations. Forecasting demand involves using quantitative or qualitative methods to identify the numbers and types of people needed to meet organizational objectives.

Supply analysis involves determining whether enough employees are available in the organization to meet demand, by using such methods as Markov analyses, staffing tables, and skills inventories. Succession planning is particularly important for leadership positions.

Organizations facing a surplus of labour have several options to restructure or downsize. Layoff decisions are usually made based on seniority or ability.

Attrition strategies or hiring freezes affect the employees least, while termination has the greatest negative impact on organizational finances, climate, and public image.

Organizations facing a shortage of labour can ask employees to work overtime, hire part-time employees, or use temporary staffing agencies.

KEY TERMS

attrition 149
benchmarking 137
cultural audits 137
hiring freeze 150
human resources planning
   (HRP) 130

management forecasts 141
Markov analysis 142
organizational capability 135
replacement charts 143
restructuring 148
severance pay 151

skill inventories 142
staffing tables 142
succession planning 143
termination 151
trend analysis 140

DISCUSSION QUESTIONS

1. Identify the three key elements of the human resources planning model, and discuss how they relate to each other.

2. Distinguish between the quantitative and the qualitative approaches to forecasting human resource requirements.

3. Distinguish between the quantitative and qualitative approaches to HR forecasting. Describe situations in which qualitative approaches would be used, and others in which quantitative approaches would be the better approach.

4. Nortel, when faced with declining demand for its products, eliminated over 50 000 jobs in the late 1990s. What downsizing options were used, and why?

5. Most students have had some experience with part-time employment. In groups, prepare a report for management that would lessen some of the limitations of part-time employment described in Figure 4.7.

Developing Managerial Skills

CUSTOMIZING HR FOR DIFFERENT TYPES OF HUMAN CAPITAL

Part of strategic planning in HR is mapping an organization's human capital. When we look at the strategic value of a person's skills, we soon discover that organizations are made up of different kinds of workers who have very different kinds of skills. Some are core knowledge workers; some are more traditional job-based employees; some are contract workers; and some are external partners. In this context, it is unlikely that we would manage all these employees the same way (as much as we might want to for fairness). There are differences in HR practices for different groups. That's not bad, but it makes the job of HR managers more difficult.

Assignment

Below are descriptions of three different employees. Describe the key characteristics of the following HR practices that you would use for each of them:

a. Job design
b. Training
c. Compensation
d. Evaluating performance

Andrea Bascomb is a highly talented computer programmer for MiniFluff, Inc. She is among the elite set of engineers in the computer industry doing leading-edge work on advanced computer modelling. In truth, CEO Bill Ding believes that the future of the company rests on the innovative work that Andrea and her team are doing. He worries that someone might lure Andrea away to work for them, so he wants to give her all the room she needs to grow and stay committed to MiniFluff.

Calvin Duff is a salesperson on the retail side of MiniFluff. He has daily contact with customers and is responsible for making sales and communicating with service personnel. Make no mistake, to many customers, Calvin and his co-workers are the "face" of MiniFluff. Always on the lookout for a better situation, Calvin has thought about working for PeachTree Computing, MiniFluff's main competitor. In truth, other salespeople have found that they can leave MiniFluff and get "up to speed" easily at other firms. Their skills are very transferable and the transition is not difficult. Bill Ding and other managers at MiniFluff recognize this fact, so they try to keep salespeople loyal and productive, recognizing that many of them do eventually leave.

Evelyn Frank is a part-time secretary for MiniFluff. She handles routine typing and filing work for the company, particularly in peak periods in the summer and around the holidays. She usually works for a few weeks at a time and then takes time off. The executives at MiniFluff have considered either outsourcing the job to an agency or automating it through a new computer system. But for now things are steady.

Case Study 1

The Federal Government

In the mid-1990s the federal government undertook the largest mass layoff in Canadian history. Roughly 20 000 employees were affected. Some of the departments announcing cuts were Transport, Natural Resources, Public Works, and Human Resources.

Everyone was scrambling. Most workers did not know who would be affected. Even the president of the Public Service Alliance of Canada (PSAC) did not know which of his 165 000 members were to be terminated. (The Treasury Board, which was responsible for downsizing the civil service, had refused to release names for fear of violating the Privacy Act.) The president of the PSAC complained to reporters, "We are in a hell of a position trying to find these people so we can provide them assistance or even guidance and advice. At the same time, because of that fear mentality that's out there, some of the individuals are saying, 'If I go to the union that might hurt my chances of keeping my job.' It's absolutely ridiculous what's going on out there, and it's another reason why we need more time."

PSAC faced the difficult task of protecting its employees from the effects of a proposed bill (C-76) that would override the key job security provisions of the union's labour contracts. Under the old legislation, government employees had the right to another job in the public service if their positions were eliminated. The new legislation gives public employees whose jobs are terminated sixty days to choose between a generous buyout, a chance at another job, and early retirement.

The government expected about 15 000 workers to take the buyout and another 4000 (over age fifty) to accept early retirement programs. The buyouts cost $1 billion. In a novel twist, PSAC wanted to open up the incentive package so that affected workers who did not want to leave the government could swap their packages with employees who wanted to leave but whose positions were not terminated. Many workers in the Ministry of Transport were transferred to the soon-to-be privatized airports and ports.

Government workers had good reason to worry. According to psychologists, people who work in huge organizations do not develop networks of external contacts that may lead to new jobs. Their skills are very narrow because of the volumes of work. For example, a clerk in the government might spend his or her entire year processing a form unique to the government. Many of these individuals have worked for only one employer and have no job search skills. Public perceptions about the easy working life of civil servants may work against their employability. And while government workers in the 1990s were waiting for the axe to fall, they were expected to continue to work.

Source: This case was developed from information in newspapers, including *The Globe and Mail*, May 2, 1995: A13, and May 26, 1995: A1.

QUESTIONS

1. What downsizing strategies did the federal government adopt? What were the limitations of these strategies?
2. What should the government have done to help laid-off workers find new jobs?
3. What should the government have done to manage survivor sickness?
4. If you were a federal employee about to be laid off, what would you do to optimize your chances of re-employment?

Case Study 2

Filling the Shoes

Bata Ltd. is a multinational shoe company, headquartered in Canada, that has more than 55 000 employees worldwide, located in sixty-seven subsidiaries. Every single subsidiary has a succession plan in place. Each senior position has three possible successors: a person who could fill the job immediately; a second who could be ready in two years; and a third who could be considered in five years. There are developmental plans for each employee on the chart; these plans are contained in a master file that lists such things as the highest position the employee can be expected to attain, the training programs completed, and areas that need improvement.

The methods for developing these senior managers are varied. For example, Bata has four levels of management training: (1) for high-potential middle managers; (2) for potential company managers; (3) for executive managers who are ready to lead the company now; and (4) for existing company managers. Employees know who is on the chart.

For those not currently part of the management succession plan, there are annual opportunities to earn a place. Formal appraisal programs identify those who are doing well and make recommendations for further training. Another method for developing managers is to offer them temporary "testing" assignments. Managers can replace people on vacation for trial periods to test and upgrade their skills. A system like this one runs the risk of simply repeating the managerial styles and thinking of the previous generation. So Bata, very conscious of the need to look for new blood (i.e., new ways of thinking and acting), also identifies people who have suggested new business opportunities and who are open to divergent perspectives.

Source: Adapted from D. Brown, "You Have to Become Deputy Before You Become Sheriff," *Canadian HR Reporter*, February 14, 2000: 9.

QUESTIONS

1. Bata Ltd. has a plan for replacing senior managers. Should this plan be extended to lower levels? Would the plan be similar, or does the training of supervisors and middle managers require different selection criteria and developmental methods?
2. What are the advantages and disadvantages of making employees aware who is part of the succession chart?

CAREER COUNSEL

To learn about job search strategies, visit the *Managing Human Resources* website (www.belcourt4e.nelson.com).

NOTES AND REFERENCES

1. Roger Moncarz and Azure Reaser, "The 2000–10 Job Outlook in Brief," *Occupational Outlook Quarterly* 46, no. 1 (Spring 2002): 2–47.

2. Statistics Canada, CANSIM II, table 282-0002, http://www.statcan.ca/english/Pgdb/labor20a.htm; Laura Cassiani, "Labour Shortages Stunts Manufacturing Growth," *Canadian HR Reporter* 13, no. 18 (October 23, 2000): 2.

3. Stephenie Overman, "Gearing Up for Tomorrow's Workforce," *HRFocus* 76, no. 2 (February 1999): 1, 15; Rick Mullin and Sylvia Pfeifer, "Hiring Becomes a Star Search," *Chemical Week* 159, no. 19 (May 14, 1997): 40–1; Douglas T. Hall, "Executive Careers and Learning: Aligning Selection, Strategy, and Development," *Human Resource Planning* 18, no. 2 (1995): 14–23.

4. James Walker, "Human Capital: Beyond HR?" *Human Resource Planning* 24, no. 2: 4–5; Gary Kesler, "Four Steps to Building an HR Agenda for Growth: HR Strategy Revisited," *Human Resource Planning* 23, no. 3: 24–37.

5. Justin Hibard, "Web Service: Ready or Not," *Informationweek* 709 (November 16, 1998): 18–20; Dunstan Prial, "On-Line: Barnes & Noble Books: An IPO for Web Unit," *The Wall Street Journal*, August 21, 1998: B1; Chris Clark, "Trying to Sell Books over the Internet? Yeah, Right," *MC Technology Marketing Intelligence* 18, no. 8 (August 1998): 62.

6. Bill Leonard, "GM Drives HR to the Next Level," *HRMagazine* 47, no. 3: 46–51; William James, "Best HR Practices for Today's Innovation Management," *Research Technology Management* 45, no. 1 (January/February 2002): 57–60.

7. James W. Walker, "Integrating the Human Resource Function with the Business," *Human Resource Planning* 14, no. 2 (1996): 59–77; James W. Walker, "Perspectives," *Human Resource Planning* 25, no. 1 (2002): 12–14.

8. Carol Stephenson, "Corporate Values Drive Global Success at Lucent Technologies," *Canadian Speeches* 13, no. 5 (November–December 1999): 23–7.

9. Patrick Wright, Gary McMahan, Scott Snell, and Barry Gerhart, "Comparing Line and HR Executives' Perceptions of HR Effectiveness: Services, Roles, and Contributions," *Human Resource Management* 40, no. 2 (2001): 111–23; Ryan Langlois, "Fairmont Hotels: Business Strategy Starts with People," *Canadian HR Reporter* 14, no. 19 (November 5, 2001): 19–25.

10. D. P. Lepak and S. A. Snell, "The Human Resource Architecture: Toward a Theory of Human Capital Development and Allocation," *Academy of Management Review* 24, no. 1 (1999): 31–48; David Lepak and Scott Snell, "Examining the Human Resource Architecture: The Relationship among Human Capital, Employment, and Human Resource Configurations," *Journal of Management,* forthcoming.

11. Brian Becker, Mark Huselid, and Dave Ulrich, *The HR Scorecard: Linking People, Strategy, and Performance* (Cambridge, MA: Harvard Business School Press, 2001). See also Shari Caudron, "How HR Drives Profits," *Workforce* 80, no. 12 (December 2001): 26–31.

12. P. M. Wright and S. A. Snell, "Toward a Unifying Framework for Exploring Fit and Flexibility in Strategic Human Resource Management," *Academy of Management Review* 22, no. 4 (1998): 756–72; Scott A. Snell, Mark Shadur, and Patrick Wright, "Human Resources Strategy: The Era of Our Ways," in M. A. Hitt, R. E. Freeman, and J. S. Harrison (eds.), *Handbook of Strategic Management* (Oxford: Blackwell Publishing, 2002): 627–49; Patrick Wright, Ben Dunford, and Scott Snell, "Human Resources and the Resource-Based View of the Firm," *Journal of Management* 27, no. 6 (2001): 701–21.

13. R. Sanchez, "Strategic Flexibility in Product Competition," *Strategic Management Journal* 16 (1995): 135–59; Wright and Snell, "Toward a Unifying Framework."

14. Eileen Abels, "Hot Topics: Environmental Scanning," *Bulletin of the American Society for Information Science* 28, no. 3 (February/March 2002): 16–17; William M. James, "Best HR Practices for Today's Innovation Management," *Research Technology Management* 45, no. 1 (January/February 2002): 57–60; Robert W. Rowden, "Potential Roles of the Human Resource Management Professional in the Strategic Planning Process," *S.A.M. Advanced Management Journal* 64, no. 3 (Summer 1999): 22–27.

15. Janet Wiscombe, "Creative Hiring on the Green," *Workforce* 81, no. 2 (February 2002): 21; Geoffrey Brewer, "Older Workers Are Thriving in Tight Job Market," *The New York Times,* June 21, 2000, C1.

16. Jennifer Laabs, "The HR Side of Sears' Comeback," *Workforce* 78, no. 3 (March 1999): 24–29; Odette Pollar, "A Diverse Workforce Requires Balanced Leadership," *Workforce* extra (December 1998); 4–5; Anthony Early, Jr., "A Passion for Personal Success," *Vital Speeches of the Day* 65, no. 6 (January 1, 1999): 184–87.

17. Ray Brillinger, "Best Practices: Human Resources Benchmarking," *Canadian HR Reporter* 14, no. 12 (June 18, 2001): 12; Chris Mahoney, "Benchmarking Your Way to Smarter Decisions," *Workforce* 79, no. 10 (October 2000): 100–103.

18. Terry Wagar, "Factors Influencing Permanent Workforce Reduction: Evidence from Large Canadian Companies," *Canadian Journal of Administrative Studies* 14, no. 3 (1997): 303–14.

19. "The Rebirth of IBM: Blue Is the Colour," *The Economist* 347, no. 8071 (June 6, 1998): 65–68; Ronald Henkoff, "Getting beyond Downsizing," *Fortune,* January 10, 1994: 58–64; Susan Caminiti, "What Happens to Laid-Off Managers?" *Fortune,* June 13, 1994: 68–78; Del Jones, "Kodak to Eliminate 10,000 Jobs by '96," *USA Today,* August 19, 1993: B1; Tim Jones, "Retooling Unleashes Huge Wave of Layoffs," *Chicago Tribune,* June 22, 1994: 11.

20. G. Keenan, "GM Slashing 1400 Quebec Jobs," *The Globe and Mail,* June 3, 1995: B1.

21. Linda Gutri, "Survivor Skills," *Human Resource Professional* 9, no. 3 (March 1995): 13–15.

22. Anneli Legault, "Aging Disgracefully," *Human Resources Professional* 10, no. 11 (December 1993): 10–11.

23. David McCabe, "Improvising the Future," *Human Resources Professional* 10, no. 11 (December 1993): 17–19.

24. William Soukup, Miriam Rothman, and Dennis Briscoe, "Outplacement Services: A Vital Component of Personnel Policy," *SAM Advanced Management Journal,* Autumn 1987: 19–23.

25. Margot Gibb-Clark, "Survivors Also Suffer in Downsizing: Expert," *The Globe and Mail,* May 23, 1995: B5.

26. D. Worrel, W. Davidson, and V. Sharma, "Lay-off Announcements and Shareholder Wealth," *Academy of Management Journal* 34 (1991): 662–78.

27. T.H. Wagar, "Downsizing or Dumbsizing? Possible Consequences of Permanent Workforce Reduction," *Proceedings of the Administrative Sciences Association of Canada, Annual Conference* 15, no. 9, 1994.

28. W. Casco, "Downsizing? What Do We Know? What Have We Learned?" *The Executive* 7 (1993): 95–104.

29. A. Tomlinson, "Enron, WorldCom Leave Employees Bitter," *Canadian HR Reporter,* November 18, 2002: 3.

30. Gibb-Clark, "Survivors Also Suffer in Downsizing: Expert."

31. Gutri, "Survivor Skills."

32. D. Brown, "Losing Your Brand," *Canadian HR Reporter* 15, no. 8 (April 22, 2002): 7.

33. Chris Lee, "After the Cuts," *Training* 29, no. 7 (July 1992): 17–23.

34. Bruce Tucker, "Downsizing Has Killed Loyalty," *Human Resource Management in Canada Report* 124 (June 1993): 17–23.

35. Mary Anne Lesperance, "Strategic Staffing," *Human Resource Professional,* May 2001.

36. John W. Medcof and Brent Needham, "The Supra-Organizational HRM System," *Business Horizons,* 41, no. 1 (January-February), 1998; L. Duxbury and C. Higgins, *National Work-Life Conflict Study,* Health Canada, 2001.

37. Barb Cole Gomolski, "Recruiters Lure Temps with Free IT Training," *Computerworld* 33, no. 31 (August 2, 1999): 10.

38. Karen Bannan, "Breakaway (A Special Report)—Getting Help—Together: By Bundling Job-Recruiting Efforts, Small Firms Seek Attention—and Leverage," *The Wall Street Journal,* April 23, 2001: 12.

Calculating Turnover and Absenteeism

Throughout this chapter we have emphasized that HRP depends on having an accurate picture of both the supply of and the demand for employees. Two factors, employee turnover and absenteeism, have a direct impact on HR planning and recruitment processes. In this appendix we discuss in depth both turnover and absenteeism, and methods for measuring them, and suggest ways to manage their impact.

EMPLOYEE TURNOVER RATES

"Employee turnover" refers simply to the movement of employees out of an organization. It is often cited as one of the reasons why Canadian productivity rates have failed to keep pace with those of foreign competitors. It is also one of the chief determinants of labour supply. Even if everything else about an organization stays the same, as employees turn over, the supply of labour goes down. This has both direct and indirect costs to the organization.

Computing the Turnover Rate

One formula for computing turnover rates is

$$\frac{\text{Number of separations during the month}}{\text{Total number of employees at midmonth}} \times 100$$

Thus, if there were 25 separations during a month and the total number of employees at midmonth was 500, the turnover rate would be

$$\frac{25}{500} \times 100 = 5\%$$

Turnover rates are computed on a regular basis to compare specific units (departments, divisions, work groups, etc.). Often, comparisons are made with data provided by other organizations.

Another method for computing the turnover rate reflects only the avoidable separations (S). This rate is computed by subtracting unavoidable separations (US) — such as pregnancy, return to school, death, marriage—from all separations. The formula for this method is as follows:

$$\frac{S - US}{M} \times 100$$

where M represents the total number of employees at midmonth. For example, if there were 25 separations during a month, 5 of which were US, and the total number of employees at midmonth (M) was 500, the turnover rate would be

$$\frac{25 - 5}{500} \times 100 = 4\%$$

In looking at the impact of turnover on HR planning and recruitment, it is vitally important to recognize that quantitative rates of turnover are not the only factor to be considered: the quality of employees who leave an organization is equally important. If poor employees leave—what experts refer to as "functional turnover"—this can benefit the organization. The costs of keeping unproductive workers may be far more than the costs of recruiting and training new, more effective performers.

Determining the Costs of Turnover

Replacing an employee is time-consuming and expensive. Costs can generally be broken down into three categories: separation costs for the departing employee, replacement costs, and training costs for the new employee. These costs are conservatively estimated at two to three times the monthly salary of the departing employee and do not include indirect costs such as low productivity prior to quitting and lower morale and overtime for other employees because of the vacated job. Consequently, reducing turnover could result in significant savings to an organization. Highlights in HRM 4A.1 details one organization's costs associated with the turnover of a single computer programmer. Note that the major expense is the cost involved in training a replacement.

EMPLOYEE ABSENTEEISM RATES

How often employees are absent from their work—the absenteeism rate—is also directly related to HR planning and recruitment. When employees miss work, the organization incurs direct costs of lost wages and decreased productivity. It is not uncommon for organizations to hire extra workers just to make up for the number of absences totalled across all employees. Besides these direct costs, there are indirect costs that may underlie excessive absenteeism. A certain amount of absenteeism is, of course, unavoidable. There will always be some who must be absent from work because of sickness, accidents, or serious family problems, or for other legitimate reasons. However, chronic absenteeism may signal some deeper problems in the work environment.

Highlights in HRM 4A.1

COSTS ASSOCIATED WITH THE TURNOVER OF ONE EMPLOYEE

Turnover costs = Separation costs + Replacement costs + Training costs

Separation Costs

1. Exit interview = Cost for salary and benefits of both interviewer and departing employee during the exit interview
2. Administrative and record-keeping action

Separation costs = 1 + 2

Replacements Costs

1. Advertising for job opening
2. Pre-employment administrative functions and record-keeping action
3. Selection interview
4. Employment tests
5. Meetings to discuss candidates (salary and benefits of managers while participating in meetings)

Replacement costs = 1 + 2 + 3 + 4 + 5

Training Costs

1. Booklets, manuals, and reports
2. Education = Cost per day for new employee's salary and benefits times days for workshops, seminars, or courses
3. One-to-one coaching = ($/day/new employee + $/day/staff coach or job expert) × 20 days of one-to-one coaching
4. Salary and benefits of new employee until he or she gets "up to par" = Costs per day for salary and benefits × 20 days

Training costs = 1 + 2 + 3 + 4

Total turnover costs = Separation + Replacement + Training

Source: Adapted from Michael W. Mercer, *Turning Your Human Resources Department into a Profit Center* (New York: AMACOM, 1993). Copyright 1993 Michael W. Mercer, The Mercer Group, Inc., Chicago.

Computing Absenteeism Rates

Managers should determine the extent of the absenteeism problem, if any, by maintaining individual and departmental attendance records and by computing absenteeism rates. There is no universally accepted definition of "absence," nor is there a standard formula for computing absenteeism rates. However, the method most often used is

$$\frac{\text{Number of worker-days lost through job absence during period}}{\text{Average number of employees} \times \text{Number of workdays}} \times 100$$

If 300 worker-days are lost through job absence during a month having 25 scheduled working days at an organization that employs 500 workers, the absenteeism rate for that month is

$$\frac{300}{500 \times 25} \times 100 = 2.4\%$$

Job absence can be defined as the failure of employees to report to work when their schedules require it, whether or not such failure to report is excused. Scheduled vacations, holidays, and prearranged leaves of absence are not counted as job absence.

Comparing Absenteeism Data

The Vancouver-based Saratoga Institute regularly monitors absenteeism rates and for a fee can provide comparison rates. HR managers in a number of sectors, including health care, collect and share absenteeism rates. The Conference Board of Canada and Statistics Canada publish absenteeism data.

Costs of Absenteeism

Traditional accounting and information systems often do not generate data that reflect the costs of absenteeism. Consequently, their usefulness in HR planning is often limited. To accentuate the impact of absenteeism on organizational performance, managers should translate the data into dollar costs. A system for computing absenteeism costs for an individual organization is available. Organizations with computerized absence-reporting systems should find this additional information easy and inexpensive to generate. The cost of each person-hour lost to absenteeism is based on the hourly weighted average salary, costs of employee benefits, supervisory costs, and incidental costs.

For example, XYZ Company, with 1200 employees, has 78 000 person-hours lost to absenteeism per year; the total absence cost is $560 886. When this figure is divided by 1200 employees, the cost per employee is $467.41 annually. (In this example, we are assuming that the absent workers are paid. If absent workers are not paid, their salary figures are omitted from the computation.) A Nova Scotia government audit of sick leave revealed that employees took an average of 10.8 sick days per year, compared to the national average of 7.3 days for public sector employees and 6.6 days for all Canadian workers. The cost of sick leave was estimated to be $25 million in one year alone. Current absenteeism rates for the Canadian workforce are 6.7 days; the public sector rate is 8.1 days.*

*Sources: Conference Board of Canada, *Compensation Planning Outlook*, chart 17, 2003; A. Jeffers, "Our Civil Servants Sickest in Country," *Chronicle-Herald* (Halifax), December 12, 1994: A1, A2; L. Kelly, "Attendance Management: An Issue of the 90's," *Worklife* 8, no. 5 (1992): 12–14.

Absenteeism and HR Planning

While an employer may find that the overall absenteeism rate and costs are within an acceptable range, it is still advisable to study the statistics to determine whether there are patterns in the data. Rarely does absenteeism spread itself evenly across an organization. It is very likely that employees in one area (or occupational group) may have nearly perfect attendance records, while others in a different area may be absent frequently. By monitoring these differential attendance records, managers can assess where problems may exist and, more importantly, begin planning ways to address underlying causes. For example, incentives could be provided for perfect attendance. Alternatively, progressive discipline procedures could be used with employees who are regularly absent.

chapter 5

Recruitment and Selection

After studying this chapter, you should be able to

objective 1
Explain the advantages and disadvantages of recruiting from within the organization.

objective 2
Describe the advantages and disadvantages of recruiting from the external labour market.

objective 3
Describe methods for improving the effectiveness of recruiting.

objective 4
Explain the objectives of the personnel selection process.

objective 5
Identify the various sources of information used for personnel selection.

objective 6
Compare the value of different types of employment tests.

objective 7
Illustrate the different approaches to conducting an employment interview.

objective 8
Describe the various decision strategies for selection.

There is perhaps no more important topic in HRM than employee recruitment and selection. If it is true that organizations succeed or fail on the basis of talents of employees, then managers directly influence that success by the people they hire. Regardless of whether the company is large or small, hiring the best and the brightest employees lays a strong foundation for excellence. Alternatively, it is common to hear managers who don't recognize this point lament the inordinate amount of time they spend trying to fix bad selection decisions. In addition, equal employment opportunity legislation (discussed in Chapter 2) has also provided an impetus for making sure that the selection process is done well. The bottom line is, good selection decisions make a difference. So do bad ones.

RECRUITING WITHIN THE ORGANIZATION

objective

Recruitment is the process of locating potential applicants and encouraging them to apply for existing or anticipated job openings. During this process, efforts are made to inform the applicants fully about the qualifications required to perform the job and the career opportunities the organization can offer its employees. Whether a particular job vacancy will be filled by someone from within the organization or from outside will, of course, depend on the availability of personnel, the organization's HR policies, and the requirements of the job to be staffed. Highlights in HRM 5.1 outlines hotel chain Marriott's principles for recruiting.

Advantages of Recruiting from Within

Most organizations try to follow a policy of filling job vacancies above the entry-level position through promotions and transfers. By filling vacancies in this way, an organization can capitalize on the investment it has made in recruiting, selecting, training, and developing its current employees. Promotion serves to reward employees for past performance and is intended to encourage them to continue their efforts. It also gives other employees reason to anticipate that similar efforts by them will lead to promotion, thus improving morale within the organization. This is particularly true for members of the designated groups who have encountered difficulties in finding employment and have often faced even greater difficulty in advancing within an organization. Most organizations have integrated promotion policies as an essential part of their employment equity programs.

If an organization's promotion policy is to have maximum motivational value, employees must be made aware of that policy. The following is an example of a policy statement that an organization might prepare:

> "Promotion from within" is generally recognized as a foundation of good employment practice, and it is the policy of our museum to promote from within whenever possible when filling a vacancy. The job vacancy will be posted for five calendar days to give all qualified full- and part-time personnel an equal opportunity to apply.

Highlights in HRM 5.1

MARRIOTT'S RECRUITMENT PRINCIPLES

1. **Get It Right the First Time.** Marriott "hires friendly" and "trains technical." It's better to hire people with "the spirit to serve" and train them to work than hire people who know business and try to teach them to enjoy serving guests. Marriott hires cooks who love to cook and housekeepers who love to clean. They have learned that this approach works both for delivering excellent service and for retaining their employees.

2. **Money Is a Big Thing, But ...** The top concern of Marriott associates is total compensation. But intangible factors taken together, such as work-life balance, leadership quality, opportunity for advancement, work environment, and training, far outweigh money in their decisions to stay or leave. Pay matters less and the other factors matter more the longer someone works for Marriott. From flexible schedules to tailored benefit packages and development opportunities, Marriott has built systems to address these nonmonetary factors.

3. **A Caring Workplace Is a Bottom-Line Issue.** When employees come to work, they feel safe, secure, and welcome. Committed associates are less likely to leave. And associate work commitment is one of the key generators of guest satisfaction. Managers are accountable for associate satisfaction ratings and for turnover rates. Every day, associates in each of Marriott's full service hotels participate in a fifteen-minute meeting to review basic values such as respect. Managers also encourage associates to raise their personal concerns. They take the time to celebrate birthdays and anniversaries. Marriott calls this the loyalty program, because it builds loyalty among associates and repeat business from customers. The result is that everyone has a stake in making the hotel a success.

4. **Promote from Within.** More than 50 percent of Marriott's current managers have been promoted from within. All associates are given the opportunity to advance as far as their abilities will carry them. Elevating veterans to positions of leadership helps Marriott pass on the soul of its business—its corporate culture—from one generation to the next. In addition, promoting from within is a powerful tool for recruitment and retention. Associates cite "opportunity for advancement" as a key factor in their decisions to stay with Marriott. (Accompanying that is the company's $100-million-a-year commitment to training.)

5. **Build the Employment Brand.** Marriott attracts employees the same way it attracts customers. Just as consumers buy experiences, not just products, potential employees are looking for a great work experience when they shop for jobs. Communicating the promise of a great work experience is what employment branding is all about. It's basically a value proposition. According to CEO J. W. Marriott, "For more than seventy years, we've lived by a simple motto: If we take care of our associates they'll take care of our guests. That isn't just a sentiment. It's a strategy—one all businesses must adopt to remain competitive in an environment where our most valuable resource, human capital, drives economic value for our company."

Sources: J. W. Marriott, "Competitive Strength," *Executive Excellence* 18, no. 4 (April 2001): 3–4; J. W. Marriott, "Our Competitive Strength: Human Capital," *Executive Speeches* 15, no. 5 (April/May 2001): 18–21.

While a transfer lacks the motivational value of a promotion, it sometimes can serve to protect employees from layoff or to broaden their job experiences. Furthermore, the transferred employee's familiarity with the organization and its operations can eliminate the orientation and training costs that recruitment from the outside would entail. Most important, the transferee's performance record is likely to be a more accurate predictor of the candidate's success than the data gained about outside applicants.

Methods of Locating Qualified Job Candidates

The effective use of internal sources requires a system for locating qualified job candidates and for enabling those who consider themselves qualified to apply for the opening. Qualified job candidates within the organization can be located by computerized record systems, by job posting and bidding, and by looking to those who have been laid off.

Human Resources Information Systems

As discussed in Chapter 1, information technology has made it possible for organizations to create databases that contain the complete records and qualifications of each employee within an organization. Combined with increasingly user-friendly search engines, managers can access this information and identify potential candidates for available jobs. Organizations have developed resumé-tracking systems that allow managers to query an online database of resumés. Companies such as PeopleSoft and SAP are leaders in developing automated staffing and skills management software. Similar to the skills inventories mentioned earlier, these information systems allow an organization to rapidly screen its entire workforce to locate suitable candidates to fill an internal opening. These data can also be used to predict the career paths of employees and to anticipate when and where promotion opportunities may arise. Since the value of the data depends on its being kept up to date, the systems typically include provisions for recording changes in employee qualifications and job placements as they occur.[1]

Job Posting and Bidding

Job posting and bidding
Posting vacancy notices and maintaining lists of employees for upgraded positions

Organizations may communicate information about job openings through a process referred to as **job posting and bidding.** In the past, this process has consisted largely of posting vacancy notices on bulletin boards. In addition, it may also include use of designated posting centres, employee publications, special handouts, direct mail, and public-address messages. Increasingly, companies such as Xerox are developing computerized job posting systems and maintaining voluntary lists of employees looking for upgraded positions. As a position becomes available, the list of employees seeking that position is retrieved from the computer, and the records of these employees are reviewed to select the best-qualified candidate.[2] Highlights in HRM 5.2 provides some guidelines for setting up an online job posting system.

The system of job posting and bidding can provide many benefits to an organization. However, these benefits may not be realized unless employees believe the system is being administered fairly. Furthermore, job bidding is more effective when it is part of a career development program in which employees are made aware of opportuni-

Highlights in HRM 5.2

GUIDELINES FOR SETTING UP AN ONLINE JOB POSTING SYSTEM

Below is a list of best practices for online recruitment:

▶ Links to careers from the home page
▶ About the company: benefits
▶ About the company: culture
▶ A university recruiting section
▶ Job search by job category
▶ Job search by key word
▶ Urgent-needs jobs highlighted
▶ Complete job description
▶ One click to apply
▶ Pre-assessment tool customized for each position

▶ Choice of cut-and-paste form or resumé builder
▶ Attachment of formatted resumé
▶ Application automatically connected to a job
▶ Anonymous application
▶ E-mail to a friend
▶ Profiling
▶ Reuse of candidate information for multiple applications
▶ Online user feedback

To begin building an electronic job posting system, organizations need an e-mail software program with the capability to display job postings and accept recruiting requests for available openings.

Designing and Administering the System

To design and administer the system, organizations need

▶ An automated process to enter job postings into the system and to delete listings once they are filled
▶ The capability to automatically calculate each listing's expiration date
▶ A system that automatically assigns numbers to job postings
▶ The capability to preschedule job positions for future postings
▶ A way for coordinators to revise and delete postings after they are on the system
▶ Security measures that allow access to authorized users only

Source: "Canadian Employers Lagging behind in Use of Corporate Websites for Recruitment," *Canadian HR Reporter*, November 19, 2001. Condensed from Sharon M. Tarrant, "Setting Up an Electronic Job-Posting System," *Training and Development,* January 1994, 39–42.

ties available to them within the organization. For example, HR departments may provide new employees with literature on job progression that describes the lines of job advancement, training requirements for each job, and skills and abilities needed as they move up the job-progression ladder.

Limitations of Recruiting from Within

Sometimes certain jobs at the middle and upper levels that require specialized training and experience cannot be filled from within the organization and must be filled from the outside. This is especially common in small organizations. Also, for certain openings it may be necessary to hire individuals from the outside who have gained from another employer the knowledge and expertise required for these jobs.

Even though HR policy encourages job openings to be filled from within the organization, potential candidates from the outside should be considered in order to prevent the inbreeding of ideas and attitudes. Applicants hired from the outside, particularly for certain technical and managerial positions, can be a source of new ideas and may bring with them the latest knowledge acquired from their previous employers. Indeed, excessive reliance on internal sources can create the risk of "employee cloning." Furthermore, it is not uncommon for firms in high-tech industries such as chemicals and electronics to attempt to gain secrets from competitors by hiring away their employees. Dow recently sued GE over just such an issue.[3]

RECRUITING OUTSIDE THE ORGANIZATION

Unless there is to be a reduction in the workforce, a replacement from outside must be found to fill a vacancy when a job holder moves to a new slot in the organization. Thus, when the president or CEO of the organization retires, a chain reaction of promotions may subsequently occur. This creates other managerial openings throughout the organization. The question therefore is not whether to bring people into the organization, but rather at which level they are to be brought in.

In the past few years, organizations such as 3M, Home Depot, and Air Canada have brought in outsiders to be their new CEOs. In fact, an astounding share of Fortune 500 companies who replace their CEOs do so by hiring executives from outside their companies. In many of these cases, hiring someone from the outside is seen as essential for revitalizing the organizations.[4]

The Labour Market

Labour market
Area from which applicants are recruited

The **labour market,** or the area from which applicants are to be recruited, will vary with the type of position to be filled and the amount of compensation to be paid. Recruitment for executives and technical personnel who require a high degree of knowledge and skill may be national or even international in scope. Most colleges and universities, for example, conduct national employment searches to fill top administrative positions. Recruitment for jobs that require relatively little skill, however, may encompass only a small geographic area. The reluctance of people to relocate may cause them to turn down offers of employment, thereby eliminating them from employment consideration beyond the local labour market. However, by offering an attractive level of compensation and by helping to defray moving costs, employers may induce some applicants to move.[5]

The ease with which employees can commute to work will also influence the boundaries of the labour market. Insufficient public transportation or extreme traffic congestion on the streets and freeways can limit the distance employees are willing to travel to work, particularly to jobs of low pay. Also, population migration from the cities to the suburbs has had its effect on labour markets. If suitable employment can be obtained near where they live or if they can work at home, many suburbanites are less likely to accept or remain in jobs in the central city.

Outside Sources of Recruitment

The outside sources from which employers recruit will vary with the type of position to be filled. A computer programmer, for example, is not likely to be recruited from the same source as a machine operator. Trade schools can provide applicants for entry-level positions, though these recruitment sources are not as useful when highly skilled employees are needed.

The condition of the labour market may also help to determine which recruiting sources an organization will use. During periods of high unemployment, organizations may be able to maintain an adequate supply of qualified applicants from unsolicited resumés alone. A tight labour market, one with low unemployment, may force the employer to advertise heavily and/or seek assistance from local employment agencies. How successful an organization has been in reaching its employment goals may be still another factor in determining the sources from which to recruit. Typically, an employer at any given time will find it necessary to utilize several recruitment sources. Figure 5.1 shows how 201 HR executives in one study rated the effectiveness of nine different recruiting methods.

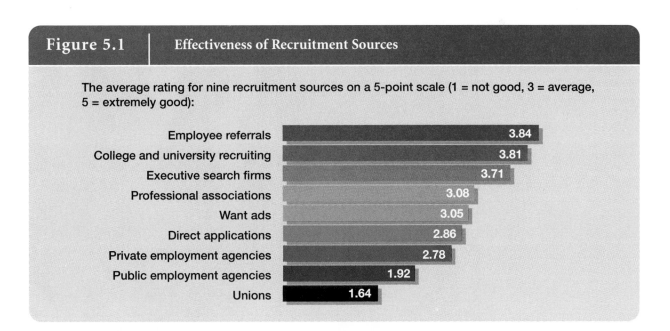

| Figure 5.1 | Effectiveness of Recruitment Sources |

The average rating for nine recruitment sources on a 5-point scale (1 = not good, 3 = average, 5 = extremely good):

Employee referrals	3.84
College and university recruiting	3.81
Executive search firms	3.71
Professional associations	3.08
Want ads	3.05
Direct applications	2.86
Private employment agencies	2.78
Public employment agencies	1.92
Unions	1.64

Source: "The Search for Effective Methods" from *HRFocus*, May 1996. ©1996 American Management Association International.

Several other studies have suggested that an employee's recruitment source can affect that employee's subsequent tenure and job performance in both large and small organizations.[6] In general, applicants who find employment through referral by a current employee tend to remain with the organization longer and give higher-quality performance than those employees recruited through the formal recruitment sources of advertisements and employment agencies. Informal recruiting sources may also yield higher selection rates than formal sources. Employers are cautioned, however, that relying on only one or two recruitment sources to secure job applicants could have an adverse effect on protected classes.

Advertisements

One of the most common methods of attracting applicants is through advertisements. While newspapers and trade journals are the media used most often, radio, television, billboards, posters, and electronic mail are also utilized. Advertising has the advantage of reaching a large audience of possible applicants. Some degree of selectivity can be achieved by using newspapers and journals directed toward a particular group of readers. Professional journals, trade journals, and publications of unions and various fraternal or nonprofit organizations fall into this category.

The preparation of recruiting advertisements is not only time-consuming, it also requires creativity in developing design and message content. Well-written advertisements highlight the major assets of the position while showing the responsiveness of the organization to the job and career needs of the applicants. Also, there appears to be a correlation between the accuracy and completeness of information provided in advertisements and the recruitment success of the organization. Among the information typically included in advertisements is that the recruiting organization is an equal opportunity employer.

Five thousand applicants vie for one of 500 lucrative positions at an IBM job fair in Markham, Ontario. Four hundred prospects were identified in twenty-four hours.

CP (STEVE RUSSELL)

Advertising can sometimes place a severe burden on an organization's employment office. Even though the specifications for the openings are described thoroughly in the advertisement, many applicants who know they do not meet the job requirements may still be attracted. They may apply with the hope that the employer will not be able to find applicants who do meet the specifications.

Unsolicited Applications and Resumés

Many employers receive unsolicited applications and resumés from individuals who may or may not be good prospects for employment.[7] Even though the percentage of acceptable applicants from this source may not be high, it is a source that cannot be ignored. In fact, it is often believed that individuals who contact the employer on their own initiative will be better employees than those recruited through college placement services or newspaper advertisements.

Good public relations dictates that any person contacting an organization for a job be treated with courtesy and respect. If there is no possibility of employment in the organization at present or in the future, the applicant should be tactfully and frankly informed of this fact. Telling an applicant to "fill out an application, and we will keep it on file," when there is no hope for his or her employment, is not fair to the applicant.

Internet Recruiting

According to a Society for Human Resource Management study, 96 percent of all job seekers use the Internet, making it their most commonly used search tactic, whereas 88 percent of recruiters use the Internet to get the word out about new positions. Companies and applicants find the approach cheaper, faster, and potentially more effective. A variety of websites are available where applicants can submit their resumés and potential employers can check for qualified applicants. Applicant tracking systems can match the job requirements with the experiences and skills of applicants. Estimates are that more than 2500 websites exist that contain job postings, and more than 1.5 million resumés are currently online.[8]

But online recruiting has become more than just matching candidates with companies. The next generation of web-based tools includes online job fairs in which companies can "meet" candidates in a virtual environment and chat with them online. The method is often cost-effective as well. The Employee Management Association estimates that the cost per hire is about $377, compared to $3295 using print media.[9]

USING THE INTERNET

Internet recruiting consulting firm Recruitsoft offers a good selection of research, reports, tools, and articles on recruitment, most of it for online recruitment.

www.recruitsoft.com

Employee Referrals

The recruitment efforts of an organization can be aided by employee referrals, or recommendations made by current employees. Managers have found that the quality of employee-referred applicants is normally quite high, since employees are generally hesitant to recommend individuals who might not perform well. Keith Swenson, a human resources consultant with William H. Mercer, suggests several ways to increase the effectiveness of employee referral programs.

▶ *Up the ante.* Companies pay high commissions to employment agencies and search firms, so why not do the same thing with employees when they provide a good referral? Other recruitment incentives used by organizations include complimentary dinners, discounts on merchandise, all-expense-paid trips, and free insurance. When employers pay higher bonuses for "hot" skills, employees are more likely to focus on people they know in that area.

▶ *Pay for performance.* It is sometimes a good idea to save part of the referral bonus until the new hire has stayed for six months. This encourages referring employees to help the new hires succeed.

▶ *Tailor the program.* Companies typically need more of certain types of skills than others, but the referral programs do not always reflect this. Part of a good referral program is educating employees about the kinds of people the organization wants to hire. This includes some communication of the skills required, but also a reaffirmation of the values and ethics sought in applicants.

▶ *Increase visibility.* One of the best ways to publicize a referral program is to celebrate successes. Some companies use novel approaches such as "job of the month" or "celebrity endorsements" from managers. The idea is to keep everyone thinking about bringing in good people.

▶ *Keep the data.* Even if a referral does not get the job, it might be a good idea to keep the resumé on file just in case another vacancy arises.

▶ *Rethink your taboos.* Some companies are reluctant to take on certain potential hires, such as former employees, relatives, and the like. In a tight labour market, it is a good idea to broaden the search.

▶ *Widen the program.* Just as it may make sense to consider hiring former employees, it may make sense to ask them for referrals even if they are not candidates for the jobs themselves. Most companies have mailing lists of "corporate friends" that can be used to seek out potential candidates.

▶ *Measure results.* No surprise here. After the program is implemented, managers need to take a hard look at the volume of referrals, the qualifications of candidates, and the success of new hires on the job. These results are then fed back to fine-tune the program.[10]

As noted previously, some potential negative factors are associated with employee referrals. They include the possibility of inbreeding and the violation of employee equity guidelines. Since employees and their referrals tend to have similar backgrounds, employers who rely heavily on employee referrals to fill job openings may intentionally or unintentionally screen out, and thereby discriminate against, members of designated groups. Furthermore, organizations may choose not to employ relatives of current employees. The practice of hiring relatives, referred to as **nepotism,** can invite charges of favouritism, especially in appointments to desirable positions.[11]

Nepotism
A preference for hiring relatives of current employees

Executive Search Firms

In contrast to public and private employment agencies, which help job seekers find the right job, executive search firms (often called "headhunters") help employers find the right person for a job. Firms such as Korn/Ferry and the Caldwell Partners seek out candidates with qualifications that match the requirements of the positions their client firm is seeking to fill. Executive search firms do not advertise in the media for job candidates, nor do they accept a fee from the individual being placed.

The fees charged by search firms may range from 30 to 40 percent of the annual salary for the position to be filled. For the recruitment of senior executives, this fee is paid by the client firm, whether or not the recruiting effort results in a hire. It is for this practice that search firms receive the greatest criticism.

Nevertheless, as noted earlier, it is an increasingly common occurrence that new chief executive officers (CEOs) are brought in from outside the organization. A large number of these new CEOs are placed in those positions through the services of an executive search firm. Since high-calibre executives are in short supply, a significant number of the nation's largest corporations use search firms to fill their top positions.

Figure 5.2 shows the results of a study by McKinsey and Company that investigated the key factors that determine the likelihood executives would want to work for a particular company.

Figure 5.2	Factors That Motivate Top Talent

Working for a great company and having a great job are more important to most executives than compensation.*

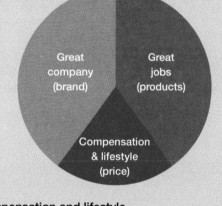

Great company (brand)

Values and culture	58%
Well managed	50%
Exciting challenges	38%
Strong performance	29%
Industry leader	21%
Many talented people	20%
Good at development	17%
Inspiring mission	16%
Fun with colleagues	11%
Job security	8%

Great jobs (products)

Freedom and autonomy	56%
Exciting challenges	51%
Career advancement and growth	39%
Fit with boss I admire	29%

Compensation and lifestyle (price)

Differentiated compensation	29%
High total compensation	23%
Geographic location	19%
Respect for lifestyle	14%
Acceptable pace and stress	1%

*Each number represents the percentage of the top 200 executives who agreed each factor was important.

Source: Adapted from E.G. Chambers, H. Hanafield-Jones, S.M. Hankin, and E.G. Michaels, III, "Win the War for Top Talent," *Workforce* 77, no. 12 (December 1998): 50–56. Used with permission of McKinsey & Co.

Educational Institutions

Educational institutions typically are a source of young applicants with formal training but with relatively little full-time work experience. High schools are usually a source of employees for clerical and blue-collar jobs. Community colleges, with their various types of specialized training, can provide candidates for technical jobs. These institutions can also be a source of applicants for a variety of white-collar jobs, including those in the sales and retail fields. Some management-trainee jobs are also staffed from this source.

For technical and managerial positions, colleges and universities are generally the primary source. However, the suitability of college graduates for open positions often depends on their major field of study. Organizations seeking applicants in the technical and professional areas, for example, are currently faced with a shortage of qualified candidates. To attract graduates in areas of high demand, managers employ innovative recruitment techniques such as work-study programs, internships, low-interest loans, and scholarships.

Some employers fail to take full advantage of college and university resources because of a poor recruitment program.[12] Consequently, their recruitment efforts fail to attract many potentially good applicants. Another common weakness is the failure to maintain a planned and continuing effort on a long-term basis. Furthermore, some recruiters sent to college campuses are not sufficiently trained or prepared to talk to interested candidates about career opportunities or the requirements of specific openings. Attempts to visit too many campuses instead of concentrating on selected institutions and the inability to use the campus placement office effectively are other recruiting weaknesses. Mismanagement of applicant visits to the organization's headquarters and the failure to follow up on individual prospects or to obtain hiring commitments from higher management are among other mistakes that have caused employers to lose well-qualified prospects.

Professional Organizations

Many professional organizations and societies offer a placement service to members as one of their benefits. Listings of members seeking employment may be advertised in their journals or publicized at their national meetings. A placement centre is usually established at national meetings for the mutual benefit of employers and job seekers. The Human Resources Professionals Association of Ontario, for example, helps employers and prospective HR employees come together through a program called the Hire Authority.

Unions

Unions can be a principal source of applicants for blue-collar and some professional jobs. Some unions, such as those in the maritime, printing, and construction industries, maintain hiring halls that can provide a supply of applicants, particularly for short-term needs. Employers wishing to use this recruitment source should contact the local union under consideration for employer-eligibility requirements and applicant availability.

To start a job search, consult Jobs, Workers, Training & Careers, which posts job openings across Canada and offers advice for finding and getting work:

www.jobsetc.ca/toolbox/job_search/jobSearch.do?lang=e

Your organization may qualify for help from the federal government in filling your recruitment needs:

http://employers.ic.gc.ca/gol/hrmanagement/interface.nsf/engdocBasic/0.html.

Public Employment Agencies

Each province maintains an employment agency that is responsible for administering its unemployment insurance program. The agency is called the Department of Human Resources Development, or similar, and maintains local public employment offices in most communities of any size. Individuals who become unemployed must register at one of these offices and be available for "suitable employment" before they can receive their weekly unemployment cheques. This requirement means that public employment agencies are able to refer to employers with job openings those applicants with the required skills who are available for employment.

HRDC has developed a nationwide computerized job bank that lists job openings, and provincial employment offices are connected to this job bank. The computerized job bank helps facilitate the movement of job applicants to different geographic areas. Most of these offices now have a local job bank book that is published as a daily computer printout. Job openings are listed along with other pertinent information, such as number of openings, pay rates, and job specifications. The local job bank makes it possible for the agency's employment interviewers to keep a list of all the job openings in the geographic area for which the applicants assigned to them might qualify. Also, applicants looking for a specific job can review the computer printout and apply directly to the organization that has the opening. HRDC provides all kinds of labour market information including occupational profiles, industry profiles, and job outlooks.

In addition to matching unemployed applicants with job openings, public employment agencies may assist employers with employment testing, job analysis, evaluation programs, and community wage surveys.

Private Employment Agencies

Charging a fee enables private employment agencies to tailor their services to the specific needs of their clients. However, it is common for agencies to specialize in serving a specific occupational area or professional field. Depending on who is receiving the most service, the fee may be paid by either the employer or the job seeker or both. It is not uncommon for private employment agencies to charge an employer a 25 to 30 percent fee, based on the position's annual salary, if the employer hires an applicant found by the agency.

Private employment agencies differ in the services they offer, their professionalism, and the calibre of their counsellors. If counsellors are paid on a commission basis, their desire to do a professional job may be offset by their desire to earn a commission. Thus they may encourage job seekers to accept jobs for which they are not suited. Because of this, job seekers would be wise to take the time to find a recruiter who is knowledgeable, experienced, and professional. When talking with potential recruiters, individuals should discuss openly their philosophies and practices with regard to recruiting strategies, including advertising, in-house recruiting, screening procedures, and costs for these efforts. They should try to find a recruiter who is flexible and who will consider their needs and wants.[13]

A large-scale Statistics Canada survey of over 25 000 employees found that the most frequent source leading to employment was family and friends, followed by personal initiative (see Highlights in HRM 5.3). Obviously the use of the Internet has increased since the 1999 study; another study found that 12 percent of Canadians who found jobs in 2003 found them on the web, a higher rate than any other country, and much higher than the global average of 3 percent.[14]

Improving the Effectiveness of External Recruitment

According to a Conference Board of Canada survey, four out of five executives were concerned about the effectiveness of their organization's recruitment practices. The most successful methods of recruitment of top talent were the augmentation of student programs through partnerships with educational institutions, forecasting HR needs, and the use of employee referrals.[15] With all the uncertainties inherent in external recruiting, it is sometimes difficult to determine whether an organization's efforts to locate promising talent are effective and/or cost-efficient. However, man-

Highlights in HRM 5.3

SOURCES OF INFORMATION LEADING TO EMPLOYEES' CURRENT EMPLOYMENT

Type of Source	% of those who used source to find current employment N = 24 983
Family/friends	37.7
Personal initiative	21.6
Help wanted ads	17.7
Directly recruited by employer	10.7
Other	8.7
Used more than one	4.0
Canada Employment Centre HRDC	3.0
Recruitment agency	2.2
On-campus recruitment	2.0
Union posting	0.5
News story	0.2
Job fair	0.2
Internet	0.2
Did not respond	8.0

Source: A Bissonnette and V.M. Catano, "Revisiting the Efficacy of Recruitment Methods," Poster presented at the 11th European Workshop on Organizational Psychology Congress, Lisbon, Portugal, May 2003.

agers can do several things to maximize the probability of success. These include calculating yield ratios on recruiting sources, training organizational recruiters, and conducting realistic job previews.

Yield Ratios

Yield ratio

Percentage of applicants from a recruitment source that make it to the next stage of the selection process

Yield ratios help indicate which recruitment sources are most effective at producing qualified job candidates. Quite simply, a **yield ratio** is the percentage of applicants from a particular source that make it to the next stage in the selection process. For example, if 100 resumés were obtained from an employment agency, and 17 of the applicants submitting those resumés were invited for an on-site interview, the yield ratio for that agency would be 17 percent (17/100). This yield ratio could then be recalculated for each subsequent stage in the selection process (for example, after the interview and again after the final offer), which would result in a cumulative yield ratio. By calculating and comparing yield ratios for each recruitment source, it is possible to find out which sources produce qualified applicants.

Costs of Recruitment

The cost of various recruiting procedures can be computed using a fairly simple set of calculations. For example, the average source cost per hire (SC/H) can be determined by the following formula:

$$\frac{SC}{H} = \frac{AC + AF + RB + NC}{H}$$

where AC = advertising costs, total monthly expenditure (example: $28 000)
AF = agency fees, total for the month (example: $19 000)
RB = referral bonuses, total paid (example: $2300)
NC = no-cost hires, walk-ins, nonprofit agencies, etc. (example: $0)
H = total hires (example: 119)

Substituting the example numbers into the formula gives

$$\frac{SC}{H} = \frac{\$28\ 000 + \$19\ 000 + \$2300 + \$0}{119}$$

$$= \frac{\$49\ 300}{119}$$

$$= \$414 \text{ (source cost of recruits per hire)}$$

Organizational Recruiters

Who performs the recruitment function depends mainly on the size of the organization. For large employers, professional HR recruiters are hired and trained to find new employees. In smaller organizations, recruitment may be done by an HR generalist; if the organization has no HR position, recruitment may be carried out by managers and/or supervisors. At companies such as Shell, members of work teams take part in the selection of new team members.

Regardless of who does the recruiting, it is imperative that these individuals have a good understanding of the knowledge, skills, abilities, experiences, and other characteristics required for the job. All too often, a new person in the HR department or a line manager may be given a recruitment assignment, even before that person has been given interview training, before he or she fully understands the job, and before he or she fully comprehends the values and goals of the organization.

It is important to remember that recruiters have an influence on an applicant's job decision. Because recruiters can often enhance the perceived attractiveness of a job and an organization, they are often a main reason why applicants select one organization over another. A study by Derek Chapman, a professor at the University of Calgary, has demonstrated that applicants viewed the recruiters as cues to what it would be like to work in the organizations they represented.[16] On this basis we can conclude that personable, enthusiastic, and competent recruiters have an impact on the success of an organization's recruitment program.

Realistic Job Previews

Realistic job preview (RJP)
Informing applicants about all aspects of the job, both desirable and undesirable

Another way organizations may be able to increase the effectiveness of their recruitment efforts is to provide job applicants with a **realistic job preview** (**RJP**). An RJP informs applicants about all aspects of the job, including both its desirable and undesirable facets. In contrast, a typical job preview presents the job in only positive terms. The RJP may also include a tour of the working area, combined with a discussion of any negative health or safety considerations. Proponents of the RJP believe that applicants who are given realistic information regarding a position are more likely to remain on the job and be successful, because there will be fewer unpleasant surprises. In fact, a number of research studies on RJP report these positive results:

▶ Improved employee job satisfaction
▶ Reduced voluntary turnover
▶ Enhanced communication through honesty and openness
▶ Realistic job expectations[17]

Like other HR techniques, however, RJPs must be tailored to the needs of the organization and should include a balanced presentation of positive and negative job information.

MATCHING PEOPLE AND JOBS

Selection
Process of choosing individuals who have relevant qualifications to fill existing or projected job openings

In conjunction with the recruiting process, which is designed to increase the number of applicants whose qualifications meet job requirements and the needs of the organization, **selection** is the process of reducing that number and choosing from among those individuals who have the relevant qualifications.

Figure 5.3 shows in broad terms that the overall goal of selection is to maximize "hits" and avoid "misses." Hits are accurate predictions and misses are inaccurate ones. The cost of one type of miss would be the direct and indirect expense of hiring an employee who turns out to be unsuccessful. The cost of the other type of miss is an opportunity cost—someone who could have been successful didn't get a chance.

While the overall selection program is often the formal responsibility of the HR department, line managers typically make the final decision about hiring people in their unit. It is important therefore that managers understand the objectives, policies, and practices used for selection. In that way, they can be highly involved in the process from the very beginning. Those responsible for making selection decisions should

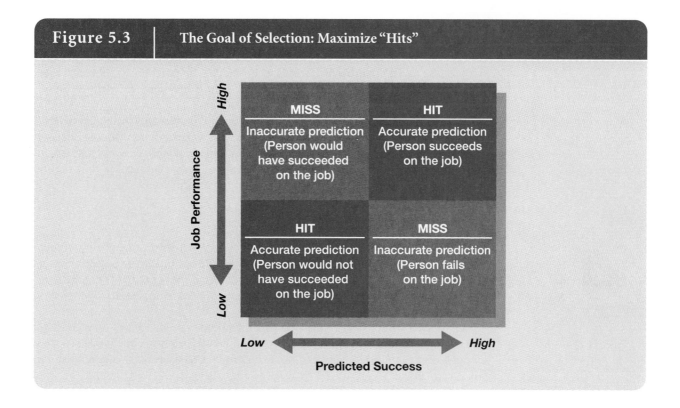

Figure 5.3 | **The Goal of Selection: Maximize "Hits"**

have adequate information upon which to base their decisions. Information about the jobs to be filled, knowledge of the ratio of job openings to the number of applicants, and as much relevant information as possible about the applicants themselves are essential for making sound decisions.

Person-Job Fit: Beginning with Job Analysis

In Chapter 3 we discussed the process of analyzing jobs to develop job descriptions and specifications. Job specifications, in particular, help identify the *individual competencies* employees need for success—the knowledge, skills, abilities, and other factors (KSAOs) that lead to superior performance. By identifying competencies through job analysis, managers can then use selection methods such as interviews, references, psychological tests, and the like to measure applicant KSAOs against the competencies required for the job. This is often referred to as *person-job fit*. Research has demonstrated that complete and unambiguous specification of required competencies (via job analysis) reduces the influence of racial and gender stereotypes and helps the interviewer to differentiate between qualified and unqualified applicants.[18]

Person-Organization Fit

In addition to the requirements of the job, many organizations also place a priority on finding individuals that meet broader organizational requirements. Companies such as Intuit and Starbucks place a high priority on selecting individuals who match the values and culture of the organization. Although there are at times potential concerns that this may create an overly uniform workforce (and raises diversity concerns), the need for teamwork and flexibility has created a keen interest in this type of person-organization fit. In many instances, managers will pass up potential employees if they don't embrace the values of the organization—even if they have excellent technical skills for the job.[19]

Ordinarily, managers are well acquainted with the requirements pertaining to skill, physical demands, and other factors for jobs in their organizations. Interviewers and other members of the HR department who participate in selection should maintain a close liaison with the various departments so that they can become thoroughly familiar with the jobs and competencies needed to perform them.

The Selection Process

In most organizations, selection is an ongoing process. Turnover inevitably occurs, leaving vacancies to be filled by applicants from inside or outside the organization or by individuals whose qualifications have been assessed previously. It is common to have a waiting list of applicants who can be called when permanent or temporary positions become open.

The number of steps in the selection process and their sequence will vary, not only with the organization but also with the type and level of jobs to be filled. Each step should be evaluated for its contribution. The steps that typically make up the selection process are shown in Figure 5.4. Not all applicants will go through all these steps. Some may be rejected after the preliminary interview, others after taking tests, and so on.

As shown in Figure 5.4, organizations use several different means to obtain information about applicants. These include application blanks, interviews, tests, and background investigations. Regardless of the method used, it is essential that it

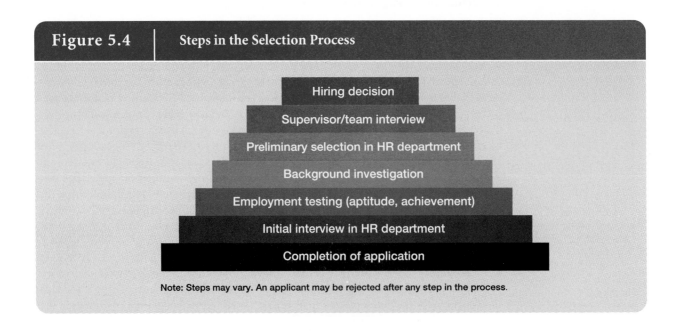

Figure 5.4 | **Steps in the Selection Process**

Hiring decision
Supervisor/team interview
Preliminary selection in HR department
Background investigation
Employment testing (aptitude, achievement)
Initial interview in HR department
Completion of application

Note: Steps may vary. An applicant may be rejected after any step in the process.

conform to accepted ethical standards, including privacy and confidentiality, as well as legal requirements. Above all, it is essential that the information obtained be sufficiently reliable and valid.

Obtaining Reliable and Valid Information

Reliability
Degree to which interviews, tests, and other selection procedures yield comparable data over time and alternative measures

The degree to which interviews, tests, and other selection procedures yield comparable data over a period of time is known as **reliability**. For example, unless interviewers judge the capabilities of a group of applicants to be the same today as they did yesterday, their judgments are unreliable (that is, unstable). Likewise, a test that gives widely different scores when it is administered to the same individual a few days apart is unreliable.

Reliability also refers to the extent to which two or more methods (interviews and tests, for example) yield similar results or are consistent. Inter-rater reliability—agreement between two or more raters—is one measure of a method's consistency. Unless the data upon which selection decisions are based are reliable, in both stability and consistency, they cannot be used as predictors.

Validity
Degree to which a test or selection procedure measures a person's attributes

In addition to having reliable information pertaining to a person's suitability for a job, the information must be as valid as possible. **Validity** refers to what a test or other selection procedure measures and how well it measures it. In the context of personnel selection, validity is essentially an indicator of the extent to which data from a procedure (interview or test, for example) are predictive of job performance. Like a new medicine, a selection procedure must be validated before it is used. There are two reasons for validating a procedure. First, validity is directly related to increases in employee productivity, as we will demonstrate later. Although we commonly refer to "validating" a test or interview procedure, validity in the technical sense refers to the inferences made from the use of a procedure, not to the procedure itself.

Three recognized approaches to validation are criterion-related validity, content validity, and construct validity.

Criterion-Related Validity

Criterion-related validity
Extent to which a selection tool predicts, or significantly correlates with, important elements of work behaviour

The extent to which a selection tool predicts, or significantly correlates with, important elements of work behaviour is known as **criterion-related validity**. Performance on a test, for example, is compared with actual production records, supervisory ratings, training outcomes, and other measures of success that are appropriate to each type of job. In a sales job, for example, it is common to use sales figures as a basis for comparison. In production jobs, quantity and quality of output may provide the best criteria of job success.

Concurrent validity
The extent to which test scores (or other predictor information) match criterion data obtained at about the same time from current employees

There are two types of criterion-related validity, concurrent and predictive. **Concurrent validity** involves obtaining criterion data from *current employees* at about the same time that test scores (or other predictor information) are obtained. For example, a supervisor is asked to rate a group of clerical employees on the quantity and quality of their performance. These employees are then given a clerical aptitude test, and the test scores are compared with the supervisory ratings to determine the degree of relationship between them. **Predictive validity**, on the other hand, involves testing *applicants* and obtaining criterion data *after* those applicants have been hired and have been on the job for some indefinite period. For example, applicants are given a clerical aptitude test, which is then filed away for later study. After the individuals

Predictive validity
Extent to which applicants' test scores match criterion data obtained from those applicants/employees after they have been on the job for some indefinite period

have been on the job for several months, supervisors, who should not know the employees' test scores, are asked to rate them on the quality and quantity of their performance. Test scores are then compared with the supervisors' ratings.

Regardless of the method used, cross-validation is essential. **Cross-validation** is a process in which a test or battery of tests is administered to a different sample (drawn from the same population) for the purpose of verifying the results obtained from the original validation study.

Correlational methods are generally used to determine the relationship between predictor information such as test scores and criterion data. The correlation scatter plots in Figure 5.5 illustrate the difference between a selection test of zero validity (A) and one of high validity (B). Each dot represents a person. Note that in scatter plot A there is no relationship between test scores and success on the job; in other words, the validity is zero. In scatter plot B, those who score low on the test tend to have low success on the job, whereas those who score high on the test tend to have high success on the job, indicating high validity. In actual practice we would apply a statistical formula to the data to obtain a coefficient of correlation referred to as a *validity coefficient*. Correlation coefficients range from 0.00, denoting a complete absence of relationship, to +1.0 and to −1.1, indicating a perfect positive and perfect negative relationship, respectively.

A thorough survey of the literature shows that the averages of the maximum validity coefficients are 0.45 where tests are validated against *training* criteria and 0.35 where tests are validated against job *proficiency* criteria. These figures represent the predictive power of single tests.[20] A higher validity may be obtained by combining two or more tests or other predictors (interview or biographical data, for instance), using the appropriate statistical formulas. The higher the overall validity, the greater the

Cross-validation
Verifying the results obtained from a validation study by administering a test or test battery to a different sample (drawn from the same population)

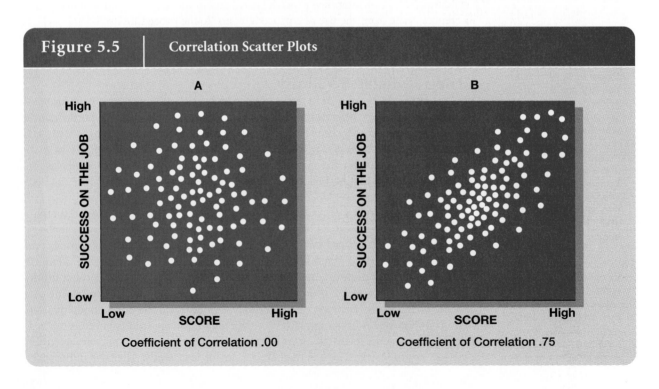

Figure 5.5   **Correlation Scatter Plots**

A
High
SUCCESS ON THE JOB
Low
Low   SCORE   High
Coefficient of Correlation .00

B
High
SUCCESS ON THE JOB
Low
Low   SCORE   High
Coefficient of Correlation .75

chances of hiring individuals who will be the better performers. The criterion-related method is generally preferred to other validation approaches because it is based on empirical data.

For several decades, personnel psychologists believed that validity coefficients had meaning only for the specific situation (job and organization). More recently, as a result of several research studies—many involving clerical jobs—it appears that validity coefficients can often be generalized across situations, hence the term **validity generalization**. Where there are adequate data to support the existence of validity generalization, the development of selection procedures can become less costly and time-consuming. The process involves analyzing jobs and situations and, on the basis of these analyses, consulting tables of generalized validities from previous studies using various predictors in similar circumstances. It is advisable for organizations to employ the services of an industrial-organizational psychologist experienced in test validation to develop the selection procedures.[21]

Validity generalization
Extent to which validity coefficients can be generalized across situations

Content Validity

Where it is not feasible to use the criterion-related approach, often because of limited samples of individuals, the content method is used. **Content validity** is assumed to exist when a selection instrument, such as a test, adequately samples the knowledge and skills needed to perform a particular job.

The closer the content of the selection instrument is to actual work samples or behaviours, the greater its content validity. For example, a civil service examination for accountants has high content validity when it requires the solution of accounting problems representative of those found on the job. Asking an accountant to lift a sixty-pound box, however, is a selection procedure that has content validity only if the job description indicates that accountants must be able to meet this requirement.

Content validity is the most direct and least complicated type of validity to assess. It is generally used to evaluate job knowledge and skill tests, to be described later. Unlike the criterion-related method, content validity is not expressed in correlational terms. Instead, an index is computed (from evaluations of an expert panel) that indicates the relationship between the content of the test items and performance on the job.[22] While content validity does have its limitations, it has made a positive contribution to job analysis procedures and to the role of expert judgment in sampling and scoring procedures.

Content validity
Extent to which a selection instrument, such as a test, adequately samples the knowledge and skills needed to perform a particular job

Construct Validity

The extent to which a selection tool measures a theoretical construct, or trait, is known as **construct validity**. Typical constructs are intelligence, mechanical comprehension, and anxiety. They are in effect broad, general categories of human functions that are based on the measurement of many discrete behaviours. For example, the Bennett Mechanical Comprehension Test consists of a wide variety of tasks that measure the construct of mechanical comprehension.

Measuring construct validity requires showing that the psychological trait is related to satisfactory job performance and that the test accurately measures the psychological trait. There is a lack of literature covering this concept as it relates to employment practices, probably because it is difficult and expensive to validate a construct and to show how it is job-related.[23]

Construct validity
Extent to which a selection tool measures a theoretical construct or trait

Sources of Information about Job Candidates

objective

Many sources of information are used to provide as reliable and valid a picture as possible of an applicant's potential for success on the job. The selection process at The Bay, outlined in Reality Check, illustrates the most important sources of information. Figure 5.6 shows the results of a recent survey that asked HR executives to evaluate the effectiveness of various selection techniques. In this section, we will study the potential contributions of application forms; biographical information blanks; background investigations; polygraph, or lie detector, tests; honesty and integrity tests; graphology; and medical examinations. Because interviewing plays such a major role in selection and because testing presents unique challenges, there will be expanded discussions of these sources of information later in the chapter. Assessment centres, which are often used in managerial selection, will be discussed in Chapter 7.

Application Forms

Most organizations require application forms to be completed because they provide a fairly quick and systematic means of obtaining a variety of information about the applicant. Application forms serve several purposes. They provide information for deciding whether an applicant meets the minimum requirements for experience, education, and so on. They provide a basis for questions the interviewer will ask about the applicant's background. They also offer sources for reference checks. For certain jobs,

Figure 5.6	The Effectiveness of Selection Methods

In a survey of 201 HR executives, participants were asked which selection methods produce the best employees. The mean rating for nine methods on a 5-point scale (1 = not good, 3 = average, 5 = extremely good):

Work samples	3.68
References/recommendations	3.49
Unstructured interviews	3.49
Structured interviews	3.42
Assessment centres	3.42
Specific aptitude tests	3.08
Personality tests	2.93
General cognitive ability tests	2.89
Biographical information blanks	2.84

Source: Excerpted from IOMA's *HRFocus* publication and reprinted with permission of IOMA (the Institute of Management & Administration). Copyright © 2003. For more information about IOMA or to subscribe to IOMA newsletters such as *HRFocus*, please contact 212-244-0360 x245, or e-mail to: contact@ioma.com or visit our website at www.ioma.com.

Reality Check

SELECTION AT THE BAY

Canada's oldest corporation and largest department store retailer is the Hudson's Bay Company, which was established in 1670 and operates as The Bay and Zellers. Tina Peacock, human resources manager for Merchandise Services & Corporate Offices, has been with HBC for more than twenty years. She helps the company achieve its goals by carefully applying selection methods to identify key potential candidates for many different positions, such as merchandise buyer, financial manager, and systems manager.

"In addition to succession planning," states Peacock, "we follow established trends, such as growth in our business units, turnover, and performance results, to identify those positions that may become vacant during the year. Through a number of training programs provided in-house, we are able to fill our positions internally. In fact, 80 percent are staffed from internal promotions. For the other 20 percent, we hire externally. As a proactive measure in anticipation of those openings, we run recruiting ads so that we always have a 'stable' of competent candidates.

"It is important that we work closely with the managers because they know what is needed to run their business. My role is to provide them with qualified candidates who possess the basic job knowledge with the right competencies to work in our fast-paced, changing environment. For instance, a number of managers are tapped into the marketplace, so they are able to get the ball rolling by identifying candidates in the industry before an ad is placed. Our role is to pre-screen those candidates to ensure they have the attributes needed to successfully perform in our environment.

"We work very closely with an ad agency to assist us in preparing the ad and to provide advice on the marketing strategies of where and when to place the ad. They save you a lot of time, especially when they understand your business. Running our ads for a particular position yields us other qualified candidates for other positions we had not counted on.

"Many of our ads yield as many as 250 resumés. Based on the competencies required for a position, we prescreen the resumés. It is not uncommon for me to receive over fifty phone calls per day when an ad is running. If I can delegate some of those calls, I do; however, if they have asked me for something specific, I make an effort to call them back because they are our customers and they are important to us. Once I have determined a short list, I then conduct a pretty thorough telephone interview before bringing in any candidates. Questions regarding salary expectations, any information that may be missing on the resumé, and some very job-specific questions are reviewed. We are always looking to improve our systems. Our next ad will incorporate a voice response system that has been developed internally by our Information Services Department. Candidates who wish to apply to an ad will be asked to call our system and respond to some basic job-related questions. At the end of the session, the candidate will be advised whether they possess the basic requirements of the job and whether they should apply to this position.

(continued on following page)

"The questions we ask during the face-to-face interview are open-ended questions that look for behavioural attributes specific to the competencies and key job requirements. For example, we want the candidates to demonstrate how they have gone about performing their job duties in the past. For those candidates who proceed to a final interview, we ask each of them to complete a communications survey. Using an outside consultant, we have developed a prediction performance program profile that has identified benchmark attributes for our buyers, merchandising trainees, and store managers. The results are graphed and compared against the benchmark. This profile is not used as a basis for determining whether we should hire a candidate or not. It provides us with another opportunity to fully assess the individual's capabilities by asking more focused questions. In this way, it ensures that we have fully investigated the individual's background and credentials. We provide each of our candidates with a written assessment of the report, whether they are hired or not, and ask them to comment on the accuracy of the results. Based on these responses, the report has been assessed at an accuracy of over 90 percent."

Peacock says in closing: "Systems in the workplace will continue to change, but the bottom line is that we need the best people to technically do the job and, most importantly, they must be customer focused."

a short application form is appropriate. For example, McDonald's uses a form that is quite brief but asks for information that is highly relevant to job performance. For scientific, professional, and managerial jobs, a more extended form is likely to be used.

Even when applicants come armed with elaborate resumés, it is important that they complete an application form early in the process. Individuals frequently exaggerate or overstate their qualifications on a resumé. However, the consequences of falsifying information on applications and resumés are frequently high. But candidates not only exaggerate; in a tight labour market, candidates sometimes delete advanced qualifications, as described in Ethics in HRM.

Other cases highlight the importance of integrity in job applications. Some observers estimate that at least 33 percent of applicants "stretch" the truth on their resumés. Ethics in HRM also describes these situations. One technique for anticipating problems of misrepresentation is to ask applicants to transcribe specific resumé material onto a standardized application form. The applicant is then asked to sign a statement that the information contained on the form is true and that he or she accepts the employer's right to terminate the candidate's employment if any of the information is subsequently found to be false.[24]

Many managers remain unclear about the questions they can ask on an application blank. While most know they should steer clear of issues such as age, race, marital status, and sexual orientation, other issues are less clear. The following are some suggestions for putting together an application form:

▶ *Application date.* The applicant should date the application. This helps managers know when the form was completed and gives them an idea of the time limit (for example, one year) that the form should be on file.

Ethics in HRM

WRITING IT WRONG

Most candidates for white-collar jobs prepare a resumé and submit it to prospective employers. They also complete the application form, answering questions required by employers for comparison purposes. Some recruitment agencies noticed during the last recession that resumé padding increased. Applicants were "stretching" the dates of their employment, misleading employers about the nature of their duties, and misrepresenting their salaries. While you are writing a resumé, adding three months to your previous employment, saying you were a night auditor instead of clerk, and adding $950 to your last salary seem like relatively harmless lies.

What are the facts? Studies of "creative" resumé writing indicate that about 30 percent of resumés report incorrect dates, 11 percent misrepresent reasons for leaving, and others exaggerate education attainments or omit criminal records. The probability is that about two-thirds of employers check references. Some former employers give only dates of employment and previous salary ranges.

Most organizations require you to sign a statement saying that the information you supply is true, and that if it is not you will be dismissed. Some cases of resumé padding have been heavily publicized. A Toronto Stock Exchange manager was dismissed for lying about having a master's degree. A Member of Parliament listed an ILB on his resumé, which normally stands for International Baccalaureate of Law, but which he claimed stood for Incomplete Baccalaureate of Law. In one heart-wrenching case, a person who was ready to retire was found to have lied about his age decades earlier to get a job. On discovery, he was dismissed and lost his pension. In another case, a Canadian businessman was sentenced to eight months in jail in New Zealand for lying on his resumé, by listing false qualifications such as an MBA.

In a labour market where there are too many people chasing too few jobs, candidates will also lie on their resumés, but do so by dropping experience and educational qualifications. This practice, called "stripping," is used because job seekers are ready to take any job in order to survive or to hold them over until the jobs they really want are available. Knowing that graduate degrees will act as barriers to jobs as labourers or administrative assistants, applicants simply don't list the degrees or previous professional jobs. Understandably, employers don't want to hire those who are overqualified and who would soon quit for better jobs.

Sources: E. Urquhart, "Should We Edit Our Job Skills?" *The Globe and Mail*, June 20, 2003: C1; P. Waldie, "Davy Sentenced to Eight Months in N.Z. Court," *The Globe and Mail*, May 30, 2002: B6; J. Schilder, "Trial by Hire," *Human Resource Professional* 11, no. 2 (March 1994): 21–23.

▶ *Educational background.* The applicant should also provide grade school, high school, college, and university attendance—but not the dates attended, since that can be connected with age.

▶ *Experience.* Virtually any questions that focus on work experience related to the job are permissible.

▶ *Arrests and criminal convictions.* Questions about arrests, convictions, and criminal records are to be avoided. If bonding is a requirement, the candidate can be asked if she or he is eligible.

▶ *Country of citizenship.* Such questions are not permitted. It is allowable to ask if the person is legally entitled to work in Canada.

▶ *References.* It is both permissible and advisable that the names, addresses, and phone numbers of references be provided. (We will cover this in more detail later.)

▶ *Disabilities.* Employers should avoid asking about disabilities, hospitalization, and if candidates have received worker's compensation.

Many of these issues will be addressed again, particularly in the section on employment interviews.

Some organizations use what is referred to as a *weighted application blank (WAB)*. The WAB involves the use of a common standardized employment application that is designed to distinguish between successful and unsuccessful employees. If managers can identify application items (such as where someone went to school) that have predicted employee success in the past, they may use that information to screen other applicants. Some evidence suggests that use of the WAB has been especially helpful for reducing turnover costs in the hospitality industry.

Online Applications

As noted earlier, many organizations now help individuals apply online for jobs that are posted on the Internet. The practice speeds up the application process for potential employees, and importantly, allows the organization to track applicants, combine information, and disseminate possible leads to managers more quickly and efficiently than before.

Discount broker Charles Schwab modified its application process so that applicants could provide job-relevant information that can be matched against predefined selection criteria for a variety of jobs. This change reduced the firm's average time to fill a job to a week. Other firms such as Home Depot and Hollywood Video have introduced similar systems in the past few years. Home Depot's system, called the Job Preference Program, has been essential for keeping pace with the company's rapid growth. While the original impetus for the system was a class-action lawsuit by women who were not being considered for higher-paying jobs, the staffing system has helped to ensure a broader pool of applicants. The added benefit is that the system helps the company to rapidly identify candidates with the right qualifications.[25]

Biographical Information Blanks

One of the oldest methods for predicting job success uses biographical information about job applicants. As early as 1917, the Life Insurance Agency Management Association constructed and validated a biographical information blank (BIB) for life insurance salespeople. BIBs cover such issues as family life, hobbies, club memberships, sales experience, and investments. Like application blanks, BIBs reveal information about a person's history that may have shaped his or her behaviour. Sample questions from a BIB might include the following:

▶   At what age did you leave home?

▶   How large was the town/city in which you lived as a child?

▶   Did you ever build a model airplane that flew?

▶   Were sports a big part of your childhood?

▶   Do you play any musical instruments?

Both the BIB and the application form can be scored like tests. And because biographical questions rarely have obviously right or wrong answers, BIBs are difficult to fake. The development of a scoring system requires that the items that are valid predictors of job success (positively or negatively correlated) be identified and that weights be established for different responses to these items. By totalling the scores for each item, it is possible to obtain a composite score on the BIB as a whole for each applicant. Studies have shown that an objective scoring of BIB and application forms is one of the most potentially valid methods of predicting job success. This method has been useful in predicting all types of behaviour, including employee theft, turnover, and performance in jobs such as sales, nursing, and management.[26]

Background Investigations

When the interviewer is satisfied that the applicant is potentially qualified, information about previous employment as well as other information provided by the applicant is investigated. Former employers, school and college officials, credit bureaus, and individuals named as references may be contacted for verification of pertinent information such as length of time on the job, type of job, performance evaluation, highest wages, and academic degrees earned. Most of this information is now readily available on existing computer databases. Figure 5.7 shows the results of a Society for Human Resource Management (SHRM) study on how managers check applicant backgrounds.

Figure 5.7	How HR Uses Background Investigations

Percentage of respondents conducting the following checks:

Contact references provided by candidate	75%
Verify schools attended and degrees earned	62%
Contact people suggested by references	42%
Check driving records	41%
Verify reference letters provided by candidate	30%
Run credit checks	25%

Source: Society for Human Resource Management (SHRM).

Checking References

Organizations use both the mail and the telephone to check references. But while references are commonly used to screen and select employees, they have not proved successful for predicting employee performance. Written letters of reference are notoriously inflated, and this limits their validity. Generally, telephone checks are preferable because they save time and provide for greater candour. At Intuit, the Edmonton, Alberta, software company that produces Quicken, managerial applicants are asked to provide between five and nine references who are then called and asked specific job-related questions. The most reliable information usually comes from supervisors, who are in the best position to report on an applicant's work habits and performance. Written verification of information relating to job titles, duties, and pay levels from the former employer's HR office is also very helpful.[27]

An employer has no legal obligation to provide a former employee with a reference. To avoid liability, many employers are providing a perfunctory letter of reference, which supplies only the name, employment dates, last position with the company, and final salary. New privacy legislation being enacted by provinces will make employers even more cautious. However, inadequate reference checking can contribute to high turnover, employee theft, and white-collar crime. By using sources in addition to former employers, organizations can obtain valuable information about an applicant's character and habits. Telephone interviews are most effective and one key question that is particularly effective in screening is to ask "Would you re-hire this employee?" Some employers prefer to outsource reference checking to professional firms such as Intelysis Employment Screening Services in Toronto, Ontario. The most common problems found by reference checkers, in about 40 percent of the cases, are candidates listing family members as former supervisors, gaps in employment not shown on resumé, incorrect start and end dates, false academic credentials, and incorrect job titles.[28]

Using Credit Reports

The use of consumer credit reports by employers as a basis for establishing an applicant's eligibility for employment has become more restricted. For positions of trust, such as those involving financial instruments in banks, credit reports must be used. Applicants must agree in writing to a credit report and have the right to review its contents. More importantly, the reason for the credit report must be job-related.

Polygraph Tests

The polygraph, or lie detector, is a device that measures the changes in breathing, blood pressure, and pulse of a person who is being questioned. It consists of a rubber tube around the chest, a cuff around the arm, and sensors attached to the fingers that record the physiological changes in the examinee as the examiner asks questions that call for an answer of yes or no. Questions typically cover such items as whether a person uses drugs, has stolen from an employer, or has committed a serious undetected crime. The use of lie detector tests for employment purposes is prohibited under the Employment Standards Acts in Ontario and New Brunswick. Check provincial legislation before considering the use of polygraphs.

Honesty and Integrity Tests

Many employers have increased their use of pencil-and-paper honesty and integrity tests. These tests have commonly been used in settings such as retail stores where employees have access to cash or merchandise. Common areas of inquiry include beliefs about frequency and extent of theft in our society, punishment for theft, and perceived ease of theft. For example, Payless ShoeSource has used a paper-and-pencil honesty test to reduce employee theft. When the company began its program, losses totalled nearly $21 million per year among its 4700 stores. Within only one year of implementing its screening program, inventory shrinkage fell by 20 percent to less than 1 percent of sales.[29]

Potential items that might be used on an integrity test are shown in Figure 5.8. A comprehensive analysis of honesty tests reveals that they are valid for predicting job performance as well as a wide range of disruptive behaviours such as theft, disciplinary problems, and absenteeism.[30]

Graphology

Graphology, a term that refers to a variety of systems of handwriting analysis, is used by some employers to make employment decisions. Graphologists obtain a sample of handwriting and then examine such characteristics as the size and slant of letters, amount of pressure applied, and placement of the writing on the page. From their observations, graphologists draw inferences about such things as the writer's personality traits, intelligence, energy level, organizational abilities, creativity, integrity, emotional maturity, self-image, people skills, and entrepreneurial tendencies. Graphology is used extensively in France, Germany, Switzerland, Israel, and the United Kingdom in making employment decisions.[31] Companies such as Ford and General Electric have used it for selection.

Organizations using handwriting analysis say they prefer it to typical personality tests because it requires only that job candidates take a few minutes to jot down a short essay. By contrast, a battery of personality tests and interviews with psychologists can take several hours and can cost thousands of dollars. In addition, the available evidence shows graphology to be a reliable predictor of personality when compared with other psychological tests. However, its predictive validity for job performance and occupational success remains questionable. In the academic community, where formal and rigorous validity studies are customary, use of graphology for employment decisions has been viewed with considerable skepticism.[32]

EMPLOYMENT TESTS

The formal introduction of psychological selection techniques into the Canadian Army in 1941 represented both a pragmatic response to the exigencies of war and an attempt to make selection processes more democratic. Prior to 1941, entry into officer training was often based on social rank or monetary favours (as opposed to proven ability).

Figure 5.8	Integrity Test Question Examples

To Test Tendency to	Description
Protect	Contains items that require individuals to indicate whether they would protect friends or co-workers who had engaged in counterproductive behaviours.
	Example: I would turn in a fellow worker I saw stealing money.
Be lenient	Contains items in which test takers indicate whether they would be lenient with respect to the wrongdoings of others.
	Example: An employee should be fired if the employer finds out the employee lied on the application blank.
Admit thought	Includes items that require test takers to indicate the degree to which they would engage in counterproductive thoughts or behaviours.
	Example: I've thought about taking money from an employer without actually doing it.
Admit behaviour	Contains items in which individuals admit to directly participating in actual counterproductive behaviours.
	Example: Over the last three years, what's the total amount of money you've taken without permission from your employer?
Consider common	Includes items that require the individual to indicate the extent to which theft and other misbehaviours are common.
	Example: Most people I've worked with have stolen something at one time or another.
Excuse	Contains items in which individuals indicate whether there are excuses or justifi-cations for stealing or performing other questionable behaviours.
	Example: Someone who steals because his family is in need should not be treated the same as a common thief.
Lie	Contains items that measure the extent to which the test taker is responding in a socially desirable manner.
	Example: Never in my whole life have I wished for anything I was not entitled to.

Note: The number of items in each tendency category was 2, 8, 13, 9, 17, 8, and 7 respectively.

Source: Stephen Dwight and George Alliger, "Reactions to Overt Integrity Test Items," *Educational and Psychological Measurement* 57, no. 6 (December 1977): 937–48, copyright © 1997. Reprinted by permission of Sage Publications, Inc.

Because of the practical need for efficiency, and to reduce selection errors, new selection procedures were adopted to optimize the use of "manpower." This in turn led to the establishment of selection and assessment centres in Canada. Tests have played a more important part in government HR programs, in which hiring on the basis of merit is required by law. With their testing programs, government agencies have faced the same types of problems as organizations in the private sector. However, their staffs have been forced to improve their testing programs rather than abandon them. The federal government has a highly regarded testing program, which is administered by the Personnel Psychology Centre of the Public Service Commission.

A recent American Management Association survey showed that 43 percent of responding firms assess applicants with basic math and/or literacy tests; 60 percent required specific job-skill testing of applicants; and 31 percent use psychological tests. More specific information about job skill testing in different industries is provided in Figure 5.9.[33] In part, this indicates both that employers today are less fearful of lawsuits challenging the soundness of their tests and that there is a return to a focus on individual competence. Objective standards are coming back in both education and employment. Concurrently, methodological changes have made it easier to demonstrate test validity.[34] Too often employers have relied exclusively on the interview to measure or predict skills and abilities that can be measured or predicted more accurately by tests.

Tests have played a more important part in government HR programs where hiring on the basis of merit is required by law. Government agencies experienced the same types of problems with their testing programs as did organizations in the private sector. However, their staffs were forced to improve their testing programs rather than to abandon them.

While it is often advisable to use consultants, especially if an organization is considering the use of personality tests, managers should have a basic understanding of the technical aspects of testing and the contributions that tests can make to the HR program.

Nature of Employment Tests

An employment test is an objective and standardized measure of a sample of behaviour that is used to gauge a person's knowledge, skills, abilities, and other characteristics (KSAOs) in relation to other individuals.[35] The proper sampling of behaviour—

Figure 5.9	Percentage of Job Skills Testing in Selected Industries	
	Test All Job Applicants	Only Select Industry Job Categories
Manufacturing	7%	49%
Financial Services	4%	68%
Wholesale and Retail	0%	53%
Business and Professional Services	2%	57%
Other Services	6%	63%

Source: American Management Association: "Job Skills Testing Questionnaire," 1998.

PHOTODISC

Some employers use tests, such as keyboarding or Dictaphone, to help reach a selection decision.

Aptitude tests
Measures of a person's capacity to learn or acquire skills

Achievement tests
Measures of what a person knows or can do right now

whether verbal, manipulative, or some other type—is the responsibility of the test author. It is also the responsibility of the test author to develop tests that meet accepted standards of reliability.[36] Data concerning reliability are ordinarily presented in the manual for the test. While high reliability is essential, it offers no assurance that the test provides the basis for making valid judgments. It is the responsibility of the HR staff to conduct validation studies before a test is adopted for regular use. Other considerations are cost, time, ease of administration and scoring, and the apparent relevance of the test to the individuals being tested—commonly referred to as "face validity." While face validity is desirable, it is no substitute for technical validity, described earlier in this chapter. Adopting a test just because it appears relevant is bad practice; many a "good-looking" test has poor validity.

Classification of Employment Tests

Employment tests may be classified in different ways. Generally, they are viewed as measuring either aptitude or achievement. **Aptitude tests** measure a person's capacity to learn or acquire skills. **Achievement tests** measure what a person knows or can do right now.

Cognitive Ability Tests

Cognitive ability tests measure mental capabilities such as general intelligence, verbal fluency, numerical ability, and reasoning ability. A host of paper-and-pencil tests measure cognitive abilities, including the General Aptitude Test Battery (GATB), the Scholastic Aptitude Test (SAT), the Graduate Management Aptitude Test (GMAT), and the Bennett Mechanical Comprehension Test. Figure 5.10 shows some items that could be used to measure different cognitive abilities.

Although cognitive ability tests can be developed to measure very specialized areas such as reading comprehension and spatial relations, many experts believe that the validity of cognitive ability tests simply reflects their connection to general intelligence. Measures of general intelligence (such as IQ) have been shown to be good predictors of performance across a wide variety of jobs.[37]

Personality and Interest Inventories

Whereas cognitive ability tests measure a person's mental capacity, personality tests measure disposition and temperament. Years of research show that five dimensions can summarize personality traits. The "Big Five" factors are the following:

1. *Extroversion*—the degree to which someone is talkative, sociable, active, aggressive, and excitable

Figure 5.10	Is That Your Final Answer?

Verbal

1. What is the meaning of the word "surreptitious"?

   a. covert   c. lively

   b. winding   d. sweet

2. How is the noun clause used in the following sentence? "I hope that I can learn this game."

   a. subject   c. direct object

   b. predicate nominative   d. object of the preposition

Quantitative

3. Divide 50 by 0.5 and add 5. What is the result?

   a. 25   c. 95

   b. 30   d. 105

4. What is the value of 144^2?

   a. 12   c. 95

   b. 30   d. 20736

Reasoning

5. _____ is to *boat* as *snow* is to _____.

   a. Sail, ski   c. Water, ski

   b. Water, winter   d. Engine, water

6. Two women played 5 games of chess. Each women won the same number of games, yet there were no ties. How can this be?

   a. There was a forfeit.   c. They played different people.

   b. One player cheated.   d. One game is still in progress.

Mechanical

7. If gear A and gear C both are turning counterclockwise, what is happening to gear B?

   a. It is turning counterclockwise.   c. It remains stationary.

   b. It is turning clockwise.   d. The whole system will jam.

A   B   C

Answers: 1. a, 2. c, 3. d, 4. d, 5. c, 6. c, 7. b.

2. *Agreeableness*—the degree to which someone is trusting, amiable, generous, tolerant, honest, cooperative, and flexible

3. *Conscientiousness*—the degree to which someone is dependable and organized and perseveres in tasks

4. *Neuroticism*—the degree to which someone is secure, calm, independent, and autonomous

5. *Openness to experience*—the degree to which someone is intellectual, philosophical, insightful, creative, artistic, and curious[38]

Figure 5.11 illustrates facets and sample items from the well-known California Psychological Inventory (CPI). The predictive validity of personality and interest inventories historically has been quite low. However, when used in combination with cognitive ability tests, measures of personality traits (such as conscientiousness) can lead to better prediction of job performance.[39]

It is important to note that personality tests can be problematic if they inadvertently discriminate against individuals who would otherwise perform effectively. Demonstrating job relatedness and validity of some personality characteristics is not always easy. The use of personality tests may also be seen as an invasion of privacy.[40] Beyond the initial hiring decision, personality and interest inventories may be most useful for helping with occupational selection and career planning. Interest tests, such as the Kuder Inventory, measure an applicant's preferences for certain activities over others (such as sailing versus poker).

Physical Ability Tests

In addition to learning about a job candidate's mental capabilities, employers frequently need to assess a person's physical abilities. These types of tests are reportedly being used more widely today for selection than ever before. Particularly for demanding and potentially dangerous jobs like those held by firefighters and police officers, physical abilities such as strength and endurance tend to good predictors not only of performance, but of accidents and injuries.[41]

Despite their potential value, physical ability tests tend to work to the disadvantage of women and disabled job applicants, a tendency that has led to several recent lawsuits. Evidence suggests that the average man is stronger, faster, and more powerful than the average woman, but women tend to have better balance, manual dexterity, flexibility, and coordination than men. For example, applicants who take the RCMP's Physical Fitness Abilities Requirement Evaluation (PARE) are required to run 350 metres, complete a standing broad jump of about 2 metres, and pick up and carry a heavy bag for 15 metres. According to one RCMP officer, "If you're a bigger person, the PARE test is easier, no doubt." The fact that women fail the test in greater numbers than men has resulted in a complaint before the Canadian Human Rights Commission. The RCMP is defending the PARE test on the grounds that it simulates common police activities such as chasing a suspect on foot, carrying an injured person, and forcing open a door.[42] On the basis of these differences, it is clear that (as with other methods for screening potential employees) the use of physical ability tests should be carefully validated on the basis of the essential functions of the job.[43]

Figure 5.11	CPI Personality Facets and Sample Items

Agreeableness

▶ Consideration—I like to do little things for people to make them feel good.
▶ Empathy—I take other people's circumstances and feelings into consideration before making a decision.
▶ Interdependence—I tend to put group goals first and individual goals second.
▶ Openness—I do not have to share a person's values to work well with that person.
▶ Thought agility—I think it is vital to consider other perspectives before coming to conclusions.
▶ Trust—I believe people are usually honest with me.

Conscientiousness

▶ Attention to detail—I like to complete every detail of tasks according to the work plans.
▶ Dutifulness—I conduct my business according to a strict set of ethical principles.
▶ Responsibility—I can be relied on to do what is expected of me.
▶ Work focus—I prioritize my work effectively so the most important things get done first.

Extroversion

▶ Adaptability—For me, change is exciting.
▶ Competitiveness—I like to win, even if the activity isn't very important.
▶ Desire for achievement—I prefer to set challenging goals, rather than aim for goals I am more likely to reach.
▶ Desire for advancement—I would like to attain the highest position in an organization some day.
▶ Energy level—When most people are exhausted from work, I still have energy to keep going.
▶ Influence—People come to me for inspiration and direction.
▶ Initiative—I am always looking for opportunities to start new projects.
▶ Risk-taking—I am willing to take big risks when there is potential for big returns.
▶ Sociability—I find it easy to start up a conversation with strangers.
▶ Taking charge—I actively take control of situations at work if no one is in charge.

Neuroticism

▶ Emotional control—Even when I am very upset, it is easy for me to control my emotions.
▶ Negative affectivity—I am easily displeased with things at work.
▶ Optimism—My enthusiasm for living life to its fullest is apparent to those with whom I work.
▶ Self-confidence—I am confident about my skills and abilities.
▶ Stress tolerance—I worry about things that I know I should not worry about.

Openness to Experience

▶ Independence—I tend to work on projects alone, even if others volunteer to help me.
▶ Innovativeness/creativity—I work best in an environment that allows me to be creative and expressive.
▶ Social astuteness—I know what is expected of me in different social situations.
▶ Thought focus—I quickly make links between causes and effects.
▶ Vision—I can often foresee the outcome of a situation before it unfolds.

Source: Mark J. Schmit, Jenifer A. Kihm, and Chet Robie, "Development of a Global Measure of Personality," *Personnel Psychology* 53, no. 1 (Spring 2000): 153–93.

For jobs that are physically demanding or potentially dangerous, employers need to assess the physical abilities of job candidates.

PHOTODISC

Job Knowledge Tests

Government agencies and licensing boards usually develop job knowledge tests, a type of achievement test designed to measure a person's level of understanding about a particular job. Most civil service examinations, for example, are used to determine whether an applicant possesses the information and understanding that will permit placement on the job without further training.[44] They should be considered useful tools for private and public organizations.

Work Sample Tests

Work sample tests, or job sample tests, require the applicant to perform tasks that are actually a part of the work required on the job. Like job knowledge tests, work sample tests are constructed from a carefully developed outline that experts agree includes the major job functions; the tests are thus considered content-valid. Organizations that are interested in moving toward *competency-based selection*—that is, hiring based on observation of behaviours previously shown to distinguish successful employees—increasingly use work samples to see potential employees "in action."[45]

Work samples have been devised for many diverse jobs: a map-reading test for traffic control officers, a lathe test for machine operators, a complex coordination test for pilots, an in-basket test for managers, a group discussion test for supervisors, and a judgment and decision-making test for administrators, to name a few. In an increasing number of cases, work sample tests are aided by computer simulations, particularly when testing a candidate might prove dangerous. The reports are that this type of test is cost-effective, reliable, valid, fair, and acceptable to applicants.[46]

THE EMPLOYMENT INTERVIEW

Traditionally, the employment interview has a central role in the selection process—so much so that it is rare to find an instance in which an employee is hired without some sort of interview. Depending on the type of job, applicants may be interviewed by one person, members of a work team, or other individuals in the organization. While researchers have raised some doubts about its validity, the interview remains a mainstay of selection because (1) it is especially practical when there are only a small number of applicants; (2) it serves other purposes, such as public relations; and (3) interviewers maintain great faith and confidence in their judgments. Nevertheless, the interview can be plagued by problems of subjectivity and personal bias. In those instances, the judgments of different interviewers may vary dramatically and the quality of the hire can be called into serious question.

In this section, we review the characteristics, advantages, and disadvantages of various types of employment interviews. We highlight the fact that the structure of the interview and the training of interviewers strongly influence the success of the hiring process.[47]

Interviewing Methods

Interview methods differ in several ways, most significantly in the amount of structure, or control, exercised by the interviewer. In highly structured interviews, the interviewer determines the course that the interview will follow as each question is

Figure 5.12	I Really Want to Work Here

▶ After answering the first few questions, the candidate called his parents on his cell phone to let them know that the interview was going well.

▶ One candidate handcuffed himself to the desk during the interview, while another sent lottery tickets with her resumé.

▶ After being complimented on his choice of university and the GPA (grade point average) he had achieved there, the candidate replied, "I am glad that got your attention. I really didn't go there."

▶ When asked by the hiring manager why she was leaving her current job, the candidate replied, "My manager is a jerk. All managers are jerks."

▶ When told that she would meet with another interviewer, the candidate took out a large bag from her briefcase and proceeded to re-apply her makeup and hairspray, all in the first interviewer's office.

▶ When asked why he wanted to work for the company, the candidate replied, "That is a really good question. I really haven't given it much thought."

Sources: "Candidates Say the Darnedest Things," *Canadian HR Reporter* 15, no. 19 (November 4, 2002): 4; "But I Really Want to Work Here," *Canadian HR Reporter* 15, no. 22 (December 16, 2002): 4.

asked. In the less structured interview, the applicant plays a larger role in determining the course the discussion will take. An examination of the different types of interviews from the least structured to the most structured reveals these differences.

The Nondirective Interview

In the **nondirective interview,** the interviewer carefully refrains from influencing the applicant's remarks. The applicant is allowed the maximum amount of freedom in determining the course of the discussion. The interviewer asks broad, open-ended questions—such as "Tell me more about your experiences on your last job"—and permits the applicant to talk freely with a minimum of interruption. Generally, the nondirective interviewer listens carefully and does not argue, interrupt, or change the subject abruptly. The interviewer also uses follow-up questions to allow the applicant to elaborate, makes only brief responses, and allows pauses in the conversation; the pausing technique is the most difficult for the beginning interviewer to master.

The greater freedom afforded to the applicant in the nondirective interview is particularly valuable in bringing to the interviewer's attention any information, attitudes, or feelings that may often be concealed by more structured questioning. However, because the applicant determines the course of the interview and no set procedure is followed, little information that comes from these interviews enables interviewers to cross-check agreement with other interviewers. Thus the reliability and validity of the nondirective interview may be expected to be minimal. This method is most likely to be used in interviewing candidates for high-level positions and in counselling, which we will discuss in Chapter 13.

The Structured Interview

More attention is being given to the structured interview as a result of employment equity requirements and a concern for maximizing validity of selection decisions.[48] Because a **structured interview** has a set of standardized questions (based on job analysis) and an established set of answers against which applicant responses can be rated, it provides a more consistent basis for evaluating job candidates. For example, staff members of Weyerhaeuser Company's HR department have developed a structured interviewing process with the following characteristics:

1. The interview process is based exclusively on job duties and requirements critical to job performance.
2. It uses four types of questions: situational questions, job knowledge questions, job sample/simulation questions, and worker requirements questions.
3. There are sample (benchmark) answers, determined in advance, to each question. Interviewee responses are rated on a five-point scale relative to those answers.
4. The process involves an interview committee so that interviewee responses are evaluated by several raters.
5. It consistently follows the same procedures in all instances to ensure that each applicant has exactly the same chance as every other applicant.

The interviewer takes notes and documents the interview for future reference and in case of legal challenge.[49]

Nondirective interview
An interview in which the applicant is allowed the maximum amount of freedom in determining the course of the discussion, while the interviewer carefully refrains from influencing the applicant's remarks

Structured interview
An interview in which a set of standardized questions having an established set of answers is used

A structured interview is more likely to provide the type of information needed for making sound decisions. It also helps to reduce the possibility of legal charges of unfair discrimination. Employers must be aware that the interview is highly vulnerable to legal attack and that more litigation in this area can be expected in the future.

Most employment interviewers will tend toward either a nondirected or a structured format. However, within the general category of structured interviews, there are more specific differences that relate to the format of questions. These include the situational interview and behavioural description interview, discussed next.

The Situational Interview

Situational interview
An interview in which an applicant is given a hypothetical incident and asked how he or she would respond to it

One variation of the structured interview is called the **situational interview**. With this approach, an applicant is given a *hypothetical* incident and asked how he or she would respond to it. The applicant's response is then evaluated relative to pre-established benchmark standards. Interestingly, many organizations are using the situational interview to select new college graduates. Highlights in HRM 5.4 shows a sample question from a situational interview used to select systems analysts at a chemical plant.

Highlights in HRM 5.4

SAMPLE SITUATIONAL INTERVIEW QUESTION

QUESTION:
It is the night before your scheduled vacation. You are all packed and ready to go. Just before you get into bed, you receive a phone call from the plant. A problem has arisen that only you can handle. You are asked to come in to take care of things. What would you do in this situation?

RECORD ANSWER:

_____

_____

_____

_____

SCORING GUIDE:
Good: "I would go in to work and make certain that everything is okay. Then I would go on vacation."
Good: "There are no problems that *only* I can handle. I would make certain that someone qualified was there to handle things."
Fair: "I would try to find someone else to deal with the problem."
Fair: "I would go on vacation."

The Behavioural Description Interview

Behavioural description interview (BDI)
An interview in which an applicant is asked questions about what he or she actually did in a given situation

In contrast to a situational interview, which focuses on hypothetical situations, a **behavioural description interview (BDI)** focuses on *actual* work incidents in the interviewee's past. The BDI format asks the job applicant what he or she actually did in a given situation. For example, to assess a potential manager's ability to handle a problem employee, an interviewer might ask, "Tell me about the last time you disciplined an employee." Such an approach to interviewing, based on a critical-incidents job analysis, assumes that past performance is the best predictor of future performance. It also may be somewhat less susceptible to applicant faking. The Business Case for behaviourally based interviews is presented on page 211. In addition, recent research indicates that the behavioural description interview is more effective than the situational interview for hiring higher-level positions such as general managers and executives.[50]

The Panel Interview

Panel interview
An interview in which a board of interviewers questions and observes a single candidate

Another type of interview involves a panel of interviewers who question and observe a single candidate. In a typical **panel interview** the candidate meets with three to five interviewers who take turns asking questions. After the interview the interviewers pool their observations to reach a consensus about the suitability of the candidate. HRM specialists using this method report that panel interviews provide several significant advantages over traditional one-to-one interviews, including higher reliability because of multiple inputs, greater acceptance of the decision, and shorter decision time.[51]

The Computer Interview

With advances in information technology, more and more organizations are using computers and the Internet to help with the interviewing process. Typically, a computer interview requires candidates to answer a series (75 to 125) of multiple-choice questions tailored to the job. These answers are compared either with an ideal profile or with profiles developed on the basis of other candidates' responses. Commercially available systems allow organizations to generate printed reports that contain applicant response summaries, itemized lists of contradictory responses, latency response reports (time delays for each answer), summaries of potentially problematic responses, and lists of structured interview questions for the job interviewer to ask.[52]

A few years ago, Pic 'n Pay Shoe Stores created a computerized interview that could be conducted over the phone using an 800 number. The interview focused on honesty, work attitude, drug use, candour, dependability, and self-motivation. After implementing the system, the company cut turnover by 50 percent and reduced employee theft by almost 40 percent.

In addition to the benefits of objectivity, some research evidence suggests that applicants may be less likely to engage in "impression management" in computerized interviews than in face-to-face interviews. So far, organizations have used the computer mainly as a complement to, rather than as a replacement for, conventional interviews.[53]

The Business Case

BEHAVIOURAL INTERVIEWS BRING BIG RETURNS

Fairmont Hotels, formerly Canadian Pacific Hotels, with nearly 31 000 employees at eighty-one hotels in six countries, measures the effectiveness of selection tools. Using a Gallup selection tool, Fairmont Hotels has tracked the performance of sales personnel, by selecting those who matched the characteristics of the best performers. Those superior employees produce two to three times more revenue than others. A financial organization decided to assess the ROI (Return on Investment) of competency-based behavioural interviewing. They focused first on the sales and marketing function, which employed about 100 people, with average annual salaries of $135 000 ($90 000 plus a variable bonus of 50 percent for on-target performance). Turnover was about 20 percent a year. Elementary statistics suggests that the output of a group of workers forms a bell-shaped distribution, resulting in a small portion (about 10 percent) of staff working at above or below acceptable performance, while the majority worked in the acceptable range. The recruiters decided to delineate the competencies that differentiated the superior performers from the average performers and to use these to improve the selection procedure.

Here is how the ROI was calculated:

Assume twenty new recruits a year.

Two recruits, on average, would be superior performers under the current recruiting system.

Under the new system, all twenty would be superior, for a net increase of eighteen new superior employees.

Performing above average is worth about 48 percent of the average annual salary to the company.

Therefore: $18 \times (\$135\ 000 \times .48) = \$1\ 166\ 000$

But the recruitment process is not perfect, and so must be discounted by .545 (the consultants' estimate of how good they were at selecting superior candidates and rejecting inferior candidates).

$.545 \times \$1\ 166\ 000 = \$635\ 000$

The *cost* of the competency project for sales and marketing was $130 000.

The *benefit* was $635 000 for an ROI of 488 percent.

The long-term ROI may be higher, as superior recruits may have lower turnover, shorter learning curves, and increasingly effective performance.

Interviews must be as valid as tests, because they are so expensive. The average cost per hire of an executive is $43 000, a manager or professional $17 000, a technical person $13 000 and clerical and administrative support around $3000.

Sources: Adapted from A. Davis, "What Is the Cost of Hiring?" *Canadian HR Reporter* 16, no. 11 (June 2, 2003): 12; T. Tritch, "Fairmont's Talent Strategy Delivers Results," *Gallup Management Journal*, www.gmj.gallup.com, May 13, 2003; Lionel LaRoche and Stephen Martin, "Demonstrating the Bottom-Line Impact of HR: A Competencies Case Study," *Canadian HR Reporter* 13, no. 22 (December 18, 2000): 29–31.

Video Interviews

Companies such as Shell Oil and Nike are using videoconference technologies to evaluate job candidates. While some use their own in-house systems, others use outside service partners. Kinko's, for example, rents videoconferencing rooms at a quarter of its nine hundred stores for about $150 per hour. National Career Centers has partnered with Radisson and Hilton to offer videoconferencing to customers in hotels.

Video interviews have several potential advantages related to flexibility, speed, and cost. Employers can make preliminary assessments about candidates' technical abilities, energy level, appearance, and the like before incurring the costs of a face-to-face meeting. The goal of course is to enable faster, higher-quality decisions at lower cost.

Guidelines for Employment Interviewers

Apart from the characteristics of the interviews themselves, there are several important tips for interviewers. Organizations should be cautious in selecting employment interviewers. Qualities that are desirable include humility, the ability to think objectively, maturity, and poise. Given the importance of diversity in the workforce, experience in associating with people from a variety of backgrounds is also desirable. Qualities to avoid in interviewers include overtalkativeness, extreme opinions, and biases.

A Review of the Best

There have been several reviews of research studies on the employment interview.[54] Each of these reviews discusses and evaluates numerous studies concerned with such questions as "What traits can be assessed in the interview?" and "How do interviewers reach their decisions?" Highlights in HRM 5.5 presents some of the major findings of these studies. It shows that information is available that can be used to increase the validity of interviews.

Figure 5.13 summarizes the variables and processes involved in the employment interview. The figure shows that a number of applicant characteristics may influence the perception of the interviewer and thus the hiring decision. In addition, many interviewer and situational factors may also influence the perceptual and judgmental processes. For example, the race and sex of an applicant may shape the expectations, biases, and behaviours of an interviewer, which in turn may affect the interview outcome. Even a limited understanding of the variables shown in Figure 5.13 can help increase the interviewing effectiveness of managers and supervisors.

Interviewer Training

Training has been shown to dramatically improve the competence of interviewers.[55] If not done on a continuing basis, training should at least be done periodically for managers, supervisors, and HR representatives who conduct interviews. Interviewer training programs should include practice interviews conducted under guidance. Practice interviews may be recorded on videotape and evaluated later in a group training session. Some variation in technique is only natural. However, the following list presents ten ground rules for employment interviews that are commonly accepted and supported by research findings. Their apparent simplicity should not lead one to underestimate their importance.

Highlights in HRM 5.5

SOME MAJOR FINDINGS FROM RESEARCH STUDIES ON THE INTERVIEW

1. Structured interviews are more reliable than unstructured interviews.
2. Interviewers are influenced more by unfavourable than by favourable information.
3. Inter-rater reliability is increased when there is a greater amount of information about the job to be filled.
4. A bias is established early in the interview, and this tends to be followed by either a favourable or an unfavourable decision.
5. Intelligence is the trait most validly estimated by an interview, but the interview information adds nothing to test data.
6. Interviewers can explain why they feel an applicant is likely to be an unsatisfactory employee but not why the applicant may be satisfactory.
7. Factual written data seem to be more important than physical appearance in determining judgments. This increases with interviewing experience.
8. An interviewee is given a more extreme evaluation (positive/negative) when preceded by an interviewee of opposing value (positive/negative).
9. Interpersonal skills and motivation are probably best evaluated by the interview.
10. Allowing the applicant time to talk makes rapid first impressions less likely and provides a larger behaviour sample.
11. Nonverbal as well as verbal interactions influence decisions.
12. Experienced interviewers rank applicants in the same order, although they differ in the proportion that they will accept. Experienced interviewers tend to be more selective than less experienced ones.

1. *Establish an interview plan.* Examine the purposes of the interview and determine the areas and specific questions to be covered. Review job requirements, application-form data, test scores, and other available information before seeing the applicant.

2. *Establish and maintain rapport.* This is accomplished by greeting the applicant pleasantly, by explaining the purpose of the interview, by displaying sincere interest in the applicant, and by listening carefully.

3. *Be an active listener.* Strive to understand, comprehend, and gain insight into what is only suggested or implied. A good listener's mind is alert, and face and posture usually reflect this fact.

4. *Pay attention to nonverbal cues.* An applicant's facial expressions, gestures, body position, and movements often provide clues to that person's attitudes and feelings. Interviewers should be aware of what they themselves are communicating nonverbally.

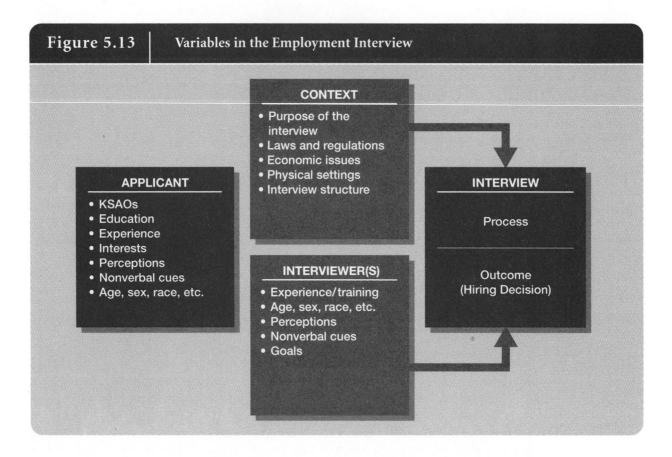

Figure 5.13 | Variables in the Employment Interview

5. *Provide information as freely and honestly as possible.* Answer fully and frankly the applicant's questions. Present a realistic picture of the job.

6. *Use questions effectively.* To elicit a truthful answer, questions should be phrased as objectively as possible, giving no indication of what response is desired.

7. *Separate facts from inferences.* During the interview, record factual information. Later, record your inferences or interpretations of the facts. Compare your inferences with those of other interviewers.

8. *Recognize biases and stereotypes.* One typical bias is for interviewers to consider strangers who have interests, experiences, and backgrounds similar to their own to be more acceptable. Stereotyping involves forming generalized opinions of how people of a given gender, race, or ethnic background appear, think, feel, and act. The influence of sex-role stereotyping is central to sex discrimination in employment. Avoid the influence of "beautyism." Discrimination against unattractive people is a persistent and pervasive form of employment discrimination. Also avoid "halo error," or judging an individual favourably or unfavourably overall on the basis of only one strong point (or weak point) on which you place high value.

9. *Control the course of the interview.* Establish an interview plan and stick to it. Provide the applicant with ample opportunity to talk, but maintain control of the situation in order to reach the interview objectives.

10. *Standardize the questions asked.* To increase reliability and avoid discrimination, ask the same questions of all applicants for a particular job. Keep careful notes; record facts, impressions, and any relevant information, including what was told to the applicant.

Diversity Management: Are Your Questions Legal?

The entire subject of pre-employment questioning is complex. Federal and provincial requirements sometimes vary in the types of questions that may be asked during the interview. However, all jurisdictions forbid direct questions about race, sex, colour, age, religion, and national origin, and most look with disapproval on indirect questions dealing with the same topics. Some of the questions that interviewers once felt free to ask can be potentially hazardous. Human rights commissions have severely limited the areas of questioning. In general, if the question is job-related, is asked of everyone, and does not discriminate against a certain class of applicants, it is likely to be acceptable to government authorities. Readers who are interested in a more comprehensive discussion should consult Catano et al., *Recruitment and Selection in Canada* 2nd edition (2002).

Particular care has to be given to questions asked of female applicants about their family responsibilities. It is inappropriate, for example, to ask, "Who will take care of your children while you are at work?" or "Do you plan to have children?" or "What is your husband's occupation?" or "Are you engaged?" It is, in fact, inappropriate to ask applicants of either gender questions about matters that have no relevance to job performance.

Employers have found it advisable to provide interviewers with instructions on how to avoid potentially discriminatory questions in their interviews. The examples of appropriate and inappropriate questions shown in Highlights in HRM 5.6 may serve as guidelines for application forms as well as pre-employment interviews. Complete guidelines may be developed from current information available from provincial human rights commissions. Once an individual is hired, the information needed but not asked in the interview may be obtained if there is a valid need for it and if it does not lead to discrimination.

USING THE INTERNET

Current regulations can be found on the Canadian Human Rights Commission website:

www.chrc-ccdp.ca

Medical Examination

A medical examination is generally given to ensure that the health and fitness of applicants is adequate to meet the job requirements. It also provides a baseline against which subsequent medical examinations can be compared and interpreted. The last objective is especially important for determining work-caused disabilities under workers' compensation law.

Highlights in HRM 5.6

APPROPRIATE AND INAPPROPRIATE INTERVIEW QUESTIONS

	Appropriate Questions	Inappropriate Questions
National or ethnic origin	Are you legally entitled to work in Canada?	Where were you born?
Age	Have you reached the minimum or maximum age for work, as defined by the law?	How old are you?
Sex	How would you like to be referred to during the interview?	What are your child care arrangements?
Marital status	As travel is part of the requirements of our position, would you foresee any problems meeting this obligation?	What does your spouse do for a living? Is there travel involved? Who takes care of the children when you are away?
Disabilities	Do you have any conditions that could affect your ability to do the job?	Do you use drugs or alcohol?
Height and weight	(Ask nothing)	How tall are you? How much do you weigh?
Address	What is your address?	What were your addresses outside Canada?
Religion	Would you be able to work the following schedules?	What are your religious beliefs?
Criminal record	Our job requires that our employees be bonded. Are you bondable?	Have you ever been arrested?
Affiliations	As an engineer, are you a member of the engineering society?	What religious associations do you belong to?

In the past, requirements for physical characteristics such as strength, agility, height, and weight were often determined by the employer's invalidated notions of what should be required. Many requirements that tend to discriminate against women have been questioned and modified so as to represent typical job demands.

Medical examinations and inquiries about a candidate directed to medical professionals can be conducted only after an offer (preferably written) of employment has been made. The offer can be made conditional on the applicant's ability to perform the essential duties of the job as determined by a job-related medical examination. Any medical inquiries must be directly related to assessing the candidate's abilities to perform the essential duties of the job.[56] This allows the applicant with a disability the opportunity to be considered exclusively on merits during the selection process. Before human rights legislation was introduced, employers would screen out applicants with disabilities based on medical information requested on application forms or obtained through pre-employment medical examinations. These methods are now deemed discriminatory.

An employer may ask a candidate if she or he has any disability-related needs that would require accommodation to enable performance of the essential duties of the job. The interviewer should be cautioned about probing as to the nature of the disability. Later employment-related decisions may be perceived to be based on this information and thereby characterized as discriminatory. To ensure neutrality, and to avoid the possibility of a complaint to the Canadian Human Rights Commission, such information should remain exclusively with the examining physician, not in the personnel file.

If the employee has a disability, the employer has a duty to accommodate his or her needs. The accommodation can be accomplished either by changing some of the essential duties of the position or by providing the appropriate equipment. To determine whether an individual can do the essential duties of a particular position, the employer should conduct a physical demands analysis, checklists for which are available through most provincial ministries of labour.[57]

As mentioned earlier, requirements for physical characteristics such as height were in the past often determined by an employer's notion of what should be required. Under human rights legislation, employers are prohibited from imposing their own standards where it has the effect of excluding members of the designated groups, unless it can be shown that the requirements are reasonable and bona fide. Such standards are often based on the vital statistics of the average white Anglo-Saxon male. There is little evidence to demonstrate that characteristics such as height and weight constitute bona fide occupational requirements.[58]

Drug Testing

The Canadian Human Rights Commission and some of its provincial counterparts have issued policies on employment-related drug testing. Addiction to drugs or alcohol is considered a handicap, and the employer is to be guided by legislation and by practices such as workplace accommodation. The medical examination cannot be conducted until a conditional offer of employment is made in writing, and the examination can determine only the individual's ability to perform the essential duties.

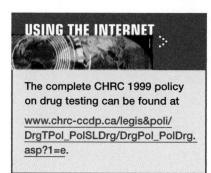

USING THE INTERNET

The complete CHRC 1999 policy on drug testing can be found at

www.chrc-ccdp.ca/legis&poli/ DrgTPol_PolSLDrg/DrgPol_PolDrg. asp?1=e.

Syncor Canada, a world leader in mining and extracting crude oil, feels that drug testing of heavy equipment operators could be justified on safety grounds, but not for those in an office environment.[59]

If the employer has established that drug testing is job-related—typically, this involves safety issues—the candidate must be informed that job offers are conditional on the successful passing of a drug test and that this test will be required during the course of employment. The employer then has the right to demand a medical examination. If an employee refuses, he or she can be dismissed. In one situation, a Canadian Pacific conductor who had been charged by the police with cultivating marijuana (he had received a prior conviction for possession) was asked by his employer to submit to a drug test. He refused. He was then terminated, and the decision was upheld by an arbitrator.[60] Toronto-Dominion Bank, Imperial Oil, and the Federal Transport Department all use drug testing.

There is widespread opposition to drug testing in the workplace, which is why only about 2 percent of companies in Canada do it, compared to about 80 percent of American companies. The Canadian Civil Liberties Association takes the position that "no person should be required to share urine with a stranger" as a condition of employment.[61] Employee Assistance Programs (EAPs) play an important role in helping employees with drug and alcohol problems. EAPs will be discussed in Chapter 12. Figure 5.14 shows the relative popularity of various selection methods in Canada.

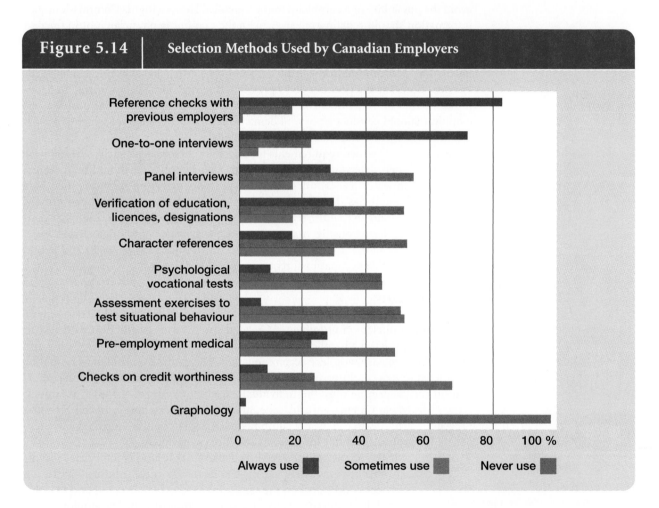

Figure 5.14 | **Selection Methods Used by Canadian Employers**

Note: Some method percentages do not total to 100 percent because of rounding.
Source: Murray Axmith and Associates, 1997. (Courtesy of Right Axmith, a division of Right Management Consultants.)

REACHING A SELECTION DECISION

objective 8

While all of the steps in the selection process are important, the most critical step is the decision to accept or reject applicants. Because of the cost of placing new employees on the payroll, the short probationary period in many organizations, and employment equity considerations, the final decision must be as sound as possible. Thus it requires systematic consideration of all the relevant information about applicants. It is common to use summary forms and checklists to ensure that all the pertinent information has been included in the evaluation of applicants.

Summarizing Information about Applicants

Fundamentally, an employer is interested in what an applicant can do and will do. An evaluation of candidates on the basis of assembled information should focus on these two factors, as shown in Figure 5.15. The "can-do" factors include knowledge and skills, as well as the aptitude (the potential) for acquiring new knowledge and skills. The "will-do" factors include motivation, interests, and other personality characteristics. Both factors are essential to successful performance on the job. The employee who has the ability (can do) but is not motivated to use it (will not do) is little better than the employee who lacks the necessary ability.

It is much easier to measure what individuals can do than what they will do. The can-do factors are readily evident from test scores and verified information. What the individual will do can only be inferred. Responses to interview and application-form questions may be used as a basis for obtaining information for making inferences about what an individual will do.

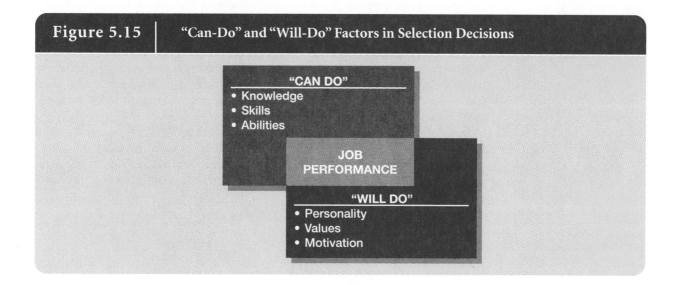

| Figure 5.15 | "Can-Do" and "Will-Do" Factors in Selection Decisions |

"CAN DO"
- Knowledge
- Skills
- Abilities

JOB PERFORMANCE

"WILL DO"
- Personality
- Values
- Motivation

Decision Strategy

The strategy used for making personnel decisions for one category of jobs may differ from that used for another category. The strategy for selecting managerial and executive personnel, for example, will differ from that used in selecting clerical and technical personnel. While many factors are to be considered in hiring decisions, the following are some of the questions that managers must consider:

1. Should the individuals be hired according to their highest potential or according to the needs of the organization?
2. At what grade or wage level should the individual be started?
3. Should initial selection be concerned primarily with an ideal match of the employee to the job, or should potential for advancement in the organization be considered?
4. To what extent should those who are not qualified but are qualifiable be considered?
5. Should overqualified individuals be considered?
6. What effect will a decision have on meeting affirmative action plans and diversity considerations?

Final Decision

After a preliminary selection has been made in the employment department, those applicants who appear to be most promising are then referred to departments having vacancies. There they are interviewed by the managers or supervisors, who usually make the final decision and communicate it to the employment department. Because of the weight that is usually given to their choices, managers and supervisors should be trained so that their role in the selection process does not negate the more rigorous efforts of the HR department staff.

In large organizations, notifying applicants of the decision and making job offers is often the responsibility of the HR department. This department should confirm the details of the job, working arrangements, wages, and so on, and specify a deadline by which the applicant must reach a decision. If, at this point, findings from the medical examination are not yet available, an offer is often made contingent upon the applicant's passing the examination.

In government agencies, the selection of individuals to fill vacancies is made from lists or registers of eligible candidates. Ordinarily, three or more names of individuals at the top of the register are submitted to the requisitioning official. This arrangement provides some latitude for those making a selection and, at the same time, preserves the merit system.

SUMMARY

Employers usually find it advantageous to use internal promotion and transfer to fill as many openings as possible above the entry level. By recruiting from within, an organization can capitalize on previous investments made in recruiting, selecting, training, and developing its current employees. Further, internal promotions can reward employees for past performance and send a signal to other employees that their future efforts will pay off. However, potential candidates from the outside should occasionally be considered in order to prevent the inbreeding of ideas and attitudes.

Filling jobs above the entry level often requires managers to rely on outside sources. These outside sources are also utilized to fill jobs with special qualifications, to avoid excessive inbreeding, and to acquire new ideas and technology. Which outside sources and methods are used in recruiting will depend on the recruitment goals of the organization, the conditions of the labour market, and the specifications of the jobs to be filled.

Employers wanting to maximize the effectiveness of their recruitment programs should calculate a yield ratio, train organizational recruiters, and conduct realistic job previews.

The selection process should provide as much reliable and valid information as possible about applicants so that their qualifications can be carefully matched with job specifications. The information that is obtained should be clearly job-related or predictive of success on the job and free from potential discrimination. Reliability refers to the consistency of test scores over time and across measures. Validity refers to the accuracy of measurement. Validity can be assessed by whether the measurement is based on a job specification (content validity), whether test scores correlate with performance criteria (predictive validity), and whether the test accurately measures what it purports to measure (construct validity).

Interviews are customarily used in conjunction with application forms, biographical information blanks, references, background investigations, medical examinations, cognitive ability tests, job knowledge tests, and work sample tests.

While the popularity of tests had declined somewhat with the passage of employment equity laws, in recent years there has been a dramatic resurgence of testing. The value of tests should not be overlooked since they are more objective than the interview and can provide a broader sampling of behaviour. Cognitive ability tests are especially valuable for assessing verbal, quantitative, and reasoning abilities. Personality and interest tests are perhaps best for placement. Physical ability tests are most useful for predicting job performance, accidents, and injuries, particularly for demanding work. Job knowledge and work sample tests are achievement tests that are useful for determining if a candidate can perform the duties of the job without further training.

The interview is an important source of information about job applicants. It can be unstructured, wherein the interviewer is free to pursue whatever approach and sequence of topics might seem appropriate. Alternatively, an interview can be structured, wherein each applicant receives the same set of questions, which have pre-established answers. Some interviews are situational and can focus on hypothetical situations or actual behavioural descriptions of previous work experiences. Interviews can be conducted by a single individual, by a panel, or via a computer interface. Regardless of the technique chosen, those who conduct interviews should receive special training to acquaint them with interviewing methods and employment equity considerations. The training should also make them more aware of the major findings from research studies on the interview and how they can apply these findings.

In the process of making decisions, all "can-do" and "will-do" factors should be assembled and weighted systematically so that the final decision can be based on a composite of the most reliable and valid information.

KEY TERMS

achievement tests 202
aptitude tests 202
behavioural description interview
  (BDI) 210
concurrent validity 189
construct validity 191
content validity 191
criterion-related validity 189

cross-validation 190
job posting and bidding 174
labour market 176
nepotism 180
nondirective interview 208
panel interview 210
predictive validity 189
realistic job preview (RJP) 186

reliability 189
selection 186
situational interview 209
structured interview 208
validity 189
validity generalization 191
yield ratio 185

DISCUSSION QUESTIONS

1. What are the advantages and disadvantages of filling openings from internal sources?

2. In what ways do executive search firms differ from the traditional employment agencies?

3. Form groups of about five people. Have each person review the job sites of Internet recruitment organizations. As a group develop a list of features that encourage you to stay on the site, and a second list of features that make you want to apply for a job through that site. Compare your lists to the suggestions outlined in Highlights in HRM 5.2.

4. Explain how realistic job previews (RJPs) operate. Why do they appear to be an effective recruitment technique?

5. What is meant by the term *criterion* as it is used in personnel selection? Give some examples of criteria used for jobs with which you are familiar.

6. What are some of the problems that arise in checking references furnished by job applicants? Are there any solutions to these problems?

7. What characteristics do job knowledge and job sample tests have that often make them more acceptable to the examinees than other types of tests?

8. Personality tests, like other tests used in employee selection, have been under attack for several decades. What are some of the reasons applicants find personality tests objectionable? On what basis could their use for selection purposes be justified?

9. In groups, discuss and label employment interviews that each student has experienced. How valid was each from an employer's perspective? How effective was each type in attracting you, as a candidate, to the recruiting organization?

10. If you were starting a company, which selection strategy (hire for potential or hire for current knowledge and skills) would you employ for the following positions:
    Accountant   Sales personnel
    Receptionist   Information technology
                    personnel

Developing Managerial Skills

DESIGNING SELECTION CRITERIA AND METHODS

Making hiring decisions is one of the most important—and difficult—decisions a manager makes. Without good information, the manager has almost no chance of making the right choice. They might as well be using a ouija board. The process begins with a sound understanding of the job: the tasks, duties, and responsibilities required and the knowledge, skills, and abilities needed to do it. Job analysis is very helpful in making certain that all the information is needed to ensure a person-job fit, but it may not be enough. Other information about company values, philosophy, and the like may be required to ensure person-organization fit.

Assignment

1. Working in teams of four to six individuals, choose a job with which you are familiar and identify the most important knowledge, skills, abilities, and other characteristics needed for someone to perform well.
2. Next, identify which methods you would use to tap these qualities. Would you use applications, interviews, psychological tests, work samples, or something else? Explain why you would use these methods and justify the cost and time required.
3. After you have identified your selection criteria and methods, do a "reality check" in a real organization. Interview a manager who employs someone in that job. For example, if the job you selected is salesperson, go to a local business to learn how it selects individuals for sales jobs. Compare what you thought would be a good selection approach with what you learned in the company you visited.
4. Identify the reasons for any discrepancies between your approach and theirs. Are the reasons justified and sound?

Case Study 1

Searching for Spies

The Canadian Security Intelligence Service (CSIS) is a civilian-run agency, formerly the Security Services of the RCMP. Its role is defensive—to protect Canada from terrorists and foreign spies. It does not send armed spies overseas. Selecting spies used to be a secret process. There was no public knowledge about how spies were recruited, what the job description was, and what the selection criteria and methods were.

Each year CSIS receives 3000 unsolicited applicants for about 100 openings. However, most of these applications are from unqualified James Bond wanna-be's. CSIS wants highly qualified, well-educated, multilingual, multiskilled employees. It recruits openly, and its selection criteria and processes are public.

If you want to apply: CSIS looks for Canadian citizens who are university graduates, preferably with advanced degrees. You must have a driver's licence and be able to relocate anywhere in Canada at any time. You will have lived or studied abroad, be proficient in English and French, and have a third or fourth language. CSIS looks for generalists—people who are knowledgeable about international and political issues and who have investigative and analytical skills. As a CSIS employee, you will not be able to discuss your work with outsiders at any time.

CSIS recruits at government job fairs. As an applicant, you must go through the following selection process:

▶ Submit a resumé
▶ Complete a twelve-page application, which also involves writing a 500-word essay explaining why you want to become an intelligence officer
▶ Attend a group information session, where recruiters and intelligence officers answer questions
▶ Attend a suitability interview, where your motivation and verbal and people skills are judged
▶ Take a battery of psychological and aptitude tests
▶ Have your language skills tested
▶ Attend a national assessment panel—veterans will assess your motivation, knowledge of CSIS, and general awareness of public affairs
▶ Be submitted to security clearance procedures (including a polygraph test, fingerprints, lie detector test, credit check, criminal record check, and references back to teen years), which takes three months and costs thousands of dollars
▶ Go to a final interview

This is a multiple-hurdle model of selection. As a candidate you will have to pass each hurdle before being allowed to continue to the next. If successful, you will be on probation for five years, undergo twelve weeks of classroom training and language training, and spend two or three years at an operations desk at headquarters, before being transferred to the field under the guidance of a mentor.

Source: Adapted from J. Sallot, "The Spy Masters' Talent Hunt Goes Public," *The Globe and Mail*, June 22, 1999: A1, A10. Reprinted by permission of *The Globe and Mail*.

QUESTIONS

1. Do you think the selection system used by CSIS is valid? Using your knowledge of validity, rate each step in this process.
2. One reason CSIS went public was to increase the representation of women from 10 percent to a target of 50 percent. Are there any possible problems with discrimination in this selection system? Discuss.

Case Study 2

Aptitude Tests at an Electronics Corporation

An electronics plant in Midland, Ontario, has begun using aptitude tests as part of its selection process. Before they will be considered for new job openings and for promotions, new candidates must pass eight different aptitude tests. One test for manual dexterity requires applicants to move small metal pegs from holes on one side of a board to holes on the other side as fast as they can. In another test, employees are shown pictures of two cows—one white and the other spotted—and asked, "Which cow would be easier to see from an airplane?"

The company's employees see no relationship between their jobs and the cow test; they also find it humiliating to have to move pegs on a board in order to qualify for jobs they have been doing for years. In one testing session, 80 percent of employees failed. The price of failure is exclusion from higher-paying and more desirable jobs. Even more shameful is the fact that people with less seniority and little plant experience are passing the aptitude tests.

The dispute is deeply rooted. The union feels that the tests are allowing management to replace experienced workers with new hires who work for less pay. The fact that test results are almost always confidential has led to suspicions that the results are being manipulated in some way. After seeing their colleagues fail the tests, some workers are so discouraged that they don't even try for new jobs or promotions. Other changes that have been introduced along with the tests include twelve-hour rotating shifts, the "flexible" replacement of workers, and new computerized inspection systems.

Management defends the testing, claiming that new plants and new work methods require aptitudes such as problem solving and flexible thinking. These skills are not usually associated with the stereotype of the senior blue-collar worker. In the past, young people had no need to even graduate from high school if there was a plant in town offering big paycheques for manual labour. The tests that have been introduced discriminate against older workers with less formal education. In demand today are employees who can do many jobs, solve problems, make decisions, provide creative solutions, and function effectively as part of an empowered work team.

Source: Reprinted by permission of the author Megan Terepocki.

QUESTIONS

1. Do you see any problems with the way the company's testing program is being managed? Discuss.

2. Suggest how the program might be modified.

3. The union is fighting to eliminate the testing. On what grounds could the union base its arguments?

4. If an employee files a complaint with the Ontario Human Rights Commission on the grounds that the test discriminated against him as an older worker, what kinds of information will have to be gathered to determine the validity of his claim?

CAREER COUNSEL

The resumé preparation exercises on the *Managing Human Resources* website (www.belcourt4e.nelson.com) will help you tailor your resumé to the position.

NOTES AND REFERENCES

1. Interested readers can check out the websites of these companies at http://www.peoplesoft.com and http://www.sap.com. Also see Natasha Wanchek, "People Who Need PeopleSoft," *MC Technology Marketing Intelligence* 18, no. 5 (May 1998): 22–29; Paul Gosling, "The Computer Is Going through Your CV Now," *The Independent,* August 23, 1998, 2.

2. Gillian Flynn, "Texas Instruments Engineers a Holistic HR," *Workforce* 77, no. 2 (February 1998): 30–35; Gillian Flynn, "Internet Recruitment Limits Demographic Scope," *Workforce* 79, no. 4 (April 2000): 85–87; Vivian Marino, "A Traffic Jam of Resumes," *The New York Times,* December 16, 2001, 3: 10.

3. Micheline Maynard and Del Jones, "Keeping Secrets: High-Tech Tools Usher in Stolen-Information Age," *USA Today,* April 10, 1997: B1, B4.

4. Rekha Balu and L. Amante, "Kellogg Co. Shakes Up Management: Financial Officer among Those Quitting," *The Wall Street Journal,* March 4, 1999: B14; George Lazarus, "Pepsi Bottlers May Look Outside for New Chief," *Chicago Tribune,* February 12, 1999: 3; Joann S. Lublin, "Albertsons Picks an Outsider—GE Veteran Johnston—for Top Posts," *The Wall Street Journal,* April 24, 2001: B1.

5. Jennifer Laabs, "Cool Relo Benefits to Retain Top Talent," *Workforce* 78, no. 3 (March 1999): 89–94; Nancy Wong, "Do More Than Make a Move," *Workforce* 78, no. 3 (March 1999): 95–97.

6. Herbert G. Heneman III and Robyn A. Berkley, "Applicant Attraction Practices and Outcomes among Small Businesses," *Journal of Small Business Management* 27, no. 1 (January 1999): 53–74; James Breaugh and Mary Starke, "Research on Employee Recruitment: So Many Studies, So Many Remaining Questions," *Journal of Management* 26, no. 3 (2000): 405–34.

7. For additional sources on writing resumés, see Martin Yates, *Knock 'Em Dead 2002* (Avon, MA: Adams Media Corporation, 2001); Arthur Rosenberg and David Hizer, *The Resumé Handbook: How to Write Outstanding Resumés and Cover Letters for Every Situation,* 3rd ed.

(Avon, MA: Adams Media Corporation, 1996); Joyce Lain Kennedy, *Resumés for Dummies* (New York: John Wiley and Sons, 2000).

8. Sarah Fister Gale, "Internet Recruiting: Better, Cheaper, Faster," *Workforce* 80, no. 12 (December 2001): 74–77.

9. Samuel Greengard, "Putting Online Recruiting to Work," *Workforce* 77, no. 8 (August 1998): 73–76; Richard Ream, "Rules for Electronic Resumes," *Information Today* 17, no. 8 (September 2000): 24–25; Pat Curry, "Log On for Recruits," *Industry Week* 249, no. 17 (October 16, 2000): 46–54.

10. Keith Swenson, "Maximizing Employee Referrals," *HRFocus* 76, no. 1 (January 1999): 9–10; Thomas A. Stewart, "In Search of Elusive Tech Workers," *Fortune* (February 16, 1998): 171–72; Thomas Love, "Smart Tactics for Finding Workers," *Nation's Business* (January 1998): 20.

11. Steven Berglas, "Hiring In-Laws: The Kiss of Death," *Inc.* 20, no. 16 (November 1998): 31–33; Paulette Thomas, "Workplace: An Ohio Design Shop Favors Family Ties," *The Wall Street Journal,* September 8, 1998, B1; Chad Kaydo, "Does Nepotism Work?" *Sales and Marketing Management* 150, no. 7 (July 1998): 161; Brenda Paik Sunoo, "Nepotism—Problem or Solution?" *Workforce* 77, no. 6 (June 1998): 17; James Olan Hutcheson, "Negotiating Nepotism: A Written Employment Policy Statement for Your Client's Family Business Will Keep the Business Efficient and Family Members on the Same Page," *Financial Planning* (February 1, 2002): 75–76.

12. Audrey Bottjen, "The Benefits of College Recruiting," *Sales and Marketing Management* 153, no. 4 (April 2001): 12; Rhea Nagel and Jerry Bohovich, "College Recruiting in the 21st Century," *Journal of Career Planning & Employment* 61, no. 1 (Fall 2000): 36–37.

13. Michelle Neely Martinez, "Working With an Outside Recruiter? Get It in Writing," *HRMagazine* 46, no. 1 (January 2001): 98–105.

14. V. Galt, "Canadians Lead World in Job Hunting on Line," *The Globe and Mail,* April 5, 2003: B5.

15. "Innovative Recruitment and Retention Critical, Bosses Say," *Human Resources Management in Canada*, Report Bulletin, 206, April 2000: 3.

16. D. Chapman, "Recruiting: More Art than Science?" *HR Professional* 19, no. 2 (April/May 2002): 42–43.

17. Robert D. Bretz Jr. and Timothy A. Judge, "Realistic Job Previews: A Test of the Adverse Self-Selection Hypothesis," *Journal of Applied Psychology* 83, no. 2 (April 1998): 330–37.

18. George Callaghan and Paul Thompson, "'We Recruit Attitude': The Selection and Shaping of Routine Call Centre Labour," *Journal of Management Studies* 39, no. 2 (March 2002): 233–54; Terry Beehr, Lana Ivanitskaya, Curtiss Hansen, Dmitry Erofeev, and David Gudanoski, "Evaluation of 360-Degree Feedback Ratings: Relationships with Each Other and with Performance and Selection Predictors," *Journal of Organizational Behavior* 22, no. 7 (November 2001): 775–88.

19. Dan Cable and Charles Parsons, "Socialization Tactics and Person-Organization Fit," *Personnel Psychology* 54, no. 1 (Spring 2001): 1–23; Amy Kristof-Brown, "Perceived Applicant Fit: Distinguishing between Recruiters' Perceptions of Person-Job and Person-Organization Fit," *Personnel Psychology* 53, no. 3 (Autumn 2000): 643–71.

20. Frank J. Landy, "Test Validity Yearbook," *Journal of Business Psychology* 7, no. 2 (1992): 111–257. See also Edwin E. Ghiselli, "The Validity of Aptitude Tests in Personnel Selection," *Personnel Psychology* 26, no. 4 (Winter 1973): 461–77; J. E. Hunter and R. H. Hunter, "Validity and Utility of Alternative Predictors of Job Performance," *Psychological Bulletin* 96 (1984): 72–98; Ivan Robertson and Mike Smith, "Personnel Selection," *Journal of Occupational and Organizational Psychology* 74, no. 4 (November 2001): 441–72.

21. Calvin C. Hoffman and S. Morton McPhail, "Exploring Options for Supporting Test Use in Situations Precluding Local Validation," *Personnel Psychology* 51, no. 4 (Winter 1998): 987–1003; Leaetta Hough and Frederick Oswald, "Personnel Selection: Looking toward the Future— Remembering the Past," *Annual Review of Psychology* 51 (2000): 631–64.

22. S. Messick, "Foundations of Validity: Meaning and Consequences in Psychological Assessment," *European Journal of Psychological Assessment* 10 (1994): 1–9; Michael Lindell and Christina Brandt, "Assessing Interrater Agreement on the Job Relevance of a Test: A Comparison of the CVI, T, $r^{WG(J)}$, and $r\star^{WG(J)}$ Indexes," *Journal of Applied Psychology* 84, no. 4 (August 1999): 640–47.

23. D. Brent Smith and Lill Ellingson, "Substance versus Style: A New Look at Social Desirability in Motivating Contexts," *Journal of Applied Psychology* 87, no. 2 (April 2002): 211–19; Ken Craik et al., "Explorations of Construct Validity in a Combined Managerial and Personality Assessment Programme," *Journal of Occupational and Organizational Psychology* 75, no. 2 (June 2002): 171–93.

24. Tammy Prater and Sara Bliss Kiser, "Lies, Lies, and More Lies," *A.A.M. Advance Management Journal* 67, no. 2 (Spring 2002): 9–14.

25. Scott R. Kaak, Hubert S. Field, William F. Giles, and Dwight R. Norris, "The Weighted Application Blank," *Cornell Hotel and Restaurant Administration Quarterly* 39, no. 2 (April 1998): 18–24; Brad Bingham, Sherrie Ilg, and Neil Davidson, "Great Candidates Fast: Online Job Application and Electronic Processing: Washington State's New Internet Application System," *Public Personnel Management* 31, no. 1 (Spring 2002): 53–64; Sarah Fister Gale, "Internet Recruiting: Better, Cheaper, Faster," *Workforce* 80, no. 12 (December 2001): 74–77; Tim Armes, "Internet Recruiting," *Canadian Manager* 24, no. 1 (Spring 1999): 21–22; "Top Firms Recruit on Web," *USA Today*, September 22, 2000: A1; Cora Daniels, "To Hire a Lumber Expert, Click Here," *Fortune* 141, no. 7 (April 3, 2000): 267–70.

26. Margaret A. McManus and Mary L. Kelly, "Personality Measures and Biodata: Evidence Regarding Their Incremental Predictive Value in the Life Insurance Industry," *Personnel Psychology* 52, no. 1 (Spring 1999): 137–48; Andrew J. Vinchur, Jeffrey S. Schippmann, Fred S. Switzer III, and Philip L. Roth, "A Meta-Analytic Review of Predictors of Job Performance for Salespeople," *Journal of Applied Psychology* 83, no. 4 (August 1998): 586–97; Gary R. Kettlitz, Imad Zbib, and Jaideep Motwani, "Validity of Background Data as a Predictor of Employee Tenure among Nursing Aides in Long-Term Care Facilities," *Health Care Supervisor* 16, no. 3 (March 1998): 26–31; Yen Chung, "The Validity of Biographical Inventories for the Selection of Salespeople," *International Journal of Management* 18, no. 3 (September 2001): 322–29; Teri Elkins and James Phillips, "Job Context, Selection Decision Outcome, and the Perceived Fairness of Selection Tests: Biodata as an Illustrative Case," *Journal of Applied Psychology* 85, no. 3 (June 2000): 479–84; Herschel Chait, Shawn Carreher, and M. Ronald Buckley, "Measuring Service Orientation with Biodata," *Journal of Managerial Issues* 12, no. 1 (Spring 2000): 109–20.

27. Samuel Greengard, "Are You Well Armed to Screen Applicants?" *Personnel Journal* (December 1995): 84–95; "The Final Rung: References," *Across the Board* (March 1996): 40; Judith Howlings, "Staff Recruitment: Your Rights and Obligations," *People Management* (May 30, 1996): 47; "Read between the Lines," *Management Today*

(February 1996): 14; Diane Domeyer, "Reference Checks Offer Valuable Insight," *Women in Business* 51, no. 4 (July/August 1999): 32.

28. T. Humber, "Name, Rank and Serial Number," *Canadian HR Reporter* 15, no. 10 (May 19, 2003): 1.

29. Constance L. Hays, "Tests Are Becoming Common in Hiring," *The New York Times,* November 28, 1997, D1. See also Gregory M. Lousig-Nont, "Avoid Common Hiring Mistakes with Honesty Tests," *Nation's Restaurant News* 31, no. 11 (March 17, 1997): 30; "If the Shoe Fits," *Security Management* 40, no. 2 (February 1996): 11; Michelle Cottle, "Job Testing: Multiple Choices," *The New York Times,* September 5, 1999, 3: 10.

30. D.S. Ones, C. Viswesvaran, and F.L. Schmidt, "Comprehensive Meta-Analysis of Integrity Test Validities: Findings and Implications for Personnel Selection and Theories of Job Performance," *Journal of Applied Psychology* 78 (August 1993): 679–703. See also Deniz S. Ones and Chockalingam Viswesvaran, "Gender, Age and Race Differences on Overt Integrity Tests: Results across Four Large-Scale Job Applicant Data Sets," *Journal of Applied Psychology* 83, no. 1 (February 1998): 35–42; Lynn McFarland and Ann Marie Ryan, "Variance in Faking across Noncognitive Measures," *Journal of Applied Psychology* 85, no. 5 (October 2000): 812–21.

31. Bill Leonard, "Reading Employees," *HRMagazine* 44, no. 4 (April 1999): 67–73; Steven Thomas and Steve Vaught, "The Write Stuff: What the Evidence Says about Using Handwriting Analysis in Hiring," *S.A.M. Advanced Management Journal* 66, no. 4 (Autumn 2001): 31–35.

32. Dirk D. Steiner and Stephen W. Gilliland, "Fairness Reactions to Personnel Selection Techniques in France and the United States," *Journal of Applied Psychology* 81, no. 2 (April 1996): 134–41.

33. Gillian Flynn, "A Legal Examination of Testing," *Workforce* 81, no. 6 (June 2002): 92–94; Gillian Flynn, "Pre-Employment Testing Can Be Unlawful," *Workforce* 78, no. 7 (July 1999): 82–83; Gilbert Nicholsen, "Screen and Glean: Good Screening and Background Checks Help Make the Right Match for Every Open Position," *Workforce* 79, no. 10 (October 2000): 70–72.

34. Kathryn Tyler, "Put Applicants' Skills to the Test," *HRMagazine* 45, no. 1 (January 2000): 74–80. For a counterargument, see Kevin R. Murphy and Ann Harris Shiarella, "Implications of the Multidimensional Nature of Job Performance for the Validity of Selection Tests: Multivariate Frameworks for Studying Test Validity," *Personnel Psychology* 50, no. 4 (Winter 1997): 823–54.

35. For books with comprehensive coverage of testing, including employment testing, see Catano et al., *Recruitment and Selection in Canada,* 2nd ed., Toronto: Nelson Thomson Learning, 2001; Anne Anastasi and Susana Urbina, *Psychological Testing,* 7th ed. (New York: Macmillan, 1997); Gary Groth-Marnat, *Handbook of Psychological Assessment* (New York: John Wiley and Sons, 1996); Lee J. Cronbach, *Essentials of Psychological Testing,* 5th ed. (New York: HarperCollins, 1990).

36. Standards that testing programs should meet are described in *Standards for Educational and Psychological Tests* (Washington, DC: American Psychological Association, 1986). HR managers who want to examine paper-and-pencil tests should obtain specimen sets that include a test manual, a copy of the test, an answer sheet, and a scoring key. The test manual provides the essential information about the construction of the test; its recommended use; and instructions for administering, scoring, and interpreting the test. Test users should not rely entirely on the material furnished by the test author and publisher. A major source of consumer information about commercially available tests—the *Mental Measurements Yearbook (MMY)*—is available in most libraries. Published periodically, the *MMY* contains descriptive information plus critical reviews by experts in the various types of tests. The reviews are useful in evaluating a particular test for tryout in employment situations. Other sources of information about tests include *Test Critiques,* a set of volumes containing professional reviews of tests, and *Tests: A Comprehensive Reference for Assessments in Psychology, Education, and Business.* The latter describes more than 3100 tests published in the English language. Another source, *Principles for the Validation and Use of Personnel Selection Procedures,* published by the Society for Industrial and Organizational Psychology, is a valuable guide for employers who use tests. Other publications present detailed information on how to avoid discrimination and achieve fairness in testing.

37. Harold W. Goldstein, Kenneth P. Yusko, Eric P. Braverman, D. Brent Smith, and Beth Chung, "The Role of Cognitive Ability in the Subgroup Differences and Incremental Validity of Assessment Center Exercises," *Personnel Psychology* 51, no. 2 (Summer 1998): 357–74; Sara Rynes, Amy Colbert, and Kenneth Brown, "HR Professionals' Beliefs about Effective Human Resource Practices: Correspondence between Research and Practice," *Human Resource Management* 41, no. 2 (Summer 2002): 149–74; Mary Roznowski, David Dickter, Linda Sawin, Valerie Shute, and Sehee Hong, "The Validity of Measures of Cognitive Processes and Generability for Learning and Performance on Highly Complex Computerized Tutors: Is the g Factor of Intelligence even More General?" *Journal of Applied Psychology* 85, no. 6 (December 2000): 940–55.

38. Timothy Judge and Joyce Bono, "Five-Factor Model of Personality and Transformational Leadership," *Journal of Applied Psychology* 85, no. 5 (October 2000): 751–65; J. Michael Crant and Thomas S. Bateman, "Charismatic Leadership Viewed from Above: The Impact of Proactive Personality," *Journal of Organizational Behavior* 21, no. 1 (February 2000): 63–75.

39. Gregory Hurtz and John Donovan, "Personality and Job Performance: The Big Five Revisited," *Journal of Applied Psychology* 85, no. 6 (December 2000): 869–79.

40. In the case of *Soroka v Dayton Hudson Corporation* (1993), plaintiffs sued on the grounds that the selection test violated California's Fair Employment laws and that certain items, especially MMPI items, constituted an unlawful invasion of privacy. Although the case was settled out of court, the California state appellate court, in a preliminary injunction, found that certain questions violated the plaintiffs' rights to privacy and that Target Stores had not shown these questions to be job-related. See Stephen Dwight and George Alliger, "Reactions to Overt Integrity Test Items," *Educational and Psychological Measurement* 57, no. 6 (December 1977); Daniel P. O'Meara, "Personality Tests Raise Questions of Legality and Effectiveness," *HRMagazine* 39, no. 1 (January 1994): 97–100; Jeffrey A. Mello, "Personality Tests and Privacy Rights," *HRFocus* 73, no. 3 (March 1996): 22–23.

41. Walter C. Borman, Mary Ann Hanson, and Jerry W. Hedge, "Personnel Selection," *Annual Review of Psychology* 48 (1997): 299–337; Charles Sproule and Stephen Berkley, "The Selection of Entry-level Corrections Officers: Pennsylvania Research," *Public Personnel Management* 30, no. 3 (Fall 2001): 377–418.

42. M. Brewster, "RCMP Ease Fitness Rules for Women," *The Globe and Mail*, July 14, 1997: A4.

43. Alisha Berger, "Physical Fitness as a Job Yardstick," *The New York Times*, June 29, 1999: 8; Charles Anderson, "Can Employees Physically Do the Job?" *Human Resources* 7, no. 5 (September/October 1994): 3–5.

44. It may be interesting to note that the origins of the civil service system go back to 2200 B.C., when the Chinese emperor examined officials every three years to determine their fitness for continuing in office. In 1115 B.C. candidates for government posts were examined for their proficiency in music, archery, horsemanship, writing, arithmetic, and the rites and ceremonies of public and private life.

45. Leonard D. Goodstein and Alan D. Davidson, "Hiring the Right Stuff: Using Competency-Based Selection," *Compensation & Benefits Management* 14, no. 3 (Summer 1998): 1–10.

46. Linda Marsh, "By Their Actions Shall Ye Know Them," *Works Management* 50, no. 11 (November 1997): 52–53; Florence Berger and Ajay Ghei, "Employment Tests: A Facet of Hospitality Hiring," *Cornell Hotel and Restaurant Administration Quarterly* 36, no. 6 (December 1995): 28–31; Malcolm James Ree, Thomas R. Carretta, and Mark S. Teachout, "Role of Ability and Prior Job Knowledge in Complex Training Performance," *Journal of Applied Psychology* 80, no. 6 (December 1995): 721–30.

47. Cynthia Kay Stevens, "Antecedents of Interview Interactions, Interviewers' Ratings, and Applicants' Reactions," *Personnel Psychology* 51, no. 1 (Spring 1998): 55–85; Laura Gollub Williamson, James E. Campion, Stanley B. Malos, and Mark V. Roehling, "Employment Interview on Trial: Linking Interview Structure with Litigation Outcomes," *Journal of Applied Psychology* 82, no. 6 (December 1997): 900–12; Richard A. Posthuma, Frederick Morgeson, and Michael Campion, "Beyond Employment Interview Validity: A Comprehensive Narrative Review of Recent Research and Trends over Time," *Personnel Psychology* 55, no. 1 (Spring 2002): 1–8; Frank Schmidt and Mark Rader, "Exploring the Boundary Conditions for Interview Validity: Meta-Analytic Validity Findings for a New Interview Type," *Personnel Psychology* 52, no. 2 (Summer 1999): 445–64.

48. Schmidt and Rader, "Exploring the Boundary Conditions for Interview Validity: Meta-Analytic Validity Findings for a New Interview Type"; Williamson, Campion, Malos, and Roehling, "Employment Interview on Trial"; Jennifer R. Burnett and Stephan J. Motowidlo, "Relations between Different Sources of Information in the Structured Selection Interview," *Personnel Psychology* 51, no. 4 (Winter 1998): 963–83. See also Geoffrey Colvin, "Looking to Hire the Very Best? Ask the Right Questions. Lots of Them," *Fortune* (June 21, 1999): 192–94; "Recruiting Practices That Get the EEOC's Attention," *HRMagazine* 42, no. 11 (November 1997): 60.

49. For an excellent review of research on the structured interview, see Michael A. Campion, David K. Palmer, and James E. Campion, "A Review of Structure in the Selection Interview," *Personnel Psychology* 50, no. 3 (Autumn 1997): 655–702. See also Karen van der Zee, Arnold Bakker, and Paulien Bakker, "Why Are Structured Interviews So Rarely Used in Personnel Selection?" *Journal of Applied Psychology* 87, no. 1 (February 2002): 176–84.

50. Todd Maurer, Jerry Solamon, and Deborah Troxtel, "Relationship of Coaching with Performance in Situational Employment Interviews," *Journal of Applied Psychology* 83, no. 1 (February 1998): 128–36; Allen Huffcutt, Jeff Weekley, Willi Wiesner, Timothy Degroot, and Casey Jones, "Comparison of Situational and Behavior Description Interview Questions for Higher-Level Positions," *Personnel Psychology* 54, no. 3 (Autumn 2001): 619–44.

51. Amelia J. Prewett-Livingston, John G. Veres III, Hubert S. Feild, and Philip M. Lewis, "Effects of Race on Interview Ratings in a Situational Panel Interview," *Journal of Applied Psychology* 81, no. 2 (April 1996): 178–86. See also Damodar Y. Golhar and Satish P. Deshpande, "HRM Practices of Large and Small Canadian Manufacturing Firms," *Journal of Small Business Management* 35, no. 3 (July 1997): 30–38; Philip L. Roth and James E. Campion, "An Analysis of the Predictive Power of the Panel Interview and Pre-Employment Tests," *Journal of Occupational and Organizational Psychology* 65 (March 1992): 51–60.

52. Peter C. Sawyers, "Structured Interviewing: Your Key to the Best Hires," *Personnel Journal,* Special supplement, December 1992. See also Bob Smith, "Pinkerton Keeps Its Eye on Recruitment," *HRFocus* 70, no. 9 (September 1993): 1, 8; Elizabeth Daniele, "PC-Based Screening Passes the Test at Cigna," *Insurance & Technology* 17 (January 1992): 15, 18. For more information about Interactive Information Services, see their website at http://www.iiserve.com/about.html.

53. Linda Thornburg, "Computer-Assisted Interviewing Shortens Hiring Cycle," *HRMagazine* 43, no. 2 (February 1998): 73–79; Dan Hanover, "Hiring Gets Cheaper and Faster," *Sales and Marketing Management* 152, no. 3 (March 2000): 87; Jessica Clark Newman et al., "The Differential Effects of Face-to-Face and Computer Interview Modes," *American Journal of Public Health* 92, no. 2 (February 2002): 294; David Mitchell, "ijob.com Recruiting Online," *Strategic Finance* 80, no. 11 (May 1999): 48–51.

54. Posthuma, Morgeson, Campion, "Beyond Employment Interview Validity"; Schmidt and Rader, "Exploring the Boundary Conditions for Interview Validity."

55. Burnett and Motowidlo, "Relations between Different Sources"; Allen Huffcutt and David Woehr, "Further Analysis of Employment Interview Validity: A Quantitative Evaluation of Interviewer-Related Structuring Methods," *Journal of Organizational Behavior* 20, no. 4 (July 1999): 549–60; "LIMRA Offers New Recruiting, Assessment, and Retention Technologies," *LIMRA's MarketFacts* 19, no. 3 (May/June 2000): 15. See also Mike Frost, "Interviewing ABCs," *HRMagazine* 42, no. 3 (March 1997): 32–34.

56. "Discrimination Because of Handicap," *Ontario Human Rights Commission*, Ontario Human Rights Commission, Government of Ontario, May 1991: 5.

57. See, for example, *Ontario Human Rights Commission Policy on Employment-Related Medical Information*, Ontario Human Rights Commission, Government of Ontario, March 1991: 1–2.

58. *Ontario Human Rights Commission Policy on Height and Weight Requirements*, Ontario Human Rights Commission, Government of Ontario, 1989: 1.

59. "Alberta's Suncor Says It's Reviewing Drug Testing after Human Rights Ruling," *Canada Press Newswire*, January 12, 2002.

60. C. Hoglund, "Mandatory Drug Testing," *Human Resource Professional* 8, no. 1 (January 1992): 21–22.

61. Hoglund, "Mandatory Drug Testing."

Training and Development

After studying this chapter, you should be able to

1
objective

List some of the characteristics of an effective orientation program.

5
objective

Identify the types of training methods used for managers and nonmanagers.

2
objective

Discuss the systems approach to training and development.

6
objective

Discuss the advantages and disadvantages of various evaluation criteria.

3
objective

Describe the components of training-needs assessment.

7
objective

Describe the special training programs that are currently popular.

4
objective

Identify the principles of learning and describe how they facilitate training.

Training has become increasingly vital to the success of modern organizations. Recall that in Chapter 1 we noted that organizations often compete on competencies—the core sets of knowledge and expertise that give them an edge over their competitors. Training plays a central role in nurturing and strengthening these competencies, and in this way has become part of the backbone of strategy implementation. In addition, rapidly changing technologies require that employees continuously hone their knowledge, skills, and abilities (KSAs) to cope with new processes and systems. Jobs that require little skill are rapidly being replaced by jobs that require technical, interpersonal, and problem-solving skills. Other trends toward empowerment, total-quality management, teamwork, and international business make it necessary for managers, as well as employees, to develop the skills that will enable them to handle new and more demanding assignments.

ORIENTATION

objective

Orientation
Formal process of familiarizing a new employee with the organization, the new job, and the new work unit

To get new employees off to a good start, organizations offer formal orientation programs. **Orientation** is the formal process of familiarizing a new employee with the organization, the new job, and the new work unit. It enables new employees to get "in sync" so that they start becoming productive members of the organization.

Benefits of Orientation

In some organizations, formal, new-hire orientation programs are almost nonexistent or, if they do exist, are performed in a casual manner. Some readers may remember showing up the first day on a new job, being told to work, and receiving no instructions, introductions, or support. This is unfortunate, since well-run orientation programs have a number of very practical, cost-effective benefits. As reported by employers, these include the following:

▶ Lower turnover
▶ Higher productivity
▶ Improved employee morale
▶ Lower recruiting and training costs
▶ Facilitation of learning
▶ Reduction of the new employee's anxiety

The more time and effort an organization devotes to making new employees feel welcome, the more likely those employees are to identify with the organization and become valuable members of it. Unlike training, which emphasizes the *what* and the *how*, orientation stresses the *why*. It is designed to develop in employees a particular attitude about the work they will be doing and their role in the organization. It explains the philosophy behind the rules and provides a framework for job-related tasks.

For a well-integrated orientation program, cooperation between line staff and the HR department is important. The HR department is responsible for coordinating orientation activities and for providing new employees with information about pay, benefits, conditions of employment, and other areas not directly under a supervisor's direction. However, the supervisor plays the most important role in the orientation program. New employees are interested mainly in what the supervisor says and does and what their new co-workers are like. Before a new employee arrives, the supervisor should inform the work group that a new worker is joining the unit. Often, supervisors or other managerial personnel recruit co-workers to serve as volunteer "sponsors" for incoming employees. Besides providing practical help to newcomers, this approach conveys an emphasis on teamwork. At Sofitel's hotel in Montreal, new employees receive knapsacks, filled with Sofitel products and a passport that training session leaders sign as they move through each phase of the orientation program. To orient new employees, GM's financial group puts students behind the wheels of a virtual GM vehicle. New employees can drive their way through video clips on GM, details on organizational structure and functions, and employee benefits.

Given the immediate and lasting impact of orientation programs, careful planning—with emphasis on program goals, topics to be covered, and methods of organizing and presenting them—is essential. In many cases, organizations devise checklists for use by those responsible for conducting orientations. Highlights in HRM 6.1 lists items that should be included in an orientation checklist for supervisors. Orientation should focus on matters of immediate concern, such as important aspects of the job and the organization's rules for behaviour (e.g., attendance and safety).

Highlights in HRM 6.1

SUPERVISORY ORIENTATION CHECKLIST

1. A formal greeting, including introduction to colleagues.
2. Explanation of job procedures, duties, and responsibilities.
3. Training to be received (when and why).
4. Supervisor and organization expectations regarding attendance and behaviour norms.
5. Job standards and production/service levels.
6. Performance appraisal criteria, including estimated time frame for achieving peak performance.
7. Conditions of employment, including hours of work, benefits, union contracts, pay periods, and overtime requirements.
8. Organization and work unit rules, regulations, and policies.
9. Safety regulations.
10. Those to notify or turn to if problems or questions arise.
11. Chain of command for reporting purposes.
12. An overall explanation of the organization's operations and purpose.
13. Offers of help and encouragement, including a specific time each week (in the early stages of employment) for questions or coaching.

In orientation sessions, new employees are often given a packet of materials to read at their leisure. Some of the materials these packets might include are noted in Highlights in HRM 6.1. It is possible that statements regarding such matters as tenure, basis for dismissal, and benefits might be viewed by employees and the courts as legally binding on the employer, so it is advisable to have the legal department review the packet and write a disclaimer to the effect that it does not constitute an employment contract.

Those who are planning an orientation program should take into account the anxiety that employees feel during their first few days on the job. It is natural to experience some anxiety, but if employees are too anxious, training costs, turnover, absenteeism, and even production costs may increase. Early in the orientation program, steps should be taken to reduce the anxiety of new employees. This can be accomplished by establishing specific times during which the supervisor will be available for questions and/or coaching. It is also worthwhile to reassure newcomers that they will attain the performance levels they are observing among their co-workers within a predetermined time frame, based on experiences with other newcomers. This reassurance is especially important for employees with limited work experience who are learning new skills.

Some employers think it does no harm to allow new employees to be oriented by their peers. But there is a danger to this practice: Unsafe work practices and unacceptable behaviours that conflict with the organization's policies can be perpetuated if the supervisors themselves do not conduct the orientation. The behaviours these employees develop can undermine the organization's policies and procedures.

Highlights in HRM 6.2 describes the way Intuit Canada treats employees from the initial contact to the first day on the job.

Scope of Training

Many new employees come equipped with most of the KSAs needed to start work. Others may require extensive training before they are ready to make much of a contribution to the organization. Almost any employee, however, needs some type of ongoing training to maintain effective performance or to adjust to new ways of work.

The term *training* is often used casually to describe almost any effort initiated by an organization to foster learning among its members. However, many experts distinguish between *training,* which tends to be more narrowly focused and oriented toward short-term performance concerns, and *development,* which tends to be oriented more toward broadening an individual's skills for the future responsibilities. The two terms tend to be combined into a single phrase—*training and development*—to recognize the combination of activities used by organizations to increase the skill base of employees.

The primary reason that organizations train new employees is to bring their KSAs up to the level required for satisfactory performance. As these employees continue on the job, additional training provides opportunities for them to acquire new knowledge and skills. As a result of this training, employees may be even more effective on the job and may be able to perform other jobs in other areas or at higher levels.

Highlights in HRM 6.2

WOWING THE CANDIDATE

Intuit Canada, headquartered in Edmonton, Alberta, is a leading developer of financial software, including personal finance management, small business accounting and tax preparation, with products such as Quicken. Intuit, like other organizations profiled in this report, is a top employer; it is ranked number two in Canada by the *Globe and Mail* survey and forty-fifth of the 100 Best Companies to Work for in America by *Fortune* magazine in 2002. What makes Intuit special is its success in a highly competitive industry. There are many factors, but evidence of its success is its low attrition rate of 3 percent, which is remarkable in a sector where the average turnover is 20 percent. Ninety-four percent of its employees report that Intuit is a "great place to work," according to their annual surveys.

Intuit is very careful about the first few days of a new employee's work life. There are too many stories about employees in other organizations showing up very excited about their new job, only to discover that no one remembers they are hired, supplies and offices are not ready, and the reporting manager is absent. Intuit is committed to wowing the candidate—now employee—on the first day. Upon arriving at work, new employees are greeted by name by the receptionist who gives them a stainless steel coffee mug engraved with their names. The hiring manager is called and arrives promptly. He knows the candidate and takes him to the workstation, showing him the computer, telephone, and office supplies. The next step is to introduce the new employee to colleagues and other team members and a "buddy" who has volunteered to guide the new employee and answer all questions for the next three weeks. New employees often struggle with simple questions such as how does the photocopier work? Do most people bring their lunches to work? The IT person arrives next and helps set up voice mail, e-mail, Internet access, etc. Intuit considers it vital that when the new employee goes home that night, he should be able to answer the universal question "How was your first day on the job?" with "Wow, am I ever glad that I took this job!"

This informal orientation is completed by a formal orientation, in which information about the strategy, vision, plans, history, including war stories and all the successes is shared. A key part of this orientation is a discussion of Intuit values. At the end of the first week, and again at the end of the first month, feedback about the new employee's experiences is solicited. What worked, what was frustrating, how can the orientation be improved?

Source: M. Belcourt and S. Taggar, "Making Government the Best Place to Work: Building Commitment," IPAC, New Directions Series, no. 8, 2002.

Investments in Training

According to *Training Magazine*'s ongoing industry report, U.S. businesses spend an average of about $1115 per employee for training, compared to Canadian employers, who spend about $859 per employee. Overall, the average expenditure in Canada on training and development was 1.8 percent of payroll, and organizations annually provided about thirty hours of training per employee.[1] The BMO Financial Group is one organization that does better than the average—it has an annual training budget of $71 million, which is 2.5 percent of payroll. Its employees receive on average forty-one hours of annual training.[2] Ethics in HRM describes the debate surrounding decisions to force organizations to provide training and to force employees to take training. Figure 6.1 shows some of the training programs offered most frequently to employees. The importance of technical training, particularly related to information technology, has of course increased a great deal over the past decade. While a good deal of money is spent on executive development and management training, Figure 6.2 shows that by far the greatest proportion of training is spent on rank-and-file employees and supervisors.[3]

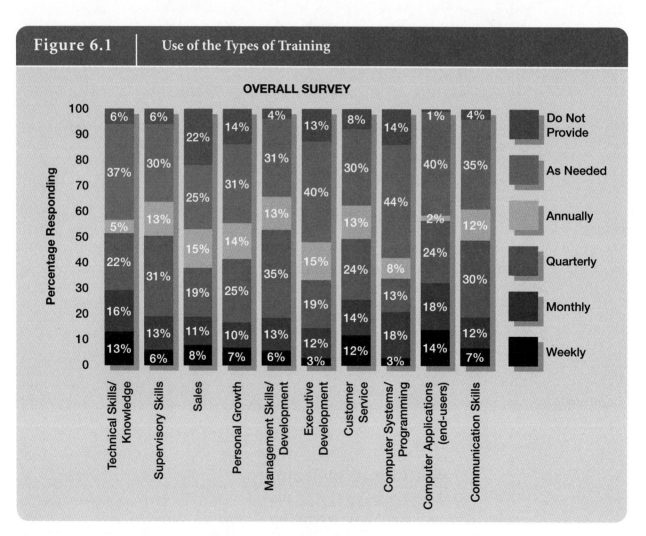

Figure 6.1 | **Use of the Types of Training**

Source: Tammy Galvin, "The Methods," *Training* 38, no. 10 (October 2991): 48–56.

Ethics in HRM

MANDATORY OR VOLUNTARY?

There is only one payroll training tax in North America. The Quebec government program that forces employers to spend 1 percent of payroll on training may not have the intended consequences of increasing training investments in employees. Using data from a Statistics Canada survey, Alan Saks of the University of Toronto and Robert Haccoun of the Université de Montréal matched Quebec employers with Ontario employers and found that there were no differences in amounts spent on training. The paperwork is so cumbersome that many employers prefer to pay the 1 percent tax rather than go through the thick guidebooks necessary to report the training.

If there is little effect gained by forcing employers to provide training, are there benefits by forcing employees to attend training? The answer is not clear: Some studies report some slight benefits in outcomes (such as improved job performance) when employees voluntarily attend courses; other studies see no differences.

There may be more serious problems than performance results created by forcing employees to attend courses. Half of the twenty-four employees of SaskTel who participated in a training program on process re-engineering required psychological counselling, or stress leave, or both in its aftermath. Trainees said they were subjected to a greenhouse environment: Windows were papered over, employees were not allowed to communicate with one another, and all were subjected to verbal abuse from the training consultants. As the president of the Ontario Society for Training and Development commented: "That's not training, that's assault."

Seagulls Pewter and Silversmiths of Pugwash, Nova Scotia, sent its employees to seminars based on the controversial Est therapy. Employees complained to their union that the seminars, in which participants were encouraged to delve into painful emotions, often drove participants to breakdowns. In another example, a large insurance company hired a consultant to conduct management training for hundreds of supervisors and managers. The company did not realize that the consultant was a member of L. Ron Hubbard's Church of Scientology and was teaching management principles developed by Scientologists. Critics contend that Scientology is a cult, not a religion. Employees resented being subjected to psychological concepts based on "tones" that catalogue emotions; to the ruthless devotion to ferreting out and firing problem employees; and to "religious scriptures."

The employees in these organizations were required to participate in programs that caused them undue stress and sometimes violated their moral or religious beliefs. Those who organized the programs believed that employees with the "right" attitudes would be more effective.

Sources: K. Harding, "A Taxing Way to Train Staff," *The Globe and Mail*, June 4, 2003: C1; D. Brown, "Legislated Training, Questionable Results," *Canadian HR Reporter* 15, no. 9, May 6, 2002: 1; A. Thomlinson, "Mandatory or Voluntary?" *Canadian HR Reporter* 15, no. 6 (March 25, 2002): 1; Edward Kay, "Trauma in Real Life," *The Globe and Mail Report on Business Magazine*, November 1996: 82–92; J. Saunders, "How Scientology's Message Came to Allstate," *The Globe and Mail*, April 24, 1995: B1; R. Sharpe, "Agents of Intimidation," *The Globe and Mail*, March 28, 1995: B8.

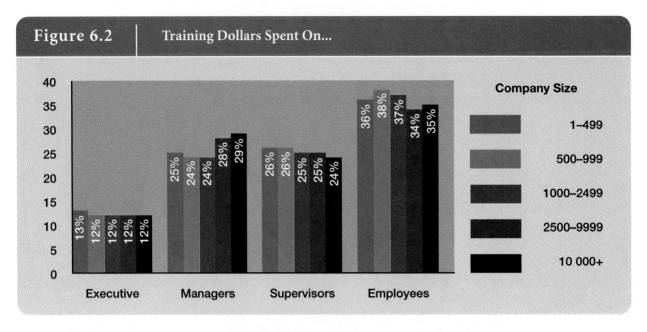

| Figure 6.2 | Training Dollars Spent On... |

Source: Tammy Galvin, "The Methods," *Training* 38, no. 10 (October 2991): 48–64.

In addition to formal training, more than $180 billion is spent on informal instruction that goes on every day in organizations everywhere. These investments are directed at a variety of programs, ranging from basic computer skills to customer service. In today's organizations, fully one-third of all training is information-technology-based. We discuss this trend later in the chapter.

A Systems Approach to Training

From the broadest perspective, the goal of training is to contribute to the organization's overall goals. Training programs should be developed with this in mind. Managers should keep a close eye on organizational goals and strategies and orient training accordingly. Unfortunately, many organizations never make the connection between their strategic objectives and their training programs. Instead, fads, fashions, or "whatever the competition is doing" can sometimes be the main drivers of an organization's training agenda. As a result, much of an organization's investment can be wasted—training programs are often misdirected, poorly designed, inadequately evaluated—and these problems directly affect organizational performance.

To make certain that investments in training and development have maximum impact on individual and organizational performance, a systems approach to training should be used. The systems approach involves four phases: (1) needs assessment, (2) program design, (3) implementation, and (4) evaluation. A model that is useful to designers of training programs is presented in Figure 6.3. We will use this model as a framework for organizing the material throughout this chapter.

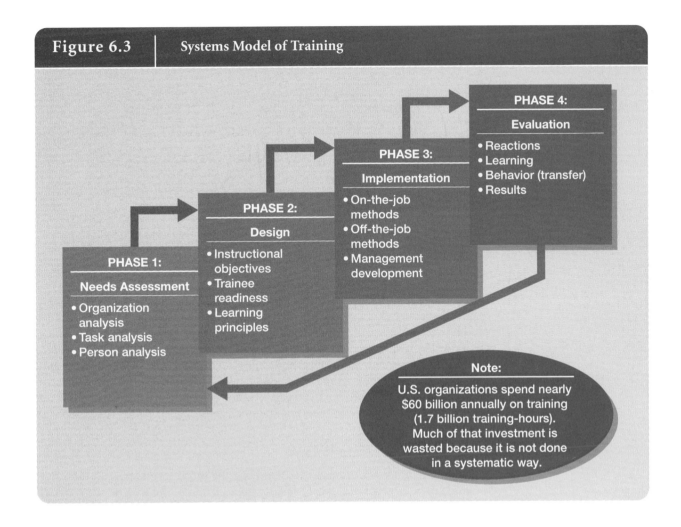

| Figure 6.3 | Systems Model of Training |

PHASE 1:

Needs Assessment

- Organization analysis
- Task analysis
- Person analysis

PHASE 2:

Design

- Instructional objectives
- Trainee readiness
- Learning principles

PHASE 3:

Implementation

- On-the-job methods
- Off-the-job methods
- Management development

PHASE 4:

Evaluation

- Reactions
- Learning
- Behavior (transfer)
- Results

Note:

U.S. organizations spend nearly $60 billion annually on training (1.7 billion training-hours). Much of that investment is wasted because it is not done in a systematic way.

PHASE 1: CONDUCTING THE NEEDS ASSESSMENT

objective 3

Managers and HR staffs should stay alert to the kinds of training that are needed, where they are needed, who needs them, and which methods will best deliver needed KSAs to employees. If workers consistently fail to achieve productivity objectives, this might be a signal that training is needed. Likewise, if organizations receive an excessive number of customer complaints, this too might suggest inadequate training. To make certain that training is timely and focused on priority issues, managers should approach needs assessment systematically by utilizing the three different types of analysis shown in Figure 6.4: organization analysis, task analysis, and person analysis. Each of these is discussed next.

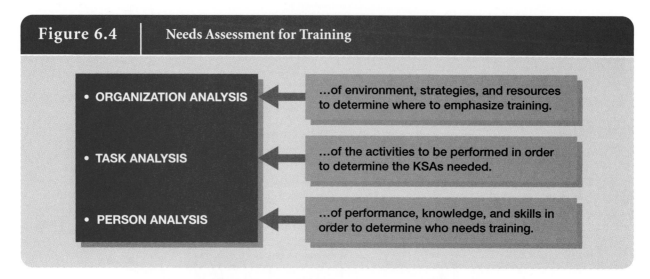

Figure 6.4 | **Needs Assessment for Training**

- ORGANIZATION ANALYSIS
  - ...of environment, strategies, and resources to determine where to emphasize training.

- TASK ANALYSIS
  - ...of the activities to be performed in order to determine the KSAs needed.

- PERSON ANALYSIS
  - ...of performance, knowledge, and skills in order to determine who needs training.

A study by the American Society for Training and Development (ASTD) found that, unfortunately, because of the costs, expertise, and time required, organizations conduct needs assessment less than 50 percent of the time before initiating a training program. Too frequently, managers lament that they simply don't have time to conduct needs assessment. Ironically, as the speed of change increases, and time and resources are at a premium, the need for good needs assessment actually increases. In these cases, the process need not be so daunting and laborious.[4] Highlights in HRM 6.3 provides some tips for rapidly assessing training needs.

Organization Analysis

The first step in needs assessment is identifying the broad forces that can influence training needs. **Organization analysis** is an examination of the environment, strategies, and resources of the organization to determine where training emphasis should be placed.

Economic and public policy issues influence training needs. For example, since the September 11 attacks, training of airport security personnel has increased substantially. It has also increased for flight crews of airlines, employees in the transportation industry, workers in nuclear power plants, and even security staff at theme parks.

According to Chris Rogers, senior consultant for loss control at Aon Corporation's National Entertainment Practices Group, there is an emphasis today on training theme park security in a tactic called "aggressive hospitality," which calls for staff to greet people and look them in the eye and offer to assist, rather than waiting to be approached by visitors. "This is one of the best and simplest security measures," he says. When staff members engage visitors, they become more aware of them. This heightened level of attention also discourages troublemakers from coming to the facility, because they generally go where they can remain anonymous.[5]

Other training issues tend to revolve around the strategic initiatives of an organization. Mergers and acquisitions, for example, frequently require that employees take on new roles and responsibilities and adjust to new cultures and ways of conducting business. Nowhere is this more prevalent than in grooming new leaders within organiza-

Organization analysis
Examination of the environment, strategies, and resources of the organization to determine where training emphasis should be placed

Highlights in HRM 6.3

NOTES ON RAPID NEEDS ASSESSMENT

NOTE 1: Look at Problem Scope. Common sense suggests that small, local matters may require less information gathering than big problems with a major impact on the organization. Ask managers a series of questions about the nature of the problem and its impact on the organization and gear your analysis accordingly.

NOTE 2: Do Organizational Scanning. Stay connected with what is going on in the organization in order to anticipate upcoming training needs. If a new technology is about to be launched, the need for training should take no one by surprise. In short, needs assessment isn't an event with a start-and-stop switch. It is the process of being engaged in your business.

NOTE 3: Play "Give and Take." Get the information you need, but don't drag your feet with excessive analysis before reporting back to managers. Show them that you are sensitive to their need for action by giving them updates on the information you have collected. If necessary, explain that better value may be gained by further analysis.

NOTE 4: Check "Lost and Found." Often, information gathered for a different purpose may bear on your training issue. Performance data (such as errors, sales, customer complaints) and staffing data (such as proficiency testing, turnover, absenteeism) can be very helpful as a starting point.

NOTE 5: Use Plain Talk. Instead of using clinical terms such as "analysis" or "assessment," use straight talk with managers that tells them what you are doing: (1) Identify the problem, (2) identify alternative ways to get there, (3) implement a solution based on cost/benefit concerns, and (4) determine the effectiveness and efficiency of the solution.

NOTE 6: Use the Web. Information technology allows you to communicate with others, perhaps setting up an electronic mailing list to post questions, synthesize responses, share resources, get feedback, gather information on trends, and the like.

NOTE 7: Use Rapid Prototyping. Often the most effective and efficient training is that which is "just-in-time, just enough, and just for me." Create a rapid prototype of a training program, evaluating and revising as you implement and learn more about the problems.

NOTE 8: Seek Out Exemplars. Find those in the organization who currently demonstrate the performance the organization wants. Bring others together with them to talk about the performance issues, and let the exemplars share their experiences and insights. This avoids the risk of packaging the wrong information, and people learn just what they need to know from each other.

Source: Condensed from Ron Zemke, "How to Do a Needs Assessment When You Think You Don't Have Time," *Training* 35, no. 3 (March 1998): 38–44. Bill Communications, Inc., Minneapolis, MN.

tions. Other issues such as technological change, globalization, re-engineering, and total quality management all influence the way work is done and the types of skills needed to do it. A study of 6000 Canadian organizations reported that about one-third had adopted new technology and about 40 percent had implemented an organizational change, primarily by re-engineering and downsizing.[6] Still other concerns may be more tactical but no less important in their impact on training. Organizational restructuring, downsizing, empowerment, and teamwork, for example, have immediate training requirements. Finally, trends in the workforce itself have an impact on training needs. As we mentioned in Chapter 1, employees increasingly value self-development and personal growth, and with this has come an enormous desire for learning. At the same time, as older workers near retirement, younger workers need to focus on gaining the skills and knowledge needed to take their place. Because no company in the private sector can count on stable employment levels, organizations as diverse as Inco and Boeing are facing situations in which they need to prepare the next generations of employees as the current groups approach retirement.

Side by side with forces that influence training needs, organization analysis involves close examination of the resources—technological, financial, and human—that are available to meet training objectives. Organizations typically collect data to use in the analysis, data such as information on direct and indirect labour costs, quality of goods or services, absenteeism, turnover, and number of accidents. The availability of potential replacements and the time required to train them are other important factors in organization analysis.

In recent years, as organizations continue to keep a tight rein on costs, training budgets are often constrained—even while organizations recognize the need for more and better training. To cope with resource constraints while contributing to strategic imperatives, managers have to be more focused and efficient with their training budgets. Companies such as Motorola, Ford, and Merck have found that by using information technology wisely, they cut their training budget by as much as 30 to 50 percent while keeping service levels high. In order to "do more with less," managers have to plan carefully where they will spend their training dollars, and this means doing rigorous organization analysis.

Other companies have outsourced their training programs to external partners in order to cut costs. However, evidence suggests that while many companies find they can provide equal or better service to employees in this way, surprisingly few actually reduce their training costs as a result.[7]

Task Analysis

Task analysis
Process of determining what the content of a training program should be on the basis of a study of the tasks and duties involved in the job

The second step in training-needs assessment is task analysis. **Task analysis** involves reviewing the job description and specification to identify the activities performed in a particular job and the KSAs needed to perform them. Task analysis often becomes more detailed than job analysis, but the overall purpose is to determine the exact content of the training program.

The first step in task analysis is to list all the tasks or duties included in the job. The second step is to list the steps performed by the employee to complete each task. Once the job is understood thoroughly, the type of performance required (such as speech, recall, discrimination, manipulation), along with the skills and knowledge necessary for performance, can be defined. For example, in the task of taking a chest x-ray, a radiologist correctly positions the patient (manipulation), gives special instructions (speech), and checks the proper distance of the x-ray tube from the patient (discrimination). The types of performance skills and knowledge that trainees need can be determined by observing and questioning skilled job holders and/or by reviewing job descriptions. This information helps trainers select program content and choose the most effective training method.

However, like job analysis, task analysis appears to be shifting from an emphasis on a fixed sequence of tasks to the more flexible sets of competencies required for superior performance. Companies such as the RBC Financial Group have found that as jobs change to a teamwork orientation, flexibility requires that employees adjust their behaviour as needed. **Competency assessment** focuses on the sets of skills and knowledge employees need to be successful, particularly for decision-oriented and knowledge-intensive jobs. While training programs based on work-oriented task analysis can become dated as work undergoes dynamic change, training programs based on competency assessment are more flexible and perhaps have more durability. The practice has been adopted extensively in the health care industry. Highlights in HRM 6.4 shows an example of a competency assessment used for designing training programs for public health professionals. The American Public Health Service has adopted the model as an infrastructure for training universal skills.[8]

Competency assessment
Analysis of the sets of skills and knowledge needed for decision-oriented and knowledge-intensive jobs

Person analysis
Determination of the specific individuals who need training

Person Analysis

Along with organization and task analyses, it is necessary to perform a person analysis. **Person analysis** involves determining which employees require training and, equally important, which do not. In this regard, person analysis is important for several reasons. First, thorough analysis helps organizations avoid the mistake of sending all employees into training when some do not need it. In addition, person analysis helps managers determine what prospective trainees are able to do when they enter training so that the programs can be designed to emphasize the areas in which they are deficient.

Companies such as Hewlett-Packard use performance appraisal information as an input for person analysis. However, while performance appraisals may reveal who is not meeting expectations, it typically does not reveal why. If performance deficiencies are due to ability problems, training is likely a good intervention. However, if performance deficiencies are due to poor motivation or factors outside an employee's control, training may not be the answer. Ultimately, managers have to sit down with employees to talk about areas for improvement so that they can jointly determine the developmental approaches that will have maximum benefit.[9]

PHOTODISC

Person analysis helps determine the abilities of trainees before entering a training program.

Highlights in HRM 6.4

COMPETENCY ASSESSMENT FOR TRAINING PUBLIC HEALTH WORKERS

▶ Analytic discipline
　Determining appropriate use of data and statistical methods
　Making relevant inferences from data
▶ Communications discipline
　Communicating effectively both in writing and orally
　Presenting accurately and effectively demographic, statistical, programmatic, and scientific information for professional and lay audiences
▶ Policy and program-planning discipline
　Developing mechanisms to monitor and evaluate programs (effectiveness, quality)
▶ Culture discipline
　Developing and adapting approaches that take into account cultural differences
▶ Basic science discipline
　Understanding research methods in all basic public health sciences
　Applying the basic public health sciences, including behavioural and social sciences, biostatistics, epidemiology, environmental public health, and prevention of chronic and infectious diseases and injuries
▶ Finance and management discipline
　Monitoring program performance
▶ Orientation to public health
　Public health process
　Core functions and essential services
　Ethics and values of public health
　Legal basis of public health

Source: Margaret Potter, Christine Pistella, Carl Fertman, and Virginia Dato, "Needs Assessment and a Model Agenda for Training the Public Health Workforce," *American Journal of Public Health* 90, no. 8 (August 2000): 1294–96.

PHASE 2: DESIGNING THE TRAINING PROGRAM

Once the training needs have been determined, the next step is to design the type of learning environment necessary to enhance learning. The success of training programs depends on more than the organization's ability to identify training needs. Success hinges on taking the information gained from needs analysis and utilizing it to design first-rate training programs. Experts believe that training design should focus on at least four related issues: (1) instructional objectives, (2) trainee readiness and motivation, (3) principles of learning, and (4) characteristics of instructors.

Instructional Objectives

As a result of conducting organization, task, and person analyses, managers will have a more complete picture of the training needs. On the basis of this information, they can more formally state the desired outcomes of training through written instructional objectives. Generally, **instructional objectives** describe the skills or knowledge to be acquired and/or the attitudes to be changed. One type of instructional objective, the performance-centred objective, is widely used because it lends itself to an unbiased evaluation of results. For example, the stated objective for one training program might be "Employees trained in team methods will be able to perform these different jobs within six months." Performance-centred objectives typically include precise terms, such as "to calculate," "to repair," "to adjust," "to construct," "to assemble," and "to classify."

Robert Mager, an internationally known training expert, emphasizes the importance of instructional objectives by noting that "before you prepare for instruction, before you select instructional procedures or subject matter or material, it is important to be able to state clearly just what you intend the results of that instruction to be. A clear statement of instructional objectives will provide a sound basis for choosing methods and materials and for selecting the means for assessing whether the instruction will be successful."[10]

Instructional objectives
Desired outcomes of a training program

Trainee Readiness and Motivation

Two preconditions for learning affect the success of those who are to receive training: readiness and motivation. *Trainee readiness* refers to both maturity and experience factors in the trainee's background. Prospective trainees should be screened to determine that they have the background knowledge and the skills necessary to absorb what will be presented to them. Recognizing individual differences in readiness is as important in organizational training as it is in any other teaching situation. It is often desirable to group individuals according to their capacity to learn, as determined by test scores, and to provide an alternative type of instruction for those who need it.

The receptiveness and readiness of participants in training programs can be increased by having them complete questionnaires about why they are attending training and what they hope to accomplish. Participants may also be asked to give copies of their completed questionnaires to their managers.

The other precondition for learning is *trainee motivation*. Individuals who are conscientious, goal-oriented, self-disciplined, and persevering are more likely to perceive a link between the effort they put into training and higher performance on the job. For optimum learning to take place, trainees must recognize the need for new knowledge or skills, and they must maintain a desire to learn as training progresses. By focusing on the trainees themselves rather than on the trainer or training topic, managers can create a training environment that is conducive to learning. Six strategies can be essential:

1. Use positive reinforcement.
2. Eliminate threats and punishment.
3. Be flexible.
4. Have participants set personal goals.
5. Design interesting instruction.
6. Break down physical and psychological obstacles to learning.[11]

While most employees are motivated by certain common needs, they differ from one another in the relative importance of these needs at any given time. For example, new college graduates often have a high desire for advancement, and they have established specific goals for career progression. Training objectives that are clearly related to trainees' individual needs will increase the motivation of employees to succeed in training programs. Some employees are so motivated that they take training on their own time, often at their own costs. About 80 percent of organizations have a tuition reimbursement program, and only 25 percent of these require that the employee stay with the company after completion of the program. Most employers feel that these programs enhance retention of employees.[12]

Principles of Learning

As we move from needs assessment and instructional objectives to employee readiness and motivation, we shift from a focus on the organization to a focus on employees. Ultimately, training has to build a bridge between employees and the organization. One important step in this transition is giving full consideration to the psychological principles of learning, that is, the characteristics of training programs that help employees grasp new material, make sense of it in their own lives, and transfer it back to the job.

Because the success or failure of a training program is frequently related to certain principles of learning, managers as well as employees should understand that different training methods or techniques vary in the extent to which they utilize these principles. All things considered, training programs are likely to be more effective if they incorporate the principles of learning shown in Figure 6.5.

Goal Setting

The value of goal setting for focusing and motivating behaviour extends into training. When trainers take the time to explain the goals and objectives to trainees—or when trainees are encouraged to set goals on their own—the level of interest, understanding, and effort directed toward training is likely to increase. In some cases, goal setting can simply take the form of a "road map" of the course or program, its objectives, and learning points.[13]

Meaningfulness of Presentation

One principle of learning is that the material to be learned should be presented in as meaningful a manner as possible. Quite simply, trainees are better able to learn new information (from training) if they can connect it with things that are already familiar to them. Trainers frequently use colourful examples to which trainees can relate. The examples make the material meaningful. In addition, material should be arranged so that each experience builds upon preceding ones. In this way, trainees are able to integrate the experiences into a usable pattern of knowledge and skills.

Modelling

The old saying "A picture is worth a thousand words" applies to training. Just as examples increase the meaningfulness of factual material or new knowledge in a training environment, modelling increases the salience of behavioural training. Work by Albert Bandura and others on social learning theory underscores the point that we learn vic-

Figure 6.5	Principles of Learning

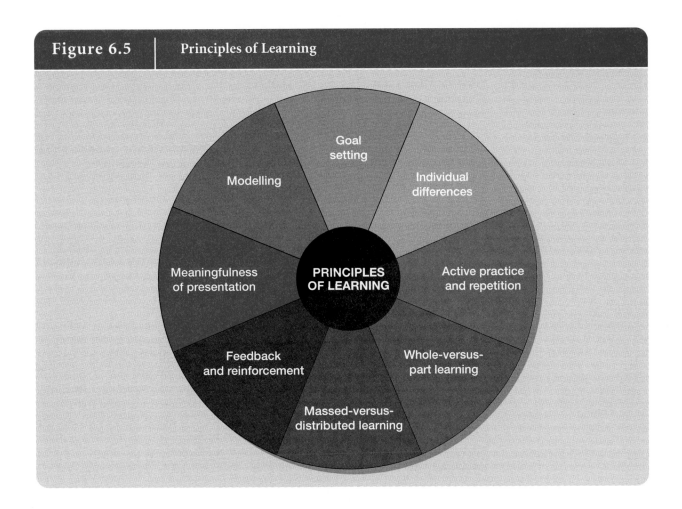

ariously. Quite simply, we learn by watching. For example, if you were learning to ride a horse, it would be much easier to watch someone do it—and then try it yourself—than to read a book or listen to a lecture and hope you can do it right.[14]

Modelling can take many forms. For example, real-life demonstrations or video-tapes are often helpful; even pictures and drawings can get the visual message across. The point is that modelling demonstrates the desired behaviour or method to be learned. In some cases, modelling the wrong behaviour can even be helpful if it shows trainees what not to do and then clarifies the appropriate behaviour.

Individual Differences

People learn at different rates and in different ways. For example, some individuals can remember new information after hearing it only once (echoic memory) or seeing it only once (iconic memory). Others may have to work longer or find other techniques for retrieving the information, but this may have nothing to do with their intelligence. Some students do horribly in large lecture settings but then excel in small discussion classes. Others may have the opposite ability. To the extent possible, training programs should try to account for and accommodate these individual differences in order to facilitate each person's style and rate of learning.[15]

Active Practice and Repetition
Those things we do daily become a part of our repertoire of skills. Trainees should be given frequent opportunity to practise their job tasks in the way that they will ultimately be expected to perform them. The individual who is being taught how to operate a machine should have an opportunity to practise on it. The manager who is being taught how to train should be given supervised practice in training.

In some cases, the value of practice is that it causes behaviours to become second nature. For example, when you first learned to drive a car, you focused a great deal on the mechanics: "Where are my hands, where are my feet, how fast am I going?" As you practised driving, you began to think less about the mechanics and more about the road, the weather, and the traffic. Other forms of learning are no different—by practising, a trainee can forget about distinct behaviours and concentrate on the subtleties of how they are used.

Whole-versus-Part Learning
Most jobs and tasks can be broken down into parts that lend themselves to further analysis. Determining the most effective manner for completing each part then provides a basis for giving specific instruction. Typing, for example, is made up of several skills that are part of the total process. The typist starts by learning the proper use of each finger; eventually, with practice, the individual finger movements become integrated into a total pattern. Practice by moving individual fingers is an example of part learning. In evaluating whole-versus-part learning, it is necessary to consider the nature of the task to be learned. If the task can be broken down successfully, it probably should be broken down to facilitate learning; otherwise, it should probably be taught as a unit.

Massed-versus-Distributed Learning
Another factor that determines the effectiveness of training is the amount of time devoted to practice in one session. Should trainees be given training in five two-hour periods or in ten one-hour periods? It has been found in most cases that spacing out the training will result in faster learning and longer retention. This is the principle of *distributed learning*. Since the efficiency of the distribution will vary with the type and complexity of the task, managers should refer to the rapidly growing body of research in this area when they require guidance in designing a specific training situation.

Feedback and Reinforcement
Can any learning occur without feedback? Some feedback comes from self-monitoring while other feedback comes from trainers, fellow trainees, and the like. As an employee's training progresses, feedback serves two related purposes: (1) knowledge of results and (2) motivation.

The informational aspects of feedback help individuals focus on what they are doing right and what they are doing wrong. In this way, feedback serves a "shaping" role in helping individuals approach the objectives of training. Think about when you first learned how to throw a baseball, ride a bicycle, or swim. Someone, perhaps a parent, told you what you were doing right and what things to correct. As you did, you perhaps got better.

In addition to its informational aspects, feedback also serves an important motivational role. At times, progress in training, measured by either mistakes or successes, may be plotted on a chart commonly referred to as a "learning curve." Figure 6.6 presents an example of a learning curve common in the acquisition of many job skills. In many learning situations there are times when progress does not occur. Such periods show up on the curve as a fairly straight horizontal line called a *plateau*. A plateau may be the result of reduced motivation or of ineffective methods of task performance. It is a natural phenomenon of learning, and there is usually a spontaneous recovery, as Figure 6.6 shows.

Verbal encouragement or more extrinsic rewards may help to reinforce desired behaviour over time. At times, reinforcement is simply the feeling of accomplishment that follows successful performance. (In some cases it may be impossible to distinguish between feedback and rewards.) Reinforcement is generally most effective when it occurs immediately after a task has been performed.

Behaviour modification
Technique that operates on the principle that behaviour that is rewarded, or positively reinforced, will be exhibited more frequently in the future, whereas behaviour that is penalized or unrewarded will decrease in frequency

In recent years some work organizations have used **behaviour modification,** a technique that operates on the principle that behaviour that is rewarded—positively reinforced—will be exhibited more frequently in the future, whereas behaviour that is penalized or unrewarded will decrease in frequency. For example, in safety training it is possible to identify "safe" behavioural profiles—that is, actions that ensure fewer accidents—as well as unsafe profiles. As a follow-up to training, or as part of the training itself, managers can use relatively simple rewards to encourage and maintain desired behaviour. Companies have found that nothing more than words of encouragement and feedback are needed to strengthen the behaviours required and desired from training. Other more formal rewards such as awards and ceremonies may prove useful as well. However, the idea with behaviour modification is that behaviour can be motivated and gradually shaped toward the desired profile using reinforcement.[16]

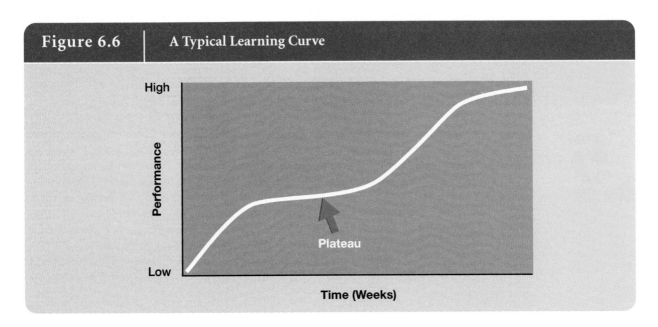

Figure 6.6 | **A Typical Learning Curve**

Characteristics of Instructors

The success of any training effort will depend in large part on the teaching skills and personal characteristics of those responsible for conducting the training. What separates good trainers from mediocre ones? Often a good trainer is one who shows a little more effort or demonstrates more instructional preparation. However, training is also influenced by the trainer's personal manner and characteristics. Here is a short list of desirable traits:

1. *Knowledge of subject.* Employees expect trainers to know their job or subject thoroughly. Furthermore, they are expected to demonstrate that knowledge (what some experts call "active intelligence").

2. *Adaptability.* Some individuals learn faster or slower than others, and instruction should be matched to the trainee's learning ability.

3. *Sincerity.* Trainees appreciate sincerity in trainers. Along with this, trainers need to be patient with trainees and demonstrate tact in addressing their concerns.

4. *Sense of humour.* Learning can be fun; very often a point can be made with a story or anecdote.

5. *Interest.* Good trainers have a keen interest in the subject they are teaching; this interest is readily conveyed to trainees.

6. *Clear instructions.* Naturally, training is accomplished more quickly and retained longer when trainers give clear instructions.

7. *Individual assistance.* When training more than one employee, successful trainers always provide individual assistance.

8. *Enthusiasm.* A dynamic presentation and a vibrant personality show trainees that the trainer enjoys training; employees tend to respond positively to an enthusiastic climate.[17]

For training programs to be most successful, organizations should reward managers who prove to be excellent trainers. Too often managers are not recognized for their contributions to this important aspect of HRM. Likewise, training specialists in the HR function should be recognized for their role in the training program.

Phase 3: Implementing the Training Program

objective

Despite the importance of needs assessment, instructional objectives, principles of learning, and the like, choices regarding instructional methods are where "the rubber meets the road" in implementing a training program. A major consideration in choosing among various training methods is determining which ones are appropriate for the KSAs to be learned. For example, if the material is mostly factual, methods such as lecture, classroom, or programmed instruction may be fine. However, if the training involves a large behavioural component, other methods such as on-the-job training, simulation, or computer-based training might work better.[18]

In order to organize our discussion of various training methods, we will break them down into two primary groups: those used for nonmanagerial employees and those used for managers.

Training Methods for Nonmanagerial Employees

A wide variety of methods are available for training employees at all levels. Some methods have a long history of usage. Newer methods have emerged over the years out of a greater understanding of human behaviour, particularly in the areas of learning, motivation, and interpersonal relationships. More recently, technological advances, especially in computer hardware and software, have resulted in training devices that in many instances are more effective and economical than the traditional training methods.

On-the-Job Training

On-the-job training (OJT)
Method by which employees are given hands-on experience with instructions from their supervisor or other trainer

By far, the most common method used for training nonmanagerial employees is **on-the-job training (OJT)**. In fact, one estimate suggests that organizations spend three to six times more on OJT than on classroom training. OJT has the advantage of providing hands-on experience under normal working conditions and an opportunity for the trainer—a manager or senior employee—to build good relationships with new employees. As time becomes a critical resource—and "just-in-time training" is needed most—OJT is viewed by some to be potentially the most effective means of facilitating learning in the workplace.[19]

Although it is used by all types of organizations, OJT is often one of the most poorly implemented training methods. Three common drawbacks are (1) the lack of a well-structured training environment, (2) poor training skills of managers, and (3) the absence of well-defined job performance criteria. To overcome these problems, training experts suggest the following:

1. Develop realistic goals and/or measures for each OJT area.
2. Plan a specific training schedule for each trainee, including set periods for evaluation and feedback.
3. Help managers establish a nonthreatening atmosphere conducive to learning.
4. Conduct periodic evaluations, after training is completed, to prevent regression.[20]

Highlights in HRM 6.5 shows the basic steps of an OJT program. The method is used frequently in organizations to ensure that new employees have adequate guidance before taking on work responsibilities on their own. For example, KLM Royal Dutch Airlines uses OJT to train cabin attendants in customer service. The airline started an experimental program that places cabin attendant trainees in the classroom for a certain period and then gives them additional training during an evaluation flight. On these flights, experienced cabin attendants provide the trainees with OJT, based on a list of identified job tasks. Some tasks, such as serving meals and snacks, are demonstrated during the actual delivery of services to passengers. Other tasks are presented to trainees away from passengers between meal service.[21]

Apprenticeship Training

Apprenticeship training
System of training in which a worker entering the skilled trades is given thorough instruction and experience, both on and off the job, in the practical and theoretical aspects of the work

An extension of OJT is **apprenticeship training**. With this method, individuals entering an industry, particularly in the skilled trades such as machinist, laboratory technician, or electrician, are given thorough instruction and experience, both on and

Highlights in HRM 6.5

THE PROPER WAY TO DO ON-THE-JOB TRAINING

P

Prepare. Decide what employees need to be taught. Identify the best sequence or steps of the training. Decide how best to demonstrate these steps. Have materials, resources, and equipment ready.

R

Reassure. Put each employee at ease. Learn about his or her prior experience, and adjust accordingly. Try to get the employee interested, relaxed, and motivated to learn.

O

Orient. Show the employee the correct way to do the job. Explain why it is done this way. Discuss how it relates to other jobs. Let him or her ask lots of questions.

P

Perform. When employees are ready, let them try the job themselves. Give them an opportunity to practise the job and guide them through rough spots. Provide help and assistance at first, then less as they continue.

E

Evaluate. Check the employees' performance, and question them on how, why, when, and where they should do something. Correct errors; repeat instructions.

R

Reinforce and Review. Provide praise and encouragement, and give feedback about how the employee is doing. Continue the conversation and express confidence in his or her doing the job.

off the job, in the practical and theoretical aspects of the work. Many former fishermen left the declining East Coast fishery to join in a seafarers' training program funded by several companies, the federal government, and the Nova Scotia government to learn new skills working in the engine rooms of larger vessels. Magna International, the auto parts giant, pays students $8 to $15 per hour to train as millwrights and tool and die makers. Learning is offered variously in shops, laboratories, and classrooms.

Cooperative Training, Internships, and Governmental Training

Cooperative training
Training program that combines practical on-the-job experience with formal educational classes

Similar to apprenticeships, **cooperative training** programs combine practical on-the-job experience with formal classes. However, the term *cooperative training* is typically used in connection with high school and college programs that incorporate part- or full-time experiences. In recent years there has been an increased effort to expand opportunities that combine on-the-job skill training with regular classroom training so that students can pursue either technical work or a college degree program. Workplace education programs developed jointly by employers and unions can have a number of benefits as outlined in Highlights in HRM 6.6.

Highlights in HRM 6.6

WORKFORCE DEVELOPMENT

Joint training programs give workers, employers, and unions a wide range of benefits.

Benefits for the Employer	Benefits for the Union	Benefits for the Workers
Improved customer service	Improved quality of work	Improved quality of work
Improved quality of work	Improved attitude toward the union	Fewer errors
Increased productivity	Greater appreciation of learning	Increased productivity
Fewer errors	Better communication with other union members	Better communication with co-workers and managers
Better understanding of job tasks	Increased application of skills in union activities	Better understanding of job tasks
Greater appreciation of learning	Better understanding of union activities	Greater appreciation of learning

Source: M. Bloom and A. Campbell, *Success by Design: What Works in Workforce Development*, The Conference Board of Canada, December 2002.

Internship programs
Programs jointly sponsored by colleges, universities, and other organizations that offer students the opportunity to gain real-life experience while allowing them to find out how they will perform in work organizations

Internship programs, jointly sponsored by colleges, universities, and a variety of organizations, offer students the chance to get real-world experience while finding out how they will perform in work organizations. Highlights in HRM 6.7 shows how to make the most from internship opportunities.[22]

Classroom Instruction

When most people think about training, they think about classrooms. There is good reason for this. Beyond its pervasiveness in education, classroom training enables the maximum number of trainees to be handled by the minimum number of instructors. This method lends itself particularly to training in areas where information can be presented in lectures, demonstrations, films, and videotapes or through computer instruction. Where it is not possible to obtain videotapes, audiotapes can be very valuable. For example, to instruct flight-crew trainees, airlines might play a cockpit tape taken from a doomed aircraft. After listening to the tape, the trainees discuss the behaviour of the crew during the crisis. By listening to the recorded statements of others and observing their failure to operate as a team, pilot trainees will develop an understanding of the need for balancing their sense of self-reliance with an ability to listen to subordinates.

A special type of classroom facility is used in *vestibule training*. Trainees are given instruction in the operation of equipment like that found in operating departments. Perhaps you have been given instructions on using a new computer system in a classroom/lab setting. In this way, vestibule training emphasizes instruction rather than production.

USING THE INTERNET

Career Edge helps students with the transition from school to work by arranging paid internships:

http://overview.careeredge.ca/index.asp?FirstTime=True&context=0&FromContext=1&language=1

Highlights in HRM 6.7

MAKING THE MOST OF INTERNSHIPS

Today, many colleges and universities encourage students to apply for internships as part of the curriculum. Done well, internships provide advantages to students, universities, and potential employers.

Benefits for Students
Those who intern with organizations before graduation have higher starting salaries, more job offers, a shorter time to obtain their first position, faster movement into jobs with more prestige, greater challenges and financial rewards, and faster promotion. They are better prepared for the world of work.

Benefits for Community Colleges and Universities
Internships help colleges get in touch with the marketplace. As students succeed in the workplace, student recruitment improves. Strong internship programs increase the retention of students and their placement after graduation.

Benefits for Potential Employers
Interns can provide your organization with competent assistance without a large financial outlay. Internships also let organizations evaluate a prospective employee nearly risk-free. At the end of the internship, there are no obligations to continue the relationship, but if it's a good match the organization has a leg up on hiring the person—it eliminates recruitment expenses and greatly reduces the cost per hire.

How to Increase the Value of Interns
To increase the internal value of your internship programs, take the following steps:
1. Assign the intern to projects that are accomplishable, and provide training as required.
2. Involve the intern in the project planning process.
3. Appoint a mentor or supervisor to guide the intern.
4. Invite project suggestions from other staff members.
5. Ask interns to keep a journal of their work activities.
6. Rotate interns throughout the organization.
7. Explain the rationale behind work assignments.
8. Hold interns accountable for projects and deadlines.
9. Treat interns as part of the organizational staff, and invite them to staff meetings.
10. Establish a process for considering interns for permanent hire.

Source: Condensed from John Byrd and Rob Poole, "Highly Motivated Employees at No Cost? It's Not an Impossible Dream," *Nonprofit World* 19, no. 6 (November/December 2001): 312–32.

Programmed Instruction

One method of instruction that is particularly good for allowing individuals to work at their own pace is programmed instruction. Programmed instruction—increasingly referred to as *self-directed learning*—involves the use of books, manuals, or computers to break down subject matter content into highly organized, logical sequences that demand continuous response on the part of the trainee. After being presented with a small segment of information, the trainee is required to answer a question, either by writing it in a response frame or by pushing a button. If the response is correct, the trainee is told so and is presented with the next step (frame) in the material. If the response is incorrect, further explanatory information is given and the trainee is told to try again.

A major advantage of programmed instruction is that it incorporates a number of the established learning principles discussed earlier in the chapter. With programmed instruction, training is individualized, trainees are actively involved in the instructional process, and feedback and reinforcement are immediate. While programmed instruction may not increase the amount an individual learns, it typically increases the speed at which he or she learns.[23]

Audiovisual Methods

To teach skills and procedures for many production jobs, certain audiovisual devices can be used. At the simplest level, videotapes are often used to illustrate the steps in a procedure such as assembling electronic equipment or working with a problem employee. Using camcorders permits trainers and trainees to view an on-the-spot recording and to get immediate feedback about progress toward learning objectives. Golf and tennis coaches frequently tape their students to let them see their mistakes. RBC Financial Group uses videoconferencing extensively, broadcasting about forty hours of programming per month. All 1300 branches across Canada are hooked by satellite, and the employees can listen to the keynote speaker, see slides and video presentations, ask questions, and take multi-choice tests.[24]

Other technologies, such as CDs and DVDs, take audiovisual technology further by providing trainees with interactive capability. Students can access any segment of the instructional program, which is especially useful for individualized instruction when employees have different levels of knowledge and ability. Such technology is currently used to teach doctors to diagnose illness, to help dairy farmers increase productivity, and to teach CPR trainees to revive victims of heart attacks. More recent applications tackle the difficult managerial skills of leadership, supervision, and interpersonal relations.

Computer-Based Training and E-Learning

As development of technology proceeds at a rapid pace and the cost of computers continues to decline, technology-based training methods are finding increased use in industry, academia, and the military. In 2001, about four out of ten organizations were using e-learning, and there are estimates that 90 percent of all new training will be Internet-based by 2005. Forty percent of employees said they preferred e-learning to classroom training. E-learning has helped cut Bell Nexxia's annual training budget by about 40 percent, largely because of savings in the cost of developing courses, and

Computer-assisted instruction (CAI)
    System that delivers instructional materials directly through a computer terminal in an interactive format

Computer-managed instruction (CMI)
    System normally employed in conjunction with CAI that uses a computer to generate and score tests and to determine the level of training proficiency

paying for travel and accommodations. Courses that once consumed eight hours of class time can be taught in ninety minutes, leaving employees more time to spend at work.[25] Computer-based training (CBT) encompasses two distinct techniques: computer-assisted instruction and computer-managed instruction. A **computer-assisted instruction (CAI)** system delivers training materials directly through a computer terminal in an interactive format. Computers make it possible to provide drill and practice, problem solving, simulation, gaming forms of instruction, and certain very sophisticated forms of individualized tutorial instruction.

A **computer-managed instruction (CMI)** system is normally used in conjunction with CAI, thereby providing an efficient means of managing the training function. CMI uses a computer to generate and score tests and to determine the level of trainee proficiency. CMI systems can also track the performance of trainees and direct them to appropriate study material to meet their specific needs. With CMI, the computer takes on some of the routine aspects of training, freeing the instructor to spend time on course development or individualized instruction. Additionally, when the CBT is structured in a way that makes it available to employees on the job whenever they need it, it is referred to as "just-in-time" training.

Increasingly, organizations are using the Internet or their own intranet to conduct training online. Known more generally as *e-learning,* web-based training programs are beginning to replace stand-alone CBT systems. (An e-learning version of this course can be purchased at www.captus.com.) Merck has developed a "blended" approach that combines traditional classroom experiences with web-based e-learning opportunities. In association with Forum Corporation, Merck piloted the use of an online 360-degree diagnostic tool called Performance Compass for its Leadership Development Program. The tool helps managers assess their developmental needs and then connects them to a wide array of external training and educational resources. Similarly, Merck worked with Developmental Dimensions International (DDI) to implement the On-line Performance and Learning (OPAL) system, which provides coaching tips and learning tools and resources for employees and managers.[26]

Systems such as these don't necessarily replace conventional learning experiences, but they transform the learning process in several ways. First, individuals can search through a virtual sea of information and customize their own learning. This dramatically reduces employee research time, not to mention the cost savings associated with producing and distributing typical hard-copy reference material. But more important, systems such as these facilitate just-in-time skill development by bringing the training to the employees, rather than vice versa. In their most advanced forms, *performance support systems (PSSs)* use artificial intelligence and hypermedia to provide just the help a performer needs to do a job, just when the performer needs it, and in just the form in which he or she needs it.

Although systems can be very sophisticated, they need not be overly expensive. Web-based training can be revised rapidly, thereby providing continuously updated training material. This not only makes it easier and cheaper to revise training curricula, it saves travel and classroom costs. When combined with other communications technology such as e-mail, teleconferencing, videoconferencing, groupware, and the like, web-based training becomes almost indistinguishable from real-time management. A summary of these advantages includes the following:

▶ Learning is self-paced.
▶ Training comes to the employee.
▶ Training is interactive.
▶ New employees do not have to wait for a scheduled training session.
▶ Training can focus on specific needs as revealed by built-in tests.
▶ Trainees can be referred to online help or written material.
▶ It is easier to revise a computer program than to change classroom-training materials.
▶ Record keeping is facilitated.
▶ The program can be linked to video presentations.
▶ The training can be cost-effective if used for a large number of employees.

One caveat of web-based training applications bears mentioning: Some have suggested there is a potential downside in that Internet users, in general, tend to "surf." Given the sometimes nondirect format of the Internet, it may be a challenge to focus trainee interaction. Of course, this could be an advantage as well. The Internet requires that users become adept at searching, comparing, and making sense of a large amount of information. These skills are particularly important for building other skills: troubleshooting, problem solving, and analytical thinking.

Simulation Method

Sometimes it is either impractical or unwise to train employees on the actual equipment used on the job. An obvious example is training employees to operate aircraft, spacecraft, and other highly technical and expensive equipment. The simulation method emphasizes realism in equipment and its operation at minimum cost and maximum safety. For example, before the launch of its first edition, the *National Post* used simulations to train a new workforce, by requiring them to produce a mock newspaper with real content and deadlines.

Air Canada uses a technologically advanced simulator to train its pilots. The sophistication of simulation training centres such as Air Canada's are certainly impressive, but as information technology becomes more powerful the distinction between simulation and the simpler CBT is beginning to blur. For example, a simulation developed by Wicat in partnership with Airbus and Singapore Airlines runs on a PC and replicates a cockpit with control displays and throttle/flap controls. Even though the PC-based simulation is relatively inexpensive, it is powerful. Pilots are taken through a self-paced program that simulates "taxi, takeoff, climb, cruise, descent, approach, landing, and go-around." These types of technologies are making it easier to offer training in new and different ways. Denny Schmidt, director of training and development for Delta Airlines, has stated that his company's goal is to deliver simulation training to employees at their homes. Given advances in telecommunications, the possibilities seem limitless.[27]

USING THE INTERNET

The Canadian Society for Training and Development (formerly the Ontario Society for Training and Development) has an online training tool kit:

www.ostd.ca/resources/tca_specs.html

The simulation method replicates reality.

© ROGER RESSMEYER/CORBIS/MAGMAPHOTO.COM

Training Methods for Management Development

While many of the methods used to train first-level employees are also used to train managers and supervisors, other methods tend to be reserved for management development. Recall that development differs somewhat from training in that its purpose is to broaden an individual's experience and provide a longer-term view of that individual's role in the organization. Over the past decade, the importance of management development has grown as organizations attempt to compete through people. Organizational change and strategic revitalization depend on talented leaders, managers, and supervisors. Management development is instrumental for giving managers the skills and perspectives they need to be successful.[28]

As with training for nonmanagerial employees, the methods used for management development differ in the principles of learning they incorporate and their appropriateness for delivering various KSAs.

On-the-Job Experiences

Some skills and knowledge can be acquired just by listening and observing or by reading. But others must be acquired through actual practice and experience. By presenting managers with the opportunities to perform under pressure and to learn from their mistakes, on-the-job development experiences are some of the most powerful and commonly used techniques.

However, just as on-the-job training for first-level employees can be problematic if not well planned, on-the-job management development should be well organized, supervised, and challenging to the participants. Methods of providing on-the-job experiences include the following:

1. *Coaching* involves a continuing flow of instructions, comments, and suggestions from the manager to the subordinate. (*Mentoring,* discussed in Chapter 7, is a similar approach to personal and informal management development.)

2. *Understudy assignments* groom an individual to take over a manager's job by gaining experience in handling important functions of the job.

3. *Job rotation* provides, through a variety of work experiences, the broadened knowledge and understanding required to manage more effectively.

4. *Lateral transfer* involves horizontal movement through different departments, along with upward movement in the organization.

5. *Special projects* and *junior boards* provide an opportunity for individuals to become involved in the study of current organizational problems and in planning and decision-making activities.

6. *Action learning* gives managers release time to work full-time on projects with others in the organization. In some cases, action learning is combined with classroom instruction, discussions, and conferences.

7. *Staff meetings* enable participants to become more familiar with problems and events occurring outside their immediate area by exposing them to the ideas and thinking of other managers.

8. *Planned career progressions* (discussed in Chapter 7) use all these different methods to provide employees with the training and development necessary to progress through a series of jobs requiring higher and higher levels of knowledge and/or skills.[29]

Although these methods are used most often to develop managers for higher-level positions, they also provide valuable experiences for those who are being groomed for other types of positions in the organization. And while on-the-job experiences constitute the core of management training and development, other off-the-job methods of development can be used to supplement these experiences.

Seminars and Conferences

Seminars and conferences, like classroom instruction, are useful for bringing groups of people together for training and development. In management development, seminars and conferences can be used to communicate ideas, policies, or procedures, but they are also good for raising points of debate or discussing issues (usually with the help of a qualified leader) that have no set answers or resolutions. In this regard, seminars and conferences are often used when attitude change is a goal. Nearly every provincial HR association offers seminars and conferences to ensure that their members are current.

Case Studies

A particularly useful method used in classroom learning situations is the case study. Using documented examples, participants learn how to analyze (take apart) and synthesize (put together) facts, to become conscious of the many variables on which management decisions are based, and, in general, to improve their decision-making skills. Experienced educators and trainers generally point out that the case study is most appropriate where

1. Analytic, problem-solving, and critical thinking skills are most important.
2. The KSAs are complex and participants need time to master them.
3. Active participation is desired.
4. The process of learning (questioning, interpreting, and so on) is as important as the content.
5. Team problem solving and interaction are possible.[30]

Even in situations in which case studies may be appropriate, they are often mismanaged. As with any other development technique, implementation is crucial for effectiveness.

Management Games

Training experiences have been brought to life and made more interesting through the development of management games, where players are faced with the task of making a series of decisions affecting a hypothetical organization. The effects that every decision has on each area within the organization can be simulated with a computer programmed for the game. A major advantage of this technique is the high degree of participation it requires.

Games are now widely used as a management development method. Many of them have been designed for general use but more recently have been adapted for specific industries. Bell Canada has its managers play the game of TeleSim, a computer simulation for the telecommunications industry developed by Thinking Tools Inc. and Coopers & Lybrand Consulting to teach executives how to act in an increasingly open, competitive market.[31]

As the development of industry-specific games has increased, there are now simulations for a wide variety of organizations. For example, Lufthansa Airlines has partnered with Unicon Management Systems to develop a management game called General Airline Management Simulation. The three-day event is used as part of a management development program to teach participants business issues related to competition. Managers working in teams compete with one another running fictitious airline companies and have to balance issues of routing, schedules, costs, profits, and the like.[32] Practitioners in the area of management training have come to realize that extensive preparation, planning, and debriefing are needed to realize the potential benefits of this method.

Role Playing

Role playing consists of assuming the attitudes and behaviour—that is, playing the role—of others, often a supervisor and a subordinate who are involved in a particular problem. By acting out another's position, participants in the role playing can improve their ability to understand and cope with others. Role playing should also help them to learn how to counsel others by helping them see situations from a different point of view. Role playing is used widely in training health care professionals to be empathic and sensitive to the concerns of patients. It is also used widely in training managers to handle employee issues relating to absenteeism, performance appraisal, and conflict situations.

At times, participants may be hesitant to try role playing. Successful role play takes planning. Instructors should

1. Ensure that members of the group are comfortable with each other.
2. Select and prepare the role players by introducing a specific situation.
3. Help participants prepare by asking them to describe potential characters.
4. Realize that volunteers make better role players.
5. Prepare the observers by giving them specific tasks (such as evaluation or feedback).
6. Guide the role-play enactment through its bumps (since it is not scripted).
7. Keep it short.
8. Discuss the enactment and prepare bulleted points of what was learned.[33]

Role play is a versatile teaching model, applicable to a variety of training experiences. Planned and implemented correctly, role play can bring realism and insight into dilemmas and experiences that otherwise might not be shared.

Behaviour Modelling

One technique that combines several different training methods, and therefore various principles of learning, is the behaviour modelling technique. **Behaviour modelling** involves four basic components:

Behaviour modelling
Approach that demonstrates desired behaviour and gives trainees the chance to practise and role-play those behaviours and receive feedback

1. *Learning points.* At the beginning of instruction, the essential goals and objectives of the program are enumerated. In some cases, the learning points are a sequence of behaviours that are to be taught. For example, the learning points might describe the recommended steps for giving employees feedback.
2. *Model.* Participants view films or videotapes in which a model manager is portrayed dealing with an employee in an effort to improve his or her performance. The model shows specifically how to deal with the situation and demonstrates the learning points.
3. *Practice and role play.* Trainees participate in extensive rehearsal of the behaviours demonstrated by the models. The greatest percentage of training time is spent in these skill-practice sessions.
4. *Feedback and reinforcement.* As the trainee's behaviour increasingly resembles that of the model, the trainer and other trainees provide social reinforcers such as praise, approval, encouragement, and attention. Videotaping behaviour rehearsals provides feedback and reinforcement. Emphasis throughout the training period is placed on transferring the training to the job.

Does behaviour modelling work? Several controlled studies have demonstrated success in helping managers interact with employees, handle discipline, introduce change, and increase productivity.[34]

PHASE 4: EVALUATING THE TRAINING PROGRAM

objective

Training, like any other HRM function, should be evaluated to determine its effectiveness. A variety of methods are available to assess the extent to which training programs improve learning, affect behaviour on the job, and have an impact on the bottom-line performance of an organization. Unfortunately, few organizations adequately evaluate their training programs. In many ways, this goes beyond poor management; it is poor business practice. Given the substantial monetary stake that organizations have in training, it would seem prudent that managers would want to maximize the return on that investment.

Figure 6.7 shows that four basic criteria are available to evaluate training: (1) reactions, (2) learning, (3) behaviour, and (4) results. Some of these criteria are easier to measure than others, but each is important in that it provides different information about the success of the programs. The combination of these criteria can give a total picture of the training program in order to help managers decide where problem areas lie, what to change about the program, and whether to continue with a program.[35]

Criterion 1: Reactions

One of the simplest and most common approaches to training evaluation is assessing participant reactions. Happy trainees will be more likely to want to focus on training principles and to utilize the information on the job. However, participants can do more than tell you whether they liked a program or not. They can give insights into the content and techniques they found most useful. They can critique the instructors or make suggestions about participant interactions, feedback, and the like. Potential questions might include the following:

▶ What were your learning goals for this program?
▶ Did you achieve them?
▶ Did you like this program?
▶ Would you recommend it to others who have similar learning goals?
▶ What suggestions do you have for improving the program?
▶ Should the organization continue to offer it?

While evaluation methods based on reactions are improving, too many conclusions about training effectiveness are still based on broad satisfaction measures that lack specific feedback. Furthermore, it should be noted that positive reactions are no guarantee that the training has been successful. It may be easy to collect glowing comments from trainees, but gratifying as this information is to management, it may not

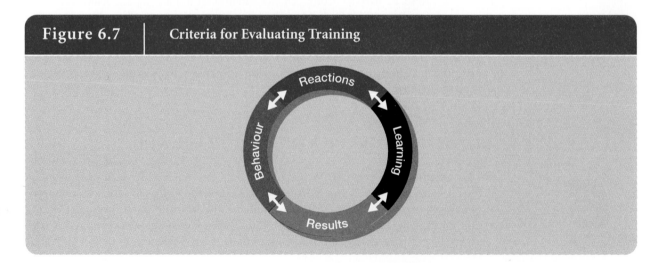

Figure 6.7   Criteria for Evaluating Training

be useful to the organization unless it somehow translates into improved behaviour and job performance. In the final analysis, reaction measures should not stop with assessing the training's entertainment value.[36]

Criterion 2: Learning

Beyond what participants *think* about the training, it might be a good idea to see whether they actually learned anything. Testing knowledge and skills before beginning a training program gives a baseline standard on trainees that can be measured again after training to determine improvement. However, in addition to testing trainees before and after training, parallel standards can be measured for individuals in a control group to compare with those in training to make certain that improvements are due to training and not some other factor (such as change in jobs, compensation, and the like). The control group should be made up of employees who have not received the training but who match the trainees in such areas as experience, past training, and job level.

Earlier in this chapter we discussed the principles of learning that are key ingredients of a well-designed training program. Revisiting those principles (such as goal setting, modelling, individual differences, practice, and feedback) should be done routinely as an element of evaluation. It is not enough to just know that learning did (or did not) occur; evaluation of training will, it is hoped, uncover "why."[37]

Criterion 3: Behaviour

You might be surprised to learn that much of what is learned in a training program never gets used back on the job. It's not that the training was necessarily ineffective. In fact, on measures of employee reactions and learning, the program might score quite high. But for several reasons, trainees may not demonstrate behaviour change back on the job. **Transfer of training** refers to the effective application of principles learned to what is required on the job. To maximize transfer, managers and trainers can take several approaches:

1. *Feature identical elements.* Transfer of training to the job can be facilitated by having conditions in the training program come as close as possible to those on the job.
2. *Focus on general principles.* In cases where jobs change or where the work environment cannot be matched exactly, trainers often stress the general principles behind the training rather than focusing on rote behaviour. This approach helps trainees learn how to apply the main learning points to varying conditions on the job.
3. *Establish a climate for transfer.* In some cases, trained behaviour is not implemented because old approaches and routines are still reinforced by other managers, peers, and employees. To prevent this kind of problem, the manager should ensure that the work environment supports, reinforces, and rewards the trainee for applying the new skills or knowledge.
4. *Give employees transfer strategies.* Particularly in settings that are not conducive to transfer, managers should also provide trainees with strategies and tactics for dealing with their transfer environment. One approach, called *relapse prevention (RP),* teaches individuals how to anticipate and cope with the inevitable setbacks

Transfer of training
Effective application of principles learned to what is required on the job

they will encounter back on the job—that is, a relapse into former behaviours. By identifying high-risk situations that jeopardize transfer and developing coping strategies, relapse prevention can help employees gain better control over maintaining learned behaviours.[38]

There are several methods for assessing transfer of learned skills back to the job. At Xerox, for example, managers use several methods, including observations of trainees once they return to their regular positions, interviews with the trainees' managers, and examination of trainees' post-training performance appraisals. They combine these indices to ascertain whether training and development has affected job behaviours. Booster sessions, in which trainees discuss their training experiences and support one another, have also had a positive effect on transfer; so has the submission of post-training progress reports by trainees. Supervisors can reinforce transfer by providing trainees with opportunities to practise their recently acquired KSAs, and by offering positive feedback when they do. The organization can use promotions or bonuses to reward and motivate trainees who successfully implement the KSAs.[39]

Criterion 4: Results

Training managers are coming under additional pressure to show that their programs produce "bottom-line" results. Some of the results-based criteria used in evaluating training include increased productivity, fewer employee complaints, decreased costs and waste, and profitability.[40]

The Business Case provides some examples of organizations focusing on ROI.

Reality Check describes how one organization measures all four levels: reaction, learning, behaviour, and results.

Utility and Return on Investment

In addition to results criteria, many organizations are beginning to think about the utility of the training programs. *Utility* refers to the benefits derived from training relative to the costs incurred. Motorola has conducted several studies to assess the value training brings to the company. In one such study, Motorola found that for every $1 spent on training, $33 was returned to the company. Based on a calculation of the dollar payoff, if the cost of training is high and the benefits are low, or if employees leave their jobs for other ones, the utility of training may be low.[41]

Increasingly, organizations with sophisticated training systems look to training to support long-term strategy and change more than they look for short-term financial returns from their investments. Instead of looking for a "payback," organizations view training in relation to the extent to which it provides knowledge and skills that create a competitive advantage and a culture that is ready for continuous change.[42]

Benchmarking

Benchmarking
Process of measuring one's own services and practices against the recognized leaders in order to identify areas for improvement

As training and development are increasingly viewed from a strategic standpoint, there is increased interest in **benchmarking** developmental services and practices against those of recognized leaders in industry. While no single model for exact benchmarking exists, the simplest models are based on the late W. Edwards Deming's classic four-step process. The four-step process advocates that managers do the following:

The Business Case

RETURN ON TRAINING INVESTMENT

Organizations spend about 2 percent of payroll on training, an estimated $750 billion around the globe. Most organizations (four out of five) do not measure the ROI on their training dollars, citing barriers such as the difficulty of doing so, the cost, lack of training, and lack of experience. However, at TD Bank, which has 1500 branches, 45 000 employees, and 30 different businesses, a focus on measuring the ROI of training captures results such as revenues and profitability. TD has a front-end process—that is, the business units determine the business results expected, the job performance that will generate these results, and the role that training plays.

According to the Conference Board of Canada, a positive relationship exists between formal training expenditures and performance indicators, such as employee productivity and company profitability. H.J. Heinz Company Canada provided training for its staff in response to increased competition and the need for new technologies. The training costs of $869 000 were repaid within twenty months due to increased productivity, reduced absenteeism, and fewer damaged containers.

A useful tool for developing Return on Training Investment (ROTI) can be found at the website of FutureEd Inc.: www.futured.com/audited/returned.htm.

Sources: S. Carrigan, "Training: Investment in the Future," *Canadian HR Reporter* 14, no. 11 (June 4, 2001): G1; "What Should You Expect from Your Investment in Training?" Strategis, Industry Canada, "Canadian Training Solutions," www.strategis.gc.ca.

1. *Plan.* Conduct a self-audit to define internal processes and measurements; decide on areas to be benchmarked and choose the comparison organization.
2. *Do.* Collect data through surveys, interviews, site visits, and/or historical records.
3. *Check.* Analyze data to discover performance gaps and communicate findings and suggested improvements to management.
4. *Act.* Establish goals, implement specific changes, monitor progress, and redefine benchmarks as a continuous improvement process.

To use benchmarking successfully, managers must clearly define the measures of competency and performance and must objectively assess the current situation and identify areas for improvement. To this end, experts in this area are attempting to work out ways of measuring what training departments do. Three broad areas that most HR training and developmental practitioners consider essential to measure are the following:

1. *Training activity:* How much training is occurring?
2. *Training results:* Do training and development achieve their goals?
3. *Training efficiency:* Are resources utilized in the pursuit of this mission?

Reality Check

A CLASSIC FOUR-LEVEL EVALUATION

CONEXUS is the largest credit union in Saskatchewan with assets of $1.1 billion. According to Gayle Johnson, CHRP, EVP Human Resources and Corporate Secretary, its training and development budget for its 465 employees is 6 percent of payroll. Three percent is spent on university education, and the other 3 percent is spent on training. Its largest training program is one that develops financial service representatives (their title is to be changed to "relationship managers"). The training consists of several steps and each is measured.

In-house and classroom-based modules teach content, such as computer literacy, cash duties, and introduction to CONEXUS's products and services, and progresses through to more advanced training, such as consumer lending practices, estates, and minimal mortgage lending. Each three- to five-day module is followed by a work period of three to twelve months, so that employees can apply their knowledge. The four levels of measurement of the effectiveness of training are the following:

1. Reaction: "Smile sheets" are completed by each participant at the end of the classroom training, asking questions such as "What did you get from this session?"
2. Comprehensive Review: Exams are given after each module and the results are fed back to the employees and managers.
3. Employee Performance Competencies: Every job family has a number of job-specific competencies, and managers are asked to rate the participants on these performance competencies. The changes in ratings are tracked.
4. Results: These vary by module. For example, after the cash-lending module, the performance tracked would be the number of call-outs to customers and the number of sales.

The American Society for Training and Development (ASTD) and its Institute for Workplace Learning have established a project that allows organizations to measure and benchmark training and development activities against each other. This benchmarking forum, which shares findings from over eight hundred companies, compares data on training costs, staffing, administration, design, development, and delivery of training programs. Not only do initiatives such as these help organizations evaluate their training programs, but the process serves as a feedback loop to reinitiate needs assessment and design of future training.[43] Highlights in HRM 6.8 shows several aspects of training that can be benchmarked against organizations considered superior in the training function.

Highlights in HRM 6.8

BENCHMARKING HR TRAINING

MEASUREMENT NAME	MEASUREMENT TYPE	HOW TO CALCULATE	EXAMPLE
Percent of payroll spent on training	Training activity	Total training expenditures ÷ total payroll	U.S. average = 2.0 percent of payroll spent on training per year.
Training dollars spent per employee	Training activity	Total training expenditures ÷ total employees served	Leading firms spent $1616 per employee on training in 1997.
Average training hours per employee	Training activity	Total number of training hours (hours x participants) ÷ total employees served	U.S. average for large firms (1001 employees) = 35 hours per employee in 1997.
Percent of employees trained per year	Training activity	Total number of employees receiving training ÷ total employee population	Leading firms trained an average of 96.4 percent of their work- forces in 1997.
HRD staff per 1000 employees	Training activity	Number of HRD staff ÷ total employee population × 1000	Leading firms had an average of 1 HRD staff member per 146 employees.
Cost savings as a ratio of training expenses	Training results: Bottom line	Total savings in scrap or waste ÷ dollars invested in training	A Baldrige winner report- ed saving $30 for every $1 spent on TQM train- ing (for an ROI of 30:1).
Profits per employee per year	Training results: Bottom line	Total yearly gross profits ÷ total number of employees	An electronics firm earned average profits per employee of $21 000 in 1990.
Training costs per student hour	Training efficiency	Total costs of training ÷ total number of hours of training	Three Baldrige winners reported $27 in average training costs per hour of training in 1990.

Sources: Adapted from "The Latest Data on Expenditures, Types of Training, and More," *HRFocus* 77, no. 4 (April 2000): 10–13; Donald J. Ford, "Benchmarking HRD," *Training and Development,* 1993, 36–41; and Leslie F. Overmyer Day, "Benchmarking Training," *Training and Development,* November 1995, 26–30.

SPECIAL TOPICS IN TRAINING AND DEVELOPMENT

While we have focused almost exclusively on the processes underlying a systems model of training—needs assessment, principles of learning, implementation methods, evaluation—it may be useful to discuss some of the more popular topics that are covered in these training programs. As we noted in the beginning of this chapter, there are a wide variety of training programs. In addition to the training that addresses KSAs reflecting the demands of a particular job, many employers develop training programs to meet the needs of a broader base of employees. In this final section, we summarize some of these programs, including basic skills training, team training, and diversity training. Global training will be covered in Chapter 15.

Basic Skills Training

The National Literacy Secretariat and Human Resources Development Canada finds that 42 percent of Canadians have literacy skills below the level they need to succeed. Experts define an illiterate individual as one having a sixth-grade education or less. Working adults who improve their literacy skills gain better pay and more promotions and are employed for longer periods of time. Employers launch literacy training in order to improve productivity. Avon Foods in Nova Scotia and Palliser's Furniture in Manitoba created workplace education programs to give workers easy access to skills upgrading.[44]

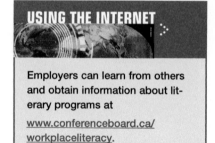

USING THE INTERNET

Employers can learn from others and obtain information about literary programs at

www.conferenceboard.ca/workplaceliteracy.

These figures have important implications for society at large and for organizations that must work around these skill deficiencies. Never has this been more true, given tight labour markets on the one hand and increasing skill requirements (related to advances in technology) on the other. Basic skills have become essential occupational qualifications, having profound implications for product quality, customer service, internal efficiency, and workplace and environmental safety. Canadian employers report that the top five skills they need in employees today are the ability to

- read and understand information;
- listen, ask questions, and understand;
- work in teams;
- assess situations and identify problems;
- share information orally and work with others.

But grown-ups don't learn the way kids do, so many of the traditional basic skills training techniques are not successful with adults. To implement a successful program in basic and remedial skills, managers should

1. Explain to employees why and how the training will help them in their jobs.
2. Relate the training to the employees' goals.
3. Respect and consider participant experiences, and use these as a resource.
4. Use a task-centred or problem-centred approach so that participants "learn by doing."
5. Give feedback on progress toward meeting learning objectives.

Adult learners may prefer to learn on the job.

DICK HEMINGWAY

A workplace education program in the City of Charlottetown won an award of excellence for Municipal Workplace Literacy Achievements in 2003, by following these principles. The key to developing a successful basic-skills program is *flexibility,* reinforcing the principle of individual differences while acknowledging the reality of work and family constraints.

Team Training

As we discussed in Chapter 3, organizations rely on teams to attain strategic and operational goals. Whether the team is an aircrew, a research team, or a manufacturing or service unit, the contributions of the individual members of the team are not only a function of the KSAs of each individual but of the interaction of the team members. The teamwork behaviours that differentiate effective teams are shown in Figure 6.8. They include both process dynamics and behavioural dynamics. The fact that these behaviours are observable and measurable provides a basis for training team members to function more effectively in the pursuit of their goals.[45]

Coca-Cola has developed team training for its manufacturing employees. The program focuses on three skill categories: (1) technical, (2) interpersonal, and (3) team action. The technical component is called Four-Deep Training, which implies that each individual should learn four different jobs to allow for team flexibility. The interpersonal skills component is called Adventures in Attitudes, and it focuses on listening, conflict resolution, influence, and negotiation. Team-action training focuses on team leadership, management of meetings, team roles, group dynamics, and problem solving—all skills needed to function effectively as a team. The training has not only increased quality and customer satisfaction, it has helped decrease costs and has set up a model for preparing employees for the future.[46]

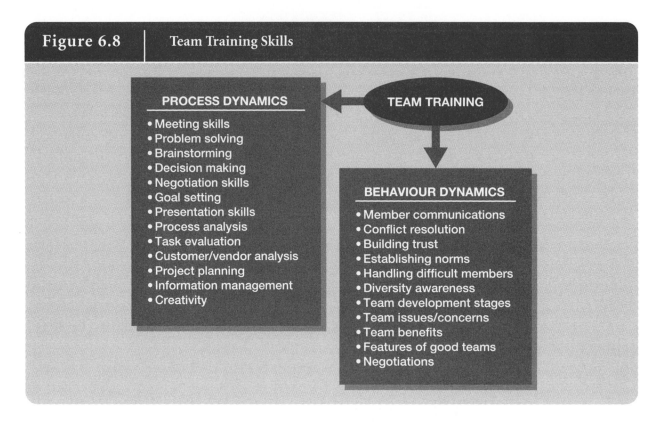

Figure 6.8 | Team Training Skills

Source: George Bohlander and Kathy McCarthy, "How to Get the Most from Team Training," *National Productivity Review*, Autumn 1996, 25–35.

In the last few years other organizations have developed exercises to generate enthusiasm and enhance team participation. Managers who want to design team training for their organization should keep the following points in mind:

1. Team building is a difficult and comprehensive process. Since many new teams are under pressure to produce, there is little time for training. You cannot cover everything in a twenty-four-hour blitz. Team training works best when it is provided over time and parallels team development.

2. Team development is not always a linear sequence of "forming, storming, norming, and performing." Training initiatives can help a team work through each of these stages, but managers must be aware that lapses can occur.

3. Additional training is required to assimilate new members. Large membership changes may result in teams reverting to a previous developmental stage.

4. Behavioural and process skills need to be acquired through participative exercises. Team members cannot internalize subjects such as conflict resolution through passive listening. Hands-on experiences are much better.[47]

Diversity Training

Many organizations sponsor some sort of diversity training. This emphasis is sparked by an awareness of the varied demographics of the workforce, the challenges of employment equity, the dynamics of stereotyping, the changing values of the workforce, and the potential competitive payoffs from bringing different people together for a common purpose. There are basically two types of diversity training: (1) awareness building, which helps employees appreciate the benefits of diversity, and (2) skill building, which provides the KSAs necessary for working with people who are different. For example, a skill-building diversity program might teach managers how to conduct performance appraisals with people from different cultures or teach male supervisors how to coach female employees toward better career opportunities. All the diverse dimensions—race, gender, age, disabilities, lifestyles, culture, education, ideas, and backgrounds—should be considered in the design of a diversity training program.[48]

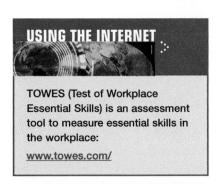

TOWES (Test of Workplace Essential Skills) is an assessment tool to measure essential skills in the workplace:

www.towes.com/

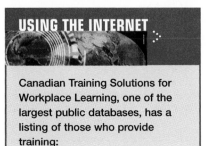

Canadian Training Solutions for Workplace Learning, one of the largest public databases, has a listing of those who provide training:

www.strategis.gc.ca/training

Connaught Laboratories has won a host of awards for its diversity training program. About eight hundred employees participated in a three-hour program that covered topics such as government policies, trends in demographics, terminology, designated groups, and the benefits of a new work environment. In addition, managers attended a one-day workshop on learning to manage diversity.

Highlights in HRM 6.9 shows some characteristics of effective diversity training programs. Increasingly, diversity training is being combined with other training programs, an occurrence that some believe represents the "mainstreaming" of diversity with other strategic issues facing organizations. Honeywell, for example, subsumes diversity training within a week-long advanced management program and as part of its sales training programs. General Electric trains mentors and protégés in a program that isn't explicitly a diversity initiative but nevertheless clearly helps women and ethnic minorities.

Organizations that have been successful with diversity training realize that it is a long-term process that requires the highest level of skill. Ineffective training in this area can be damaging and can create more problems than it solves. Unfortunately, many consulting firms have added diversity training to their list of programs without adequate personnel to handle the assignment. To avoid the pitfalls of substandard diversity training, managers will want to do the following:

1. *Forge a strategic link.* Begin by establishing the reasons for diversity training. Clarify the links between diversity and business goals in order to provide a context for training. Employment equity and valuing diversity are not the same thing. Ultimately diversity enhances differences and unites those differences toward a common goal.

2. *Check out consultant qualifications.* Recognize that there are no certification criteria for consultants, so make certain they are qualified. Background and experience checks are essential.

3. *Don't settle for "off the shelf" programs.* Each company has somewhat different goals, and the training should reflect this.

4. *Choose training methods carefully.* Most diversity training is really education (awareness building). Managers may hope they are developing skills, but this requires more in-depth training. Employees may benefit from either awareness or skill building, but they are not the same.

5. *Document individual and organizational benefits.* Diversity training, when done well, can enhance communications, improve responsiveness to social issues, reduce lawsuits, create a climate of fairness, improve productivity on complex tasks, and increase revenues and profits. These criteria extend beyond affirmative action goals and support the competitive capability of the organization.

Highlights in HRM 6.9

CHARACTERISTICS OF EFFECTIVE DIVERSITY TRAINING PROGRAMS

▶ Steering committee represents all levels of the organization and a mix of races, ages, and gender.
▶ Workshops include the following:
  – Top executives demonstrate their commitment by early participation.
  – Each participant is given a workbook with support materials.
  – Participants are made aware of key topics and company policies.
  – Participants are asked to describe specific steps they would take to support diversity.
  – Create a list of diversity ground rules or behavioural norms.
  – Have managers discuss and revise rules for their areas.
  – Link diversity training to other HR initiatives such as recruitment and selection, career management, and compensation.
▶ Hold managers accountable for achieving goals of diversity training.

SUMMARY

objective
Orientation training begins and continues throughout an employee's service with an organization. By participating in a formal orientation program, employees acquire the knowledge, skills, and attitudes that increase the probabilities of their success with the organization. To make an orientation effective, there should be close cooperation between the HR department and other departments in all phases of the program, from initial planning through follow-up and evaluation.

objective
Today we find that organizational operations cover a broad range of subjects and involve personnel at all levels, from orientation through management development. In addition to providing the training needed for effective job performance, employers offer training in such areas as personal growth and wellness. In order to have effective training programs, the systems approach is recommended. This approach consists of four phases: (1) needs assessment, (2) program design, (3) implementation, and (4) evaluation.

objective
Needs assessment begins with organization analysis. Managers must establish a context for training by deciding where training is needed, how it connects with strategic goals, and how organizational resources can best be used. Task analysis is used to identify the knowledge, skills, and abilities that are needed. Person analysis is used to identify which people need training.

objective
In designing a training program, managers must consider the two fundamental preconditions for learning: readiness and motivation. In addition, principles of learning should be considered in order to create an environment that is conducive to learning. These principles include goal setting, meaningfulness of presentation, modelling, individual differences, active practice and repetition, whole-versus-part learning, massed-versus-distributed learning, and feedback and reinforcement.

objective
In the training of nonmanagerial personnel, a wide variety of methods are available. On-the-job training is one of the most commonly used methods because it provides the advantage of hands-on experience and an opportunity to build a relationship between supervisor and employee. Apprenticeship training and internships are especially effective because they provide both on- and off-the-job experiences. Other off-the-job methods include the conference or discussion method, classroom training, programmed instruction, computer-based training, e-learning and simulation. All of these methods can make a contribution to the training effort with relatively little cost vis-à-vis the number of trainees who can be accommodated.

The training and development of managers is a multibillion-dollar business. As with nonmanagerial personnel, a wide variety of training methods are used for developing managers. On-the-job experiences include coaching, understudy assignment, job rotation, lateral transfer, project and committee assignments, and staff meetings. Off-the-job experiences include analysis of case studies, management games, role playing, and behaviour modelling.

objective
Evaluation of a training program should focus on several criteria: participant reactions, learning, behaviour change on the job, and bottom-line results. Transfer of training is measured via examination of the degree to which trained skills are demonstrated back on the job. Benchmarking and utility analysis help evaluate the impact of training and provide the information for further needs assessment.

objective
Special issues in training involve programs that are important to a broad range of employees. Basic skills training, team training, and diversity training are also critically important in today's organizations.

KEY TERMS

apprenticeship training 251
behaviour modelling 261
behaviour modification 249
benchmarking 264
competency assessment 243
computer-assisted instruction
    (CAI) 256

computer-managed instruction
    (CMI) 256
cooperative training 252
instructional objectives 245
internship programs 253
on-the-job training (OJT) 251
organization analysis 240

orientation 232
person analysis 244
task analysis 242
transfer of training 263

DISCUSSION QUESTIONS

objective 1

1. Why is employee orientation an important process? What are some benefits of a properly conducted orientation program?

objective 1

2. A new employee is likely to be anxious the first few days on the job. What are some of the possible causes of this anxiety? How can the anxiety be reduced?

objective 2

3. Providing training to employees is a significant retention tool in a tight labour market. In groups, discuss the benefits of training for individuals and organizations. Debate this resolution: "Employees should be required to repay education program benefits if they leave the organization before a specific amount of time (one year)."

objective 3

4. What analyses should be made to determine the training needs of an organization? After the needs are determined, what is the next step?

objective 4

5. Which principles of learning do you see demonstrated in your own class? In what ways might you bring other principles into the class?

objective 5

6. Indicate what training methods you would use for each of the following jobs. Give reasons for your choices.
    a. File clerk
    b. Computer operator
    c. Automobile service station attendant
    d. Pizza maker
    e. Nurse's aide

objective 5

7. Compare computer-assisted instruction with the lecture method in regard to the way the two methods involve the different psychological principles of learning.

objective 5

8. Suppose that you are the manager of an accounts receivable unit in a large company. You are switching to a new system of billing and record keeping and need to train your three supervisors and twenty-eight employees in the new procedures. What training method(s) would you use? Why?

objective 6

9. Participants in a training course are often asked to evaluate the course by means of a questionnaire. What are the pros and cons of this approach? Are there better ways of evaluating a course?

objective 7

10. You have probably worked on several class projects as a member of a team. As a group, develop a list of the kinds of skills that make a team function effectively. Rank these skills in order of importance. Take the top three skills, and design a training program to teach these skills to your group.

Developing Managerial Skills

TRAINING AND LEARNING PRINCIPLES

It is surprising how many training programs don't explicitly incorporate principles of learning into their design (such as goal setting, modelling, individual differences, and feedback). It is not that difficult to build learning principles into the training process, even for very simple instructional programs. To prove this point, do the following assignment for building a paper airplane.

Assignment

1. Form teams of four to six members. Identify someone on the team who knows how to make a paper airplane. That person will be the *trainer*.
2. Identify someone who will be the *observer/recorder*. That person will not participate in the training, but will write down how many (and how effectively) principles of learning are used in the instruction:
   a. Goal-setting
   b. Modelling
   c. Meaningfulness
   d. Individual differences
   e. Whole-versus-part learning
   f. Distributed learning
   g. Active practice
   h. Feedback
3. Give the trainer ten to fifteen minutes to train the group in making a paper airplane. The observer will keep notes of effective and ineffective training techniques (demonstrated learning principles).
4. Have someone from each team—not the trainer—volunteer to come before the class for a friendly competition. The instructor will give each team member two minutes to make a paper airplane. And then just for fun, they can compete by seeing which one flies the farthest. As always, no wagering, please.
5. To finish up the exercise, the observer/recorders will lead a discussion of the learning principles that were demonstrated. Discuss also, if they were done in this setting, why they might not be done in other training settings.

Service at the Chateau Whistler

The Chateau Whistler in Whistler, British Columbia, is one of the world's leading hotels and has been named the number one ski resort in North America for the past eight years. The 557-room hotel opened in 1989 and currently has 650 full-time employees.

The orientation program for new employees at the Chateau Whistler reflects the same standards that guests enjoy at the hotel. New recruits have raw talents such as energy and enthusiasm but have to be trained quickly in the art of excellent service.

On Day One of the orientation program, an "Orientation Game" is played; then the employees are introduced to the hotel (the types of rooms, the amenities, etc.). Then the following are discussed:

▶ Salary and benefits, including health care, pension plan, discounted ski passes, staff meals, food discounts, discounted rates at other properties, and health club access

▶ Employment standards, human rights, and labour relations (although the hotel is not unionized)

▶ Health and safety, including WHMIS (Workplace Hazardous Material Information System) and MSDS (Material Safety Data Sheets) and the environmental program

▶ Harassment policy

▶ The wellness program

▶ The incentive program

New employees also receive a tour of the town of Whistler, so that they can talk to guests about the key attractions and establish a network of friends.

Day Two is devoted to the Service Plus Program. The Service Plus Code is spelled out this way:

S	support
E	empathy
R	responsiveness
V	valuing differences
I	interdependence
C	caring
E	expectations

The Day Two program focuses on the guest–employee interaction and strives to teach employees how to provide excellent service, deal empathetically and effectively with problems reported by guests, and solve problems creatively. Training consists of role plays such as "handling the difficult guest." Specifically, the new recruits gain an understanding of the CP Hotel's mission statement and commitment to service, the changing service culture, and the high service expectations of the guests.

The third component of the orientation program is "Guest for a Night," during which employees who have been working at the hotel for three months eat at the restaurants, enjoy the facilities, and spend one night in the hotel as a guest. According to David Roberts, the hotel's general manager, the goal of the Guest for a Night program is to ensure that employees can talk knowledgeably about guest rooms, restaurants, and other facilities, and understand the level of quality that the hotel provides.

As part of this program, employees are asked to fill out a feedback survey, just like a guest. Also at this time, employees are invited to be part of a focus group to express concerns and provide feedback about their work experiences.

Through these orientation and training programs, employees develop knowledge and skills in service excellence. More importantly, they develop a commitment to the company. At a ten-year reunion party given for 600 people, 599 said it was the best working experience of their lives.

QUESTIONS

1. Compare the Chateau Whistler's orientation program to the list of activities presented in Highlights in HRM 6.1. Would you add anything?
2. The hospitality sector has high turnover rates among employees. Why does the Chateau Whistler invest so much time, money, and energy into its orientation program?
3. Describe the activities in the orientation and training programs that would ensure a high degree of transfer of training to the job.
4. How would you measure the success of this program? What results criteria would you try to measure?

Case Study 2

People Development Strategies at Credit Union Central of Saskatchewan

There are 128 credit unions in Saskatchewan, with assets ranging from less than $1 million to more than a billion dollars. All of these are affiliated with Credit Union Central of Saskatchewan, which facilitates cooperation among credit unions and provides consulting services, trade association functions, and liquidity management.

Credit Union Central, together with the four largest Saskatchewan credit unions, developed a plan to implement a comprehensive human resource management system to produce, first, a better alignment of employee performance to organizational objectives and, second, more focused training to produce desired business results and an enhanced ability to retain employees through opportunities for professional development. Working with Hay Management Consultants, the first step was to develop a competency glossary, followed by performance management processes and tools, selection and staffing tools, and then succession planning.

Competencies can be defined as attitudes, skills, knowledge or behaviours that are essential to perform at work and that differentiate superior performers. The competency glossary defines core competencies, which apply to all roles within the organization, and role-specific competencies. Competency target levels indicating superior performance are set for each role.

An example of a core competency, based on the key values and strategies of the organization, is "results orientation":

When your employee tried to improve his/her own performance he/she

1. identified areas of waste or inefficiency but didn't take any action.

2. made some changes to work methods in order to reach particular goals that had been set for him/her.

3. made specific changes in the system and his/her own work methods in order to improve performance beyond goals set.

4. set own challenging goals that were accomplished with a significant amount of planning, analysis, and effort.

5. set individual goals by thinking through the costs and benefits, and explicitly considered potential profits, risks, and return on investment, in order to make decisions that ended up having a positive organizational impact.

6. took a calculated entrepreneurial risk and committed significant organizational resources to act on an idea that ended up significantly improving performance.

A role-specific competency might be "concern for order, quality, and compliance" defined as follows:

When your employee demonstrated attention to detail in his/her work, he/she...

1. checked on the work to ensure it was accurate, complied with all relevant regulations, and followed all standard practices and procedures.

2. monitored the accuracy and quality of his/her own work and others' work consistently and systematically and kept a detailed record of work when it was necessary.

3. during the project, monitored the progress of the project against milestones and deliverables, took action to ensure the procedures put in place were effective, and quickly corrected any weaknesses or deficiencies.

4. established and utilized a procedure and/or system to facilitate work efficiency and ensure high-quality output; modified and improved the procedure and/or system when a weakness was identified, in order to ensure that high-quality work was being produced.

Managers work with employees to assess competency levels. The competency glossary and a competency assessment questionnaire enable managers and employees to discuss skills, abilities, and behaviours using a common framework. Training and development plans are based on gaps between target performance and actual performance. A developmental resource kit, which includes training courses, seminars, books, and work opportunities, all classified by competency, assists with building development plans.

This approach has resulted in clear direction on performance and development plans to move employees toward optimum performance levels.

QUESTIONS

1. Describe the advantages of the approach used to identify performance gaps.
2. Why would managers resist or support this approach?
3. Describe methods that you would use to evaluate the effectiveness of this approach at level 2 (learning), level 3 (behaviour), and level 4 (organizational results).

CAREER COUNSEL

Complete the training list on the *Managing Human Resources* website (www.belcourt4e.nelson.com).

NOTES AND REFERENCES

1. A. Thomlinson, "T& D Spending up in US as Canada Lags Behind," *Canadian HR Reporter* 15, no. 6 (March 25, 2002): 1; Industry Canada, "Canadian Training Solutions," http://strategix.ic.gc.ca/epic/internet.
2. Training Magazine, "Feature Stories," www.trainingmag. com. March 2003.
3. Tammy Galvin, "Industry Report," *Training* 38, no. 10 (October 2001): 2; "Training Is Up, Especially in Technical Areas," *HRFocus* 78, no. 5 (May 2001): 8.
4. Bob Rosner, "Training Is the Answer ... But What Was the Question?" *Workforce* 78, no. 5 (May 1999): 42–52; see also Irwin L. Goldstein and J. Kevin Ford, *Training in Organizations: Needs Assessment, Development and Evaluation,* 4th ed. (Belmont, CA: Wadsworth, 2002). For the classic citation on needs assessment, see William McGehee and Paul W. Thayer, *Training in Business and Industry* (New York: John Wiley and Sons, 1961).
5. Tracy Mauro, "Helping Organizations Build Community," *Training and Development* 56, no. 2 (February 2002): 25–29; Liam Lahey, "RFIDs Touted as Standard for Airport Security," *Computing Canada* 28, no. 13 (June 21, 2002): 21; Caroline Wilson, "Ensuring a Smooth Ride," *Security Management* 46, no. 8 (August 2002): 92.
6. N. Leckie, A. Leonard, J. Turcotte, and D. Wallanc, *The Evolving Workplace Series: Employer and Employee Perspectives on Human Resources Practices,* Statistics Canada/Human Resources Development Canada, September 2001.
7. Thomas Gainey, Brian Klaas, and Darla Moore, "Outsourcing the Training Function: Results from the Field," *Human Resource Planning* 25, no. 1 (2002): 16; Sarah Fister Gale, "Creative Training: Doing More with Less," *Workforce* 80, no. 10 (October 2001): 82–88.
8. Ron Zemke and Susan Zemke, "Putting Competencies to Work," *Training* 36, no. 1 (January 1999): 70–76; Catherine Robbins, Elizabeth Bradely, Maryanne Spicer, and Gary Mecklenburge, "Developing Leadership in Healthcare Administration: A Competency Assessment Tool/Practitioner Application," *Journal of Healthcare Management* 46, no. 3 (May/June 2001): 188–202; Margaret Potter, Christine Pistella, Carl Fertman, and Virginia Dato, "Needs Assessment and a Model Agenda for Training the Public Health Workforce," *American Journal of Public Health* 90, no. 8 (August 2000): 1294–96.
9. Elwood Holton, Reid Bates, and Sharon Naquin, "Large-Scale Performance-Driven Training Needs Assessment: A Case Study," *Public Personnel Management* 29, no. 2 (Summer 2000): 249–67.
10. Robert Mager, *What Every Manager Should Know about Training: An Insider's Guide to Getting Your Money's Worth from Training* (Atlanta, GA: Center for Effective Performance, 1999).
11. Jason A. Colquitt and Marcia J. Simmering, "Conscientiousness, Goal Orientation, and Motivation to Learn during the Learning Process: A Longitudinal Study," *Journal of Applied Psychology* 83, no. 4 (August 1998): 654–65; Sherry Ryan, "A Model of the Motivation for IT Retraining," *Information Resources Management Journal* 12, no. 4 (October–December 1999): 24–32; Kimberly A. Smith-Jentsch, Florian G. Jentsch, Stephanie C. Payne, and Eduardo Salas, "Can Pretraining Experiences Explain Individual Differences in Learning?" *Journal of Applied Psychology* 81, no. 1 (February 1996): 110–16.
12. T. Humber, "Tuition Assistance," *Canadian HR Reporter* 15, no. 20 (November 18, 2002): G1.
13. J. Kevin Ford, Eleanor M. Smith, Daniel A. Weissbein, Stanley M. Gully, and Eduardo Salas, "Relationships of Goal Orientation, Metacognitive Activity, and Practice Strategies with Learning Outcomes and Transfer," *Journal of Applied Psychology* 83, no. 2 (April 1998): 218–33; Annette Towler and Robert Dipboye, "Effects of Trainer Expressiveness, Organization, and Trainee Goal Orientation on Training Outcomes," *Journal of Applied Psychology* 86, no. 4 (August 2001): 664–73; Steve Kozlowski, Stanley Gully, Kenneth Brown, and Eduardo Salas, "Effects of Training Goals and Goal Orientation Traits on Multidimensional Training Outcomes and Performance Adaptability," *Organizational Behavior and Human Decision Processes* 85, no. 1 (May 2001): 1–31.
14. The classics by Albert Bandura here include *Social Foundations of Thought and Action: A Social Cognitive Theory* (Englewood Cliffs, NJ: Prentice Hall, 1986) and *A*

Social Learning Theory (Englewood Cliffs, NJ: Prentice Hall, 1977). See also Melesa Altizer Bolt, Larry Killough, and Hian Chye Koh, "Testing the Interaction Effects of Task Complexity in Computer Training Using the Social Cognitive Model," *Decision Sciences* 32, no. 1 (Winter 2001): 1–20.

15. M. K. Kacmar, P. W. Wright, and G. C. McMahan, "The Effect of Individual Differences on Technological Training," *Journal of Managerial Issues* 9, no. 1 (Spring 1997): 104–20; Stanley Gully, Stephanie Payn, K. Lee Kiechel Koles, and John-Andrew Whiteman, "The Impact of Error Training and Individual Differences on Training Outcomes: An Attribute-Treatment Interaction Perspective," *Journal of Applied Psychology* 87, no. 1 (February 2002): 143–55; Steven John Simon, "The Relationship of Learning Style and Training Method to End-User Computer Satisfaction and Computer Use: A Structural Equation Model," *Information Technology, Learning, and Performance Journal* 18, no. 1 (Spring 2000): 41–59.

16. Don Hartshorn, "Reinforcing the Unsafe Worker," *Occupational Hazards* 62, no. 10 (October 2000): 125–28; Jean M. Patterson, "Smart Training," *Occupational Health & Safety* 68, no. 10 (October 1999): 216–21; Fred Luthan and Alexander Stajkovic, "Reinforce for Performance: The Need to Go beyond Pay and Even Rewards," *Academy of Management Executive* 13, no. 2 (May 1999): 49–57.

17. For recent discussions on the desired characteristics of trainers as well as their effects on training, see Greg Hopkins, "How to Design an Instructor Evaluation," *Training and Development* 53, no. 3 (March 1999): 51–52; Beth Thomas, "How to Hire Instructors Who Love Training," *Training and Development* 53, no. 3 (March 1999): 14–15; John L. Bennett, "Trainers as Leaders of Learning," *Training and Development* 55, no. 3 (March 2001): 42–45; Ruth Palombo Weiss, "Deconstructing Trainers' Self-Image," *Training and Development* 55, no. 12 (December 2001): 34–39.

18. Eduardo Salas and Janis Cannon-Bowers, "The Science of Training: A Decade of Progress," *Annual Review of Psychology* 52 (2001): 471–99.

19. Diane Walter, *Training on the Job* (Alexandria, VA: American Society for Training and Development, 2001); Toni Hodges, *Linking Learning and Performance: A Practical Guide to Measuring Learning and On the Job Application* (Burlington, MA: Butterworth-Heinemann, 2001); Gary Sisson, *Hands-On Training: A Simple and Effective Method for On-the-Job Training* (San Francisco: Barrett-Koehler, 2001).

20. Alison Booth, Yu-Fu Chen, and Gylfi Zoega, "Hiring and Firing: A Tale of Two Thresholds," *Journal of Labor Economics* 20, no. 2 (April 2002): 217–48; Sherrill Tapsell,

"Train to Retain," *New Zealand Management* 46, no. 7 (August 1999): 49–53; Gary Sisson, "HOT Training," *Executive Excellence* 19, no. 3 (March 2002): 15; Holly Ann Suzik, "On-the-Job Training: Do It Right!" *Quality* 38, no. 12 (November 1999): 84.

21. Ronald L. Jacobs and Michael J. Jones, "Teaching Tools: When to Use On-the-Job Training," *Security Management* 41, no. 9 (September 1997): 35–39.

22. John Byrd and Rob Poole, "Highly Motivated Employees at No Cost? It's Not an Impossible Dream," *Nonprofit World* 19, no. 6 (November/December 2001): 312–32.

23. K. M. Kritch and D. E. Bostow, "Degree of Constructed-Response Interaction in Computer-Based Programmed Instruction," *Journal of Applied Behavior Analysis* 31, no. 3 (Fall 1998): 387–98; Glenn Kelly and John Crosbie, "Immediate and Delayed Effects of Imposed Postfeedback Delays in Computerized Programmed Instruction," *Psychological Record* 47, no. 4 (Fall 1997): 687–98.

24. S. Wintroe, "Satellites Present Cost Savings," *Financial Post*, June 16, 2003: FE 6.

25. "What Is the Impact of Learning Technologies," Industry Canada, at Strategis.gc.ca; R. Ray, "Employers, Employees Embrace E-Learning," *The Globe and Mail*, May 25, 2001, E2.

26. Scott A. Snell, Donna Stueber, and David P. Lepak, "Virtual HR Departments: Getting out of the Middle," in R. L. Heneman and D. B. Greenberger (eds.), *Human Resource Management in Virtual Organizations* (Greenwich, CT: Information Age Publishing, 2002).

27. For other applications of simulation in training used at Boeing and Eastman Kodak, see George Tischelle, "E-Learning Gets a Dose of Reality," *InformationWeek* 895 (July 1, 2002): 57. For applications of simulation training used in the U.S. Navy, see John Flink, "This Is Really Neat Stuff," *United States Naval Institute Proceedings* 128, no. 7 (July 2002): 68–69. For applications of simulation training used in medical schools, see David Noonan, "Is the Cadaver Dead?" *Newsweek* 139, no. 25 (June 24, 2002): 62. For applications of simulation training used in the police force, see Jim Weiss and Mickey Davis, "Deadly Force Decision-Making," *Law and Order* 50, no. 6 (June 2002): 58–62.

28. Martin Delahoussaye, Kristine Ellis, and Matt Bolch, "Measuring Corporate Smarts," *Training* 39, no. 8 (August 2002): 20–35; Daniel Crepin, "From Design to Action: Developing a Corporate Strategy," *Quality Progress* 35, no. 2 (February 2002): 49–56; Brad Miller, "Making Managers More Effective Agents of Change," *Quality Progress* 34, no. 5 (May 2001): 53–57.

29. Joseph Alutto, "Just-in-Time Management Education in the 21st Century," *HRMagazine* 44, no. 11 (1999): 56–57; Gordon Dehler, M. Ann Welsh, and Marianne W. Lewis,

"Critical Pedagogy in the 'New Paradigm,'" *Management Learning* 493, no. 4 (December 2001): 493–511.

30. Chris Whitcomb, "Scenario-Based Training to the F.B.I.," *Training and Development* 53, no. 6 (June 1999): 42–46; Anne Hoag, Dale Brickley, and Joanne Cawley, "Media Management Education and the Case Method," *Journalism and Mass Communication Educator* 55, no. 4 (Winter 2001): 49–59.

31. Jenny C. McCune, "The Game of Business," *Management Review* 87, no. 2 (February 1998): 56–58; Phaedra Brotherton, "Let the Games Begin," *American Gas* 81, no. 3 (April 1999): 19–20; A. J. Faria, "The Changing Nature of Business Simulation/Gaming Research: A Brief History," *Simulation and Gaming* 32, no. 1 (March 2001): 97–110.

32. Leonard Hill, "Games People Play," *Air Transport World* 37, no. 3 (March 2000): 97–98.

33. Sandra J. Balli, "Oh No ... Not Role Play Again," *Training and Development* 49, no. 2 (February 1995): 14–15; Rick Sullivan, "Lessons in Smallness," *Training and Development* 56, no. 3 (March 2002): 21–23; James W. Walker, "Perspectives," *Human Resource Planning* 23, no. 3 (2000): 5–7; Richard Sappey and Jennifer Sappey, "Different Skills and Knowledge for Different Times: Training in an Australian Retail Bank," *Employee Relations* 21, no. 6 (1999): 577.

34. Jon M. Werner, Anne O'Leary-Kelly, Timothy T. Baldwin, and Kenneth N. Wexley, "Augmenting Behavior-Modeling Training: Testing the Effects of Pre- and Post-Training Interventions," *Human Resource Development Quarterly* 5, no. 2 (Summer 1994): 169–83; Gary May and William Kahnweiler, "The Effect of a Mastery Practice Design on Learning and Transfer in Behavior Modeling Training," *Personnel Psychology* 53, no. 2 (Summer 2000): 353–73.

35. Donald Kirkpatrick, "Great Ideas Revisited: Revisiting Kirkpatrick's Four-Level Model," *Training and Development* 50, no. 1 (January 1996): 54–57; Martin Delahoussaye, "Show Me the Results," *Training* 39, no. 3 (March 2002): 28–29; Reinout van Brakel, "Why ROI Isn't Enough," *Training and Development* 56, no. 6 (June 2002): 72–74.

36. James Pershing and Jana Pershing, "Ineffective Reaction Evaluation," *Human Resource Development Quarterly* 12, no. 1 (Spring 2001): 73–90.

37. Kozlowski, Gully, Brown, and Salas, "Effects of Training Goals and Goal Orientation Traits on Multidimensional Training Outcomes and Performance Adaptability"; Mike Miller, "Evaluate Training on These Four Levels," *Credit Union Magazine* 65, no. 5 (May 1999): 25–26; Donna Abernathy, "Thinking outside the Evaluation Box," *Training and Development* 53, no. 2 (February 1999): 18–23.

38. Jathan Janove, "Use It or Lose It," *HR Magazine* 47, no. 4 (April 2002): 99–104; Max Montesino, "Strategic Alignment of Training, Transfer-Enhancing Behaviors, and Training Usage: A Posttraining Study," *Human Resource Development Quarterly* 13, no. 1 (Spring 2002): 89–108; Siriporn Yamnill and Gary McLean, "Theories Supporting Transfer of Training," *Human Resource Development Quarterly* 12, no. 2 (Summer 2001): 195–208.

39. Alan M. Saks and Monica Belcourt, "Post-Training Activities and the Transfer of Training," *Canadian Learning Journal*, April 1998.

40. Delahoussaye, "Show Me the Results"; van Brakel, "Why ROI Isn't Enough."

41. Miller, "Evaluate Training on These Four Levels"; Dean R. Spitzer, "Embracing Evaluation," *Training* 36, no. 6 (June 1999): 42–47; van Brakel, "Why ROI Isn't Enough"; Sarah Fister Gale, "Measuring the ROI of E-Learning," *Workforce* 81, no. 8 (August 2002): 74–77; Earl Honeycutt, Kiran Karande, Ashraf Attia, and Steven Maurer, "A Utility Based Framework for Evaluating the Financial Impact of Sales Force Training Programs," *Journal of Personal Selling and Sales Management* 21, no. 3 (Summer 2001): 229–38.

42. Richard Lee, "The 'Pay-Forward' View of Training," *People Management* 2, no. 3 (February 8, 1996): 30–32; Terry Sloan, Paul Hyland, and Ron Beckett, "Learning as a Competitive Advantage: Innovative Training in the Australian Aerospace Industry," *International Journal of Technology Management* 23, no. 4 (2002): 341–52.

43. Ellen Drost, Colette Frayne, Keven Lowe, and J. Michael Geringer, "Benchmarking Training and Development Practices: A Multi-Country Comparative Analysis," *Human Resource Management* 41, no. 1 (Spring 2002): 67–86; Daniel McMurrer, Mark Van Buren, and William Woodwell, "Making the Commitment," *Training and Development* 54, no. 1 (January 2000): 41–48.

44. A. Thomlinson, "Math, Reading Skills Holding Employees Back," *Canadian HR Reporter* 15, no. 8 (October 21, 2002).

45. "What Makes Teams Work?" *HRFocus* 79, no. 4 (April 2002): S1–S3; John Annett, David Cunningham, and Peter Mathias-Jones, "A Method for Measuring Team Skills," *Ergonomics* 43, no. 8 (August 2000): 1076–94; Alan Auerbach, "Making Decisions under Stress: Implications for Individual and Team Training," *Personnel Psychology* 52, no. 4 (Winter 1999): 1050–53.

46. Sandra N. Phillips, "Team Training Puts Fizz in Coke Plant's Future," *Personnel Journal* 75, no. 1 (January 1996): 87–92.

47. George W. Bohlander and Kathy McCarthy, "How to Get the Most from Team Training," *National Productivity Review,* Autumn 1996, 25–35; Howard Prager, "Cooking Up Effective Team Building," *Training and Development* 52, no. 12 (December 1999): 14–15.

48. Gary Stern, "Small Slights Bring Big Problems," *Workforce* 81, no. 8 (August 2002): 17; Bill Leonard, "Ways to Tell If a Diversity Program Is Measuring Up," *HRMagazine* 47, no. 7 (July 2002): 21.

Career Development

After studying this chapter, you should be able to

objective

Explain how a career development program integrates individual and organizational needs.

objective

Cite the ways in which employers can facilitate the career development of women.

objective

Describe the conditions that help make a career development program successful.

objective

Discuss the ways in which employers can facilitate the career development of members of minority groups and of dual-career couples.

objective

Discuss how job opportunities can be inventoried and employee potential assessed.

objective

Describe the various aspects of personal career development that one should consider.

objective

Compare the methods used for identifying and developing managerial talent.

We have noted at several different points in this text—and in several different ways—that the ground rules for managing people are changing dramatically in today's working world. To be competitive over the long run, organizations have to be adaptive. Jobs are becoming more flexible to cope with change, and organizations are embracing alternative ways of designing work that take into account the diverse interests and backgrounds of potential employees. The need for innovation and technological change means that skills that are valuable today may be obsolete tomorrow. Flatter organization structures mean that there are fewer positions for promotion, so individuals must look for advancement opportunities outside the firm. At the same time, increased competition for talent means that some individuals will be lured away to work for other firms. As economic cycles lead organizations first to hire—then to lay off—then to hire again, employment security can be assured only when individuals take control of their own careers. Options and opportunities are perhaps more likely to exist across firms rather than within only one. The upshot from this is that individuals are less likely to work in the same job for extended periods and, in fact, most are unlikely to spend their entire careers with only one firm.[1]

Whoa! All these changes are going on at once, so it's small wonder that the topic of career management is one of the most important to new employees and old employees as well as to those of you who are just now thinking about entering the workforce. The desire to make the most of their knowledge and skills is something that individuals and organizations have in common. On one hand, the task has perhaps never been more challenging. On the other hand, organizations and employees are both perhaps more focused on it than ever before. In this chapter we not only cover career development as an HRM function, we also provide some suggestions that you may wish to consider in your own career development.

ELEMENTS OF CAREER DEVELOPMENT PROGRAMS

Organizations have traditionally engaged in human resources planning and development. As we noted in Chapter 4, this activity involves charting the moves of large numbers of employees through various positions in an organization and identifying future staffing and development needs. Career development programs, with their greater emphasis on the individual, introduce a personalized aspect to the process.

A common approach to establishing a career development program is to integrate it with the existing HR functions and structures in the organization. Integrating career development with other HR programs creates synergies in which all aspects of HR reinforce one another. Figure 7.1 illustrates how HR structures relate to some of the essential aspects of the career management process. For example, in planning careers, employees need organizational information—information that strategic planning, forecasting, succession planning, and skills inventories can provide. Similarly, as they obtain information about themselves and use it in career planning, employees need to know the career paths within the organization and how management views their performance.[2]

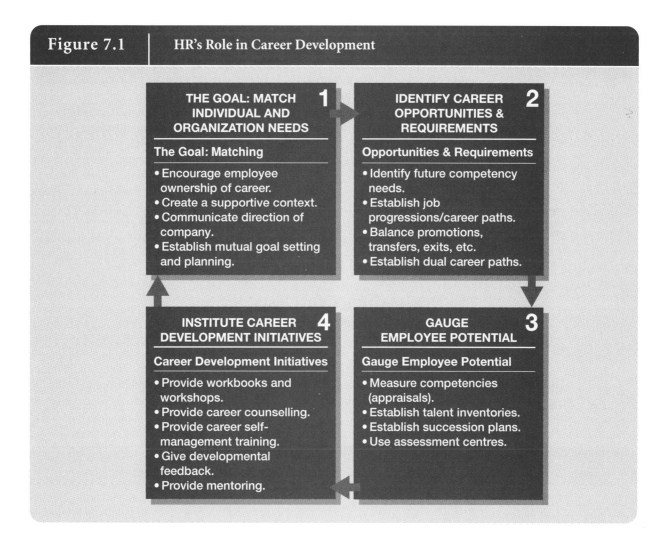

| Figure 7.1 | HR's Role in Career Development |

THE GOAL: MATCH INDIVIDUAL AND ORGANIZATION NEEDS 1

The Goal: Matching

- Encourage employee ownership of career.
- Create a supportive context.
- Communicate direction of company.
- Establish mutual goal setting and planning.

IDENTIFY CAREER OPPORTUNITIES & REQUIREMENTS 2

Opportunities & Requirements

- Identify future competency needs.
- Establish job progressions/career paths.
- Balance promotions, transfers, exits, etc.
- Establish dual career paths.

INSTITUTE CAREER DEVELOPMENT INITIATIVES 4

Career Development Initiatives

- Provide workbooks and workshops.
- Provide career counselling.
- Provide career self-management training.
- Give developmental feedback.
- Provide mentoring.

GAUGE EMPLOYEE POTENTIAL 3

Gauge Employee Potential

- Measure competencies (appraisals).
- Establish talent inventories.
- Establish succession plans.
- Use assessment centres.

The Goal: Matching Individual and Organizational Needs

In the final analysis, a career development program should be viewed as a dynamic process that matches the needs of the organization with the needs of employees.

The Employee's Role

In today's organizations, individuals are responsible for initiating and managing their own career planning. It is up to each individual to identify his or her own knowledge, skills, abilities, interests, and values and seek out information about career options in order to set goals and develop career plans. Managers should encourage employees to take responsibility for their own careers, offering continuing assistance in the form of feedback on individual performance and making available information about the organization, about the job, and about career opportunities that might be of interest.

The organization is responsible for supplying information about its mission, policies, and plans and for providing support for employee self-assessment, training, and development. Significant career growth can occur when individual initiative combines with organizational opportunity. Career development programs benefit managers by giving them increased skill in managing their own careers, greater retention of valued employees, increased understanding of the organization, and enhanced reputations as people-developers. As with other HR programs, the inauguration of a career development program should be based on the organization's needs as well.

Assessment of needs should take a variety of approaches (surveys, informal group discussions, interviews, and so on) and should involve personnel from different groups, such as new employees, managers, plateaued employees, minority employees, and technical and professional employees. Identifying the needs and problems of these groups provides the starting point for the organization's career development efforts. As shown in Figure 7.2, organizational needs should be linked with individual career needs in a way that joins personal effectiveness and satisfaction of employees with the achievement of the organization's strategic objectives.

The Organization's Role: Establishing a Favourable Context

If career development is to succeed, it must receive the complete support of top management. Ideally, senior line managers and HR department managers should work together to design and implement a career development system. The system should reflect the goals and culture of the organization, and the HR philosophy should be woven throughout. An HR philosophy can provide employees with a clear set of

Figure 7.2   Balancing Individual and Organizational Needs

ORGANIZATION'S NEEDS		INDIVIDUAL'S NEEDS	
Strategic	**Operational**	**Personal**	**Professional**
• Current competencies	• Employee turnover	• Age/tenure	• Career stage
• Future competencies	• Absenteeism	• Family concerns	• Education & training
• Market changes	• Talent pool	• Spouse employment	• Promotion aspirations
• Mergers, etc.	• Outsourcing	• Mobility	• Performance
• Joint ventures	• Productivity	• Outside interests	• Potential
• Innovation			• Current career path
• Growth			
• Downsizing			
• Restructuring			

CAREER MANAGEMENT

expectations and directions for their own career development. For a program to be effective, managerial personnel at all levels must be trained in the fundamentals of job design, performance appraisal, career planning, and counselling.

One of the most important indicators of management support comes in the form of mentoring. This is true regardless of whether it is done formally as part of an ongoing program or informally as merely a kind gesture to a less experienced employee. Dealing with uncertainty is one of the biggest challenges any individual faces in his or her career. Receiving advice and counsel from someone who has gone through similar experiences can prove to be invaluable to employees. We discussed mentoring briefly in Chapter 6 "Training and Development," and devote an entire section to the topic later in this chapter.

Blending Individual and Organizational Goals

Before individuals can engage in meaningful career planning, not only must they have an awareness of the organization's philosophy, but they must also have a good understanding of the organization's more immediate goals. Otherwise, they may plan for personal change and growth without knowing if or how their own goals match those of the organization. For example, if the technology of a business is changing and new skills are needed, will the organization retrain to meet this need or hire new talent? Is there growth, stability, or decline in the number of employees needed? How will turnover affect this need? Clearly, an organizational plan that answers these kinds of questions is essential to support individual career planning.

At the same time, it would be unrealistic to expect that individuals can establish their career goals with *perfect* understanding of where they are going or—for that matter—where the organization is going. Individuals change over time, and because of that, their needs and interests change. Similarly, organizations also change their directions and adjust their strategies to cope with change. So while goal setting is critical, building in some flexibility is probably a good idea.

Identifying Career Opportunities and Requirements

While career development integrates a number of related HR activities, those who direct the process have to keep a steady watch on the needs and requirements of the organization. This involves an analysis of the competencies required for jobs, the progression among related jobs, and the supply of ready (and potential) talent available to fill those jobs.

Competency Analysis

It is important for an organization to study its jobs carefully in order to identify and assign weights to the knowledge and skills that each one requires. This can be achieved with job analysis and evaluation systems such as those used in compensation programs. The system used at Sears measures three basic competencies for each job: know-how, problem solving, and accountability. Know-how is broken down into three types of job knowledge: technical, managerial, and human relations. Problem solving and accountability also have several dimensions. Scores for each of these three major competencies are assigned to each job, and a total value is computed for each job. For any planned job transfer, the amount of increase (or decrease) the next job represents in each of the skill areas, as well as in the total point values, can be computed. This information is then used to make certain that a transfer to a different job is a move that requires growth on the part of the employee.

Sears designs career development paths to provide the following experiences: (1) an increase in at least one skill area on each new assignment, (2) an increase of at least 10 percent in total points on each new assignment, and (3) assignments in several different functional areas.[3]

Job Progressions

Once the skill demands of jobs are identified and weighted according to their importance, it is then possible to plan **job progressions**. A new employee with no experience is typically assigned to a "starting job." After a period of time in that job, the employee can be promoted to one that requires more knowledge and/or skill. While most organizations concentrate on developing job progressions for managerial, professional, and technical jobs, progressions can be developed for all categories of jobs. These job progressions then can serve as a basis for developing **career paths**—the lines of advancement within an organization—for individuals.

Figure 7.3 illustrates a typical line of advancement in the human resources area of a large multinational corporation. It is apparent that one must be prepared to move geographically in order to advance very far in HRM with this firm. This would also be true of other career fields within the organization.

Many organizations prepare interesting and attractive brochures to describe the career paths that are available to employees. General Motors has prepared a career development guide that groups jobs by fields of work such as engineering, manufacturing, communications, data processing, financial, HR, and scientific. These categories give employees an understanding of the career possibilities in the various fields.

Although these analyses can be quite helpful to employees—and are perhaps essential for organizations—a word of caution is appropriate here for readers. Many successful careers are not this methodical, nor do they proceed in a lockstep manner. In today's working world, career progressions often occur as much through creating and capitalizing on arising opportunities as they do through rational planning. So while it is a good idea for organizations to map out a career path, and individuals would do well to establish a strategy for advancement, many successful individuals readily admit that their career paths are quite idiosyncratic to their circumstances. These people often note that they have been fortunate to be "in the right place at the right time." Of course, others describe them as being extremely career savvy.

Lots of Possibilities

It used to be that career development and planning systems were primarily focused on promotions and hierarchical advancement. However, in today's flatter organizations and more dynamic work environment, an individual's career advancement can occur along several different paths: transfers, demotions—even exits—as well as promotions. HR policies have to be flexible enough to adapt as well as helpful enough to support the career change.

As illustrated in Figure 7.4, a **promotion** is a change of assignment to a job at a higher level in the organization. The new job normally provides an increase in pay and

Job progressions
Hierarchy of jobs a new employee might experience, ranging from a starting job to jobs that successively require more knowledge and/or skill

Career paths
Lines of advancement in an occupational field within an organization

Promotion
Change of assignment to a job at a higher level in the organization

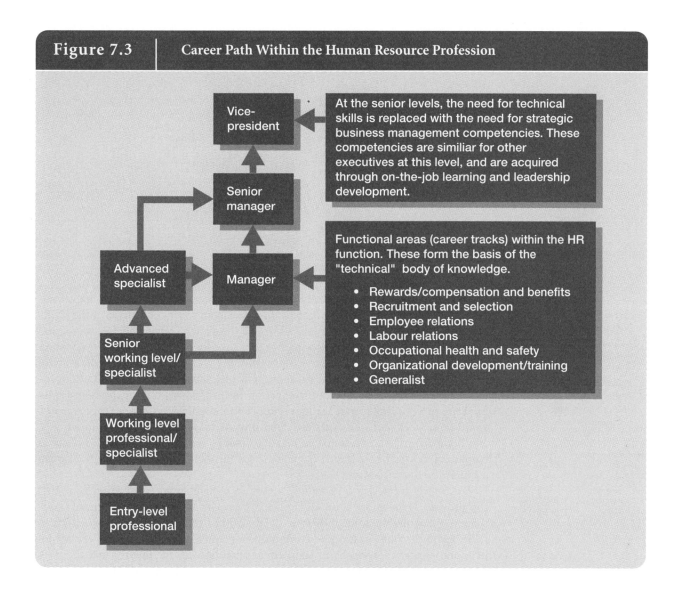

Figure 7.3 **Career Path Within the Human Resource Profession**

Vice-president

At the senior levels, the need for technical skills is replaced with the need for strategic business management competencies. These competencies are similiar for other executives at this level, and are acquired through on-the-job learning and leadership development.

Senior manager

Advanced specialist

Manager

Functional areas (career tracks) within the HR function. These form the basis of the "technical" body of knowledge.

- Rewards/compensation and benefits
- Recruitment and selection
- Employee relations
- Labour relations
- Occupational health and safety
- Organizational development/training
- Generalist

Senior working level/ specialist

Working level professional/ specialist

Entry-level professional

status and demands more skill or carries more responsibility. Promotions enable an organization to utilize the skills and abilities of its personnel more effectively, and the opportunity to gain a promotion serves as an incentive for good performance. The three principal criteria for determining promotions are merit, seniority, and potential. Often the problem is to determine how much consideration to give to each factor. A common problem in organizations that promote primarily on past performance and seniority is called the Peter Principle. This refers to the situation in which individuals are promoted as long as they have done a good job in their previous job. Trouble is, this continues until someone does poorly in his or her new job. Then he or she no longer promoted. This results in people being promoted to their level of incompetence.[4]

Figure 7.4 | **Alternative Career Moves**

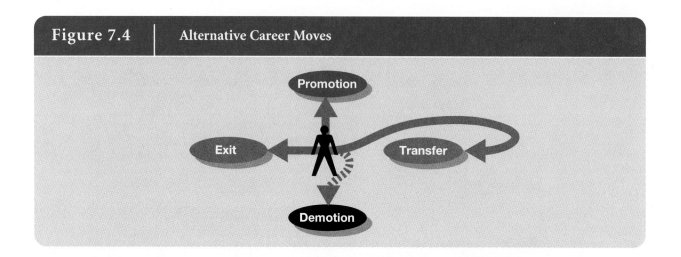

Transfer
Placement of an individual in another job for which the duties, responsibilities, status, and remuneration are approximately equal to those of the previous job

In flatter organizations, there are fewer promotional opportunities and many individuals have found career advancement through lateral moves. A **transfer** is the placement of an employee in another job for which the duties, responsibilities, status, and remuneration are approximately equal to those of the previous job (although as an incentive, organizations may offer a salary adjustment). Individuals who look forward to change or want a chance to learn more may seek out transfers. In addition, transfers frequently provide a broader foundation for individuals to prepare them for an eventual promotion. A transfer may require the employee to change work group, workplace, work shift, or organizational unit; it may even necessitate moving to another geographic area. Transfers make it possible for an organization to place its employees in jobs where there is a greater need for their services and where they can acquire new knowledge and skills.

A downward transfer, or *demotion,* moves an individual into a lower-level job that can provide developmental opportunities. Although such a move is ordinarily considered unfavourable, some individuals actually may request it in order to return to their "technical roots." It is not uncommon, for example, for organizations to appoint temporary leaders (especially in team environments) with the proviso that they will eventually step down from this position to reassume their former position.

Transfers, promotions, and demotions require individuals to adjust to new job demands and usually to a different work environment. A transfer that involves moving to a new location within Canada or abroad places greater demands on an employee, because it requires that employee to adapt not only to a new work environment but also to new living conditions. The employee with a family has the added responsibility of helping family members adjust to the new living arrangements. Even though some employers provide all types of **relocation services**—including covering moving expenses, helping to sell a home, and providing cultural orientation and language training—there is always some loss of productive time. Pretransfer training, whether related to job skills or to lifestyle, has been suggested as one of the most effective ways to reduce lost productivity.

When one considers the numerous changes that may accompany a career move within an organization, it should come as no surprise that many individuals are

Relocation services
Services provided to an employee who is transferred to a new location, which might include help in moving, in selling a home, in orienting to a new culture, and/or in learning a new language

Relocating to another city or country is an issue for dual-career people.

PHOTODISC

opting to accept career changes that involve *organizational exit*. Given limited career opportunities within firms, coupled with the need for talent in other companies, many individuals are discovering that their best career options may involve switching companies.

While some employees leave voluntarily, some employees are forced to leave. Even so, many organizations now provide **outplacement services** to help terminated employees find a job elsewhere. These services can be used to enhance a productive employee's career as well as to terminate an employee who is unproductive. If an organization cannot meet its career development responsibilities to its productive workers, HR policy should provide for assistance to be given them in finding more suitable career opportunities elsewhere. Jack Welch, chairman of General Electric, was one of the first executives to make a commitment to employees that while the company could no longer guarantee lifetime employment, it would try to ensure *employability*. That is, GE has committed to providing employees with the skills and support they would need to find a job in another organization.[5]

Outplacement services
Services provided by organizations to help terminated employees find a new job

Dual Career Paths

One of the most obvious places where career paths have been changing is in technical and professional areas. One of the ironies of organizations in the past has been that the most successful engineers, scientists, and professionals were often promoted right out of their area of specialization into management. Instead of doing what they were good at, they were promoted into a job they often didn't understand and often didn't enjoy. It has become apparent that there must be another way to compensate such individuals without elevating them to a management position. The solution has been to develop dual career paths, or tracks, that provide for progression in special areas such as information technology, finance, marketing, and engineering, with compensation that is comparable to that received by managers at different levels.

Many organizations have found that this is the solution to keeping employees with valuable knowledge and skills performing tasks that are as important to the organization as those performed by managers. Highlights in HRM 7.1 shows the dual career path devised by Xenova Corporation, a biopharmaceutical company, to recognize both the scientific and the managerial paths of employees.

Highlights in HRM 7.1

ROLES WITHIN THE XENOVA SYSTEM

Scientist (RS 1/2)
Plans and undertakes laboratory work to achieve agreed project goals, using inputs from colleagues, the external scientific community, literature, and suppliers.

Senior Scientist (RS 3/4)
Plans and undertakes experimental programs and laboratory to achieve agreed project or scientific goals, using inputs from and providing outputs to colleagues, community, and suppliers.

Research Associate (RS 5/6)
Provides expertise and direction to programs and projects through in-depth understanding of a scientific specialism; leads or forms part of a scientific team with the main purpose of providing a specialist's expertise in a scientific discipline.

Principal Scientist (RS 7/8)
Provides scientific expertise and understanding of the highest level to ensure scientific leadership and direction; maintains a personal standing as a world-recognized and highly respected scientist and uses this to further the aims of the company through science.

Section Leader (SM 4/5)
Leads and manages a team of scientists from both a science and an operational management standpoint; makes a significant contribution to the management of groups of scientists and the general management of the department.

Department Head (SM 3)
Leads and manages a department of scientists to provide Xenova with a well-managed and motivated scientific resource; makes a significant contribution to the general management of the company or division of the company.

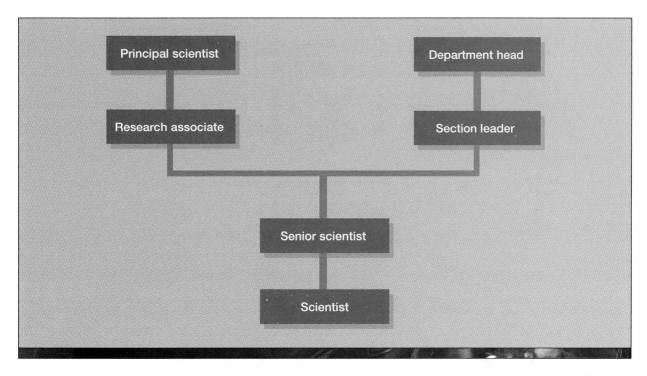

Source: Adapted from Alan Garmonsway and Michael Wellin, "Creating the Right Natural Chemistry," *People Management* 1, no. 19 (September 21, 1995): 36–9.

The Boundaryless Career

A generation ago, the "organization man" served as a popular career icon. Career success was synonymous with ascending a corporate hierarchy over the course of a lifetime spent in a single firm. Today, however, individuals pursuing *boundaryless careers* may prefer to see themselves as self-directed "free agents" who develop a portfolio of employment opportunities by proactively moving from employer to employer, simultaneously developing and utilizing their marketable skills. As shown in Figure 7.5, it is possible to map the different career profiles. Employees pursuing boundaryless careers develop their human capital along dimensions of industry and occupational knowledge. That is, they may be experts in computer programming or have great insights into trends in the banking industry. In contrast, individuals pursuing more traditional careers develop their knowledge in ways specific to a given firm.[6]

Both approaches can be beneficial, but they are not the same. Under the new boundaryless career model, success depends on continually learning new skills, developing new relationships, and capitalizing on existing skills and relationships. These individuals place a premium on flexibility and the capacity to do several different types of tasks, to learn new jobs, to adjust quickly to different group settings and organizational cultures, and to move from one firm, occupation, or industry to another. Their employment security depends on their marketable skills rather than their dedication to one organization over time.

| Figure 7.5 | Human Capital Profiles for Two Different Careers |

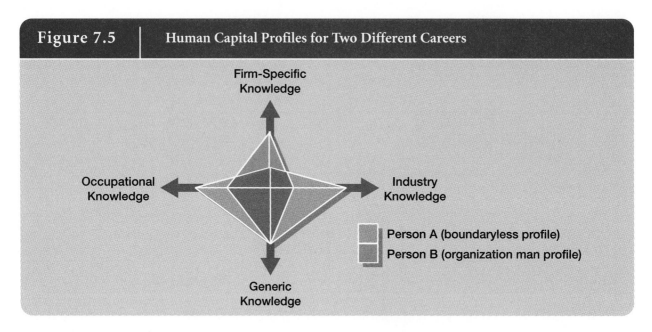

Source: Scott Snell, Cornell University.

Gauging Employee Potential

Side by side with mapping the career opportunities and requirements with their organizations, managers must also establish a clear understanding of the talent base they have at their disposal. This typically begins with the use of performance appraisal and moves into other potentially sophisticated methods.

Using Performance Appraisals

Performance appraisals are discussed more fully in the next chapter (Chapter 8). For our purposes here, we want to note that managers measure and evaluate an employee's performance for several reasons, none more important than for making developmental and career decisions. Successful performers are often good candidates for a promotion. In contrast, poorly performing employees may need—and benefit from—a transfer to another area or even a demotion.

Identifying and developing talent in individuals is a role that all managers should take seriously. As they conduct formal appraisals, they should be concerned with their subordinates' potential for managerial or advanced technical jobs and encourage their growth in that direction. In addition to immediate managers, others in the organization should have the power to evaluate, nominate, and sponsor employees with promise.

Inventorying Management Talent

As we discussed in Chapter 4, skill inventories are an important tool for succession planning. These inventories provide an indication of the skills employees have as well as their interests and experiences. In this way, they help managers pay better attention to the developmental needs of employees, both in their present jobs and in managerial jobs to which they may be promoted. An equally important part of this process is identifying high-potential employees who may be groomed as replacements for managers who are reassigned, retire, or otherwise vacate a position.

Unfortunately, many companies do a poor job of managing their talent. In a study conducted by McKinsey and Company, three-quarters of corporate officers said their companies were chronically short of talent. At the same time, half of the respondents to a similar survey acknowledged that they were not doing effective succession planning and were unprepared to replace key executives.[7]

Organizations that emphasize developing human assets as well as turning a profit typically have the talent they need and some to spare. Some companies—GE, Xerox, and Intel, to name a few—have become "academy" companies that unintentionally provide a source of talented managers to organizations that lack good management career development programs of their own.

Using Assessment Centres

There are other very effective ways to assess a person's career potential. Pioneered in the mid-1950s by Douglas Bray and his associates at AT&T, assessment centres are considered one of the most valuable methods for evaluating personnel. An **assessment centre** is a process (not a place) by which individuals are evaluated as they participate in a series of situations that resemble what they might be called upon to handle on the job. The popularity of the assessment centre can be attributed to its capacity for increasing an organization's ability to select employees who will perform successfully in management positions or to assist and promote the development of skills for their current position. These centres may use in-basket exercises, leaderless group discussions, and approaches discussed in Chapter 6:

▶ **In-basket training.** This method is used to simulate a problem situation. The participants are given several documents, each describing some problem or situation requiring an immediate response. They are thus forced to make decisions under the pressure of time and also to determine what priority to give each problem.

▶ **Leaderless group discussions.** With this activity, trainees are gathered in a conference setting to discuss an assigned topic, either with or without designated group roles. The participants are given little or no instruction in how to approach the topic, nor are they told what decision to reach. Leaderless group trainees are evaluated on their initiative, leadership skills, and ability to work effectively in a group setting.

The various activities of the Public Service Commission assessment centre are shown in Highlights in HRM 7.2. Participation in these activities provides samples of behaviour that are representative of what is required for advancement. At the end of the assessment-centre period, the assessors' observations are combined and integrated to develop an overall picture of the strengths and needs of the participants. A report is normally submitted to senior management, and feedback is given to the participants.

Increasing attention is being given to the validity of assessment-centre procedures. As with employment tests, the assessments provided must be valid. Before the assessment centre is run, the characteristics or dimensions to be studied should be determined through job analyses. The exercises used in the centre should reflect the job for

Assessment centre Process by which individuals are evaluated as they participate in a series of situations that resemble what they might be called upon to handle on the job

In-basket training Assessment-centre process for evaluating trainees by simulating a real-life work situation

Leaderless group discussions Assessment-centre process that places trainees in a conference setting to discuss an assigned topic, either with or without designated group roles

Highlights in HRM 7.2

THE ASSESSMENT CENTRE PROGRAM OF THE PUBLIC SERVICE COMMISSION

The first step in the use of an assessment centre is to work with managers, who are asked by psychologists to keep a diary of their daily activities and problems. They are then questioned about their work in order to identify the major problems that a manager might face. The focus is on identifying the abilities needed to resolve these problems. This information is used to develop the simulation exercises.

Candidates for managerial positions, playing the role of a manager, are asked to respond to a series of letters, memos, and variance reports (reports detailing how the results varied from the planned results). They then present, in oral and written forms, the approach they would use to resolve the problem. These approaches include the establishment of priorities, plans, solutions, and decisions.

The selection board, composed of the hiring manager, at least one outside manager, and a staffing officer, is trained to understand the simulation and the various effective approaches. The candidates are evaluated on how well they got their ideas across and on how well they plan, monitor, and control programs.

Everyone involved strongly identifies with the realistic nature of the simulation. Candidates get so involved in the simulation that they forget it is a test, and managers feel they can actually visualize these people at work. Even unsuccessful candidates claim they learn about themselves in the process.

Source: The Personal Psychology Centre, Public Service Commission, Government of Canada, Ottawa.

which the person is being evaluated; that is, the exercises should have content validity. While the assessment-centre methodology lends itself readily to content validation, predictive validity has also been observed in many instances. A strong positive relationship is found between assessments and future performance on the job.[8]

While assessment centres have proved quite valuable in identifying managerial talent and in helping with the development of individuals, it should be noted that the method tends to favour those who are strong in interpersonal skills and have the ability to influence others. Some individuals find it difficult to perform at their best in a situation that for them is as threatening as taking a test. The manner in which assessment-centre personnel conduct the exercises and provide feedback to the participants will play a major role in determining how individuals react to the experience.

Career Development Initiatives

Although career management involves a good deal of analysis and planning, the reality is that it needs to provide a set of tools and techniques that help employees gauge their potential for success in the organization. Informal counselling by HR staff

The University of Waterloo offers a complete career development e-site:

www.cdm.uwaterloo.ca/

and supervisors is used widely. Many organizations give their employees information on educational assistance, employment equity programs and policies, salary administration, and job requirements. Career planning workbooks and workshops are also popular means of helping employees identify their potential and the strength of their interests.

In a recent study undertaken by Drake Beam Morin, a management consulting firm, the six most successful career-management practices used within organizations are the following:

▶ Placing clear expectations on employees so that they know what is expected of them throughout their careers with the organization.

▶ Giving employees the opportunity to transfer to other office locations, both domestically and internationally.

▶ Providing a clear and thorough succession plan to employees.

▶ Encouraging performance through rewards and recognition.

▶ Giving employees the time and resources they need to consider short- and long-term career goals.

▶ Encouraging employees to continually assess their skills and career direction.

In contrast, organizations also need to be mindful of the internal barriers that inhibit employees' career advancement. Generally, these barriers can include such things as the following:

▶ Lack of time, budgets, and resources for employees to plan their careers and to undertake training and development.

▶ Rigid job specifications, lack of leadership support for career management, and a short-term focus.

▶ Lack of career opportunities and pathways within the organization for employees.[9]

Career Planning Workbooks

Several organizations have prepared workbooks to guide their employees individually through systematic self-assessment of values, interests, abilities, goals, and personal development plans. General Motors' *Career Development Guide* contains a section called "What Do You Want Your Future to Be?" in which the employee makes a personal evaluation. General Electric has developed an extensive set of career development programs, including workbooks to help employees explore life issues that affect career decisions.

Some organizations prefer to use workbooks written for the general public. Popular ones include Richard N. Bolles's *What Color Is Your Parachute?*, Andrew H. Souerwine's *Career Strategies: Planning for Personal Growth,* John Holland's *Self-Directed Search,* and John W. Slocum and G. Scott King's *How to Pack Your Career Parachute.*[10] These same books are recommended to students for help in planning their careers.

Career Planning Workshops

Workshops offer experiences similar to those provided by workbooks. However, they have the advantage of providing a chance to compare and discuss attitudes, concerns, and plans with others in similar situations. Some workshops focus on current job performance and development plans. Others deal with broader life and career plans and values.

As mentioned earlier, employees should be encouraged to assume responsibility for their own careers. A career workshop can help them do that. It can also help them learn how to make career decisions, set career goals, create career options, seek career planning information, and at the same time build confidence and self-esteem.[11]

Career Counselling

Career counselling
Process of discussing with employees their current job activities and performance, their personal and career interests and goals, their personal skills, and suitable career development objectives

Career counselling involves talking with employees about their current job activities and performance, their personal and career interests and goals, their personal skills, and suitable career development objectives. While some organizations make counselling a part of the annual performance appraisal, career counselling is usually voluntary. Career counselling may be provided by the HR staff, managers and supervisors, specialized staff counsellors, or outside consultants. Several techniques for career counselling are outlined at the end of this chapter. (See the section titled "Personal Career Development.") The obligations of employees to return the corporate investment in their development are discussed in Ethics in HRM.

As employees approach retirement, they may be encouraged to participate in preretirement programs, which often include counselling along with other helping activities. Preretirement programs will be discussed in Chapter 11.

Supporting career development activities can help the organization achieve retention and productivity goals, as outlined in The Business Case.[12]

Determining Individual Development Needs

Because the requirements of each position and the qualifications of each person are different, no two individuals will have identical developmental needs. For one individual, self-development may consist of developing the ability to write reports, give talks, and lead conferences. For another, it may require developing interpersonal skills

Ethics in HRM

INDIVIDUAL INVESTMENT OR ORGANIZATIONAL INVESTMENT?

Organizations such as Procter & Gamble and IBM invest a great deal of time and money in developing their professional sales staff and management personnel. Similarly, the federal government offers new university recruits up to six months of language training and tuition-paid university courses, as well as several weeks of skills training, within the first two years on the job.

Other organizations refuse to invest in the long-term development of their employees. They cite statistics suggesting that over one-third of university recruits will quit within the first year. In addition, they argue that other corporations will raid these highly trained personnel.

Do employees who have received the benefit of extensive development programs at the employer's expense have an obligation to remain with the organization so that it can realize a return on its investment?

The Business Case

THE HIDDEN VALUE OF CAREER DEVELOPMENT PROGRAMS

Career development programs may not appear to offer the obvious return on investments that absenteeism or safety management programs offer. However, employers should start to measure the following in order to make the business case for career development:

Attraction: Do organizations establish reputations as "academies" that develop talent through solid career development and mentoring programs?

Retention: Do units with strong career development programs have higher retention rates of top talent than those without?

Employability: If organizations cannot guarantee lifetime employment, do they have a moral responsibility to provide career development programs that ensure that employees are employable?

Commitment: In those organizations with career development programs, is there a correlation between employee commitment and productivity?

in order to communicate and relate more effectively with a diverse workforce. Periodic performance appraisals can provide a basis for determining each manager's progress. Conferences in which these appraisals are discussed are an essential part of self-improvement efforts.

In helping individuals plan their careers, it is important for organizations to recognize that younger employees today seek meaningful training assignments that are interesting and involve challenge, responsibility, and a sense of empowerment. They also have a greater concern for the contribution that their work in the organization will make to society. Unfortunately, they are frequently given responsibilities they view as rudimentary, boring, and composed of too many "make-work" activities. Some organizations are attempting to retain young managers with high potential by offering a **fast-track program** that enables them to advance more rapidly than those with less potential. A fast-track program may provide for a relatively rapid progression—lateral transfers or promotions—through a number of managerial positions requiring exposure to different organizational functions; it may also provide opportunities to make meaningful decisions.

Fast-track program
Program that encourages young managers with high potential to remain with an organization by enabling them to advance more rapidly than those with less potential

Career Self-Management Training

In response to the growing view that employees should assume greater responsibility for their own career management, many organizations are establishing programs for employees on how they can engage in *career self-management*. The training focuses on two major objectives: (1) helping employees learn to continuously gather feedback and information about their careers and (2) encouraging them to prepare for mobility.

The training is not geared to skills and behaviours associated with a specific job, but rather toward their long-term personal effectiveness. Employees typically undertake self-assessments to increase awareness of their own career attitudes and values. In addition, they are encouraged to widen their viewpoint beyond the next company promotion to broader opportunities in the marketplace. For many, these external opportunities have not been seen as viable options, much less something the company would acknowledge. Participants might be encouraged to engage in career networking or to identify other means to prepare for job mobility, such as hearing reports from employees who made transitions to new job opportunities both within and outside the organization.[13]

Mentoring

When one talks with men and women about their employment experiences, it is common to hear them mention individuals at work who influenced them. They frequently refer to immediate managers who were especially helpful as career developers. But they also mention others at higher levels in the organization who provided guidance and support to them in the development of their careers. These executives and managers who coach, advise, and encourage employees of lesser rank are called **mentors.**

At times, individuals can be overly restrictive in their definitions of who constitutes a mentor or what that mentor can do. The top ten myths about mentors are shown in Figure 7.6. In reality, informal mentoring goes on daily within every type of organization. Generally, the mentor initiates the relationship, but sometimes an employee will approach a potential mentor for advice. Most mentoring relationships develop over time on an informal basis. However, proactive organizations emphasize formal mentoring plans that assign a mentor to those employees considered for upward movement in the organization. Under a good mentor, learning focuses on goals, opportunities, expectations, standards, and assistance in fulfilling one's potential.[14]

Figure 7.7 shows a list of the most effective features of mentors as well as partners. In order to form an effective mentoring relationship, individuals should follow a few general guidelines:

Mentors
Executives who coach, advise, and encourage individuals of lesser rank

1. *Research the person's background.* Do your homework. The more you know about your potential mentor, the easier it will be to approach him or her and establish a relationship that will work for both of you.
2. *Make contact with the person.* Have a mutual friend or acquaintance introduce you, or get involved with your potential mentor in business settings. That will help the mentor see your skills in action.
3. *Request help on a particular matter.* Let the mentor know that you admire him or her, and ask for help in that arena. For example, you might say, "You're good at dealing with customers. Would it be okay if I came to you for advice on my customers?" Keep your request simple and specific.
4. *Consider what you can offer in exchange.* Mentoring is a two-way street. If you can do something for your potential mentor, then by all means, tell him or her.
5. *Arrange a meeting.* Once your specific request has been accepted, you're ready to meet with your potential mentor. Never go into this meeting cold. Set goals, identify your desired outcomes, and prepare a list of questions. Listen attentively. Then ask your prepared questions and request specific suggestions.

Figure 7.6	Top Ten Myths about Mentors

Myth 1: *Mentors exist only for career development.* Sometimes the mentor focuses on formal career development. Sometimes the mentor is teacher, counsellor, and friend. Some mentors assume all these roles. This enhances both personal and professional development.

Myth 2: *You need only one mentor.* We can have multiple mentors in our lives. Different mentors provide different things and tap different facets of our lives.

Myth 3: *Mentoring is a one-way process.* Learning flows both ways. The mentor often learns from the protégé, so the growth is reciprocal.

Myth 4: *A mentor has to be older than the protégé.* Age does not matter. Experience and wisdom matter. Don't deprive yourself of learning opportunities from others who have rich experiences.

Myth 5: *A mentor has to be the same gender and race as the protégé.* The purpose of mentoring is to learn. Don't deprive yourself. Seek mentors who are different from you.

Myth 6: *Mentor relationships just happen.* Being in the right place at the right time can help, but the key to selecting a good mentor is what (not whom) you need. Don't be afraid to actively seek a mentor.

Myth 7: *Highly profiled people make the best mentors.* Prestige and success can be good, but good advice, leadership styles, work ethics, and the like vary by individuals. Good mentors are people who challenge you according to your needs, readiness, and aspirations.

Myth 8: *Once a mentor, always a mentor.* Over time, the mentor should pull back and let the protégé go his or her own way. Although the two may maintain contact, the relationship changes over time.

Myth 9: *Mentoring is a complicated process.* The most complicated part is getting out of a bad mentor relationship. If the relationship is not productive, find a tactful way to disengage.

Myth 10: *Mentor-protégé expectations are the same for everyone.* Individuals seek mentors for the same reasons: resources, visibility, enhanced skills, and counsel. But each individual brings different expectations. The key is understanding where the protégé is *now,* not where he or she *should be.*

Figure 7.7	Mentoring Functions

Good Mentors . . .
- Listen and understand
- Challenge and stimulate learning
- Coach
- Build self-confidence
- Provide wise counsel
- Teach by example
- Act as role model
- Share experiences
- Offer encouragement

SUCCESSFUL MENTORING

Good Partners . . .
- Listen
- Act on advice
- Show commitment to learn
- Check ego at the door
- Ask for feedback
- Are open-minded
- Are willing to change
- Are proactive

Source: Matt Starcevich and Fred Friend, "Effective Mentoring Relationships from the Mentee's Perspective," *Workforce*, supplement (July 1999): 2–3. Center for Coaching and Mentoring, Inc., http://coachingandmentoring.com/.

6. *Follow up.* After the meeting, try some of your potential mentor's suggestions and share the results. Express appreciation by identifying something in particular that was significant to you.

7. *Ask to meet on an ongoing basis.* After your potential mentor has had a chance to not only meet and interact with you, but also to see the value of what he or she can provide, you're in a good position to request an ongoing relationship. Suggest that you meet with him or her regularly, or ask permission to get help on an ad hoc basis.[15]

Highlights in HRM 7.3 shows a checklist of some of the qualities an individual should look for in a mentor.

Organizations with formal mentoring programs include Shell International, Sun Microsystems, Johnson & Johnson, and the Bank of Montreal. Alternatively, given the importance of the issue, a number of mentoring organizations have begun to spring up. About 70 percent of Canadian organizations have formal or informal mentoring programs.[16] When done well, the mentoring process is beneficial for both the pupil and the mentor. A new form of mentoring, sponsored by the MS Foundation for Women, provides an opportunity for girls nine to fifteen years old to spend a day with mothers or friends on the job. The program is designed to give young women more attention and to provide them with career role models. Many large organizations, including Nike, DuPont, Ford, and Valvoline, have participated in this program, and it has grown to include boys of the same age. Other groups, such as the Girl Scouts in the Washington, D.C., area, have longer-term mentoring plans where young women age twelve to eighteen spend up to a month during one year in the offices of women scientists, accountants, and other professionals. It is hoped that through such programs, young women will think more broadly in their career planning.[17]

USING THE INTERNET

You can download a complete mentoring tool kit from

www.mentoring.org/training/TMT/Mentor_training_toolkit.pdf

Not surprisingly, mentoring is also being done over the Internet. Known as *e-mentoring,* the process is mediated via websites that bring experienced business professionals together with individuals needing counselling. A few examples include the following:

▶ *Women in Technology International (WITI)* is an association that has assembled thousands of women in technology fields who act as online mentors to visitors to its website.

▶ *Canada Info Net* is an online mentoring program that includes a twelve-week virtual training program to help immigrants receive support and adapt to the Canadian job market.

▶ *NursingNet* is an online nursing forum that has mentoring programs for those in health care. The site hooks up experienced nurses with those who need guidance.[18]

Even though participants in e-mentoring typically never meet in person, many form long-lasting e-mail connections that tend to be very beneficial. Still, most participants see these connections as supplements to—rather than substitutes for—in-company mentors. Highlights in HRM 7.4 discusses the advantages of e-mail mentoring.

Highlights in HRM 7.3

MENTOR CHECKLIST

Successful mentoring is built on a common understanding of interests and "ground rules." Here are some to consider before establishing a mentor–protégé relationship:

1. Formalize the expectations with a written agreement that outlines the behaviours of each person.
2. Understand that either party can withdraw from the relationship at any time, and it is not necessary to provide an explanation.
3. All documents exchanged, such as company plans or resumés, will be treated as confidential.
4. The mentor cannot be solicited for a job. Doing so is grounds for breaking the relationship.
5. Respect each other's time. Arrive on time and prepared with a list of questions or topics to be discussed.
6. Provide feedback honestly. For example, the protégé could state, "This is not the kind of information I need at this stage" or the mentor might advise, "You should not skip meetings just because they are tedious; it is an important part of this company's culture to be visible at these meetings."

Networking

As the number of contacts grows, mentoring broadens into a process of *career networking*. As a complement to mentoring, where relationships are more selective, networking relationships tend to be more varied and temporary. The networks can be internal to a particular organization or connected across many different organizations.

According to the Monster.com Career Center (http://content.monster.com/career/networking/), networking contacts can be identified in many ways. Some of the best places to consider are the following:

▶ Your college or university alumni association or career office networking lists
▶ Your own extended family
▶ Your friends' parents and other family members
▶ Your professors, advisors, coaches, tutors, clergy
▶ Your former bosses and your friends' and family members' bosses
▶ Members of clubs, religious groups, and other organizations to which you belong
▶ All the organizations near where you live or go to school

Through networking, individuals often find out about new jobs, professional trends, and other opportunities.

Highlights in HRM 7.4

E-MENTORING

Virtual mentoring is often an excellent way for busy mentors (and equally busy protégés) to deal with time constraints. Those who are comfortable with e-mail and the Internet say that both have many advantages over real-time meetings. Because there are no geographic boundaries to e-mentoring (i.e., no need for the mentor and the protégé to be in the same city), a wider range of possible mentors is accessible. Scheduling is easier, since either party can log on at any time to ask questions or offer counsel. Because the mentor can take time to consider the answers to questions, the individual being mentored gets more reasoned responses. People seeking advice often maintain a log of their questions and the answers to them; these can be shared later with others in similar situations. Because e-mentoring is more efficient in many ways, mentors can advise more people. The technology can even help match mentors and protégés.

IBM Canada runs a pilot e-mentoring program in which forty girls from grades seven and eight have been matched with computer programmers, sales personnel, and administrators, the goal being to stimulate their interest in technology careers.

The downside is that e-mentoring uses "flat" technology and so cannot convey emotions or facial expressions that in a face-to-face interaction often alert the mentor to underlying problems. That being said, the advantages of e-mentoring—quick feedback, well-considered responses, and more informal communication—make it one of the more popular ways for employees to build organizational know-how.

DIVERSITY MANAGEMENT AND CAREER DEVELOPMENT

Today some organizations offer extensive career development programs that include programs geared to special groups, such as women, minorities, and dual-career couples. Let's examine some of these special programs more closely.

Career Development for Women

In Chapter 4 we discussed some of the current trends in the employment of women in jobs that until recently were held predominantly by men. Included among these jobs are management-level positions. Organizations are continually concerned, as a result of employment equity requirements and because of the need for strong leadership, about increasing the proportion of women they employ as managers.

Eliminating Barriers to Advancement
Women in management have been at a disadvantage because they were not part of the so-called old boys' network, an informal network of interpersonal relationships that has traditionally provided a means for senior (male) members of the organization to

pass along news of advancement opportunities and other career tips to junior (male) members. Women have typically been outside the network, lacking role models to serve as mentors. Figure 7.8 lists some of the do's and don'ts of networking.

To combat their difficulty in advancing to management positions, women in several organizations have developed their own women's networks. The Bank of Montreal has a women's network that any female employee can join in order to facilitate career development. Corporate officers are invited to regularly scheduled network meetings to discuss such matters as planning, development, and company performance. Network members view these sessions as an opportunity to let corporate officers know of women who are interested in and capable of furthering their careers. Employees who have had a senior manager take an interest in their careers have received more promotions and compensation than those who have not.[19]

As we mentioned previously, there are several online e-mentoring networks available. One that is expressly devoted to working women is Advancing Women (www.advancingwomen.com). In addition, an organization devoted to helping employers break down barriers to upward mobility for women is Catalyst, a not-for-profit organization. Catalyst (www.catalystwomen.org/) not only courts corporate officers but also offers career advice, job placement, continuing education, and related professional development for women of all ages.[20]

The advancement of women in management has been hindered by a series of sex-role stereotypes that have shaped the destiny of women, working women in particular. (See Chapter 4.) Fortunately, there is substantial evidence that stereotyped attitudes toward women are changing. As women pursue career goals assertively and attitudes continue to change, the climate for women in management will be even more

Figure 7.8	Rules of Networking

Barbara Moses, president of BBM Human Resource Consultants and the author of *Career Intelligence: Mastering the New Work and Personal Realities*, states that networking is an increasingly important career skill. Networking is not about using someone to get ahead; rather, it is about expanding relationships and developing mutually supportive ones. Here are some do's and don'ts of networking:

▶ Don't call once a year, feigning friendship and concern, when it is obvious that the rest of the year you don't care if this person exists.

▶ Do keep in touch throughout the year, giving information about mergers and moves, or anything that might benefit the other person.

▶ Don't approach everyone you meet as a potential business lead. People you meet at parties or on planes should be appreciated for their characteristics, not for what they can do for you. Make new friends, not new contacts. Too often, people hang out in herds, actors with actors; bankers with bankers. Parties and planes offer the opportunity to add breadth to your world.

▶ Don't use information interviewing. Some guru suggested that calling someone and saying, "I am currently exploring careers. Can I meet with you to discuss your business?" is now seen as the transparent and tired job-search technique that it is. Volunteer work and internships will impress an employer more.

Source: Adapted from Barbara Moses, "The Right and Wrong Ways to Network," *The Globe and Mail*, September 4, 1997, B10.

favourable. Research has shown that newer male managers tend to be more receptive to the advancement of women managers. A study commissioned by the Women's Executive Network in Canada revealed that the majority of women executives feel that they have hit the glass ceiling—that they face more barriers than similarly qualified men. Women hold only 14 percent of corporate officer positions in Canada's 500 largest corporations.[21]

Glass-Ceiling Audits

The glass ceiling can be described as "those artificial barriers based on attitudinal or organizational bias that prevent qualified individuals from advancing upward in their organizations into management level positions."[22] "Glass-ceiling reviews," also known as "corporate reviews," are conducted to identify practices that appear to hinder the upward mobility of qualified women (and minorities) and to be limiting their access to

▶ Upper-level management and executive training
▶ Rotational assignments
▶ International assignments
▶ Opportunities for promotion
▶ Opportunities for executive development programs at universities
▶ Desirable compensation packages
▶ Opportunities to participate on high-profile project teams
▶ Upper-level special assignments

These audits can document any ceilings and the reasons they exist. Self-audits are one step to tapping the potentials of a diversified workforce.

Artificial barriers or "glass ceilings" are being shattered by successful women executives.

PHOTODISC

Preparing Women for Management

As noted earlier, opportunities for women to move into management positions are definitely improving. In addition to breaking down the barriers to advancement, the development of women managers demands a better understanding of women's needs and the requirements of the management world.

Business today needs all the leadership, talent, quality, competence, productivity, innovation, and creativity it can get, as Canadian firms face more-demanding world-wide competition. Companies committed to equal opportunities for women and men will undoubtedly keep the best talent available. A list of actions organizations can take to maximize the human resource represented by women is presented in Highlights in HRM 7.5.[23]

Many employers now offer special training to women who are on a management career path. They may use their own staff or outside firms to conduct this training. Opportunities are also available for women to participate in seminars and workshops that provide instruction and experiences in a wide variety of management topics.

In addition to formal training opportunities, women today are provided with a wealth of information and guidance in books and magazines. Business sections in bookstores are stocked with numerous books written especially for women who want a better idea of the career opportunities available to them. Many books are devoted to the pursuit of careers in specific fields.[24]

Popular magazines that contain many articles about women and jobs include *Working Woman, New Woman, Savvy, The Executive Female,* and *Enterprising Women.* These magazines are also recommended reading for men who want a better understanding of the problems that women face in the world of work.

Accommodating Families

One of the major problems women have faced is that of having both a managerial career and a family. Women managers whose children are at an age requiring close parental attention often experience conflict between their responsibility to the children and their duty to the employer. If the conflict becomes too painful, they may decide to forgo their careers, at least temporarily, and leave their jobs. Companies with three hundred or more employees lose an average of $88 000 a year because of absenteeism, shortened workdays, and lost work hours due to child care problems.[25]

USING THE INTERNET

Many organizations today realize the importance of families to both male and female managers. See how quality-of-life and family resource programs are included in career planning at DuPont.

www.dupont.com/careers/vs_work
life/index.html

In recent years many employers, including CIBC, have inaugurated programs that are mutually advantageous to the career-oriented woman and the employer. These programs, which include alternative career paths, extended leave, flextime, job sharing, and telecommuting, provide new ways to balance career and family. The number of employers moving to protect their investment in top-flight women is still small, but more of them are defining a separate track for women managers.[26]

Nevertheless, there is still a fairly controversial debate about the so-called mommy track, a separate track designed to help women be productive but not necessarily upwardly mobile. Many women, as well as men, criticize the use of a separate track as perpetuating the inequities of a double standard and as pitting women against women—those with children against those without. On the other hand, there are those who believe that this approach at least gives women choices.[27]

Highlights in HRM 7.5

MAXIMIZING THE HUMAN RESOURCES OF FEMALE MANAGERS

1. Ensure that women receive frequent and specific feedback on their job performance. Women need and want candid reviews of their work. Clearly articulated suggestions for improvement, standards for work performance, and plans for career advancement will make women feel more involved in their jobs and help make them better employees.

2. Accept women as valued members of the management team. Include them in every kind of communication. Listen to their needs and concerns, and encourage their contributions.

3. Give talented women the same opportunities given to talented men to grow, develop, and contribute to company profitability. Give them the responsibility to direct major projects and to plan and implement systems and programs. Expect them to travel and relocate and to make the same commitment to the company as men aspiring to leadership positions.

4. Give women the same level of counselling on professional career advancement opportunities as that given to men.

5. Identify women as potential managers early in their employment and facilitate their advancement through training and other developmental activities.

6. Assist women in strengthening their assertion skills. Reinforce strategic career planning to encourage women's commitment to their careers and long-term career plans.

7. Accelerate the development of qualified women through fast-track programs. Either formally or informally, this method will provide women with the exposure, knowledge, and positioning for career advancement.

8. Provide opportunities for women to develop mentoring or sponsoring relationships with employees. Women do not often have equal or easy access (compared with their male colleagues) to senior employees. The overall goal should be to provide advice, counsel, and support to promising female employees by knowledgeable, senior-level men and women.

9. Encourage company co-ed management support systems and networks. Sharing experiences and information with other men and women who are managers provides invaluable support to peers. These activities provide the opportunity for women to meet and learn from men and women in more advanced stages of their careers—a helpful way of identifying potential mentors or role models.

10. Examine the feasibility of increasing participation of women in company-sponsored planning retreats, use of company facilities, social functions, and so forth. With notable exceptions, men are still generally more comfortable with other men, and as a result, women miss many of the career and business opportunities that arise during social functions. In addition, women may not have access to information about the company's informal political and social systems. Encourage male managers to include women when socializing with other business associates.

Source: Adapted from R. M. Wentling, "Women in Middle Management: Their Career Development and Aspirations," from *Business Horizons,* January/February 1992, the Foundation for the School of Business at Indiana University.

objective

Career Development for Minorities

Many organizations have specific career planning programs for minority employees. These programs are intended to equip employees with career planning skills and development opportunities that will help them compete effectively for advancement.

We observed in Chapter 4 that many employers make a special effort to recruit minorities. Once individuals from minority groups are on the job, it is important for employers to provide opportunities for them to move ahead in the organization as they improve their job skills and abilities.

Advancement of Minorities to Management

The area of employment that has been the slowest to respond to employment equity appeals is the advancement of minorities to middle- and top-management positions. While visible minorities tend to be better educated, they continue to have higher rates of unemployment and fewer executive positions.[28]

Visible minorities who aspire to higher levels in an organization are likely to find that their careers will start off like rockets but that as they reach the middle ranks a barrier makes it very difficult to move to the top. Visible minorities, including aboriginals, tend to have reduced access to job interviews, higher rates of unemployment and lower compensation.[29] Given the talent shortages existing in most industries, few organizations can afford to neglect the development of potential managers.

While minority managers do play a part in creating a better climate for groups that are discriminated against in advancement opportunities, top management and the HR department have the primary responsibility to create conditions in the organization that are favourable for recognizing and rewarding performance on the basis of objective, nondiscriminatory criteria.

Providing Internships

One approach to helping minority students prepare for management careers is to give them employment experiences while they are still in school. Most employers work with educational institutions to place and train interns, who are then frequently hired on a permanent basis after their schooling is finished. The Canadian Association for Internships was created to increase the number of internships available within Canadian organizations.[30]

Organizing Training Courses

As part of diversity management programs some organizations offer specialized programs to facilitate the promotion of visible minority employees. For example, the Department of Citizenship and Immigration has established a development program "for individuals in a visible minority whose potential to progress to senior (feeder groups) and executive levels would have been identified as early as possible in their career. The program features individual coaching, a career map, and a training and development path for each individual, with milestones and regular checkpoints. Developmental assignments, internship programs and education leave are used to round up the development of these employees of high potential. Assessment of the program, by both the participating visible minorities and the implicated managers is mandatory." [31]

Dual-Career Couples

As discussed throughout this book, the employment of both members of a couple has become a way of life in North America. Economic necessity and social forces have encouraged this trend to the point that over 80 percent of all marriages are now **dual-career partnerships** in which both members follow their own careers and actively support each other's career development.

As with most lifestyles, the dual-career arrangement has its positive and negative sides. A significant number of organizations are concerned with the problems facing dual-career couples and offer assistance to them. Flexible working schedules are the most frequent organizational accommodation to these couples. Other arrangements include leave policies where either parent may stay home with a newborn, policies that allow work to be performed at home, day care on organization premises, and job sharing.

The difficulties that dual-career couples face include the need for quality child care, the time demands, and the emotional stress. However, the main problem these couples face is the threat of relocation. Many large organizations now offer some kind of job-finding assistance for spouses of employees who are relocated, including payment of fees charged by employment agencies, job counselling firms, and executive search firms. Organizations are also developing networking relationships with other employers to find jobs for the spouses of their relocating employees. These networks can provide a way to "share the wealth and talent" in a community while simultaneously assisting in the recruitment efforts of the participating organizations.[32]

Relocating dual-career couples to foreign facilities is a major issue that international employers face. Fewer employees are willing to relocate without assistance for their spouses. Many employers have developed effective approaches for integrating the various allowances typically paid for overseas assignments when husband and wife work for the same employer. Far more complex are the problems that arise when couples work for two different employers. The problems associated with overseas assignments of dual-career couples will be examined in greater detail in Chapter 15.

Dual-career partnerships
Couples in which both members follow their own careers and actively support each other's career development

PERSONAL CAREER DEVELOPMENT

objective

We have observed that there are numerous ways for an employer to contribute to an individual employee's career development and at the same time meet the organization's HR needs. The organization can certainly be a positive force in the development process, but the primary responsibility for personal career growth still rests with the individual. One's career may begin before and often continue after a period of employment with an organization. To help employees achieve their career objectives, managers and HRM professionals should understanding the stages one goes through in developing a career and the actions one should take to be successful.

Stages of Career Development

Knowledge, skills, abilities, and attitudes as well as career aspirations change as one matures. While the work that individuals in different occupations perform can vary significantly, the challenges and frustrations that they face at the same stage in their careers are remarkably similar. A model describing these stages is shown in Figure 7.9. The stages are (1) preparation for work, (2) organizational entry, (3) early career, (4) midcareer, and (5) late career. The typical age range and the major tasks of each stage are also presented in the figure.

The first stage—preparation for work—encompasses the period prior to entering an organization, often extending until age twenty-five. It is a period in which individuals must acquire the knowledge, abilities, and skills they will need to compete in the marketplace. It is a time when careful planning, based on sound information, should be the focus. Reality Check describes a service that helps new entrants obtain their first job experiences. The second stage, typically from ages eighteen to twenty-five, is devoted to soliciting job offers and selecting an appropriate job. During this period one may also be involved in preparing for work. The next three stages entail fitting into a chosen occupation and organization, modifying goals, making choices, remaining productive, and finally, preparing for retirement. In the remainder of the chapter we will examine some of the activities of primary concern to the student, who is likely to be in the early stages. Retirement planning will be discussed in Chapter 11.

Figure 7.9	Stages of Career Development

Stage 5: Late Career (ages 55–retirement):

Remain productive in work, maintain self-esteem, prepare for effective retirement.

Stage 4: Midcareer (ages 40–55):

Reappraise early career and early adulthood goals, reaffirm or modify goals, make choices appropriate to middle adult years, remain productive.

Stage 3: Early Career (ages 25–40):

Learn job, learn organizational rules and norms, fit into chosen occupation and organization, increase competence, pursue goals.

Stage 2: Organizational Entry (ages 18–25):

Obtain job offer(s) from desired organization(s), select appropriate job based on complete and accurate information.

Stage 1: Preparation for Work (ages 0–25):

Develop occupational self-image, assess alternative occupations, develop initial occupational choice, pursue necessary education.

Developing Personal Skills and Competencies

In planning a career, one should attend to more than simply acquiring specific job knowledge and skills. Job know-how is clearly essential, but one must develop other skills to be successful as an employee. To succeed as a manager, one must achieve a still-higher level of proficiency in such major areas as communication, time management, self-motivation, interpersonal relationships, and the broad area of leadership.

Hundreds of self-help books have been written on these topics, and myriad opportunities to participate in workshops are available, often sponsored by one's employer.[33] One should not overlook sources of valuable information such as articles in general-interest magazines and professional journals. For example, the pointers on the basic skills of successful career management listed in Highlights in HRM 7.6 are taken from a competency assessment conducted at Caterpillar.

Reality Check

CAREER EDGE MAKING A DIFFERENCE

Career Edge is Canada's youth internship program that helps university, college, and high school graduates launch their careers as full-time paid interns. For recent graduates with no work experience, obtaining that first job can be difficult. They are caught in the cycle of "no experience, no job; no job, no experience." Career Edge helps graduates obtain that first job, which then leads, in most cases, to a permanent job. Career Edge also operates Ability Edge, a national internship program for graduates with disabilities. Career Edge contacts host organizations, who agree to provide an internship combining four elements: employment experience, learning, coaching, and networking. Because the interns are employed by Career Edge, employers do not have to fight for additional positions (a very difficult task in any organization), but can employ the interns from contract budgets. The interns are paid a stipend of $1500 per month.

All job posting is done electronically. Employers post internships on the Career Edge website (www.careeredge.org). Underemployed or unemployed graduates can sign on and search for internships by sector, company, educational discipline, recency, city, length of internship desired, and so on. When a fit is found, the full job description is made available. The site also offers information on job search skills such as resumé and interview preparation.

Frances Randle, the former president and CEO of Career Edge, says: "The contact is made directly between the candidate and the host organization, because these students have to learn how to market themselves, and companies have to commit to the intern directly. Interns are looking for practical experience, increased confidence in their abilities, learning about their fields, getting experience in that field, having challenging work, developing a network, and getting feedback on performance, in that order. Companies want recent university graduates who are enthusiastic, flexible, interested in learning, yet with some technical skills and the ability to communicate."

Since opening for business in October 1996, when the youth unemployment rate was nearly 18 percent, Career Edge has placed 5500 interns at 850 companies. About 50 percent of the interns find full-time work with their host organizations.

Highlights in HRM 7.6

CAREER COMPETENCIES AT CATERPILLAR

During the Caterpillar business unit's career development training process in Joliet, Illinois, the company compiled the following competencies as necessary for success within the reorganized, changing organization:

▶ *Interpersonal skills:* Possesses team-building and leadership skills; can effectively lead groups and facilitate group interaction
▶ *Problem-solving skills:* Can analyze and use problem-solving approaches
▶ *Communication skills:* Able to verbalize articulately, make presentations, and write cogently
▶ *Leadership skills:* Is recognized by peers as a natural leader; accomplishes results without formal authority
▶ *Organization and planning skills:* Able to manage time; sets and achieves goals
▶ *Technical skills:* Possesses education specific to assignments and job content; understands and uses appropriate level of technical skills
▶ *Responsibility:* Takes initiative; accepts accountability for own work and additional tasks for the good of the group
▶ *Assertiveness:* Able and comfortable with communicating openly and directly; demonstrates self-confidence and awareness of others' perceptions
▶ *Flexibility:* Able to adapt to organizational changes and changing market needs; willingly considers new ideas and implements new ways of doing things
▶ *Judgment:* Able to determine level of risk and appropriate action; accepts accountability for significant decisions

Source: Peggy Simonsen and Cathy Wells, "African Americans Take Control of Their Careers," *Personnel Journal* 73, no. 4 (April 1994): 99–108. See also David Dubois, "The Seven Stages of One's Career," *Training and Development* 54, no. 12 (December 2000): 45–50.

Choosing a Career

Many years ago, when Peter Drucker was asked about career choice, he said, "The probability that the first job choice you make is the right one for you is roughly one in a million. If you decide your first choice is the right one, chances are that you are just plain lazy."[34] The implications of this statement are just as true today. One must often do a lot of searching and changing to find a career path that is psychologically and financially satisfying. The 2001 Statistics Canada Census said that the single fastest-growing occupation grouping was customer service and call centre jobs, followed by IT and financial officers (everyone from people who handle the organization's financial investments to those in the finance sector who advise on investments).[35]

Use of Available Resources

A variety of resources are available to aid in the process of choosing a satisfying career. Counsellors at colleges and universities, as well as those in private practice, are equipped to assist individuals in evaluating their aptitudes, abilities, interests, and values as they relate to career selection. There is broad interest among business schools in a formal instructional program in career planning and development, and other units in the institutions, such as placement offices and continuing education centres, offer some type of career planning assistance.

Accuracy of Self-Evaluation

Successful career development depends in part on an individual's ability to conduct an accurate self-evaluation. In making a self-evaluation, one needs to consider those factors that are personally significant. The most important internal factors are one's academic aptitude and achievement, occupational aptitudes and skills, social skills, communication skills, leadership abilities, and interests and values. The latter should include consideration of salary level, status, opportunities for advancement, and growth on the job. External factors that should be assessed include family values and expectations, economic conditions, employment trends, job market information, and perceived effect of physical or psychological disabilities on success.

Significance of Interest Inventories

Psychologists who specialize in career counselling typically administer a battery of tests such as those mentioned in Chapter 5. The *Strong Vocational Interest Blank (SVIB)*, developed by E. K. Strong, Jr., was among the first of the interest tests.[36] Somewhat later, G. Frederic Kuder developed inventories to measure degree of interest in mechanical, clerical, scientific, and persuasive activities, among others. Both the Strong and the Kuder interest inventories have been used widely in vocational counselling.

Strong found that there are substantial differences in interests that vary from occupation to occupation and that a person's interest pattern, especially after age twenty-one, tends to become quite stable. By taking his test, now known as the *Strong Interest Inventory*, one can learn the degree to which his or her interests correspond with those of successful people in a wide range of occupations. Personality type can also be obtained by using a special scoring key on an individual's *Strong Interest Inventory* answer sheet. This key, developed by John Holland, provides scores on six personality types: (1) realistic, (2) investigative, (3) artistic, (4) social, (5) enterprising, and (6) conventional. These categories characterize not only a type of personality, but also the type of working environment that a person would find most satisfying. In the actual application of Holland's theory, combinations of the six types are examined. For example, a person may be classified as realistic-investigative-enterprising (RIE). Jobs in the RIE category include mechanical engineer, lineperson, and air-traffic controller.[37]

Another inventory that measures both interests and skills is *the Campbell Interest and Skill Survey (CISS)*.[38] The CISS can be used not only to assist employees in exploring career paths and options but to help organizations develop their employees or to reassign them because of major organizational changes. In completing the inventory, individuals report their levels of interest and skill using a six-point response scale on 200 interest items and 120 skill items. CISS item responses are translated into seven orientations—influencing, organizing, helping, creating, analyzing, producing,

and adventuring—and further categorized into twenty-nine basic scales such as leadership and supervision, to identify occupations that reflect today's workplace.

Highlights in HRM 7.7 shows a sample profile for one individual. Note that at the top of the profile the range of scores is from 30 to 70, with 50 in the midrange. Corresponding verbal descriptions of scores range from very low to very high. Also note that on the profile two types of scores are profiled: interest (a solid diamond ◆) and skill (an open diamond ◇). The interest score ◆ shows how much the individual likes the specified activities; the skill score ◇ shows how confident the individual feels about performing these activities.

There are four noteworthy patterns of combinations of the interest and skill scores as shown in Figure 7.10: Pursue, Develop, Explore, and Avoid. For the individual whose scores are profiled in Highlights in HRM 7.7, one would interpret the scores on the seven orientation scales (as shown in the right-hand column of the profile) as follows:

Influencing	Pursue
Organizing	Indeterminate
Helping	Pursue
Creating	Avoid
Analyzing	Avoid
Producing	Indeterminate
Adventuring	Develop

On the basis of such profiles, individuals can see how their interests and skills compare with those of a sample of people happily employed in a wide range of occupations. Completed answer sheets can be mailed to a scoring centre, or software is available and may be obtained for in-house scoring.

Evaluation of Long-Term Employment Opportunities

In making a career choice, one should attempt to determine the probable long-term opportunities in the occupational fields one is considering. While even the experts can err in their predictions, one should give at least some attention to the opinions that are available. Human Resources Development Canada provides valuable information about the labour market, with many links to career planning sites. Many libraries also have publications that provide details about jobs and career fields. In recent years, a considerable amount of computer software has been developed to facilitate access to information about career fields and to enable individuals to match their abilities, aptitudes, interests, and experiences with the requirements of occupational areas.

Choosing an Employer

Once an individual has made a career choice, even if only tentatively, the next major step is deciding where to work. The choice of employer may be based primarily on location, on immediate availability of a position, on starting salary, or on other basic considerations. However, the college graduate who has prepared for a professional or managerial career is likely to have more sophisticated concerns. Douglas Hall, a psychologist specializing in careers, proposes that people frequently choose an organization on the basis of its climate and how it appears to fit their needs. According to Hall,

Highlights in HRM 7.7

CAMPBELL INTEREST AND SKILL SURVEY: INDIVIDUAL PROFILE

SAMPLE   ORIENTATIONS AND BASIC SCALES   DATE SCORED 10/20/2003

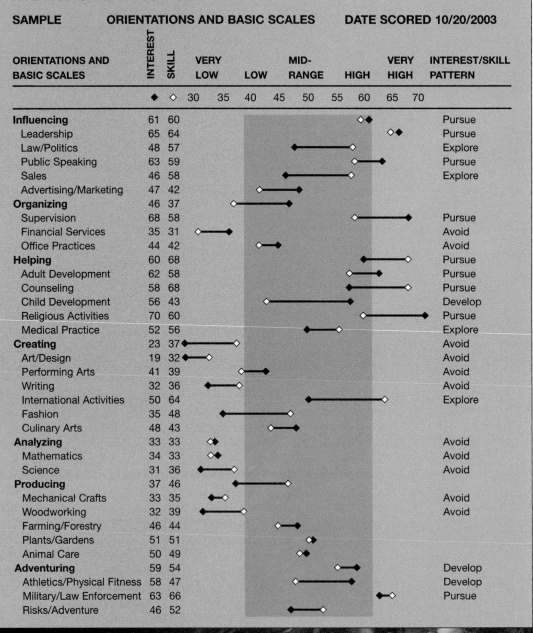

ORIENTATIONS AND BASIC SCALES	INTEREST ◆	SKILL ◇	VERY LOW	LOW	MID-RANGE	HIGH	VERY HIGH	INTEREST/SKILL PATTERN
Influencing	61	60						Pursue
Leadership	65	64						Pursue
Law/Politics	48	57						Explore
Public Speaking	63	59						Pursue
Sales	46	58						Explore
Advertising/Marketing	47	42						
Organizing	46	37						
Supervision	68	58						Pursue
Financial Services	35	31						Avoid
Office Practices	44	42						Avoid
Helping	60	68						Pursue
Adult Development	62	58						Pursue
Counseling	58	68						Pursue
Child Development	56	43						Develop
Religious Activities	70	60						Pursue
Medical Practice	52	56						Explore
Creating	23	37						Avoid
Art/Design	19	32						Avoid
Performing Arts	41	39						Avoid
Writing	32	36						Avoid
International Activities	50	64						Explore
Fashion	35	48						
Culinary Arts	48	43						
Analyzing	33	33						Avoid
Mathematics	34	33						Avoid
Science	31	36						Avoid
Producing	37	46						
Mechanical Crafts	33	35						Avoid
Woodworking	32	39						Avoid
Farming/Forestry	46	44						
Plants/Gardens	51	51						
Animal Care	50	49						
Adventuring	59	54						Develop
Athletics/Physical Fitness	58	47						Develop
Military/Law Enforcement	63	66						Pursue
Risks/Adventure	46	52						

Scale markers: 30 35 40 45 50 55 60 65 70

Figure 7.10 | **Combination of Career Interests and Skill Survey**

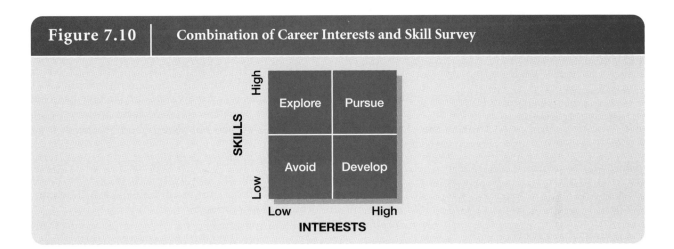

---

people with high needs for achievement may choose aggressive, achievement-oriented organizations. Power-oriented people may choose influential, prestigious, power-oriented organizations. Affiliative people may choose warm, friendly, supportive organizations. We know that people whose needs fit with the climate of an organization are rewarded more and are more satisfied than those who fit in less well, so it is natural to reason that fit would also be a factor in one's choice of an organization. As noted at the outset of this chapter, it is increasingly unlikely that individuals will remain with only one organization for their entire career. The old model of "the organization man" who starts and stays with the same company is being replaced by a more flexible career model that Hall calls a "protean" career (based on the Greek god Proteus, who could change shape at will).[39]

The Plateauing Trap

Career plateau
Situation in which for either organizational or personal reasons the probability of moving up the career ladder is low

Judith Bardwick, a professor of management who specializes in career development, was the first to label the plateauing phenomenon.[40] A **career plateau** is a situation in which for either organizational or personal reasons the probability of moving farther up the career ladder is low. According to Bardwick, only 1 percent of the labour force will not plateau in their working lives. There are three types of plateaus: structural, content, and life. A *structural plateau* marks the end of promotions; one will now have to leave the organization to find new opportunities and challenges. A *content plateau* occurs when a person has learned a job too well and is bored with day-to-day activities. A *life plateau* is more profound and may feel like a midlife crisis. People who experience life plateaus often have allowed work or some other major factor to become the most significant aspect of their lives, and they experience a loss of identity and self-esteem when there is no longer success in that area.

Organizations can help individuals cope with plateaus by providing opportunities for lateral growth where opportunities for advancement do not exist. Career enrichment programs, for example, help people learn more about what gives them satisfaction within a company, as well as what kinds of opportunities will make them happiest if they go elsewhere. These programs are similar to the self-management approaches discussed earlier.

Becoming an Entrepreneur

At the opening of the new century, no discussion of careers would be complete if entrepreneurship opportunities were not mentioned. Being an **entrepreneur**—one who starts, organizes, manages, and assumes responsibility for a business or other enterprise—offers a personal challenge that many individuals prefer over being an employee. Small businesses are typically run by entrepreneurs who accept the personal financial risks that go with owning a business but who also benefit directly from the success of the business.[41]

Canadian small businesses also offer career development opportunities for their employees, through training and mentoring programs. Nearly half provide on average 113 hours of informal training that includes on-the-job training, tutoring, and mentoring.[42]

Since the details of organizing a business are beyond the scope of this book, Figure 7.11 is presented to provide an overview of the basic steps in starting a new business.[43]

Entrepreneur
One who starts, organizes, manages, and assumes responsibility for a business or other enterprise

USING THE INTERNET

For assistance in starting a small business, visit Canadian Business gateway at

http://businessgateway.ca/en/hi/.

Keeping a Career in Perspective

For most people, work is a primary factor in the overall quality of their lives. It provides a setting for satisfying practically the whole range of human needs and is thus of considerable value to the individual. Nevertheless, it is advisable to keep one's career in perspective so that other important areas of life are not neglected.

Off-the-Job Interests

Satisfaction with one's life is a product of many forces. Some of the more important ingredients are physical health, emotional well-being, financial security, harmonious interpersonal relationships, freedom from too much stress, and achievement of one's goals. While a career can provide some of the satisfaction that one needs, most people

Becoming an entrepreneur can lead to great personal satisfaction as the business grows and prospers.

PHOTODISC

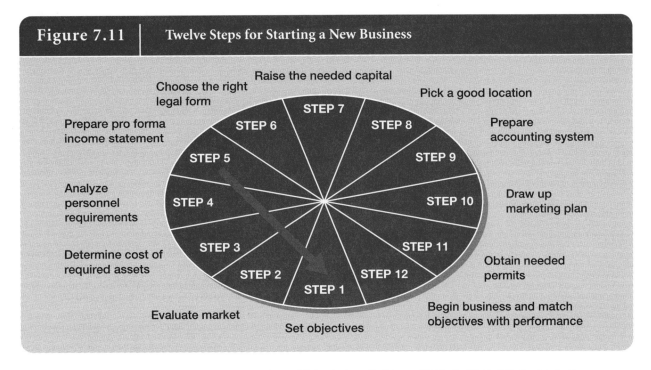

Figure 7.11 | **Twelve Steps for Starting a New Business**

Raise the needed capital

Choose the right legal form

Pick a good location

Prepare pro forma income statement

Prepare accounting system

Analyze personnel requirements

Draw up marketing plan

Determine cost of required assets

Obtain needed permits

Evaluate market

Begin business and match objectives with performance

Set objectives

STEP 1, STEP 2, STEP 3, STEP 4, STEP 5, STEP 6, STEP 7, STEP 8, STEP 9, STEP 10, STEP 11, STEP 12

Source: From *Business in a Changing World*, 3rd edition, by W. Cunningham, R. Aldag, and S. Block: 139. © 1993. Reprinted with permission of South-Western, a division of Thomson Learning: www.thomsonrights.com. Fax 800-730-2215.

find it necessary to turn to interests and activities outside their career. Off-the-job activities not only provide a respite from daily work responsibilities but also offer satisfaction in areas unrelated to work.

Marital and/or Family Life

The career development plans of an individual as well as of an organization must take into account the needs of spouses and children. As we have said, the one event that often poses the greatest threat to family needs is relocation. Conflict between a desire to advance in one's career and a desire to stay in one place and put down family roots often borders on the disastrous. Many employers now provide assistance in this area, including relocation counselling, in an effort to reduce the severity of the pain that can accompany relocations.

While relocation may be the most serious threat to employees with families, there are also other sources of conflict between career and family. Some work-related sources of conflict are number of hours worked per week, frequency of overtime, and the presence and irregularity of shift work. In addition, ambiguity and/or conflict within the employee's work role, low level of leader support, and disappointments due to unfulfilled expectations affect one's life away from the job. Some family-related sources of conflict include the need to spend an unusually large amount of time with the family and its concerns, spouse employment patterns, and dissimilarity in a couple's career orientations.

Planning for Retirement

While retirement appears to be a long way off for the individual who is still in the early stages of a career, it is never too early to plan for it. In order to enjoy retirement one should prepare for it by giving careful attention to health, finances, family, and interpersonal relationships throughout one's adult life. While most large organizations have preretirement programs, many participants in those programs are unfortunately already too close to actual retirement. Thus it is each individual's responsibility to plan early in order to have time to set the stage for a healthy and satisfying retirement as free as possible from worries—especially those that could have been avoided or minimized earlier in life. While employer-sponsored preretirement programs are usually considered very helpful by the participants, as we will see in Chapter 11, they are not a substitute for continual personal concern for oneself.

Maintaining a Balance

According to a 2003 survey of Canadians, an appropriate work-life balance was the top indicator of personal career success.[44] Those who are "married" to their jobs to the extent that they fail to provide the attention and caring essential to marriage and family relationships can be said to lack an appreciation for the balance needed for a satisfying life. One should always be aware that "to be a success in the business world takes hard work, long hours, persistent effort, and constant attention. To be a success in marriage takes hard work, long hours, persistent effort, and constant attention. The problem is giving each its due and not shortchanging the other."

SUMMARY

 A career development program is a dynamic process that should integrate individual employee needs with those of the organization. It is the responsibility of the employee to identify his or her own KSAs as well as interests and values and to seek out information about career options. The organization should provide information about its mission, policies, and plans and what it will provide in the way of training and development for the employee.

 In order to be successful, a career development program must receive the support of top management. The program should reflect the goals and the culture of the organization, and managerial personnel at all levels must be trained in the fundamentals of job

design, performance appraisal, career planning, and counselling. Employees should have an awareness of the organization's philosophy and its goals; otherwise they will not know how their goals match those of the organization. HRM policies, especially those concerning rotation, transfers, and promotions, should be consistent with the goals. The objectives and opportunities of the career development program should be announced widely throughout the organization.

 Job opportunities may be identified by studying jobs and determining the knowledge and skills each one requires. Once that is accomplished, it is possible to plan job progressions. These progressions can then serve as a basis for developing career paths. Once career paths are developed and employees are identified on the career ladders, it is possible to inventory the jobs and determine where individuals with the required skills and knowledge are needed or will be needed.

 Identifying and developing managerial talent is a responsibility of all managers. In addition to immediate superiors, there should be others in the organization who can nominate and sponsor employees with promise. Many organizations use assessment centres to identify managerial talent and recommend developmental experiences in order that each individual may reach her or his full potential. Mentoring has been found to be valuable for providing guidance and support to potential managers.

 The first step in facilitating the career development of women is to eliminate barriers to advancement. Formation of women's networks, providing special training for women, accepting women as valued members of the organization, providing mentors for women, and accommodating families have been found to be effective ways to facilitate a woman's career development.

 While a diversified workforce is composed of many different groups, an important segment is minority groups. In addition to creating conditions that are favourable for recognizing and rewarding performance, many organizations have special programs such as internships that provide hands-on experience as well as special training opportunities. Another group that requires the attention of management is composed of dual-career couples who often need to have flexible working schedules.

 In choosing a career, one should use all available resources. Consideration should be given to internal factors such as academic aptitude and achievement, occupational aptitudes and skills, communication skills, leadership abilities, and interests and values. External factors such as economic conditions, employment trends, and job market information must also be considered. In choosing a career, one should make use of interest and skill inventories. Long-term employment opportunities in an occupational field should be assessed by consulting various publications, including those published by the government. Keeping a career in perspective so as to have a balanced life is desirable. While work is usually a primary factor in overall quality of life, one should give proper attention to physical health, harmonious family and interpersonal relationships, and interests and activities outside of one's career.

KEY TERMS

assessment centre 295	entrepreneur 318	mentors 300
career counselling 298	fast-track program 299	outplacement services 291
career paths 288	in-basket training 295	promotion 288
career plateau 317	job progressions 288	relocation services 290
dual-career partnerships 310	leaderless group discussions 295	transfer 290

DISCUSSION QUESTIONS

 1. Give some reasons for the trend toward increased emphasis on career development programs. What role do the following work trends play in the development of a career plan: contract work; outsourcing; restructuring and early retirement?

 2. The TD Bank maintains a special suite of offices at its world headquarters in Toronto for its retired executives.
   a. Of what value is this arrangement to the corporation? To the individuals?

b. How might retired executives in any organization assist in the career development of current employees?

3. What contributions can a career development program make to an organization that is forced to downsize its operations?

4. More than 50 percent of all MBAs leave their first employer within five years. While the change may mean career growth for the individuals, it represents a loss to the employers. What are some of the probable reasons an MBA would leave his or her first employer?

5. Your partner has just received an exciting job offer, which requires relocation to a small town in another province. The new job represents significant career advancement for your partner, but it is unlikely you will be able to find a comparable job in the new location. In groups, discuss the issues and possible solutions to this dual career couple challenge.

6. How are the career challenges of minorities both similar to and different from those of women?

7. List the advantages and disadvantages of being an entrepreneur.

8. In your opinion, what personal characteristics are employers looking for in individuals whom they are considering for long-term employment and probable advancement in the organization? To what extent can one develop these characteristics?

9. One recruiter has said, "Next to talent, the second most important factor in career success is taking the time and effort to develop visibility." What are some ways of developing visibility?

Developing Managerial Skills

CAREER PROGRESSION INTERVIEWS

We often think that successful people plan their careers in advance and then work toward their goals in a very logical, sequential manner. Although some successes are designed and implemented this way, others are created through insight, preparedness, and taking advantages of opportunities as they arise.

Assignment

1. Form teams of four to six members. Identify three different people to interview about their careers. One person should be in the early stages of his or her career; one should be in midcareer; and one should be in the final stages of his or her career.
2. Ask each person to identify his or her career goals and how they have changed or are expected to change over time.
3. Ask each person to describe the sequence of events that led to where he or she is. How well does that story align with the traditional model of careers?
4. Ask each person what (if anything) he or she would do differently. Ask what advice he or she has for you about how to approach your career.

Case   Study   1

UPS Delivers the Goods

When Jordan Colletta joined UPS in 1975, fresh out of school and newly married, he wasn't thinking about building a career. He just wanted some security. Now not only is he still a faithful UPS employee, but the former tracing clerk has come a long way— he's vice-president of the shipper's e-commerce sales team. His advancement in the company was steady, the result of careful planning through UPS's career-development programs. By putting resources into such programs and helping reps set goals and develop skills, businesses can allow employees to grow within their organization and reduce turnover rates in the process, as UPS has found: Its turnover rate among full-time managers is 4 percent.

Developing salespeople starts with a clear mission. At UPS, employees meet annu-ally with managers to identify their strengths and decide what skills they need for a new job within the company. "We lay the foundation for future development and map out immediate, midterm, and future goals," Colletta says. "When I was a tracing clerk, I told my supervisor that my goal was to become a district sales manager. I then became a driver, then a salesperson, and in 1986 I reached my goal."

Career development entails implementing training programs and Internet career centres that can help companies grow their staffs. Employees take courses in order to acquire the pedigree that will make them candidates for management positions. But learning isn't just in the classroom. Mentoring programs in which managers coach lower-level employees are also valuable. "Mentors are especially important," Colletta says. "They help you understand the opportunities that are out there. They helped me see what I couldn't because I couldn't look that far ahead yet."

Progress must be routinely monitored. Employee reviews and 360-degree reports are good ways to track improvement. So is a manager's involvement. "Have an open door policy to keep the communication lines open," he says.

Finally, when it comes to encouraging participation in these programs, companies should highlight successes. Colletta announces promotions during weekly calls with UPS directors and immediately sends messages to his employees throughout the country. "It can't be about talk," Colletta says. "You can't say, 'We have opportunities to develop you' and then look around and not see anyone getting ahead. You have to celebrate it."

Source: Adapted from Eduardo Javier Canto, "Rising through the Ranks," *Sales and Marketing Management* 153, no. 7 (July 2001): 66. Copyright © 2001. Reprint Management Services.

QUESTIONS

1. What do you think are the main strengths of UPS's career development program?
2. What are the key outcomes that UPS wants to achieve?
3. What suggestions do you have for improving the program?

Case Study 2

Careers—Dead or Alive

The management of a career can be a full-time job in itself. Here is some advice on how to manage a career:

▶ *Competence counts.* It's not who you know but what you know. Until you can prove your ability to do the work, and are seen as adding value, there is no point in discussing transfers or promotions.

▶ *Establish a network.* It's not only what you know, after all, but who you know.

▶ *Do what you love.* Work is focusing more and more on issues broader than money. Once you have determined what motivates you, your career will evolve. A career does not simply mean getting ahead, or moving vertically up a career ladder.

▶ *Volunteer in not-for-profit organizations.* This will help you kick-start your career and establish a network. The number of volunteers from the fifteen to twenty-four age group increased from 18 percent in 1987 to 33 percent in 1997. These people say they learned job skills and gained experience by working as volunteers.

QUESTIONS

1. Mergers, downsizings, and bankruptcies demonstrate dramatically that jobs are not forever. Is career management a dead concept?

2. The advice given by career experts and managers is often contradictory: "It's who you know" versus "It's what you know"; "Become a generalist" versus "Stay a specialist"; "Work hard and focus on your own job" versus "Act strategically with your eye on the next job." Why does advice vary so much? List some factors (demographic, labour market, sector, etc.) that influence the advice given to those seeking to develop a career plan.

CAREER COUNSEL

Visit the *Managing Human Resources* Website (www.belcourt4e.nelson.com) for assistance in preparing a career plan.

NOTES AND REFERENCES

1. Brent B. Allred, Charles C. Snow, and Raymond E. Miles, "Characteristics of Managerial Careers in the 21st Century," *Academy of Management Executive* 10, no. 4 (1996): 17–27; Sherry Sullivan, "The Changing Nature of Careers: A Review and Research Agenda," *Journal of Management* 25, no. 3 (1999): 457–84; Steve Prentice, "A Game Plan for Career Survival," *Canadian HR Reporter* 15, no. 11 (June 3, 2002): 27–28.

2. Ellen Ernst Kossek, Karen Roberts, Sandra Fisher, and Beverly Demarr, "Career Self-Management: A Quasi-Experimental Assessment of the Effects of a Training Intervention," *Personnel Psychology* 51, no. 4 (Winter 1998): 935–62; Shelly Green, "Attracting Top Talent Despite Business Challenges," *Journal of Career Planning and Employment* 62, no. 4 (Summer 2002): 24–28; Cynthia Jones, "Step by Step: Creating a Strategic Management System for Career Services Delivery," *Journal of Career Planning and Employment* 62, no. 3 (Spring 2002): 21–27.

3. Peg O'Herron and Peggy Simonsen, "Career Development Gets a Charge at Sears Credit," *Personnel Journal* 74, no. 5 (May 1995): 103–6. See also Jules Abend, "Behind the Scenes at: Sears," *Bobbin* 39, no. 11 (June 1998): 22–26; Shari Caudron, "The De-Jobbing of America," *Industry Week* 243, no. 16 (September 5, 1994): 30–36; Edward E. Lawler III, "From Job-Based to Competency-Based Organizations," *Journal of Organizational Behavior* 15, no. 1 (January 1994): 3–15; Douglas T. Hall, "Accelerate Executive Development—At Your Peril!" *Career Development International* 4, no. 4 (1999): 237–39.

4. Laurence J. Peter and Raymond Hull, *The Peter Principle* (Cutchogue, NY: Buccaneer Books, 1996); James Fairburn and James Malcomson, "Performance, Promotion, and the Peter Principle," *Review of Economic Studies* 68, no. 234 (January 2001): 45–66.

5. Sumantra Ghoshal, Christopher A. Bartlett, and Peter Moran, "A New Manifesto for Management," *Sloan Management Review* 40, no. 3 (Spring 1999): 9–20; Elizabeth Craig, John Kimberly, and Hamid Bouchikhhi, "Can Loyalty Be Leased?" *Harvard Business Review* 80, no. 9 (September 2002): 24–34; Edward Potter, "Improving Skills and Employability in the 21st Century," *Industrial and Labor Relations Review* 55, no. 4 (July 2002): 739–45.

6. P. Monique Valcour and Scott A. Snell, "The Boundaryless Career and Work Force Flexibility: Developing Human and Social Capital or Organizational and Individual Advantage," paper presented at the annual meeting of the Academy of Management, Denver, Colorado, 2002; Robert Lewellyn, "The Four Career Concepts," *HRMagazine* 47, no. 9 (September 2002): 121–26.

7. Robert J. Grossman, "Heirs Unapparent," *HRMagazine* 44, no. 2 (February 1999): 36–44; Amy Barrett, "How to Keep Rising Stars from Straying," *Business Week* (June 7, 1999): 80.

8. Peter Carrick and Richard Williams, "Development Centres—A Review of Assumptions," *Human Resource Management Journal* 9, no. 2 (1999): 77–92; Paul Jansen and Bert Stoop, "The Dynamics of Assessment Center Validity: Results of a 7-Year Study," *Journal of Applied Psychology* 86, no. 4 (August 2001): 741–53; Filip Lievens, "Trying to Understand the Different Pieces of the Construct Validity Puzzle of Assessment Centers: An Examination of Assessor and Assessee Effects," *Journal of Applied Psychology* 87, no. 4 (August 2002): 675–86.

9. Larry Cambron, "Career Development Pays," *Far Eastern Economic Review* 164, no. 42 (October 25, 2001): 83.

10. For up-to-date career information and guidance as well as an opportunity for self-analysis, see Richard Bolles, *What Color Is Your Parachute 2003: A Practical Manual for Job-Hunters & Career-Changers* (Berkeley, CA: Ten Speed Press, 2002); James D. Porterfield, *Business Career Planning Guide* (Cincinnati, OH: South-Western Publishing, 1993); and Julie Griffin Levitt, *Your Career—How to Make It Happen,* 3rd ed. (Cincinnati, OH: South-Western Publishing, 1995). Interested readers might also wish to obtain a copy of the video "Planning Your Career," TMW/Media Group (1998) (run time: 22 minutes).

11. Shari Caudron, "Marriott Trains Managers to Become Partners in Career Development," *Personnel Journal* 73, no. 4 (April 1994): 641. [Also published as "Marriott Trains Managers to Become Partners in Career Development," *Business Credit* 97, no. 9 (September 1995): 22.] See also Susan Wells, "Smoothing the Way," *HRMagazine* 46, no. 6 (June 2001): 52–58; "Leadership: The Practicalities," *Business Europe* 39, no. 14 (July 14, 1999): 4–5.

12. Suzan Butyn, "Mentoring Your Way to Improved Retention," *Canadian HR Reporter* 16, no. 2 (January 27, 2003): 13.

13. Ellen Ernst Kossek, Karen Roberts, Sandra Fisher, and Beverly Demarr, "Career Self-Management: A Quasi-Experimental Assessment of the Effects of a Training Intervention," *Personnel Psychology* 51, no. 4 (Winter 1998): 935–62; Zella King, "Career Self-Management: A Framework for Guidance of Employed Adults," *British*

Journal of Guidance and Counselling 29, no. 1 (February 2001): 65–78; Cyndi Maxey, "No More Mister Nice Guy," *Training and Development* 53, no. 6 (June 1999): 17–18.

14. Matt Starcevich and Fred Friend, "Effective Mentoring Relationships from the Mentee's Perspective," *Workforce*, supplement, July 1999, 2–3; Kenn Fracaro, "Mentoring: Tool for Career Guidance," *SuperVision* 63, no. 9 (September 2002): 10–12.

15. Kathleen Barton, "Will You Mentor Me?" *Training and Development* 56, no. 5 (May 2002): 90–92.

16. Suzan Butyn, "Mentoring Your Way to Improved Retention," *Canadian HR Reporter* 16, no. 2 (January 27, 2003): 13.

17. Audrey L. Mathews, "The Diversity Connections: Mentoring and Networking," *Public Manager* 23, no. 4 (Winter 1994/1995): 23–26; Barbara Addison Reid, "Mentorships Ensure Equal Opportunity," *Personnel Journal* 73, no. 11 (November 1994): 122–23.

18. Stephanie Armour, "Mentoring with a Twist: Workers Connect On-line," *USA Today,* August 18, 1999, 1B; Rhea Borija, "E-Mentors Offer Online Support, Information for Novice Instructors," *Education Week* 21, no. 29 (April 3, 2002): 12.

19. Audrey J. Merrell and Erika Hayes James, "Gender and Diversity in Organizations: Past, Present and Future Directions," *Sex Roles* 45, no. 5/6 (September 2001): 243.

20. Headquarters for Catalyst is at 250 Park Avenue South, 5th floor, New York, NY 10003-8900. Articles that summarize research sponsored by Catalyst include Sheila Wellington, "Advancing Women in Business: You've Come a Long Way—Maybe!" *Vital Speeches of the Day* 65, no. 20 (August 1, 1999): 637–39; Robert W. Thompson, "More Women Are Expected to Ascend Corporate Ladder," *HRMagazine* 44, no. 1 (January 1999): 10; Elaine McShulskis, "Women's Progress in Corporate Leadership," *HRMagazine* 41, no. 6 (June 1996): 21–22.

21. Asha Tomlinson, "Is There a War of the Sexes? It Depends on Who You Ask," *Canadian HR Reporter* 15, no. 18 (October 21, 2002): 3; David Brown, "Progress Slow, Incremental for Women," *Canadian HR Reporter* 16, no. 7 (April 7, 2003): 11.

22. A host of reports on glass ceiling issues can be found on the U.S. Department of Labor's website at http://www.dol.gov/.

23. Rose Mary Wentling, "Women in Middle Management: Their Career Development and Aspirations," *Business Horizons* 35, no. 1 (January–February 1992): 47–54. See also Mary Mallong and Catherine Cassell, "What Do Women Want? The Perceived Development Needs of Women Managers," *Journal of Management Development* 18, no. 2 (1999): 137–54.

24. The interested reader should find the following books very informative: Johanna Hunsaker and Phillip Hunsaker, *Strategies and Skills for Managerial Women* (Cincinnati, OH: South-Western Publishing, 1991); Marian Ruderman and Patricia Ohlott, *Standing at the Crossroads: Next Steps for High-Achieving Women* (New York: John Wiley and Sons, 2002).

25. Nancy Hatch Woodward, "Child Care to the Rescue," *HRMagazine* 44, no. 8 (August 1999): 82–88.

26. Stephenie Overman, "Make Family-Friendly Initiatives Fly," *HRFocus* 76, no. 7 (July 1999): 1–14; "Work-Family Concern Tops List," *HRFocus* 76, no. 7 (July 1999): 4; Kathleen Cannings and William Lazonick, "Equal Employment Opportunity and the 'Managerial Woman,'" *Industrial Relations* 33, no. 1 (January 1994): 44–69.

27. Alison Stein Wellner, "Future Perfect?" *Working Woman* 26, no. 8 (September 2001): 70–72; Jane Bryant Quinn, "Revisiting the Mommy Track," *Newsweek* 136, no. 3 (July 27, 2000): 44.

28. Statistics Canada, "Census of Population: Earnings, Level of Schooling; Field of Study and School Attendance," http://www.statcan.ca/Daily/English/030311/d030311a.htm, http://www.statcan.ca/english/Pgdb/labor20a.htm table 282-0002, Statistics Canada, CANSIM II, table 282-0002; Sharon Collins-Lowry, *Black Corporate Executives: The Making and Breaking of a Black Middle Class* (Philadelphia: Temple University Press, 1996).

29. Statistics Canada, "Census of Population."

30. University of Alberta, Canadian Association for Internship Programs, http://www.cs.ualberta.ca/~cafip/.

31. Treasury Board of Canada Secretariat, "Employment Equity," http://www.tbs-sct.gc.ca/ee/pmp/promo/cic-vm-mv2_e.asp.

32. Valerie Frazee, "Expert Help for Dual-Career Spouses," *Workforce* 4, no. 2 (March 1999): 18–20; Charlene Marmer Solomon, "One Assignment, Two Lives," *Personnel Journal* 75, no. 5 (May 1996): 36–74; Gillian Flynn, "Heck No—We Won't Go!" *Personnel Journal* 75, no. 3 (March 1996): 37–43.

33. A selection of self-help publications on a variety of topics may be found in any bookstore. College and university bookstores typically have a wide selection in their trade or general books department. Two particularly useful books might be Edward Crip and Richard Mansfield, *The Value-Added Employee: 31 Competencies to Make Yourself Irresistible to Any Company* (London: Butterworth-Heinemann, 2001); Daniel Goleman, *Emotional Intelligence* (New York: Bantam Books, 1995).

34. Mary Harrington Hall, "A Conversation with Peter Drucker," *Psychology Today* (March 1968): 22.

35. Uyen Vu, "Labour Force Growth Depends on Immigrants," *Canadian HR Reporter* 16, no. 5 (March 10, 2003): 3.

36. E. K. Strong, Jr., of Stanford University, was active in the measurement of interests from the early 1920s until his death in 1963. Since then his work has been carried on by the staff of the Measurement Research Center, University of Minnesota. The *Strong Interest Inventory* is distributed by Consulting Psychologists Press, Inc., P. O. Box 60070, Palo Alto, CA 94306, to qualified people under an exclusive licence from the publisher, Stanford University Press.

37. Gary D. Gottfredson and John L. Holland, *Dictionary of Holland Occupational Codes* (Lutz, FL: Psychological Assessment Resources, December 1996).

38. The *Campbell Interest and Skill Survey* (copyright 1992) is published and distributed by NCS Assessments, P.O. Box 1416, Minneapolis, MN 55440. For recent research in this area, see David Lubinski, Camilla P. Benbow, and Jennifer Ryan, "Stability of Vocational Interests among the Intellectually Gifted from Adolescence to Adulthood: A 15-Year Longitudinal Study," *Journal of Applied Psychology* 80, no. 1 (February 1995): 196–200.

39. Douglas T. Hall and Jonathan E. Moss, "The New Protean Career Contract: Helping Organizations and Employees Adapt," *Organizational Dynamics* 26, no. 3 (Winter 1998): 22–37. See also Douglas T. Hall, *The Career Is Dead, Long Live the Career: A Relational Approach to Careers* (San Francisco: Jossey-Bass, 1996); Douglas T. Hall, "Protean Careers of the 21st Century," *Academy of Management Executive* 10, no. 4 (1996): 8–16; Douglas T. Hall and Associates, *Career Development in Organizations* (San Francisco: Jossey-Bass, 1986); Yue-Wah Chay and Samuel Aryee, "The Moderating Influence of Career Growth Opportunities on Careerist Orientation and Work Attitudes: Evidence of the Protean Career Era in Singapore," *Journal of Organizational Behavior* 20, no. 5 (September 1999): 613–23.

40. Judith Bardwick, *The Plateauing Trap* (New York: AMACOM, 1986). See also Judith Bardwick, *Danger in the Comfort Zone: From Boardroom to Mailroom—How to Break the Entitlement Habit That's Killing American Business* (New York: AMACOM Book Division, 1995). See also Max Messmer, "Moving beyond a Career Plateau," *National Public Accountant* 45, no. 7 (September 2000): 20–21.

41. Abraham Sagie and Dov Abraham, "Achievement Motive and Entrepreneurial Orientation: A Structural Analysis," *Journal of Organizational Behavior* 20, no. 3 (May 1999): 375–87; Eleni T. Stavrous, "Succession in Family Businesses: Exploring the Effects of Demographic Factors on Offspring Intentions to Join and Take Over the Business," *Journal of Small Business Management* 37, no. 3 (July 1999): 43–61; Julie Rose, "The New Risk Takers," *Fortune Small Business* 12, no. 2 (March 2002): 28–34.

42. David Brown, "Small Business Getting Better at Training Staff," *Canadian HR Reporter* 16, no. 9 (May 13, 2003): 1.

43. For information on starting a business, the interested reader might look into Bob Adams, *Adams Streetwise Small Business Startup* (Holbrook, MA: Adams Media Corporation, 1996); Linda Pinson and Jerry Jinnett, *Anatomy of a Business Plan: Starting Smart, Building a Business and Securing Your Company's Future* (Chicago: Upstart Publishing, 1996); Kenneth Cook, AMA *Complete Guide to Strategic Planning for Small Business* (Lincolnwood, IL: NTC Business Books, 1995); Priscilla Y. Huff, *101 Best Small Businesses for Women* (Rocklin, CA: Prima Publishing, 1996); Constance Jones, *The 220 Best Franchises to Buy: The Sourcebook for Evaluating the Best Franchise Opportunities* (New York: Bantam Doubleday Dell, 1993).

44. Christopher Caggiano, "Married ... with Companies," *Inc.* 17, no. 6 (May 1995): 68–76; Sue Shellenbarger, "Sustaining a Marriage When Job Demands Seem to Be Endless," *The Wall Street Journal*, December 8, 1999: B1; Katherine Harding "Balance Tops List of Job Desires," *The Globe and Mail*, May 7, 2003: C1.

Appraising and Improving Performance

After studying this chapter, you should be able to

1
objective

Explain the purposes of performance appraisals and the reasons they fail.

2
objective

Identify the characteristics of an effective appraisal program.

3
objective

Describe the different sources of appraisal information.

4
objective

Explain the various methods used for performance evaluation.

5
objective

Outline the characteristics of an effective performance appraisal interview.

In the preceding chapters we have discussed some of the most effective methods available to managers for acquiring and developing top-notch employees. But talented employees are not enough—a successful organization is especially adept at engaging its workforce to achieve goals that benefit both it and its employees. In this chapter we turn to performance appraisal programs. These are some of the most helpful tools an organization can use to maintain and enhance productivity and facilitate progress toward strategic goals. While we will focus mainly on formal procedures, they can be informal as well. All managers monitor how employees work and assess their performance against organizational needs. They form impressions about the relative value of employees to the organization and seek to maximize every individual's contribution. Yet while these ongoing informal processes are vitally important, most organizations also have a formal performance appraisal once or twice a year.

The success or failure of a performance appraisal program depends on the philosophy underlying it, its connection with business goals, and the attitudes and skills of those responsible for its administration. Many different methods can be used to gather information about employee performance. However, gathering information is only one step in the appraisal process. The information must be evaluated in the context of organizational needs, and then communicated to employees so that it will result in high levels of performance.[1]

PERFORMANCE APPRAISAL PROGRAMS

Advocates for formal performance appraisal programs see these HR programs as excellent ways to appraise, develop, and use the knowledge and abilities of employees. However, more and more observers are pointing out that performance appraisals often fall short of their potential.[2]

The push toward teamwork, continuous improvement, learning, and the like has caused numerous organizations to rethink their approach to appraisal. Some argue that performance appraisal discourages teamwork because it frequently focuses on individual achievement and produces a self-focus rather than a team focus. Others contend that appraisals are useful only at the extremes—highly effective or highly ineffective employees—and are not as useful for the majority of employees in the middle. Others point out that appraisals may focus on short-term achievements rather than long-term improvement and learning. They are sometimes too subjective or inconsistent or autocratic in that they create a distance between manager and employee rather than creating a team environment. Companies such as Xerox, Motorola, and Procter & Gamble have modified their performance appraisals to better acknowledge the importance of teamwork, continuous improvement, quality, and the like. Each of these issues is discussed at greater length throughout the chapter.[3]

Purposes of Performance Appraisal

It might seem at first glance that performance appraisals have a rather narrow purpose—to evaluate who is doing a good job (or not). But in reality, performance appraisals are among the most versatile tools available to managers, and can serve many purposes that benefit both the organization and the employee whose performance is being appraised.

Figure 8.1 shows the most common uses of performance appraisals. In general, these can be classified as either *administrative* or *developmental*.

Administrative Purposes

From the standpoint of administration, appraisal programs provide input that can be used for the entire range of HRM activities. Performance appraisals are used most often as a basis for compensation decisions.[4] The practice of "pay for performance" is found in all types of organizations. Performance appraisal is also directly related to a number of other important HR functions, such as promotion, transfer, and layoff decisions. Performance appraisal data can also be used in HR planning, to determine the relative worth of jobs under a job evaluation program and as criteria for validating selection tests. Performance appraisals also provide a "paper trail" for documenting HRM actions that may result in legal action. Because of employment equity programs, employers should maintain accurate and objective records of employee performance; that way, they will be able to defend themselves against possible charges of discrimination in connection with HRM actions such as promotion, salary

Figure 8.1	Purposes for Performance Appraisal

DEVELOPMENTAL	ADMINISTRATIVE
Provide performance feedback	Document personnel decisions
Identify individual strengths/weaknesses	Determine promotion candidates
Recognize individual performance	Determine transfers and assignments
Assist in goal identification	Identify poor performance
Evaluate goal achievement	Decide retention or termination
Identify individual training needs	Decide on layoffs
Determine organizational training needs	Validate selection criteria
Reinforce authority structure	Meet legal requirements
Allow employees to discuss concerns	Evaluate training programs/progress
Improve communication	Personnel planning
Provide a forum for leaders to help	Make reward/compensation decisions

determination, and termination. Finally, it is important to recognize that the success of the entire HR program depends on knowing how the performance of employees compares with the goals established for them. This knowledge is best derived from a carefully planned and administered HR appraisal program. Appraisal systems are capable of influencing employee behaviour and can lead directly to an improvement in organizational performance.[5]

Developmental Purposes

From the standpoint of individual development, appraisal provides the feedback that is essential when discussing an employee's strengths and weaknesses with the goal of improving performance. Whatever the employee's level of performance, the appraisal process provides an opportunity to identify issues for discussion, to eliminate any potential problems, and to set new goals for achieving high performance. Newer approaches to performance appraisal emphasize training, development, and growth plans for employees. A developmental approach to appraisal recognizes that the purpose of a manager is to improve job behaviour, not simply to evaluate past performance. One of the major benefits of an appraisal program is that it provides a sound basis for improving performance.

Companies such as Best Buy and EDS have redesigned their performance appraisal systems to focus more on employee development and learning. EDS, for example, integrated its performance appraisal system to work in concert with learning and career management objectives. The new system, called the Career Resource System, includes a detailed job description, a performance review, and a career planner to track long-term goals, as well as access to the company's automated career library. The system is ultimately linked to the company's succession policies. By creating this overall system, EDS hopes to shift the role of manager from that of "judge" to one of "coach."[6]

Reasons Appraisal Programs Sometimes Fail

In actual practice, and for a number of reasons, formal performance appraisal programs sometimes yield disappointing results. Figure 8.2 shows that the primary culprits include lack of top-management information and support, unclear performance standards, rater bias, too many forms to complete, and use of the program for conflicting purposes. For example, if an appraisal program is used to provide a written appraisal for salary action and at the same time to motivate employees to improve their work, the administrative and developmental purposes may be in conflict. As a result, the appraisal interview may become a discussion about salary in which the manager seeks to justify the action taken. In such cases, the discussion might have little influence on the employee's future job performance.

As with all HR functions, if the support of top management is lacking, the appraisal program will not succeed. Even the best-conceived program will not work in an environment where appraisers are not encouraged by their superiors to take the program seriously. To underscore the importance of this responsibility, top management should announce that effectiveness in appraising subordinates is a standard by which the appraisers themselves will be evaluated.

Other reasons performance appraisal programs sometimes fail to yield the desired results include the following:

Figure 8.2 | Let Me Count the Ways...

There are many reasons why performance appraisal systems might not be effective. Some of the most common problems include the following:

▶ Inadequate preparation on the part of the manager.

▶ Employee is not given clear objectives at the beginning of performance period.

▶ Manager may not be able to observe performance or have all the information.

▶ Performance standards may not be clear.

▶ Inconsistency in ratings among supervisors or other raters.

▶ Rating personality rather than performance.

▶ The halo effect, contrast effect, or some other perceptual bias.

▶ Inappropriate time span (either too short or too long).

▶ Overemphasis on uncharacteristic performance.

▶ Inflated ratings because managers do not want to deal with "bad news."

▶ Subjective or vague language in written appraisals.

▶ Organizational politics or personal relationships cloud judgments.

▶ No thorough discussion of causes of performance problems.

▶ Manager may not be trained at evaluation or giving feedback.

▶ No follow-up and coaching after the evaluation.

Sources: Patricia Evres, "Problems to Avoid during Performance Evaluations," *Air Conditioning, Heating & Refrigeration News* 216, no. 16 (August 19, 2002): 24–26; Clinton Longnecker and Dennis Gioia, "The Politics of Executive Appraisals," *Journal of Compensation and Benefits* 10, no. 2 (1994): 5–11; "Seven Deadly Sins of Performance Appraisals," *Supervisory Management* 39, no. 1 (1994): 7–8.

1. Managers feel that little or no benefit will be derived from the time and energy spent in the process.
2. Managers dislike the face-to-face confrontation of appraisal interviews.
3. Managers are not sufficiently adept in providing appraisal feedback.
4. The judgmental role of appraisal conflicts with the helping role of developing employees.

In many organizations, performance appraisal is a once-a-year activity in which the appraisal interview becomes a source of friction for both managers and employees. An important principle of performance appraisal is that continual feedback and employee coaching must be a positive daily activity. The annual or semiannual performance review should be a logical extension of the day-to-day supervision process.

One of the main concerns of employees is the fairness of the performance appraisal system, since the process is central to so many HRM decisions. Employees who believe the system is unfair may consider the appraisal interview a waste of time and leave the interview with feelings of anxiety or frustration. Also, they may view compliance with the appraisal system as perfunctory and thus play only a passive role during the interview process. By addressing these employee concerns during the planning stage of the appraisal process, the organization will help the appraisal program to succeed in reaching its goals.[7]

Finally, organizational politics can introduce a bias even in fairly administered employee appraisals.[8] For example, managers may inflate evaluations because they desire higher salaries for their employees or because higher subordinate ratings make them look good as managers. Alternatively, managers may want to get rid of troublesome employees, passing them off to another department by inflating their ratings. A survey of over 2000 Canadian workers indicated that only 60 percent understood the measures being used to evaluate their performance, 57 percent thought their performance had been evaluated fairly, and even fewer (39 percent) found that the performance review was helpful. The next section describes how performance appraisal processes can be improved.[9]

DEVELOPING AN EFFECTIVE APPRAISAL PROGRAM

The HR department ordinarily has the main responsibility for overseeing and coordinating appraisal programs. Managers from the operating departments must also be actively involved, especially in helping establish the program's objectives. Furthermore, employees are more likely to accept and be satisfied with the performance appraisal program when they have the chance to participate in its development. Their concerns about fairness and accuracy in determining raises, promotions, and the like tend to be alleviated somewhat when they have been involved at the planning stages and have helped develop the performance standards themselves.

What Are the Performance Standards?

Before appraisals are conducted, the standards by which performances are to be evaluated must be clearly defined and communicated to the employees. These standards should be based on job-related requirements derived from job analysis and reflected in the job descriptions and job specifications (see Chapter 3). When performance standards are properly established, they help translate organizational goals and objectives into job requirements that convey acceptable and unacceptable levels of performance to employees.

As shown in Figure 8.3, there are four basic considerations in establishing performance standards: strategic relevance, criterion deficiency, criterion contamination, and reliability.

Strategic Relevance

Strategic relevance refers to the extent to which standards relate to the strategic objectives of the organization. For example, if an organization has established a standard that "95 percent of all customer complaints are to be resolved in one day," then it is relevant for the customer service representatives to use such a standard for their evaluations. Companies such as 3M and Rubbermaid have strategic objectives that 25 to

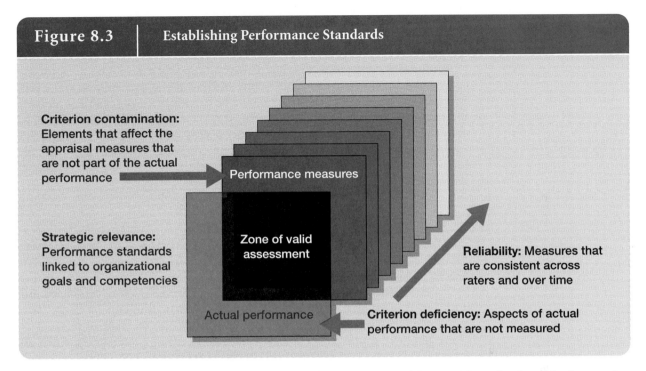

Figure 8.3   Establishing Performance Standards

Criterion contamination: Elements that affect the appraisal measures that are not part of the actual performance

Performance measures

Strategic relevance: Performance standards linked to organizational goals and competencies

Zone of valid assessment

Reliability: Measures that are consistent across raters and over time

Actual performance

Criterion deficiency: Aspects of actual performance that are not measured

30 percent of their sales are to be generated from products developed in the past five years. These objectives are translated into performance standards for their employees. General Motors and Whirlpool include other objectives such as cost, quality, and speed. They develop metrics to identify and compare performance around the world on the measures.[10]

Criterion Deficiency

A second consideration in establishing performance standards is the extent to which those standards capture the entire range of an employee's responsibilities. When performance standards focus on a single criterion (e.g., sales revenues) to the exclusion of other important but less quantifiable performance dimensions (e.g., customer service), the appraisal system is said to suffer from criterion deficiency.[11]

Criterion Contamination

Performance criteria can be "contaminated." In other words, there are factors outside an employee's control that can influence his or her performance. Thus, the performance appraisals of production workers should not be contaminated by the fact that some use newer machines than others. In the same vein, the performance appraisals of travelling salespeople should not be contaminated by the fact that territories vary in sales potential.[12]

Reliability

As discussed in Chapter 5, reliability refers to the stability or consistency of a standard, or the extent to which individuals tend to maintain a certain level of performance over time. Reliability can be measured by correlating two sets of ratings made by a single rater or by two different raters. For example, two managers can rate the same individual and estimate his or her suitability for a promotion. Their ratings can then be compared to determine inter-rater reliability.

Performance standards will permit managers to specify and communicate precise information to employees about the quality and quantity of their output. When performance standards are written, they should be defined in quantifiable and measurable terms. For example, "ability and willingness to handle customer orders" is not as good a performance standard as "all customer orders will be filled in four hours with a 98 percent accuracy rate." When standards are expressed in specific terms, and the employee's performance is measured against a clear standard, a more justifiable appraisal results.

Legal Issues

Since performance appraisals are used as one basis for HRM actions, they must meet certain legal requirements. HR professionals and their lawyers often face the situation where a manager has fired an employee for poor performance, but has also left a paper trail of glowing performance reviews over the years. In circumstances like this it is difficult for the employer to argue that the employee was dismissed for cause. As a common result, the employer must assume legal liability for wrongful dismissal.

An employer can also face a legal challenge to its appraisal system when an appraisal indicates acceptable or above-average performance but the employee is later passed over for promotion, or disciplined for poor performance, or discharged, or laid off. In these situations a performance appraisal can undermine the legitimacy of the later personnel decision. Intel was recently taken to court by a group of former employees on the grounds that the performance appraisal system (used for layoff decisions) was unreliable and invalid. In light of court cases like this one, performance appraisals should meet the following guidelines:

▶ Performance ratings must be job-related, with performance standards developed through job analysis.

▶ Employees must be given a written copy of their job standards in advance of appraisals.

▶ Managers who conduct the appraisal must be able to observe the behaviour they are rating. This involves having a measurable standard against which to compare employee behaviour.

▶ Supervisors should be trained to use the appraisal form correctly. They should be instructed in how to apply appraisal standards when making judgments.

Appraisals should be discussed openly with employees. Counselling or corrective guidance should be offered to help poor performers improve their performance.

There should be an appeals procedure to enable employees to express disagreement with the appraisal.

Employers must make sure that managers and supervisors document appraisals and reasons for subsequent HRM actions (see Chapter 12 on documentation). This information may prove decisive should an employee take legal action. An employer's credibility is strengthened when it can support performance appraisal ratings by documenting instances of poor performance.

objective 3

Who Should Appraise Performance?

Just as there are many standards for evaluating performance, so are there many candidates for appraising performance. Given the complexity of today's jobs, it is often unrealistic to expect one person to fully observe and evaluate a given employee's performance. As shown in Figure 8.4, raters can include supervisors, peers, team members, subordinates, customers, and the employee (i.e., self-evaluation). Each of these alternatives has at least some relevance to the administrative and developmental purposes we discussed earlier. The Canadian Institute of Chartered Accountants and the Ontario Ministry of Northern Development and Mines have begun using multiple-rater approaches (i.e., 360-degree appraisal) to evaluate employee performance. We will talk more about 360-degree appraisal at the end of this section.

Manager/Supervisor Appraisal

Manager and/or supervisor appraisal has been the traditional approach to evaluating an employee's performance. In most instances, supervisors are in the best position to perform this function, although it may not always be possible for them to do so. Managers often complain that they do not have the time to fully observe the performance of their employees. These managers must then rely on performance records to evaluate an employee's performance. When reliable and valid measures are not available, the appraisal may well be less than accurate. (Recall our earlier discussion of criterion deficiency and contamination.)

When a supervisor appraises employees independently, provision is often made for a review of the appraisals by the supervisor's superior. Having appraisals reviewed by a supervisor's superior reduces the chance of superficial or biased evaluations. Reviews by superiors generally are more objective and provide a broader perspective of employee performance than do appraisals by immediate supervisors.

Self-Appraisal

Sometimes employees are asked to evaluate themselves on a self-appraisal form. **Self-appraisal** can be useful when managers are trying to increase the employee's involvement in the review process. A self-appraisal system requires the employee to

---

Manager and/or supervisor appraisal
Performance appraisal done by an employee's manager and often reviewed by a manager one level higher

Self-Appraisal
Performance appraisal done by the employee being evaluated, generally on an appraisal form completed by the employee to the performance review

---

Figure 8.4 | **Alternative Sources of Appraisal**

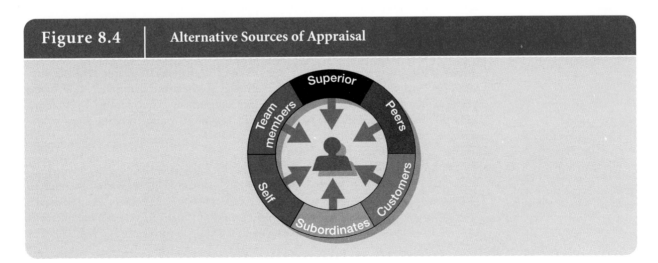

complete the appraisal form before the performance interview. At a minimum, this gets the employee thinking about his or her strengths and weaknesses; this in turn can lead to discussions about barriers to effective performance. During the performance interview, the manager and the employee discuss job performance and agree on a final appraisal.

This approach can work well when the manager and the employee jointly establish future performance goals or employee development plans. Critics of self-appraisal argue that self-raters are more lenient than managers in their assessments and tend to present themselves in a highly favourable light. For this reason, self-appraisals may be best for developmental purposes rather than for administrative decisions. When used in conjunction with other methods, self-appraisals can be a valuable source of appraisal information.[13]

Electronic Performance Monitoring

The most controversial practice in performance appraisal is electronic performance monitoring. Nowadays it is easy to track workers by audiotaping their conversations, videotaping their activities, counting their computer keystrokes electronically, and so on. Employee performance can be measured objectively by these means. However, employees must be told they are being monitored, and all dimensions of job performance should be included in the performance appraisal.

Subordinate Appraisal

Some organizations use **subordinate appraisal** to give managers feedback on how their subordinates view them. Subordinates are in a good position to evaluate their managers, since they are in frequent contact with them and occupy a unique position from which to observe many performance-related behaviours. The performance dimensions judged most appropriate for subordinate appraisals include leadership, oral communication, delegation of authority, coordination of team effort, and interest in subordinates. The manager at Victoria-based B.C. Buildings Corporation appreciated the specific feedback received from her subordinates that she could be providing them with more guidance.[14] However, dimensions related to managers' specific job tasks, such as planning and organizing, budgeting, creativity, and analytical ability, are not usually appropriate for subordinate appraisal.

Since subordinate appraisals give employees power over their bosses, managers may be hesitant to endorse such a system, especially when it might be used as a basis for compensation decisions. However, when the information is used for developmental purposes, managers tend to be more open to the idea. Available evidence suggests that when managers heed the advice of their subordinates, their own performance can improve substantially. Nevertheless, to avoid potential problems, subordinate appraisals should be submitted anonymously and combined across several individual raters.[15]

Peer Appraisal

Individuals of equal rank who work together are being asked more and more often to evaluate one another. A **peer appraisal** often differs to some degree from a supervisor's appraisal, since peers see different dimensions of performance. Peers can readily identify a co-worker's leadership and interpersonal skills, along with various other strengths

Subordinate appraisal
Performance appraisal of a superior by an employee, which is more appropriate for developmental than for administrative purposes

Peer appraisal
Performance appraisal done by one's fellow employees, generally on forms that are compiled into a single profile for use in the performance interview conducted by the employee's manager

and weaknesses. A desk sergeant asked to rate a foot patrol officer on a dimension such as "dealing with the public" may not have had much opportunity to observe it. Fellow officers will have had the opportunity to observe this behaviour regularly.

One advantage of peer appraisals is the belief that they often furnish more accurate and valid information than appraisals by superiors. The supervisor often sees employees putting their best foot forward; those who work with their fellow employees on a regular basis will have gained a more realistic picture. With peer appraisals, co-workers complete an evaluation on the employee. The forms are then usually compiled into a single profile, which is given to the supervisor for use in the final appraisal.[16]

Despite evidence that peer appraisals are possibly the most accurate method of judging employee behaviour, there are reasons why they are not used more often.[17] These reasons are commonly cited:

1. Peer ratings are simply a popularity contest.
2. Managers are reluctant to give up control over the appraisal process.
3. Those receiving low ratings might retaliate against their peers.
4. Peers rely on stereotypes in ratings.

When peers are in competition with one another (e.g., sales associates), peer appraisals may not be advisable for administrative decisions such as those relating to salary or bonuses. Also, employers who use peer appraisals must make sure to safeguard confidentiality in handling the review forms. A breach of confidentiality can create interpersonal rivalries or hurt feelings and foster hostility among fellow employees.

Team Appraisal

Team appraisal
Performance appraisal, based on TQM concepts, that recognizes team accomplishment rather than individual performance

An extension of the peer appraisal is the **team appraisal**. Peers of equal standing often do not work closely together. In a team setting it may be nearly impossible to separate out an individual's contribution. Advocates of team appraisal argue that individual appraisal can be dysfunctional in a team environment, since it detracts from the critical issues of the team.

A company's interest in team appraisals is often driven by its commitment to TQM principles and practices. At its root, TQM is a control system that involves setting standards (based on customer requirements), measuring performance against those standards, and identifying opportunities for continuous improvement. In this regard TQM and performance appraisal are perfectly complementary. However, a basic tenet of TQM is that performance is best understood at the level of the system as a whole, whereas performance appraisal traditionally has focused on individual performance. Team appraisals represent one way to break down barriers between individuals and to encourage their collective effort.[18] Often, the system is complemented by team incentives or group variable pay (see Chapters 10 and 16).

Customer Appraisal

Customer appraisal
Performance appraisal, which, like team appraisal, is based on TQM concepts and seeks evaluation from both internal and external customers

More and more organizations are using internal and external **customer appraisal** as a source of performance appraisal information. This form of appraisal is also driven by TQM concerns. External customers' evaluations have long been used to appraise restaurant personnel. However, companies such as Sears have begun utilizing external customers as well. Sears customers receive a coupon asking them to call a

Team appraisals are one way a company can practise TQM, break down barriers between individuals, and encourage collective effort.

PHOTODISC

1-800 number within a week of making a purchase. In exchange for answering prerecorded questions on a touchtone phone, the customers receive $5 off their next purchase. Each call can be linked to a particular transaction (and sales associate) based on the receipt number. With 468 million transactions a year, enough survey data are generated for each sales associate to provide meaningful feedback on performance measures such as service and product knowledge. Customer appraisals can also tell an organization if employees are following procedures. Secret shoppers at the Radisson Hotel Saskatoon provided feedback to hotel management that employees were failing to provide accurate accounting on some customers' bills.

Managers establish customer service measures (CSMs) and set goals for employees that are linked to company goals. Often the CSM goals are linked to employee pay through incentive programs. Customer survey data are then incorporated into the performance evaluation. By including CSMs in their performance reviews, managers hope to produce more objective evaluations, more effective employees, more satisfied customers, and better business performance.[19]

In contrast to external customers, *internal* customers include anyone inside the organization who depends on an employee's work output. For example, managers who rely on the HR department for selection and training services are candidates for conducting internal customer evaluations of that department. For both developmental and administrative purposes, internal customers can provide extremely useful feedback about the value being added by an employee or team of employees.

Putting It All Together: 360-Degree Appraisal

As mentioned previously, many companies are combining various sources of performance appraisal information to create multirater—or 360-degree—appraisal and feedback systems. Jobs are multifaceted, and different people see different things. As

the name implies, 360-degree feedback is intended to provide employees with as accurate a view of their performance as possible by getting input from all angles: supervisors, peers, subordinates, customers, and the like. Although in the beginning, 360-degree systems were purely developmental and were restricted mainly to management and career development, they have migrated to performance appraisal and other administrative applications. Over 90 percent of Fortune 1000 companies have implemented some form of 360-degree feedback system for career development, performance appraisal, or both. Because the system combines more information than a typical performance appraisal, it can become administratively complex. For that reason, organizations have recently begun using web technology (Internet, intranet) to compile and aggregate the information.[20] For example, PerformancePro.net is an online system developed by Exxceed that provides managers and employees with the ability to develop performance plans, goals, and objectives, and then track progress over time. The planning process includes an online "wizard" that helps users establish SMART goals (Specific, Measurable, Achievable, Results-oriented, and Time-bound) and then allows employees to submit revised goals and action steps for approval. Using the tracking module, managers can see all of an employee's goals and action steps on a single screen. The program then combines self-appraisal and multiple-rater inputs in a 360-degree format. After rating an employee's performance on each goal, raters can provide summary comments in three categories: victories and accomplishments, setbacks and frustrations, and general comments. To ensure security, a user ID and password are required and all the data are captured and saved in the employee's history file.[21]

Figure 8.5 lists some pros and cons of 360-degree appraisal. Although 360-degree feedback can be useful for both developmental and administrative purposes, most companies start with an exclusive focus on development. Often, employees are understandably nervous about people ganging up on them in their evaluations. When an organization starts with only developmental feedback (i.e., feedback that isn't tied to compensation, promotions, and the like), its employees become accustomed to the process and learn to value the input they get from various parties. Reality Check provides a description of 360-degree feedback at Canadian Tire.

When Intel established a 360-degree system, it followed these safeguards to ensure maximum quality and acceptance:

▶ *It ensured anonymity.* It made certain that no employee ever knew how any evaluation-team member responded. (The supervisor's rating was an exception to this rule.)

▶ *It made respondents accountable.* Supervisors were instructed to discuss each evaluation team member's input, letting each member know whether she or he used the rating scales appropriately, whether their responses were reliable, and how other participants rated the employee.

▶ *Steps were taken to prevent "gaming" the system.* Some individuals will try to help or hurt an employee by giving either too high or too low an evaluation. Or team members will attempt to collude with one another by agreeing to give each other uniformly high ratings. Supervisors were instructed to check for obviously invalid responses.

Figure 8.5	Pros and Cons of 360-Degree Appraisal

PROS

▶ The system is more comprehensive in that responses are gathered from many perspectives.

▶ The quality of information is better. (Quality of respondents is more important than quantity.)

▶ It complements TQM (Total Quality Management) initiatives by emphasizing internal/external customers and teams.

▶ It may lessen bias/prejudice since feedback comes from more people, not one individual.

▶ Feedback from peers and others may increase employee self-development.

CONS

▶ The system is complex in combining all the responses.

▶ Feedback can be intimidating and cause resentment if employee feels the respondents have "ganged up."

▶ There may be conflicting opinions, though they may all be accurate from the respective standpoints.

▶ The system requires training to work effectively.

▶ Employees may collude or "game" the system by giving invalid evaluations to one another.

▶ Appraisers may not be accountable if their evaluations are anonymous.

Sources: Compiled from David A. Waldman, Leanne E. Atwater, and David Antonioni, "Has 360-Degree Feedback Gone Amok?" *Academy of Management Executive* 12, no. 2 (May 1998): 86–94; Bruce Pfau, Ira Kay, Kenneth Nowak, and Jai Ghorpade, "Does 360-Degree Feedback Negatively Affect Company Performance?" *HRMagazine* 47, no. 6 (June 2002): 54–59; Maury Peiperl, "Getting 360-Degree Feedback Right," *Harvard Business Review* 79, no. 1 (January 2001): 142–47; Jack Kondrasuk, Mary Riley, and Wang Hua, "If We Want to Pay for Performance, How Do We Judge Performance?" *Journal of Compensation and Benefits* 15, no. 2 (September/October 1999): 35–40; Mary Graybill, "From Paper to Computer," *The Human Resource Professional* 13, no. 6 (November/December 2000): 18–19; David W. Bracken, Lynn Summers, and John Fleenor, "High-Tech 360," *Training and Development* 52, no. 8 (August 1988): 42–45; Gary Meyer, "Performance Reviews Made Easy, Paperless," *HRMagazine* 45, no. 10 (October 2000): 181–84.

▶ *It used statistical procedures.* Weighted averages or other quantitative approaches were applied to combine evaluations. Supervisors were careful about using subjective combinations of data that might undermine the system.

▶ *It identified and quantified biases.* Prejudices or preferences related to age, gender, ethnicity, or other group factors were checked for.[22]

Based on the experiences of companies like Canadian Tire described in Reality Check, 360-degree feedback can be a valuable approach to performance appraisal. Its success, as with any appraisal technique, depends on how managers use the information and how fairly employees are treated.

Training Appraisers

A weakness of many performance appraisal programs is that managers and supervisors are not adequately trained for the appraisal task and provide little meaningful feedback to subordinates. Because they lack precise standards for appraising

Reality Check

CANADIAN TIRE 360-DEGREE MATRIX

"Accentuate the positive; build on leadership strengths" is the principal theme of leadership performance evaluation and development conducted by the Canadian Tire Corporation as described by Janice Wismer, vice-president of Human Resources. Canadian Tire is a network of interrelated businesses with retail, financial, and petroleum interests. About 45 000 employees work in 1000 retail stores across Canada.

The customized 360-degree feedback process used at Canadian Tire is research-based and designed to build a cadre of great leaders. The first step in the design of the 360-degree feedback instrument was to benchmark other organizations that had effective 360-degree feedback processes. Twenty-seven key employees at Canadian Tire were interviewed to identify the attributes of their great leaders as measured by the standards of the organization. These key leadership attributes were then discussed and evaluated in workshops with important stakeholders. A total of sixteen competencies were identified: seven related to "who one is"—characteristics such as trustworthy, passionate, and curious. Nine others focused on "what one can do for the team, business, and enterprise"—such as make strategic choices, motivate and celebrate, communicate authentically.

To date, about 170 managers have been assessed by an average of nine colleagues, including peers, subordinates, and bosses. Colleagues complete a self-survey, and all feedback assessment is analyzed relative to their own organization and to industry standards, which are maintained in a database. A confidential feedback report is given to each individual.

In addition to the generation of individual reports, an aggregate one-page executive summary is produced. The report, presented as a matrix, provides a visual summary colour-coded under each competency comparing aggregate feedback data for all individuals in a defined business unit. The sample 360-degree matrix shown below lists key attributes across the horizontal axis and the employee's feedback along the vertical axis. In order to maintain confidentiality, identifiers are assigned to the supervisors and managers so that they can see their relative standing but without knowing the identity of the other employees. In the colour-coding, red signifies a weak performance, yellow is an average performance, and green indicates exceptional strengths. By using this 360-degree matrix, HR can identify areas where groups of employees need professional development, thus investing training dollars where it matters most. In the example, Executives A, B, and C are perceived as generally excellent across most of the eight areas of interest, while Executives M, N, and O are experiencing considerable difficulty. In addition, most of the executive team performed well in areas 1, 2, 3, having most difficulty in area 8. In this case, individual development plans may work well for executives having problems in areas 1, 2, and 3 while a group development solution may be best designed for area 8.

According to Ed Haltrecht, Ph.D., CHRP, who specializes in measurement and organizational leadership development, in most organizations when performance feedback is presented, both the employee and the manager focus on the reds—the weaknesses—and try to work out

(continued on following page)

Executive	1. Treats others with respect.	2. Gives credit to others who have contributed or performed well.	3. Shows consistency between words and action.	4. Models the core values of the corporation; leads by example.	5. Treats team members as individuals based on knowledge of their strengths and development needs.	6. Takes actions that build a high level of commitment to work group goals and objectives.	7. Obtains resources so that the team has the knowledge, skills, and experience required to deliver results.	8. Where there is underlying conflict, helps parties involved bring up their issues and get to the heart of the problem.	Mean
A	5.0	4.9	4.9	4.6	4.8	4.6	4.6	4.5	4.7
B	5.0	4.8	4.9	4.9	4.9	4.8	4.3	3.7	4.7
C	5.0	4.7	4.5	4.7	4.7	4.7	4.5	4.2	4.6
D	4.8	4.6	4.2	4.7	4.3	4.3	4.6	4.1	4.4
E	4.7	5.0	4.7	4.0	3.7	4.0	4.3	4.3	4.4
F	4.8	4.3	4.3	4.5	4.4	4.3	4.1	3.2	4.2
G	4.6	4.2	4.2	4.2	4.2	4.1	4.2	3.9	4.2
H	4.5	4.4	4.1	4.2	4.3	3.9	3.9	4.1	4.2
I	4.4	3.8	4.0	4.3	4.0	4.3	4.5	3.7	4.2
J	4.4	4.3	4.5	4.2	4.1	4.2	3.9	4.0	4.2
K	4.6	4.2	4.5	4.0	4.5	4.2	3.6	4.3	4.1
L	3.8	4.4	4.3	4.3	3.7	4.1	4.5	3.9	4.1
M	4.4	4.2	4.4	4.1	4.2	4.0	4.0	4.2	4.1
N	4.3	3.8	4.1	3.9	4.0	4.0	3.5	2.9	3.9
O	3.3	4.1	4.0	3.6	3.8	3.8	3.9	3.3	3.6
Mean	4.5	4.3	4.4	4.2	4.2	4.2	4.1	3.9	4.2

methods of development to improve this area. What is unique about Canadian Tire is that the focus is on the positive. It has found that improvements in weak areas (provided it is not a fundamental flaw) do not affect overall performance, while improvements in areas of strength bring managers from good to extraordinary. The goal is to identify and strengthen attributes so employees will distinguish and present themselves as extraordinary. Individuals first address any "fundamental flaws"—either a very weak attribute of the individual or, more importantly, elements regarded as critical to the organization. In the sample 360-degree matrix, Executives I, L, N, and O have potential fundamental flaws in areas 1 and 2. If there are no fundamental flaws, then development focuses on building strengths. This combination has resulted in measurable gains in performance.

This approach is research based. A recently published book, *The Extraordinary Leader: Turning Good Managers into Great Leaders* by John Zenger and Joseph Folkman, presents several significant findings based on 225 000 evaluations of 20 000 people. Poor leaders were identified as those scoring in the bottom 10 percent; extraordinary leaders scored in the top 10 percent. Employee turnover in a call centre was 19 percent for the units managed by the poor managers, 14 percent for the middle group, and 9 percent for the extraordinary leaders. In another case that looked at a bank, net incomes for the bank generated by those groups whose managers were extraordinary, average, and poor were $7 million, $3.7 million, and $1.9 million respectively. Employee satisfaction indices were at the 80th percentile for top managers compared to the 18th percentile for the bottom-scoring managers. Likewise Union Vulnerability indices, which measures how attractive the organization is to a union's membership drive, reflected the 91st percentile for the top-scoring managers compared to the 10th percentile for the poor managers—that is, poorer managers are more likely to attract union interest. Although the pay structure was the same across different departments, those led by the top-scoring managers had employees who were at the 65th percentile in satisfaction with company pay and job security; the employees of average managers were in the 50th percentile; and poor managers' employees scored at the 37th percentile for satisfaction with company pay and job security.

Canadian Tire's leadership development system also recognizes two other significant research findings: first, extraordinary leaders have about three competencies that they excel at and developing a few strengths to very high performance levels has a greater impact than improving several competencies from poor to average. Second, competencies travel together and improvement in one leads to significant progress in others. Identifying these companion competencies has proven to be extremely worthwhile. In a nutshell, these are the findings: start with the right set of competencies or attributes; focus on strengths; eliminate any fundamental flaws; and pay attention to companion attributes.

The assessment feedback process at Canadian Tire is seen as a tool for dialogue and for focusing on what makes a great company and what matters in leadership. Those employees who try to improve are given a developmental opportunities guidebook. Canadian Tire has discovered that the best development methods are stretch challenging assignments, coaching and mentoring, personal feedback, talks with consultants, and training programs.

subordinates' performance and have not developed the necessary observational and feedback skills, their appraisals become nondirective and meaningless. Training appraisers can vastly improve the performance appraisal process.

Establishing an Appraisal Plan

Training programs are most effective when they follow a systematic process that begins with explaining the objectives of the performance appraisal system.[23] It is important for the rater to know what the appraisal is to be used for. For example, using the appraisal for compensation decisions rather than development purposes may affect how the rater evaluates the employee and may change the rater's opinion of how the appraisal form should be completed. The mechanics of the rating system—how often the appraisals are to be conducted, who will conduct them, what the standards of performance are, and so on—should also be explained. In addition, appraisal training should alert raters to the weaknesses and problems of appraisal systems so they can be avoided.

Eliminating Rater Error

Appraisal training should focus on eliminating subjective errors in the rating process. Gary Latham of the University of Toronto and Kenneth Wexley, an American industrial psychologist, stress the importance of performance appraisal training by noting

> Regardless of whether evaluations are obtained from multiple appraisers or from only the employee's immediate superior, all appraisers should be trained to reduce errors of judgment that occur when one person evaluates another. This training is necessary because to the degree to which a performance appraisal is biased, distorted, or inaccurate, the probability of increasing the productivity of the employee is greatly decreased. Moreover, wrong decisions could be made regarding whom to promote, retain, or replace, which in turn will penalize the organization's bottom line. In addition, when a performance appraisal is affected by rating errors, the employee may be justified in filing a discrimination charge.[24]

With any rating method, certain types of errors can arise that should be considered. The "halo error," discussed in Chapter 5, is common with respect to rating scales, especially those that do not include carefully developed descriptions of the employee behaviours that are being rated.[25] Provision for comments on the rating form tends to reduce halo error.

Some types of rating errors are *distributional errors* in that they involve a group of ratings given across various employees. For example, raters who are reluctant to assign either extremely high or extremely low ratings commit the **error of central tendency**. In this case, all employees are rated about average. To such raters it is a good idea to explain that, among large numbers of employees, one should expect to find significant differences in behaviour, productivity, and other characteristics.

It is also common for some raters to give unusually high or low ratings. For example, a manager may erroneously assert, "All my employees are excellent," or "None of my people are good enough." These beliefs give rise to what is called **leniency or strictness error**.[26] One way to reduce this error is to clearly define the characteristics or dimensions of performance and to provide meaningful descriptions of behaviour, known as "anchors," on the scale. Another approach is to require ratings

Error of central tendency
Performance rating error in which all employees are rated about average

Leniency or strictness error
Performance rating error in which the appraiser tends to give employees either unusually high or unusually low ratings

Contrast error can occur when rating two employees simultaneously.

PHOTODISC

Recency error
Performance rating error in which the appraisal is based largely on the employee's most recent behaviour rather than on the behaviour throughout the appraisal period

Contrast error
Performance rating error in which an employee's evaluation is biased either upward or downward because of comparison with another employer just recently evaluated

to conform to a *forced distribution*. Managers appraising employees under a forced distribution system are required to place a certain percentage of employees into various performance categories. For example, it may be required that 10 percent of ratings be poor (or excellent). This is similar to the requirement in some schools that instructors grade on a curve. However, while a forced distribution may solve leniency and strictness error, it may also create other errors in the accuracy of ratings—especially if most employees are performing above standard.

Some rating errors are *temporal* in that the performance review is biased either favourably or unfavourably, depending how performance information is selected, evaluated, and organized by the rater over time. For example, when the appraisal is based largely on the employee's recent behaviour, good or bad, the rater has committed the **recency error**. Managers who give higher ratings because they believe an employee is "showing improvement" may unwittingly be committing recency error. Without work record documentation for the entire appraisal period, the rater is forced to recall recent employee behaviour to establish the rating. Having the rater routinely document employee accomplishments and failures throughout the whole appraisal period can minimize the recency error. Rater training also helps reduce this error.

Contrast error occurs when an employee's evaluation is biased either upward or downward because of another employee's performance that was evaluated just previously. For example, an average employee can appear especially productive when compared with a poor performer; yet that same employee can appear unproductive when compared with a star performer. Contrast errors are most likely to occur when raters are required to rank employees from best to poorest. Employees are evaluated against one another, usually on the basis of some organizational standard or guideline. For example, they may be compared on the basis of their ability to meet production standards or on their "overall" ability to perform their job. As with other types of rating error, contrast error can be reduced through training that focuses on using objective standards and behavioural anchors to appraise performance.[27]

Similar-to-me error occurs when appraisers inflate the evaluations of people with whom they have something in common. For example, if both the manager and the employee are from small towns, the manager may unwittingly have a more favourable impression of the employee. The effects of a similar-to-me error can be powerful, and when the similarity is based on race, religion, gender, or some other protected category, it may result in discrimination.

Furthermore, raters should be aware of any stereotypes they may hold toward particular groups (e.g., male/female, white/black), because the observation and interpretation of performance can be clouded by these stereotypes. Results from a study

Similar-to-me error
Performance rating error in which an appraiser inflates the evaluation of an employee because of a mutual personal connection

examining how stereotypes of women affect performance ratings suggested that women evaluated by raters who hold traditional stereotypes of women are at a disadvantage when it comes to obtaining merit pay increases and promotion. This problem is aggravated when employees are appraised on the basis of poorly defined performance standards and subjective performance traits.

Avenor, a Montreal-based pulp and paper company, developed formal training programs to reduce the subjective errors commonly made during the rating process. This type of training can pay off, especially when participants have the opportunity to (1) observe other managers making errors, (2) actively participate in discovering their own errors, and (3) practise job-related tasks to reduce the errors they tend to make.[28]

Feedback Training

Finally, a training program for raters should provide some general points to consider for planning and conducting the feedback interview. The interview not only provides employees with knowledge of the results of their evaluation, but also allows the manager and employee to discuss current problems and set future goals.

Training in specific skills should cover at least three basic areas: communicating effectively, diagnosing the root causes of performance problems, and setting goals and objectives.[29] Supervisors can use a checklist to help them prepare for the appraisal interview. A checklist suggested by AT&T is provided in Highlights in HRM 8.1. The AT&T checklist reflects the growing tendency of organizations to have employees assess their own performance prior to the appraisal interview. Performance appraisal interviews will be discussed in more depth later in the chapter.

PERFORMANCE APPRAISAL METHODS

In the discussion that follows, we examine in some detail some methods that have found widespread use, and we briefly touch on other methods that are used less often. Broadly speaking, performance appraisal methods measure traits, or behaviours, or results. *Trait* approaches are still the most popular despite their inherent subjectivity. *Behavioural* approaches provide more action-oriented information to employees and for that reason may be best for development. *Results-oriented* approaches are gaining popularity because they focus on the measurable contributions that employees make to the organization.

Trait Methods

Trait approaches to performance appraisal are designed to measure the extent to which an employee possesses certain characteristics—dependability, creativity, initiative, leadership, and so on—that are viewed as important for the job and for the organization in general. Trait methods are the most popular mainly because they are so easy to develop. However, if they are not designed carefully on the basis of job analysis, they can be severely biased and subjective.

Highlights in HRM 8.1

SUPERVISOR'S CHECKLIST FOR THE PERFORMANCE APPRAISAL

Scheduling

1. Schedule the review and notify the employee ten days or two weeks in advance.
2. Ask the employee to prepare for the session by reviewing his or her performance, job objectives, and development goals.
3. Clearly state that this will be the formal annual performance appraisal.

Preparing for the Review

1. Review the performance documentation collected throughout the year. Concentrate on work patterns that have developed.
2. Be prepared to give specific examples of above- or below-average performance.
3. When performance falls short of expectations, determine what changes need to be made. If performance meets or exceeds expectations, discuss this and plan how to reinforce it.
4. After the appraisal is written, set it aside for a few days and then review it again.
5. Follow whatever steps are required by your organization's performance appraisal system.

Conducting the Review

1. Select a location that is comfortable and free of distractions. The location should encourage a frank and candid conversation.
2. Discuss each item in the appraisal one at a time, considering both strengths and shortcomings.
3. Be specific and descriptive, not general or judgmental. Report occurrences rather than evaluating them.
4. Discuss your differences and resolve them. Solicit agreement with the evaluation.
5. Jointly discuss and design plans for taking corrective action for growth and development.
6. Maintain a professional and supportive approach to the appraisal discussion.

Graphic Rating Scales

Graphic rating scale method

A trait approach to performance appraisal whereby each employee is rated according to a scale of characteristics

In the **graphic rating scale method**, each trait or characteristic to be rated is represented by a scale on which a rater indicates the degree to which the employee possesses that trait or characteristic. An example of this type of scale is shown in Highlights in HRM 8.2. There are many variations of the graphic rating scale. The differences lie mainly in (1) the characteristics or dimensions on which individuals are rated, (2) the degree to which the performance dimensions are defined for the rater, and (3) how clearly the points on the scale are defined. In Highlights in HRM 8.2 the dimensions are defined

Highlights in HRM 8.2

GRAPHIC RATING SCALE WITH PROVISION FOR COMMENTS

Appraise employee's performance in PRESENT ASSIGNMENT. Check (✔) most appropriate square. Appraisers are *urged to freely use* the "Remarks" sections for significant comments descriptive of the individual.

1. KNOWLEDGE OF WORK: Understanding of all phases of his/her work and related matters

Needs instruction or guidance	Has required knowledge of own and related work	Has exceptional knowledge of own and related work
☐	☐ ☐	✔✔ ☐

Remarks: *Is particularly good on gas engines.*

2. INITIATIVE: Ability to originate or develop ideas and to get things started

Lacks imagination	Meets necessary requirements	Unusually resourceful
☐	✔✔ ☐	☐ ☐

Remarks: *Has good ideas when asked for an opinion, but otherwise will not offer them. Somewhat lacking in self-confidence.*

3. APPLICATION: Attention and application to his/her work

Wastes time Needs close supervision	Steady and willing worker	Exceptionally industrious
☐	☐ ✔✔	☐ ☐

Remarks: *Accepts new jobs when assigned.*

4. QUALITY OF WORK: Thoroughness, neatness, and accuracy of work

Needs improvement	Regularly meets recognized standards	Consistently maintains highest quality
☐	☐ ☐	☐ ✔✔

Remarks: *The work he turns out is always of the highest possible quality.*

5. VOLUME OF WORK: Quantity of acceptable work

Should be increased	Regularly meets recognized standards	Unusually high output
☐	☐ ✔✔	☐ ☐

Remarks: *Would be higher if he did not spend so much time checking and rechecking his work.*

briefly, and some attempt is made to define the points on the scale. Subjectivity bias is reduced somewhat when the dimensions on the scale and the scale points are defined as precisely as possible. This can be achieved by training raters and by including descriptive appraisal guidelines in a performance appraisal reference packet.[30]

Also, the rating form should provide sufficient space for comments on the behaviour associated with each scale. These comments improve the accuracy of the appraisal because they require the rater to think about observable employee behaviours and also to provide specific examples to discuss with the employee during the appraisal interview.

Mixed-Standard Scales

Mixed-standard scale method

A trait approach to performance appraisal similar to other scale methods but based on comparison with (better than, equal to, or worse than) a standard

The **mixed-standard scale method** is a modification of the basic rating scale method. Instead of evaluating traits according to a single scale, the rater is given three specific descriptions of each trait. These descriptions reflect three levels of performance: superior, average, and inferior. After the three descriptions for each trait are written, they are randomly sequenced to form the mixed standard scale. As shown in Highlights in HRM 8.3, supervisors evaluate employees by indicating whether their performance is better than, equal to, or worse than the standard for each behaviour.

Forced Choice Method

Forced choice method

A trait approach to performance appraisal that requires the rater to choose from statements designed to distinguish between successful and unsuccessful performance

The **forced choice method** requires the rater to choose from statements, often in pairs, that appear equally favourable or equally unfavourable. The statements, however, are designed to distinguish between successful and unsuccessful performance. The rater selects one statement from the pair without knowing which statement correctly describes successful job behaviour. For example, forced choice pairs might include the following:

1. _____ a) Works hard.   _____ b) Works quickly.
2. _____ a) Shows initiative   _____ b) Is responsive to customers.
3. _____ a) Produces poor quality.   _____ b) Lacks good work habits.

The forced choice method is not without limitations, the primary one being the cost of establishing and maintaining its validity. Because it has been a source of frustration to many raters, it has sometimes been eliminated from appraisal programs. In addition, it is not as good as some other methods at helping employees develop their skills and strengths. Some organizations force the raters to place only 10 percent of their employees in the top category, which can sometime result in problems as described in The Business Case.

Essay Method

Essay method

A trait approach to performance appraisal that requires the rater to compose a statement describing employee behaviour

Rating scale methods provide a structured form of appraisal; in contrast, the **essay method** requires the appraiser to compose a statement that best describes the employee being appraised. The appraiser is usually instructed to describe the employee's strengths and weaknesses and to make recommendations for his or her

Highlights in HRM 8.3

EXAMPLE OF MIXED STANDARD SCALE

DIRECTIONS: Please indicate whether the individual's performance is above (+), equal to (0), or lower (–) than each of the following standards.

1. _____ Employee uses good judgment when addressing problems and provides workable alternatives; however, at times does not take actions to prevent problems. (medium PROBLEM SOLVING)

2. _____ Employee lacks supervisory skills; frequently handles employees poorly and is at times argumentative. (low LEADERSHIP)

3. _____ Employee is extremely cooperative; can be expected to take the lead in developing cooperation among employees; completes job tasks with a positive attitude. (high COOPERATION)

4. _____ Employee has effective supervision skills; encourages productivity, quality, and employee development. (medium LEADERSHIP)

5. _____ Employee normally displays an argumentative or defensive attitude toward fellow employees and job assignments. (low COOPERATION)

6. _____ Employee is generally agreeable but becomes argumentative at times when given job assignments; cooperates with other employees as expected. (medium COOPERATION)

7. _____ Employee is not good at solving problems; uses poor judgment and does not anticipate potential difficulties. (low PROBLEM SOLVING)

8. _____ Employee anticipates potential problems and provides creative, proactive alternative solutions; has good attention to follow-up. (high PROBLEM SOLVING)

9. _____ Employee displays skilled direction; effectively coordinates unit activities; is generally a dynamic leader and motivates employees to high performance. (high LEADERSHIP)

development. Often the essay method is combined with other rating methods. Essays can provide additional descriptive information on performance that is not obtained with a structured rating scale, for example.

The essay method provides an excellent opportunity to point out the unique characteristics of the employee being appraised. This aspect of the method is heightened when the supervisor is instructed to describe specific points about the employee's promotability, special talents, skills, strengths, and weaknesses. A major limitation of the essay method is that composing an essay that covers all of an employee's essential characteristics is a very time-consuming task (though when combined with other methods, this method does not require a lengthy statement). Another disadvantage of the essay method is that the quality of the performance appraisal may be influenced by the supervisor's writing skills and composition style. Good writers often produce more favourable appraisals. A final drawback of this appraisal method is that it tends to be subjective and may not focus on relevant aspects of job performance.

The Business Case

RANK AND YANK

Research shows that performance appraisals can have a positive financial impact, but there is the potential to lose money if the wrong system is chosen. Goodyear Tire & Rubber Co. abandoned a performance-rating system for salaried employees just as discrimination attorneys were planning to file a class-action lawsuit over it. Goodyear said it was dropping major parts of its program, including its so-called 10-80-10 feature, which essentially graded all salaried employees on a curve. The top 10 percent were rated A, the middle 80 percent were rated B, and the bottom 10 percent were rated C. Those falling in the bottom 10 percent weren't eligible for raises or bonuses and were warned that they might lose their jobs.

The lawsuit alleged that the workers who got C ratings were humiliated and stigmatized among their peers and managers. The legal arm of the AARP, formerly known as the American Association of Retired Persons, joined the lawsuit as co-counsel. Most of the plaintiffs in the case were Goodyear employees who were over fifty years old and who got C rankings. "This case will send a clear message that performance rating schemes that target older workers for unfair treatment are illegal and will not be tolerated," said Laurie McCann of AARP.

Jack McGilvrey, a fifty-nine-year-old salaried employee, was one of those named in the suit. He claimed that he always received ratings of at least "good/effective performer" in his formal performance reviews up through the late 1990s. In 2000, he was ranked "highly effective." But in February 2001, he was transferred to a new department and shortly thereafter was given a C rating in his performance review. The suit asserted that Mr. McGilvrey didn't deserve the rating and received it as part of Goodyear's plan to discriminate against older employees. He was later dismissed.

The lawsuit against Goodyear has many parallels to one filed in 2001 against Ford Motor Co. In that case, also joined by AARP, the company modified its plans in the face of a legal challenge. The Ford case was eventually settled.

In modifying its white-collar ranking system, Goodyear said it would replace those A, B, and C rankings with the terms *exceeds expectations, meets expectations,* and *unsatisfactory.* There will be no requirement to assign those ratings to set percentages of employees. The company also said it was stepping up training for managers so they learn to do a better job of conducting performance reviews. Goodyear has about 28 000 salaried employees around the world.

Source: Timothy Aeppel, "Goodyear Ends Ratings System ahead of Discrimination Suit," *The Wall Street Journal,* September 12, 2002: B8. Copyright © 2002 Dow Jones. Reprinted by permission of the publisher, Dow Jones, via Copyright Clearance Center.

Behavioural Methods

As mentioned earlier, one of the potential drawbacks of trait-oriented performance appraisals is that traits tend to be vague and subjective. We discussed earlier that one way to improve a rating scale is to have descriptions of behaviour along a scale, or continuum. These descriptions permit the rater to readily identify the point where a particular employee falls on the scale. Behavioural methods have been developed to state specifically which actions should (or should not) be exhibited on the job. These methods are often more useful for providing employees with developmental feedback.

Critical Incident Method

Critical incident method
Job analysis method by which important job tasks are identified for job success

The **critical incident method**, described in Chapter 3 in connection with job analysis, is also used as a method of appraisal. Recall that a critical incident occurs when employee behaviour results in unusual success or unusual failure in some part of the job. Example of a *favourable* critical incident: A janitor observed that a file cabinet containing classified documents had been left unlocked at the close of business. The janitor called the security officer, who took the necessary action to correct the problem. Example of an *unfavourable* critical incident: A mail clerk failed to deliver an Express Mail package immediately, instead putting it in with regular mail to be routed two hours later.

One advantage of the critical incident method is that it covers the entire appraisal period (and therefore may guard against recency error). And because the behavioural incidents are specific, they can facilitate employee feedback and development. However, unless both favourable and unfavourable incidents are discussed, employees who are appraised may have negative feelings about this method. Some employees have been known to refer to it as the "little black book" approach. Perhaps its greatest contribution is in developing job specifications and in constructing other types of appraisal procedures (see below).[31]

Behavioural Checklist Method

One of the oldest appraisal techniques is the behavioural checklist method, which consists of the rater checking those statements on a list that he or she believes are characteristic of the employee's performance or behaviour. A checklist developed for computer salespeople might include a number of statements such as the following:

_____ Is able to explain equipment clearly.
_____ Keeps abreast of new developments in technology.
_____ Tends to be a steady worker.
_____ Reacts quickly to customer needs.
_____ Processes orders correctly.

Behaviourally Anchored Rating Scale (BARS)

Behaviourally anchored rating scale (BARS)
A behavioural approach to performance appraisal that consists of a series of vertical scales, one for each important dimension of job performance

A **behaviourally anchored rating scale (BARS)** consists of a series of five to ten vertical scales, one for each important dimension of performance identified through job analysis. These dimensions are anchored by behaviours identified through a critical incidents job analysis. The critical incidents are placed along the scale and are assigned point values according to the opinions of experts. A BARS for the job of firefighter is shown in Highlights in HRM 8.4. Note that this particular scale is for the dimension described as "Firefighting Strategy: Knowledge of Fire Characteristics."

Typically, a BARS is developed by a committee that includes both subordinates and managers. The committee's task is to identify all the relevant characteristics or dimensions of the job. Behavioural anchors in the form of statements are then established

Highlights in HRM 8.4

EXAMPLE OF A BARS FOR MUNICIPAL FIRE COMPANIES

FIREFIGHTING STRATEGY: Knowledge of Fire Characteristics. This area of performance concerns the ability of a firefighter to use his or her knowledge of fire characteristics to develop the best strategy for fighting a fire. It involves the following activities: Observe fire and smoke conditions and locate source of fire. Size up fire and identify appropriate extinguishing techniques and ventilation procedures. Consult preplan reports. Apply knowledge of heat and fluid mechanics to anticipate fire behaviour. Identify and screen or saturate potential exposures using direct or fog streams or water curtains. Identify and remove or protect flammable or hazardous materials.

HIGH	7	
	6	— Finds the fire when no one else can — Correctly assesses the best point of entry for fighting fire — Uses type of smoke as indicator of type of fire
	5	
		— Understands basic hydraulics
AVERAGE	4	
	3	— Cannot tell the type of fire by observing the colour of the flame
	2	— Cannot identify location of the fire — Will not change firefighting strategy in spite of flashbacks and other signs that accelerants are present
LOW	1	

Source: Adapted from Landy, Jacobs, and Associates.

for each of the job dimensions. Several participants are asked to review the anchor statements and indicate which job dimension each anchor illustrates. The only anchors retained are those that at least 70 percent of the group agree belong with a particular dimension. Finally, anchors are attached to their job dimensions and placed on the appropriate scales according to values that the group assigns to them.

At present there is no strong evidence that a BARS reduces all the rating errors mentioned earlier. However, some studies have shown that scales of this type can yield more accurate ratings.[32] One major advantage of a BARS is that personnel outside the HR department participate with HR staff in its development. Employee participation can lead to greater acceptance of the performance appraisal process and of the performance measures it uses.

The procedures followed in developing a BARS also result in scales with a high degree of content validity. Canadian Pacific Hotels launched a performance management system called REACH, in which each job skill was described at each of three levels: developing, succeeding, and mastering. An employee at the developing level of customer service might miss opportunities to improve service, while one at the mastering level might anticipate future guests' needs.[33] The main disadvantage of a BARS is that it requires considerable time and effort to develop. Also, because the scales are specific to particular jobs, a scale designed for one job may not apply to another.

Behaviour Observation Scales (BOS)

A **behaviour observation scale (BOS)** is similar to a BARS in that both are based on critical incidents. However, as Highlights in HRM 8.5 shows, rather than asking the evaluator to choose the most representative behavioural anchor, BOS is designed to measure how often each of the behaviours has been observed.

The value of BOS is that it enables the appraiser to play the role of observer rather than judge. In this way, he or she can more easily provide constructive feedback to the employee. Users of the system often prefer it over BARS or trait scales for (1) maintaining objectivity, (2) distinguishing good from poor performers, (3) providing feedback, and (4) identifying training needs.[34]

Results Methods

Rather than looking at the traits of employees or the behaviours they exhibit on the job, many organizations evaluate employee accomplishments—the results they achieve through their work. Advocates of results appraisals contend that they are more objective and empowering for employees. Looking at results such as sales figures, production output, and the like is less subjective and so may be less open to bias. Furthermore, results appraisals often give employees responsibility for their outcomes, while giving them discretion over the methods they use to accomplish them (within limits). This is empowerment in action.

Productivity Measures

A number of results measures are available to evaluate performance. Salespeople are evaluated on the basis of their sales volume (both the number of units sold and the dollar amount in revenues). Production workers are evaluated on the basis of the number of units they produce and perhaps on the scrap rate or number of defects that are detected. Purchasing agents at Gaines Pet Foods in Cobourg, Ontario, use performance measurements such as managing the purchasing cycle time. Executives are often evaluated on the basis of company profits or growth rate. Each of these measures directly links what employees accomplish to results that benefit the organization. In this way, results appraisals can directly align employee and organizational goals.

Behaviour observation scale (BOS)

A behavioural approach to performance appraisal that measures the frequency of observed behaviour

Highlights in HRM 8.5

SAMPLE ITEMS FROM BEHAVIOUR OBSERVATION SCALE

Instructions: Please consider the sales representative's behaviour on the job in the past rating period. Read each statement carefully, then circle the number that indicates the extent to which the employee has demonstrated this effective or ineffective behaviour.

For each behaviour observed, use the following scale:

5 represents almost always   95–100% of the time
4 represents frequently   85–94% of the time
3 represents sometimes   75–84% of the time
2 represents seldom   65–74% of the time
1 represents almost never   0–64% of the time

SALES PRODUCTIVITY	ALMOST NEVER				ALMOST ALWAYS
1. Reviews individual productivity results with manager	1	2	3	4	5
2. Suggests to peers ways of building sales	1	2	3	4	5
3. Formulates specific objectives for each contact	1	2	3	4	5
4. Focuses on product rather than customer problem	1	2	3	4	5
5. Keep account plans updated	1	2	3	4	5
6. Keeps customer waiting for service	1	2	3	4	5
7. Anticipates and prepares for customer concerns	1	2	3	4	5
8. Follows up on customer leads	1	2	3	4	5

But there are some problems with results appraisals. First of all, recall our earlier discussion of criteria contamination. Results appraisals are easily contaminated by external factors that employees cannot influence. Sales representatives who have extremely bad markets and production employees who can't get the materials will not be able to perform up to their abilities. It may be unfair to hold these employees accountable for results that are contaminated by circumstances beyond their control.

Furthermore, results appraisals may inadvertently encourage employees to "look good" on a short-term basis, while ignoring the long-term ramifications. For example, line supervisors may let their equipment suffer to reduce maintenance costs. If the appraisal focuses on a narrow set of results criteria to the exclusion of other important process issues, the system may suffer from criterion deficiency and may unintentionally foster the attitude that "what gets measured gets done." In fact, in any job involving interaction with others, it is not enough to simply look at production or sales figures. Factors such as cooperation, adaptability, initiative, and concern for human relations may be important to job success. If these factors are important job standards, they should be added to the appraisal review. Thus, to be realistic, both the results and the methods or processes used to achieve them should be considered.[35]

Management by Objectives

Management by objectives (MBO)

Philosophy of management that rates performance on the basis of employee achievement of goals set by mutual agreement of employee and manager

One method that attempts to overcome some of the limitations of results appraisals is **management by objectives (MBO)**. MBO is a philosophy of management first proposed by Peter Drucker in 1954 that has employees establish objectives (e.g., production costs, sales per product, quality standards, profits) through consultation with their superiors and then uses these objectives as a basis for evaluation.[36] MBO is a system involving a cycle (Figure 8.6) that begins with setting the organization's common goals and objectives and ultimately returns to that step. The system acts as a goal-setting process whereby objectives are established for the organization (step 1), departments (step 2), and individual managers and employees (step 3).

As Figure 8.6 illustrates, a significant feature of the cycle is that specific goals are established by the employee, but those goals are based on a broad statement of employee responsibilities prepared by the supervisor. Employee-established goals are discussed with the supervisor and jointly reviewed and modified until both parties are satisfied with them (step 4). The goal statements are accompanied by a detailed account of the actions the employee proposes to take in order to reach the goals. During periodic reviews, as objective data are made available, the progress the employee is making toward the goals is assessed (step 5). Goals can be changed at this time as new or additional data are received. After a period of time (usually six months

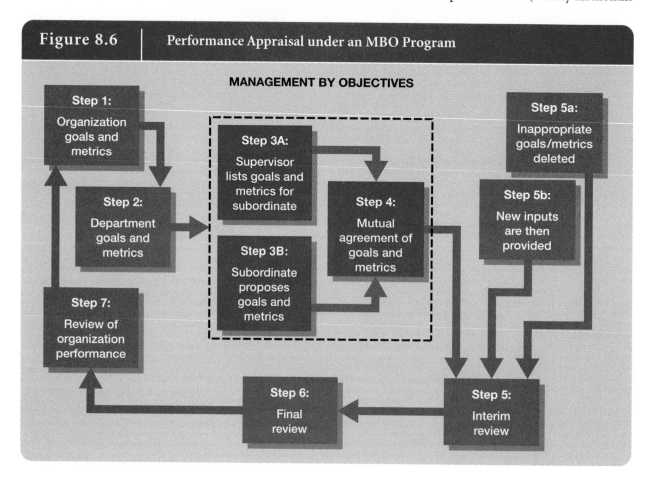

Figure 8.6   Performance Appraisal under an MBO Program

MANAGEMENT BY OBJECTIVES

Step 1: Organization goals and metrics

Step 2: Department goals and metrics

Step 3A: Supervisor lists goals and metrics for subordinate

Step 3B: Subordinate proposes goals and metrics

Step 4: Mutual agreement of goals and metrics

Step 5a: Inappropriate goals/metrics deleted

Step 5b: New inputs are then provided

Step 7: Review of organization performance

Step 6: Final review

Step 5: Interim review

or one year), the employee makes a self-appraisal of what she or he has accomplished, substantiating the self-appraisal with factual data wherever possible. The "interview" is an examination of the employee's self-appraisal by the supervisor and the employee together (step 6). The final step (step 7) is reviewing the connection between individual and organizational performance.

MBO programs should be viewed as part of a total system for managing, not as merely an addition to the manager's job. Managers must be willing to empower employees to accomplish their objectives on their own, giving them discretion over the methods they use but also holding them accountable for outcomes. The following guidelines can be especially helpful:

1. Managers and employees must be willing to establish goals and objectives together. Goal setting has been shown to improve employee performance, typically by 10 to 25 percent. Goal setting works because it helps employees focus on important tasks and makes them accountable for completing these tasks. It also establishes an automatic feedback system that aids learning, since employees can regularly evaluate their performance against their goals.[37]

2. Objectives should be quantifiable and measurable for the long and short term. However, goal statements should be accompanied by a description of how that goal will be accomplished.

3. Expected results must be under the employee's control. Recall our early discussion of criterion contamination.

4. Goals and objectives must be consistent for each level (top executive, manager, and employee).

5. Managers and employees must establish specific times when goals are to be reviewed and evaluated.

The Balanced Scorecard

One of the most enthusiastically adopted performance management innovations over the past decade has been the Balanced Scorecard (BSC). Developed by Harvard professors Robert Kaplan and David Norton, the BSC is a measurement framework that helps managers translate strategic goals into operational objectives. The generic model, shown in Highlights in HRM 8.6, has four related categories: (1) financial, (2) customer, (3) processes, and (4) learning. The logic of the BSC is that learning and people management help organizations improve their internal processes. These internal processes—product development, service, and the like—are critical for creating customer satisfaction and loyalty. Customer value creation in turn is what drives financial performance and profitability.

Similar in some ways to MBO, the BSC enables managers to translate broad corporate goals into divisional, departmental, and team goals in a cascading fashion. Highlights in HRM 8.7 shows an example of a personal scorecard used for this process. The value of this is that each individual can see more clearly how his or her performance ties into the overall performance of the firm.

Although a recent study found that over 40 percent of North American companies have adopted the BSC, it is neither a flawless nor a simple performance management system. Some recommendations for ensuring its successful application include the following:

Highlights in HRM 8.6

THE BALANCED SCORECARD

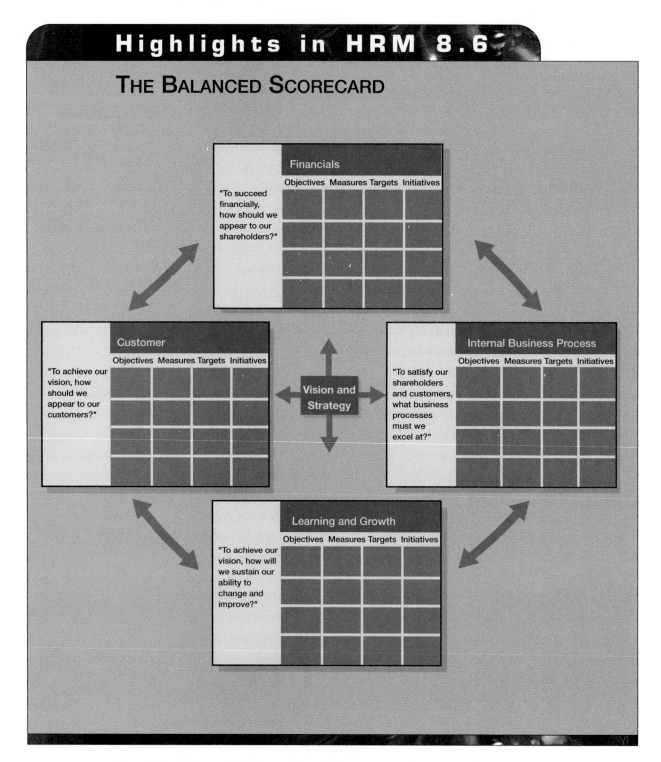

Source: Robert Kaplan and David Norton, "Strategic Learning and the Balanced Scorecard," *Strategy & Leadership* 24, no. 5 (September/October 1996): 18–24.

▶ *Translate the strategy into a scorecard of clear objectives.* As the BSC process begins with strategic objectives, unless these are clear the rest of the system is doomed to ambiguity and potential failure. By translating a strategy into objectives, managers and front-line employees are provided with goals that are more understandable and attainable. Typically, having fewer goals adds clarity and focus.

▶ *Attach measures to each objective.* In order for managers and employees to know if and when the objectives are achieved, clear measures must be attached to each goal. Each objective should be given at least one metric that can be measured either by a pre-existing system or manually within an organization.

Highlights in HRM 8.7

PERSONAL SCORECARD

CORPORATE OBJECTIVES

- Double our corporate value in seven years.
- Increase our earnings by an average of 20% per year.
- Achieve an internal rate of return 2% above the cost of capital.
- Increase both production and reserves by 20% in the next decade.

☑ Corporate
☐ Business Unit
☐ Team/Individual

CorporateTargets				Scorecard Measures	Bus. Unit Targets				Team/Individual Objectives
2001	2002	2003	2004		2001	2002	2003	2004	1.
				Financial					
100	120	160	180	Earnings (millions of dollars)					
100	450	200	210	Net cash flow					
100	85	75	70	Overhead and operating costs					2.
				Operating					
100	75	73	70	Production costs/barrel					
100	97	93	90	Development costs/barrel					
100	105	108	110	Total annual production					3.

Team/Individual Measures	Targets				
1.					
2.					4.
3.					
4.					

Source: Robert Kaplan and David Norton, "Strategic Learning and the Balance Scorecard," *Strategy Leadership* 24, no. 5 (September/October 1996): 75–85.

▶ *Cascade scorecards to the front line.* It is often said that the real strategic work happens at the front line. In order for all employees to understand how their roles and job duties are aligned with higher-level goals, scorecards should be cascaded to the individual level. By cascading scorecards, strategy then becomes "everyone's" job.

▶ *Provide performance feedback based on measures.* As with other performance management systems, unless managers provide employees with solid feedback on how they are doing, the system is likely to be ineffective. As part of this process, employees must know that they are accountable for achieving their objectives, and providing explanation when they do not hit their targets.

▶ *Empower employees to make performance improvements.* Individuals on their own, or working in teams, may understand ways of achieving higher performance. One of the benefits of a results-based system such as the BSC is that it gives employees the latitude to continuously improve best-practices methods.

▶ *Reassess strategy.* One of the key benefits of the BSC is that it is a continuous-loop process. Managers should monitor performance and use this information to reassess the strategy and make continuous adjustments. Those who have had the best success with the BSC argue that the system helps improve communication and learning rather than fixing in place a mechanical set of controls.[38]

Which Performance Appraisal Method to Use?

The choice of method should be based largely on the purpose of the appraisal. Figure 8.7 lists some of the strengths and weaknesses of trait, behaviour, and results approaches to appraisal. Note that the simplest and least expensive techniques often yield the least accurate information. However, research has not always supported a clear choice among appraisal methods.[39] While researchers and HR managers generally believe that the more sophisticated and more time-consuming methods offer more useful information, this may not always be the case. Managers must make cost-benefit decisions about which methods to use.

The bigger picture here focuses on how the performance appraisal systems are used. Having a first-rate method does no good if the manager simply "shoves it in a drawer." Alternatively, even a rudimentary system, when used properly, can initiate a discussion between managers and employees that genuinely brings about superior performance. These issues are discussed below under the topic of performance appraisal interviews.

APPRAISAL INTERVIEWS

The appraisal interview is perhaps the most important part of the entire performance appraisal process. The appraisal interview gives a manager the opportunity to discuss a subordinate's performance record and to explore areas of possible improvement and growth. It also provides an opportunity to identify the subordinate's attitudes and feelings more thoroughly and thus to improve communication.

Figure 8.7	Summary of Various Appraisal Methods

	ADVANTAGES	DISADVANTAGES
Trait methods	1. Are inexpensive to develop 2. Use meaningful dimensions 3. Are easy to use	1. Have high potential for rating errors 2. Are not useful for employee counselling 3. Are not useful for allocating rewards 4. Are not useful for promotion decisions
Behavioural methods	1. Use specific performance dimensions 2. Are acceptable to employees and superiors 3. Are useful for providing feedback 4. Are fair for reward and promotion decisions	1. Can be time-consuming to develop/use 2. Can be costly to develop 3. Have some potential for rating error
Results method	1. Has less subjectivity bias 2. Is acceptable to employees and superiors 3. Links individual performance to organizational performance 4. Encourages mutual goal setting 5. Is good for reward and promotion decisions	1. Is time-consuming to develop/use 2. May encourage short-term perspective 3. May use contaminated criteria 4. May use deficient criteria

Unfortunately, the interviewer can become overburdened by attempting to discuss too much, such as the employee's past performance and future development goals. Dividing the appraisal interview into two sessions, one for the performance review and the other for the employee's growth plans, can alleviate time pressures. Moreover, by separating the interview into two sessions, the interviewer can give each session the proper attention it deserves. It can be difficult for a supervisor to perform the role of both evaluator and counsellor in the same review period. Dividing the sessions can also improve communication between the parties, thereby reducing stress and defensiveness.

The format for the appraisal interview is determined in large part by the purpose of the interview, the type of appraisal system used, and the organization of the interview form. Most appraisal interviews attempt to give feedback to employees on how well they are performing their jobs and on planning for their future development. Interviews should be scheduled far enough in advance to allow the interviewee, as well as the interviewer, to prepare for the discussion. Ten days to two weeks is usually enough lead time.

Three Types of Appraisal Interviews

The individual who has studied different approaches to performance appraisal interviews most thoroughly is probably Norman R.F. Maier. In his classic book *The Appraisal Interview*, he analyzes the cause-and-effect relationships in three types of appraisal interviews: tell-and-sell, tell-and-listen, and problem solving.[40]

Tell-and-Sell Interview

The skills required in the tell-and-sell interview include the ability to persuade an employee to change in a prescribed manner. This may require the development of new behaviours on the part of the employee and skilful use of motivational incentives on the part of the appraiser/supervisor.

Tell-and-Listen Interview

In the tell-and-listen interview the skills required include the ability to communicate the strong and weak points of an employee's job performance during the first part of the interview. During the second part of the interview, the employee's feelings about the appraisal are thoroughly explored. The supervisor is still in the role of appraiser, but the method requires listening to disagreement and coping with defensive behaviour without attempting to refute any statements. The tell-and-listen method assumes that the opportunity to release frustrated feelings will help to reduce or remove those feelings.

Problem-Solving Interview

The skills associated with the problem-solving interview are consistent with the nondirective procedures of the tell-and-listen method. Listening, accepting, and responding to feelings are essential elements of the problem-solving interview. However, this method goes beyond an interest in the employee's feelings. It seeks to stimulate growth and development in the employee by discussing the problems, needs, innovations, satisfactions, and dissatisfactions the employee has encountered on the job since the last appraisal interview. Maier recommends this method, since the objective of appraisal is normally to stimulate growth and development in the employee.

Managers should not assume that only one type of appraisal interview is appropriate for every review session. Rather, they should be able to use one or more of the interview types, depending on the topic being discussed or on the behaviour of the employee being appraised. The interview should be seen as requiring a flexible approach.[41]

Conducting the Appraisal Interview

While there are probably no hard-and-fast rules for how to conduct an appraisal interview, there are some guidelines for increasing the employee's acceptance of the feedback, satisfaction with the interview, and intention to improve in the future. Many of the principles of effective interviewing discussed in Chapter 5 apply to performance appraisal interviews as well. Here are some other guidelines that should also be considered.

Ask for a Self-Assessment

As noted earlier in the chapter, it is useful to have employees evaluate their own performance prior to the appraisal interview. Even if this information is not used formally, the self-appraisal starts the employee thinking about his or her accomplishments. Self-appraisal also ensures that the employee knows which criteria he or she is being evaluated against; this eliminates any potential surprises.

Recent research evidence suggests that employees are more satisfied and view the appraisal system as providing more *procedural justice* when they have input into the process. When the employee has evaluated his or her own performance, the interview can be used to discuss those areas where the manager and the employee have reached different conclusions—not so much to resolve the "truth," but to work toward a resolution of problems.[42]

Invite Participation

The core purpose of a performance appraisal interview is to initiate a dialogue that will help the employee improve her or his performance. The more the employee is an active participant in that discussion, the more likely it is that the root causes of problems and obstacles to satisfactory performance will be uncovered, and the more likely it is that constructive ideas for improvement will be raised. Research suggests that participation is strongly related to the employee's satisfaction with the appraisal feedback, to the extent to which that feedback is perceived as fair and useful, and to the strength of the employee's intention to improve performance.[43] As a rule of thumb, supervisors should spend only about 30 to 35 percent of their time talking during the interview. The rest of the time they should be listening to employees respond to questions.

Express Appreciation

Praise is a powerful motivator, and especially in an appraisal interview, employees are seeking positive feedback. It is frequently beneficial to start the appraisal interview by expressing appreciation for what the employee has done well. In this way, he or she may be less defensive and more likely to talk about aspects of the job that are not going so well. However, try to avoid obvious use of the "sandwich technique," in which positive statements are followed by negative ones, which are then followed by positive ones. This approach may not work for several reasons. Praise often alerts the employee that criticism will be coming. Positive comments following the criticism then suggest to the employee that no more negative comments will be coming for a while. If managers follow an appraisal form, the problem of the sandwich technique can often be avoided. Furthermore, if employees are kept informed of their behaviour on a regular basis, there will be no need for this appraisal technique to be used.

Minimize Criticism

Employees who have a good relationship with their managers may be able to handle criticism better than those who do not. However, even the most stoic employees can absorb only so much criticism before they start to get defensive. If an employee has many areas in need of improvement, managers should focus on those few objective issues that are most severely in need of improvement or most important to the job. Some tips for using criticism constructively include the following:

▶ *Consider whether it is really necessary.* Frustration with performance problems sometimes leads to criticism that is little more than a manager "letting off steam." Make certain that the criticism focuses on a recurrent problem or a consistent pattern of behaviour.

▶ *Don't exaggerate.* Even managers who dislike criticizing may find that once they get started, they tend to overdo it. Sometimes we overstate problems in order to be convincing or to demonstrate our concern. Try to keep criticism simple, factual, and to the point. Avoid using terms like "always, completely, or never."

▶ *Make improvement your goal.* "Laying it on the line" is not likely to be useful unless it clarifies a path to improved performance. Criticism needs to be complemented with managerial support. This point is elaborated on below.[44]

Change the Behaviour, not the Person

Managers frequently try to play psychologist, to "figure out" why an employee has acted a certain way. When dealing with a problem area in particular, remember that it is not the person who is bad, but the actions exhibited on the job. Avoid suggestions about personal traits to change; instead suggest more acceptable ways of performing. For example, instead of focusing on the employee's "unreliability," the manager might focus on the fact that the employee "has been late to work seven times this month." It is difficult for employees to change who they are; it is usually much easier for them to change how they act.

Focus on Solving Problems

In addressing performance issues, it is often tempting to get into the "blame game," in which both manager and employee enter into a potentially endless discussion of why a situation has arisen. Solving problems often requires an analysis of the causes, but ultimately the appraisal interview should be directed at devising a solution to the problem.

Specific, measurable job standards help remove vagueness and subjectivity from performance appraisals.

PHOTODISC

Be Supportive

One of the better techniques for engaging an employee in the problem-solving process is for the manager to ask, "What can I do to help?" Employees often attribute performance problems to either real or perceived obstacles (such as bureaucratic procedures or inadequate resources). By being open and supportive, the manager conveys to the employee that he or she will try to eliminate external roadblocks and work with the employee to achieve higher standards.

Establish Goals

Since a major purpose of the appraisal interview is to make plans for improvement, it is important to focus the interviewee's attention on the future rather than the past. In setting goals with an employee, the manager should observe the following points:

▶ Emphasize strengths that the employee can build on rather than weaknesses to overcome.

▶ Concentrate on opportunities for growth that exist within the framework of the employee's current position.

▶ Limit plans for growth to a few important items that can be accomplished within a reasonable period of time.

▶ Establish specific action plans that spell out how each goal will be achieved. These action plans can include lists of contacts and resources as well as timetables for follow-up.

▶ Some supervisors may be tempted to establish difficult goals with their subordinates. The ethical issues surrounding unreasonable goals are discussed in Ethics in HRM.

Supervisors play a critical role in performance evaluation, but those being evaluated can play a more active role in ensuring that the process is fair and they receive the feedback necessary to improve and advance. Highlights in HRM 8.8 lists the questions that subordinates should be asking.

Follow Up Day to Day

Ideally, performance feedback should be an ongoing part of a manager's job. Feedback is most useful when it is immediate and specific to a particular situation. Unfortunately, both managers and employees are often happy to finish the interview and file away the appraisal form. A better approach is to have informal talks periodically to follow up on the issues raised in the appraisal interview. Levi Strauss explicitly includes informal feedback and coaching sessions on an ongoing basis. The process, referred to as the Partners in Performance Program, helps Levi Strauss managers adopt more of a coaching role (as opposed to that of a judge) and is designed to enhance continuous improvement and business objectives.

Improving Performance

In many instances, the appraisal interview provides the basis for noting deficiencies in employee performance and for making plans for improvement. Unless these deficiencies are brought to the employee's attention, they are likely to continue until they

Ethics in HRM

STRETCH GOALS

Employees are being asked to set performance goals, labelled "stretch goals," that ask them to do such things as double their sales or increase response time to customers threefold. Research has shown that the establishment of goals results in higher productivity. So if goals are good, are super goals better?

"Not necessarily," says Steve Kerr, General Electric's chief learning officer. In his opinion, most managers don't know how to manage stretch targets. Companies set ambitious goals for their employees but fail to provide them with the resources they need to achieve them. They are saying, in effect, "We aren't going to give you any more people or money, so your solution is to work smarter and be creative." The only resource left to employees is their personal time, and so North Americans are working harder than employees in any other developed country. They are working evenings and weekends, with fewer vacations. "That's immoral," says Kerr. "Companies have a moral obligation to provide the tools to meet tough goals."

How should stretch goals be managed? The goal must be seen as achievable, and not provoke a reaction of "You've got to be kidding." People must also realize that creative energy can be increased. For example, in one innovation training program, teams are given an orange and told that each person must handle the orange, but that the orange must end up in the hands of the person who started with it. All teams start by throwing the orange to team members; this takes nine seconds. They try to reduce the time to seven seconds by throwing faster or in tighter circles. When told that it is possible to do this task in one second, they get creative: they stack their hands and the first person drops the orange through the stacked but open hands and catches it at the bottom.

If the stretch goals aren't achieved, then punishment should not be used. Be careful with high achievers who are already stretching, or these winners will feel like losers if they can't meet impossible goals. Provide the tools; asking people to double their quota without ensuring backup is demoralizing. Finally, share the wealth. If the achievement results in additional funds flowing to the organization, split the incremental savings or gains.

Some employees, masters at the politics of organizations, play games with stretch goals. They negotiate hard for modest, achievable goals, while arguing that these are stretch targets. Others, with high needs for achievement, accept the stretch targets. At bonus time, the modest goal setters have met or surpassed their goals and receive merit increases. Having failed to achieve impossible targets, the less Machiavellian employees receive nothing.

Source: Adapted from S. Sherman, "Stretch Goals: The Dark Side of Asking for Miracles," *Fortune*, November 13, 1995: 231.

Highlights in HRM 8.8

THE TOUGH QUESTIONS

Performance appraisals can be improved when subordinates receive answers to these tough questions:

1. Was my performance rated against a specific written job description and defined standards of performance?

asks? How would you rate my performance on these

r my performance?
d placed in my file?
ork on to improve my performance.
my performance (coaching, training, etc.)?
onuses) be based on this evaluation? How does my
thers'?
why not?

ions?" *Supervision* 64, no. 1 (January 2003): 20–22.

mes underperformers may not understand exactly what
r, once their responsibilities are clarified, they are in a
e action needed to improve their performance.

of Ineffective Performance

several factors, which perhaps can be boiled down to
notivation, and environment. Every individual has a
nd weaknesses that play a part. But talented employees
kely to succeed. Also, other factors in the work environ-
al environment, which includes personal, family, and
ect performance positively or negatively. Figure 8.8 sug-
(ability, motivation, and environment) can influence

iagnosis of poor employee performance focus on these
hown in Figure 8.8, if an employee's performance is not
up to standards, the cause could be a skill problem (knowledge, abilities, technical
competencies), an effort problem (motivation to get the job done), and/or some

YOUR ACCESS CERTIFICATE

ISBN # 0176103872

This certificate contains your serial number for access to the online version of *Canadian HR Reporter*. Your access begins when the registration is complete and lasts for four months.

How to register Your Serial Number:

Go to www.hrreporter.com/students

Click the "register" button to enter your serial number.

Enter the serial number exactly as it appears here and create a unique user ID and password.

Record your user ID and password in a secure location.

Once registered, return to the above URL and enter your user ID and password.

Serial number: JC4FE532

Figure 8.8 | Factors that Influence Performance

Perf $= f\,(A,M,E)$

MOTIVATION	ENVIRONMENT	ABILITY
• Career ambition	• Equipment/materials	• Technical skills
• Employee conflict	• Job design	• Interpersonal skills
• Frustration	• Economic conditions	• Problem-solving skills
• Fairness/satisfaction	• Unions	• Analytical skills
• Goals/expectations	• Rules and policies	• Communication skills
	• Management support	• Physical limitations
	• Laws and regulations	

---

problem in the external conditions of work (poor economic conditions, supply shortages, difficult sales territories).[45] Any one of these problem areas could cause performance to suffer.

Performance Diagnosis

Although performance appraisal systems can often tell us who is not performing well, they typically cannot reveal why. Unfortunately, research evidence suggests that managers often make wrong attributions for poor performance. They often assume that poor performance is first due to lack of ability, second to poor motivation, and then to external constraints. Ironically, research evidence also suggests that we tend to make just the opposite attributions about our own performance. We first attribute poor performance to external constraints such as bad luck or factors out of our control. If the problem is internal, then we typically attribute it to temporary factors such as motivation or energy ("I had a bad day") and only as a last resort admit that it might be due to ability.

So what can be done to diagnose the real reasons for poor performance? More specifically, how can managers identify the root causes and get to work on a solution that improves performance? By comparing different performance measures, managers can begin to get an idea of the underlying causes of performance problems. For example, as shown in Highlights in HRM 8.9, results measures cannot distinguish between ability, motivation, or situational determinants of performance. So if someone is not achieving desired results it could be due to ability, motivation, or external constraints. On the other hand, behavioural measures are less affected by external constraints. So if someone is demonstrating all the desired behaviours but is not achieving the desired results, logic suggests that it may be due to factors beyond his or her control.

Other kinds of diagnoses are possible by comparing different measures of performance. And only by correctly diagnosing the causes of performance problems can managers—and employees—hope to improve them.

Highlights in HRM 8.8

THE TOUGH QUESTIONS

Performance appraisals can be improved when subordinates receive answers to these tough questions:

1. Was my performance rated against a specific written job description and defined standards of performance?
2. What do you consider my top priority tasks? How would you rate my performance on these tasks?
3. How do I rate against my peers? Why?
4. What can I do to improve my ranking or my performance?
5. Will this evaluation be documented and placed in my file?
6. Tell me what specific areas I need to work on to improve my performance.
7. What help can you give me to improve my performance (coaching, training, etc.)?
8. Will my compensation (i.e., raises or bonuses) be based on this evaluation? How does my change in compensation compare to others'?
9. Am I assessed as promotable? Why or why not?

Source: David K. Lindo, "Can You Answer Their Questions?" *Supervision* 64, no. 1 (January 2003): 20–22.

become quite serious. Sometimes underperformers may not understand exactly what is expected of them. However, once their responsibilities are clarified, they are in a position to take the corrective action needed to improve their performance.

Identifying Sources of Ineffective Performance

Performance is a function of several factors, which perhaps can be boiled down to three primary ones: ability, motivation, and environment. Every individual has a unique pattern of strengths and weaknesses that play a part. But talented employees with low motivation are not likely to succeed. Also, other factors in the work environment—or even in the external environment, which includes personal, family, and community concerns—can affect performance positively or negatively. Figure 8.8 suggests how these three factors (ability, motivation, and environment) can influence performance.

It is recommended that a diagnosis of poor employee performance focus on these three interactive elements. As shown in Figure 8.8, if an employee's performance is not up to standards, the cause could be a skill problem (knowledge, abilities, technical competencies), an effort problem (motivation to get the job done), and/or some

Figure 8.8	Factors that Influence Performance

$$\text{Perf} = f\,(A, M, E)$$

MOTIVATION	ENVIRONMENT	ABILITY
• Career ambition • Employee conflict • Frustration • Fairness/satisfaction • Goals/expectations	• Equipment/materials • Job design • Economic conditions • Unions • Rules and policies • Management support • Laws and regulations	• Technical skills • Interpersonal skills • Problem-solving skills • Analytical skills • Communication skills • Physical limitations

problem in the external conditions of work (poor economic conditions, supply shortages, difficult sales territories).[45] Any one of these problem areas could cause performance to suffer.

Performance Diagnosis

Although performance appraisal systems can often tell us who is not performing well, they typically cannot reveal why. Unfortunately, research evidence suggests that managers often make wrong attributions for poor performance. They often assume that poor performance is first due to lack of ability, second to poor motivation, and then to external constraints. Ironically, research evidence also suggests that we tend to make just the opposite attributions about our own performance. We first attribute poor performance to external constraints such as bad luck or factors out of our control. If the problem is internal, then we typically attribute it to temporary factors such as motivation or energy ("I had a bad day") and only as a last resort admit that it might be due to ability.

So what can be done to diagnose the real reasons for poor performance? More specifically, how can managers identify the root causes and get to work on a solution that improves performance? By comparing different performance measures, managers can begin to get an idea of the underlying causes of performance problems. For example, as shown in Highlights in HRM 8.9, results measures cannot distinguish between ability, motivation, or situational determinants of performance. So if someone is not achieving desired results it could be due to ability, motivation, or external constraints. On the other hand, behavioural measures are less affected by external constraints. So if someone is demonstrating all the desired behaviours but is not achieving the desired results, logic suggests that it may be due to factors beyond his or her control.

Other kinds of diagnoses are possible by comparing different measures of performance. And only by correctly diagnosing the causes of performance problems can managers—and employees—hope to improve them.

Highlights in HRM 8.9

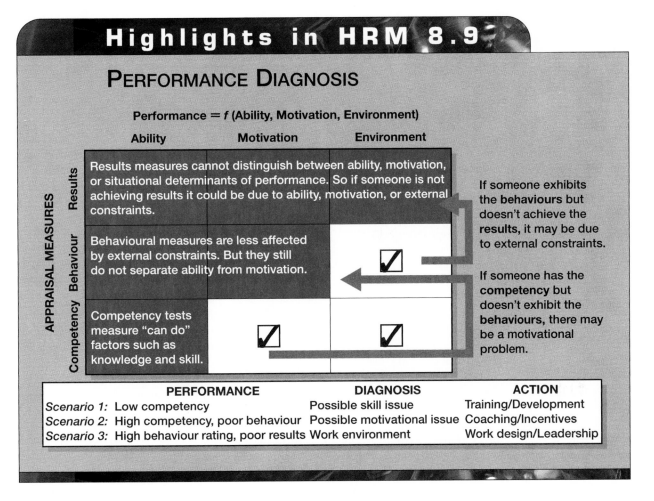

PERFORMANCE DIAGNOSIS

Performance = *f* (Ability, Motivation, Environment)

		Ability	Motivation	Environment
APPRAISAL MEASURES	**Results**	Results measures cannot distinguish between ability, motivation, or situational determinants of performance. So if someone is not achieving results it could be due to ability, motivation, or external constraints.		
	Behaviour	Behavioural measures are less affected by external constraints. But they still do not separate ability from motivation.	✓	
	Competency	Competency tests measure "can do" factors such as knowledge and skill.	✓	✓

If someone exhibits the **behaviours** but doesn't achieve the **results**, it may be due to external constraints.

If someone has the **competency** but doesn't exhibit the **behaviours**, there may be a motivational problem.

	PERFORMANCE	DIAGNOSIS	ACTION
Scenario 1:	Low competency	Possible skill issue	Training/Development
Scenario 2:	High competency, poor behaviour	Possible motivational issue	Coaching/Incentives
Scenario 3:	High behaviour rating, poor results	Work environment	Work design/Leadership

Source: Scott Snell, Cornell University.

Managing Ineffective Performance

Once the sources of performance problems are known, a course of action can be planned. This action may lie in providing training in areas that would increase the knowledge and/or skills needed for effective performance. A transfer to another job or department might give an employee a chance to become a more effective member of the organization. In other situations, greater attention may have to be focused on ways to motivate the individual.

If ineffective performance persists, it may be necessary to transfer the employee, take disciplinary action, or discharge the person from the organization. Whatever action is taken to cope with ineffective performance, it should be done with objectivity, fairness, and a recognition of the feelings of the individual involved.

SUMMARY

Performance appraisal programs serve many purposes, which in general terms fall into two categories: administrative and developmental. *Administrative purposes* relate to who will be promoted, transferred, or laid off, and compensation decisions. *Developmental purposes* relate to improving and enhancing an individual's capabilities (e.g., identifying a person's strengths and weaknesses, eliminating external performance obstacles, and establishing training needs). These two purposes of performance appraisal reflect HRM's larger role, which is to integrate the individual with the organization.

In many organizations, performance appraisals are seen as a necessary evil. Many managers avoid conducting appraisals because they dislike playing the role of judge. As a consequence, they conduct appraisals reluctantly once a year and then forget about them. As a result, they do not develop good feedback skills. Furthermore, when managers are not adequately trained, subjectivity and organizational politics can distort the reviews.

The success of an organization depends largely on the performance of its human resources. To determine the contributions of each individual, it is necessary to have a formal appraisal program with clearly stated objectives. Carefully defined performance standards that are reliable, strategically relevant, and free from either criterion deficiency or contamination are essential foundations for evaluation. Appraisal systems must also comply with the law. Appraisals should be treated with the same concerns for validity as are selection tests. For example, ratings must be job-related, employees must understand their performance standards in advance, appraisers must be able to observe job performance, appraisers must be trained, feedback must be given, and an appeals procedure must be established.

Using several raters is frequently a good idea because different individuals see different facets of an employee's performance. The supervisor, for example, has legitimate authority over an employee and is in a good position to discern whether he or she is contributing to the goals of the organization. Peers and team members, on the other hand, often have an unfiltered view of an employee's work activity, particularly related to issues such as cooperation and dependability. Subordinates often provide good information about whether an employee is facilitating their work, and customers (both internal and external) can convey the extent to which an employee adds value and meets their requirements. Self-appraisal is useful, if for no other reason than it encourages employees to think about their strengths, weaknesses, and future goals. An increasing number of organizations are using several raters—or 360-degree appraisal—to get a more comprehensive picture of employee performance. Regardless of the source of appraisal information, appraisers should be thoroughly trained in the particular methods they will use in evaluating their subordinates. Participation in developing rating scales, such as a BARS, automatically provides such training.

Several methods can be used for performance appraisal. These include trait approaches (graphic rating scales, mixed standard scales, forced choice forms, and essays), behavioural methods (critical incident ratings, checklists, BARS, and BOS), and results methods (MBO). Which method is chosen depends on the purpose of the appraisal. Trait appraisals are simple to develop and complete, but have problems of subjectivity and are not useful for feedback. Behavioural methods provide more specific information for feedback but can be time-consuming and costly to develop. Results appraisals are more objective and can link individual performance to the organization as a whole, but they may encourage a short-term perspective (e.g., annual goals) and may not include subtle yet important aspects of performance.

The degree to which the performance appraisal program benefits the organization and its members is directly related to the quality of the appraisal interviews. Interviewing skills are best developed through instruction and supervised practice. Research suggests that while there are various approaches to interviews, employee participation and goal-setting exercises lead to higher satisfaction and improved performance. It is also helpful to discuss problems, show support, minimize criticism, and reward effective performance. In the interview, deficiencies in employee performance can be discussed and plans for improvement can be made.

KEY TERMS

behaviour observation scale
  (BOS) 356
behaviourally anchored rating
  scale (BARS) 354
contrast error 347
critical incident method 354
customer appraisal 339
error of central tendency 346

essay method 351
forced choice method 351
graphic rating scale method 349
leniency or strictness error 346
management by objectives
  (MBO) 358
manager and/or supervisor
  appraisal 337

mixed-standard scale method 351
peer appraisal 338
recency error 347
self-appraisal 337
similar-to-me error 347
subordinate appraisal 338
team appraisal 339

DISCUSSION QUESTIONS

 1. What are the major purposes of performance appraisal? In what ways might these purposes be contradictory?

 2. Describe the relationships among performance appraisal and selection, training, and development.

 3. How can performance appraisals be adjusted to include the principles underlying total quality management?

 4. Describe the characteristics of the ideal appraisal system.

 5. What guidelines must performance appraisals follow if they are to be legally defensible?

 6. What sources could evaluate the performance of people working in the following jobs?
   a. sales representative
   b. TV repairer
   c. director of nursing in a hospital

   d. HR manager
   e. air traffic controller

 7. In many organizations, evaluators submit ratings to their immediate superiors for review before discussing them with the individual employees they have rated. What advantages are there to this procedure?

 8. What are the pros and cons of trait, behaviour, and results appraisals?

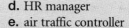 9. Three types of appraisal interviews are described in this chapter.
   a. What different skills are required for each type of appraisal interview? What reactions can one expect to the use of these different skills?
   b. How can one develop the skills needed for the problem-solving type of interview?
   c. Which method do you feel is the least desirable? Explain.

Developing Managerial Skills

PERFORMANCE DIAGNOSIS

Managing performance is an important—yet delicate—process for managers to undertake. They need to make tough calls at times regarding who is performing well or not. Also, they need to play the role of coach to help each employee improve his or her performance. One of the toughest aspects of performance management is making an assessment of why someone is not performing well. Although it may be easy to spot who is not performing well, it is not always easy to diagnose the underlying causes of poor performance (such as motivation, ability, and external constraints). But without a correct diagnosis, it is nearly impossible to cure the problem.

Assignment

Below are descriptions of three different employees. Describe the potential causes of poor performance in each case. And for each potential cause, identify appropriate solutions to enhance performance.

1. *Carl Spackler* is the assistant greens-keeper at Bushwood Country Club. Over the past few months, members have been complaining that gophers are destroying the course and digging holes in the greens. Although Carl has been working evenings and weekends to address the situation, the problem persists. Unfortunately, his boss is interested only in results, and because the gophers are still there, he contends that Carl is not doing his job. He has accused Carl of "slacking off" and threatened his job.

2. *Clark Griswold* works in research and development for a chemical company that makes non-nutritive food additives. His most recent assignment has been the development of a nonstick aerosol cooking spray, but the project is way behind schedule and seems to be going nowhere. CEO Frank Shirley is decidedly upset and has threatened that if things don't improve, he will suspend bonuses again this year like he did last year. Clark feels dejected, because without the bonus he won't be able to take his family on vacation.

3. *Bonnie Malloy* is the host of a local television talk show called *Morning Chicago*. Although she is a talented performer and comedienne, Bonnie has an unacceptable record of tardiness. The show's producer, David Bellows, is frustrated, because the problem has affected the quality of the show. On several occasions, Bonnie was unprepared when the show went on the air. Bellows has concluded that Bonnie is not a morning person and has thought about replacing her with a different host.

Case Study 1

Workload Worries

A hotel's receiving department is responsible for checking deliveries of food and beverages, checking what has been received against what has been ordered, and verifying the quality of the merchandise received. In May 2000 an employee of the Westin Ottawa failed to check a case of vegetables, which had started to rot. The receiver, who had been with the hotel for seventeen years, admitted that he had not checked the vegetables. As a result, his supervisor gave him a written warning. The employee grieved, stating that he was too busy because the work load was excessive.

There was an investigation, which indicated that the grievor had not worked any overtime, nor had he requested permission to work any overtime. It was also noted that during the receiver's vacation period, the replacement worker had been able to perform the job without any difficulty. There was also evidence that the receiver was taking excessive breaks.

As a result of this investigation, the grievance was denied. In addition, the employee was sent a letter reminding him of his job responsibilities and of the need to restrict himself to the scheduled breaks. As a last step he was given a procedure to follow if he believed that the work was becoming excessive.

QUESTIONS

1. Discuss how a performance appraisal system might have prevented this grievance.
2. Which performance appraisal method would you recommend for this type of job?

Case Study 2

The Bank of Montreal's Balanced Scorecard

In 1990, when Matthew W. Barrett became the Bank of Montreal's chairman and Tony Comper became its president, they had one main goal: to focus the entire workforce on success. It's a simple idea, but not so easy to execute. How would they get entry-level tellers to think of their work not just as a means to a paycheque, but as a direct contribution to BMO shareholders? How would they remind corporate executives that their jobs were not just to boost the bottom line, but to charm entire communities?

The answer was a balanced scorecard approach. To be competitive, executives decided, the bank had to meet the needs of four stakeholders: BMO shareholders, customers, employees, and communities.

Executives translated that idea into four goals: shareholders needed a return on equity, customers needed good service, employees needed to feel loyal and satisfied, and communities needed to feel that the bank made a difference in their neighbourhoods. Return on investment would determine satisfaction for shareholders; surveys and feedback would determine satisfaction for customers, employees, and communities.

So far, so good. But every single department and every employee in every department had to understand how their work contributed to achieving those four goals. So each employee's and department's performance ratings now are dependent on their contribution toward each goal. Employees in the customer service department, for instance, are rated by their return on equity (judged by their cost-effectiveness), their customer satisfaction (judged by customer feedback), and their community involvement (judged by any outreach programs or increase in customers).

Departments may be assigned a specific stakeholder. HR is charged with the employee piece—that is, with providing competent, committed workers in a cost-effective way. Harriet Stairs, senior vice-president of HR, uses training and education to ensure competency and work-life and career development programs to boost commitment. Knowing that she's rated on the cost-effectiveness of all this, she also keeps her eye on the price tag: "It encourages everyone to do his or her job with the exact same issues in mind," she says.

At the end of the year, the scores from everyone's performance ratings are translated into indexes, with ratings from 1 to 10. The index for the employee stakeholder piece is determined by ratings for competency, commitment, and cost-effectiveness. The four indexes—for BMO shareholders, customers, employees, and communities— are then rolled up into one figure of merit. At the end of each year, these results are presented to the board of directors, who use them to determine bonuses.

Source: "How the Bank of Montreal Keeps Score on Success" by Gillion Flynn, copyright December 1997. ACC Communications/Workforce, Costa Hesa, CA. http://www.workforce.com.

QUESTIONS

1. What are the strengths and weaknesses of a balanced scorecard approach to performance appraisal?
2. Do you think such an approach would integrate well with an MBO system? Explain.
3. Do you believe that a balanced scorecard approach would be more effective for the administrative or developmental purposes of appraisal?

CAREER COUNSEL

Obtain a rating of your performance by consulting www.belcourt4e.nelson.com.

NOTES AND REFERENCES

1. Brian D. Cawley, Lisa M. Keeping, and Paul E. Levy, "Participation in the Performance Appraisal Process and Employee Reactions: A Meta-Analytic Review of Field Investigations," *Journal of Applied Psychology* 83, no. 4 (August 1998): 615–33; Susan Scherreik, "Your Performance Review: Make It Perform," *Business Week,* no. 3762 (December 17, 2001): 139; Dick Grote, "Performance Evaluations: Is It Time for a Makeover?" *HRFocus* 77, no. 11 (November 2000): 6–7.

2. Philip Schofield, "Do Appraisals Need Review?" *Works Management* 52, no. 2 (February 1999): 24–26; Marilyn Moats Kennedy, "The Case against Performance Appraisals," *Across the Board* 36, no. 1 (January 1999): 51–52; Matthew Boyle, "Performance Reviews: Perilous Curves Ahead," *Fortune* 143, no. 11 (May 28, 2001): 187–88; Susanne Scott and Walter Einstein, "Strategic Performance Appraisal in Team-Based Organizations: One Size Does Not Fit All," *Academy of Management Executive* 15, no. 2 (May 2001): 107–16.

3. Jonathan A. Segal, "86 Your Appraisal Process?" *HRMagazine* 45, no. 10 (October 2000): 199–206; Barry Witcher and Rosie Butterworth, "Honshin Kanri: How Xerox Manages," *Long Range Planning* 32, no. 3 (June 1999): 323–32.

4. Matt Bloom, "The Performance Effects of Pay Dispersion on Individuals and Organizations," *Academy of Management Journal* 42, no. 1 (February 1999): 25–40; Donald J. Campbell, Kathleen M. Campbell, and Ho-Beng Chia, "Merit Pay, Performance Appraisal, and Individual Motivation: An Analysis and Alternative," *Human Resource Management* 37, no. 2 (Summer 1998): 131–46; Janet Wiscombe, "Can Pay for Performance Really Work?" *Workforce* 80, no. 8 (August 2001): 28–34.

5. David Allen and Rodger Griffeth, "Test of a Mediated Performance-Turnover Relationship Highlighting the Moderating Roles of Visibility and Reward Contingency," *Journal of Applied Psychology* 86, no. 5 (October 2001): 1014–21; Charles Pettijohn, Linda Pettijohn, and Michael D'Amico, "Characteristics of Performance Appraisals and Their Impact on Sales Force Satisfaction," *Human Resource Development Quarterly* 12, no. 2 (Summer 2001): 127–46; Scott and Einstein, "Strategic Performance Appraisal in Team-Based Organizations."

6. Donna Doldwasser, "Me a Trainer?" *Training* 38, no. 4 (April 2001): 60–66; Rebecca Ganzel, "Mike Carter," *Training* 38, no. 7 (July 2001): 28–30; Carla Joinson, "Making Sure Employees Measure Up," *HRMagazine* 46, no. 3 (March 2001): 36–41.

7. Ronald J. Deluga, "The Quest for Justice on the Job: Essays and Experiments," *Journal of Occupational and Organizational Psychology* 72, no. 1 (March 1999): 122–24; Kathryn Bartol, Cathy Durham, and June Poon, "Influence of Performance Evaluation Rating Segmentation on Motivation and Fairness Perceptions," *Journal of Applied Psychology* 86, no. 6 (December 2001): 1106–19; Elizabeth Douthitt and John Aiello, "The Role of Participation and Control in the Effects of Computer Monitoring on Fairness Perceptions, Task Satisfaction, and Performance," *Journal of Applied Psychology* 86, no. 5 (October 2001): 867–74.

8. Robert Bookman, "Tools for Cultivating Constructive Feedback," *Association Management* 51, no. 2 (February 1999): 73–79; Clinton O. Longnecker and Dennis A. Gioia, "The Politics of Executive Appraisals," *Journal of Compensation and Benefits* 10, no. 2 (September/October 1994): 5–11; John Newman, J. Mack Robinson, Larry Tyler, David Dunbar, and Joseph Zager, "CEO Performance Appraisal: Review and Recommendations/Practitioner Application," *Journal of Healthcare Management* 46, no. 1 (January/February 2001): 21–38.

9. T. Davis and M.J. Landa, "A Contrary Look at Performance Appraisal," *Canadian Manager* 24, no. 3 (Fall 1999): 18, 19.

10. "Strategic Planning Viewed from the Bottom Up," *The Futurist* 32, no. 4 (May 1998): 46; Michael Arndt, "3M: A Lab for Growth?" *Business Week,* no. 3766 (January 21, 2002): 50–51; "General Motors and Whirlpool: Two Approaches for Developing Performance Benchmarks," *HRFocus* 77, no. 6 (June 2000): 7–10; Doug Cederblom, "From Performance Appraisal to Performance Management: One Agency's Experience," *Public Personnel Management* 31, no. 2 (Summer 2002): 131–40; Sean Way and James Thacker, "The Successful Implementation of Strategic Human Resource Management Practices: A Canadian Survey," *International Journal of Management* 18, no. 1 (March 2001): 25–32.

11. Gregory D. Streib and Theodore H. Poister, "Assessing the Validity, Legitimacy, and Functionality of Performance Measurement Systems in Municipal Governments," *American Review of Public Administration* 29, no. 2 (June 1999): 107–23; Margaret A. McManus and Steven H. Brown, "Adjusting Sales Results Measures for Use as Criteria," *Personnel Psychology* 48, no. 2 (Summer 1995): 391–400.

12. Joel Lefkowitz, "The Role of Interpersonal Affective Regard in Supervisory Performance Ratings: A Literature Review and Proposed Causal Model," *Journal of Occupational and Organizational Psychology* 73, no. 1 (March 2000): 67–85.

13. Adrian Furnham and Paul Stringfield, "Congruence in Job-Performance Ratings: A Study of 360-Degree Feedback Examining Self, Manager, Peers, and Consultant Ratings," *Human Relations* 51, no. 4 (April 1998): 517–30; Bob Rosner, "Squeezing More Respect out of Your Team," *Workforce* 79, no. 7 (July 2000): 80; Dick Grote, "The Secrets of Performance Appraisal: Best Practices from the Masters," *Across the Board* 37, no. 5 (May 2000): 14–20.

14. Paddy Kamen, "360-Degree Review a New Spin for Managers," *The Globe and Mail*, September 22, 2002: B13.

15. Alan G. Walker and James W. Smither, "A Five-Year Study of Upward Feedback: What Managers Do with Their Results Matters," *Personnel Psychology* 52, no. 2 (Summer 1999): 393–423; Joan Brett and Leanne Atwater, "360-Degree Feedback: Accuracy, Reactions, and Perceptions of Usefulness," *Journal of Applied Psychology* 86, no. 5 (October 2001): 930–42.

16. Donald B. Fedor, Kenneth L. Bettenhausen, and Walter Davis, "Peer Reviews: Employees' Dual Roles as Raters and Recipients," *Group & Organization Management* 24, no. 1 (March 1999): 92–120.

17. Vanessa Urch Druskat and Steven B. Wolff, "Effects and Timing of Developmental Peer Appraisals in Self-Managing Work Groups," *Journal of Applied Psychology* 84, no. 1 (February 1999): 58–74; John Drexler, Jr., Terry Beehr, and Thomas Stetz, "Peer Appraisals: Differentiation of Individual Performance on Group Tasks," *Human Resource Management* 40, no. 4 (Winter 2001): 333–45.

18. Bradley Kirkman and Benson Rosen, "Powering Up Teams," *Organizational Dynamics* 28, no. 3 (Winter 2000): 48–66; Matthew Valle and Kirk Davis, "Teams and Performance Appraisal: Using Metrics to Increase Reliability and Validity," *Team Performance Management* 5, no. 8 (1999): 238–43.

19. Michael Cohn, "Best Buy Beefs Up Customer Value at the Call Center," *Internet World* 8, no. 6 (June 2002): 42–43; Joe Kohn, "Isuzu Has IDEA for Boosting Sales," *Automotive News* 76, no. 5973 (March 4, 2002): 41; D. L. Radcliff, "A New Paradigm of Feedback," *Executive Excellence* 19, no. 4 (April 2002): 20.

20. Bruce Pfau, Ira Kay, Kenneth Nowak, and Jai Ghorpade, "Does 360-Degree Feedback Negatively Affect Company Performance?" *HRMagazine* 47, no. 6 (June 2002): 54–59; Maury Peiperl, "Getting 360-Degree Feedback

Right," *Harvard Business Review* 79, no. 1 (January 2001): 142–47; Jack Kondrasuk, Mary Riley, and Wang Hua, "If We Want to Pay for Performance, How Do We Judge Performance?" *Journal of Compensation and Benefits* 15, no. 2 (September/October 1999): 35–40; Matt Graybill, "From Paper to Computer," *The Human Resource Professional* 13, no. 6 (November/December 2000): 18–19.

21. David W. Bracken, Lynn Summers, and John Fleenor, "High-Tech 360," *Training and Development* 52, no. 8 (August 1998): 42–45; Gary Meyer, "Performance Reviews Made Easy, Paperless," *HRMagazine* 45, no. 10 (October 2000): 181–84.

22. David A. Waldman, Leanne E. Atwater, and David Antonioni, "Has 360-Degree Feedback Gone Amok?" *Academy of Management Executive* 12, no. 2 (May 1998): 86–94.

23. Gary E. Roberts, "Perspectives on Enduring and Emerging Issues in Performance Appraisal," *Public Personnel Management* 27, no. 3 (Fall 1998): 301–20; William Hubbartt, "Bring Performance Appraisal Training to Life," *HRMagazine* 40, no. 5 (May 1995): 166, 168; Filip Lievens, "Assessor Training Strategies and Their Effects on Accuracy, Interrater Reliability, and Discriminant Validity," *Journal of Applied Psychology* 86, no. 2 (April 2001): 255–64; Dick Grote, "Performance Appraisals: Solving Tough Challenges," *HRMagazine* 45, no. 7 (July 2000): 145–50.

24. Gary P. Latham and Kenneth N. Wexley, *Increasing Productivity through Performance Appraisal*, 2nd ed. (Reading, MA: Addison-Wesley, 1994), 137.

25. Lefkowitz, "The Role of Interpersonal Affective Regard in Supervisory Performance Ratings"; Gordon Cheung, "Multifaceted Conceptions of Self-Other Ratings Disagreement," *Personnel Psychology* 52, no. 1 (Spring 1999): 1–36.

26. Deidra J. Schleicher and David V. Day, "A Cognitive Evaluation of Frame-of-Reference Rater Training: Content and Process Issues," *Organizational Behavior and Human Decision Processes* 73, no. 1 (January 1998): 76–101; Wanda Smith, K. Vernard Harrington, and Jeffery Houghton, "Predictors of Performance Appraisal Discomfort: A Preliminary Examination," *Public Personnel Management* 29, no. 1 (Spring 2000): 21–32.

27. Lisa Keeping and Paul Levy, "Performance Appraisal Reaction: Measurement, Modeling, and Method Bias," *Journal of Applied Psychology* 85, no. 5 (October 2000): 708–23.

28. Wendy Boswell and John Boudreau, "Employee Satisfaction with Performance Appraisals and Appraisers: The Role of Perceived Appraisal Use," *Human Resource Development Quarterly* 11, no. 3 (Fall

2000): 283–99; James W. Smither, *Performance Appraisal: State of the Art in Practice* (San Francisco: Jossey-Bass, 1998); Donald Fedor, Kenneth Bettenhausen, and Walter Davis, "Peer Reviews: Employees' Dual Roles as Raters and Recipients," *Group & Organization Management* 24, no. 1 (March 1999): 92–120.

29. Terry Gillen, "Why Appraisal Should Climb the Skills Agenda," *People Management* 2, no. 9 (May 2, 1996): 43.

30. Stephen C. Behrenbrinker, "Conducting Productive Performance Evaluations in the Assessor's Office," *Assessment Journal* 2, no. 5 (September/October 1995): 48–54; Aharon Tziner, Christine Joanis, and Kevin Murphy, "A Comparison of Three Methods of Performance Appraisal with Regard to Goal Properties, Goal Perception, and Ratee Satisfaction," *Group & Organization Management* 25, no. 2 (June 2000): 175–90.

31. Joseph Maiorca, "How to Construct Behaviorally Anchored Rating Scales (BARS) for Employee Evaluations," *Supervision* 58, no. 8 (August 1997): 15–18; Jeffrey M. Conte, Frank J. Landy, and John E. Mathieu, "Time Urgency: Conceptual and Construct Development," *Journal of Applied Psychology* 80, no. 1 (February 1995): 178–85; Elaine Pulakos, Sharon Arad, Michelle Donovan, and Kevin Plamondon, "Adaptability in the Workplace: Development of a Taxonomy of Adaptive Performance," *Journal of Applied Psychology* 85, no. 4 (August 2000): 612–24.

32. For a comprehensive review of the research on BARS, see Chapter 6 in H. John Bernadin and Richard W. Beatty, *Performance Appraisal: Assessing Human Behavior at Work* (Boston: Kent, 1984). Also see Latham and Wexley, *Increasing Productivity*; Kevin R. Murphy and Jeanette N. Cleveland, *Understanding Performance Appraisal* (Thousand Oaks, CA: Sage, 1995).

33. S. Nador, "A Properly Crafted Performance Management Program Aids Professional Development," *Canadian HR Reporter,* May 17, 1999: 10.

34. Latham and Wexley, *Increasing Productivity*; Tziner, Joanis, and Murphy, "A Comparison of Three Methods of Performance Appraisal"; Simon Taggar and Travor Brown, "Problem-Solving Team Behaviors: Development and Validation of BOS and a Hierarchical Factor Structure," *Small Group Research* 32, no. 6 (December 2001): 698–726.

35. Daniel Bachrach, Elliot Bendoly, and Philip Podsakoff, "Attributions of the 'Causes' of Group Performance as an Alternative Explanation of the Relationship between Organizational Citizenship Behavior and Organizational Performance," *Journal of Applied Psychology* 86, no. 6 (December 2001): 1285–93; Susan Leandri, "Measures That Matter: How to Fine-Tune Your Performance Measures," *Journal for Quality and Participation* 24, no. 1 (Spring 2001): 39–41.

36. Peter F. Drucker, *The Practice of Management* (New York: Harper & Brothers, 1954). Reissued by HarperCollins in 1993.

37. E. Locke and G. Latham, *A Theory of Goal Setting and Task Performance* (Englewood Cliffs, NJ: Prentice Hall, 1990). See also John J. Donovan and David J. Radosevich, "The Moderating Role of Goal Commitment on the Goal Difficulty-Performance Relationship: A Meta-Analytic Review and Critical Reanalysis," *Journal of Applied Psychology* 83, no. 2 (April 1998): 308–15; Don Vande Walle, Steven P. Brown, William L. Cron, and John W. Slocum Jr., "The Influence of Goal Orientation and Self-Regulation Tactics on Sales Performance: A Longitudinal Field Test," *Journal of Applied Psychology* 84, no. 2 (April 1999): 249–59; Douglas Smith, *Make Success Measurable!: A Mindbook-Workbook for Setting Goals and Taking Action* (New York: John Wiley and Sons, 1999); Tony Moglia, *Partners in Performance: Successful Performance Management* (Menlo Park, CA: Crisp Publications, 1998).

38. Jack Steele, "Transforming the Balanced Scorecard into Your Strategy Execution System," *Manage* 53, no. 1 (September/October 2001): 22–23. See also Robert Kaplan and David Norton, "Strategic Learning and the Balanced Scorecard," *Strategy & Leadership* 24, no. 5 (September/October 1996): 18–24; Robert Kaplan and David Norton, "Using the Balanced Scorecard as a Strategic Management System," *Harvard Business Review* (January–February 1996): 75–85.

39. Deloris McGee Wanguri, "A Review, an Integration, and a Critique of Cross-Disciplinary Research on Performance Appraisals, Evaluations, and Feedback," *Journal of Business Communications* 32, no. 3 (July 1995): 267–93; Tziner, Joanis, and Murphy, "A Comparison of Three Methods of Performance Appraisal."

40. Norman R. F. Maier, *The Appraisal Interview* (New York: John Wiley and Sons, 1958); Norman R.F. Maier, *The Appraisal Interview—Three Basic Approaches* (San Diego: University Associates, 1976).

41. John F. Kikoski, "Effective Communication in the Performance Appraisal Interview: Face-to-Face Communication for Public Managers in the Culturally Diverse Workplace," *Public Personnel Management* 28, no. 2 (Summer 1999): 301–22; Howard J. Klein and Scott A. Snell, "The Impact of Interview Process and Context on Performance Appraisal Interview Effectiveness," *Journal of Managerial Issues* 6, no. 2 (Summer 1994): 160–75.

42. David E. Bowen, Stephen W. Gilliland, and Robert Folger; "HRM and Service Fairness: How Being Fair with Employees Spills Over to Customers," *Organizational Dynamics* 27, no. 3 (Winter 1999): 7–23; Audrey M. Korsgaard and Loriann Roberson, "Procedural Justice in Performance Evaluation: The Role of Instrumental and Non-Instrumental Voice in Performance Appraisal Discussions," *Journal of Management* 21, no. 4 (1995): 657–69; Susan M. Taylor, Kay B. Tracy, Monika K. Renard, J. Kline Harrison, and Stephen J. Carroll, "Due Process in Performance Appraisal: A Quasi-Experiment in Procedural Justice," *Administrative Science Quarterly* 40, no. 3 (September 1995): 495–523; Fran Rees, "Reaching High Levels of Performance through Team Self-Evaluation," *Journal for Quality and Participation* 22, no. 4 (July/August 1999): 37–39.

43. Martin Geller, "Participation in the Performance Appraisal Review: Inflexible Manager Behavior and Variable Worker Needs," *Human Relations* 51, no. 8 (August 1998): 1061–83; Cawley, Keeping, and Levy, "Participation in the Performance Appraisal Process"; Douthitt and Aiello, "The Role of Participation and Control in the Effects of Computer Monitoring on Fairness Perceptions, Task Satisfaction, and Performance."

44. Kwok Leung, Steven Su, and Michael Morris, "When Is Criticism Not Constructive? The Roles of Fairness Perceptions and Dispositional Attributions in Employee Acceptance of Critical Supervisory Feedback," *Human Relations* 54, no. 9 (September 2001): 1155–87; Donald Klein and Suzanne Crampton, "Helpful Hints for Sending Criticism," *Workforce* extra (March 1999): p. 9.

45. Scott A. Snell and Kenneth N. Wexley, "Performance Diagnosis: Identifying the Causes of Poor Performance," *Personnel Administrator* 30, no. 4 (April 1985): 117–27.

Managing Compensation

After studying this chapter, you should be able to

objective

Explain employer concerns in developing a strategic compensation program.

objective

Indicate the various factors that influence the setting of wages.

objective

Differentiate the mechanics of each of the major job evaluation systems.

objective

Explain the purpose of a wage survey.

objective

Define the wage curve, pay grades, and rate ranges as parts of the compensation structure.

objective

Identify the major provisions of the laws affecting compensation.

objective

Discuss the current issues of equal pay for work of equal value and pay compression.

A n extensive review of the literature indicates that important work-related variables leading to job satisfaction include challenging work, interesting job assignments, equitable rewards, competent supervision, and rewarding careers.[1] It is doubtful, however, whether many employees would continue working were it not for the money they earn. Employees desire compensation systems that they perceive as being fair and commensurate with their skills and expectations. Pay, therefore, is a major consideration in HRM because it provides employees with a tangible reward for their services, as well as a source of recognition and livelihood. Employee compensation includes all forms of pay and rewards received by employees for the performance of their jobs. *Direct compensation* encompasses employee wages and salaries, incentives, bonuses, and commissions. *Indirect compensation* comprises the many benefits supplied by employers, and *nonfinancial compensation* includes employee recognition programs, rewarding jobs, organizational support, work environment, and flexible work hours to accommodate personal needs.

Both managers and scholars agree that the way compensation is allocated among employees sends a message about what management believes is important and the types of activities it encourages. Furthermore, for an employer, the payroll constitutes a sizable operating cost. In manufacturing firms compensation is seldom as low as 20 percent of total expenditures, and in service enterprises it often exceeds 80 percent. A strategic compensation program, therefore, is essential so that pay can serve to motivate employee production sufficiently to keep labour costs at an acceptable level. This chapter will be concerned with the management of a compensation program, job evaluation systems, and pay structures for determining compensation payments. Included will be a discussion of federal regulations that affect wage and salary rates. Chapter 10 will review financial incentive plans for employees. Employee benefits that are part of the total compensation package are then discussed in Chapter 11.

STRATEGIC COMPENSATION PLANNING

objective

What is strategic compensation planning? Simply stated, it is the compensation of employees in ways that enhance motivation and growth while, at the same time, aligning their efforts with the objectives, philosophies, and culture of the organization. Strategic compensation planning goes beyond determining what market rates to pay employees—although market rates are one element of compensation planning—to purposefully linking compensation to the organization's mission and general business objectives.[2] Commenting on the importance of strategic compensation planning to organizational success, Gerald Ledford and Elizabeth Hawk, two compensation specialists, note, "Companies throughout the economy have begun to rethink their compensation systems in search for competitive advantage."[3]

Additionally, strategic compensation planning serves to mesh the monetary payments made to employees with specific functions of the HR program. For example, in the recruitment of new employees, the rate of pay for jobs can increase or limit the supply of applicants. A compensation specialist speaking to one of the authors noted, "The linkage of pay levels to labour markets is a strategic policy issue because it serves to attract or retain valued employees while affecting the organization's relative payroll budget."

Many fast-food restaurants, such as Burger King and Taco Bell—traditionally low-wage employers—have needed to raise their starting wages to attract a sufficient number of job applicants to meet staffing requirements. If rates of pay are high, creating a large applicant pool, then organizations may choose to raise their selection standards and hire better-qualified employees. This in turn can reduce employer training costs. When employees perform at exceptional levels, their performance appraisals may justify an increased pay rate. For these reasons and others, an organization should develop a formal HR program to manage employee compensation.[4]

We will discuss three important aspects of strategic compensation planning: linking compensation to organizational objectives, the pay-for-performance standard, and motivating employees through compensation.

Linking Compensation to Organizational Objectives

Compensation has been revolutionized by heightened domestic competition, globalization, increased employee skill requirements, and new technology. Therefore, an outcome of today's dynamic business environment is that managers have needed to change their pay philosophies from paying for a specific position or job title to rewarding employees on the basis of their individual competencies or group contributions to organizational success. A recent study showed that 81 percent of responding organizations listed *improving employee's focus on achieving business goals* as a significant objective influencing pay and reward changes (see Figure 9.1).

Increasingly, compensation specialists speak of value-added compensation.[5] A **value-added compensation** program, also called value-chain compensation, is one in which the components of the compensation package (benefits, base pay, incentives, and so on), both separately and in combination, create value for the organization and its employees. Using a value-added viewpoint, managers will ask questions such as "How does this compensation practice benefit the organization?" and "Does the benefit offset the administrative cost?" Payments that fail to advance either the employee or the organization are removed from the compensation program.

It is not uncommon for organizations to establish very specific goals for joining their organizational objectives to their compensation program.[6] Formalized compensation goals serve as guidelines for managers to ensure that wage and benefit policies achieve their intended purpose. The more common goals of a strategic compensation policy include the following:

1. To reward employees' past performance
2. To remain competitive in the labour market
3. To maintain salary equity among employees
4. To mesh employees' future performance with organizational goals
5. To control the compensation budget
6. To attract new employees[7]
7. To reduce unnecessary turnover[8]

Value-added compensation Evaluating the individual components of the compensation program to see if they advance the needs of employees and the goals of the organization

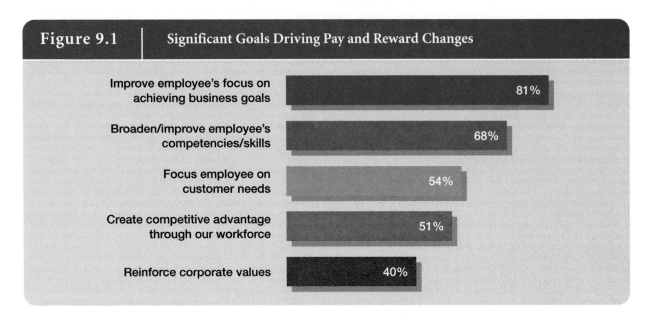

Figure 9.1 | **Significant Goals Driving Pay and Reward Changes**

Source: Towers Perrin and Duncan Brown, "Reward Strategies for Real: Moving from Intent to Impact," *WorldatWork Journal* 10, no. 3 (2001): 43. Used with permission.

To achieve these goals, policies must be established to guide management in making decisions. Formal statements of compensation policies typically include the following:

1. The rate of pay within the organization and whether it is to be above, below, or at the prevailing community rate
2. The ability of the pay program to gain employee acceptance while motivating employees to perform to the best of their abilities
3. The pay level at which employees may be recruited and the pay differential between new and more senior employees
4. The intervals at which pay raises are to be granted and the extent to which merit and/or seniority will influence the raises
5. The pay levels needed to facilitate the achievement of a sound financial position in relation to the products or services offered

The Pay-for-Performance Standard

Pay-for-performance standard
> Standard by which managers tie compensation to employee effort and performance

To raise productivity and lower labour costs in today's competitive economic environment, organizations are increasingly setting compensation objectives based on a **pay-for-performance standard**.[9] It is agreed that managers must tie at least some reward to employee effort and performance. Without this standard, motivation to perform with greater effort will be low, resulting in higher wage costs to the organization. Additionally, most employees believe that their compensation should be directly linked to their relative performance.

The term "pay for performance" refers to a wide range of compensation options, including merit-based pay, bonuses, salary commissions, job and pay banding, team/group incentives, and various gainsharing programs.[10] (Gainsharing plans are

USING THE INTERNET

A variety of wage and benefit information can be obtained at www.worldatwork.org.

discussed in Chapter 10.) Each of these compensation systems seeks to differentiate between the pay of average performers and outstanding performers. In 2000, when Pfizer acquired Warner-Lambert Company, creating the world's largest pharmaceutical company, it created a pay-for-performance compensation strategy that linked an employee's pay level to performance of the company, their division, and their team, and to personal contributions.[11] Interestingly, productivity studies show that employees will increase their output by 15 to 35 percent when an organization installs a pay-for-performance program.

Unfortunately, designing a sound pay-for-performance system is not easy. Considerations must be given to how employee performance will be measured. For example, measuring an employee's output on an assembly line may be relatively easy and objective but more difficult (and subjective) when the employee works in a service environment.[12] Other concerns include the monies to be allocated for compensation increases, which employees to cover, the payout method, and the periods when payments will be made. A critical issue concerns the size of the monetary increase and its perceived value to employees.[13] Richard Long of the University of Saskatchewan has written about the advantages and disadvantages of different pay systems in the text *Compensation in Canada: Strategy, Practices and Issues*.[14] While differences exist as to how large a wage or salary increase must be before it is perceived as meaningful, a pay-for-performance program will lack its full potential when pay increases only approximate rises in the cost of living.

Motivating Employees through Compensation

Pay constitutes a quantitative measure of an employee's relative worth. For most employees, pay has a direct bearing not only on their standard of living, but also on the status and recognition they may be able to achieve both on and off the job. Since pay represents a reward received in exchange for an employee's contributions, it is essential, according to the equity theory, that the pay be equitable in relation to those contributions. It is essential also that an employee's pay be equitable in relation to what other employees are receiving for their contributions.

Pay Equity

Simply defined, equity embraces the concept of fairness. Equity theory, also referred to as *distributive fairness*, is a motivation theory that explains how people respond to situations in which they feel they have received less (or more) than they deserve.[15] Central to the theory is the role of perception in motivation and the fact that individuals make comparisons. It states that individuals form a ratio of their inputs (abilities, skills, experiences) in a situation to their outcomes (salary, benefits) in that situation. They then compare the value of that ratio with the value of the input/output ratio for other individuals in a similar class of jobs either internal or external to the organization. If the value of their ratio equals the value of another's, they perceive the situation as equitable and no tension exists. However, if they perceive their input/output ratio as inequitable relative to others', this creates tension and motivates them to eliminate or reduce the inequity. The strength of their motivation is proportional to the magnitude of the perceived inequity. Figure 9.2 illustrates pay equity and feelings of being fairly paid.

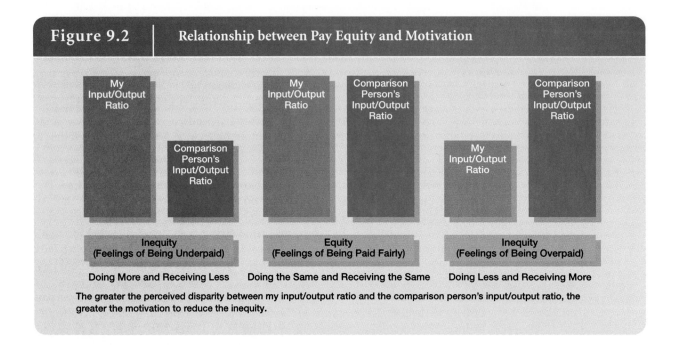

Figure 9.2 | Relationship between Pay Equity and Motivation

The greater the perceived disparity between my input/output ratio and the comparison person's input/output ratio, the greater the motivation to reduce the inequity.

Pay equity

An employee's perception that compensation received is equal to the value of the work performed

For employees, **pay equity** is achieved when the compensation received is equal to the value of the work performed. Research clearly demonstrates that employees' perceptions of pay equity, or inequity, can have dramatic effects on their motivation for both work behaviour and productivity.[16] Managers must therefore develop strategic pay practices that are both internally and externally equitable. Compensation policies are *internally* equitable when employees believe that the wage rates for their jobs approximate the job's worth to the organization. Perceptions of *external* pay equity exist when the organization is paying wages that are relatively equal to what other employers are paying for similar types of work.

Expectancy Theory and Pay

The expectancy theory of motivation predicts that one's level of motivation depends on the attractiveness of the rewards sought and the probability of obtaining those rewards.[17] The theory has developed from the work of psychologists who consider humans as thinking, reasoning people who have beliefs and anticipations concerning future life events. Expectancy theory therefore holds that employees should exert greater work effort if they have reason to expect that it will result in a reward that is valued.[18] To motivate this effort, the value of any monetary reward should be attractive. Employees also must believe that good performance is valued by their employer and will result in their receiving the expected reward.

Figure 9.3 shows the relationship between pay-for-performance and the expectancy theory of motivation. The model predicts, first, that high effort will lead to high performance (expectancy). For example, if an employee believes she has the skills and abilities to perform her job, and if she works hard (effort), then her performance will improve or be high. Second, high performance should result in rewards that are appreciated (valued). Elements of the compensation package are said to have

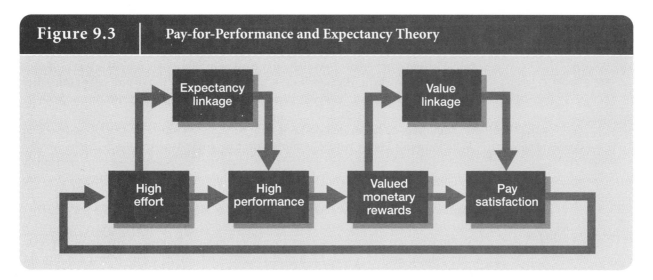

Figure 9.3 | **Pay-for-Performance and Expectancy Theory**

instrumentality when an employee's high performance leads to monetary rewards that are valued. Since we previously stated that pay-for-performance leads to a feeling of pay satisfaction, this feeling should reinforce one's high level of effort.

Thus, how employees view compensation can be an important factor in determining the motivational value of compensation. Furthermore, the effective communication of pay information together with an organizational environment that elicits employee trust in management can contribute to employees having more accurate perceptions of their pay. The perceptions employees develop concerning their pay are influenced by the accuracy of their knowledge and understanding of the compensation program's strategic objectives.

Pay Secrecy

Misperceptions by employees concerning the equity of their pay and its relationship to performance can be created by secrecy about the pay that others receive. There is reason to believe that secrecy can generate distrust in the compensation system, reduce employee motivation, and inhibit organizational effectiveness. Yet pay secrecy seems to be an accepted practice in many organizations in both the private and the public sector.

Managers may justify secrecy on the grounds that most employees prefer to have their own pay kept secret. Probably one of the reasons for pay secrecy that managers may be unwilling to admit is that it gives them greater freedom in compensation management, since pay decisions are not disclosed and there is no need to justify or defend them. Employees who are not supposed to know what others are being paid have no objective base for pursuing complaints about their own pay. Secrecy also serves to cover up inequities existing within the internal pay structure. Furthermore, secrecy surrounding compensation decisions may lead employees to believe that there is no direct relationship between pay and performance.

Managers wishing to maintain pay secrecy among employees may encounter problems with Internet salary survey data. Ready access to free online salary surveys gives employees an approximate idea of how their salary compares to others nationally or locally.[19] This information could put managers "on the spot" should employees discover that their salaries are lower than those of other employees at comparable organizations.

The Bases for Compensation

Hourly work
Work paid on an hourly basis

Piecework
Work paid according to the number of units produced

Work performed in most private, public, and not-for-profit organizations has traditionally been compensated on an hourly basis. It is referred to as **hourly work**, in contrast to **piecework**, in which employees are paid according to the number of units they produce. Hourly work, however, is far more prevalent than piecework as a basis for compensating employees.

Employees compensated on an hourly basis are classified as *hourly employees,* or wage earners. Those whose compensation is computed on the basis of weekly, biweekly, or monthly pay periods are classified as *salaried employees.* Hourly employees are normally paid only for the time they work. Salaried employees, by contrast, are generally paid the same for each pay period, even though they occasionally may work more hours or fewer than the regular number of hours in a period. They also usually receive certain benefits not provided to hourly employees.

Employment practices are a provincial jurisdiction, and each province has its own employment standards act. Each of these acts contains a provision that requires the employer to reimburse the employee at a specified rate after he or she has worked the minimum required hours. This rate is usually 1.5 times the employee's base hourly rate of pay. A number of employers offer overtime pay that is more generous than what the act specifies. Some acts provide for time in lieu of overtime; thus, four hours of overtime paid at 1.5 would be the equivalent of six hours in either pay or time off in lieu of payment. Supervisory and management personnel are not usually paid overtime; still other personnel work overtime for free (see Ethics in HRM). Each of the employment standards acts includes a list of people who are exempt from the overtime provision.

Because so many American companies are operating in Canada, the terms *exempt* (to describe employees not covered in the overtime provisions of the U.S. Fair Labor Standards Act) and *nonexempt* (to described employees covered by the overtime provisions of the U.S. Fair Labor Standards Act) are often heard, although neither has any relevance in Canadian legislation. These terms are used specifically to denote *supervisory* and *nonsupervisory* roles. U.S. legislation stipulates that only nonexempt (i.e., nonsupervisory) workers are entitled to overtime pay.

DETERMINING COMPENSATION—THE WAGE MIX

objective

Employees may inquire of their managers, "How are the wages for my job determined?" In practice, a combination of *internal* and *external* factors can influence, directly or indirectly, the rates at which employees are paid. Through their interaction these factors constitute the wage mix, as shown in Figure 9.4. For example, the area wage rate for administrative assistants might be $9.75 per hour. However, one employer may elect to pay its administrative assistants $11.50 per hour because of their excellent performance. Pay systems always take into consideration the context of internal factors, including organizational strategies and external factors such as the labour market.[20] The influence of government legislation on the wage mix will be discussed later in the chapter.

Ethics in HRM

Working for Free

Two restaurants in Ontario, one in Port Hope and the other in Belleville, were benefiting from the services of more than twenty people (called volunteers or agents) who were not being paid wages but made their money on the tips customers left for them. The province's Employment Standards Act stipulated that waiters must be paid $5.95 an hour (less than the minimum wage, due to tips), and that every employer must pay a minimum wage. The restaurants argued that they provided a location where workers could act as service agents and undertake their business, relying on tips for income. Were the waiters working for free?

Elaine Chu worked at a local fast-food restaurant to earn enough money to support herself while she attended university part-time. Her job title was night manager, and she worked the 4 p.m. to 11 p.m. shift. During this shift she was the only employee on duty, and she did much of the food preparation, serving, and cleanup. Most nights, customers arrived after the movies (around 11 p.m.), and Chu was expected to work into the next shift until the crowd dispersed. She received no overtime pay for these extra hours because employers were not required to pay overtime for managers. Did Chu's employer misuse the title "manager" in order to circumvent its obligations with respect to overtime pay? To be deemed a true manager, an individual should have staff reporting to him or her, should have responsibility for a major aspect of the business, and should provide counselling to more junior staff through performance appraisal. Was Chu working for free?

According to a Statistics Canada survey, one-fifth of all employees put in extra hours at work, and 60 percent of these are unpaid, with workers averaging nine unpaid hours per week. White-collar employees are working for free, and they know why: they are afraid of losing their jobs.

Sources: Bruce Little, "Canadians Work Overtime for Free," *The Globe and Mail*, July 14, 1997: B6; Susan Bourette, "Volunteer Waiters Work Only for Tips," *The Globe and Mail*, July 27, 1997: A7.

Internal Factors

The internal factors that influence wage rates are the employer's compensation strategy, the worth of a job, an employee's relative worth in meeting job requirements, and an employer's ability to pay.

Employer's Compensation Strategy

Highlights in HRM 9.1 illustrates the compensation strategies of two organizations, Tri Star Performance and Preventive Health Care. The pay strategy of Preventive Health Care is to be an industry pay leader, while Tri Star Performance seeks to be wage-competitive. Both employers strive to promote a compensation policy that is internally fair.

Figure 9.4 | Factors Affecting the Wage Mix

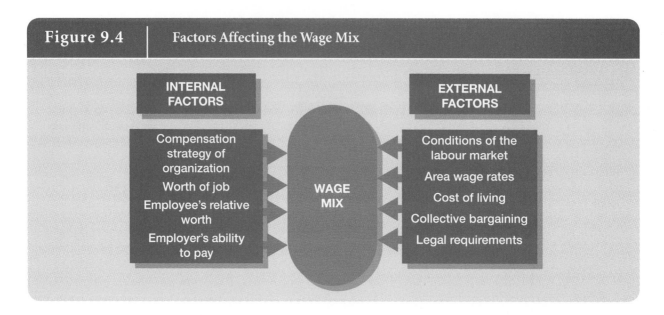

Tri Star Performance and Preventive Health Care, like other employers, will establish numerous compensation objectives that affect the pay employees receive. As a minimum, both large and small employers should set pay policies reflecting (1) the internal wage relationship among jobs and skill levels, (2) the external competition or an employer's pay position relative to what competitors are paying, (3) a policy of rewarding employee performance, and (4) administrative decisions concerning elements of the pay system such as overtime premiums, payment periods, and short-term or long-term incentives.[21]

Worth of a Job

Organizations without a formal compensation program generally base the worth of jobs on the subjective opinions of people familiar with the jobs. In such instances, pay rates may be influenced heavily by the labour market or, in the case of unionized employers, by collective bargaining. Organizations with formal compensation programs, however, are more likely to rely on a system of *job evaluation* to aid in rate determination. Even when rates are subject to collective bargaining, job evaluation can assist the organization in maintaining some degree of control over its wage structure.

The use of job evaluation is widespread in both the public and the private sectors. The City of Mississauga and Star Data Systems use job evaluation in establishing wage structures. The jobs covered most frequently by job evaluation are clerical, technical, and various blue-collar groups, whereas those jobs covered least frequently are managerial and top-executive positions.

Employee's Relative Worth

In both hourly and salary jobs, employee performance can be recognized and rewarded through promotion and with various incentive systems. (The incentive systems used most often will be discussed in the next chapter.) Superior performance can also be rewarded by granting merit raises on the basis of steps within a rate range established for a job class. If merit raises are to have their intended value, however,

Highlights in HRM 9.1

COMPARISON OF COMPENSATION STRATEGIES

Compensation strategies and objectives can differ widely across large and small employers as well as across employers in the private and public sectors. Here are the compensation strategies at Tri Star Performance and Preventive Health Care.

Tri Star Performance

▶ Promote pay-for-performance practices
▶ Pay market-competitive compensation
▶ Achieve internal and external pay equity
▶ Achieve simplicity in compensation programs
▶ Strive for employee commitment and a collaborative work environment
▶ Promote gender fairness in pay and benefits
▶ Comply with all governmental compensation regulations
▶ Minimize increased fixed costs

Preventive Health Care

▶ Be a pay leader in the health care industry
▶ Promote open and understandable pay practices
▶ Ensure fair employee treatment
▶ Offer benefits promoting individual employee needs
▶ Offer compensation rewarding employee creativity and achievements
▶ Offer compensation to foster the strategic mission of the organization
▶ Obtain employee input when developing compensation practices
▶ Emphasize performance through variable pay and stock options

they must be determined by an effective performance appraisal system that differentiates between employees who deserve the raises and those who do not. This system, moreover, must provide a visible and credible relationship between performance and any raises received. Unfortunately, too many so-called merit systems provide for raises to be granted automatically. As a result, employees tend to be rewarded more for merely being present than for being productive on the job.

Employer's Ability to Pay

Pay levels are limited by earned profits and other financial resources available to employers. Thus an organization's ability to pay is determined in part by the productivity of its employees. This productivity is a result not only of their performance, but also of the amount of capital the organization has invested in labour-saving equipment. Generally, increases in capital investment reduce the number of employees required to perform the work and increase an employer's ability to provide higher pay for those it employs.

How would you rate the worth of a rescue worker's job?

PHOTODISC

Economic conditions and competition faced by employers can also significantly affect the rates they are able to pay. Competition and recessions can force prices down and reduce the income from which compensation payments are derived. In such situations, employers have little choice but to reduce wages and/or lay off employees, or, even worse, to go out of business.

External Factors

The major external factors that influence wage rates include labour market conditions, area wage rates, cost of living, collective bargaining if the employer is unionized, and legal requirements. The legal requirements of compensation will be discussed later in the chapter.

Labour Market Conditions

The labour market reflects the forces of supply and demand for qualified labour within an area. These forces help influence the wage rates required to recruit or retain competent employees. It must be recognized, however, that counterforces can reduce the full impact of supply and demand on the labour market. The economic power of unions, for example, may prevent employers from lowering wage rates even when unemployment is high among union members. Government regulations also may prevent an employer from paying at a market rate less than an established minimum. In regions where unemployment is high, workers may be willing to accept lower wages in exchange for the assurance of stable employment. For example, letter carriers in Saint John, New Brunswick, accepted a contract with a modest 1 percent pay increase because it included a no-layoff clause and a guarantee that employees would not be relocated outside a forty-kilometre radius.

Area Wage Rates

A formal wage structure should provide rates that are in line with those being paid by other employers for comparable jobs within the area. Data pertaining to area wage rates may be obtained from local wage surveys. Wage survey data can also be obtained from compensation consulting firms such as Mercer Management Consulting and for free from some companies such as Monster.ca. Smaller employers use government or local board of trade surveys to establish rates of pay for new and senior employees. Many organizations conduct their own surveys. Others engage in a cooperative exchange of wage information or rely for these data on various professional associations such as the Professional Engineers Association. The Conference Board of Canada also conducts an annual compensation survey.

Wage surveys (discussed fully later in the chapter) serve the important function of providing external wage equity between the surveying organization and other organizations competing for labour in the surrounding labour market. Importantly, data from area wage surveys can be used to prevent the rates for jobs from drifting too far above or below those of other employers in the region. When rates rise above existing area levels, an employer's labour costs may become excessive. Conversely, if they drop too far below area levels, it may be difficult to recruit and retain competent personnel. Wage-survey data must also take into account indirect wages paid in the form of benefits.

USING THE INTERNET

Monster.ca offers a free tool for calculating salaries by occupation and by region at

http://salary.monster.ca.

Cost of Living

Because of inflation, compensation rates have had to be adjusted upward periodically to help employees maintain their purchasing power. Employers make these changes with the help of the **consumer price index (CPI)**. The CPI is a measure of the average change in prices over time in a fixed "market basket" of goods and services.[22] The consumer price index is based on prices of food, clothing, shelter, and fuels; transportation fares; charges for health and personal care ; and prices of other goods and services that people buy for day-to-day living. Statistics Canada collects price information on a monthly basis and calculates the CPI for Canada as a whole and for various Canadian cities. Separate indexes are published by size of city and by region of the country. Employers in a number of communities monitor changes in the CPI as a basis for compensation decisions.

Changes in the CPI can have important effects on pay rates. Granting wage increases solely on the basis of the CPI helps compress pay rates within a pay structure, thereby creating inequities among those who receive the wage increase. Inequities also result from the fact that adjustments are made on a cents-per-hour rather than a percentage basis. For example, a cost-of-living adjustment of 50 cents represents a 7.1 percent increase for an employee earning $7 per hour, but only a 4.2 percent increase for one earning $12 per hour. Unless adjustments are made periodically in employee base rates, the desired differential between higher- and lower-paying jobs will gradually be reduced. The incentive to accept more-demanding jobs will also be reduced.

Employees who work under a union contract may receive wage increases through **escalator clauses** found in their collective agreements. These clauses provide for quarterly cost-of-living adjustments (COLA) in wages based on changes in the CPI. The most common adjustments are 1 cent per hour for each 0.3- or 0.4-point change in the CPI. COLAs are favoured by unions during particularly high periods of inflation.

Consumer price index (CPI)

Measure of the average change in prices over time in a fixed "market basket" of goods and services

Escalator clauses

Clauses in collective agreements that provide for quarterly cost-of-living adjustments in wages, basing the adjustments on changes in the consumer price index

Compensation can be adjusted to account for changes in the cost of living.

PHOTODISC

Collective Bargaining

One of the primary functions of a labour union, as emphasized in Chapter 14, is to bargain collectively over conditions of employment, the most important of which is compensation.[23] The union's goal in each new agreement is to achieve increases in **real wages**—wage increases larger than the increase in the CPI—thereby improving the purchasing power and standard of living of its members. This goal includes gaining wage settlements that equal or exceed the pattern established by other unions within the area.

The agreements negotiated tend to establish rate patterns within the labour market. As a result, wages are generally higher in areas where organized labour is strong. To recruit and retain competent personnel and avoid unionization, nonunion employers must either meet or exceed these rates. The "union scale" also becomes the prevailing rate that all employers must pay for work performed under government contract. The impact of collective bargaining therefore extends beyond that segment of the labour force that is unionized.

Real wages
Wage increases larger than rises in the consumer price index; that is, the real earning power of wages

JOB EVALUATION SYSTEMS

objective

As we discussed earlier, one important component of the wage mix is the worth of the job. Organizations formally determine the value of jobs through the process of job evaluation. **Job evaluation** is the systematic process of determining the *relative* worth of jobs in order to establish which jobs should be paid more than others within the organization. Job evaluation helps establish internal equity between various jobs. The relative worth of a job may be determined by comparing it with others within the organization or by comparing it with a scale that has been constructed for this purpose. Each method of comparison, furthermore, may be made on the basis of the jobs as a whole or on the basis of the parts that constitute the jobs.

NEL

Job evaluation
Systematic process of determining the relative worth of jobs in order to establish which jobs should be paid more than others within an organization

Four methods of comparison are shown in Figure 9.5. They provide the basis for the principal systems of job evaluation. We will begin by discussing the simpler, nonquantitative approaches and conclude by reviewing the more popular, quantitative systems. Regardless of the methodology used, it is important to remember that all job evaluation methods require varying degrees of managerial judgment.

Job Ranking System

Job ranking system
Simplest and oldest system of job evaluation by which jobs are arrayed on the basis of their relative worth

The simplest and oldest system of job evaluation is the **job ranking system,** which arrays jobs on the basis of their relative worth. One technique used to rank jobs consists of having the raters arrange cards listing the duties and responsibilities of each job in order of the importance of the jobs. Job ranking can be done by a single individual knowledgeable about all jobs or by a committee composed of management and employee representatives.

Another common approach to job ranking is the paired-comparison method. Raters compare each job with all other jobs by means of a paired-comparison ranking table that lists the jobs in both rows and columns, as shown in Figure 9.6. To use the table, raters compare a job from a row with the jobs from each of the columns. If the row job is ranked higher than a column job, an X is placed in the appropriate cell. After all the jobs have been compared, raters total the Xs for row jobs. The total number of Xs for a row job will establish its worth relative to other jobs. Differences in rankings should then be reconciled into a single rating for all jobs. After jobs are evaluated, wage rates can be assigned to them through use of the salary survey discussed later in the chapter.

The basic disadvantage of the job ranking system is that it does not provide a very precise measure of each job's worth. Another weakness is that the final ranking of jobs indicates the relative importance of the job, not the differences in the degree of importance that may exist between jobs. A final limitation of the job ranking method is that it can only be used with a small number of jobs, probably no more than fifteen. Its simplicity, however, makes it ideal for use by smaller employers.

Job Classification System

Job classification system
System of job evaluation in which jobs are classified and grouped according to a series of predetermined wage grades

In the **job classification system**, jobs are classified and grouped according to a series of predetermined grades. Successive grades require increasing amounts of job responsibility, skill, knowledge, ability, or other factors selected to compare jobs.

Figure 9.5	Different Job Evaluation Systems	
	SCOPE OF COMPARISON	
Basis for Comparison	**Job as a Whole (Nonquantitative)**	**Job Parts or Factors (Quantitative)**
Job vs. job	Job ranking system	Factor comparison system
Job vs. scale	Job classification system	Point system

Figure 9.6	Paired-Comparison Job Ranking Table

Row Jobs \ Column Jobs	Senior Administrative Secretary	Data-Entry Operator	Data-Processing Director	File Clerk	Systems Analyst	Programmer	Total
Senior Administrative Secretary	—	X		X		X	3
Data-Entry Operator		—		X			1
Data-Processing Director	X	X	—	X	X	X	5
File Clerk				—			0
Systems Analyst	X	X		X	—	X	4
Programmer		X		X		—	2

Directions: Place an X in the cell where the value of a row job is higher than that of a column job.

For example, Grade GS-1 from the federal government grade descriptions reads as follows:

GS-1 includes those classes of positions the duties of which are to perform, under immediate supervision, with little or no latitude for the exercise of independent judgment (A) the simplest routine work in office, business, or fiscal operations; or (B) elementary work of a subordinate technical character in a professional, scientific, or technical field.

The descriptions of each of the job classes constitute the scale against which the specifications for the various jobs are compared. Managers then evaluate jobs by comparing job descriptions with the different wage grades in order to "slot" the job into the appropriate grade. While this system has the advantage of simplicity, it is less precise than the point and factor comparison systems (discussed in the next sections) because the job is evaluated as a whole.

Point System

Point system
Quantitative job evaluation procedure that determines the relative value of a job by the total points assigned to it

The **point system** is a quantitative job evaluation procedure that determines a job's relative value by calculating the total points assigned to it. It has been successfully used by high-visibility organizations such as Boeing, Honeywell, and many other public and private organizations, both large and small. Although point systems are rather complicated to establish, once in place they are relatively simple to understand and use. The principal advantage of the point system is that it provides a more refined basis for making judgments than either the ranking or classification systems and thereby can produce results that are more valid and less easy to manipulate.

The point system permits jobs to be evaluated quantitatively on the basis of factors or elements—commonly called *compensable factors*—that constitute the job. The skills, efforts, responsibilities, and working conditions that a job usually entails are the more common major compensable factors that serve to rank one job as more or less important than another. The number of compensable factors an organization uses depends on the nature of the organization and the jobs to be evaluated. Once selected, compensable factors will be assigned weights according to their relative importance to the organization. For example, if responsibility is considered extremely important to the organization, it could be assigned a weight of 40 percent. Next, each factor will be divided into a number of degrees. Degrees represent different levels of difficulty associated with each factor.

The point system requires the use of a *point manual*. The point manual is, in effect, a handbook that contains a description of the compensable factors and the degrees to which these factors may exist within the jobs. A manual also will indicate—usually by means of a table (see Highlights in HRM 9.2)—the number of points allocated to each factor and to each of the degrees into which these factors are divided. The point value assigned to a job represents the sum of the numerical degree values of each compensable factor that the job possesses.

Developing a Point Manual

A variety of point manuals have been developed by organizations, trade associations, and management consultants. An organization that seeks to use one of these existing manuals should make certain that the manual is suited to its particular jobs and conditions of operation. If necessary, the organization should modify the manual or develop its own to suit its needs.

The job factors illustrated in Highlights in HRM 9.2 represent those covered by the American Association of Industrial Management point manual. Each of the factors listed in this manual has been divided into five degrees. The number of degrees into which the factors in a manual are to be divided, however, can be greater or smaller than this number, depending on the relative weight assigned to each factor and the ease with which the individual degrees can be defined or distinguished.

After the job factors in the point manual have been divided into degrees, a statement must be prepared defining each of these degrees, as well as each factor as a whole. The definitions should be concise and yet distinguish the factors and each of their degrees. Highlights in HRM 9.3 represents another portion of the point manual used by the American Association of Industrial Management to describe each of the degrees for the education factor. These descriptions enable those conducting a job evaluation to determine the degree to which the factors exist in each job being evaluated.

The final step in developing a point manual is to determine the number of points to be assigned to each factor and to each degree within these factors. Although the total number of points is arbitrary, 500 points is often the maximum.

Highlights in HRM 9.2

POINT VALUES FOR JOB FACTORS OF THE AMERICAN ASSOCIATION OF INDUSTRIAL MANAGEMENT

FACTORS	1ST DEGREE	2ND DEGREE	3RD DEGREE	4TH DEGREE	5TH DEGREE
Skill					
1. Education	14	28	42	56	70
2. Experience	22	44	66	88	110
3. Initiative and ingenuity	14	28	42	56	70
Effort					
4. Physical demand	10	20	30	40	50
5. Mental or visual demand	5	10	15	20	25
Responsibility					
6. Equipment or process	5	10	15	20	25
7. Material or product	5	10	15	20	25
8. Safety of others	5	10	15	20	25
9. Work of others	5	10	15	20	25
Job Conditions					
10. Working conditions	10	20	30	40	50
11. Hazards	5	10	15	20	25

Source: Reproduced with permission of the American Association of Industrial Management, Springfield, Mass.

Using the Point Manual

Job evaluation under the point system is accomplished by comparing the job descriptions and job specifications, factor by factor, against the various factor-degree descriptions contained in the manual. Each factor within the job being evaluated is then assigned the number of points specified in the manual. When the points for each factor have been determined from the manual, the total point value for the job as a whole can be calculated. The relative worth of the job is then determined from the total points that have been assigned to that job.

Factor comparison system
Job evaluation system that permits the evaluation process to be accomplished on a factor-by-factor basis by developing a factor comparison scale

Factor Comparison System

The **factor comparison system,** like the point system, permits the job evaluation process to be accomplished on a factor-by-factor basis. It differs from the point system, however, in that the compensable factors of the jobs to be evaluated are compared against the compensable factors of *key jobs* within the organization that serve as

Highlights in HRM 9.3

DESCRIPTION OF EDUCATION FACTOR AND DEGREES OF THE AMERICAN ASSOCIATION OF INDUSTRIAL MANAGEMENT

1. EDUCATION
This factor measures the basic trades training, knowledge or "scholastic contact" essential as background or training preliminary to learning the job duties. This job knowledge or background may have been acquired either by formal education or by training on jobs of lesser degree or by any combination of these approaches.

1st Degree   14 points
Requires the use of simple writing, adding, subtracting, whole numbers and the carrying out of instructions; and the use of fixed gauges and direct reading instruments and devices in which interpretation is not required.

2nd Degree   28 points
Requires the use of commercial English, grammar and arithmetic such as addition, subtraction, multiplication and division, including decimals and fractions; simple use of formulas, charts, tables, drawings, specifications, schedules, wiring diagrams, together with the use of adjustable measuring instruments, graduates and the like requiring interpretation in their various applications; or the posting, preparation, interpretation, use and checking of reports, forms, records and comparable data.

3rd Degree   42 points
Requires the use of shop mathematics together with the use of complicated drawings, specifications, charts, tables, various types of adjustable measuring instruments and the training generally applicable in a particular or specialized occupation. Equivalent to 1 to 3 years applied trades training.

4th Degree   56 points
Requires the use of advanced shop mathematics, together with the use of complicated drawings, specifications, charts, tables, handbook formulas, all varieties of adjustable measuring instruments and the uses of broad training in a recognized trade or craft. Equivalent to complete, accredited, indentured apprenticeship or equivalent to high school plus a 2-year technical college education.

5th Degree   70 points
Requires the use of higher mathematics involved in the application of engineering principles and the performance of related, practical operations, together with a comprehensive knowledge of the theories and practices of mechanical, electrical, chemical, civil or like engineering field. Equivalent to complete 4 years of technical college or university education.

Source: Reproduced with permission of the American Association of Industrial Management, Springfield, Mass.

the job evaluation scale. Key jobs can be defined as those jobs that are important for wage-setting purposes and are widely known in the labour market. Key jobs have the following characteristics:

1. They are important to employees and the organization.
2. They vary in their job requirements.
3. They have relatively stable job content.

They are used in salary surveys for wage determination.

Key jobs are evaluated against five compensable factors—skill, mental effort, physical effort, responsibility, and working conditions—resulting in a ranking of the different factors for each key job. Normally a committee is selected to rank the criteria across key jobs. Committee members must also assign monetary rates of pay to each compensable factor for each key job. When this task is completed, a factor comparison scale is developed for use in evaluating all other jobs. Highlights in HRM 9.4 describes how one company used this system to achieve its compensation objectives.

Highlights in HRM 9.4

PROVEN METHODS IN JOB EVALUATION

Star Data Systems of Markham, Ontario, is a company that produces software programs and currently employs around 500 people. To facilitate Star Data's growth, the director of human resources implemented a job evaluation program as a means of "paying people fairly and equitably, complying with pay equity legislation, and being able to attract high-calibre candidates."

Following proven models, all employees were required to complete job questionnaires. The process involved having the employees answer questions that related to the compensable factors chosen for the job evaluation process. Of the ninety-two descriptions prepared, forty-seven were deemed benchmark positions and forty-five were deemed nonbenchmark positions. Examples of benchmark positions at Star Data included marketing coordinator, network support technicians, assistant controller, and shipper/receiver. Among the nonbenchmark positions were exchange reporter, product specialist, and technical sales analyst.

To ensure fairness and equity in the evaluation process, Star Data formed a job evaluation committee made up of employees from various levels in the organization. An outside consultant was hired to train committee members to evaluate positions in an unbiased manner. Job evaluation was used to determine the relative value placed on all positions in the organization. A point-factor method was applied. The focus of the evaluations was the requirements of the job. Each job was measured against four compensable factors: skill, which included the subfactors of knowledge and experience; working conditions, which involved consideration of work environment factors; responsibility, which focused on interpersonal skills, communications, judgment, problem solving, scope of responsibility, and impact of results; and effort. All these compensable factors, along with their subfactors, were tailor-made to fit Star Data's business needs.

Weightings were determined for each of the compensable factors in the evaluation process based on the value of the particular factor to the organization, the value placed on the factors by other companies in the industry, the requirements of pay equity legislation, and input from the consulting group. Since working conditions and effort were not deemed to be deterrents for completing the work, only a 5 percent weight was assigned to that factor; in contrast, skill received a 40 percent weighting.

Having completed its evaluation of the positions, the committee assigned a point total to each position, which allowed a hierarchy to be developed. Based on the point totals, the positions were divided into groups to form twelve salary grades. Using the benchmark positions found in each salary grade, salary and pay information was collected from competitors and other organizations to arrive, via salary surveys, at an average market salary as the midpoint. This methodology ensured that the plan was competitive with the external marketplace.

Star Data, with a new salary grade format, was in a position to analyze internal salaries against the new ranges and to review any pay equity issues. All employees in the organization knew their own salary ranges, their position within the range, and whether salary adjustments would be necessary.

In the future, Star Data will ensure that the system is maintained in a bias-free manner, that the salary administration program remains competitive with the external marketplace, and that salaries are administered fairly and consistently. The company plans to remain competitive by participating in annual surveys and by making necessary salary and range adjustments as conditions warrant. The ultimate responsibility rests with the managers to provide constructive and timely performance reviews and salary increases that are tied directly to performance.

Job Evaluation for Management Positions

Because management positions are more difficult to evaluate and involve certain demands not found in jobs at the lower levels, some organizations do not attempt to include them in their job evaluation programs. Employers that do evaluate these positions, however, may extend their regular system of evaluation to include such positions, or they may develop a separate evaluation system for management positions.

Several systems have been developed especially for the evaluation of executive, managerial, and professional positions. One of the better-known is the **Hay profile method,** developed by Edward N. Hay. The three broad factors that constitute the evaluation in the "profile" include knowledge (or know-how), mental activity (or problem solving), and accountability.[24] The Hay method uses only three factors because it is assumed that these factors represent the most important aspects of all executive and managerial positions. The profile for each position is developed by determining the percentage value to be assigned to each of the three factors. Jobs are then ranked on the basis of each factor, and point values that make up the profile are assigned to each job on the basis of the percentage-value level at which the job is ranked.

Hay profile method
Job evaluation technique using three factors—knowledge, mental activity, and accountability—to evaluate executive and managerial positions

The Compensation Structure

Job evaluation systems provide for internal equity and serve as the basis for wage-rate determination. They do not in themselves determine the wage rate. The evaluated worth of each job in relation to its rank, class, points, or monetary worth must be converted into an hourly, daily, weekly, or monthly wage rate. The compensation tool used to help set wages is the wage and salary survey.

Wage and Salary Surveys

objective 4

Wage and salary survey
Survey of the wages paid to employees of other employers in the surveying organization's relevant labour market

The **wage and salary survey** is a survey of the wages paid by employers in an organization's relevant labour market—local, regional, or national, depending on the job. The labour market is frequently defined as that area from which employers obtain certain types of workers. The labour market for office personnel would be local, whereas the labour market for engineers would be national. It is the wage and salary survey that permits an organization to maintain external equity, that is, to pay its employees wages equivalent to the wages similar employees earn in other establishments.

When job evaluation and wage-survey data are used jointly, they serve to link the likelihood of both internal and external equity. Although surveys are primarily conducted to gather competitive wage data, they can also collect information on employee benefits or organizational pay practices (such as overtime rates or shift differentials).

Collecting Survey Data

While many organizations conduct their own wage and salary surveys, a variety of "preconducted" pay surveys are available to satisfy the requirements of most public and not-for-profit or private employers. Companies such as Watson Wyatt (www.watsonwyatt.com), Hewitt Associates (www.hewittassoc.com), Mercer Human Resource Consulting (www.mercerHR.com) and Hay Management Consultants (www.haygroup.com) conduct annual compensation surveys. Of course, these general surveys are not particularly useful when employers are looking for salary information about highly specialized jobs such as chemical process-control engineers.[25] Highlights in HRM 9.5 describes the results of compensation surveys for those working in human resources management.

USING THE INTERNET

Statistics Canada offers a variety of useful links to various databases that contain information on pay:

www.statcan.ca

Many provinces and cities conduct surveys and make them available to employers. Besides these government surveys, boards of trade and professional associations conduct special surveys tailored to their members' needs. Employers with global operations can purchase international surveys through large consulting firms. While all of these third-party surveys provide certain benefits to their users, they also have various limitations. Two problems with all published surveys are that (1) they are not always compatible with the user's jobs and (2) the user cannot specify what specific data to collect. To overcome these problems, organizations may collect their own compensation data.

HRIS and Salary Surveys

Wage and benefits survey data can be found on numerous websites, including the previously mentioned Monster.ca. The rule of thumb is that only 10 percent to 15 percent

Highlights in HRM 9.5

COMPENSATION SURVEYS FOR HR PROFESSIONALS

According to the 2002/2003 Watson Wyatt survey, the average weighted salaries (base level plus bonus) for human resources positions are the following: human resources assistant, $37 000; human resources generalist, $53 200; human resources specialist, $66 300; human resources manager, $76 400; and human resources executive, $145 500. The Toronto Board of Trade also conducted a survey and rates were slightly higher, primarily because of the Toronto location: human resources assistant can expect to earn $41 000; human resources specialist/generalist, $53 000; human resources manager, $80 000; and human resources executive, $146 000. The HRDC website (www.jobfutures.ca) lists the hourly earnings for HR managers as $28.89 compared to $16.91 for an average of all other occupations.

A study done by the Human Resources Professionals Association of Ontario showed the value of professional certification. Those people working in HR who had achieved the CHRP (Certified Human Resources Professional) earned on average $67 000, compared to the average annual earnings of $50 000 for those without a CHRP. Clearly, the CHRP has an economic value in employers' minds.

Sources: D. Brown, "More Respect, Better Pay for HR: Toronto Study," *Canadian HR Reporter* 15, no. 20 (November 18, 2002): 2; M. Belcourt and A. Templer, "The CHRP Edge," *HR Professional,* April/May 2002: 30; M. Belcourt and A. Templer, "The CHRP Edge: Part 2," *HR Professional*, December 2002/January 2003: 36.

of jobs should be surveyed, and that is sufficient to provide estimates and ranges for all jobs in an organization. Managers and compensation specialists can search for applicable surveys for either purchase or participation.[26]

Employer-Initiated Surveys

Employers wishing to conduct their own wage and salary survey must first select the jobs to be used in the survey and identify the organizations with which they actually compete for employees.[27] Since it is not feasible to survey all the jobs in an organization, normally only key jobs, also called benchmark jobs, are used. The survey of key jobs will usually be sent to ten or fifteen organizations that represent a valid sample of other employers likely to compete for the employees of the surveying organization. A diversity of organizations should be selected—large and small, public and private, new and established, and union and nonunion—since each classification of employer is likely to pay different wage rates for surveyed jobs.

After the key jobs and the employers to be surveyed have been identified, the surveying organization must decide what information to gather on wages, benefit types, and pay policies. For example, when requesting pay data, it is important to specify whether hourly, daily, or weekly pay figures are needed. In addition, those conducting surveys must state if the wage data are needed for new hires or for senior employees.

Precisely defining the compensation data needed will greatly increase the accuracy of the information received and the number of purposes for which it can be used. Once the survey data are tabulated, the compensation structure can be completed.

The Wage Curve

objective

Wage curve
Curve in a scattergram representing the relationship between relative worth of jobs and wage rates

The relationship between the relative worth of jobs and their wage rates can be represented by means of a **wage curve**. This curve may indicate the rates currently paid for jobs within an organization, the new rates resulting from job evaluation, or the rates for similar jobs currently being paid by other organizations within the labour market. A curve may be constructed graphically by preparing a scattergram consisting of a series of dots that represent the current wage rates. As shown in Figure 9.7, a freehand curve is then drawn through the cluster of dots in such a manner as to leave approximately an equal number of dots above and below the curve. The wage curve can be relatively straight or curved. This curve can then be used to determine the relationship between the value of a job and its wage rate at any given point on the line.

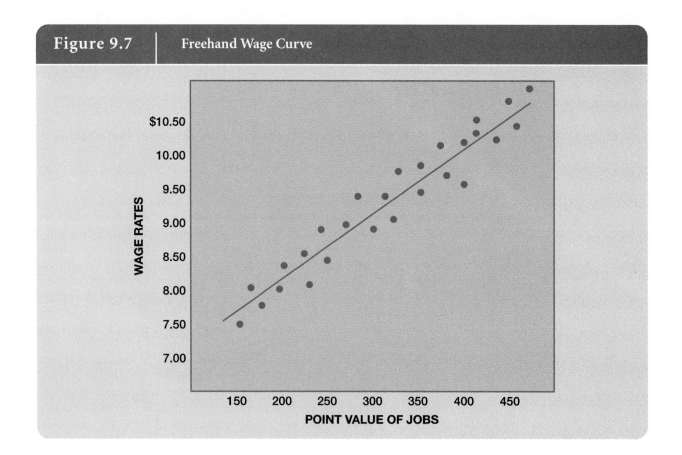

| Figure 9.7 | Freehand Wage Curve |

Pay Grades

Pay grades
Groups of jobs within a particular class that are paid the same rate

From an administrative standpoint, it is generally preferable to group jobs into **pay grades** and to pay all jobs within a particular grade the same rate or rate range. When the classification system of job evaluation is used, jobs are grouped into grades as part of the evaluation process. When the point and factor comparison systems are used, however, pay grades must be established at selected intervals that represent either the point or the evaluated monetary value of these jobs. The graph in Figure 9.8 illustrates a series of pay grades designated along the horizontal axis at fifty-point intervals.

The grades within a wage structure may vary in number. The number is determined by such factors as the slope of the wage curve, the number and distribution of the jobs within the structure, and the organization's wage administration and promotion policies. The number utilized should be sufficient to permit difficulty levels to be distinguished, but not so great as to make the distinction between two adjoining grades insignificant.

| **Figure 9.8** | **Single Rate Structure** |

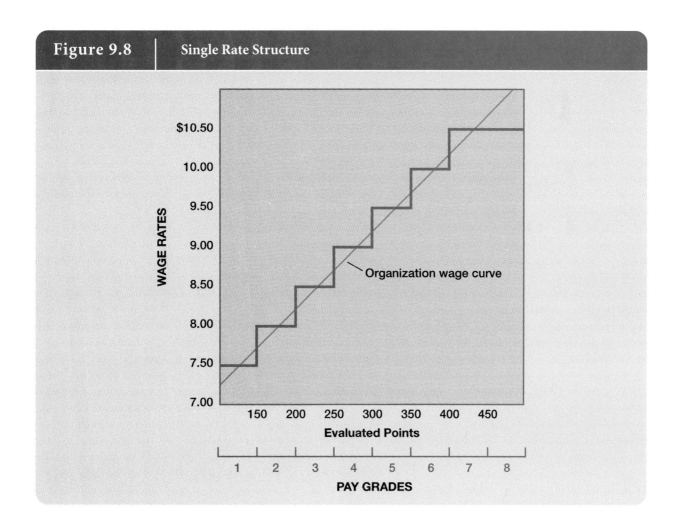

Rate Ranges

Although a single rate may be created for each pay grade, as shown in Figure 9.8, it is more common to provide a range of rates for each pay grade. The rate ranges may be the same for each grade or proportionately greater for each successive grade, as shown in Figure 9.9. Rate ranges constructed on the latter basis provide a greater incentive for employees to accept a promotion to a job in a higher grade.

Rate ranges generally are divided into a series of steps that permit employees to receive increases up to the maximum rate for the range on the basis of merit or seniority or a combination of the two. Most salary structures provide for the ranges of adjoining pay grades to overlap. The purpose of the overlap is to permit an employee with experience to earn as much as or more than a person with less experience in the next-higher job classification.

| Figure 9.9 | Wage Structure with Increasing Rate Ranges |

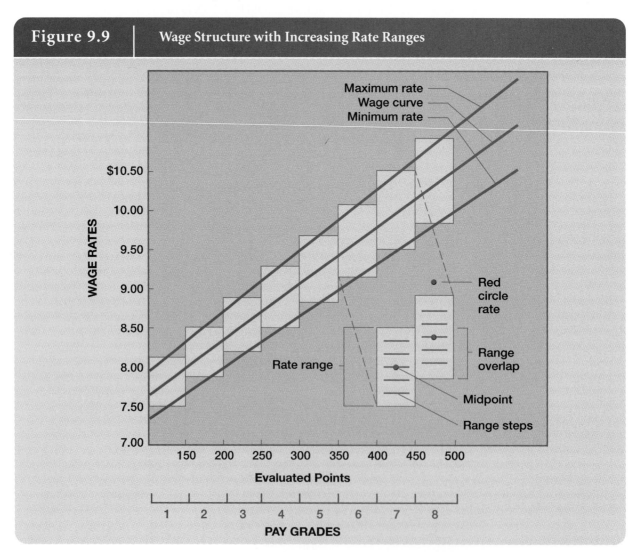

The final step in setting up a wage structure is to determine the appropriate pay grade into which each job should be placed on the basis of its evaluated worth. Traditionally, this worth is determined on the basis of job requirements without regard to the performance of the person in that job. Under this system, the performance of those who exceed the requirements of a job may be acknowledged by merit increases within the grade range or by promotion to a job in the next-higher pay grade.

Organizations may pay individuals above the maximum of the pay range when employees have high seniority or promotional opportunities are scarce. Wages paid above the range maximum are called **red circle rates**. Because these rates are exceptions to the pay structure, employers will often "freeze" these rates until all ranges are shifted upward through market wage adjustments.

Red circle rates
Payment rates above the maximum of the pay range

Competence-Based Pay

The predominant approach to employee compensation is still the job-based system.[28] Unfortunately, such a system often fails to reward employees for their skills or the knowledge they possess or to encourage them to learn a new job-related skill. Additionally, job-based pay systems may not reinforce an organizational culture stressing employee involvement or provide increased employee flexibility to meet overall production or service requirements. Therefore, organizations such as Nortel Networks and Honeywell have introduced competence-based pay plans.

Competence-based pay, also referred to as skill-based pay or knowledge-based pay, compensates employees for the different skills or increased knowledge they possess rather than for the job they hold in a designated job category. Regardless of the name, these pay plans encourage employees to earn higher base wages by learning and performing a wider variety of skills (or jobs) or displaying an array of competencies that can be applied to a variety of organizational requirements. For example, in a manufacturing setting, new tasks might include various assembly activities carried out in a particular production system or a variety of maintenance functions. Within service organizations, employees might acquire new knowledge related to advanced computer systems or accounting procedures.[29] Organizations will grant an increase in pay after each skill or knowledge has been mastered and can be demonstrated according to a predetermined standard.[30]

Competence-based pay
Pay based on an employee's skill level, the variety of skills possessed, or increased job knowledge of the employee

Competence-based pay systems represent a fundamental change in the attitude of management regarding how work should be organized and how employees should be paid for their work efforts. The most frequently cited benefits of competence-based pay include greater productivity, increased employee learning and commitment to work, improved staffing flexibility to meet production or service demands, and the reduced effects of absenteeism and turnover, since managers can assign employees where and when needed. Competence-based pay also encourages employees to acquire training when new or updated skills are needed by an organization.

Unfortunately, competence-based plans bring some long-term difficulties. Some plans limit the amount of compensation employees can earn, regardless of the new skills or competencies they acquire. Thus, after achieving the top wage, employees may be reluctant to continue their educational training. Perhaps the greatest challenge in paying individuals for their skills, knowledge, and competencies is developing

Continuous training and upgrading of skills has become a necessity in today's labour market.

PHOTODISC

appropriate measures. It is difficult to write specific knowledge and skill descriptions for jobs that employees perform and then establish accurate measures of acquired skills or knowledge. According to Robert Carow, director of corporate compensation at American International Group, Inc., "Teasing out the value of individual skills such as specific computer programming knowledge or the level of financial modelling knowledge is problematic."[31]

Broadbanding

Organizations that adopt a competency-based or skill-based pay system frequently use *broadbanding* to structure their compensation payments to employees. Broadbanding simply collapses many traditional salary grades into a few wide salary bands. Broadbands may have midpoints and quartiles or they may have extremely wide salary ranges or no ranges at all.[32] Banding encourages lateral skill building while addressing the need to pay employees performing several jobs with different skill-level requirements. Additionally, broadbands help eliminate the obsession with grades and, instead, encourage employees to move to jobs where they can develop in their careers and add value to the organization. Paying employees through broadbands enables organizations to consider job responsibilities, individual skills and competencies, and career mobility patterns in assigning employees to bands.

GOVERNMENTAL REGULATION OF COMPENSATION

Compensation management, like the other areas of HRM, is subject to provincial and federal regulations. In each province there is an employment standards act that establishes minimum requirements with respect to wages, hours of work, and overtime. Provincial as well as federal minimum requirements can be obtained by contacting the appropriate federal or provincial office.

The Canada Labour Code

USING THE INTERNET

Canada's Labour Code can be found on
http://laws.justice.gc.ca.

Part III of the Canada Labour Code and the Canada Labour Standards Regulations set minimum labour standards for all employees and employers in works or undertakings that fall within federal jurisdiction, including interprovincial highway and rail transportation, pipelines, telecommunications, air transport, fishing, and banking. Federal Crown corporations are covered by the Canada Labour Code, but federal public service employees are not. Employees working under these classifications are subject to a forty-hour work week. Managerial and professional

Reality Check

PAY EQUITY

Linda Sullivan, program specialist, Ontario Pay Equity Commission, talks about current issues in pay equity: "Most private sector employers should have implemented pay equity by now, and our role is to monitor them for compliance. However, organizations with ten to ninety-nine employees have the highest rate of noncompliance because they do not have resources, including a dedicated HR professional, and some positions are held by family members. Last year we monitored the food services sector. A family-owned bakery, for example, would need to identify female and male jobs, compare them, and make the required pay adjustments. In these family-owned enterprises, one can find the traditional breakdown where, for example, the bakers are male, and the customer service positions (i.e., the [people] working at the counter) are female. The bakers are paid more than positions in customer service. The multitude of tasks needed in customer service, such as communication skills, organizational skills, dealing with people who are upset, dealing with customers quickly are typically overlooked in female-dominated jobs and are not credited. These tasks within each job must be carefully identified and compensated.

"Smaller organizations in the public sector have different types of problems. In the public sector, it is difficult to do pay equity in a lot of organizations, because these organizations only have jobs held by women. For example, women usually hold all jobs in a day care centre. These organizations can't compare male and female jobs because there are no male jobs. So, in 1993, when the pay equity act was amended, another method of comparing jobs for these types of organizations was added: a proxy comparison method. The proxy comparison method allowed organizations to take key jobs, such as a day care supervisor or an early childhood educator, and compare these to similar jobs in a larger public sector employer, such as a large municipal day care centre. The municipal sector had already done pay equity, comparing male and female jobs in the day care centre to male jobs in the municipality. The small day care centre could compare the early childhood educator job and borrow their pay equity results, i.e., through a proxy comparison method.

"A third issue is, without a doubt, the degree of emotion felt by those who believe that they are being paid unfairly. For example, I had an e-mail from a woman about her work situation, where she had been hired and was doing what she felt was an equivalent job to a male colleague, but was being paid less. So she went to her manager and raised the issue with her, and a change was made to her wage, which she felt was justified. Then she realized once again, while they had raised her wage, she was still being paid considerably less than her male colleague doing work of equal or less value. The employer has not done pay equity. To me, what was striking about this situation was how emotional and betrayed the woman felt. The employers don't realize that employees feel so strongly about this unfair treatment. In a lot of these situations, women end up looking for other work, leaving the organization and costing the employer thousands of dollars required to recruit and train new employees."

employees are not covered by the hours-of-work provisions and may be required to exceed those hours. Revisions are constantly being made to these standards; HR managers must keep abreast of these changes to ensure compliance in the workplace.

Employment Standards Acts

The Employment Standards Acts of each province and territory establish minimum standards with a view to protecting both employees and employers in certain employment situations. Collective agreements are permitted to override the provisions of these acts as long as employees are not being provided with less than what the acts have stipulated, and as long as these overrides benefit the employee. Employers who operate in more than one province must become fully informed of the different requirements that exist in each province. This information is generally available on the Internet.

Each province's act contains a provision that stipulates that an overtime rate of 1.5 times the base rate must be paid for all hours worked in excess of the set minimum prescribed in the province. For example, if an employee works forty-five hours in a province that legislates the minimum work week as forty hours, he or she is entitled to overtime for the extra five hours at 1.5 times his or her base rate. Particular groups, including lawyers, doctors, engineers, and managers, are exempt from overtime requirements.

Other Legislation

Employment equity is under federal jurisdiction for all federally regulated companies, as well as for companies not covered under the Canada Labour Code that have dealings with federally legislated companies. Pay equity is covered provincially where applicable. As we discussed in Chapter 2, legislation relating to employment equity and pay equity is designed to ensure that fair employment practices are applied to all members of designated groups.

SIGNIFICANT COMPENSATION ISSUES

As with other HR activities, compensation management operates in a dynamic environment. For example, as managers strive to reward employees in a fair manner, they must consider controls over labour costs, legal issues regarding male and female wage payments, and internal pay equity concerns. Each of these concerns is highlighted in four important compensation issues: equal pay for comparable worth, wage-rate compression, living-wage laws, and low salary budgets.

Equal Pay for Work of Equal Value

One of the most important gender issues in compensation is equal pay for work of equal value. (In Ontario, the definition is "equal pay for work of equal or comparable value.") The issue stems from the fact that jobs performed predominantly by women are paid less than those performed by men. This practice results in what critics term *institutionalized sex discrimination*, causing women to receive lower pay for jobs that may be different from but comparable in worth to those performed by men. The issue of **equal pay for work of equal value** goes beyond providing equal pay for jobs that involve the same duties for women as for men. It is not concerned with whether a female secretary should receive the same pay as a male secretary. Rather, the argument for comparable worth is that jobs held by women are not compensated the same as those held by men, even though both job types may contribute equally to organizational success.

Equal pay for work of equal value

The concept that male and female jobs that are dissimilar, but equal in value or worth to the employer, should be paid the same

Measuring Comparability

Advocates of comparable worth argue that the difference in wage rates for predominantly male and female occupations rests in the undervaluing of traditional female occupations. To remedy this situation, they propose that wages should be equal for jobs that are "somehow" equivalent in total worth or compensation to the organization. Unfortunately, there is no consensus on a comparable worth standard by which to evaluate jobs, nor is there agreement on the ability of current job evaluation techniques to remedy the problem.[33] Indeed, organizations may dodge the comparable worth issue by using one job evaluation system for clerical and secretarial jobs and another system for other jobs. Furthermore, the advocates of comparable worth argue that current job evaluation techniques simply serve to continue the differences in pay between the sexes. However, others believe that job evaluation systems can be designed to measure different types of jobs, in the same way that apples and oranges can be compared (see Figure 9.10). Two large settlements have resulted from pay equity issues, as described in The Business Case.

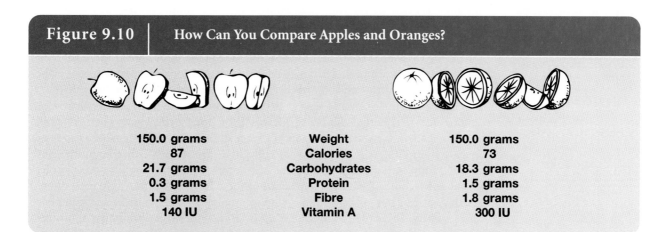

Figure 9.10	How Can You Compare Apples and Oranges?

150.0 grams	Weight	150.0 grams
87	Calories	73
21.7 grams	Carbohydrates	18.3 grams
0.3 grams	Protein	1.5 grams
1.5 grams	Fibre	1.8 grams
140 IU	Vitamin A	300 IU

Source: M. Belcourt, "Human Resource Management" in *Introduction to Canadian Business*, edited by J. Plinuissen (Toronto: McGraw-Hill Ryerson and Captus Press, 1994): 410.

The Business Case

CASHING OUT

Bell Canada had to pay out $178 billion in cash and added pension benefits to settle a pay equity dispute, started in the early 1990s. The union argued that thousands of Bell employees, who are mostly women, were underpaid, compared with those in male-dominated positions. The request for salary adjustments was based on a study of the work performed by telephone operators, clerical staff, sales associates, and others. Most of those employees were women. Their salaries were compared with other job functions that were dominated by men.

In July 1998, the Canadian Human Rights Tribunal ruled that there was a substantial and illegal wage gap between job categories dominated by men and those jobs dominated by women in the federal government. The tribunal determined that the federal government had underpaid those mainly female workers in administrative support occupational categories. Each employee was entitled to about $30 000 in pay retroactive to March 1985. The Public Service Alliance of Canada, the union representing the workers affected by the tribunal ruling, calculates that the average annual pension of workers from these groups is only $10 000 per year. The pay equity settlement would make an important difference in the standard of living for these workers and their families now and in the future.

Wage-rate compression
Compression of differentials between job classes, particularly the differential between hourly workers and their managers

Earlier, when we discussed the compensation structure, it was noted that the primary purpose of the pay differentials between the wage classes is to provide an incentive for employees to prepare for and accept more-demanding jobs. Unfortunately, this incentive is being significantly reduced by **wage-rate compression**—the reduction of differences between job classes. Wage-rate compression is largely an internal pay-equity concern. The problem occurs when employees perceive that there is too narrow a difference between their compensation and that of colleagues in lower-rated jobs. It can cause low employee morale, leading to issues of reduced employee performance, higher absenteeism and turnover, and even delinquent behaviour such as employee theft.

There is no single cause of wage-rate compression. For example, it can occur when unions negotiate across-the-board increases for hourly employees but managerial personnel are not granted corresponding wage differentials. Such increases can result in part from COLAs provided for in collective agreements. Other inequities have resulted from the scarcity of applicants in computers, engineering, and other professional and technical fields. Job applicants in these fields frequently have been offered starting salaries not far below those paid to employees with considerable experience and seniority. This situation is occurring now due to the critical shortages of business professors, where new Ph.D.s in business are being offered higher starting salaries than those with many years of experience. Wage-rate compression often occurs when organizations grant pay adjustments for lower-rated jobs without providing commensurate adjustments for occupations at the top of the job hierarchy.

Identifying wage-rate compression and its causes is far simpler than implementing organizational policies to alleviate its effect. Organizations wishing to minimize the problem may incorporate the following ideas into their pay policies:

1. Give larger compensation increases to more-senior employees.
2. Emphasize pay-for-performance and reward merit-worthy employees.
3. Limit the hiring of new applicants seeking exorbitant salaries.
4. Design the pay structure to allow a wide spread between hourly and supervisory jobs or between new hires and senior employees.
5. Provide equity adjustments for selected employees hardest hit by pay compression.

Other options include permitting more flexibility in employees' work schedules, including four-day work weeks and work at home.

SUMMARY

objective 1

Establishing compensation programs requires both large and small organizations to consider specific goals—employee retention, compensation distribution, and adherence to a budget, for instance. Compensation must reward employees for past efforts (pay-for-performance) while serving to motivate employees' future performance. Internal and external equity of the pay program affects employees' concepts of fairness. Organizations must balance each of these concerns while still remaining competitive. The ability to attract qualified employees while controlling labour costs is a major factor in allowing organizations to remain viable in the domestic or international markets.

objective 2

The basis on which compensation payments are determined, and the way they are administered, can significantly affect employee productivity and the achievement of organizational goals. Internal influences include the employer's compensation policy, the worth of the job, the performance of the employee, and the employer's ability to pay. External factors influencing wage rates include labour market conditions, area wage rates, cost of living, the outcomes of collective bargaining, and legal requirements.

objective 3

Organizations use one of four basic job evaluation techniques to determine the relative worth of jobs. The job ranking system arranges jobs in numerical order on the basis of the importance of the job's duties and responsibilities to the organization. The job classification system slots jobs into pre-established grades. Higher-rated grades will require more responsibilities, working conditions, and job duties. The point system of job evaluation uses a point scheme based on the compensable job factors of skill, effort, responsibility, and working conditions. The more compensable factors a job possesses, the more points are assigned to it. Jobs with higher accumulated points are considered more valuable to the organization. The factor comparison system evaluates jobs on a factor-by-factor basis against key jobs in the organization.

objective 4

Wage surveys determine the external equity of jobs. Data obtained from surveys will facilitate establishing the organization's wage policy while ensuring that the employer does not pay more, or less, than needed for jobs in the relevant labour market.

objective 5

The wage structure is composed of the wage curve, pay grades, and rate ranges. The wage curve depicts graphically the pay rates assigned to jobs within each pay grade. Pay grades represent the grouping of similar jobs on the basis of their relative worth. Each pay grade will include a rate range. Rate ranges will have a midpoint and minimum and maximum pay rates for all jobs in the pay grade.

The federal and provincial governments through the Canada Labour Code, Employment Standards Acts, Child Labour provisions, and employment equity/pay equity legislation regulate compensation. The concept of equal pay for work of equal value seeks to overcome the fact that jobs held by women are compensated at a lower rate than those performed by men.

 This happens even though both types of jobs may contribute equally to organizational productivity. Wage-rate compression largely affects managerial and senior employees as the pay given to new employees or the wage increases gained through collective agreements erode the pay differences between these groups.

KEY TERMS

competence-based pay 407
consumer price index (CPI) 393
equal pay for work of equal value 411
escalator clauses 393
factor comparison system 398
Hay profile method 401
hourly work 388

job classification system 395
job evaluation 394
job ranking system 395
pay equity 386
pay-for-performance standard 384
pay grades 405
piecework 388

point system 396
real wages 394
red circle rates 407
value-added compensation 383
wage and salary survey 402
wage curve 404
wage-rate compression 412

DISCUSSION QUESTIONS

 1. Tomax Corporation has 400 employees and wishes to develop a compensation policy to correspond to its dynamic business strategy. The company wishes to employ a high-quality workforce capable of responding to a competitive business environment. Suggest different compensation objectives to match Tomax's business goals.

 2. Since employees may differ in their job performance, would it not be more feasible to determine the wage rate for each employee on the basis of his or her relative worth to the organization? Explain.

 3. What is job evaluation? Describe the two nonquantitative and two quantitative approaches to job evaluation.

 4. Describe the basic steps in conducting a wage and salary survey. What are some factors to consider?

 5. One of the objections to granting wage increases on a percentage basis is that the lowest-paid employees, who are having the most trouble making ends meet, get the smallest increase, while the highest-paid employees get the largest increase. Is this objection a valid one? Explain.

 6. Federal laws governing compensation raise important issues for both employers and employees. Discuss the following:
   a. The effect of mandatory overtime
   b. The effects of raising the minimum wage

 7. What are some of the problems of developing a pay system based on equal pay for work of equal value?

Develop Managerial Skills

WHY THIS SALARY?

A question frequently asked is "Why is that person paid more than I am when we both perform the same job?" The answer to this question lies in understanding the components of the wage mix as discussed in this chapter. While we may disapprove of the idea that someone is paid more or less than we are for similar work, nevertheless, factors both internal and external to the organization influence the final salary paid to a job or a specific person. Often we have little control over the wage mix factors. However, at other times, we can improve our wage by gaining additional job experience or seniority, or by obtaining increases in job knowledge or skills. This project is designed to give you experience in understanding why jobs are paid different salaries.

Assignment

The website of Monster.ca (http://salary.monster.ca) provides a salary calculator for the Canadian market, giving you salary ranges for jobs and a comparison tool to graph it beside the national average. At the time this text was written, a Financial Analyst I working in Toronto, Ontario, earned a median base salary of $53 168. Half the people in this job earn between $46 991 and $59 503.

Go the site to research the salaries paid to the following occupations in the city in which you live and then answer the questions that follow. (You can choose other occupations that are of more interest to your group.) Relate your answers to the internal and external factors of the wage mix that are discussed in the text.

Occupation	Median Base Salary	Low	High
▶ Financial Analyst I (Toronto)	$53 168	$46 991	$59 503
▶ Librarian			
▶ Construction labourer			
▶ Computer services manager			
▶ Police officer			
▶ Motel desk clerk			
▶ Lawyer			

1. What factors may account for the wide differences among salaries for different occupations?
2. Now check on the compensation rates in Toronto, Calgary, Charlottetown, and Moose Jaw, Saskatchewan, for the jobs you have chosen. What factors may account for the differences among salaries for identical occupations in different cities?
3. What factors may account for the differences among salaries for identical occupations in different organizations?

   You may work individually or in teams to complete this skill-building exercise.

Case Study 1

Canada Post

Canada Post Corporation employs 67 000 workers, which makes it one of Canada's largest employers. In 1997 it revised its job evaluation system for postmasters and assistants. The old system, which had been in place since 1976, did not take into account changes that had arisen since 1981, when Canada Post became a Crown corporation.

A human resources consulting firm, Watson Wyatt Worldwide, was hired to assist with the entire process. According to Linda Tremblay of Organization Planning and Development, Canada Post, the job evaluation system was revised to incorporate employee input, to be responsive to federal pay equity legislation, and—most importantly—to reflect corporate culture and values.

The new job evaluation system measured the content and relative value of jobs. The system evaluated jobs according to their "typical" or "normal" components—that is, tasks that were done on a regular basis. These compensable factors were a function of the job itself, not of the performance of the person doing the job.

The four factors considered and their relative weights were as follows:

A   Responsibilities—What type of responsibilities does the job entail? 60%

B   Skills—What particular skills are needed to accomplish the job? 25%

C   Working Conditions—What working conditions apply to the job? 11%

D   Effort—What amount of effort does the job require? 4%

Total 100%

An example of an item under C: Working Conditions:

This factor measures the surroundings or physical conditions under which your work must be done and the extent to which they make your job disagreeable. Consider whether elements such as those listed are present, and the relative amount and continuity of exposure:

Place a checkmark beside all those that apply:

▶   adverse weather conditions

▶   confined work space

▶   dirt/dust

▶   fumes

▶   inadequate lighting

▶   lack of privacy

▶   noisy conditions

▶   temperature extremes

▶   verbal abuse/public harassment

▶   other

Job evaluation criteria, such as in the above example, were used in each of the four areas and are summarized as below:

Job Evaluation Criteria

Compensable factors	Components
Responsibilities	Internal and external contacts
	Decision making
	Supervision of employees
	Responsibility for property maintenance
	Responsibility for rural routes, suburban services and/or stage services
	Points of call
	Responsibility for contractor invoices
	Responsibility for a till and/or authorized allowance
Skills	Knowledge areas (such as budget process, collective agreement, contacted services in mail operations or property management, financial practices, procedures knowledge, product knowledge, primary sortation, final sortation, sales and customer service techniques, personnel management techniques)
	Job-related experience
Working conditions	Physical work environment
	Travel
Effort	Physical effort
	Multiple demands

Employees completed the job evaluation questionnaire for their own jobs. The completed questionnaires were reviewed by supervisors, managers, and human resources staff.

Total points were then allocated to each job, which corresponded to one of six job bands. Collective agreement negotiations were used to set the rates of pay for each of the six job bands.

Source: Interview and correspondence with Linda Tremblay, Canada Post Corporation.

QUESTIONS

1. What type of job evaluation system did Canada Post use?
2. What are the advantages and limitations of this system?
3. If you were asked to review both the questionnaire and the process used to obtain the job information, what recommendations would you make?

Case Study 2

Pay Decisions at Performance Sports

Katie Perkins's career objective while attending Durham College was to earn a degree in small business management and then start her own business. Her ultimate desire was to combine her love of sports with her strong interest in marketing and start a mail-order golf equipment business aimed specifically at beginning golfers.

In February 1998, after extensive development of a strategic business plan and a loan of $75 000 from the Federal Business Development Bank, she established Performance Sports. Based on a marketing plan that stressed fast delivery, error-free customer service, and deep discount pricing, the company grew rapidly. Currently, Performance Sports employs sixteen people: eight customer service reps earning between $9.75 and $11.25 per hour; four shipping and receiving associates earning between $8.50 and $9.50 per hour; two clerical staff, each earning $8.75 per hour; an assistant manager earning $13.10 per hour, and a general manager with a wage of $15 per hour. Both the manager and the assistant manager are former customer service representatives.

Perkins intends to create a new managerial position, purchasing agent, to handle the complex duties of purchasing golf equipment from the company's many suppliers. Also, the mail order catalogue from Performance Sports will soon be expanded to handle a complete line of tennis equipment. Since the position of purchasing agent is new, Perkins isn't sure how much to pay this person. She wants to employ someone with between five and eight years' experience in sports equipment purchasing.

While attending an equipment manufacturers' convention in Vancouver, Perkins learns that a competitor, East Valley Sports, pays its customer service reps on a pay-for-knowledge basis. Intrigued by this approach, Perkins asks her assistant manager, George Balkin, to research the pros and cons of this payment strategy. This request has become a priority, since only last week two customer service representatives expressed dissatisfaction with their hourly wage. Both complained that they felt underpaid relative to the large amount of skills and knowledge needed to provide excellent customer service.

QUESTIONS

1. What factors should Perkins consider when setting the wage for the purchasing agent position? What resources are available for her to consult when establishing this wage?
2. Suggest some advantages and disadvantages of a pay-for-knowledge policy for Performance Sports.
3. Suggest a new payment plan for the customer service representatives.

CAREER COUNSEL

To find out what compensation you can expect to receive in your career, visit the *Managing Human Resources* website (www.belcourt4e.nelson.com).

NOTES AND REFERENCES

1. Paul W. Mulvey, Gerald E. Ledford, Jr., and Peter V. LeBlanc, "Rewards of Work," *WorldatWork Journal* 9, no. 3 (Third Quarter 2000): 6–18.

2. For a frequently referenced book on strategic compensation planning, see Edward E. Lawler III, *Strategic Pay: Aligning Organizational Strategies and Pay Systems* (San Francisco: Jossey-Bass, 1990).

3. Gerald E. Ledford and Elizabeth J. Hawk, "Compensation Strategy: A Guide for Senior Managers," *American Compensation Journal* 9, no. 1 (First Quarter 2000): 28–38.

4. Duncan Brown, "Rewards Strategies for Real: Moving from Intent to Impact," *WorldatWork Journal* 10, no. 3 (Third Quarter 2001): 42–49.

5. Jerry M. Newman and Frank J. Krzystrofiak, "Value-Chain Compensation," *Compensation and Benefits Review* 30, no. 3 (May–June 1998): 60–66.

6. Robert L. Heneman and Katherine E. Dixon, "Reward and Organizational Systems Alignment: An Expert System," *Compensation and Benefits Review* 33, no. 6 (November–December 2001): 18–28.

7. Kenneth F. Clarke, "What Businesses Are Doing to Attract and Retain Employees—Becoming an Employer of Choice," *Employee Benefits Journal* 26, no. 1 (March 2001): 21–23.

8. Claudia Zeitz Poster, "Retaining Key People in Troubled Companies," *Compensation and Benefits Review* 34, no. 1 (January–February 2002): 7–11.

9. "The Future of Salary Management," *Compensation and Benefits Review* 33, no. 4 (July–August 2001): 7–13.

10. Michelle Brown and John S. Heywood, *Paying for Performance: An International Comparison* (Armonk, NY: M. E. Sharpe, 2002).

11. Randolph W. Keuch, "Pay-for-Performance Is Alive and Well," *WorldatWork Journal* 10, no. 3 (Third Quarter 2001): 18–23.

12. Janet Wiscombe, "Can Pay-for-Performance Really Work?" *Workforce* 80, no. 8 (August 2001): 28–34.

13. Douglas J. Friske and Beverly C. Petersen, "Paying for Performance in a Volatile Market," *Workspan* 44, no. 11 (November 2001): 20–28.

14. Richard Long, *Compensation in Canada: Strategy, Practice and Issues* 2nd ed. (Toronto: ITP Nelson, 2003), ITP Nelson Series in Human Resources Management.

15. For one of the classic articles on equity theory, see J. Stacey Adams, "Integrity in Social Exchange," in L. Berkowitz (ed.), *Advances in Experimental Social Psychology* (New York: Academic Press, 1965): 276–99.

16. Ramon J. Aldag and Loren W. Kuzuhara, *Organizational Behavior and Management* (Mason, OH: South-Western Publishing, 2002): 266–70.

17. Victor H. Vroom, *Work and Motivation* (San Francisco: Jossey-Bass, 1994). This landmark book, originally published in 1964, integrates the work of hundreds of researchers seeking to explain choice of work, job satisfaction, and job performance.

18. Aldag and Kuzuhara, *Organizational Behavior and Management,* 263–65.

19. Alison Stein Wellner, "Salaries in Site," *HR Magazine* 46, no. 5 (May 2001): 88–96.

20. T. Van Eck, and E. Konkle, "Getting to the Base of Competitive Pay," *Canadian HR Reporter* 16, no. 4 (February 24, 2003): 17, 19.

21. George T. Milkovich and Jerry M. Newman, *Compensation,* 7th ed. (Chicago: Irwin, 2002): 12–16.

22. *CPI Detailed Report,* December 2001 (Washington, DC: U.S. Department of Labor, Bureau of Labor Statistics). Published monthly.

23. John A. Fossum, *Labor Relations,* 8th ed. (Boston: McGraw-Hill Irwin, 2002): 266–68.

24. Richard I. Henderson, *Compensation Management,* 8th ed. (Englewood Cliffs, NJ: Prentice Hall, 2000).

25. Long, *Compensation in Canada: Strategy, Practice and Issues,* 458.

26. R.E. Sibson, *Compensation* (New York: American Management Association, 1990).

27. Jeremy Handel, "Dollars and Sense: Salary Surveys from A–Z," *Workspan* 44, no. 2 (February 2001): 48–49. See also Charlie Trevor and Mary E. Graham, "Deriving the Market Wage: Three Decision Areas in the Compensation Survey Process," *WorldatWork Journal* 9, no. 4 (Fourth Quarter 2000): 69–76.

28. Edward E. Lawler, "Pay Strategy: New Thinking for the New Millennium," *Compensation and Benefits Review* 32, no. 1 (January–February 2000): 7–12.

29. James R. Thompson and Charles W. LeHew, "Skill-Based Pay as an Organizational Innovation," *Review of Public Personnel Administration* 20, no. 2 (Winter 2000): 20–38.

30. David A. Hofrichter and Todd McGovern, "People, Competencies and Performance: Clarifying Means and Ends," *Compensation and Benefits Review* 33, no. 4 (July–August 2001): 34–38.

31. "The Future of Salary Management," *Compensation and Benefits Review* 33, no. 4 (July–August 2001): 11.

32. Michael Enos and Greg Limoges, "Broadbanding: Is That Your Company's Final Answer?" *WorldatWork Journal* 9, no. 4 (Fourth Quarter 2000): 61–68.

33. E. Jane Arnault, Louis Gordon, Douglas H. Joines, and G. Michael Phillips, "An Experimental Study of Job Evaluation and Comparable Worth," *Industrial and Labor Relations Review* 54, no. 4 (July 2001): 806–15.

chapter 10

Pay-for-Performance: Incentive Rewards

After studying this chapter, you should be able to

objective 1

Discuss the basic requirements for successful implementation of incentive programs.

objective 2

Identify the types of, and reasons for implementing, individual incentive plans.

objective 3

Explain why merit raises may fail to motivate employees adequately and discuss ways to increase their motivational value.

objective 4

Indicate the advantage of each of the principal methods used to compensate salespeople.

objective 5

Differentiate how gains may be shared with employees under the Scanlon, Rucker, Improshare, and earnings-at-risk gainsharing systems.

objective 6

Differentiate between profit-sharing plans and explain advantages and disadvantages of these programs.

objective 7

Describe the main types of ESOP plans and discuss the advantages of ESOP to employers and employees.

In the previous chapter we emphasized that the worth of a job is a significant factor in determining the pay rate for that job. However, pay based solely on this measure may fail to motivate employees to perform to their full capacity. Unmotivated employees are likely to meet only minimum performance standards. Recognizing this fact, diverse organizations such as BF Goodrich and Manulife Financial offer some form of incentive to workers. These organizations are attempting to get more motivational mileage out of employee compensation by tying it more closely to organizational objectives and employee performance. John Trebe, president and CEO of Waterloo Industries, describes incentive rewards as "a powerful way to connect people to the business."[1] When incentives are linked with output, workers will increasingly apply their skills and knowledge to their jobs and will be encouraged to work together as a team. Therefore, in their attempt to raise productivity, managers are focusing on the many variables that help to determine the effectiveness of pay as a motivator.

In this chapter we will discuss incentive plans with regard to the objectives they hope to achieve and the various factors that may affect their success. Since many organizations have implemented broad-based incentive programs, for discussion purposes we have grouped incentive plans into three broad categories: individual incentive plans, group incentive plans, and enterprise incentive plans, as shown in Figure 10.1.

STRATEGIC REASONS FOR INCENTIVE PLANS

objective

A clear trend in strategic compensation management is the growth of incentive plans, also called **variable pay** programs, for employees throughout the organization. Nearly three-quarters of Canadian companies offer some form of variable pay. Ken Abosch, compensation specialist with Hewitt Associates LLC, notes, "There's no question that most corporations have turned away from fixed forms of compensation in favour of variable forms. There has been an abandonment of entitlement programs."[2]

Incentive rewards are based entirely on a pay-for-performance philosophy (see Chapter 9). Incentive pay programs establish a performance "threshold" (a baseline

Figure 10.1	Types of Incentive Plans

Individual	Group	Enterprise
Piecework	Team compensation	Profit sharing
Standard hour plan	Scanlon Plan	Stock options
Bonuses	Rucker Plan	Employee stock ownership
Merit pay	Improshare	plans (ESOPs)
Lump-sum merit pay	Earnings-at-risk plans	
Sales incentives		
Incentives for professional employees		
Executive compensation		

Variable pay
Tying pay to some measure of individual, group, or organizational performance

performance level) that an employee or group of employees must reach in order to qualify for incentive payments. According to one compensation manager, "The performance threshold is the minimum level an employee must reach in order to qualify for variable pay."[3] Additionally, incentive plans emphasize a shared focus on organizational objectives by broadening the opportunities for incentives to employees throughout the organization. Incentive plans create an operating environment that champions a philosophy of shared commitment through the belief that every individual contributes to organizational performance and success.

Incentive Plans as Links to Organizational Objectives

Over the years, organizations have implemented incentive plans for a variety of reasons: high labour costs, competitive product markets, slow technological advances, and high potential for production bottlenecks. While these reasons are still cited, contemporary arguments for incentive plans focus on linking compensation rewards, both individual and group, to organizational goals.[4] By meshing compensation and organizational objectives, managers believe that employees will assume "ownership" of their jobs, thereby improving their effort and overall job performance. Incentives are designed to encourage employees to put out more effort to complete their job tasks—effort they might not be motivated to expend under hourly and/or seniority-based compensation systems. Financial incentives are therefore offered to improve or maintain high levels of productivity and quality, which in turn improves the market for Canadian goods and services in a global economy. Figure 10.2 summarizes the major advantages of incentive pay programs as noted by researchers and HR professionals.

Do incentive plans work? Various studies, along with reports from individual organizations, show a measurable relationship between incentive plans and improved organizational performance. In the area of manufacturing, productivity will often improve by as much as 20 percent after the adoption of incentive plans. Improvements, however, are not limited to goods-producing industries. Service organizations, not-for-profits, and government agencies also show productivity gains when incentives are linked to organizational goals. Taco Bell Corporation reduced food costs and improved customer service after it began an employee bonus program.

Figure 10.2	Advantages of Incentive Pay Programs

▶ Incentives focus employee efforts on specific performance targets. They provide real motivation that produces important employee and organizational gains.

▶ Incentive payouts are variable costs linked to the achievement of results. Base salaries are fixed costs largely unrelated to output.

▶ Incentive compensation is directly related to operating performance. If performance objectives (quantity and/or quality) are met, incentives are paid. If objectives are not achieved, incentives are withheld.

▶ Incentives foster teamwork and unit cohesiveness when payments to individuals are based on team results.

▶ Incentives are a way to distribute success among those responsible for producing that success.

Unfortunately, studies also show that variable pay plans may not achieve their proposed objectives or lead to organizational improvements. First, incentive plans sometimes fail to satisfy employee needs. Second, management may have failed to give adequate attention to the design and implementation of the plan. Third, employees may have little ability to affect performance standards. Furthermore, the success of an incentive plan will depend on the environment that exists within an organization. A plan is more likely to work in an organization where morale is high, employees believe they are being treated fairly, and there is harmony between employees and management.

Requirements for a Successful Incentive Plan

For an incentive plan to succeed, employees must have some desire for the plan. This desire can be influenced in part by how successful management is in introducing the plan and convincing employees of its benefits. Encouraging employees to participate in developing and administering the plan is likely to increase their willingness to accept it.

Employees must be able to see a clear connection between the incentive payments they receive and their job performance. This connection is more visible if there are objective quality or quantity standards by which they can judge their performance. Commitment by employees to meet these standards is also essential for incentive plans to succeed. This requires mutual trust and understanding between employees and their supervisors, which can only be achieved through open, two-way channels of communication. Management should never allow incentive payments to be seen as an *entitlement*. Instead, these payments should be viewed as a reward that must be earned through effort. This perception can be strengthened if the incentive money is distributed to employees in a separate cheque. Compensation specialists also note the following as characteristics of a successful incentive plan:

▶ Financial incentives are linked to valued behaviour.
▶ The incentive program seems fair to employees.
▶ Productivity and quality standards are challenging but achievable.
▶ Payout formulas are simple and understandable.

Furthermore, the best-managed incentive pay programs are clearly and continuously communicated to employees. This is true both during good and bad economic periods. According to Patricia Zingheim, compensation consultant with Schuster-Zingheim and Associates, "Every study of workforce attitudes suggests that honest and frequent communication of the facts creates improved employee understanding of the realities of how people can help a company thrive."[5] Highlights in HRM 10.1 provides one diagnostic tool for the periodic review and assessment of incentive programs.

SETTING PERFORMANCE MEASURES

Measurement is key to the success of incentive plans because it communicates the importance of established organizational goals. What gets measured and rewarded gets attention.[6] For example, if the organization desires to be a leader in quality, then performance indexes may focus on customer satisfaction, timeliness, or being error-free. If being a low-priced producer is the goal, then emphasis should be on cost reduction or increased productivity with lower acceptable levels of quality. While a

Highlights in HRM 10.1

ASSESSING INCENTIVE PROGRAM EFFECTIVENESS

MasterBrand Cabinets and Waterloo Industries, manufacturers of tool storage products, have spent several years broadly implementing incentive programs. With a hard-working and dedicated workforce, each company has identified broad-based incentives as a key element in achieving business goals. To ensure continued success with their incentive programs, managers at both organizations are expected to make periodic reviews and assessment of their incentive programs. Here is an example of one diagnostic assessment tool.

Incentive Program Assessment Tool

General Assessment	Unsure	Low	Some	High
1. To what extent do incentive program measures support business and operational objectives?	❑	❑	❑	❑
2. To what extent do employees understand how to influence program measures?	❑	❑	❑	❑
3. To what extent have employee behaviours changed as a result of the program?	❑	❑	❑	❑
4. To what extent has plant leadership actively engaged employees in improving performance?	❑	❑	❑	❑
5. To what extent is there an effective infrastructure to support the program (e.g., communications, tracking)?	❑	❑	❑	❑
6. Overall, how would you rate plant management's satisfaction with the program?	❑	❑	❑	❑
7. Overall, how would you rate employee (program participant) satisfaction with the program?	❑	❑	❑	❑

Source: Christian M. Ellis and Cynthia L. Paluso, "Blazing a Trail to Broad-Based Incentives," *WorldatWork Journal* 9, no. 4 (2000): 33–41. Used with permission, WorldatWork, Scottsdale, Arizona.

variety of performance options are available, most focus on quality, cost control, or productivity. Highlights in HRM 10.2 provides five proven guidelines on how to establish and maintain an effective performance measurement program.

For some organizations, linking incentive payments to formalized performance measures has not obtained positive results for either employees or the organization.[7] Failure can often be traced to the choice of performance measures. Therefore, measures that are quantitative, simple, and structured to show a clear relationship to improved performance are best. Overly quantitative, complex measures are to be avoided. Also, when selecting a performance measure, it is necessary to evaluate the extent to which the employees involved can actually influence the measurement. Finally, employers must guard against "ratcheting up" performance goals by continually trying to exceed previous results. This eventually leads to employee frustration and employee perception that the standards are unattainable. The result will be a mistrust of management and a backlash against the entire incentive program.

Highlights in HRM 10.2

SETTING PERFORMANCE MEASURES—THE KEYS

Both large and small organizations have established performance measures to improve operational success while rewarding employees for their performance outcomes. Establishing meaningful performance measures is one of the important and difficult challenges facing management today. Before managers or supervisors develop and implement organizational measures, they should consider the following guidelines.

▶ *Performance measures—at all organizational levels—must be consistent with the strategic goals of the organization.* Avoid nonrelevant measures that are not closely linked to the business or what employees do in their work.

▶ *Define the intent of performance measures and champion the cause relentlessly.* Demonstrate that performance measures are, in fact, good business management, and hold managers and employees accountable for their success.

▶ *Involve employees.* A critical step in any measurement program is the development of an employee involvement strategy outlining the nature of employee participation, implementation, and ongoing management of the performance management program. Segment the workforce based on nature of work and potential for impact. Consider which measurements require customization. Acceptance of a performance measurement program is heightened when employees "buy into" the process.

▶ *Consider the organization's culture and workforce demographics when designing performance measures.* For example, organizations with a more traditional hierarchical structure may need more time to introduce performance measurements compared to flatter organizations, which are more fluid and less steeped in control and command characteristics.

▶ *Widely communicate the importance of performance measures.* Performance messages are the principles and guidelines that communicate to employees about required performance levels and why the organization needs to achieve those levels of success.

Source: Adapted from Christian M. Ellis, "Improving the Impact of Performance Management," *Workspan* 45, no. 2 (February 2002): 7–8.

ADMINISTERING INCENTIVE PLANS

While incentive plans based on productivity can reduce direct labour costs, to achieve their full benefit they must be carefully thought out, implemented, and maintained. A cardinal rule is that thorough planning must be combined with a "proceed with caution" approach. Compensation managers repeatedly stress a number of points related to the effective administration of incentive plans. Three of the more important points are, by consensus, the following:

1. Incentive systems are effective only when managers are willing to grant incentives based on differences in individual, team, or organizational performance. Allowing incentive payments to become pay guarantees defeats the motivational intent of the incentive. The primary purpose of an incentive compensation plan is not to pay off under almost all circumstances, but rather to motivate performance. Thus, if the plan is to succeed, poor performance must go unrewarded.

2. Annual salary budgets must be large enough to reward and reinforce exceptional performance. When compensation budgets are set to ensure that pay increases do not exceed certain limits (often established as a percentage of payroll or sales), these constraints may prohibit rewarding outstanding individual or group performance.

3. The overhead costs associated with plan implementation and administration must be determined. These may include the cost of establishing performance standards and the added cost of record keeping. The time consumed in communicating the plan to employees, answering questions, and resolving any complaints about it must also be included in these costs.

INDIVIDUAL INCENTIVE PLANS

In today's competitive world, one word, *flexibility,* describes the design of individual incentive plans.[8] For example, technology, job tasks and duties, and/or organizational goals (such as being a low-cost producer) affect the organization's choice of incentive pay programs. Incentive payments may be determined by the number of units produced, by the achievement of specific performance goals, or by productivity improvements in the organization as a whole. In addition, in highly competitive industries such as foods and retailing, low profit margins will affect the availability of monies for incentive payouts. All these considerations suggest that tradition and philosophy, as well as economics and technology, help govern the design of individual incentive systems.

Piecework

Straight piecework
Incentive plan under which employees receive a certain rate for each unit produced

Differential piece rate
Compensation rate under which employees whose production exceeds the standard amount of output receive a higher rate for all of their work than the rate paid to those who do not exceed the standard amount

One of the oldest incentive plans is based on piecework. Under **straight piecework**, employees receive a certain rate for each unit produced. Their compensation is determined by the number of units they produce during a pay period. At Steelcase, an office furniture maker, employees can earn more than their base pay, often as much as 35 percent more, through piecework for each slab of metal they cut or chair they upholster. Under a **differential piece rate,** employees whose production exceeds the standard output receive a higher rate for *all* of their work than the rate paid to those who do not exceed the standard.

Employers include piecework in their compensation strategy for several reasons. The wage payment for each employee is simple to compute, and the plan permits an organization to predict its labour costs with considerable accuracy, since these costs are the same for each unit of output. The piecework system is more likely to succeed when units of output can be measured readily, when the quality of the product is less critical, when the job is fairly standardized, and when a constant flow of work can be maintained.

Computing the Piece Rate

Although time standards establish the time required to perform a given amount of work, they do not by themselves determine what the incentive rate should be. The incentive rates must be based on hourly wage rates that would otherwise be paid for the type of work being performed. Say, for example, the standard time for producing one unit of work in a job paying $7.50 per hour was set at twelve minutes. The piece rate would be $1.50 per unit, computed as follows:

$$\frac{60 \text{ (minutes per hour)}}{12 \text{ (standard time per unit)}} = 5 \text{ units per hour}$$

$$\frac{\$7.50 \text{ (hourly rate)}}{5 \text{ (units per hour)}} = \$1.50 \text{ per unit}$$

Piecework: The Drawbacks

Despite their obvious advantages—including their direct tie to a pay-for-performance philosophy—piecework systems have a number of disadvantages that offset their usefulness. Production standards on which piecework must be based can be difficult to develop for many types of jobs. Jobs in which individual contributions are difficult to distinguish or measure, or in which the work is mechanized to the point that the employee exercises very little control over output, also may be unsuited to piecework. Importantly, piecework incentive systems can work against an organizational culture promoting workforce cooperation, creativity, or problem solving since each of these goals can infringe on an employee's time and productivity and, therefore, total incentive earned.

One of the most significant weaknesses of piecework, as well as of other incentive plans based on individual effort, is that it may not always be an effective motivator. If employees believe that an increase in their output will provoke disapproval from fellow workers (often referred to as "rate busting"), they may avoid exerting maximum effort because their desire for peer approval outweighs their desire for more money.[9]

Piecework incentive programs have been used for many years in the garment industry.

PHOTODISC

428

Over a period of time, the standards on which piece rates are based tend to loosen, either because of peer pressure to relax the standards or because employees discover ways to do the work in less than standard time. In either case, employees are not required to exert as much effort to receive the same amount of incentive pay, so the incentive value is reduced.

Some union leaders have feared that management will use piecework or similar systems to try to speed up production, getting more work from employees for the same amount of money. Piecework may also be inappropriate where

▶ Quality is more important than quantity.
▶ Technology changes are frequent.
▶ Cross-training is desired to promote scheduling flexibility.

Standard Hour Plan

Standard hour plan
Incentive plan that sets rates based on the completion of a job in a predetermined standard time

Another common incentive technique is the **standard hour plan**, which sets incentive rates on the basis of a predetermined "standard time" for completing a job. If employees finish the work in less than the expected time, their pay is still based on the standard time for the job multiplied by their hourly rate. For example, if the standard time to install an engine in a half-ton truck is five hours and the mechanic completes the job in four and a half hours, the payment would be the mechanic's hourly rate times five hours. Standard hour plans are particularly suited to long-cycle operations or jobs or tasks that are nonrepetitive and require a variety of skills.[10]

The Wood Products Southern Division of Potlatch Corporation has successfully used a standard hour plan for the production of numerous wood products. The incentive payment is based on the standard hours calculated to produce and package 1000 feet of wood panelling. If employees can produce the panelling in less time than the standard, incentives are paid on the basis of the percentage improvement. Thus, with a 1000-hour standard and completion of the wood panelling in 900 hours, a 10 percent incentive is paid. Each employee's base hourly wage is increased by 10 percent and then multiplied by the hours worked.

While standard hour plans can motivate employees to produce more, employers must ensure that equipment maintenance and product quality do not suffer as employees strive to do their work faster to earn additional income.

Bonuses

Bonus
Incentive payment that is supplemental to the base wage

A **bonus** is an incentive payment that is given to an employee beyond one's normal base wage. It is frequently given at the end of the year and does not become part of base pay. Bonuses have the advantage of providing employees with more pay for exerting greater effort, while at the same time the employees still have the security of a basic wage. Bonus payments are common among managerial and executive employees, but recent trends show that they are increasingly given to employees throughout the organization.

Depending on who is to receive the bonus, the incentive payment may be determined on the basis of cost reduction, quality improvement, or performance criteria established by the organization. At the executive level, for example, performance criteria might include earnings growth or enterprise-specific agreed-upon objectives.

For hourly employees, a bonus payment may be based on the number of units that an individual produces, as in the case of piecework. For example, at the basic wage rate of $7 an hour plus a bonus of 15 cents per unit, an employee who produces 100 units during an eight-hour period is paid $71, computed as follows:

$$\text{(Hours} \times \text{wage rate)} + \text{(number of units} \times \text{unit rate)} = \text{Wages}$$
$$(8 \times \$7) + (100 \times 15¢) = \$71$$

When some special employee contribution is to be rewarded, a spot bonus is used. A **spot bonus,** as the name implies, is given "on the spot," normally for some employee effort not directly tied to an established performance standard. For example, a customer service representative might receive a spot bonus for working long hours to fill a new customer's large order.

Spot bonus
Unplanned bonus given for employee effort unrelated to an established performance measure

Merit Pay

A merit pay program (merit raise) links an increase in base pay to how successfully an employee performs his or her job. The merit increase is normally given on the basis of an employee's having achieved some objective performance standard—although a superior's subjective evaluation of subordinate performance may play a large role in the increase given. Merit raises can serve to motivate if employees perceive the raise to be related to the performance required to earn them.[11]

Theories of motivation, in addition to behavioural science research, provide justification for merit pay plans as well as other pay-for-performance programs.[12] For employees to see the link between pay and performance, however, their performance must be evaluated in light of objective criteria. If this evaluation also includes the use of subjective judgment by their superiors, employees must have confidence in the validity of this judgment. Most important, any increases granted on the basis of merit should be distinguishable from employees' regular pay and from any cost-of-living or other general increases. Where merit increases are based on pay-for-performance, merit pay should be withheld when performance is seen to decline.

Problems with Merit Raises

Merit raises may not always achieve their intended purpose. Unlike a bonus, a merit raise may be perpetuated year after year even when performance declines. When this happens, employees come to expect the increase and see it as being unrelated to their performance. Furthermore, employees in some organizations are opposed to merit raises because, among other reasons, they do not really trust management. What are referred to as merit raises often turn out to be increases based on seniority or favouritism, or raises to accommodate increases in cost of living or in area wage rates.

As noted by two compensation specialists, "Some subordinates have better political connections within the company than others. Subordinates who are politically, socially, and familially connected inside and outside the organization, who carry clout, and who can hurt the supervisor in some way are likely to receive a larger share of the merit pie than their performance might warrant." Even when merit raises are determined by performance, the employee's gains may be offset by inflation and higher income taxes. Compensation specialists also recognize the following problems with merit pay plans:

objective

1. Money available for merit increases may be inadequate to satisfactorily raise employees' base pay.

2. Managers may have no guidance in how to define and measure performance; there may be vagueness regarding merit award criteria.

3. Employees may not believe that their compensation is tied to effort and performance; they may be unable to differentiate between merit pay and other types of pay increases.

4. Employees may believe that organizational politics plays a significant factor in merit pay decisions, despite the presence of a formal merit pay system.

5. There may be a lack of honesty and cooperation between management and employees.

6. It has been shown that "overall" merit pay plans do not motivate higher levels of employee performance.

Probably one of the major weaknesses of merit raises lies in the performance appraisal system on which the increases are based. Even with an effective system, performance may be difficult to measure. Furthermore, any deficiencies in the performance appraisal program (these were discussed in Chapter 8) can impair the operation of a merit pay plan. Moreover, the performance appraisal objectives of employees and their superiors are often at odds. Employees typically want to maximize their pay increases, whereas superiors may seek to reward employees in an equitable manner on the basis of their performance. In some instances, employee pressures for pay increases actually may have a harmful effect on their performance appraisal.

Merit guidelines
Guidelines for awarding merit raises that are tied to performance objectives

While there are no easy solutions to these problems, organizations using a true merit pay plan often base the percentage pay raise on **merit guidelines** tied to performance appraisals. For example, Highlights in HRM 10.3 illustrates a guideline chart for awarding merit raises. The percentages may change each year, depending on various internal or external concerns such as profit levels or national economic conditions as indicated by changes in the consumer price index. Under the illustrated merit plan, to prevent all employees from being rated outstanding or above average, managers may be required to distribute the performance rating according to some pre-established formula (such as only 10 percent can be rated outstanding). Additionally, when setting merit percentage guidelines, organizations should consider individual performance along with such factors as training, experience, and current earnings.

Lump-Sum Merit Pay

Lump-sum merit program
Program under which employees receive a year-end merit payment, which is not added to their base pay

To make merit increases more flexible and visible, organizations such as Boeing, Timex, and Westinghouse have implemented a **lump-sum merit program**. Under this type of plan, employees receive a single lump-sum increase at the time of their review, an increase that is not added to their base salary. Unless management takes further steps to compensate employees, their base salary is essentially frozen until they receive a promotion.

Lump-sum merit programs offer several advantages. For employers, this innovative approach provides financial control by maintaining annual salary expenses. Merit increases granted on a lump-sum basis do not contribute to escalating base salary

Highlights in HRM 10.3

MERIT PAY GUIDELINES CHART

A merit pay guidelines chart is a "look-up" table for awarding merit increases on the basis of (1) employee performance, (2) position in the pay range, and, in a few cases, (3) time since the last pay increase. Design of any merit guidelines chart involves several concerns. Specifically,

▶ What should unsatisfactory performers be paid? Since their performance is marginal or below standard, the common response is "nothing."

▶ What should average performers be paid? Common practice is to grant increases commensurate with cost-of-living changes (see Chapter 9). The midpoint of the merit guidelines chart should equal the local or national percentage change in the consumer price index (CPI).

▶ How much should superior or outstanding performers be paid? Profit levels, compensation budgets, or psychological concerns predominate here.

The following merit pay guidelines chart shows the pay range for each pay grade as divided into five levels (quintiles), with 1 at the bottom of the pay range and 5 at the top. On the left, employee performance (as determined by the annual appraisal) is arranged in five levels from high (outstanding) to low (unsatisfactory). An employee's position in his or her salary range and performance level indicates the percentage pay increase to be awarded. For example, a person at the top of the pay range (5) who gets a performance rating of "outstanding" will be awarded a 6 percent pay increase. However, an outstanding performer at the bottom of the pay range (1) will receive a 9 percent increase.

Because the purpose of the guidelines chart is to balance conflicting pay goals, it compromises, by design, the relationship between merit increases and performance appraisal ratings. The highest-rated performers will not always be the employees with the highest percentage increase. Notice that a superior performer in quintiles 1, 2, and 3 can receive a percentage increase as much as or more than that of an outstanding performer in quintile 5. As a result, employees are likely to learn that pay increases are not determined just by performance. However, as we learned in Chapter 9, if money is to serve as a motivator, expectancy theory specifies that employees must believe there is a link between performance and pay increases if performance is to remain at a high level.

Merit Pay Guide Chart

Performance Level	Quintile (Position in Range), %				
	1	2	3	4	5
Outstanding (5)	9	9	8	7	6
Superior (4)	7	7	6	5	4
Competent (3)	5	5	4	3	3
Needs improvement (2)	0	0	0	0	0
Unsatisfactory (1)	0	0	0	0	0

levels. In addition, organizations can contain employee benefit costs, since the levels of benefits are normally calculated from current salary levels. For employees, an advantage is that receiving a single lump-sum merit payment can provide a clear link between pay and performance. For example, a 6 percent merit increase granted to an industrial engineer earning $42 000 a year translates into a weekly increase of $48.46—a figure that looks small compared with a lump-sum payment of $2520. Organizations using a lump-sum merit program will want to adjust base salaries upward after a certain period of time. This can be done yearly or after several years. These adjustments should keep pace with the rising cost of living and increases in the general market wage.

Sales Incentives

The enthusiasm and drive required in most types of sales work demand that sales employees be highly motivated. This fact, as well as the competitive nature of selling, explains why financial incentives for salespeople are widely used. These incentive plans must provide a source of motivation that will elicit cooperation and trust.[13] Motivation is particularly important for employees away from the office who cannot be supervised closely and who, as a result, must exercise a high degree of self-discipline.

Unique Needs of Sales Incentive Plans

Incentive systems for salespeople are complicated by the wide differences in the types of sales jobs.[14] These range from department store clerks who ring up customer purchases to industrial salespeople from McGraw-Edison who provide consultation and other highly technical services. Salespeople's performance may be measured by the dollar volume of their sales and by their ability to establish new accounts. Other measures are the ability to promote new products or services and to provide various forms of customer service and assistance that do not produce immediate sales revenues.[15]

Performance standards for sales employees are difficult to develop, however, because their performance is often affected by external factors beyond their control. Economic and seasonal fluctuations, sales competition, changes in demand, and the nature of the sales territory can all affect an individual's sales record.[16] Sales volume alone therefore may not be an accurate indicator of the effort salespeople have expended.

In developing incentive plans for salespeople, managers are also confronted with the problem of how to reward extra sales effort and at the same time compensate for activities that do not contribute directly or immediately to sales. Furthermore, sales employees must be able to enjoy some degree of income stability.[17]

Types of Sales Incentive Plans

Compensation plans for sales employees may consist of a straight salary plan, a straight commission plan, or a combination salary and commission plan. A **straight salary plan** permits salespeople to be paid for performing various duties not reflected immediately in their sales volume. It enables them to devote more time to providing services and building up the goodwill of customers without jeopardizing their income. The principal limitation of the straight salary plan is that it may not motivate salespeople to exert sufficient effort in maximizing their sales volume.

Straight salary plan
Compensation plan that permits salespeople to be paid for performing various duties that are not reflected immediately in their sales volume

Commission is one tool employers use to motivate people.

PHOTODISC

Straight commission plan
Compensation plan based on a percentage of sales

On the other hand, the **straight commission plan,** based on a percentage of sales, provides maximum incentive and is easy to compute and understand. For example, organizations that pay a straight commission based on total volume may use the following simple formulas:

Total cash compensation $= 2\% \times$ total volume

or

Total cash compensation $= 2\% \times$ total volume up to quota
                             $+ 4\% \times$ volume over quota

However, the straight commission plan is limited by the following disadvantages:

1.   Emphasis is on sales volume rather than on profits.
2.   Customer service after the sale is likely to be neglected.
3.   Earnings tend to fluctuate widely between good and poor periods of business, and turnover of trained sales employees tends to increase in poor periods.
4.   Salespeople are tempted to grant price concessions.

Combined salary and commission plan
Compensation plan that includes a straight salary and a commission

When a **combined salary and commission plan** is used, the percentage of cash compensation paid out in commissions (that is, incentives) is called *leverage.* Leverage is usually expressed as a ratio of base salary to commission. For example, a salesperson working under a 70/30 combination plan would receive total cash compensation paid out as 70 percent base salary and 30 percent commission. The amount of leverage will be determined after considering the constraining factors affecting performance discussed earlier and the sales objectives of the organization. The following advantages indicate why the combination salary and commission plan is so widely used:

1.   The right kind of incentive compensation, if linked to salary in the right proportion, has most of the advantages of both the straight salary and the straight commission forms of compensation.

434

2. A salary-plus-incentive compensation plan offers greater design flexibility and can therefore be more readily set up to help maximize company profits.

3. The plan can develop the most favourable ratio of selling expense to sales.

4. The field sales force can be motivated to achieve specific company marketing objectives in addition to sales volume.[18]

Incentives for Professional Employees

Like other salaried workers, professional employees—engineers and scientists, for example—may be motivated through bonuses and merit increases. In some

Reality Check

INCENTIVE COMPENSATION

Yvonne Blaszczyk, FCHRP, publisher of *Strategic Human Resources Compensation News*, suggests that when the economy is unstable, organizations look to control basic compensation and motivate employees through incentive compensation. Because markets are fragile, organizations are not achieving the profit performances that were expected, and so incentive compensation payouts for individual performers are variable and declining. How can incentive plans be structured so that not only employee results and organizational outcomes are rewarded, but so are contribution and efforts? These softer and less objective measures of contribution and effort can be measured and are important to the survival and ultimate success of organizations. For example, one company that deals with the financing and leasing of equipment has to work closely with another company that is selling the equipment. The first company cannot influence sales and therefore cannot be rewarded on the sales results. However, the company does have to service the leases and ensure customer retention. The incentive program for this company recognizes the importance of maintaining good relations with the sales company and so rewards employees based on the number of contacts, number of successfully resolved conflicts, and success in renewal of difficult contracts.

The other major change is that of the decline of merit compensation. A fixed pool of money usually distributed at the rate of 3 to 4 percent per employee is not motivating. The most common complaint heard by Blaszczyk is from high-producing employees who receive the same salary increases as average-performing employees. So companies are taking the merit money and distributing it at larger rates to only the top performers. In next decade we can expect to see companies bravely embarking on heavily weighted incentive pay, with lower base compensation. The base salary pays for day-to-day work; the incentives pay for making sure the company stays in business and is profitable. But there may be legal issues. Current employees may perceive this as a change in the implicit agreement about how they are paid.

Nonmonetary incentives are also changing. Employees who value working in flexible environments and working at home are being rewarded for performance with Blackberries and state-of-the-art laptops. Other companies give time off in lieu of compensation.

organizations, unfortunately, professional employees cannot advance beyond a certain point in the salary structure unless they are willing to take an administrative assignment. When they are promoted, their professional talents are no longer utilized fully. In the process, the organization may lose a good professional employee and gain a poor administrator. To avoid this situation, some organizations have extended the salary range for professional positions to equal or nearly equal that for administrative positions. The extension of this range provides a double-track wage system, as illustrated in Chapter 7, whereby professionals who do not aspire to become administrators still have an opportunity to earn comparable salaries.

Professional employees can receive compensation beyond base pay. For example, scientists and engineers employed by high-tech firms are included in performance-based incentive programs such as profit sharing or stock ownership. These plans encourage greater levels of individual performance. Cash bonuses can be awarded to those who complete projects on or before deadline dates. Payments may also be given to individuals elected to professional societies, granted patents, or meeting professional licensing standards.

Executive Compensation

Compensation plans for executives are unique when compared to other employees in pay-for-performance programs. One significant feature of executive pay is the opportunity to receive large incentive rewards (often obtained through stock options) relative to the executive's annual base pay. Another characteristic is the large amount of money (often in the millions of dollars) they receive for their performance. Ethics in HRM discusses executive compensation issues. Regardless, the major reasons for offering incentive rewards to executives are similar to reasons for granting incentives to other employee groups. For example, incentive plans for executives should motivate them to develop and use their abilities and contribute their energies to the fullest possible extent. Incentive plans should also facilitate the recruitment and retention of competent executive employees.

The Executive Pay Package

Organizations commonly have more than one compensation strategy for executives in order to meet various organizational goals and executive needs. For example, chief executive officers (CEOs) may have their compensation packages heavily weighted toward long-term incentives, because CEOs should be more concerned about the long-term impact of their decisions than the short-term implications. Group vice-presidents, on the other hand, may receive more short-term incentives since their decisions affect operations on a six- to twelve-month basis. Regardless of the mix, executive compensation plans consist of four basic components: (1) base salary, (2) short-term incentives or bonuses, (3) long-term incentives or stock plans, and (4) perquisites. Another important element in compensation strategy is the compensation mix to be paid to managers and executives accepting overseas assignments. (We will elaborate on this topic in Chapter 15.)

Bases for Executive Salaries. The levels of competitive salaries in the job market exert perhaps the greatest influence on executive base salaries. An organization's compensation

Ethics in HRM

THE ETHICS OF EXECUTIVE COMPENSATION

The average annual compensation for Canadian CEOs is $1 million. That is more than 150 times what the average worker makes. In the United States, the ratio is 200 to 1. The CEO of BCE, Jean Monty, was booed by striking employees at the company's annual general meeting in 1999 when union members contrasted his $17-million pay package with the company's offer of $19 per hour to telephone operators. The executives of Enron and WorldCom were granted huge numbers of stock options during their companies' rapid growth stages. As the companies went into decline, these executives then cashed in their options, making millions and leaving shareholders with worthless stock.

Is any effort—especially when it cannot be attributed to one individual—worth salaries such as the $58 million that Frank Stronach receives? What makes this issue especially sensitive is the widening gap between executive salaries and workers' wages. Bank managers are receiving millions of dollars in compensation, while bank tellers are making slightly more than the minimum wage. Executives and head hunters defend these rates on the basis of what executives contribute to their organizations.

A study of compensation practices by KPMG reveals that 35 to 40 percent of the companies listed on the Toronto Stock Exchange tie executive compensation to corporate performance. However, corporate fortunes are often beyond the control of any one individual and are more likely to be determined by external factors, including global economic conditions, new players, and changing technologies. The bottom line on executive compensation is competition. Organizations pay market rates to hire the kind of executive talent they need.

committee—normally members of the board of directors—will order a salary survey to find out what executives earn in comparable enterprises. For example, by one estimate, 96 percent of companies in the Standard & Poor's 500-stock index use a technique called *competitive benchmarking* when setting executive pay or to remain competitive for executive talent. As noted in *Business Week,* company boards reason that a CEO who doesn't earn as much as his or her peers is likely to "take a hike."[19] Comparisons may be based on organization size, sales volume, or industry groupings. Thus, by analyzing the data from published studies, along with self-generated salary surveys, the compensation committee can determine the equity of the compensation package outside the organization.[20]

Bases for Executive Short-Term Incentives. Incentive bonuses for executives should be based on the contribution the individual makes to the organization. A variety of formulas have been developed for this purpose. Incentive bonuses may be based on a percentage of a company's total profits or a percentage of profits in excess of a specific return on stockholders' investments. In other instances the payments may be tied to an annual profit plan whereby the amount is determined by the extent to which an agreed-upon profit level is exceeded. Payments may also be based on performance ratings or the achievement of specific objectives established with the agreement of executives and the board of directors.[21]

In a continuing effort to monitor the pulse of the marketplace, more organizations are tying operational yardsticks to the traditional financial gauges when computing executive pay. Called *balanced scorecards,* these yardsticks may measure things such as customer satisfaction, the ability to innovate, or product or service leadership. Notes David Cates, a compensation principal with Towers Perrin, a balanced scorecard "allows companies to focus on building future economic value, rather than be driven solely by short-term financial results." Mobil Oil uses a balanced scorecard that better indicates exactly where the company is successful and where improvement is needed.

A bonus payment may take the form of cash or stock. Also, the timing of the payment may vary. Payment can be immediate (which is frequently the case), deferred for a short term, or deferred until retirement. Most organizations pay their short-term incentive bonuses in cash (in the form of a supplemental cheque), in keeping with their pay-for-performance strategy. By providing a reward soon after the performance, and thus linking it to the effort on which it is based, they can use cash bonuses as a significant motivator.

A deferred bonus can be used to provide the sole source of retirement benefits or to supplement a regular pension plan. If they are in a lower tax bracket when the deferred benefits are ultimately received—which is not always the case—executives can realize income tax savings. Note that federal and provincial jurisdictions have income and corporate tax laws, which can influence the type of compensation offered.[22] Also, if these funds do not appreciate with inflation, participants also stand to suffer a loss from inflation.

Bases for Executive Long-Term Incentives. Short-term incentive bonuses are criticized for causing top executives to focus on quarterly profit goals to the detriment of long-term survival and growth objectives. Therefore corporations such as Sears and CIBC have adopted compensation strategies that tie executive pay to long-term performance measures.[23] Each of these organizations recognizes that, while incentive payments for executives may be based on the achievement of specific goals relating to their positions, the plans must also take into account the performance of the organization as a whole. Important to stockholders are such performance results as growth in earnings per share, return on stockholders' equity, and, ultimately, stock price appreciation. A variety of incentive plans, therefore, have been developed to tie rewards to these performance results, particularly over the long term.[24] Additionally, stock options can serve to retain key executive personnel when exercising the options is linked to a specified vesting period, say two to four years (this type of incentive is called "golden handcuffs"). As one executive at BMO commented, "These assets [the executives] have legs."[25]

Stock options are the primary long-term incentive offered to executives.[26] The principal reason for executive stock ownership is the desire of both the company and outside investors for senior managers to have a significant stake in the success of the business—to have their fortunes rise and fall with the value they create for shareholders. Stock options can also be extremely lavish for executives.[27] Managers at Sky Chef, which supplies meals on airplanes, received an average of $1.34 million each when Sky Chef was sold by Onex to Lufthansa. The managers at Sky Chef had been allowed to buy stock at book value. For every $3 of equity they bought for $1, the company arranged a bank loan of $2.[28]

Stock options are not without their critics.[29] Some object to the sheer magnitude of these incentive rewards. The link between pay and performance that options are championed to provide can also be undermined when compensation committees grant additional options to executives even when company stock prices fall or performance indexes decline. Peter Clapman, chief counsel for TIAA-CREF, the world's largest pension system, notes, "It's sort of heads you win, tails let's flip again."[30] Even worse for shareholders is the dilution problem. Every option granted to executives makes the shares of other stockholders less valuable. Compared to the United States, in Canada there is little federal support for employee ownership through purchasing stock.[31] Figure 10.3 provides definitions of the different plan types categorized into three broad categories: (1) stock price appreciation plans, (2) restricted stock and restricted cash plans, and (3) performance-based plans. Each of these broad categories includes various stock grants or cash incentives for the payment of executive performance.

Perquisites

Special benefits given to executives; often referred to as perks

Executive Perquisites. In addition to incentive programs, executive employees are often given special benefits and perquisites. **Perquisites**, or "perks," are a means of demonstrating the executives' importance to the organization while giving them an incentive to improve their performance. Furthermore, perks serve as a status symbol both inside and outside the organization. Perquisites can also provide a tax saving to executives, since some are not taxed as income. Highlights in HRM 10.4 shows the more common perks offered to executives.

Executive Compensation: The Issue of Amount

Management expert Peter F. Drucker has warned that the growing pay gap between CEOs and employees could threaten the very credibility of leadership. He believes that no leader should earn more than 20 times the company's lowest-paid employee.[32] Now consider the total direct compensation drawn in 2003 by the following executives:[33]

Frank Stronach, Magna International, $58 137 280

Richard Currie, George Weston Limited, $48 058 056

Galen Weston, George Weston Limited, $31 996 185

Pierre Lassard, Metro Inc., $28 310 200

Robert Burton, Moore Corp., $20 932 279

Given the large amount of these compensation packages, the question asked by many is "Are top executives worth the salaries and bonuses they receive?" The answer may depend on whom you ask. Corporate compensation committees justify big bonuses in the following ways:

1. Large financial incentives are a way to reward superior performance.
2. Business competition is pressure-filled and demanding.
3. Good executive talent is in great demand.
4. Effective executives create shareholder value.

Figure 10.3	Types of Long-Term Incentive Plans

STOCK PRICE APPRECIATION PLANS

Stock options	Rights granted to executives to purchase shares of their organization's stock at an established price for a fixed period of time. Stock price is usually set at market value at the time the option is granted.
Stock appreciation rights (SARs)	Cash or stock award determined by increase in stock price during any time chosen by the executive in the option period; does not require executive financing.
Stock purchase	Opportunities for executives to purchase shares of their organization's stock valued at full market or a discount price, often with the organization providing financial assistance.
Phantom stock	Grant of units equal in value to the fair market value or book value of a share of stock; on a specified date the executive will be paid the appreciation in the value of the units up to that time.

RESTRICTED STOCK/CASH PLANS

Restricted stock	Grant of stock or stock units at a reduced price with the condition that the stock not be transferred or sold (by risk of forfeiture) before a specified employment date.
Restricted cash	Grant of fixed-dollar amounts subject to transfer or forfeiture restrictions before a specified employment date.

PERFORMANCE-BASED PLANS

Performance units	Grants analogous to annual bonuses except that the measurement period exceeds one year. The value of the grant can be expressed as a flat dollar amount or converted to a number of "units" of equivalent aggregate value.
Performance shares	Grants of actual stock or phantom stock units. Value is contingent on both predetermined performance objectives over a specified period of time and the stock market.
Formula-value grants	Rights to receive units or the gain in value of units determined by a formula (such as book value or an earnings multiplier) rather than changes in market price.
Dividend units	Rights to receive an amount equal to the dividends paid on a specified number of shares; typically granted in conjunction with other grant types, such as performance shares.

Others justify high compensation as a fact of business life, reflecting market compensation trends.

Nevertheless, in an era of massive downsizing, low wage increases, and increased workloads for layoff survivors, strong criticism is voiced regarding the high monetary awards given to the senior executives.[34] Furthermore, with the large compensation packages awarded to senior managers and top-level executives, cries for performance accountability and openness abound. During the years ahead, compensation

Highlights in HRM 10.4

THE "SWEETNESS" OF EXECUTIVE PERKS

Compensation consulting firms such as Coopers and Lybrand LLP, WorldatWork, and Hewitt Associates regularly survey companies nationwide to identify the perks they provide for executives and other top managers. Below are listed popular executive perks along with some less popular perquisites.

Prevalent Perquisites

▶ Company car
▶ Company plane
▶ Financial consulting
▶ Company-paid parking
▶ Estate planning
▶ First-class air travel

▶ Physical exams
▶ Mobile phones
▶ Large insurance policies
▶ Income tax preparation
▶ Country club membership
▶ Luncheon club membership

Less Prevalent Perquisites

▶ Chauffeur service
▶ Children's education
▶ Spouse travel

▶ Personal home repairs
▶ Legal counselling
▶ Vacation cabins

Executives often receive free memberships in fitness clubs as part of their compensation packages.

PHOTODISC

professionals note several challenges facing executive compensation, including (1) performance measurement techniques that reflect individual contributions and (2) executive compensation practices that will support global value-creating strategies with well-considered incentive pay programs. Hard questions to be answered include "What exactly are the implications of global competitiveness and the corresponding strategies required to improve Canadian corporations' effectiveness?" and "How do these new strategies affect organizations and their compensation systems?"

GROUP INCENTIVE PLANS

The emphasis on cost reduction and total quality management has led many organizations to implement a variety of group incentive plans.[35] Group plans enable employees to share in the benefits of improved efficiency realized by major organizational units or various individual work teams. These plans encourage a cooperative—rather than individualistic—spirit among all employees and reward them for their total contribution to the organization. Such features are particularly desirable when working conditions make individual performance difficult, if not impossible, to measure.

Team Compensation

As production has become more automated, as teamwork and coordination among workers have become more important, and as the contributions of those engaged indirectly in production or service tasks have increased, team incentive plans have grown more popular. **Team incentive plans** reward team members with an incentive bonus when agreed-upon performance standards are met or exceeded. Furthermore, the incentive will seek to establish a psychological climate that fosters team cooperation.

One catch with setting team compensation is that not all teams are alike (see Chapter 3). For example, cross-functional teams, self-directed teams, and task force teams make it impossible to develop one consistent type of team incentive plan. And, with a variety of teams, managers find it difficult to adopt uniform measurement standards or payout formulas for team pay.[36] According to Steven Gross, Hay manager, "Each type of team requires a specific pay structure to function at its peak."

In spite of this caveat, organizations typically use the three-step approach to establishing team incentive payments.[37] First, they set performance measures upon which incentive payments are based. Improvements in efficiency, product quality, or reduction in materials or labour costs are common benchmark criteria. For example, if labour costs for a team represent 30 percent of the organization's sales dollars, and the organization pays a bonus for labour cost savings, then whenever team labour costs are less than 30 percent of sales dollars, those savings are paid as an incentive bonus to team members. Information on the size of the incentive bonus is reported to employees on a weekly or monthly basis, explaining why incentive pay was or was not earned. Second, the size of the incentive bonus must be determined. Figure 10.4 presents the commonly stated advantages and disadvantages of team incentive pay.

Team incentive plan
Compensation plan in which all team members receive an incentive bonus payment when production or service standards are met or exceeded

| Figure 10.4 | The Pros and Cons of Team Incentive Plans |

Pros

▶ Team incentives support group planning and problem solving, thereby building a team culture.

▶ The contributions of individual employees depend on group cooperation.

▶ Unlike incentive plans based solely on output, team incentives can broaden the scope of the contribution that employees are motivated to make.

▶ Team bonuses tend to reduce employee jealousies and complaints over "tight" or "loose" individual standards.

▶ Team incentives encourage cross-training and the acquiring of new interpersonal competencies.

Cons

▶ Individual team members may perceive that "their" efforts contribute little to team success or to the attainment of the incentive bonus.

▶ Intergroup social problems—pressure to limit performance (for example, team members are afraid one individual may make the others look bad) and the "free-ride" effect (one individual puts in less effort than others but shares equally in team rewards)—may arise.

▶ Complex payout formulas can be difficult for team members to understand.

Gainsharing Incentive Plans

objective 5

Gainsharing plans
Programs under which both employees and the organization share financial gains according to a predetermined formula that reflects improved productivity and profitability

Gainsharing plans are organizational programs designed to increase productivity or decrease labour costs and share monetary gains with employees.[38] These plans are based on a mathematical formula that compares a baseline of performance with actual productivity during a given period. When productivity exceeds the baseline, an agreed-upon savings is shared with employees. Inherent in gainsharing is the idea that involved employees will improve productivity through more effective use of organizational resources.

Although productivity can be measured in various ways, it is usually calculated as a ratio of outputs to inputs. Sales, pieces produced, pounds, total standard costs, direct labour dollars earned, and customer orders are common output measures. Inputs frequently measured include materials, labour, energy, inventory, purchased goods or services, and total costs. An increase in productivity is normally gained when

▶ greater output is obtained with less or equal input.
▶ equal production output is obtained with less input.

Although gainsharing is a popular reward system for employees, experience with these techniques has pointed up a number of factors that contribute to either their success or their failure. Highlights in HRM 10.5 discusses common considerations when establishing a gainsharing program.[39]

Highlights in HRM 10.5

LESSONS LEARNED: DESIGNING EFFECTIVE GAINSHARING PROGRAMS

Will your gainsharing program be successful? While there are no exact keys to success, gainsharing proponents cite the following as important components of a meaningful gainsharing plan.

▶ Enlist *total* managerial support for the gainsharing effort. While top-management support is critical, without the encouragement of middle and lower-level managers (those directly involved in program implementation), gainsharing efforts invariably fail.

▶ When developing new programs, include representatives from all groups affected by the gainsharing effort—labour, management, employees. Inclusion, not exclusion, serves to build trust and understanding of the program's intent and operation.

▶ Prevent political gamesmanship whereby involved parties are more interested in preserving their self-interests than in supporting the group effort. The political manipulation of the bonus calculation to hold down payouts is a certain obstacle to all gainsharing programs.

▶ Bonus payout formulas must be seen as fair, must be easy for employees to calculate, must offer payouts on a frequent basis, and must be large enough to encourage future employee effort. The goal is to create a pay-for-performance environment.

▶ Establish effective, fair, and precise measurement standards. Standards must encourage increased effort without being unreasonable.

▶ Be certain that employees are predisposed to a gainsharing reward system. Is there a "cultural readiness" for gainsharing? If changes are indicated, what needs to be done? Will employees need additional skills training or training in other competencies in order to make anticipated organizational improvements?

▶ Launch the plan during a favourable business period. Business downturns jeopardize payments. A plan is likely to fail if it does not pay out under normal conditions in its first two or three years of operation.

There are four unique gainsharing plans. Two plans, which bear the names of their originators, Joe Scanlon and Alan Rucker, are similar in their philosophy. Both plans emphasize participative management. Both encourage cost reduction by sharing with employees any savings resulting from these reductions. The formulas on which the bonuses are based, however, are somewhat different. The third plan, Improshare, is a gainsharing program based on the number of finished goods that employee work teams complete in an established period. The fourth plan, earnings-at-risk, encourages employees to achieve higher output and quality standards by placing a portion of their base salary at risk of loss.

The Scanlon Plan

Scanlon Plan

Bonus incentive plan using employee and management committees to gain cost-reduction improvements

The philosophy behind the **Scanlon Plan** is that employees should offer ideas and suggestions to improve productivity and, in turn, be rewarded for their constructive efforts. The plan requires good management, leadership, trust and respect between employees and managers, and a workforce dedicated to responsible decision making. When correctly implemented, the Scanlon Plan can result in improved efficiency and profitability for the organization and steady employment and high compensation for employees.

According to Scanlon's proponents, effective employee participation, which includes the use of committees on which employees are represented, is the most significant feature of the Scanlon Plan. This gives employees the opportunity to communicate their ideas and opinions and to exercise some degree of influence over decisions affecting their work and their welfare within the organization. Figure 10.5 illustrates the Scanlon Plan suggestion process, including the duties and responsibilities of two important groups—the *shop* and *screening* committees.

Financial incentives under the Scanlon Plan are ordinarily offered to all employees (a significant feature of the plan) on the basis of an established formula. This formula is based on increases in employee productivity as

USING THE INTERNET

For information about the Scanlon plan, go to

www.scanlonleader.com.

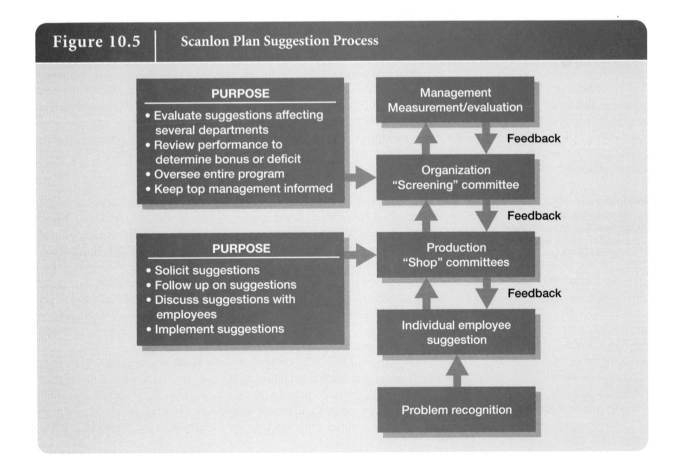

Figure 10.5   Scanlon Plan Suggestion Process

PURPOSE
- Evaluate suggestions affecting several departments
- Review performance to determine bonus or deficit
- Oversee entire program
- Keep top management informed

Management Measurement/evaluation

Feedback

Organization "Screening" committee

Feedback

PURPOSE
- Solicit suggestions
- Follow up on suggestions
- Discuss suggestions with employees
- Implement suggestions

Production "Shop" committees

Feedback

Individual employee suggestion

Problem recognition

determined by a norm that has been established for labour costs. The plan also provides for the establishment of a reserve fund into which 25 percent of any earned bonus is paid to cover deficits during the months when labour costs exceed the norm.

The Rucker Plan

Rucker Plan
Bonus incentive plan based on the historic relationship between the total earnings of hourly employees and the production value created by the employees

The share-of-production plan (SOP), or **Rucker Plan,** normally covers just production workers but may be expanded to cover all employees. As with the Scanlon Plan, committees are formed to elicit and evaluate employee suggestions. The Rucker Plan, however, uses a far less elaborate participatory structure. As one authority noted, "It commonly represents a type of program that is used as an alternative to the Scanlon Plan in firms attempting to move from a traditional style of management toward a higher level of employee involvement."

The financial incentive of the Rucker Plan is based on the historic relationship between the total earnings of hourly employees and the production value that employees create. The bonus is based on any improvement in this relationship that employees are able to realize. Thus, for every 1 percent increase in production value that is achieved, workers receive a bonus of 1 percent of their total payroll costs.[40]

Lessons from the Scanlon and Rucker Plans

Perhaps the most important lesson to be learned from the Scanlon and Rucker Plans is that any management expecting to gain the cooperation of its employees in improving efficiency must permit them to become involved psychologically as well as financially in the organization. If employees are to contribute maximum effort, they must have a feeling of involvement and identification with their organization, which does not come out of the traditional manager-subordinate relationship. Consequently, it is important for organizations to realize that while employee cooperation is essential to the successful administration of the Scanlon and Rucker Plans, the plans themselves do not necessarily stimulate this cooperation. Furthermore, the attitude of management is of paramount importance to the success of either plan. For example, where managers show little confidence and trust in their employees, the plans tend to fail.

Improshare

Improshare
Gainsharing program under which bonuses are based on the overall productivity of the work team

Improshare—improved productivity through sharing—is a gainsharing program developed by Mitchell Fain, an industrial engineer with experience in traditional individual incentive systems. Whereas individual production bonuses are typically based on how much an employee produces above some standard amount, Improshare bonuses are based on the overall productivity of the *work team*. Improshare output is measured by the number of finished products that a work team produces in a given period. Both production (direct) employees and nonproduction (indirect) employees are included in the determination of the bonus.[41] Since a cooperative environment benefits all, Improshare promotes increased interaction and support between employees and management.

The bonus is based not on dollar savings, as in the Scanlon and Rucker Plans, but on productivity gains that result from reducing the time it takes to produce a finished product. Bonuses are determined monthly by calculating the difference between standard hours (Improshare hours) and actual hours, and dividing the result by actual hours. The employees and the company each receive payment for 50 percent of the improvement. Companies such as Hinderliter Energy Equipment Corporation pay the bonus as a separate cheque to emphasize that it is extra income.

Earnings-at-Risk Plans

Earnings-at-risk incentive plans

Incentive pay plans placing a portion of the employee's base pay at risk, but giving the opportunity to earn income above base pay when goals are met or exceeded

As the name implies, **earnings-at-risk incentive plans** place a portion of an employee's base pay at risk.[42] The philosophy behind these programs is that employees should not expect substantial rewards without assuming some risk for their performance. These plans, however, allow employees to recapture lower wages, or reap additional income above full base pay when quality, service, or productivity goals are met or exceeded. An employee's base pay might be set at 90 percent (that is, 10 percent below market value—the risk part), the loss to be regained through performance. For example, at Saturn Corporation, employee total compensation is made up of base pay, risk pay, and reward pay. The risk/reward incentive encourages team members to continuously improve job performance. The risk portion of pay requires that 12 percent of base pay be withheld until specific organizational performance goals are met. When these goals are achieved, the money withheld is paid back in a quarterly lump sum. The reward portion of compensation is paid only if the risk goals are met. The maximum achievable reward is $12 500. Production rewards are paid quarterly and profitability rewards are paid annually.

ENTERPRISE INCENTIVE PLANS

Enterprise incentive plans differ from individual and group incentive plans in that all organizational members participate in the plan's compensation payout. Enterprise incentive plans reward employees on the basis of the success of the organization over an extended time period—normally one year, but the period can be longer. Enterprise incentive plans seek to create a "culture of ownership" by fostering a philosophy of cooperation and teamwork among all organizational members. Common enterprise incentive plans include profit-sharing, stock options, and employee stock ownership plans (ESOPs).

Profit-Sharing Plans

Profit sharing

Any procedure by which an employer pays, or makes available to all regular employees, in addition to base pay, special current or deferred sums based on the profits of the enterprise

Probably no incentive plan has been the subject of more widespread interest, attention, and misunderstanding than profit sharing. **Profit sharing** is any procedure by which an employer pays, or makes available to all regular employees, special current or deferred sums based on the organization's profits. As defined here, profit sharing represents cash payments made to eligible employees at designated time periods, as distinct from profit sharing in the form of contributions to employee pension funds.

Profit-sharing plans are intended to give employees the opportunity to increase their earnings by contributing to the growth of their organization's profits. These contributions may be directed toward improving product quality, reducing operating costs, improving work methods, and building goodwill rather than just increasing rates of production. Profit sharing can help stimulate employees to think and feel more like partners in the enterprise and thus to concern themselves with the welfare

Lincoln Electronic's website provides a description of its incentive management system at

www.lincolnelectric.com/corporate/career/default.asp

of the organization as a whole. Its purpose therefore is to motivate a total commitment from employees rather than simply to have them contribute in specific areas.

A popular example of a highly successful profit-sharing plan is the one in use at Lincoln Electric Company, a manufacturer of arc welding equipment and supplies. This plan was started in 1934 by J.F. Lincoln, president of the company. Each year the company distributes a large percentage of its profits to employees in accordance with their salary level and merit ratings. In recent years the annual bonus has ranged from a low of 55 percent to a high of 115 percent of annual wages. In addition, Lincoln's program includes a piecework plan with a guarantee, cash awards for employee suggestions, a guarantee of employment for thirty hours of the forty-hour work week, and an employee stock purchase plan.

The success of Lincoln Electric's incentive system depends on a high level of contribution by each employee. The performance evaluations employees receive twice a year are based on four factors—dependability, quality, output, and ideas and cooperation. There is a high degree of respect among employees and management for Lincoln's organizational goals and for the profit-sharing program.

Variations in Profit-Sharing Plans

Profit-sharing plans differ in the proportion of profits shared with employees and in the distribution and form of payment. The amount shared with employees may range from 5 to 50 percent of the net profit. In most plans, however, about 20 to 25 percent of the net profit is shared. Profit distributions may be made to all employees on an equal basis, or they may be based on regular salaries or some formula that takes into account seniority and/or merit. The payments may be disbursed in cash, deferred, or made on the basis of combining the two forms of payments.

Weaknesses of Profit-Sharing Plans

In spite of their potential advantages, profit-sharing plans are also prone to certain weaknesses. The profits shared with employees may be the result of inventory speculation, climatic factors, economic conditions, national emergencies, or other factors over which employees have no control. Conversely, losses may occur during years when employee contributions have been at a maximum. The fact that profit-sharing payments are made only once a year or deferred until retirement may reduce their motivational value. If a plan fails to pay off for several years in a row, this can have an adverse effect on productivity and employee morale.

Stock Options

Stock option programs are sometimes implemented as part of an employee benefit plan or as part of a corporate culture linking employee effort to stock performance. However, organizations that offer stock option programs to employees do so with the belief that there is some incentive value to the systems. By allowing employees to purchase stock, the organization hopes they will increase their productivity, assume a partnership role in the organization, and thus cause the stock price to rise.[43] Furthermore, stock option programs have become a popular way to boost morale of disenfranchised employees caught in mergers, acquisitions, and downsizing. The number of Canadian companies granting stock options to non-executive personnel has more than doubled from 25 percent to 59 percent from 1997 to 2002.[44]

Stock option plans grant to employees the right to purchase a specific number of shares of the company's stock at a guaranteed price (the option price) during a designated time period. Although there are many types of options, most are granted at the stock's fair market value. Not uncommon are plans for purchasing stock through payroll deductions.

Unfortunately, in the wake of the Enron Corporation collapse, employee stock option plans have come under attack (see "Bases for Executive Long-Term Incentives" earlier in this chapter).[45] Criticism largely focuses on executive abuses and faulty accounting procedures. Roger Martin, dean of the Rotman School of Management, University of Toronto, has called for an abolition of stock options.[46] Fortunately, stock options continue to be a popular and effective way to pay for the performance of employees and managers. What is needed for options is reform, not abolition.

Employee Stock Ownership Plans (ESOPs)

objective 7

Employee stock ownership plans (ESOPs)
Stock plans in which an organization contributes shares of its stock to an established trust for the purpose of stock purchases by its employees

Canadian Tire and Sears Canada have established **employee stock ownership plans (ESOPs)**—stock plans in which an organization contributes shares of its stock to an established trust for the purpose of stock purchases by its employees. Companies such as Canadian Pacific Express and Transport have been rescued by ESOP-financed employee buyouts, and Polaroid and Chevron have used ESOPs to fight hostile takeover bids. These plans take two primary forms: a stock bonus plan and a leveraged plan.[47] With a stock bonus plan, each year the organization gives stock to the ESOP or gives cash to the ESOP to buy outstanding stock. The ESOP holds the stock for employees, and they are routinely informed of the value of their accounts. Stock allocations can be based on employee wages or seniority. When employees leave the organization or retire, they can sell their stock back to the organization, or they can sell it on the open market if it is traded publicly.

Advantages of ESOPs

Employers use ESOPs to provide retirement benefits for their employees. ESOPs can also increase employees' pride of ownership in the organization, providing an incentive for them to increase productivity and help the organization prosper and grow. Federal support for ESOPs is available through labour-sponsored venture capital funds. Employees who invest in labour funds are eligible for a 30 percent federal tax credit on their investment (the maximum yearly investment is $3500). There is no federal legislation in Canada that deals exclusively with employee share ownership; the legislation that governs deferred profit sharing plans (DPSPs) and employee stock options is used as a guide. The hope is that these plans will increase productivity, improve employee-management relations, and promote economic justice.

Problems with ESOPs

Generally, ESOPs are more likely to serve their intended purposes in publicly held companies than in privately held ones. A major problem with the privately held company is its potential inability to pay back the stock of employees when they retire. These employees do not have the alternative of disposing of their stock on the open market. Even large organizations, such as Air Canada, Nortel, and Algoma Steel, have suffered financial difficulties that have lowered the value of the companies' stocks and, thus, the value of the employees' retirement plans. Requiring organizations to establish a sinking fund to be used exclusively for repurchasing stock could eliminate this problem.

Other problems with ESOPs include the following:

▶ The more an employee's pension is based on an ESOP, the more the eventual payout is going to depend on the price of the company's stock. Future retirees are vulnerable to stock market fluctuations as well as to management mistakes.

▶ Traditional pension plans are guaranteed by legislation. ESOP contributions are not. So employee pensions could vanish if the company does, or even if it simply suffers setbacks.

▶ When all pension funds are allocated to the company's stock, employees can no longer diversify their retirement options—a basic principle of investing. The risk for employees is that the ESOP will be worthless if the employer fails.[48]

Finally, though studies show that productivity improves when ESOPs are implemented, these gains are not guaranteed. ESOPs help little unless managers are willing to involve employees in organizational decision making. Unfortunately, ESOPs are sometimes set up in ways that restrict employees' access to decision making and that expose the ESOP to risk.

The effectiveness of incentive pay to meet the HR and corporate objectives is described in The Business Case.

The Business Case

ORGANIZATIONAL BENEFITS OF INCENTIVE PLANS

Incentive pay is a strategic tool used most often to attract and retain employees and to improve organizational outcomes. Organizations pay an average of 9 percent of total payroll dollars on variable compensation programs. Is this money well spent?

1. Four out of five organizations report that incentive compensation is an effective tool for attracting and retaining employees.

2. About one-third of employers reported that compensation had a positive effect on operating results. In another study, retail stores that used the Scanlon Plan had higher sales performance, more favourable customer satisfaction scores, and lower turnover than a control group. Higher-performing companies are more likely to provide stock options and feel strongly that these options influence behaviour among professional ranks. The offering of stock options is associated with improved company performance, as a Watson Wyatt study found that the more a CEO makes, the better the company performs financially.

Sources: D. Scott, WorldatWork, "Survey of Compensation Policies and Practices," www.worldatwork.org/research, March 2003; D. Scott, J. Floyd, P.G. Benson, and J.W. Bishop, "The Impact of the Scanlon Plan on Retail Store Performance," *WorldatWork Journal* 11, no. 3 (Third Quarter, 2002); D.J. Gherson, "Getting the Pay Thing Right," *Workspan* 43, no. 6 (June 2000); K.H. Van Neek and J.E. Smilko, "Variable Pay Plans," *WorldatWork Journal* 11, no. 4 (Fourth Quarter 2002).

SUMMARY

The success of an incentive pay plan depends on the organizational climate in which it must operate, employee confidence in it, and its suitability to employee and organizational needs. Importantly, employees must view their incentive pay as being equitable and related to their performance. Performance measures should be quantifiable, be easily understood, and bear a demonstrated relationship to organizational performance.

Piecework plans pay employees a given rate for each unit satisfactorily completed. Employers implement these plans when output is easily measured and when the production process is fairly standardized. Bonuses are incentive payments above base wages paid on either an individual or team basis. A bonus is offered to encourage employees to exert greater effort. Standard hour plans establish a standard time for job completion. An incentive is paid for finishing the job in less than the pre-established time. These plans are popular for jobs with a fixed time for completion.

Merit raises will not serve to motivate employees when they are seen as entitlements, which occurs when these raises are given yearly without regard to changes in employee performance. Merit raises are not motivational when they are given because of seniority or favouritism or when merit budgets are inadequate to sufficiently reward employee performance. To be motivational, merit raises must be such that employees see a clear relationship between pay and performance and the salary increase must be large enough to exceed inflation and higher income taxes.

Salespeople may be compensated by a straight salary, a combination of salary and commission, or a commission only. Paying employees a straight salary allows them to focus on tasks other than sales, such as service and customer goodwill. A straight commission plan causes employees to emphasize sales goals. A combination of salary and commission provides the advantages of both the straight salary and the straight commission form of payments.

The Scanlon, Rucker, Improshare, and earnings-at-risk gainshare plans pay bonuses to employees unrelated to profit levels. Each of these plans encourages employees to maximize their performance and cooperation through suggestions offered to improve organizational performance. The Scanlon Plan pays an employee a bonus based on saved labour cost measured against the organization's sales value of production. The bonus under the Rucker Plan is based on any improvement in the relationship between the total earnings of hourly employees and the value of production that employees create. The Improshare bonus is paid when employees increase production output above a given target level. With earnings-at-risk programs, employees earn bonuses when production quotas are met or exceeded, as well as wages that had been put at risk.

Profit-sharing plans pay to employees sums of money based on the organization's profits. Cash payments are made to eligible employees at specified times, normally yearly. The primary purpose of profit sharing is to provide employees with additional income through their participation in organizational achievement. Employee commitment to improved productivity, quality, and customer service will contribute to organizational success and, in turn, to their compensation. Profit-sharing plans may not achieve their stated gains when employee performance is unrelated to organizational success or failure. This may occur because of economic conditions, other competition, or environmental conditions. Profit-sharing plans can have a negative effect on employee morale when plans fail to consistently reward employees.

With a stock bonus ESOP, each year the organization contributes stock or cash to buy stock that is then placed in an ESOP trust. With a leveraged ESOP, the organization borrows money from a lending institution to purchase stock for the trust. With either plan, the ESOP holds the stock for employees until they either retire or leave the company, at which time the stock is sold back to the company or through a brokerage firm. Employers receive tax benefits for qualified

ESOPs; they also hope to receive their employees' commitment to organizational improvement. Employees, however, may lose their retirement income should the company fail or stock prices fall. Another drawback to ESOPs is that they are not guaranteed by any federal agency.

KEY TERMS

bonus 429

combined salary and commission plan 434

differential piece rate 427

earnings-at-risk incentive plans 447

employee stock ownership plans (ESOPs) 449

gainsharing plans 443

Improshare 446

lump-sum merit program 431

merit guidelines 431

perquisites 439

profit sharing 447

Rucker Plan 446

Scanlon Plan 445

spot bonus 430

standard hour plan 429

straight commission plan 434

straight piecework 427

straight salary plan 433

team incentive plan 442

variable pay 423

DISCUSSION QUESTIONS

1. Working individually or in groups, identify the factors for a successful incentive plan.

2. Contrast the differences between straight piecework, differential piece rate, and standard hour plans. Explain where each plan might best be used.

3. A frequently heard complaint about merit raises is that they do little to increase employee effort. What are the causes of this belief? Suggest ways in which the motivating value of merit raises may be increased.

4. What are the reasons behind the different payment methods for sales employees?

5. What are the reasons for the success of the Scanlon and Rucker Plans?

6. Because of competitive forces within your industry, you have decided to implement a profit-sharing plan for your employees. Discuss the advantages of profit sharing and identify specific characteristics that will assure success for your plan.

7. What are some of the reasons for the rapid growth of ESOPs? Cite some of the potential problems concerning their use.

Developing Managerial Skills

AWARDING SALARY INCREASES

Since pay-for-performance is an important factor governing salary increases, managers must be able to defend the compensation recommendations they make for their employees. Merit raises granted under a pay-for-performance policy must be based on objective appraisals if they are to achieve their intended purposes of rewarding outstanding employee performance. As managers know, however, other factors that can affect salary recommendations must be dealt with. These may include the opinions of the employee's peers or extenuating circumstances such as illness or family responsibilities. The purpose of this exercise is to provide you with the experience of granting salary increases to employees based on their work performance and other information.

Assignment

Following are the work records of five employees. As their supervisor, you have just completed their annual appraisal reviews and it is now time to make recommendations for their future salaries. Your department budget has $8000 allocated for salary increases. Distribute the $8000 among your employees based on the descriptions for each subordinate.

a. Janet Jenkins currently earns $35 000. Her performance appraisal rating was very high. She is respected by her peers and is felt to be an asset to the work group. She is divorced and has three young children to support.

b. Russell Watts earns a salary of $32 000. His annual performance appraisal was average. Several members of the work group have spoken to you about the difficulty involved in Russell's job. They feel that it is a tough and demanding job and that he is doing his best.

c. Jack Perkins earns $33 000. His performance appraisal was below average and he seems to have difficulty adjusting to his co-workers. Jack has had a difficult time this past year. His wife passed away early in the year and his father has recently been diagnosed as terminally ill.

d. Rick Jacobson earns $32 000. His performance appraisal was above average. He is respected by his peers and is generally considered to be a "good guy."

e. Paula Merrill earns $32 000. Her performance appraisal was very high. Her peers are upset because they feel that she is working only to provide a second income. Moreover, her peers see her as trying to "show them up."

Share your results with other class members. Be prepared to explain your allocation of money.

Case Study 1

Counter-Productive Compensation

I started worrying about the corrupting influence of incentive schemes, when in a period of one month, I was asked by three employees at three different companies to help them achieve their bonuses. The first case happened after I purchased a car and was asked by the sales representative to complete an evaluation form and give him high ratings so that he would get his bonus. The second instance took place after I had another car serviced and was told by the mechanic that I would be contacted by an agency that conducted independent ratings on employee performance, and that I had better rate him as a "10" because no other mark would get him the bonus. Then, a few days later, I wanted to move some money from one bank to another bank where I could receive a higher interest rate. I was asked by the financial advisor to delay the transfer of my money until the following month (even though it would cost me money) because her bonus was calculated at the end of the month.

Apparently my experience is not unique. At one company, employees were given a small bonus for every voluntary and spontaneous complementary letter received about their performance. Of course, employees began asking clients to send them these types of letters.

Incentives may create conflict between the best interests of employees and the best interests of customers. In order to receive commissions and bonuses, many employees engage in unethical conduct. According to one study, almost half of the respondents, who were sales personnel, had lied on a sales call, a third have made unrealistic promises, and about one-fifth had sold products that customers did not need. Another study reported that employees working in call centres, whose performance targets included handling a customer in 10 seconds, would "accidentally" disconnect those who spoke English poorly (and thus slowed the call). Sears had introduced commissions for auto-service employees, and employees began to cheat to meet their quotas. An undercover investigation revealed that customers were being charged for unnecessary repairs.

Source: Adapted from M. Choquette, "Compensation That Corrupts," *The Conference Board of Canada*, 1999: 254–99.

QUESTIONS

1. Have you ever been asked to help an employee achieve a commission or bonus? How did you feel? How did you react?

2. Many employees feel that their performance goals are unrealistic, and the pressure to meet these goals increases the probability that they will cheat. How could this problem be prevented?

3. The Royal Bank Financial Group had an incentive program whereby employees would receive a fee for referring clients across the various business units. Before starting the program the bank held focus groups to deal with the ethical implications. As a result, they have developed guidelines as to what qualifies as an appropriate referral and instituted measures to protect client privacy. What other measures could you, as an HR professional, recommend to an organization so as to minimize unethical behaviour triggered by an incentive compensation scheme?

Case Study 2

Pay-for-Performance: The Merit Question

In January 1998, the Centennial Hospital implemented a formal performance appraisal program for its 127 staff nurses. The program originally met with some resistance from a few nurses and supervisors, but generally the system was welcomed as an objective way to appraise nursing performance. Complaints centred on the increase in time it took to complete the appraisal review process and the fact that supervisors disliked having to confront nurses who disagreed with their performance review. Nursing supervisors are required to appraise employee performance annually and to forward to the HR department a copy of each appraisal form.

In July 2002, Thomas Tittle, HR manager for the hospital, reviewed all nurses' appraisals on file since the beginning of the program. From this study he concluded that the large majority (82 percent) of nurses were evaluated as performing at an "average" level, as indicated by a global rating at the bottom of the form. Approximately 10 percent were rated "above average" or "superior," and the remainder received "below standard" performance reviews. As a response to these findings, Tittle decided to base the annual raise for all nurses on the consumer price index for the hospital's metropolitan area. This, he concluded, would allow the nurses to maintain their standard of living while guaranteeing all nurses a yearly raise.

As part of the hospital's employee involvement program, Tittle holds quarterly meetings with groups of employees to solicit their feelings regarding hospital policy and their jobs. Both positive and negative opinions are expressed at these gatherings. These opinions are used to modify hospital policy. At meetings in the past year, a number of both junior and senior nurses have expressed dissatisfaction with the across-the-board pay policy for annual raises. The biggest complaint concerns the lack of motivation to increase output, since all nurses are paid the same regardless of individual performance. These comments have been numerous enough that Tittle has considered changing the nurses' compensation policy. During the past seven months, nine of the better nurses have quit to take jobs with area hospitals that award annual increases on a merit or pay-for-performance basis.

QUESTIONS

1. What are the advantages of adopting a merit pay plan for hospital nurses? Are there any disadvantages to starting a merit pay program?

2. What problems might arise with a supervisor's appraisals of nurses?

3. Develop a merit pay guideline chart based on the following levels of performance evaluation: superior, above average, average, below average, and poor. Use current cost-of-living figures for your area or salary survey data available to you to guide your merit percentage increases.

4. It is not uncommon for hospital nurses to work in teams. Explain how a team-based incentive program for nurses might be developed. What criteria might be used to evaluate team performance?

CAREER COUNSEL

Take the incentive survey on the *Managing Human Resources* website to discover what motivates you in your career: www.belcourt4e.nelson.com

NOTES AND REFERENCES

1. Christian M. Ellis and Cynthia L. Paluso, "Blazing a Trail to Broad-Based Incentives," *WorldatWork Journal* 9, no. 4 (Fourth Quarter 2000): 33–41.

2. Michelle Conlin and Robert Berner, "A Little Less in the Envelope This Week," *Business Week* (February 18, 2002): 64.

3. Sam T. Johnson, "Plan Your Organization's Reward Strategy through Pay-for-Performance Dynamics," *Compensation and Benefits Review* 30, no. 3 (May–June 1998): 67–72; J. Handel, "Variable Pay Highlights Year in Comparison," *Workspan* 44, no. 9 (September 2001).

4. Gerald E. Ledford and Elizabeth J. Hawk, "Compensation Strategy: A Guide for Senior Managers," *American Compensation Journal* 9, no. 1 (First Quarter 2000): 28–38. See also Gene Kortez, "Pay Perks Cloud the Crystal Ball," *Business Week* (September 10, 2001): 34.

5. Martha Frase-Blunt, "What Goes Up May Come Down," *HRMagazine* 46, no. 8 (August 2001): 85–90.

6. Christian M. Ellis, "Improving the Impact of Performance Management," *Workspan* 45, no. 2 (February 2002): 7–8.

7. Gregory A. Stoskopf, "Taking Performance Management to the Next Level," *Workspan* 45, no. 2 (February 2002): 26–31.

8. Ellis and Paluso, "Blazing a Trail to Broad-Based Incentives."

9. George T. Milkovich and Jerry M. Newman, *Compensation Management*, 7th ed. (Boston: McGraw-Hill Irwin, 2002): 317.

10. Milkovich and Newman, *Compensation Management*, 313.

11. Debra L. Nelson and James Quick, *Organizational Behavior*, 4th ed. (Mason, OH: South-Western Publishing, 2003).

12. Robert Vecchio, *Organizational Behavior*, 5th ed. (Mason, OH: South-Western Publishing, 2002).

13. Chad Albrecht and Mike O'Hara, "It's Not All Relative: Pitting Quotas against Other Incentive Plans to Motivate Sales Performance," *WorldatWork Journal* 10, no. 3 (Third Quarter 2001): 59–67.

14. Bill Gauthier, "The Sales Compensation Challenge: Meeting the Diverse Needs of Multiple Business Units," *Workspan* 45, no. 3 (March 2002): 34–38.

15. Brad Brown, "Rewarding Results: The Road to Sales Compensation Excellence," *Workspan* 45, no. 1 (January 2002): 26–32.

16. Tory Parks, "Fighting an Uphill Battle: Motivating a Sales Force in Tough Times," *Workspan* 45, no. 4 (April 2002): 64–67.

17. David Fiedler, "Should You Adjust Your Sales Compensation?" *HRMagazine* 47, no. 2 (February 2002): 79–82.

18. Lisa J. Riley and Arthur Anderson, "Little Things Make a Big Difference," *Workspan* 44, no. 5 (May 2001): 56–61.

19. Louis Lavelle, "The Artificial Sweetener in CEO Pay," *Business Week* (September 10, 2001): 102.

20. Steve Bates, "Executive Compensation: Salad Day May Be Over," *HRMagazine* 47, no. 1 (January 2002): 12. See also Lynn Miller, "Companies Rein in Rising Salaries—Especially for Execs," *HRMagazine* 46, no. 7 (July 2001): 16.

21. William Gerard Sanders, "Incentive Alignment, CEO Pay Level, and Firm Performance: A Case of 'Heads I Win, Tails You Lose'?" *Human Resource Management* 40, no. 2 (Summer 2001): 159–70.

22. Richard Long, *Compensation in Canada: Strategy, Practices and Issues* (Toronto: ITP Nelson, 1998): 338.

23. Scott M. Ross and Martin J. Sonelofske, "Reconsidering Stock Options for Private Companies," *WorldatWork Journal* 10, no. 2 (Second Quarter 2001): 59–63.

24. Bentham W. Stradley and Scott N. Olsen, "Options Aren't the Only Long-Term Incentive Option," *WorldatWork Journal* 10, no. 2 (Second Quarter 2001): 12–17.

25. Alison Stein Wellner, "Golden Handcuffs," *HRMagazine* 45, no. 10 (October 2000): 129–36; B. Crichely, "For Employees at the Bank of Montreal, December Can't Come Quickly Enough," *National Post*, December 5, 2002: 8.

26. Michael J. Butler, "The Worldwide Growth of the Employee Ownership Phenomenon," *WorldatWork Journal* 10, no. 2 (Second Quarter 2001): 32–36. See also Gerald E. Ledford, Jr., David Harper, and Jennifer Schuler, "Beyond Plain Vanilla: New Flavors in Stock Option Use," *WorldatWork Journal* 10, no. 2 (Second Quarter 2001): 38–43.

27. Reported in *Business Week* (May 6, 2002): 70.

28. Andrew Willis, "Sky Chefs Mid-managers Become Millionaires," *The Globe and Mail*, June 6, 2001: B1, B6.

29. Aaron Lucchetti, "Restricting Options: Key Fund Manager Gets Tough on Issues of Executive Pay," *The Wall Street Journal*, April 15, 2002, C1.

30. Louis Lavelle and Frederick F. Jespersen, "Executive Pay," *Business Week* (April 15, 2002): 80–86.

31. Long, *Compensation in Canada: Strategy, Practice and Issues*: 254.

32. John A. Byrne, "How to Fix Corporate Governance," *Business Week* (May 6, 2002): 72.

33. Janet McFarland, "Executives Saw Bonuses Slide," *The Globe and Mail*, May 1, 2003: B3.

34. Joann S. Lublin, "Under the Radar," *The Wall Street Journal*, April 22, 2002: B7.

35. Jerry McAdams and Elizabeth J. Hawk, "Making Group Incentive Plans Work," *WorldatWork Journal* 9, no. 3 (Third Quarter 2002): 28–34.

36. Milkovich and Newman, *Compensation Management*, 323.

37. Steven E. Gross, *Compensation for Teams* (New York: American Management Association, 1996).

38. Robert Mangel and Michael Useen, "The Strategic Role of Gainsharing," *Journal of Labor Research* 21, no. 2 (Spring 2000): 327–43.

39. Claire Ginther, "Incentive Programs That Really Work," *HRMagazine* 45, no. 8 (August 2000): 117–20.

40. The Rucker Plan uses a somewhat more complex formula for determining employee bonuses. For a detailed example of the Rucker bonus, see Milkovich and Newman, *Compensation*, 329.

41. The standard of Improshare's measurement system is the base productivity factor (BPF), which is the ratio of standard direct labour hours produced to total actual hours worked in a base period. The productivity of subsequent periods is then measured by enlarging standard direct labour hours earned by the BPF ratio to establish Improshare hours (IH). The IH is then compared with actual hours worked in the same period. If earned hours exceed actual hours, 50 percent of the gain is divided by actual hours worked to establish a bonus percentage for all employees in the plan.

42. Robert W. Renn, James R. Van Scotter, and W. Kevin Barksdale, "Earnings-at-Risk Incentive Plans: A Performance, Satisfaction and Turnover Dilemma," *Compensation and Benefits Review* 33, no. 4 (July–August 2001): 68–73.

43. "Don't Get Rid of Stock Options. Fix 'Em," *Business Week* (March 4, 2002): 120.

44. K. H. Van Neck and J. Smilko, "Variable Pay Plans," *WorldatWork Journal* 11, no. 4 (Fourth Quarter 2002).

45. Greg Hitt and Jacob M. Schlesinger, "Stock Options Come under Fire in Wake of Enron's Collapse," *The Wall Street Journal*, March 26, 2002: A1.

46. Burton G. Malkiel and William J. Baumol, "Stock Options Keep the Economy Afloat," *The Wall Street Journal*, April 4, 2002, A18; K. Hugessen, "Keep Options Open," *National Post*, February 13, 2003.

47. Regina Shanney-Saborsky, "ESOPs and the Employee Ownership Culture: Balancing Compensation and Equity Issues," *Compensation and Benefits Review* 32, no. 1 (January–February 2000): 72–80.

48. Ronald M. Mano and E. Devon Deppe, "The ESOP Fable: Employees Beware," *Compensation and Benefits Review* 26, no. 6 (November/December 1994): 44–48.

Employee Benefits

After studying this chapter, you should be able to

objective 1

Describe the characteristics of a sound benefits program.

objective 5

Describe those benefits that involve payment for time not worked.

objective 2

Indicate management concerns about the costs of employee benefits, and discuss ways to control those costs.

objective 6

Discuss recent trends in retirement policies and programs.

objective 3

Identify and explain the employee benefits required by law.

objective 7

Delineate the major factors involved in managing pension plans.

objective 4

Discuss ways to control the costs of health care programs.

objective 8

Describe the types of work-life benefits employers can provide.

W hat is the best-kept secret in Canada today? According to surveys, it is the hidden payroll, i.e., employee benefits. Compensation surveys indicate that most employees are unable to name accurately the benefits they receive, and about 50 percent of employees underestimate the value of their benefits.[1] Though benefits are largely undervalued and misidentified, they are still an important issue for both employers and employees. It is clear that benefits are not a "fringe" but rather an integral part of the compensation package. Additionally, since most benefits are provided voluntarily by employers, they become a significant cost and an employment advantage for employers, while providing needed psychological and physical assistance to employees. The importance of benefits to both sides cannot be overstated.

Virtually all employers provide a variety of benefits to supplement the wages or salaries they pay their workers. These benefits, some of which are required by law, must be considered a part of total compensation. Therefore, in this chapter we look at the characteristics of employee benefits programs. We will study the types of benefits required by law, the major discretionary benefits that employers offer, the employee services they provide, and the retirement programs in use. The chapter concludes with a discussion of popular and highly important work-life benefit programs.

BENEFITS PROGRAMS

objective

Employee benefits constitute an indirect form of compensation intended to improve the quality of work lives and personal lives of employees. As discussed later, benefits typically represent 40 percent of total payroll costs to employers.[2] In return, employers generally expect employees to be supportive of the organization and to be productive. Since employees have come to expect an increasing number of benefits, the motivational value of these benefits depends on how the benefits program is designed and communicated. Once viewed as a gift from the employer, benefits are now considered rights to which all employees are entitled.

HRIS and Employee Benefits

With the large number of benefits offered to employees today, administering an organization's benefits program can be both costly and time-consuming. Even for small employers with thirty to forty employees, keeping track of each employee's use of a benefit or request for a change of benefits can be cumbersome. For example, even rather straightforward tasks, such as monitoring employees' sick leave, become complex as the size of the organization grows.

Fortunately, interactive employee benefit systems are becoming mainstream for most employers. Employees at TransAlta Corporation in Calgary can obtain information about their pension plans and enroll in a flexible benefits plan by logging on to the company website whenever it is convenient for them. For the third of its employees without access to computers, TransAlta has installed kiosks on company premises. The benefits of an HRIS

USING THE INTERNET

A broad view of benefits in Canada can be found at

www.benefitscanada.ca.

Human Resources Information System (explained in Chapter 1) are reduced costs, increased efficiencies, and accuracy.[3] Online benefits programs create a form of self-service administration. One intent of online programs is to eliminate the annual open enrolment period for various benefits, thereby providing greater flexibility in benefits selection. An important advantage to an interactive benefits program is the significant savings in administration costs. Once an online system is operational, it is easy and inexpensive to adapt to employer and employee demands. However, while the Internet can be used effectively in benefits administration, security must always be a concern when transmitting benefits information.[4]

Perhaps no part of the HR function is more technologically advanced than benefits administration. A wide variety of commercially developed software packages have been developed that serve to facilitate benefits administration in such areas as pensions, variable pay, worker's compensation, health benefits, and time-off programs. Descriptions of and advertisements for a variety of benefits software programs are regularly found in HR journals such as *Canadian HR Reporter* and *Human Resource Professional*. Software programs represent a cost-effective way to manage employee benefits programs when employers lack the resources or expertise.

Requirements for a Sound Benefits Program

Too often, a particular benefit is provided because other employers are doing it, because someone in authority thinks it's a good idea, or because there is union pressure. However, the contributions that benefits will make to the HR program depend on how much attention is paid to certain basic considerations.

Strategic Benefit Planning

Like any other component of the HR program, an employee benefits program should be based on specific objectives. The objectives an organization establishes will depend on many factors, including the size of the firm; its location; its degree of unionization; its profitability; and industry patterns. Most important, these aims must be compatible with the organization's strategic compensation plan (see Chapter 9), including its philosophy and policies.

The chief objectives of most benefits programs are to

▶ Improve employee work satisfaction
▶ Meet employee health and security requirements
▶ Attract and motivate employees
▶ Reduce turnover
▶ Maintain a favourable competitive position

In a 2002 survey of job candidates who were hired, about half stated that the benefits plan was a factor in their decision to join the company, mainly because they did not want to worry about paying for health benefits not covered by their provincial plan.[5] Furthermore, these objectives must be considered within the framework of cost containment—a major issue in today's programs.

Unless the organization plans to develop a flexible benefits plan (to be discussed later), a uniform package of benefits should be developed. This involves carefully considering the various benefits that can be offered, the relative preference shown for each benefit by management and the employees, the estimated cost of each benefit, and the total amount of money available for the entire benefits package.

Allowing for Employee Involvement

Before a new benefit is introduced, the need for it should first be established. Many organizations create committees composed of managers and employees to administer, interpret, and oversee their benefits policies. Opinion surveys are also used to obtain employee input. Having employees participate in designing benefits programs helps to ensure that management is moving in the direction of satisfying employee wants. Pan Canadian Petroleum formed eleven focus groups of randomly selected employees to provide insights and valuable feedback on their pension investments.[6]

Benefits for a Diverse Workforce

To serve their intended purpose, employee benefits programs must reflect the social changes that Canada is constantly facing. Particularly significant are changes in the diversity and lifestyles of the workforce; the changes make it necessary to develop new types of benefits to meet shifting needs. Therefore, more employers are tailoring their benefit programs to be family-friendly. (Specific family-friendly benefits are discussed later in the chapter.) For example, as we have indicated throughout this book, the number of women in the workforce is continuing to grow. Which benefits are most valuable to them (and to men) will be determined largely by whether they have dependent children and whether they have a spouse who has benefits coverage.

Unfortunately, benefits plans sometimes provide little advantage to employees, limiting the organization's ability to attract and retain quality employees. For example, many employers provide unneeded medical benefits to the young and single in the form of dependants' coverage. Likewise a well-designed—and costly—defined benefits pension program may not serve the needs of employees or the employer of a predominantly younger workforce. Similarly, the employer's contribution to the

Many employers offer additional private health care insurance, above that required by law.

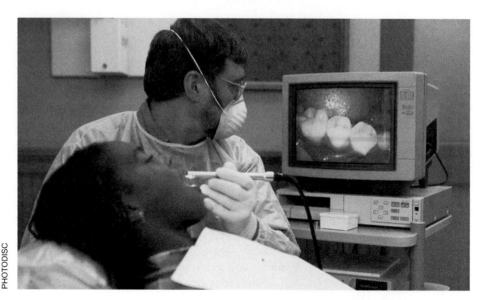

PHOTODISC

pension plan for a thirty-year-old employee is roughly one-fourth the contribution for a fifty-year-old employee for the same amount of pension commencing at age sixty-five. This difference in funds spent on older workers in effect discriminates against younger workers, although in legal terms it is not regarded as discriminatory.

Providing for Flexibility

Flexible benefits plans (cafeteria plans)

Benefits plans that enable individual employees to choose the benefits that are best suited to their particular needs

To accommodate the individual needs of employees, many organizations are embracing **flexible benefits plans**, also known as cafeteria plans. Over 90 percent of employers who responded to a survey were interested in offering flexible benefits.[7] These plans enable individual employees to choose the benefits that are best suited to their particular needs. They also prevent certain benefits from being wasted on employees who have no need for them. Typically, employees are offered a basic or core benefits package of life and health insurance, sick leave, and vacation. Requiring a core set of benefits ensures that employees have a minimum level of coverage to protect against unforeseen financial hardships. Employees are then given a specified number of credits that they may use to "buy" whatever other benefits they need. Other benefit options might include prepaid legal services, financial planning, or long-term care insurance.[8] Compensation specialists often see flexible benefits plans as ideal. Employees select the benefits of greatest value to them, while employers manage benefits costs by limiting the dollars employees have to spend.

Honeywell Canada considered three types of flexible benefits programs: cafeteria-style, whereby employees could choose any benefits they wanted; a module approach, whereby employees could select among prepackaged sets of benefits; and a core-plus-options plan, whereby employees could choose among options to augment a basic level of protection. Employees were able to select health and dental benefits that suited their life stages and that matched well with the plans their spouses had. Figure 11.1 lists the most commonly cited advantages and disadvantages of flexible benefits programs.

USING THE INTERNET

A useful tool for employers looking to maximize the value of employee compensation plans can be found at http://benefits.org.

Because cafeteria plans increase the complexity of administering the entire benefits programs, organizations may elect to outsource the handling of this function to a professional benefits vendor. About a third of Canadian firms rely on third parties to perform these types of transactional services for their plans.[9] Paying a service or contract fee to these firms may be particularly cost-effective for the smaller employer. Furthermore, benefits programs must be flexible enough to accommodate the constant flow of new laws and regulations that affect them. A number of consulting firms specializing in benefits can help managers track changes in all phases of the programs they oversee.

Communicating Employee Benefits Information

As we noted at the beginning of this chapter, employees are relatively uninformed about the benefits they receive. Therefore, it becomes critical that organizations effectively—and frequently—communicate the benefits package to employees. Court cases in Canada have established that it is the employer's responsibility to properly inform and disclose information about benefits. In *Spinks vs Canada*, an employee was not advised of certain pension options when he started with a new employer—specifically, that he was eligible to purchase past service in connection with his prior employment.

| Figure 11.1 | Flexible Benefits Plans: Advantages and Disadvantages |

Advantages

▶ Employees select benefits to match their individual needs.

▶ Benefit selections adapt to a constantly changing (diversified) workforce.

▶ Employees gain greater understanding of the benefits offered to them and the costs incurred.

▶ Employers maximize the psychological value of their benefits program by paying only for the highly desired benefits.

▶ Employers limit benefit costs by allowing employees to "buy" benefits only up to a maximum (defined) amount.

▶ Employers gain competitive advantage in the recruiting and retention of employees.

Disadvantages

▶ Poor employee benefits selection results in unwanted financial costs.

▶ There are certain added costs to establishing and maintaining the flexible plan.

▶ Employees may choose benefits of high use to them that increase employer premium costs.

The Federal Court of Appeal ruled that the employee had been poorly advised. In other cases, such as *Schmidt vs Air Products of Canada*, the courts have ruled that employee brochures, which usually aren't considered to be legal documents, may in fact be legally binding.[10]

While it is important to communicate information about employee benefits, there is no legislation that mandates how this is to be done. Various provincial pension benefits acts and federal laws regulating pension benefits state that employers operating a pension plan must provide specific information to employees. However, there are differences between provinces about what must be communicated. The sponsor of a registered retirement plan (RPP) has until six months after the end of the plan's fiscal year to provide active plan members with statements of their pension benefits. (Quebec regulations require annual pension statements for retired and deferred vested members.) The employee's name, date of birth, and date of hire must be included in the pension statement, along with the pension plan membership date, vesting date, and normal retirement date. Most provinces also require the name of the employee's spouse and/or pension plan beneficiary.[11]

Employers use a number of methods to communicate benefits to employees. In-house publications—which include employee handbooks and organization newsletters—are one popular way. The City of Regina, Saskatchewan, arranged to deliver pension presentations to all its 300 firefighters, a group of employees who are difficult to reach because of their shift work, by arranging these presentations on different days of the week at fire halls.[12] Also, the topic is usually covered in new-hire orientation programs. Managers who are conducting orientations should be allowed plenty of time to inform new employees of the benefits program and to answer any questions.

Some employers summarize benefits information on a paycheque stub as a reminder to employees of their total compensation. Highlights in HRM 11.1 provides a list of recommendations for communicating benefits.

Employee self-service systems have made it possible for employees to gather information about their benefits plans, enroll in their plans of choice, change their benefits coverage, or simply inquire about the status of their various benefit accounts without ever contacting an HR representative. Coopers & Lybrand uses a benefits information line to provide its employees with instant access to a wide variety of HR and benefits information by telephone. Employees can access their individual account information by entering a personal identification number (PIN). Other organizations use networked PCs or multimedia kiosks to the same purpose. These latter approaches enable employees to click on icons to access different benefits and to type in new

Highlights in HRM 11.1

CRAFTING AN EFFECTIVE BENEFITS COMMUNICATION PROGRAM

A well-designed benefits communication program will greatly enhance employees' appreciation of their benefits while ensuring that employers receive the intended value of these offerings. An effective program provides information to employees frequently and in a timely and cost-effective manner. Compensation specialists recommend the following when administering a benefits communication program.

An effective benefits communication program includes the following features:

▶ Design materials that are eye-catching and of high interest to employees.
▶ Develop a graphic logo for all material.
▶ Identify a theme for the benefits program.

In writing benefits materials,

▶ Avoid complex language when describing benefits. Clear, concise, and understandable language is a must.
▶ Provide numerous examples to illustrate benefit specifics.
▶ Explain all benefits in an open and honest manner. Do not attempt to conceal unpleasant news.
▶ Explain the purpose behind the benefit and the value of the benefit to employees.

In publicizing benefits information,

▶ Use all popular employee communication techniques.
▶ Maintain employee self-service (ESS) technology to disseminate benefits information and to update employee benefits selections.
▶ Use voice mail to send benefits information.
▶ Employ presentation software to present information to groups of employees.
▶ Maintain a benefits hot line to answer employee questions.

USING THE INTERNET

For information about the Certified Employee Benefit Specialist program at Dalhousie University, go to

www.dal.ca/~henson/pd/prof-des.html

information to update their records. Once an update or change has been made, the new information is permanently entered into the organization's HR information system without the need for paperwork.

It is also important for each employee to have a current statement of the status of her or his benefits. The usual means is the personalized computer-generated statement of benefits.

As the field of benefits becomes increasingly complex, and as employees become more sophisticated about financial planning, the need to hire and train benefits experts also grows. For those interested in specializing in this field, a good career move would be to become a certified employee benefit specialist (CEBS). In cooperation with the Wharton School at the University of Pennsylvania, Dalhousie University in Halifax sponsors a program leading to the CEBS designation. This ten-course program covers total compensation, health benefits, and strategic human resources.

Concerns of Management

Managing an employee benefits program requires close attention to the many forces that must be kept in balance if the program is to succeed. Management must consider union demands, the benefits other employers are offering, tax consequences, and rising costs, which are discussed in The Business Case.

USING THE INTERNET

Formerly the Canadian Compensation Association, WorldatWork looks at total compensation, including benefits. A Canadian content page on benefits can be found here:

www.worldatwork.org/canada/worldatwork-canada.jsp

The escalating cost of health care benefits is a concern to employers, who must strike an appropriate balance between offering quality benefits and keeping costs under control. The shift in benefit planning from entitlement to self-responsibility is discussed in Reality Check.

The Conference Board of Canada has published a list of cost containment strategies, which include the following:

▶ Contribution changes, such as increasing deductibles.
▶ Dollar limits, such as a dollar cap on specific benefits such as eyeglasses.
▶ Coverage changes (e.g., limits on hospital upgrades).
▶ Benefit caps (e.g., on dispensing fees).
▶ Use of preferred providers and flexible benefits.[13]

EMPLOYEE BENEFITS REQUIRED BY LAW

Legally required employee benefits amount to 11.2 percent of the benefits packages that Canadian employers provide.[14] These benefits include employer contributions to the Canada and Quebec pension plans, employment insurance, workers' compensation insurance, and (in some provinces) provincial medicare.

Canada and Quebec Pension Plans (CPP/QPP)

The Canada and Quebec pension plans cover almost all Canadian employees between the ages of eighteen and seventy. (Certain migratory and casual workers who earn less than the specified amount may be excluded.) To receive a retirement benefit, an

The Business Case

MANAGING THE COSTS OF BENEFITS

Mandatory benefits cost employers a minimum of 12 percent of payroll; when voluntary benefits are included, these costs may rise to 50 percent of payroll, up from 15 percent in the 1950s. These costs continue to increase at rates higher than inflation. For example, drug costs have been rising by 16 percent annually (higher than any other country) and drug costs represent as much as 70 percent of health care costs (excluding dental and vision care costs). These benefits represent a fixed rather than a variable cost, so management must decide whether it will be able to afford this cost in bad economic times. As managers can readily attest, if an organization is forced to discontinue a benefit, the negative effects of cutting it often outweigh any positive effects that accrued from providing it.

A current trend (and one not universally liked by employees) is for employers to require employees to pay part of the costs of certain benefits (e.g., through co-payments or higher deductibles). The Royal Bank used to pay 100 percent of benefits but now requires employees to pay a small deductible. At all times, benefit plan administrators are expected to select vendors of benefit services that have the most to offer for the cost. Furthermore, besides the actual costs of employee benefits, there are the costs of administering them, including direct labour costs, overhead charges, office space, and technology. But a big part of the escalating costs is the employee attitude of entitlement. Employees think that they are "entitled" to twelve days of sick leave, so they take it or that they since they have paid $50 for $600 of vision care, they should use it.

Sources: D. Brown, "Runaway Drug Costs Make Benefit Upgrades Impractical," *Canadian HR Reporter*, 16, no. 12 (June 16, 2003); S. Felix, "Gimme Gimme," *Benefits Canada* 24, no. 7 (July 2000): 20–21.

Reality Check

BENEFIT PLANNING: FROM ENTITLEMENT TO SELF-RESPONSIBILITY

In recent years, we have witnessed major upheavals in the area of benefits. Never before have there been such large increases in the cost of providing benefits as senior executives in companies throughout Canada try to change the "entitlement mindset" so prevalent in employees. Human resources professionals and senior executives can no longer make decisions regarding benefit plans without the assistance of benefit consultants. We met with Daphne Woolf of William H. Mercer Limited to discuss trends in benefit coverage.

(continued on following page)

Woolf specializes in the design and implementation of flexible benefit plans, strategic planning as it relates to compensation and benefits, and the design and monitoring of programs for promoting workplace health. She provides companies with extensive experience in evaluating funding, administration, and utilization for the purpose of identifying ways to contain benefit plan costs. A visionary in her own right, she leads the national and central region task forces on flexible benefits for Mercer.

"First of all, we need to look at the drivers of change. We see four things happening: our demographics are changing as people age; we have double-income families; the workplace is becoming increasingly diverse; benefits are being taxed to greater extents; and human rights legislation is changing with respect to who should be covered. Due to the high costs of providing benefit coverage, we are seeing a shift in responsibility from the provinces to third parties and individuals. The provinces are covering less, and this trend will continue to grow. The final, most important, underlying issue is increased sensitivity to the magnitude of these trends and the resulting benefit cost impacts.

"The entitlement mindset stems from the fact that, fifteen years ago, benefits were considered fringe. Now they are viewed as part of total compensation, which is a change in mentality. Employers are starting to move away from this entitlement mindset to self-responsibility. Employees are not used to making their own health care decisions, and it is a challenge for employers to educate their employees sufficiently and sway them to a different way of thinking. As the population ages, employees' needs for benefits are increasing; at the same time, the quality of their benefits must decrease in response to the high costs. Based on some of our studies, what we are seeing for the first time is that employees are making employment decisions based on benefits. Employers look at dealing with these benefit trends by revisiting their philosophy and benefits objectives. For example, does an employer pay for smoking cessation, include high deductibles, offer choice, or provide coverage for dependants?

"We are seeing an increase in flexible benefit plans. Our belief is that in five years the majority of plans will be flexible, and an employer who waits may be disadvantaged. Employers are better off as flex leaders than flex followers. You want to create your own plan, not have to base your program design on what someone else has done. Now you can 'anti-select' the benefit costs of the spouse's plan, allowing your employee to 'cash out' or allocate flex credits to stock plans or an RRSP. In the future, however, employees and their dependants may not opt out of your plan, and this would potentially increase your costs. So going flex sooner than later, if it's in keeping with corporate objectives, makes sense for many employers who have employees with spouses who work elsewhere. It is going to be a much tougher sell in the future if employees don't learn what the costs are today—they'll still be thinking entitlement when they get older and their provincial medicare does not cover as much.

"Managers have to start watching the cost of illness and absenteeism and realize the lost production costs of paying for time off. These costs add to the overall cost of benefits and should be tied to compensation so that employees can appreciate those benefits. We are also moving toward managed care. We have to look at providing the same level of health care at the same cost. That means putting caps on dispensing fees where drugs are concerned and getting second opinions to ensure that unnecessary procedures are not being administered.

"Americans have moved to a two-tiered system, and Canada is not far behind. While this is not currently a problem, it will be soon. For instance, if a patient wants a second opinion for something serious such as cancer, he or she may have to wait to see another specialist. In a two-tiered system, the patient can pay to have a second opinion immediately. This would not be reimbursed by the provincial health plan. We are beginning to see the collapse of provincial medicare as we now know it.

"There is an increase in health promotion. We are talking about wellness programs, which may focus on stress reduction, fitness in the workplace, and smoking-cessation programs. Employers are seeing the value in keeping employees healthy and productive, that is, preventing the claims costs. In one of my presentations, 'Taking the Fluff Out of Health Promotion,' I specifically outline the advantages of introducing health promotion programs to target cost pressures within the organization. Employers can yield a favourable return on investment if they ensure the right steps are taken to implement health promotion to secure effective cost containment. We are also diverging from traditional medicine to naturopathy and other paramedic services.

"In essence, employers are revisiting the extension of benefits to part-timers, retirees, and dependants. There is a movement toward providing incentive-based benefits—that is, using benefits to reward performance—and, with this, bringing things back to the overall compensation strategy. Employee expectations have become unrealistic mainly because they have not been educated. Once informed, we find that employees become a valuable resource. They need to understand the numbers. Employee focus groups are fast becoming the way to heed the transition from entitlement mindset to self-responsibility.

"[Finally], the trends are moving somewhere in the middle between the American health care system and Canada's. [In the future], flexible benefit plans will be the plan of choice so that educating the employee will be paramount if we are to move from an entitlement mindset to selfresponsibility. Your plan should be devised considering an overall philosophy with particular attention to the strategic plan of your organization. Benefits can no longer be taken for granted as the costs of providing this commodity are at a premium. What constitutes benefits must be expanded beyond the basic dental, life insurance, and drug plans. Benefits strategies cannot be short term, but rather must be long range, and in this regard benefit consultants can provide value-added advice. Selecting the right consultant to work with you is just as important as determining your overall benefits philosophy. This philosophy is key to the design of your program as it sets the stage for what your benefit plan will entail."

individual must apply to Human Resources Development Canada at least six months in advance of retirement.

Although similar in concept, the CPP and QPP differ in how much they pay out to participants. Both plans require employers to match the contributions made by employees. The revenues generated by these contributions are used to pay three main types of benefits: retirement pensions, disability benefits, and survivors' benefits. Governments do not subsidize these plans; all contributions come from employers and employees. Self-employed individuals can also contribute to the plan. With

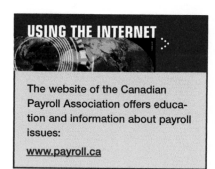

Canada's population aging, funds from the CPP will not be able to meet the needs of retirees unless those currently working, and their employers, significantly increase their contributions.

Canada has cross-border agreements with several countries to protect the acquired social security rights of people who have worked and lived in both countries and who meet the minimum qualifications for benefits from either country. A contributor's rights to benefits under CPP or QPP are not affected or impaired in any way by a change of employment or residence in Canada. All Canadian workers have "universal portability"—that is, the right to claim benefit credits wherever they are employed in Canada.

Employment Insurance (EI)

Employment insurance (EI) benefits are payable to claimants who are unemployed and are actively seeking employment. A person who becomes unemployed is usually entitled to what most Canadians still call "Unemployment Insurance" (or "UI"), which was what this program used to be called. The new name reflects a change in focus from basic income support to active employment measures.[15]

The amount of benefit paid is determined by the number of hours of employment in the past year and the regional unemployment rate. Individuals are entitled to unemployment insurance after they have contributed enough for a qualifying period and after a waiting period. The waiting period may vary with the individual's situation. Also, employees who resign from their job or who are terminated for cause may be ineligible for benefits unless they can prove there was no reasonable alternative to leaving their job. Just causes include sexual harassment, health concerns, and moving to another town or city because of a spouse's reassignment.

Additional benefits may be extended for situations involving illness, injury, or quarantine, or for maternity, parental, or adoption leave. If an organization does not offer sick leave benefits, the employee may have to apply to EI for sick benefits. The benefit amount, which is calculated on the same basis as the regular benefit, varies across jurisdictions. Sickness or disability benefits are available for up to fifteen weeks. A combination of maternity, parental, or adoptive benefits may be available up to a cumulative maximum of one year in some provinces.

Employees and employers both contribute to the EI fund. An EI premium reduction is available to employers who cover their employees under an approved wage-loss plan. The amount of the reduction depends on the supplement being given to the employee and therefore varies from company to company. Work-sharing programs have recently come into existence as a means of reducing the overall burden on EI. Under work sharing, an organization reduces the work week of all employees in a particular group instead of laying them off. The company pays for the time worked, and the employee draws EI for the rest of the work week.

Workers' compensation insurance

Insurance provided to workers to defray the loss of income and cost of treatment resulting from work-related injuries or illness

Workers' Compensation Insurance

Workers' compensation insurance is based on the theory that compensation for work-related accidents and illnesses should be considered one of the costs of doing business and should ultimately be passed on to the consumer. Individual employees

470

Injured employees have their incomes protected through sick leave provisions.

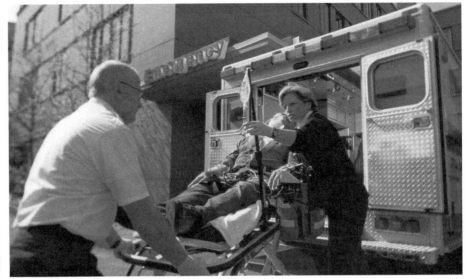

PHOTODISC

should not be required to bear the cost of their treatment or loss of income; nor should they be subjected to complicated, delaying, and expensive legal procedures.

Workers' compensation is a form of insurance. It was created by an act of Parliament to help workers injured on the job return to the workplace. Each provincial and territorial board is empowered by the relevant legislation to amend and collect assessments (i.e., insurance premiums), to determine the right to compensation, and to pay the amount due to the injured worker. This system of collective liability is compulsory. Employers' contributions are assessed as a percentage of their payroll. The percentage varies with the nature of the industry. For example, in a high-risk industry such as mining, the assessment rates are higher than in knowledge-based industries.

Workers' compensation is based on the following principles:

▶ Employers share collective liability, though contributions may vary among employers in the same industry (e.g., some provinces punish employers who do not maintain a safe and healthy work environment by levying additional fines).

▶ Injured workers are compensated regardless of the financial status of the employer, and this compensation is based on loss of earnings.

▶ The system is no-fault and nonadversarial, and thus offers no recourse to the courts.

Benefits are paid out of an employer-financed fund and include medical expenses stemming from work-related injuries, survivors' benefits (including burial expenses and pensions), and wage-loss payments for temporary, total, or partial disability. Permanent disability benefits may be disbursed as a lump-sum payment or as a permanent disability pension with rehabilitation services. The amount paid depends on the employee's earnings and provincial legislation.

Employees cannot be required either to make contributions toward a workers' compensation fund or to waive their right to receive compensation benefits. Payments made to claimants are effectively nontaxable. Premiums paid for by the employer may be deducted as expenses and are not deemed a taxable benefit for employees.

Figure 11.2	Reducing Worker's Compensation Costs: Key Areas

1. Perform an audit to assess high-risk areas in the workplace.

2. Prevent injuries by proper ergonomic design of the workplace and effective assessment of job candidates.

3. Provide quality medical care to injured employees from physicians with experience and preferably with training in occupational health.

4. Reduce litigation by ensuring effective communication between the employer and the injured worker.

5. Manage the care of the injured worker from time of injury until return to work. Keep a partially recovered employee at the worksite.

6. Provide extensive worker training in all related health and safety areas.

Figure 11.2 lists the steps that an HR department can take to control workers' compensation costs.

Provincial Hospital and Medical Services

People who have been resident in a Canadian province for three months are eligible to receive health care benefits. Applications must be made and approval given before coverage starts. Benefits include services provided by physicians, surgeons, and other qualified health professionals; hospital services such as standard ward accommodation and laboratory and diagnostic procedures; and hospital-administered drugs. Many employers offer third-party benefit coverage, which entitles their employees to additional benefits such as semi-private or private accommodation, prescription drugs, private nursing, ambulance services, out-of-country medical expenses that exceed provincial limits, vision and dental care, and paramedic services. Depending on the employer, all or just a portion of the services may be covered.

DISCRETIONARY MAJOR EMPLOYEE BENEFITS

Besides the mandated benefits, most employers offer other benefits such as health care and dental plans.

Health Care Benefits

The benefits receiving the most attention from employers today, owing to sharply rising costs and employee concerns, are health care benefits. In the past, health insurance plans covered only medical, surgical, and hospital expenses. Today employers are

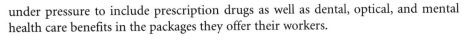

under pressure to include prescription drugs as well as dental, optical, and mental health care benefits in the packages they offer their workers.

Cost Containment

The growth in health care costs can be attributed to a number of factors, including the greater need for health care by an aging population, the costs associated with technological advances in medicine, the growing costs of health care labour, and the overuse of costly health care services.

With the significant rise in health care costs, it is understandable that employers seek relief from these expenses. The approaches used to contain the costs of health care benefits include reductions in coverage, increased deductibles or co-payments, and increased coordination of benefits to ensure that the same expense is not paid by more than one insurance reimbursement. A list of cost containment strategies is provided in Figure 11.3. Some employers seek to control the costs of benefits by providing them only to full-time employees—see Ethics in HRM. Cost containment strategies must be subject to a cost/benefit analysis.

Employee assistance programs and wellness programs can help organizations cut the costs of health care benefits. Highlights in HRM 11.2 focuses on a team approach to cost reduction.

Figure 11.3 | Cost Containment Strategies

Employers can reduce the cost of benefits in the following ways:

1. Education and Motivation
   ▶ Communicate the costs of benefits.
   ▶ Provide incentives to employees to reduce costs.
   ▶ Teach employees how to live healthy lifestyles, and how to plan for retirement.

2. Change Coverage
   ▶ Introduce dollar limits on benefits.
   ▶ Eliminate duplicate coverage for spouses.
   ▶ Remove upgrades.
   ▶ Introduce minimum fees to be paid by employees.

3. Change the System
   ▶ Form partnerships with pharmacies to provide discounts.
   ▶ Move to defined contribution plans.
   ▶ Move to a claims management approach, and audit claims.

Ethics in HRM

THE REAL VALUE OF A FULL-TIME JOB

Full-time workers get more pay (when you calculate hours worked and rate of pay per hour) and also more benefits than part-time workers. The percentages of benefits received by full-time and part-time workers differ substantially, as the following table indicates:

Benefit	Full-Time Workers	Part-Time Workers
Employer pension plan	58%	19%
Health care plan	68	18
Dental plan	63	16
Paid sick leave	66	18
Paid vacation leave	80	30

These differences have a profound impact on employees' lives: one in eight of Canada's 2.6 million part-time workers spend their spare time looking for full-time employment. If benefits are important to them, they should be looking for a large employer in a unionized environment. Unionized employees are twice as likely as their nonunionized counterparts to be covered. The probability of receiving benefits also increases if the employer is unionized, and if the job is permanent rather than temporary.

The issue of benefits for part-time workers is a concern to the government and should also concern taxpayers. Part-time workers are least able to afford their own benefits; as a result, through social transfer payments, society ends up paying for the services they need, such as health care and retirement plans. However, in a groundbreaking move, the Royal Bank of Canada now provides full benefits and bonuses to its 7500 part-time and casual workers. Should governments pass legislation to force employers to offer the same benefits to part-timers as full-timers?

Sources: "Unionization and Fringe Benefits," *Perspectives on Labour and Income* 3, no. 8, 75-001-XIE, August 2002; Bruce Little, "The Full-Scale Advantages of Full-Time Time Work," *The Globe and Mail*, July 14, 1997; Brenda Lipsett and Mark Reesor, *Job-Related Benefits for Employees*, Human Resources Development Canada, June 1997.

Other Health Benefits

In the past two decades, more and more employees have been receiving dental care insurance as a benefit. Besides their obvious purpose, dental plans encourage employees to receive regular dental attention. Typically, the insurance pays a portion of the charges and the subscriber pays the remainder.

Another fairly new benefit that many employers are offering is optical care. Typically, the coverage includes visual examinations and a percentage of the costs of lenses and frames.

Highlights in HRM 11.2

A Team Approach to Cost Containment

The University of New Brunswick (UNB) in Fredericton has long done what so many other organizations are only starting to do: it has used its employees to assist it in devising strategies to combat increases in benefit costs. In 1974, the Fringe Benefits Review Committee was established. According to Jim O'Sullivan, the university's vice-president of finance and administration, the committee was organized in "an effort to repair relations with angry faculty representatives after the university's board of governors was perceived to have unilaterally eliminated an existing benefit."

The committee, comprising management as well as unionized and nonunionized employees, has the task of reviewing the university's group file, health, and long-term disability (LTD) plans. Although the board of governors still holds the final decision-making authority, the committee alone is responsible for making benefits recommendations and working out the details; its efforts have resulted in a $3.8-million benefits surplus.

For more than twenty years, the employees have shared the costs of the university's group insurance plan, thus allowing the university to maintain effective cost control and to plan redesigns. Because the plan costs are shared, employees are aware that increasing benefits will mean higher contributions for both sides. To keep LTD claims down, employees have allowed the university to follow up directly with workers on disability claims to help them return to work faster. Compared to other universities with similar workforces, UNB has the lowest claims. For many other organizations, the price tag for health care, drug, and dental benefits has grown annually, but UNB has managed to hold benefit costs below the general rate of inflation. O'Sullivan attributes the savings to the cost-sharing partnership.

As in many other organizations, the employee assistance program is fully paid for by the employer. However, because the development of this program was discussed with the committee, employees played a major role in selling this plan to their co-workers. O'Sullivan believes that the plan is cost-effective in the long term. "Failure to seek treatment for personal problems," he notes, "would eventually affect job performance and lead to higher costs for health and LTD insurance."

The university has been self-insuring benefits—that is, paying for and managing its own risk, rather than contracting with an external insurance provider—with a pay-as-you-go philosophy, since the 1970s. Commercial insurance is purchased only to provide protection against catastrophic losses. For example, the LTD plan is self-insured for the first ten years of any claim, after which commercial insurance coverage comes into effect.

Employer and employee representative groups each have control over their half share of surplus funds. When there has been a surplus, consideration has been given to declaring contribution holidays or to implementing new benefits, but both sides, concerned that the good times

(continued on following page)

could come to an end, have decided to act conservatively. The surplus funds are invested by the university's endowment fund investment managers; investment income is used to improve employees' benefits.

"I do believe we have developed a realistic balance between the operation of a responsive and competitive benefits package and the need to maintain effective cost controls," states O'Sullivan. "In this way, we have not only helped meet our overall financial objectives but have created positive spinoffs for labour–management relations generally."

Payment for Time Not Worked

The "payment for time not worked" category of benefits includes the following: statutory holiday pay and vacation pay; time off for bereavement, jury duty, and military duty; rest periods and coffee breaks; and maternity benefits (which usually involve some form of salary continuance).

Vacations with Pay

It is generally agreed that vacation time is essential to the well-being of employees. Eligibility for vacations varies by industry, by locale, and by size of the organization. To qualify for longer vacations of three, four, or five weeks, one may expect to work for five, ten, or fifteen years.

As shown in Figure 11.4, European professional and managerial personnel tend to receive more vacation time than their Canadian, American, and Japanese counter-

Figure 11.4	Vacation Days: A Global Look

Employees of these countries are entitled to the following average vacation days:

Austria	25	
Sweden	25	Collective agreements may improve this provision.
Germany	24	Minimum statutory entitlement based on a 6-day work week.
United Kingdom	23	Fixed by collective agreement. Typical practice is 4–6 weeks. Figure is an average.
Belgium	20	For 1 year of service, based on a 5-day work week.
Ireland	20	Most employees entitled to a 4-week leave.
Canada	10	Federal provisions; 2–4 weeks depending on jurisdiction.
United States	5	1 week leave for 6 months–1 year service; 2 weeks after 1–5 years.

Note: These comparisons are intended as general guidelines and do not take into consideration age, length of service, employee level, salary unless otherwise stated.
Source: *Worldwide Benefit & Employment Guidelines 2003/2004*, Mercer Human Resource Consulting LLC.

parts. In most countries, the government requires employers to guarantee vacation time to their workers; the United States and United Kingdom are exceptions to this.

Paid Holidays

Both hourly and salaried workers can expect to be paid for statutory holidays as designated by each province. The standard statutory holidays are New Year's Day, Good Friday, Canada Day (Memorial Day in Newfoundland), Labour Day, and Christmas Day. Other holidays commonly recognized by the various provinces are Victoria Day, Thanksgiving Day, and Remembrance Day. Some provinces have their own special statutory holidays. Many employers give workers an additional one to three personal days off (i.e., personal use days).

Sick Leave

Employees who cannot work because of illness or injury are compensated in various ways. Most employers offer short-term disability and long-term disability plans. Short-term disability plans include salary continuance programs, sick leave credits, and weekly indemnity plans. Most public employees, and many in private firms—especially in white-collar jobs—receive a set number of sick leave days each year to cover such absences. Sometimes employees are permitted to accumulate the sick leave they do not use to cover prolonged absences. Accumulated vacation leave is sometimes treated as a source of income when sick leave benefits have been exhausted. Group insurance that provides income protection during a long-term disability is also becoming more common. LTD plans normally provide a disabled employee with 50 to 70 percent of pre-disability income. Yet another alternative, depending on the situation, is workers' compensation insurance, which was discussed earlier in the chapter.

Severance Pay

Severance pay
A lump-sum payment given to terminated employees by an employer at the time of an employer-initiated termination

An employee who is being terminated is sometimes given a one-time payment. Known as **severance pay**, it can amount to anywhere from a few days' wages to several months', with the exact payment depending on length of service. Only two jurisdictions (federal and Ontario) have legislation regarding severance pay. Employers that are downsizing often use severance pay to soften the impact of unexpected termination on employees. An employee is not entitled to severance pay if a reasonable offer of alternative employment is refused.

Life Insurance

Group life insurance is the benefit most commonly provided by an employer. The purpose is to provide financial security to the dependants of the employee, in case of his/her death.

Retirement Programs

Retirement is an important part of life and requires careful preparation. When convincing job applicants to come work for them, employers usually emphasize the retirement benefits that can be expected after a certain number of years of employment. As we noted earlier, it is common for each employee, once a year, to receive a personalized statement of benefits that contains information about projected retirement income from pensions and employee investment plans.

Retirement Policies

Canadian employees may retire at age fifty-five and begin drawing a reduced pension from CPP/QPP as well as funds from other sources such as RRSPs. Alternatively, some individuals can work until seventy-one in some provinces, at which time they must retire. Mandatory retirement at age sixty-five in Canada is slowly being abolished. Statistics Canada reported that sixty-one is the average age of retirement, with women leaving work at fifty-eight and men at sixty-two. The higher the household income, the lower the age of retirement.[16] Many are retiring because they have lost their jobs and cannot find other work. However, as we have seen, there is a growing trend for individuals in their golden years to take on part-time employment as a means of supplementing their income.

To avoid making layoffs and to reduce salary and benefit costs, employers often encourage early retirement. This encouragement often takes the form of increased pension benefits or cash bonuses, sometimes referred to as the **silver handshake**. Some companies, including IBM Canada, have given generously to encourage the early retirement of workers. Ontario Hydro presented its employees with various options to retire early; these included an early retirement allowance, a voluntary separation allowance, a special retirement program, and a voluntary retirement program. The incentives succeeded; most employees with twenty-five years of service opted for the special retirement program.[17] An employer can offset the cost of retirement incentives by paying lower compensation to replacements and/or by reducing its workforce.

For employees, the main factors in a decision to retire early are health, personal finances, and job satisfaction. Lesser factors include an attractive pension and the possibility of future layoffs. Highlights in HRM 11.3 summarizes the reasons that employees choose to retire.

Preretirement Programs

Most people are eager to retire; some are bitterly disappointed once they do. In an attempt to lessen the disappointment, some employers offer programs to help employees prepare for retirement. These programs typically include seminars and workshops, where lectures, videos, and printed materials are offered. Usually they cover topics such as how to live on a reduced, fixed income and how to cope with lost prestige, family conflict, and idleness. Also discussed are more concrete topics such as pension plans, health insurance coverage, retirement benefits and provincial health care, and personal financial planning.

At Consumers Gas, employees between fifty and fifty-three can attend, with their spouses, a three-day seminar that covers six subject areas: positive outlook, leisure time, health, home, financial planning, and estate planning. At other organizations, these programs have a more individual focus. CIBC, which has over 40 000 employees at 1800 different locations, provides its employees with tools such as tapes, books, videos, and computer programs. The Retirement Council of Canada recommends that 1 percent of a company's pension program be earmarked for retirement planning programs.[18]

Some organizations now offer retirement seminars to their younger employees as well. For instance, at Siemens Canada, employees as young as thirty-five are being offered the same financial sessions as employees fifty-five and over.

Silver handshake
An early retirement incentive in the form of increased pension benefits for several years or a cash bonus

Highlights in HRM 11.3

WHY RETIRE?

A 2003 survey asked people why they would want to retire (respondents could choose more than one category, so results add up to more than 100).

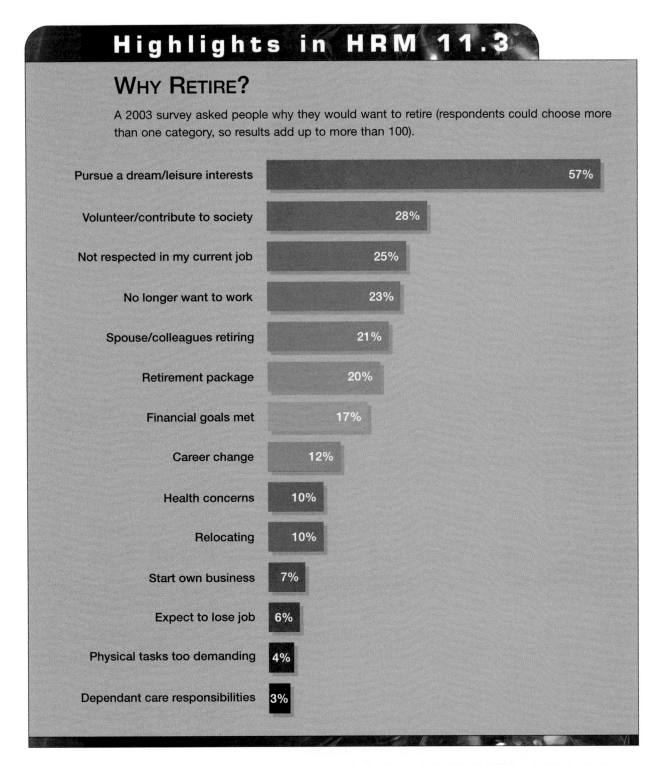

Pursue a dream/leisure interests	57%
Volunteer/contribute to society	28%
Not respected in my current job	25%
No longer want to work	23%
Spouse/colleagues retiring	21%
Retirement package	20%
Financial goals met	17%
Career change	12%
Health concerns	10%
Relocating	10%
Start own business	7%
Expect to lose job	6%
Physical tasks too demanding	4%
Dependant care responsibilities	3%

Source: U. Vu, "Wave of Retirements Coming; Few Organizations Getting Ready," *Canadian HR Reporter,* May 5, 2003: 2.

To help older workers get used to the idea of retirement, some organizations are experimenting with retirement rehearsal. Polaroid offers employees an opportunity to try out retirement through an unpaid three-month leave program. The company offers another program that permits employees to cut their hours gradually before retirement. Employees are paid only for hours worked, but receive full medical insurance and prorated pension credits. Most experts agree that preretirement planning is a much-needed, cost-effective employee benefit.[19]

Pension Plans

Originally, pensions were based on a *reward philosophy*; in other words, employers viewed pensions mainly as a reward to employees who stayed with them until retirement. Employees who quit or were terminated before retirement were not seen as deserving retirement benefits. Since then, most unions have negotiated vesting requirements into their contracts, and vesting has become required by law. Put another way, pensions are now based on an *earnings philosophy;* they are seen as deferred income that employees accumulate during their working lives; in other words, the pension belongs to the employee after a specified number of years of service, whether or not she or he remains with the employer until retirement.

Since the CPP/QPP legislation was enacted in 1966, pension plans have been used to supplement the protection provided by government-sponsored programs. Most private pension plans and a significant number of public plans now integrate their benefits with CPP/QPP benefits.

It is up to the employer whether to offer a pension plan. Because these plans are so expensive, companies are always looking for the least expensive ways to provide them to their employees.

Types of Pension Plans

Pensions can be categorized in two basic ways: according to contributions made by the employer, and according to the amount of pension benefits to be paid. In a **contributory plan**, contributions to a pension plan are made jointly by employees and employers. In a **noncontributory plan**, the contributions are made solely by the employer. Most plans in privately held organizations are contributory.

When pension plans are classified by the amount of pension benefits to be paid, there are two basic types: the defined benefit plan and the defined contribution plan. Under a **defined benefit plan**, the retirement benefit is determined according to a predefined formula. This amount is usually based on the employee's years of service, average earnings during a specific period of time, and age at time of retirement. A variety of formulas exist for determining pension benefits; the one used most often is based on the employee's average earnings (usually over a three- to five-year period immediately preceding retirement) multiplied by the number of years of service with the organization. A deduction is then made for each year the retiree is under sixty-five. As noted earlier, pension benefits are usually integrated with CPP/QPP. Very few employers introduce this type of plan, because it places them under the legal obligation to pay benefits regardless of the performance of the pension plan.

A **defined contribution plan** establishes the basis on which an employer will contribute to the pension fund. These plans come in a variety of forms: some involve profit sharing; others involve employers matching employee contributions; still others

Contributory plan
A pension plan in which contributions are made jointly by employees and employers

objective 7

Noncontributory plan
A pension plan in which contributions are made solely by the employer

Defined benefit plan
A pension plan in which the amount an employee is to receive on retirement is specifically set forth

Defined contribution plan
A pension plan that establishes the basis on which an employer will contribute to the pension fund

are employer-sponsored RRSP plans. The size of the pension the employee will get is determined by the funds in his or her account at the time of retirement and what retirement benefits (usually in the form of an annuity) these funds will purchase. These plans are not as predictable (i.e., secure) as defined benefit plans. However, even under defined benefit plans, retirees may not receive the benefits promised them if the plan is not adequately funded.

Defined benefit plans, with their fixed payouts, are falling out of use. They are less popular with employers nowadays because they cost more and because they require compliance with complicated government rules.[20] All new pension plans in Canada, such as those introduced by MacMillan Bloedel and Molson Breweries, are defined contribution plans.

Registered retirement savings plans (RRSPs) have experienced tremendous growth in recent years because the funds in these plans are allowed to accumulate tax-free until they are withdrawn. RRSPs have annual contribution limits; also, if withdrawals are made from them before retirement, tax must be paid on them. Some employers offer group RRSPs, which have some advantages over individual RRSPs: they are deducted from payroll and have mass-purchasing power.

Federal Regulation of Pension Plans

Registered pension plans (RPPs) are subject to federal and provincial regulations. The federal Income Tax Act prescribes limits and standards that affect the amount of contributions that can be deducted from income; it also mandates how pension benefits can be taxed. (It is estimated that the government loses about $5 billion a year in taxes because it does not tax private pension plans.) In the federal jurisdiction and most provincial ones, there are laws that state how pension plans must be operated. For example, the actuarial assumptions on which the funding is based must be certified by an actuary at specified intervals. An important issue to employees is vesting.

Vesting is a guarantee of accrued benefits to participants at retirement age, regardless of their employment status at that time. Vested benefits that have been earned by the employee cannot be revoked by the employer. Employees with two years of service in an organization are considered, with regard to their pension plans, fully vested and locked in.

Vesting
A guarantee of accrued benefits to participants at retirement age, regardless of their employment status at the time

Pension Portability

For a long time, most pension plans lacked portability; in other words, employees who changed jobs were unable to maintain equity in a single pension. Unions addressed this concern by encouraging multiple-employer plans. These plans cover the employees of two or more unrelated organizations in accordance with a collective agreement. They are governed by boards of trustees on which both the employers and the union are represented. Multiple-employer plans tend to be found in industries in which few companies have enough employees to justify an individual plan. They are also found often in industries in which employment tends to be either seasonal or irregular. These plans are found in the following manufacturing sectors: apparel, printing, furniture, leather, and metalworking. They are also found in nonmanufacturing industries such as mining, construction, transport, entertainment, and private higher education.

Employees who leave an organization can leave their locked-in funds in their current pension plan, or they can transfer those funds into a locked-in RRSP or into their new employer's pension plan (if one exists).

Pension Funds

A pension fund can be administered through a trusted plan or through an insured one. In a *trusted* plan, the pension contributions are placed in a trust fund. The fund is then invested and administered by trustees. The trustees are appointed by the employer; but if there is a union, the union sometimes appoints them. Contributions to an *insured* pension plan are used to purchase insurance annuities. These funds are administered by the insurance company that is providing the annuities.

Government benefits such as CPP/QPP and Old Age Security will be stretched thin as baby boomers grow older, and some private pensions may be vulnerable to poorly performing investments. It should also be noted that the pension funds of some organizations are not adequate to cover their obligations. Here is another interesting question: "Whose money is it?" When a pension fund has generated a surplus over plan (and many of them have), management tends to see this surplus as part of the organization's portfolio of assets; not surprisingly, employees tend to view it as their own money. These legal and ethical issues have yet to be addressed.

EMPLOYEE SERVICES: CREATING A WORK–LIFE SETTING

Employee services, like other benefits, represent a cost to the employer. But they are often well worth the cost. More and more different services are being offered by employers to make life at work more rewarding and to enhance the well-being of employees. "Wellness is good for business," says Ann Coll of Husky Injection Molding Systems. The employees at Husky's plant in Bolton, Ontario, enjoy a subsidized cafeteria with organic vegetarian meals, a $500 stipend for vitamins, and a fitness centre that is open around the clock.

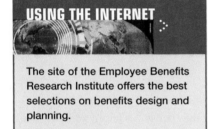

Creating a Family-Friendly Setting

Eddie Bauer, an outdoor clothing and equipment supplier, offers its employees take-out dinners and one paid "balance day" off a year. The Human Resources Professionals Association of Ontario allows a half-day of paid leave for employee birthdays. These organizations, and many others, are seeking to create a family-friendly organizational environment that allows employees to balance work and personal needs. Programs like these help employees manage their time; employers benefit by attracting good workers and by reducing the various interruptions that affect workplace productivity.[21] Figure 11.5 lists some of the more popular employer-sponsored work-life benefits.

Employee assistance programs (EAPs)
Services provided by employers to help workers cope with a wide variety of problems that interfere with the way they perform their jobs

Employee Assistance Programs

To help workers cope with a wide variety of problems that interfere with their work performance, organizations have developed **employee assistance programs (EAPs)**. Typically, an EAP provides diagnosis, counselling, and referral services for alcohol or drug problems, emotional problems, and financial or family crises. (EAPs will be discussed in more detail in Chapter 12.) It has been estimated that employees' stress

Figure 11.5	Family-Friendly Benefits: Balancing Work and Home Needs

▶ Child care/elder care referral services

▶ Time off for children's school activities

▶ Employer-paid on-site or near-site child care facilities

▶ Flexible work hours scheduling

▶ Employee-accumulated leave days for dependent care

▶ Subsidized temporary or emergency dependent care

▶ Extended leave policies for child/elder care

▶ Sick child programs (caregiver on call)

▶ Work-at-home arrangements/telecommuting

▶ Partial funding of child care costs

▶ Customized career paths

adds as much as 8 percent to payroll costs. The point of EAPs is to help employees solve their personal problems, or at least to prevent those problems from turning into crises that affect their ability to work productively. To handle crises, many EAPs offer twenty-four-hour hot lines. Between 7 and 10 percent of employees use EAPs.[22]

USING THE INTERNET

The VMC Behavioral Healthcare Services provides articles in areas such as work–life balance.

www.vmceap.com

Counselling Services

An important part of an EAP is the counselling services it provides to employees. While most organizations expect managers to counsel subordinates, some employees will have problems that require professional counselling. Most organizations refer such individual employees to outside services such as family counselling services, marriage counsellors, and mental health clinics. Some organizations have a clinical psychologist, counsellor, or comparable specialist on staff to whom employees may be referred.

Child and Elder Care

Consider these statistics:

▶ About 32 percent of Canadians have elder care responsibilities.

▶ Employees spend an average of twenty-three hours each month on elder care.[23]

In the past, working parents had to make their own arrangements with sitters or with nursery schools for pre-school children. Today, benefits may include financial assistance, alternative work schedules, and family leave. For many employees, on-site or near-site child care centres are the most visible, prestigious, and desired solutions.

Many organizations recognize the demands on working parents and ensure appropriate childcare is available.

NELSON, A DIVISION OF THOMSON CANADA LIMITED

Ontario Hydro has provided the space and is paying the occupancy costs for a program it calls Hydro Kids. This program encompasses three on-site day care centres, which are open to company employees. These nonprofit centres are operated by the parents themselves, who hire the child care staff and manage day-to-day operations. Parents pay market rates for the child care services.[24] Ford Motor of Canada offers its employees as much as $2000 a year in child care assistance.

A growing benefit offered employees with children experiencing a short illness is called mildly ill child care. Medical supervision is the primary difference between these facilities and traditional day care arrangements. Mildly ill care facilities serve children recovering from colds, flu, ear infections, chicken pox, or other mild illnesses that temporarily prevent them from attending regular school or day care. See Highlights in HRM 11.4 for the benefits of these arrangements as cited by CIBC.

Responsibility for the care of aging parents and other relatives is another fact of life for more and more employees. The term **elder care**, as used in the context of employment, refers to situations where an employee provides care to an elderly relative while remaining actively at work. Most caregivers are women.

There is no doubt that elder care responsibilities detract from work efficiency: from time lost to take a parent to the doctor, to loss of concentration due to worry, work time being spent making care arrangements, never knowing when an emergency will occur, and calls from neighbours and relatives disrupting the workday. When combined, these responsibilities lead to a situation where neither the care giver nor employee role is filled adequately. Lost productivity due to absenteeism of those caring for elders can cost a 1000-employee company without an elder care program as much as $400 000 per year. TransAmerica Corporation, an insurance and financial services organization, reported that 1600 missed workdays per year were attributed to 22 percent of its employees who were caring for an elderly relative, for an annual loss to the corporation of $250 000. For larger companies, these costs can run into the millions.[25]

Elder care
Care provided to an elderly relative by an employee who remains actively at work

Highlights in HRM 11.4

CIBC CARES

CIBC was the first Canadian corporation to open an employer-sponsored centre dedicated to backup child care. Every parent has faced the hardship of finding emergency care, when regular child care arrangements break down due to a caretaker's illness, or when schools are closed for professional development days or snow days. The CIBC Children's Centre offers special play areas for children of different ages and is licensed under the Day Nurseries Act. The centre is operated by ChildrenFirst, which designs, develops, and operates innovative backup child care facilities in North America. Nearly 600 parents used the CIBC Children's Centre in the first six months of operation, with a resultant saving of 760 employee days. At an average daily rate of about $200, the productivity saving was estimated to be about $150 000. The projected savings over five years are $1 400 000. The intangible benefits include increased attraction and retention of employees, allowing them to achieve better work-life family balance. CIBC discovered through surveys that 90 percent of Canadians want organizations to focus on more than profits, 60 percent form an impression of a company based on its social responsibility, and 17 percent have avoided a company's products because of its lack of social responsibility.

Sources: ChildrenFirst, www.childrenfirst.com; CIBC, www.cibc.com; presentation made by Joyce M. Phillips, Executive Vice-President Human Resources, CIBC in April 2003.

To reduce the negative effects of care giving on productivity, organizations can offer elder care counselling, educational fairs and seminars, printed resources, support groups, and special flexible schedules and leaves of absence. Schering-Plough, a pharmaceuticals manufacturer, uses an 800 line for elder care referrals. IBM has established a nation-wide telephone network of more than 200 community-based referral agencies. Some employers band together to come up with better solutions to the challenge of elder care.

AT&T has given grants to community organizations to recruit, train, and manage elder care volunteers where its employees live and work. Travellers Corporation, a financial services company, is part of a consortium of employers that trains family care workers; it also shares with employees the cost of three days' in-home care for family emergencies.[26] Interest in and demand for elder care programs will increase dramatically as baby boomers move into their early fifties and find themselves managing organizations and experiencing elder care problems with their own parents.

Other Services

The variety of benefits and services that employers offer today could not have been imagined a few years ago. Some are fairly standard, and we will cover them briefly. Some are unique and obviously grew out of specific concerns, needs, and interests. Figure 11.6 outlines emerging benefits. Some of the more creative and unusual

Figure 11.6 | Emerging Benefits

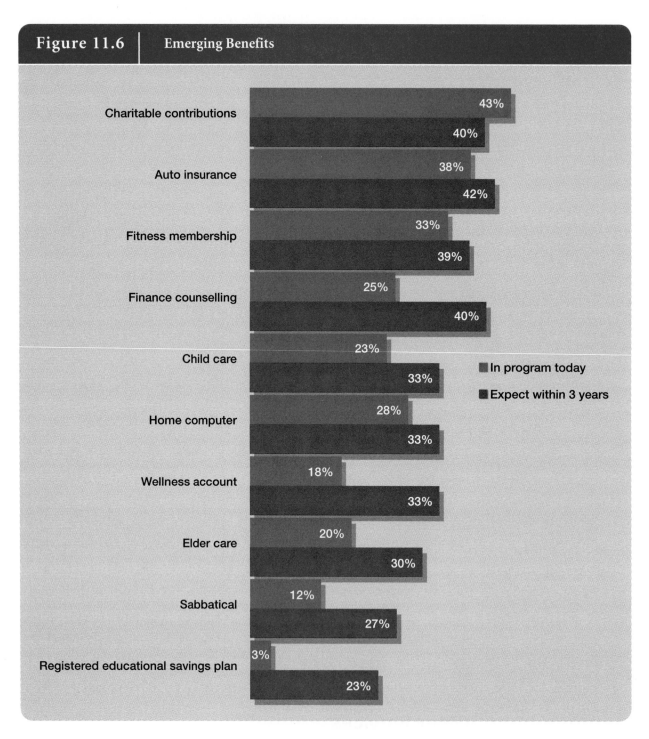

Source: T. Humber, "Perquisites No Longer a Perquisite?" *Canadian HR Reporter* 16, no. 3 (February 10, 2003): G7.

benefits are group insurance for employee pets, free baseball tickets for families and friends, summer boat cruises, and subsidized haircuts for MPs. Highlights in HRM 11.5 describes the perks at Intuit Canada.

Legal Services

Legal service plans are generally of two types: access plans and comprehensive plans. *Access plans* provide free telephone or office consultation, and document review, as well as discounts on legal fees for more complex matters. *Comprehensive plans* cover other services such as representation in divorce cases, real estate transactions, and civil and criminal trials.

Covered employees normally pay a monthly or annual fee to be enrolled in the plan. When the need for legal assistance arises, the employee may choose a lawyer from a directory of providers and incur no legal fees. Pre-paid legal programs are typically offered as part of an employer's cafeteria benefits plan.

Financial Planning

One of the newer benefits is financial planning. Primarily available to executives and middle managers, it will likely become available to more employees through flexible benefits programs. Financial planning programs cover investments, tax planning and management, estate planning, and similar.

Highlights in HRM 11.5

PERKS AT INTUIT

Intuit Canada, which develops financial software, employs about 400 employees at its Edmonton offices and is rated one of Canada's top employers. The benefits it offers employees is one of the reasons for its success. First, Intuit offers the standard benefits package, for which it pays 100 percent of the premiums. Then the fun stuff begins. There is a staff lounge with pool table, foozball, ping pong, and a gas fireplace. Down the hall, employees work out in the company gym, playing volleyball, basketball, and floor hockey. A complete fitness centre, with a free towel service, is greatly valued by employees. For the long hours and stress, Intuit even provides three nap rooms after listening to employees who said they just wanted a place to crash for an hour or two. Intuit pays for employees and their families to relax at the annual corporate retreat at Alberta's Jasper Park Lodge. For Intuit, the benefit of these benefits is the ability to attract and retain the best people.

Source: T. Humber, "Perquisites No Longer a Prerequisite," *Canadian HR Reporter* 16, no. 3 (February 10, 2003): G7-G9.

Housing and Moving Expenses

The days of "company" houses are now past, except in some remote areas and the armed forces. However, a variety of housing services is usually provided in nearly all organizations that move employees from one office or plant because of a transfer or a relocation. These services may include helping employees find living quarters, paying for travel and moving expenses, and protecting transferred employees from loss when selling their homes.

Transportation Pooling

Daily transportation to and from work is a major concern of employees. The result may be considerable time and energy devoted to organizing car pools and scrambling for parking spaces. Employer-organized van pooling is common among private and public organizations in metropolitan areas. For example, Molson Breweries introduced transportation pooling after the company consolidated its facilities and moved to a remote location. Employees appreciated the savings on expenses and the reduced commuting stress. Many employers report that tardiness and absenteeism are reduced by van pooling.

Credit Unions

Credit unions exist in many organizations to serve the financial needs of employees. They offer a variety of deposits as well as other banking services and make loans to their members. Although the employer may provide office space and a payroll deduction service, credit unions are operated by the employees under federal and provincial legislation and supervision.

Recreational and Social Services

Many organizations offer some type of sports programs in which personnel may participate on a voluntary basis. Bowling, softball, golf, baseball, and tennis are often provided as intramural programs. In addition to intramurals, many organizations have teams that represent them in competitions with other local organizations. Memberships at health clubs and fitness centres, or discounts on memberships, are also popular offerings (see Chapter 12).

Many social functions are organized for employees and their families. Employees should play a major role in the planning if these functions are to succeed. However, the employer should retain control of all events associated with the organization, because of possible legal liability. For example, employers can be held liable for injuries to third persons caused by an employee's actions arising from employment. "Employment" in this context can include attending a company party, if the employee was urged or obligated to attend it. Thus, an employee could be held responsible for an accident occurring while an employee is driving to or from an employer-sponsored event.

SUMMARY

Benefits are an established and integral part of the total compensation package. In order to have a sound benefits program, there are certain basic considerations. It is essential that a program be based on specific objectives that are compatible with the organization's philosophy and policies, as well as affordable. Through committees and surveys, a benefits package can be developed to meet employees' needs. Through the use of flexible benefit plans, employees are able to choose those benefits that are best suited to their individual needs. An important factor in how employees view the program is the full communication of benefits information through meetings, printed materials, and annual personalized statements of benefits.

Since many benefits represent a fixed cost, management must pay close attention in assuming more benefit expense. Increasingly, employers are requiring employees to pay part of the costs of certain benefits. Employers also shop for benefit services that are competitively priced.

Nearly one-quarter of the benefits packages provided by employers are legally required. These benefits include employer contributions to retirement plans, employment insurance, and workers' compensation insurance.

The cost of health care programs has become the major concern in the area of employee benefits. Several approaches can be used to contain health care costs, including reduction in coverage, increased coordination of benefits, and increased deductibles. Employee assistance programs (EAPs) and wellness programs can also help cut the costs of health care benefits.

Included in the category of benefits that involve payments for time not worked are vacations with pay, paid holidays, sick leave, and severance pay. Most Canadian workers receive 10 to 15 days' vacation leave plus statutory holidays. In addition to vacation time, most employees—especially in white-collar jobs—receive a set number of sick leave days. A one-time payment of severance pay may be given to employees who are being terminated.

Many provinces have abolished mandatory retirement, and now employees can choose when to retire. However, many employers provide incentives for early retirement in the form of increased pension benefits or cash bonuses. Some organizations now offer preretirement programs, which typically include seminars, workshops, and informational materials.

Once a pension plan has been established, it is subject to federal and provincial regulation to ensure that benefits will be available when the employee retires. While two types of plans are available—defined benefit and defined contribution—most employers now opt for the latter. The amount an employee receives on retirement is based on years of service, average earnings, and age at time of retirement. Usually, pension benefits are integrated with CPP/QPP. Pension funds are administered through either a trustee or an insurance plan.

The types of service benefits that employers typically provide include EAPs, counselling services, child care, and elder care. Other benefits are prepaid legal services, financial planning, housing and moving, transportation pooling, and credit unions, and social and recreational opportunities.

KEY TERMS

contributory plan 480
defined benefit plan 480
defined contribution plan 480
elder care 484

employee assistance programs
    (EAPs) 482
flexible benefit plans (cafeteria
    plans) 463
noncontributory plan 480

severance pay 477
silver handshake 478
vesting 481
workers' compensation insurance
    470

DISCUSSION QUESTIONS

1. You are a small employer wishing to establish a benefits program for your employees. What things should you consider to ensure that the program is a success for your employees?

2. Many organizations are concerned about the rising cost of employee benefits and question their value to the organization and to the employees.
    a. In your opinion, what benefits are of greatest value to employees? To the organization? Why?
    b. What can management do to increase the value to the organization of the benefits provided to employees?

3. Employers are required by law to provide specific benefits to employees. What laws mandate benefits to employees, and what are the provisions of those laws?

4. Identify and contrast the various ways employers can control the costs of health care.

5. Do you agree with the argument that the benefits for time not worked are the ones most readily available to reduce employer costs? Explain.

6. Employers used to prescribe a mandatory retirement age—usually sixty-five. What do you think are the advantages and disadvantages of a mandatory retirement age? What factors may affect an individual's decision to retire at a particular time, and what factors may affect his or her ability to adjust to retirement?

7. Outline the reasons why employers might prefer developing a defined contribution plan. As an employee, which plan would you prefer: defined benefit plan or defined contribution plan?

8. Working in teams of three or four, list and discuss the various benefits offered by your employer (or former employer). How were the costs of these benefits paid for?

9. Assume your team has been hired as a benefits consultant by a small business with fifty to sixty employees. What benefits do you believe this employer should offer, given its limited resources? Explain why you would offer these benefits.

Developing Managerial Skills

DESIGNING A BENEFITS PACKAGE

One measure of a successful employee benefits program is the variety of benefits available to meet employee and family needs. The popularity of cafeteria benefit plans, combined with the growing array of work-life benefits, are employer attempts to accommodate both family and job demands. For example, the benefits needs of single parents working eight-hour days will likely be entirely different when compared to the benefits needs of senior employees without child care responsibilities. With this exercise you will develop skills in benefits administration by matching benefits options to the needs of a diverse workforce.

Assignment

Below are the backgrounds of five employees. Working in teams of four to six individuals, identify those benefits you believe would serve each person's unique work-life situation. Draw on the benefits discussed in this chapter and your experience with benefits packages offered by organizations with whom you are familiar.

Note: Organizations have found it beneficial to obtain the opinions of different employee groups when designing their benefits packages. Try to form your teams with a variety of backgrounds represented.

▶ Donna Garcia is a working mother with two children, ages four and eight. As a sales representative, Donna has a job that requires her to work almost exclusively away from the office.

▶ Rod Harrison, age forty-eight, lives alone with no financial responsibilities for his adult children. Rod has recently developed an absenteeism problem that his manager believes is due to a growing dependency on alcohol.

▶ Lance Barns is a senior employee who wishes to retire in one year. Lance has raised a large family and has been unable to plan for a sound financial retirement. He has few outside hobbies or interests other than work.

▶ Patricia Hixson has three children, all in their teens. Her husband is on workers' disability insurance due to a serious construction injury.

▶ George Steigerwalt is twenty-six years old and single. He is financially secure with few monetary obligations. Both of George's parents are elderly and require frequent personal and medical assistance. George is an only child.

Case Study 1

True North Family-Friendly Benefits: The Backlash

True North Consulting Services, a provider of HR software application systems, prides itself on the variety of benefits it offers employees. In addition to extra health care, pension, and vacation benefits, the company also offers an attractive family-friendly benefits package including flexible schedules, child and elder care assistance, counselling services, adoption assistance, and extended parental leave. Unfortunately, in recent months, the company's progressive work-life policy has experienced a backlash from several employees, as the following case illustrates.

In March 2002, Teresa Wheatly was hired by True North as a software accounts manager. With excellent administrative and technical skills, as well as four years of experience at Adaptable Software, True North's main competitor, Teresa became a valued addition to the company's marketing team. As a single mother with two grade-school children, Teresa received permission to take Fridays off. She was also allowed to leave work early or come in late to meet the demands of her children. Teresa is one of eleven software account managers at True North.

The problem for True North, and particularly Janis Blancero, director of marketing, began in the fall of 2002. On September 15, Dorothy McShee, citing "personal reasons"—which she refused to discuss—requested a four-day work week for which she was willing to take a 20 percent cut in pay. When Dorothy asked for the reduced work schedule, she sarcastically quipped, "I hope I don't have to have kids to get this time off." On October 3, Juan Batista, a world-class marathon runner, requested a flexible work hours arrangement in order to accommodate his morning and afternoon training schedule. Juan is registered to run the London, England, marathon in May 2005. Just prior to Juan's request, Susan Woolf asked for, and was granted, an extended maternity leave to begin after the birth of her first child in December. If these unexpected requests were not enough, Blancero has heard comments from senior account managers about how some employees seem to get "special privileges," while the managers work long hours that often require them to meet around-the-clock customer demands. Janis has adequate reason to believe that there is hidden tension over the company's flexible work hours program. Currently, True North has no formal policy on flexible schedules. Furthermore, the company's growth in business combined with the increasing workload of software account managers and the constant service demands of some customers has made Blancero realize that she simply cannot grant all the time-off requests of her employees.

Source: Adapted from Alden M. Hayashi, "Mommy-Track Backlash," *Harvard Business Review* 79, no. 3 (March 2001): 33–42.

QUESTIONS

1. Do managers like Janis Blancero face a more complicated decision when evaluating the personal requests of employees rather than evaluating employees' individual work performance? Explain.

2. **a.** Should True North establish a policy for granting flexible work schedules? Explain.

   b. If you answered yes, what might that policy contain?

3. If you were Janis Blancero, how would you resolve this dilemma? Explain.

Case Study 2

Award-Winning Benefits Communication

The Bank of Nova Scotia, which employs 27 000 people, has created a comprehensive benefits communication package that includes a video, software, magazines, leaders' guides, and plan booklets. This information is available in English, French, and Braille. Because the bank's workforce is so diverse, much attention was paid to finding the right "voice." The bank finally decided on a friendly, conversational tone that was easy to understand. Employees were instrumental in designing the benefits program, providing input on everything from how a flexible plan should be introduced to what the magazine's content should be.

The Bank of Canada also solicited input from its employees when designing a flexible benefits program. The employees even chose the program's name: À la Carte. The full communications package included posters, information bulletins, enrolment kits (program guides, enrolment worksheets, and information about the intranet-based flex calculator), and a communications survey. A benefits hotline was established, and special forums were arranged in which groups of employees could ask questions. The flex calculator, which enabled employees to determine different benefits scenarios and target coverage to meet their personal needs, was especially popular. The number of hits on this intranet-based feature averaged 18 000 a day during the launch phase of the communications plan. The HR team that devised the plan also handed out portfolios to employees in the lobby as they arrived for work.

The impact of the communications program was measured. Nine-tenths of employees indicated that they had a clear understanding of their choices, and three-tenths chose nonstandard packages. Nineteen out of twenty met the enrolment deadline.

Source: Adapted from two articles on the Benefits Canada website: www.benefitscanada.com.

QUESTIONS

1. Compare the launch of these two communication packages to the suggestions listed in Highlights in HRM 11.1.

2. Are face-to-face meetings a more effective communication tool than an intranet-based response site? Explain.

CAREER COUNSEL

Design your own benefits package by completing the Flexible Benefits exercise on the *Managing Human Resources* website (www.belcourt4e.nelson.com).

NOTES AND REFERENCES

1. J. Taggart, "Putting Flex Benefits through Their Paces," *Canadian HR Reporter* 15, no. 21 (December 2, 2002): G3.
2. The Canadian Payroll Association, "Compensation Planning 2003," *Dialogue* [online magazine] www.payroll.ca. November/December 2002: 14–17.
3. S. Felix, "Techno Benefits," *Benefits Canada* 24, no. 1 (January 2000): 27–34.
4. Jan Everett, "Internet Security," *Employee Benefits Journal* 23, no. 3 (September 1998): 14–18. See also Alan R. Parham, "Developing a Technology Policy," *Employee Benefits Journal* 23, no. 3 (September 1998): 3–5.
5. John Tompkins and Sarah Beech, "Do Benefit Plans Attract and Retain Talent," *Benefits Canada* 26, no. 10 (2002): 49–56.
6. Dian Cohen, "Parallel Goals," *Benefits Canada* 22, no. 6 (June 1998): 98.
7. J. Taggart, "Guide to Pension and Benefits," *Canadian HR Reporter* 15, no. 21 (December 2, 2002): G3.
8. Ronald W. Perry and N. Joseph Cayer, "Cafeteria Style Health Plans in Municipal Govt.," *Public Personnel Management* 28, no. 1 (Spring 1999): 107–17; Jon J. Meyer, "The Future of Flexible Benefit Plans," *Employee Benefits Journal* 25, no. 2 (June 2000): 3–7. See also Carolyn Hirschman, "Kinder, Simpler Cafeteria Rule," *HRMagazine* 46, no. 1 (January 2001): 74–79.
9. L. Byron, L. and R. Dawson, "Flex Benefits Are More Popular Than Ever with Employers and Employees," *Benefits*, Benefits Canada, http://www.benefitscanada.com/magazine/article.jsp?content=20030624_134506_4312, April 2003.
10. "Communication Break Down: Employers Must Properly Inform Employees of Their Entitlement Benefits or Face Expensive and Time Consuming Court Challenges," *Benefits Canada* 21, no. 1 (January 1997): 27, 29.
11. M. Paterson, "Making a Statement: Are You Ready to Turn an Obligation into an Opportunity?" *Benefits Canada*, February 1995: 19–21.
12. "Great Communication Challenge," *Benefits Canada* 21, no. 9 (October 1997): 25–26.
13. J. MacBride-King, *Managing Corporate Health Care*, Conference Board of Canada, October 1995, Report 158–95: 10.
14. MacBride-King, *Managing Corporate Health Care.*
15. "FTNT Employment Insurance: More Than a New Name," *Work Life Report* 10, no. 2 (1996): 1–4, 5.
16. Dorothy Lipovenko, "Job Losses Force Early Retirement," *The Globe and Mail*, September 8, 1995: A8.
17. Doug Burn, "Wheel of Fortune: How Much Should an Organization Gamble on Early Retirement Planning?" *Human Resources Professional* 11, no. 4 (May 1994): 13–17.
18. David McCabe, "Retiring the Side: Approaches to Retirement Planning Range From the Conservative to the Revolutionary," *Human Resources Professional* 11, no. 4 (May 1994).
19. Catherine D. Fyock, "Crafting Secure Retirements," *HRMagazine* 35, no. 7 (July 1990): 30–3.
20. Larry Light, "The Power of the Pension Funds," *Business Week*, November 6, 1999: 154–58.
21. "Employers Help Workers Achieve Balance in Life," *HRFocus* 75, no. 11 (November 1998): S3.
22. T. Humber, "Stress Attack," *Canadian HR Reporter* 16, no. 3 (February 10, 2003): G1 and G10.
23. A. Tomlinson, "Trickle Down Effect of Retiring Boomers," *Canadian HR Reporter* 15, no. 11 (June 3, 2002): 1, 12.
24. Sonya Felix, "Running on Empty," *Benefits Canada* 21, no. 16 (June 1997): 109–14.
25. Elaine Davis and Mary Kay Krouse, "Elder Care Obligations Challenge the Next Generation," *HRMagazine* 41, no. 7 (July 1996): 98–103; Rodney K. Platt, "The Aging Workforce," *Workspan* 44, no. 1 (January 2001): 26.
26. Sue Shellenbarger, "Firms Try Harder, but Often Fail, to Help Workers Cope with Elder-Care Problems," *Wall Street Journal*, June 23, 1993: B1.

Safety and Health

After studying this chapter, you should be able to

objective 1
Summarize the common elements of federal and provincial occupational safety and health legislation.

objective 4
Describe the organizational services and programs for building better health.

objective 2
Describe what management can do to create a safe work environment.

objective 5
Explain the role of employee assistance programs in HRM.

objective 3
Identify the measures that should be taken to control and eliminate health hazards.

objective 6
Indicate methods for coping with stress.

O ccupational safety and health accidents are both numerous and costly to employers. Each year, about 375 000 workers are injured on the job, and nearly 1000 Canadian workers die.[1] To prevent losses such as these, employers are concerned about providing working conditions—in all areas of employment—that provide for the safety and health of their employees.

While the laws safeguarding employees' physical and emotional well-being are certainly an incentive, many employers are motivated to provide desirable working conditions by virtue of their sensitivity to human needs and rights. The more cost-oriented employer recognizes the importance of avoiding accidents and illnesses wherever possible.[2] Costs associated with sick leave, disability payments, replacement of employees who are injured or killed, and workers' compensation far exceed the costs of maintaining a safety and health program. Accidents and illnesses attributable to the workplace may also have pronounced effects on employee morale and on the goodwill that the organization enjoys in the community and in the business world.

Managers at all levels are expected to know and enforce safety and health standards throughout the organization. They must ensure a work environment that protects employees from physical hazards, unhealthy conditions, and unsafe acts of other personnel. Through effective safety and health programs, the physical and emotional well-being of employees may be preserved and even enhanced.

After discussing the legal requirements for safety and health, we shall focus in the rest of the chapter on the creation of a safe and healthy work environment and on the management of stress.

SAFETY AND HEALTH: IT'S THE LAW

Consider these facts:

▶ Every working day, three people die from a work accident or occupational disease.

▶ Every working day, more than 3000 workers are injured.

▶ In any year, approximately 16 million working days are lost because of on-the-job injuries.

▶ Each year, $5 billion is spent to compensate workers injured on the job or paid to the estates of those killed on the job. Indirect costs such as days off work, replacement workers' wages, etc. can double this figure to $10 billion.[3]

The burden on the nation's commerce as a result of lost productivity and wages, medical expenses, and disability compensation is staggering. HRDC estimates that every minute worked costs the Canadian economy about $80 000 in compensation payments to workers for accidents and injuries.[4] And there is no way to calculate the human suffering involved.

Occupational health and safety is regulated by the federal, provincial, and territorial governments. Statutes and standards vary slightly from jurisdiction to jurisdiction, although attempts have been made to harmonize the various acts and

Occupational injury
Any cut, fracture, sprain, or amputation resulting from a workplace accident or from an exposure involving an accident in the work environment

Occupational illness
Any abnormal condition or disorder, other than one resulting from an occupational injury, caused by exposure to environmental factors associated with employment

regulations. An **occupational injury** is any cut, fracture, sprain, or amputation resulting from a workplace accident. The worker's involvement in the accident can be direct, or the worker can simply be near enough to the accident to be injured as a result of it. An occupational illness is any condition or disorder (other than one resulting from an occupational injury) caused by the work environment. An **occupational illness** can be acute or chronic; it can result from inhaling, absorbing, ingesting, or directly contacting an illness-causing agent. Those working in the field agree that occupational illnesses are under-reported because few diseases are caused solely by work-related factors, and cause and effect can be difficult to determine.[5] Consider, for example, the case of a mine worker who has contracted a lung disease, but who also smokes heavily.

Acts and Regulations

All HR managers should become familiar with the occupational health and safety laws that apply to their organization. The various acts and government departments that enforce the legislation are listed in Figure 12.1.

Figure 12.1	Occupational Health and Safety in Canada	
Jurisdiction	**Legislation**	**Enforcement**
Canada	Canada Labour Code, Regulations	Labour Canada
Alberta	Occupational Health and Safety Act	Department of Labour
British Columbia	Regulations under Workers' Compensation Act	Workers' Compensation Board
Manitoba	Workplace Safety and Health Act	Department of Environment and Workplace Health and Safety
New Brunswick	Occupational Health and Safety	Occupational Health and Safety Commission
Newfoundland	Occupational Health and Safety Act	Department of Labour
Nova Scotia	Occupational Health and Safety Act	Department of Labour
Ontario	Workplace Safety and Insurance Act	Ministry of Labour
Prince Edward Island	Occupational Health and Safety Act	Department of Fisheries and Labour
Quebec	Act Respecting Occupational Health and Safety	Commission de la Santé et de la Sécurité du Travail
Saskatchewan	Occupational Health and Safety Act	Department of Labour
Northwest Territories	Safety Act	Commissioner NWT
Yukon	Occupational Health and Safety Act	Commissioner of the Yukon Territories; administered by the Workers' Compensation Board
Nunavut	Safety Act	For information only; not an official act

Duties and Responsibilities

The fundamental duty of every employer is to take every reasonable precaution to ensure employee safety. The motivating forces behind workplace legislation were effectively articulated in the landmark case *Cory vs Wholesale Travel Group*:

> Regulatory legislation is essential to the operation of our complex industrial society; it plays a legitimate and vital role in protecting those who are most vulnerable and least able to protect themselves. The extent and importance of that role has increased continuously since the onset of the Industrial Revolution. Before effective workplace legislation was enacted, labourers— including children—worked unconscionably long hours in dangerous and unhealthy surroundings that evoke visions of Dante's inferno. It was regulatory legislation with its enforcement provisions which brought to an end the shameful situations that existed in mines, factories and workshops in the nineteenth century. The differential treatment of regulatory offences is justified by their common goal of protecting the vulnerable.

Duties of Employers

Besides providing a hazard-free workplace and complying with the applicable statutes and regulations, employers must inform their employees about safety and health requirements. Employers are also required to keep certain records, to compile an annual summary of work-related injuries and illnesses, and to ensure that supervisors are familiar with the work and its associated hazards (the supervisor, in turn, must ensure that workers are aware of those hazards). An organization with many employees may have a full-time health and safety officer.

In all jurisdictions, employers are required to report to the Workers' Compensation Board accidents that cause injuries and diseases. Accidents resulting in death or critical injuries must be reported immediately; the accident must then be investigated and a written report submitted. In addition, employers must provide safety training and be prepared to discipline employees for failing to comply with safety rules. Employers are increasingly being required to prove due diligence. This includes establishing a comprehensive occupational health and safety management system; providing competent supervision, training, and instruction; and taking every reasonable precaution in the workplace for the health and safety of workers. Highlights in HRM 12.1 provides a list of health and safety procedures for new employees.

Duties of Workers

Employees are required to comply with all applicable acts and regulations, to report hazardous conditions or defective equipment, and to follow all employer safety and health rules and regulations, including those prescribing the use of protective equipment.

Workers have many rights that pertain to requesting and receiving information about safety and health conditions. They also have the right to refuse unsafe work without fear of reprisal. (Some professionals such as police, firefighters, teachers, and health care workers have only a limited

USING THE INTERNET

All the provincial Occupational Health and Safety programs can be found on the website of the Canadian Centre for Occupational Health and Safety at

www.ccohs.ca.

USING THE INTERNET

For a description of the best features of a health and safety program, go to the website for the Canadian Centre for Occupational Health and Safety and click on Basic OH&S Program Elements:

www.ccohs.ca/oshanswers/ hsprograms/basic.html

Highlights in HRM 12.1

HEALTH AND SAFETY CHECKLIST FOR NEW EMPLOYEES

By the end of a new employee's first week, an employee should be familiar with the following health and safety procedures and issues:

1. Fire Safety

    ▶ Identify the evacuation alarm sound.
    ▶ Show his/her evacuation route and assembly point, and any alternative route.
    ▶ Show where the extinguishers are in the work area.
    ▶ Explain when water and other extinguishers can/cannot be used.
    ▶ Show how to use extinguishers and what to do after use.
    ▶ Show where the alarm point is and how to sound it.
    ▶ Explain use of elevators and lifts in fire situation.

2. Housekeeping and Access

    ▶ Explain reasons for maintaining clear access.
    ▶ Explain hazards caused by obstructing gangways.

3. Smoking

    ▶ State where smoking is/is not allowed, and give reasons.

4. Accidents and Abnormal Occurrence

    ▶ Explain reporting procedure and reasons.
    ▶ Show the way to casualty (or first aid).
    ▶ Explain action in case of serious injury to oneself or another.
    ▶ Give two examples of abnormal occurrence.
    ▶ Include any hazard special to the job.

5. Lifting (manual handling)

    ▶ Demonstrate correct manual handling methods.

6. Uniforms, Overalls

    ▶ Explain issue, care, and cleaning arrangements.

7. Personal Clothing—Contamination

    ▶ Explain action in the event of clothing being contaminated (give two examples).

8. Protective Equipment

    ▶ Show how to wear equipment issued in department, and explain need for it.

(continued on following page)

9. Personal Hygiene

   ▶ Explain reasons for attention to personal hygiene.
   ▶ Give two examples of risk of cross-infection.
   ▶ Explain why it is necessary to report contact with notifiable diseases, and give examples of diseases.

10. Absence

   ▶ Know what to do in the event of sickness or other absence.
   ▶ Know to consult Occupational Health staff.

11. Electrics

   ▶ Demonstrate checks required before using electrical equipment.
   ▶ Explain action if faults found.

12. Material Hazards

   ▶ Identify any dangerous materials or objects, and explain how to handle them.
   ▶ Supply workplace hazardous information sheets.

13. Chemical Hazards

   ▶ Demonstrate safe handling methods for corrosive liquids, compressed gases, flammable solvents, other classes (appropriate to immediate workplace) (WHMIS).

14. Spillages

   ▶ Explain what must be done in the event of spillages.

15. Disposal

   ▶ Show waste/rubbish disposal system and explain hazards.

16. Machine Equipment Hazards

   ▶ Explain correct handling of equipment.
   ▶ Explain lock out/tagging procedures (appropriate to immediate workplace).

17. Health and Safety Management

   ▶ Explain the role of the Occupational Health Department.
   ▶ Identify the health and safety representatives and explain their roles.
   ▶ Explain the correct procedure if a hazard or problem is identified.
   ▶ Explain the functions of the safety committee.
   ▶ Describe the responsibilities of employees in health and safety.

Source: Adapted from B. Pomfret, "Sound Employee Orientation Program Boosts Productivity and Safety," *Canadian HR Reporter*, January 25, 1999: 17. Carswell.

right of refusal, the logic being that their work is inherently dangerous.) An employee who suspects that work conditions are hazardous can report this concern to his or her supervisor; this will trigger an investigation by the supervisor and a worker representative.

A work refusal investigation can result in either the employee's return to work or his or her continued refusal. In the latter case, the appropriate ministry is notified and an investigator is dispatched to the job site to provide a written decision. If a replacement worker is used, he or she must be notified of the previous employee's refusal to work.

Duties of Supervisors

A supervisor is generally defined as a person (with or without a title) who has charge of a workplace and authority over a worker. Occupational health and safety acts require supervisors to do the following: advise employees of potential workplace hazards; ensure that workers use or wear safety equipment, devices, or clothing; provide written instructions where applicable; and take every reasonable precaution to guarantee the safety of workers.

Duties of Joint Health and Safety Committees

Most jurisdictions require that health and safety committees be set up, with both union and management representation. The point of these joint committees is to establish a nonadversarial climate for creating safe and healthy workplaces. In Ontario, at least one management rep and one worker rep must be certified. The certification program provides training in the following subjects: safety laws, sanitation, general safety, rights and duties, and indoor air quality.

Penalties for Employer Noncompliance

The penalties for violating occupational health and safety regulations vary across provinces and territories. Most health and safety acts provide for fines up to $500 000, and offenders can be sent to jail. General Motors was fined $375 000 for failing to ensure that a machine was properly maintained, resulting in the death of an employee.[6] Under certain circumstances, the law provides for appeal by employers or employees.[7]

In certain environments, health and safety standards require the use of protective gear and equipment.

PHOTODISC

Workers' Compensation

Under workers' compensation, injured workers can receive benefits in the form of a cash payout (if the disability is permanent) or wage loss payments (if the worker can no longer earn the same amount of money). Unlimited medical aid is also provided,

USING THE INTERNET

An article written by Chubb
Corporation provides the basics of
a return-to-work program at
www.tsbic.com/rtw.htm.
Find more information at the
Ontario Workplace Safety and
Insurance Board website:
www.wsib.on.ca/wsib/wsibsite.nsf/
Public/CertificationTraining

Industrial disease
A disease resulting from
exposure to a substance
relating to a particular
process, trade, or occu-
pation in industry

along with vocational rehabilitation, which includes physical, social, and psychological services. The goal is to return the employee to his or her job (or some modification thereof) as soon as possible. Sun Life Assurance Company of Canada has a return-to-work awards program, which will give premium credits to employers that allow injured workers to change jobs or duties to enable these employees to return to work. A person who has been off work for six months has a 50 percent chance of returning; after twelve months, a 20 percent chance; and after two years, a 10 percent chance. Return-to-work models are being developed by Canadian Pacific Railway and Weyerhaeuser Canada Ltd. of Kamloops, British Columbia.[8]

Compensation has become a complex issue. The definitions of accidents and injuries have recently been expanded to include industrial diseases and stress. An **industrial disease** is a disease resulting from exposure to a substance relating to a particular process, trade, or occupation in industry.

Equally problematic is compensation for stress, which is discussed in more detail later in the chapter. Stress-related disabilities are usually divided into three groups: physical injuries leading to mental disabilities (e.g., clinical depression after a serious accident); mental stress resulting in a physical disability (ulcers or migraines); and mental stress resulting in a mental condition (anxiety over work load or downsizing leading to depression). Most claims, it should be pointed out, result from accidents or injuries.

The emphasis in workers' compensation has been shifting away from simply making assessments and payments, toward creating safety-conscious environments where there will be fewer work-related accidents, disabilities, and diseases. In some industrial sectors, employers are working together to establish rules and training programs to further the cause of accident prevention.

CREATING A SAFE WORK ENVIRONMENT

objective

We have seen that employers are required by law to provide safe working conditions for their employees. To achieve this objective, the majority of employers have a formal safety program. Typically, the HR department or the industrial relations department is responsible for the safety program. While the success of a safety program depends largely on managers and supervisors of operating departments, the HR department typically coordinates the safety communication and training programs, maintains safety records required by legislation, and works closely with managers and supervisors in a cooperative effort to make the program a success.

Organizations with formal safety programs generally have an employee-management safety committee that includes representatives from management, each department or manufacturing/service unit, and employee representatives. Committees are typically involved in investigating accidents and helping to publicize the importance of safety rules and their enforcement.

Promoting Safety Awareness

Probably the most important role of a safety awareness program is motivating managers, supervisors, and subordinates to be champions of safety considerations. In one

A starting place for setting up a workplace health and safety committee can be found at the following website—click on Certification Training:

www.wsib.on.ca

For suggestions on creating a safe work place, go the British Columbia Workers Compensation Board site:

www.worksafebc.com

study conducted by the American Institute of Plant Engineers, "survey results showed a direct correlation between an increase in management's commitment to safety in the workplace and a decrease in accidents."[9] If managers and supervisors fail to demonstrate awareness, their subordinates can hardly be expected to do so. Unfortunately, many managers and supervisors wear their "safety hats" far less often than their "production, quality control, and methods of improvement hats."

Most organizations have a safety awareness program that entails the use of several different media. Safety lectures, commercially produced films, specially developed videocassettes, and other media such as pamphlets are useful for teaching and motivating employees to follow safe work procedures. A page from one of these pamphlets is shown in Highlights in HRM 12.2. Posters have been found to be very effective because they can be displayed in strategic locations where workers will be sure to see them. For example, a shipyard found that placing posters at the work site helped reduce accidents by making employees more conscious of the hazards of using scaffolds.

The Key Role of the Supervisor

One of a supervisor's major responsibilities is to communicate to an employee the need to work safely. Beginning with new employee orientation, safety should be emphasized continually. Proper work procedures, the use of protective clothing and devices, and potential hazards should be explained thoroughly. Furthermore, employees' understanding of all these considerations should be verified during training sessions, and employees should be encouraged to take some initiative in maintaining a concern for safety. Since training by itself does not ensure continual adherence to safe work practices, supervisors must observe employees at work and reinforce safe practices. Where unsafe acts are detected, supervisors should take immediate action to find the cause. Supervisors should also foster a team spirit of safety among the work group.

Proactive Safety Training Program

What are the most popular subjects in safety training programs? One study found the most frequent topics to be (1) first aid, (2) defensive driving, (3) accident prevention techniques, (4) hazardous materials, and (5) emergency procedures.[10]

Most programs emphasize the use of emergency first-aid equipment and personal safety equipment. Furthermore, many organizations provide training in off-the-job safety—at home, on the highway, and so on—as well as in first aid. Injuries and fatalities away from the job occur much more frequently than do those on the job and are reflected in employer costs for insurance premiums, wage continuation, and interrupted production.

HR professionals, and safety directors in particular, advocate employee involvement when designing and implementing safety programs.[11] Employees can offer valuable ideas regarding specific safety and health topics to cover, instructional methods, and proper teaching techniques. Furthermore, acceptance for safety training is heightened when employees feel a sense of ownership in the instructional program.

Highlights in HRM 12.2

HARD HAT CARE

Clean the shell of your hard hat at least once a month.

Your Checklist

▶ Make sure your hat fits right. There should be approximately 1 inch between the harness and the shell so air can circulate and keep your scalp cool. If your hat is too loose, it will fall off when you bend over. Too tight and it may cause headaches.

▶ Wear a color-coded hat if you need identification. Don't paint or scratch your hard hat to identify it.

▶ Add light-attracting tape to your hat if you work at night or in darkness. This will make it easier for others to see you.

▶ Clean the shell of your hard hat at least once a month to remove oil, grease, chemicals, and sweat. Soak it for five minutes in mild detergent and water that's at least 140 degrees Fahrenheit (60 degrees Centigrade). Then wipe the hat and let the air dry it. Clean the hat according to the instructions provided.

▶ Take good care of your hat; don't drop it, throw it or drill holes in it.

▶ Sunlight and heat can rot the harness and straps. Don't leave your hard hat on the front or back window ledge of your car.

Source: Used by permission of the National Safety Council, Itasca, Illinois.

Information Technology and Safety Awareness and Training

Several reasons are advanced for the use of the Internet and information technology in safety and health training. First, enhanced delivery modes facilitate the development of both managers and employees.[12] Videos, PowerPoint presentations, and interactive CD-ROM training are ideal methods for standardized safety, environmental, and health instruction. Second, information technology allows organizations to customize their safety and health training needs.[13] At Stanley Works, Inc., the company's Internet is the number one tool for reducing health and safety problems. According to Kevin Nelson, employee health and safety director, "The Internet functions as the organization's SWAT team to develop and implement timely and efficient health and safety programs."[14]

Enforcing Safety Rules

Specific rules and regulations concerning safety are communicated through supervisors, bulletin board notices, employee handbooks, and signs attached to equipment. Safety rules are also emphasized in regular safety meetings, at new-employee orientations, and in manuals of standard operating procedures. Such rules typically refer to the following types of employee behaviours:

▶ Using proper safety devices
▶ Using proper work procedures
▶ Following good housekeeping practices
▶ Complying with accident- and injury-reporting procedures
▶ Wearing required safety clothing and equipment
▶ Avoiding carelessness and horseplay

Penalties for violation of safety rules are usually stated in the employee handbook. In a large percentage of organizations, the penalties imposed on violators are the same as those for violations of other rules. They include an oral or written warning for the first violation, suspension for repeated violations, and, as a last resort, dismissal. However, for serious violations—such as smoking around volatile substances—even the first offence may be cause for termination.

While discipline may force employees to work safely, safety managers understand that the most effective enforcement of safety rules occurs when employees willingly obey and "champion" safety rules and procedures. This can be achieved when management actively encourages employees to participate in all aspects of the organization's safety program. For example, opportunities for employee involvement include (1) jointly setting safety standards with management, (2) participation in safety training, (3) involvement in designing and implementing special safety training programs, (4) involvement in establishing safety incentives and rewards, and (5) inclusion in accident investigations. There are many workable incentives—for example, gift certificates, cash awards, trips, dinners, and gifts such as clothing or jewellery. Economy Carriers, a transportation company based in Edmonton, offers an employee points program. It audits eighteen operational areas for safety; on the basis of that audit, employees accumulate safety points, which they can use for purchases. Two researchers looked at twenty-four studies where positive reinforcement and feedback were used to enhance safe behaviour. In all the studies, incentives were found to improve safety conditions or reduce accidents.[15]

The Procter & Gamble plant in Belleville, Ontario, won an award for its novel approach to incentives. The plant manager calculated that P & G would receive a refund from workers' compensation of about $200 000 a year if injuries were eliminated at the plant. He then set up a plan that would allow this refund to go to the local hospital if the target of zero injuries was achieved. With this community-based incentive, P & G employees met the target and the hospital received a large donation.[16]

Figure 12.2 provides the steps recommended for launching a successful safety incentive program.

Accident Investigations and Records

Every accident, even those considered minor, should be investigated by the supervisor and a member of the safety committee. This investigation may determine what caused the accident and reveal what corrections are needed to prevent it from happening again. Correction may require rearranging workstations, installing safety guards or

Figure 12.2	Steps in a Successful Safety Incentive Program

- ▶ Obtain the full support and involvement of management by providing cost benefits.
- ▶ Review current injury and health statistics to determine where change is needed.
- ▶ Decide on a program of action and set an appropriate budget.
- ▶ Select a realistic safety goal such as reducing accidents by a set percentage, improving safety suggestions, or achieving a length of time without a lost-time injury. Communicate your objectives to everyone involved.
- ▶ Select incentive rewards on the basis of their attractiveness to employees and their fit with your budget.
- ▶ Develop a program that is both interesting and fun. Use kickoff meetings, posters, banners, quizzes, and/or games to spark employee interest. Give all employees a chance to win.
- ▶ Communicate continually the success of your program. Provide specific examples of positive changes in behaviour.
- ▶ Reward safety gains immediately. Providing rewards shortly after improvements reinforces changed behaviour and encourages additional support for the safety program.

Safety begins with preparedness, as these employees demonstrate in this dress rehearsal.

PHOTODISC

controls, or, more often, giving employees additional safety training and reassessing their motivation for safety.

Employers are required to keep certain records and to compile and post annual summaries of work-related injuries and illnesses. From these records, organizations can compute their incidence rates (i.e., the number of injuries and illnesses per 100 full-time employees during a given year). The standard equation for computing the incidence rate is shown below; 200 000 constitutes the base for 100 full-time workers who work 40 hours a week, 50 weeks a year:

$$\text{Incidence rate} = \frac{\text{Number of injuries and illnesses} \times 200\,000}{\text{Total hours worked by all employees during period covered}}$$

The same formula can be used to compute incidence rates for (1) the number of workdays lost because of injuries and illnesses, (2) the number of nonfatal injuries and illnesses without lost workdays, and (3) cases involving only injuries or only illnesses.

Incidence rates are useful for making comparisons between work groups, between departments, and between similar units in the same organization. They also provide a basis for making comparisons with other organizations doing similar work. The occupational health and safety departments in each province and Human Resources Development Canada compile data that employers can use to measure their safety records against those of other organizations. As noted in Ethics in HRM, organizations that report and investigate their own accidents often face more inspections, higher insurance premiums, and possible lawsuits.

Reality Check

CN CENTRE FOR OCCUPATIONAL HEALTH AND SAFETY

The CN Centre for Occupational Health and Safety is a research institute founded at Saint Mary's University in Halifax, Nova Scotia, through an endowment from CN. According to Kevin Kelloway, the director of the CN Centre, the mandate of the centre is to (a) coordinate and conduct research in occupational health and safety; (b) to build capacity for occupational health and safety research in Nova Scotia; and (c) to provide mechanisms for training and education in occupational health and safety.

Professor Kelloway, as co-author of the book *Managing Occupational Health and Safety*, says, "The hottest issue in safety is the role of human resources. We have taken engineering approaches to their limit. It is no longer the case that if we provide protective wear or put guards on equipment, that workers are safe. Engineering approaches are not sufficient. Now we are looking at these issues from a people perspective: How do we get people to work safely? What does it mean to work safely?

"There is another shift in thinking about safety and it is the recognition that compliance with legislation and standards is also not enough. We know that the old motto 'If you are compliant with the law, you have a safe workplace' is not true. Let me give you an example. WHMIS training is compulsory across Canada and all employers give WHMIS training to their employees. These organizations are fully compliant. But does that mean that the employees remember what they have learned? Does this guarantee that they pay attention to all the symbols? An employer can comply and still have unsafe work practices.

"The focus now is on safety initiative. How do we keep people and companies focused on safety? There is a role for leaders. One thing we found in our research is that active leadership which is continually promoting safety is necessary. When leaders stop talking, the minute they stop promoting safety, safety declines. There is a role for HR, to create a culture in which employees feel secure talking about safety, and mechanisms for channelling safety concerns exist. For example, do employees raise safety issues about potential safety hazards? If they raise concerns, are they treated as complainers? Is there a process to identify safety hazards? Part of the role of HR is to create that environment and provide those channels.

"It is always difficult to motivate safety, because it is the absence of something (an accident, an injury). From employees' perspective, they want to get their work done, and the organization encourages this. Of course, they want to work safely, but to get work done, shortcuts are more efficient. A good analogy is that we all want to drive safely but many of us will take risks to get home quickly. Rationally, driving safely is the most important goal, but behaviourally people drive as if saving fifteen seconds was important."

Ethics in HRM

BURY THE RECORD

A supervisor was instructing a group of new recruits in the cleaning of metal parts in an assembly plant. She was attempting to demonstrate the cleaning technique to two employees at one workstation, while at another workstation another new employee was trying to clean the parts himself. The cleaning liquid was highly toxic. The employee felt restricted by his safety gloves and so removed them. His eyes started to water, and instinctively he rubbed them with his solution-soaked hands. The pain was overwhelming, and no water was immediately available with which he could rinse his eyes. The employee suffered some temporary vision loss.

Who is to blame? The worker who started to clean without receiving full instructions and without using the issued gloves? The supervisor who could have forbidden the worker to start work until she explained the safety aspects? Or the company that failed to post warning signs about the hazardous nature of the cleaning solvent and did not have an eye-washing facility available?

Because workplace accidents increase workers' compensation premiums and the number of inspections, the company had an interest in not reporting the accident. Furthermore, because the company had instituted a reward program that provided incentives to employees for accident-free days, even the employees did not want to report the accident. Thus the supervisor and the employees agreed to "bury the record." This is illegal. Another company was fined $600 000 for misleading the Workplace Health and Safety Insurance Board after it deliberately chose not to report that injured workers had missed time at work. In a highly publicized case in 2003, a young worker fell five storeys to his death, landing just one metre from the supervisor, who was his uncle. The first thing the supervisor did was call 911, and he was overheard telling workers, "Workers' comp will be here right away, so you get that railing up right now."

CREATING A HEALTHY WORK ENVIRONMENT

From its title alone, the Occupational Safety and Health Act was clearly designed to protect the health, as well as the safety, of employees. Because of the dramatic impact of workplace accidents, however, managers and employees alike may pay more attention to these kinds of immediate safety concerns than to job conditions that are dangerous to their health. It is essential, therefore, that health hazards be identified and controlled.[17] Furthermore, pressure from the federal government and unions, as well as increased public concern, has given employers a definite incentive to provide the safest and healthiest work environment possible.

Health Hazards and Issues

At one time health hazards were associated primarily with jobs found in industrial processing operations. In recent years, however, hazards in jobs outside the plant, such as in offices, health care facilities, and airports, have been recognized and preventive methods adopted. Substituting materials, altering processes, enclosing or isolating a process, issuing protective equipment, and improving ventilation are some of the common preventions. General conditions of health with respect to sanitation, housekeeping, cleanliness, ventilation, water supply, pest control, and food handling are also important to monitor.

Chemical Hazards

When a boiler maker at Teck Cominco Ltd., a smelter plant in Trail, British Columbia, started to experience symptoms that resembled motion sickness, he never associated it with exposure to poisonous thallium metal. Like many workers, he had limited awareness of the chemicals in the workplace. It is estimated that more than 70 000 different chemicals are currently used in the workplace in places where humans can come into contact with them. Many of these chemicals are harmful, lurking for years in the body with no outward symptoms until the disease they cause is well established. Increasingly, employees are complaining of physiological reactions to low-level chemical exposures in the environment, such as headaches, dry nasal passages, and nausea. These complaints have several labels, such as total allergy symptom, twentieth-century disease, and multiple chemical sensitivity. (For a full discussion of chemical hazards, read Chapter 4 in *Management of Occupational Health and Safety* 2nd ed., by James Montgomery and Kevin Kelloway.)[18]

Test your knowledge of WHMIS at
www.whmis.net

Workplace Hazardous Materials Information Systems

In the belief that workers have the right to know about potential workplace hazards, industry, labour, and government have joined forces to develop a common information system for labelling hazardous substances. The Workplace Hazardous Materials Information System (WHMIS) is based on three elements:

1. *Labels.* Labels are designed to alert the worker that the container holds a potentially hazardous substance. The two types of labels (supplier labels and workplace labels) must contain specified and regulated information, including product identifiers and data on safe handling and material safety. WHMIS class symbols and subclass designations are shown in Figure 12.3.

2. *Material Safety Data Sheets (MSDSs).* A **Material Safety Data Sheet** identifies the product and its potentially hazardous ingredients and suggests procedures for handling the product safely. The MSDS information must be comprehensive, current, and available in English and French.

3. *Training.* Workers must be trained to check for labels and to follow specific procedures for handling spills. Training workers is part of the due diligence

Material Safety Data Sheets (MSDS)
Documents that contain vital information about hazardous substances

| Figure 12.3 | Class Symbols and Subclass Designations |

The subclass designations are shown below the class designation.

CLASS & SUBCLASS DESIGNATIONS

COMPRESSED GAS

CORROSIVE MATERIAL

OXIDIZING MATERIAL

POISONOUS AND
INFECTIOUS MATERIAL
Materials Causing
Immediate and
Serious Toxic Effects

Materials Causing
Other Toxic Effects

Biohazardous
Infectious Material

FLAMMABLE AND
COMBUSTIBLE MATERIAL
Flammable Gas
Flammable Liquid
Flammable Solid
Flammable Aerosol
Reactive Flammable Material

DANGEROUS REACTIVE
MATERIAL

Source: Solvents in the Workplace, Cat. no. B01230 (Toronto Industrial Accident Prevention Association, March).

required of employers; it also becomes an important factor in the event of a lawsuit. The Peel Board of Education in Ontario has developed a computer-based program to train workers in WHMIS. This program allows illiterate workers to respond to audio commands by touching the screen.

Indoor Air Quality

As a consequence of energy concerns, commercial and residential construction techniques have been changed to increase energy efficiency of heating, ventilating, and air-conditioning systems. This has included sealing windows, reducing outside air intake, and in general "buttoning up" buildings—thus resulting in the "sick building syndrome" (SBS) and "building related illnesses" (BRI) that give rise to such employee complaints as headaches, dizziness, disorientation, fatigue, and eye, ear, and throat irritation.[19] Popular office equipment, including photocopying machines, computer terminals, fax machines, and laser printers, contributes to these health complaints.

Four basic ways to overcome polluted buildings are to (1) eliminate tobacco smoke, (2) provide adequate ventilation, (3) maintain the ventilating system, and (4) remove sources of pollution. It is now common practice in both office and industrial settings, as well as public facilities (airports, hotels, schools, and so on), to monitor and manage the quality of indoor air.[20]

Tobacco Smoke. For the past ten years probably the most heated workplace health issue has been smoking. In a study published in the *Journal of the American Medical Association,* findings showed that "in businesses that permitted smoking, more than 60 percent of the office air samples contained nicotine levels above the 'significant risk' level of 6.8 micrograms per cubic meter."[21] Because of findings such as these, smokers have been banned from lighting up on airplanes, at work, and in restaurants and hotels. Furthermore, nonsmokers, fuelled by studies linking "passive smoking" (inhaling other people's smoke) with disease and death and irritated by smoke getting in their eyes, noses, and clothes, have demanded a smoke-free environment.

A British Columbia arbitrator has ruled recently that smoking is as addictive as cocaine and so constitutes a drug dependency. Under human rights legislation, employers may have to allow workers with a substance abuse problem to take a leave of absence to seek treatment. If nicotine addiction is accepted as a disability, companies may have to provide stop-smoking programs and refrain from disciplining addicted employees who smoke. A Labour Canada study found that employees who smoke cost companies about $2500 more per year (than nonsmoking employees) in increased absenteeism, lost productivity, and increased health and life insurance premiums.[22] It has been documented that health care costs are higher for smokers; for this reason, some employers are charging smokers more for health insurance or are reducing their benefits. Many employers, however, prefer positive reinforcement through wellness programs to encourage employees to stop smoking.

Video Display Terminals

The expanding use of computers and video display terminals (VDTs) in the workplace has generated intense debate over the possible hazards to which VDT users may be exposed. Many fears about VDT use have been shown to be unfounded, but serious health complaints remain an issue. Problems that managers have to confront in this area fall into three major groups:

1. *Visual difficulties.* VDT operators frequently complain of blurred vision, sore eyes, burning and itching eyes, and glare.

2. *Muscular aches and pains.* Pains in the back, neck, and shoulders are common complaints of VDT operators.

3. *Job stress.* Eye strain, postural problems, noise, insufficient training, excessive work loads, and monotonous work are complaints reported by three-quarters of VDT users.

To capitalize on the benefits of VDTs while safeguarding employee health, Dr. James Sheedy, a VDT and vision expert, offers these tips on how to minimize the negative effects of computer use on the eyes and body:

▶ Place the computer screen four to nine inches below eye level.

▶ Keep the monitor directly in front of you.

▶ Sit in an adjustable-height chair and use a copyholder that attaches to both the desk and the monitor.

▶ Use a screen with adjustable brightness and contrast controls.

▶ Use shades or blinds to reduce the computer-screen glare created by window lighting.

Figure 12.4 shows the common sources of emissions released by office equipment.

Cumulative Trauma Disorders

Meat cutters, fish filleters, cooks, dental hygienists, textile workers, violinists, flight attendants, office workers at computer terminals, and others whose jobs require repetitive motion of the fingers, hands, or arms are reporting injuries in growing percentages. Known as **cumulative trauma disorders** or repetitive motion injuries, these musculoskeletal disorders (MSDs) are injuries of the muscles, nerves, tendons, ligaments, joints, and spinal discs caused by repeated stresses and strains. One of the more common conditions is *carpal tunnel syndrome,* which is characterized by tingling or numbness in the fingers occurring when a tunnel of bones and ligaments in the wrist narrows and pinches nerves that reach the fingers and the base of the thumb. Without proper treatment, employees with carpal tunnel syndrome can lose complete feeling in their hands. Another cumulative trauma disorder prevalent among tennis players is tennis elbow.

In Chapter 3, we discussed job design and ergonomics considerations as one way to accommodate the capabilities and limitations of employees. Ergonomics techniques are also successfully used to improve or correct workplace conditions that cause or aggravate cumulative trauma disorders.[23] Continuous developments in office furniture, video display terminals, tool design, computer keyboards, and adjustable workstations are all attempts to make the work setting more comfortable—and, hopefully, more productive—but also to lessen musculoskeletal disorders. Mini-breaks involving exercise and the changing of work positions have been found helpful. Importantly, these kinds of injuries often go away if they are caught early. If they are not, they may require months or years of treatment or even surgical correction. Also, when cumulative trauma disorders result from work activities, they serve to lower employee productivity, increase employers' health costs, and incur workers' compensation payments.[24]

Cumulative trauma disorders
Injuries involving tendons of the fingers, hands, and arms that become inflamed from repeated stresses and strains

USING THE INTERNET

A variety of ergonomic information can be found on the Cornell University ergonomic website at http://ergo.human.cornell.edu/.

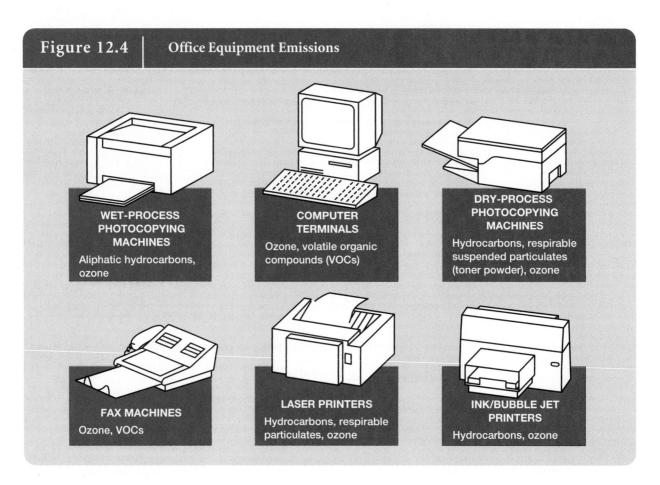

Figure 12.4 | Office Equipment Emissions

Note: Health complaints include increased perception of headache, mucous irritation; eye, nose, and throat irritation; and tight facial skin.
Source: Adapted from Air and Energy Research, EPA.

Communicable Diseases

Provisions for dealing with communicable diseases such as herpes simplex (cold sores), influenza, athlete's foot, and AIDS (acquired immune deficiency syndrome) are covered in public health legislation, not occupational health and safety legislation. In recent years, no issue has received as much attention as SARS (severe acute respiratory syndrome). SARS is a pneumonia-like and potentially fatal illness that, in 2003, infected areas such as Hong Kong, Taiwan, Singapore, and Toronto. The Centers for Disease Control advised business travellers to avoid these areas. Employers in Canada had to make decisions about travel bans, quarantines, the right to refuse work, and what constituted a safe work environment. Provincial legislation provides certain rights for employees affected by SARS, including job-protected leave, no penalties for emergency leave, payment for those not working because of quarantines, and work refusal processes. Highlights in HRM 12.3 describes how some employers coped with this crisis.

Highlights in HRM 12.3

THE SARS CRISIS

Human resource professionals, particularly those working in hospitals, faced a crisis in the spring of 2003 that none had seen in their working lifetimes. For the first time in the memory of most hospital employees at Sunnybrook and Women's College Health Sciences Centre in Toronto and London Health Sciences Centre in London, Ontario, there was a code orange crisis—in other words, the most serious level. People looked to the HR team to initiate action plans to deal with sick employees, quarantined employees, and scared employees. Unlike crises such as the events of September 11, 2001, where there is one dramatic event, SARS was an escalating event, with every day creating new problems. At Sunnybrook, the HR director took every decision with the thought "What are the repercussions? Long after SARS ends, the employees and the unions will remember how they were treated." The escalating pace was difficult. HR people had to train employees to screen 12 000 people a day and had just one weekend to design the process and hire and train staff. Communication had to be objective and immediate, not only with employees but with their worried families. For the first time, health care workers could not leave their work behind, with most having to wear masks at home and avoid contact with their families. To deal with these concerns, staff forums were held (employees had a need to talk about their concerns). The London Health Sciences Centre faced similar issues. Both vice-presidents of HR emphasized the need for visible leadership. One immediate problem that was soon evident was the folly of any absenteeism program that motivated employees to come to work sick, which of course increased the risk of communicable diseases spreading throughout the workforce. Some employees continued to come to work even when they weren't feeling well because they were worried they would lose income, so a policy that had to be developed immediately was a commitment to maintain the wages of workers in quarantine. Another unusual problem was that certain categories of workers, such as nurses, have limited rights to refuse work. When Mount Sinai Hospital in Toronto asked employees to staff screening stations, a librarian refused to do this work as she deemed it to be unsafe. A lesson learned is the importance of preparing for an emergency by stockpiling personal protective equipment and training all staff in its use.

It is not just hospitals that have to be prepared for outbreaks of communicable diseases. Hewlett-Packard has a workforce of 8000 employees, with 3200 of them at ten sites in the Greater Toronto Area. Two HP employees were hospitalized with SARS, and one site was forced to close. Fortunately, because the site had always required employees and visitors to sign in, and access was controlled with a pass card, all those known to have been at the site were easy to trace and all pass cards were revoked. Also, because HP is a high-tech company, with all employees online all the time, communication with employees was not difficult. However, the nature of the highly mobile workforce posed problems for health care officials. The public health department required lists of all employees who were absent, but HR does not track absences because most HP employees work from home or off site.

Sources: B. Orr, "SARS Outbreak Teaches Valuable Lessons on a New 'Normal' State for HR Management," *Canadian HR Reporter* 16, no. 11 (June 2, 2003): 5; Ministry of Labour, "Workplace Laws and SARS," www.gov.on.ca/LAB; A. Picard, "Mommy Are You Going to Die?", *The Globe and Mail*, April 5, 2003.

Many employers were unprepared to deal with SARS issues such as screening and employee quarantines.

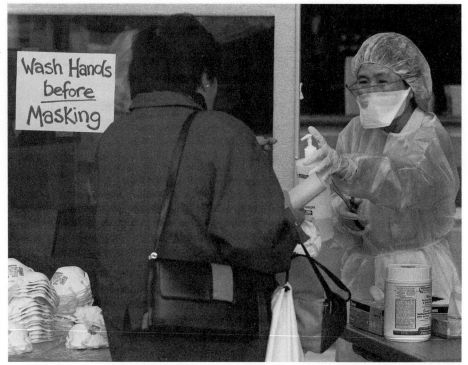

CP (KEVIN FRAYER)

Workplace Violence

The National Institute of Occupational Safety and Health (NIOSH) identified workplace homicide as one of the leading causes of workplace deaths. Manon Blanc at Queen's University and Kevin Kelloway, director of the CN Centre for Occupational Health and Safety at St. Mary's University, have identified the job characteristics that put workers at risk for aggression and violence in the workplace:

▶ Interacting with the public
▶ Making decisions that influence other people's lives (e.g., terminating an employee or assigning a failing grade) or denying the public a service or request
▶ Supervising and/or disciplining others
▶ Working nights, working alone
▶ Handling cash, handling or guarding valuables, collecting or delivering items of value
▶ Caring for the physical or emotional needs of others, going to clients' homes
▶ Serving or selling alcohol, dealing with individuals under the influence of mind-altering substances[25]

Exposure to workplace violence results in employees fearing more incidents of violence, leading to personal strains (such as stress) and organizational strains (reduced commitment, neglect of job duties).

The U.S.-based Occupational Safety and Health Administration (OSHA) has issued five recommendations for preventing workplace violence:

▶ Management commitment to and employee involvement in preventing acts of violence
▶ Analyzing the workplace to uncover areas of potential violence
▶ Preventing and controlling violence by designing safe workplaces and work practices
▶ Providing violence prevention training throughout the organization
▶ Evaluating violence program effectiveness[26]

Employers in all Canadian jurisdictions are bound to take all reasonable precautions to protect the safety and health of their workers. At this time, however, only British Columbia and Saskatchewan have specific laws requiring employers to protect their workers from violence. Managers and supervisors can be trained to recognize violence indicators such as those given in Figure 12.5. Awareness of these threatening behaviours can provide an opportunity to intervene and prevent disruptive, abusive, or violent acts.[27] Managers must effectively communicate a zero-tolerance policy for violence and encourage employees to report any possible or observed incidents of workplace violence.[28] A meaningful reporting procedure with clear lines of responsibility can ensure that management is promptly notified of potential security risks in order to take immediate steps to resolve the issues. Finally, organizations such as Garden Fresh, a growing restaurant chain, have formalized workplace violence-prevention policies, informing employees that aggressive employee behaviour will not be tolerated (see Highlights in HRM 12.4).

USING THE INTERNET

The Canadian Initiative on Workplace Violence, a social research firm, offers information at www.workplaceviolence.ca/.

Terrorism

The September 11, 2001, attacks on the World Trade Center and the Pentagon brought home to all North Americans the magnitude and horror of terrorism. Once largely confined to foreign countries, terrorism is now a major concern to North American employers, particularly those in high-target categories such as airlines, sporting facilities, energy plants and dams, high-tech companies, and public and commercial buildings. The heightened security procedures at these facilities show the importance employers place on the prevention of any terrorist attack. Although four out of five CEOs say that it is important to have safeguards in place, only about half have started the discussions necessary to put these procedures in place.[29]

Many of the points recommended to prevent workplace violence equally apply to preventing terrorism—background checks, violence prevention policy, and so on. Additionally, emergency prevention experts suggest that employers implement emergency evacuation procedures to minimize the consequences of terrorism.[30] At a minimum, these procedures would include escape routes, emergency equipment and gathering locations, and special assistance for disabled people and individuals responsible for the movement of employees.[31] Practice evacuation drills at unannounced times ensure that employees know how to respond to an evacuation while preventing unnecessary confusion should a real attack occur. Although Canadians have yet to encounter a colossal domestic catastrophe, Canadian workplaces should be prepared against such an eventuality.

Figure 12.5	Violence Indicators: Know the Warning Signs

Most people leave a trail of indicators before they become violent. Similarly, disgruntled former employees who commit acts of violence leave warning signs of their intent before and after termination. The following behaviours should be taken seriously when assessing situations of potential violence:

▶ Direct or veiled threatening statements

▶ Recent performance declines, including concentration problems and excessive excuses

▶ Prominent mood or behaviour changes; despondence

▶ Preoccupation with guns, knives, or other weapons

▶ Deliberate destruction of workplace equipment; sabotage

▶ Fascination with stories of violence

▶ Reckless or antisocial behaviour; evidence of prior assaultive behaviour

▶ Aggressive behaviour or intimidating statements

▶ Written messages of violent intent; exaggerated perceptions of injustice

▶ Serious stress in personal life

▶ Obsessive desire to harm a specific group or person

▶ Violence against a family member

▶ Substance abuse

Sources: Adapted from *Violence in the Workplace: Risk Factors and Prevention Strategies,* NIOSH Bulletin #59; Gillian Flynn, "Employers Can't Look Away from Workplace Violence," *Workforce* 79, no. 7 (July 2000): 68–70; Dannie B. Fogleman, "Minimizing the Risk of Violence in the Workplace," *Employment Relations Today* 87, no. 1 (Spring 2000): 83–98.

Crisis Management Teams

Some organizations have formal crisis management teams. These teams, composed of both hourly and managerial employees, conduct initial risk assessment surveys, develop action plans to respond to violent situations, and, importantly, perform crisis intervention during violent, or potentially violent, encounters.[32] For example, a crisis management team would investigate a threat reported by an employee. The team's mandate would be to gather facts about the threat, decide if the organization should intervene, and, if so, determine the most appropriate method of doing so. Occasionally, a member of the team or an individual manager will be called upon to intervene and calm an angry employee. When this occurs, the steps given in Figure 12.6 will help to defuse a volatile situation.

When violent incidents, such as the death of a co-worker, happen at work, employees can experience shock, guilt, grief, apathy, resentment, cynicism, and a host of other emotions.[33]

Highlights in HRM 12.4

GARDEN FRESH'S WORKPLACE VIOLENCE PREVENTION POLICY

Garden Fresh is committed to conducting its operations in a safe manner. Consistent with this policy, acts or threats (either verbal or implied) of physical violence, including intimidation, harassment, and/or coercion, which involve or affect Garden Fresh or which occur on Garden Fresh property will not be tolerated.

Acts of threats of violence include, but are not limited to, the following:

▶ All threats or acts of violence occurring on Garden Fresh premises, regardless of the relationship between Garden Fresh and the parties involved in the incident.
▶ All threats or acts of violence occurring off of Garden Fresh premises involving someone who is acting in the capacity of a representative of the company.
▶ All threats or acts of violence occurring off of Garden Fresh premises involving an employee of GFRC if the threats or acts affect the legitimate interest of Garden Fresh.
▶ Any acts or threats resulting in the conviction of an employee or agent of Garden Fresh, or of an individual performing services for Garden Fresh on a contract or temporary basis, under any criminal code provision relating to violence or threats of violence which adversely affect the legitimate interests and goals of Garden Fresh.

Specific examples of conduct which may be considered threats or acts of violence include, but are not limited to, the following:

▶ Hitting or shoving an individual.
▶ Threatening an individual or his/her family, friends, associates, or property with harm.
▶ The intentional destruction or threat of destruction of company property.
▶ Harassing or threatening phone calls.
▶ Harassing surveillance or stalking.
▶ The suggestion or intimation that violence is appropriate.
▶ Possession or use of firearms or weapons.

Garden Fresh's prohibition against threats and acts of violence applies to all persons involved in the company's operation, including Garden Fresh personnel, contract and temporary workers, and anyone else on Garden Fresh property.

Violations of this policy by any individual on Garden Fresh's property, by any individual acting as a representative of Garden Fresh while off of Garden Fresh property, or by an individual acting off of Garden Fresh's property when his/her actions affect the company's business interests will lead to disciplinary action (up to and including termination) and/or legal action as appropriate.

Employees should learn to recognize and respond to behaviors by potential perpetrators that may indicate a risk of violence.

(continued on following page)

Employees shall place safety as the highest concern, and shall report all acts or threats of violence immediately. Every employee and every person on Garden Fresh's property is encouraged to report incidents of threats or acts of physical violence of which he/she is aware. The report should be made to the Director of Human Resources, the reporting individual's immediate supervisor, or another supervisory employee if the immediate supervisor is not available.

It is the responsibility of managers and supervisors to make safety their highest concern. When made aware of a real or perceived threat of violence, management shall conduct a thorough investigation and take specific actions to help prevent acts of violence.

Nothing in this policy alters any other reporting obligation established by Garden Fresh policies or in state, federal, or other applicable law.

Source: Used with permission from Garden Fresh, 17180 Bernardo Center Drive, San Diego, Calif. 92128.

Figure 12.6	Calming an Angry Employee

If you try to defuse a tense situation, remember that anger frequently results from a person's feeling of being wronged, misunderstood, or unheard. Keep the following tips in mind to guide you.

▶ Strive to save the employee's dignity during an angry confrontation. Don't attack a person's rash statements or continue a muddled line of thinking.

▶ Hold all conversations in private. Do not allow the employee to create an embarrassing public situation for himself or herself, yourself, or other employees.

▶ Always remain calm. Anger or aggressiveness on your part will trigger a similar response in the employee.

▶ Listen to the employee with an open mind and nonjudgmental behaviour. Give the employee the benefit of hearing him or her out.

▶ Recognize the employee's legitimate concerns or feelings. Agree that the employee has a valid point and that you will work to correct the problem.

▶ If the employee is very emotional or if the engagement seems out of control, schedule a delayed meeting so people can calm down.

▶ Keep the discussion as objective as possible. Focus on the problem at hand, not the personalities of individuals. A cornerstone of conflict resolution is to "attack the problem, not the personality."

▶ If the employee appears overly aggressive, withdraw immediately and seek professional help before any further discussion with the employee.

▶ If your efforts fail to calm the employee, report the incident to your manager, security, or human resource personnel.

Source: Adapted from professional literature on crisis management and seminars attended by the authors.

Building Better Health

Along with improving working conditions that are hazardous to employee health, many employers provide health services and have programs that encourage employees to improve their health habits. It is recognized that better health not only benefits the individual, but also pays off for the organization in reduced absenteeism, increased efficiency, better morale, and other savings. An increased understanding of the close relationship between physical and emotional health and job performance has made broad health-building programs attractive to employers as well as to employees.

Ensuring Healthy Employees

The size of the organization determines the kind of health services that can be provided to employees. Small organizations are likely to have only limited facilities, such as those required to handle first aid; many larger firms offer complete diagnostic, treatment, and emergency surgical services. Since employers are required to provide medical services after an injury, larger companies usually have nurses and physicians on full-time duty. Medium-size and smaller organizations will have one or more physicians on call.

We noted in Chapter 5 that some employers give medical examinations to prospective employees after a job offer has been made. The examination should include a medical history with specific reference to previous hazardous exposures. Exposure to hazards, whose effects may be cumulative, such as noise, lead, and radiation, are especially relevant. For jobs involving unusual physical demands, the applicant's muscular development, flexibility, agility, range of motion, and cardiac and respiratory functions should be evaluated. Many organizations also give periodic examinations on a required or voluntary basis. Such examinations can help determine the effects of potential hazards in the workplace, and detect any health problems to which the employee's lifestyle or health habits may contribute.

Promoting Workplace Fitness and Health

Many organizations have developed programs that emphasize regular exercise, proper nutrition, weight control, and avoidance of substances harmful to health. Xerox gives its employees a publication called *Fitbook* that includes chapters on the hazards of smoking and the effects of alcohol and drug abuse, facts on nutrition and weight control, and guidelines for managing stress and learning to relax.

Importantly, wellness programs produce measurable cost savings to employers, as described in The Business Case. Figure 12.7 gives nine steps for launching a successful wellness program, even on a limited budget.

Employee Assistance Programs

A broad view of health includes the emotional as well as the physical aspects of one's life. While emotional problems, personal crises, alcoholism, and drug abuse are considered to be personal matters, they become organizational problems when they affect behaviour at work and interfere with job performance. Indeed only about 7 percent of employees use employee assistance programs (EAPs).[34] Supervisors are often given training and policy guidance in the type of help they can offer their subordinates. To be able to handle such problems, organizations such as RBC Financial Group and NCR in Waterloo and Mississauga, Ontario, offer an employee assistance program. Typically, such a program refers employees in need of assistance to in-house counsellors or outside professionals. However, some employees are reluctant to accept help as they risk being stigmatized. At Canadian Forces Base Winnipeg, anyone taking treatment for stress is said to be taking the Crazy Train to the North Side. Soldiers fear that they will be unjustly accused of faking post-traumatic stress disorder. Figure 12.8 outlines the type of programs offered to employees in Canada. The reasons most companies do not offer programs is the lack of resources and staff, and concerns over the cost benefits of such initiatives.[35]

The Business Case

INVESTING IN EMPLOYEE HEALTH

For the 2800 employees at Husky Injection Molding Systems of Bolton, Ontario, work seems like play as they visit their children over lunch, eat fresh healthy cafeteria food, play table tennis on their breaks, and receive an extra vacation day for staying fit. Husky spends more than $4 million a year on employee benefits, but this investment more than pays for itself in higher productivity, lower turnover, and lower absenteeism. The voluntary turnover rate is about 15 percent, which is 5 percent below the industry average. The absenteeism rate is 4 days compared to 7.3 days for the industry average. Injury claims are 1.2 for every 200 000 hours worked, compared with an industry average of 5.8. The estimated savings are $8.4 million a year.

Husky is not the only company seeing returns on investments in workplace well-being. Organizations in Atlantic Canada found that employees who participated in a three-month wellness program reduced the risk of heart disease and stroke, for an estimated return on the investment of $1.64 for every dollar spent. In one of the largest studies done on ROI of health care programs, the National Wellness program delivered wellness programs consisting of smoking cessation workshops, lifestyle and nutrition counselling, and on-site fitness to 90 000 employees in thirty locations. Those who participated had lower health care costs of between $5 and $16 per month. Even a one-time inexpensive program can show returns. TELUS introduced a flu immunization program and saw absences due to respiratory illness drop from 33 percent to 22 percent. Overall, studies of wellness programs document cost-benefit ratios of between $3 and $8 for every dollar spent. The benefits to organizations include decreased lost workdays, decreased workers' compensation costs, increased employee moral and productivity, reduced overtime costs, and reduced workplace injuries.

Sources: T. Grant, "Husky Woos Workers with Unique Perks," The Globe and Mail, August 20, 2001; S. Kee, "The Bottom Line on Wellness," Canadian Health Care Manager 9, no. 1 (Fall 2002): 23; G. Lowe, "The Dollars and Sense of Health Promotion," Canadian HR Reporter, September 23, 2002.

Figure 12.7	Tips for Starting a Successful Wellness Program

1. Conduct a health risk assessment of employees.

2. Create incentives for employees to achieve a healthy lifestyle.

3. Create opportunities for regular physical activities during the day or before or after work.

4. Provide nutritional advice from a registered dietitian.

5. Include healthy, low-fat choices among snacks and meals provided in cafeterias and through vending machines.

6. Eliminate smoking from the work setting.

7. Negotiate discounts from area health clubs.

8. Start a health and fitness newsletter.

9. Focus on reducing one or two high-risk factors among employees.

Source: Adapted from "The Surgeon General's Call to Action to Prevent and Decrease Overweight and Obesity 2001." See http://www.surgeongeneral.gov/topics/obesity.

Personal Crises

The most prevalent problems among employees are personal crises involving marital, family, financial, or legal matters. Such problems often come to a supervisor's attention. In most instances, the supervisor can usually provide the best help simply by being understanding and supportive and by helping the individual find the type of assistance he or she needs.[36] In many cases, in-house counselling or referral to an outside professional is recommended. In recent years, crisis hotlines have been set up in many communities to provide counselling by telephone for those too distraught to wait for an appointment with a counsellor.[37]

Emotional Problems

Mental health claims are the fastest growing category of disability costs in Canada today, and the cost of lost productivity alone is approximately $8 billion a year.[38] While personal crises are typically fraught with emotion, most of them are resolved in a reasonable period of time and the troubled individual's equilibrium is restored. Unfortunately, when personal crises linger, stress and tension may cause or intensify a mood disorder like depression. **Depression** is the decrease in functional activity accompanied by symptoms of low spirits, gloominess, and sadness. An estimated 1.4 million Canadians suffer from depression, and only about 6 percent have been diagnosed and are receiving proper treatment.[39] With available treatment, however, 70 percent of afflicted individuals will significantly improve, usually within a matter of weeks.

Since depression lowers individual productivity, causes morale problems, increases absenteeism, and contributes to substance abuse, it is important for managers to identify signs of depression on the job and to learn to deal with depressed employees. The more likely workplace signs of depression are decreased energy, decreased

Depression
Negative emotional state marked by feelings of low spirits, gloominess, sadness, and loss of pleasure in ordinary activities

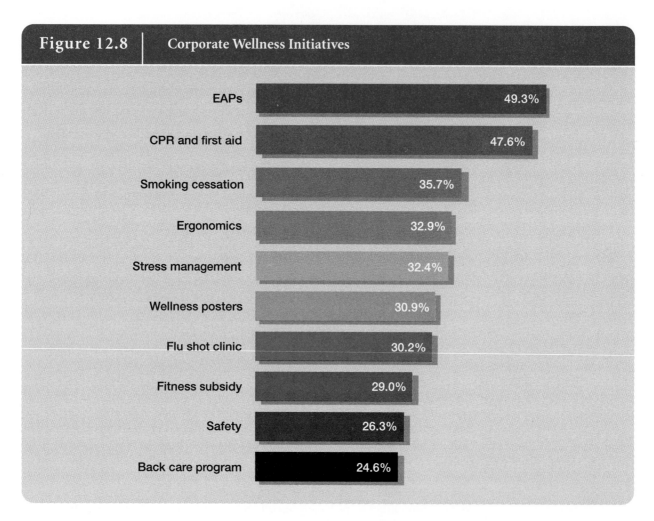

Figure 12.8 | Corporate Wellness Initiatives

Initiative	Percentage
EAPs	49.3%
CPR and first aid	47.6%
Smoking cessation	35.7%
Ergonomics	32.9%
Stress management	32.4%
Wellness posters	30.9%
Flu shot clinic	30.2%
Fitness subsidy	29.0%
Safety	26.3%
Back care program	24.6%

Source: J. Butler, "You've Invested in an EAP, Now Learn to Use It," *Canadian HR Reporter* 15, no. 11 (June 3, 2002): 7.

concentration, memory problems, guilt feelings, irritability, and chronic aches and pains that don't respond to treatment. Highlights in HRM 12.5 lists the symptoms of depression. When confronted with depressed employees, managers and supervisors are encouraged to be concerned with the employee's problem, be an active listener, and—should the depression persist—suggest professional help.[40] Under no circumstances should managers attempt to play amateur psychologist and try to diagnose an employee's condition. Mood disorders, such as depression, are complex in nature and do not lend themselves to quick diagnoses. Furthermore, in reviewing such cases, the organization should pay particular attention to workplace safety factors, since there is general agreement that emotional disturbances are primary or secondary factors in a large portion of industrial accidents and violence.[41]

Alcoholism

Alcoholism affects workers in every occupational category—blue-collar and white-collar. In confronting the problem, employers must recognize that alcoholism is a dis-

Highlights in HRM 12.5

DEPRESSION IN THE WORKPLACE

When a depressed mood persists for a few weeks, deepens, and eventually starts interfering with work and other aspects of everyday life, it has likely become an illness—or a clinical depression. In the workplace, a person with depression will exhibit many of the following signs:

Recognizing Depression

Personal Changes

▶ Irritability, hostility
▶ Hopelessness, despair
▶ Slowness of speech
▶ Chronic fatigue
▶ Withdrawal from or extreme dependency on others
▶ Alcohol or drug abuse

Workplace Changes

▶ Difficulty in making decisions
▶ Decreased productivity
▶ Inability to concentrate
▶ Decline in dependability
▶ Unusual increase in errors in work
▶ Accident proneness
▶ Frequent tardiness, increased "sick" days
▶ Lack of enthusiasm for work

Someone who has been experiencing many of these signs for a few weeks or more should seek help immediately.

Source: Reprinted by permission of Canadian Mental Health Association, Toronto.

ease that follows a rather predictable course. Thus they can take specific actions to deal with employees showing symptoms of the disease at particular stages of its progression. Alcoholism typically begins with social drinking getting out of control. As the disease progresses, the alcoholic loses control over how much to drink and eventually cannot keep from drinking, even at inappropriate times. The person uses denial to avoid facing the problems created by the abuse of alcohol and often blames others for these problems. The first step in helping the alcoholic is to awaken the person to the reality of his or her situation.

To identify alcoholism as early as possible, it is essential that supervisors monitor the performance of all personnel regularly and systematically. A supervisor should carefully document evidence of declining performance on the job and then confront the employee with unequivocal proof that the job is suffering. The employee should be assured that help will be made available without penalty. Since the evaluations are made solely with regard to lagging job performance, a supervisor can avoid any mention of alcoholism and allow such employees to seek aid as they would for any other problem.[42]

Abuse of Illegal Drugs

The abuse of drugs by employees is one of the major employment issues today. Drug abuse is now a national problem and has spread to every industry, occupation, and employee level. Estimates of the costs of substance abuse by employees vary considerably. Besides lost productivity, there are the costs of increased numbers of accidents and injuries, and rising rates of employee theft. The costs of substance abuse can have a dramatic impact on the bottom line. Drug testing remains a controversial issue. In general, pre-employment drug or alcohol testing or random testing of current employees is prohibited by human rights laws. Furthermore, human rights legislation prohibits discrimination on the basis of disability, and drug and alcohol dependency is generally considered to be a disability.

While attention is usually focused on the abuse of illegal drugs, it should be noted that the abuse of legal drugs can also pose a problem for employees. Employees who abuse legal drugs—those prescribed by physicians—often do not realize they have become addicted or how their behaviour has changed as a result of their addiction. Also, managers should be aware that some employees may be taking legal sedatives or stimulants as part of their medical treatment and that their behaviour at work may be affected by their use of these drugs.

THE MANAGEMENT OF STRESS

Many jobs require employees to adjust to conditions that place unusual demands on them. In time these demands create stresses that can affect the health of employees as well as their productivity and satisfaction. Fortunately, increasing attention is being given to ways of identifying and preventing undue stress on the job. Even greater attention must be given to identifying and removing sources of stress to protect the well-being of employees and to reduce the costs to organizations. Mental health claims now make up 25 percent of all disability claims.[43]

What Is Stress?

Stress is any demand on the individual that requires coping behaviour. Stress comes from two basic sources: physical activity and mental or emotional activity. The physical reaction of the body to both types of stress is the same. Psychologists use two separate terms to distinguish between positive and negative forms of stress, even though reactions to the two forms are the same biochemically. **Eustress** is positive stress that accompanies achievement and exhilaration. Eustress is the stress of meeting challenges such as those found in a managerial, technical, or public contact job. Eustress is regarded as a beneficial force that helps us to forge ahead against obstacles. What is

Stress
Any adjustive demand caused by physical, mental, or emotional factors that require coping behaviour

Eustress
Positive stress that accompanies achievement and exhilaration

Distress
> Harmful stress character-
> ized by a loss of feelings
> of security and adequacy

Alarm reaction
> Response to stress that
> basically involves an ele-
> vated heart rate,
> increased respiration, ele-
> vated levels of adrenaline
> in the blood, and
> increased blood pressure

harmful is **distress**. Stress becomes distress when we begin to sense a loss of our feelings of security and adequacy. Helplessness, desperation, and disappointment turn stress into distress.

The stress reaction is a coordinated chemical mobilization of the entire body to meet the requirements of fight-or-flight in a situation perceived to be stressful. The sympathetic nervous system activates the secretion of hormones from the endocrine glands that places the body on a "war footing." This response, commonly referred to as the **alarm reaction**, basically involves an elevated heart rate, increased respiration, elevated levels of adrenaline in the blood, and increased blood pressure. It persists until one's estimate of the relative threat to well-being has been re-evaluated. If distress persists long enough, it can result in fatigue, exhaustion, and even physical and/or emotional breakdown. Some research has linked stress to heart disease. Other studies have shown a connection between chronic stress and hypertension (high blood pressure). High blood pressure, the most common cause of strokes, contributes to heart disease.

Job-Related Stress

Although the body experiences a certain degree of stress (either eustress or distress) in all situations, here we are primarily concerned with the stress related to the work setting. It is in this setting that management can use some preventive approaches.

Sources of Job-Related Stress

Causes of workplace stress are many; however, high workloads, excessive job pressures, layoffs and organizational restructuring, and global economic conditions are identified as the primary factors of employee stress.[44] Additionally, disagreements

*Many Canadians report
that they experience
stress on the job.*

PHOTODISC

with managers or fellow employees are a common cause of distress, along with little or no say about how a job is performed, lack of communication on the job, and lack of recognition for a job well done. Even minor irritations such as lack of privacy, unappealing music, excessive noise, and other conditions can be distressful to one person or another.

Burnout

Burnout is the most severe stage of distress. Career burnout generally occurs when a person begins questioning his or her own personal values. Quite simply, one no longer feels that what he or she is doing is important. Depression, frustration, and a loss of productivity are all symptoms of burnout. Burnout is due primarily to a lack of personal fulfilment in the job or a lack of positive feedback about performance. In organizations that have downsized, remaining employees can experience burnout since they must perform more work with fewer co-workers. Overachievers can experience burnout when unrealistic work goals are unattainable.[45]

Burnout
> Most severe stage of distress, manifesting itself in depression, frustration, and loss of productivity

Coping with Stress

Coping with organizational stress begins by having managers recognize the universal symptoms of work stress as well as the stressful situations particular to their work unit. Major stressors include the following:

▶ Responsibility without authority
▶ Inability to voice complaints
▶ Prejudice because of age, gender, race, or religion
▶ Poor working conditions
▶ Inadequate recognition
▶ Lack of a clear job description or chain of command
▶ Unfriendly interpersonal relationships[46]

Many employers have developed stress management programs to teach employees how to minimize the negative effects of job-related stress. A typical program might include instruction in relaxation techniques, coping skills, listening skills, methods of dealing with difficult people, time management, and assertiveness. All of these techniques are designed to break the pattern of tension that accompanies stress situations and to help participants achieve greater control of their lives. Organizational techniques, such as clarifying the employee's work role, redesigning and enriching jobs, correcting physical factors in the environment, and effectively handling interpersonal factors, should not be overlooked in the process of teaching employees how to handle stress.[47]

Even though the number and severity of organizational stressors can be reduced, everyone encounters situations that may be described as distressful. Those in good physical health are generally better able to cope with the stressors they encounter. Figure 12.9 describes several ways to resolve job-related stress.

Before concluding this discussion, we should observe that stress that is harmful to some employees may be healthy for others. Most managers learn to handle distress effectively and find that it actually stimulates better performance, as it does for the CEO of Corel (See Highlights in HRM 12.6). However, there will always be those who are unable to handle stress and need assistance in learning to cope with it. The increased interest of young and old alike in developing habits that will enable them to lead happier and more productive lives will undoubtedly be beneficial to them as individuals, to the organizations where they work, and to a society where people are becoming more and more interdependent.

Figure 12.9	Tips for Reducing Job-Related Stress

▶ Build rewarding relationships with co-workers.

▶ Talk openly with managers or employees about job or personal concerns.

▶ Prepare for the future by keeping abreast of likely changes in job demands.

▶ Don't greatly exceed your skills and abilities.

▶ Set realistic deadlines; negotiate reasonable deadlines with managers.

▶ Act now on problems or concerns of importance.

▶ Designate dedicated work periods during which time interruptions are avoided.

▶ When feeling stressed, find time for detachment or relaxation.

▶ Don't let trivial items take on importance; handle them quickly or assign them to others.

▶ Take short breaks from your work area as a change of pace.

Highlights in HRM 12.6

PERSONAL POWER

Michael Cowpland, chairman, president, and CEO of software giant Corel Corp., was known for his hands-on management style—for becoming involved in every decision and having few middle managers. Virtually everyone in his company reported to him. He had no secretary and answered and returned his own mail. Cowpland regularly worked eighty-hour weeks. He read fifty industry magazines in one week (he was beyond speed-reading and into hyper-reading, he said). He played tennis five times a week and squash three times, and watched a wall of sixteen televisions all at the same time. He handled stress well. According to one stress researcher, the only factor that has any significant impact on a person's ability to withstand work pressure is "personal power"—having control over your time, resources, important information, work load, and so on. It is not the volume of work or work demands that makes people sick; it is the extent to which they can control it. Michael Cowpland is an example of a man who controlled his work environment.

Sources: "Racquet Scientist," *Canadian Business*, June 1995; P. Froiland, "What Cures Job Stress?" *Training*, December 1993: 32–36.

SUMMARY

Occupational health and safety legislation is designed to ensure, as far as is possible, safe and healthful working conditions for all working people. In general, it extends to all employers and employees. Occupational health and safety acts set standards, ensure employer and employee compliance, and provide safety and health consultation and training where needed. Both employers and employees have certain responsibilities and rights under these acts. Employers are required to provide a hazard-free work environment; they must also keep employees informed about legislative requirements and insist that they use protective equipment when necessary. In addition, employers are required to keep employees informed of hazardous substances and to instruct them in avoiding the dangers these present. Employees, for their part, are required to comply with safety standards, to report hazardous conditions, and to follow all employer safety and health regulations.

In order to provide safe working conditions for their employees, employers typically establish a formal program that, in a large percentage of organizations, is under the direction of the HR manager. The program may have many facets, including providing safety knowledge and motivating employees to use it, making employees aware of the need for safety, and rewarding them for safe behaviour. Such incentives as praise, public recognition, and awards are used to involve employees in the safety program. Maintenance of required records from accident investigations provides a basis for information that can be used to create a safer work environment.

Job conditions that are dangerous to the health of employees are now receiving much greater attention than in the past. There is special concern for toxic chemicals that proliferate at a rapid rate and may lurk in the body for years without outward symptoms. Concern for health hazards other than those found in industrial processing operations—indoor air pollution, video display terminals, and cumulative trauma disorders—present special problems that must be addressed. Today tobacco smoke is rarely tolerated in the work environment.

Along with providing safer and healthier work environments, many employers establish programs that encourage employees to improve their health habits. Some of the larger employers have opened primary care clinics for employees and their dependants to provide better health care service and to reduce costs. Wellness programs that emphasize exercise, nutrition, weight control, and avoidance of harmful substances serve employees at all organizational levels.

Virtually all the larger organizations and many of the smaller ones have found that an employee assistance program is beneficial to all concerned. While emotional problems, personal crises, alcoholism, and drug abuse are often viewed as personal matters, it is apparent that they affect behaviour at work and interfere with job performance. An employee assistance program typically provides professional assistance by in-house counsellors or outside professionals where needed.

An important dimension to health and safety is stress that comes from physical activity and mental or emotional activity. While stress is an integral part of being alive, when it turns into distress it becomes harmful. We have seen that many sources of stress are job-related. In recognizing the need for reducing stress, employers can develop stress management programs to help employees learn techniques for coping with stress. In addition, organizations need to redesign and enrich jobs, clarify the employee's work role, correct physical factors in the environment, and take any other actions that will help reduce stress on the job.

KEY TERMS

alarm reaction 527
burnout 528
cumulative trauma disorders 513
depression 523
distress 527

eustress 526
industrial disease 502
Material Safety Data Sheets
   (MSDSs) 510

occupational illness 497
occupational injury 497
stress 526

DISCUSSION QUESTIONS

1. What effects have occupational health and safety laws had on employer and employee behaviour?

2. Play a safety game that quizzes users on the dangers in the workplace at www.buildingfutures.ca. Another educational site, especially useful for summer students, can be found at the website of the Education Safety Association of Ontario: www.esao.on.ca.

3. An unhealthy work environment can lower productivity, contribute to low morale, and increase medical and workers' compensation costs. Working individually or in teams, list specific ways managers can
   a. Improve indoor air quality
   b. Accommodate the desires of smokers and nonsmokers
   c. Reduce the harmful affects of VDTs
   d. Address employee fears caused by violence

4. To live a healthier life, medical professionals say we need to identify those things we cur-

rently do that either impair or contribute to our health. Prepare a list of those activities you do that are beneficial or harmful to your overall health. Discuss with others a way to develop a lifetime program for a healthy lifestyle.

5. Go to the website of Human Resources Development Canada, and discover what the experts (including your authors!) have to say about work-life family balance, and what organizations are doing about this: http://labour.hrdc-drhc.gc.ca/worklife/ innovative-practices-en.cfm#4. Prepare a list of the key initiatives that would make your life as an employee less stressful.

6. Identify the sources of stress in an organization.
   a. In what ways do they affect the individual employee? The organization?
   b. What can managers and supervisors do to make the workplace less stressful?

Developing Managerial Skills

REDUCING EMPLOYEE STRESS

Job stress and its negative effect on both employees and the organization are a growing concern for managers and supervisors. As the text discusses, employee distress costs employers staggering amounts of money in lost productivity, absenteeism, turnover, increased workers' compensation claims, and health care costs. The cost of distress on the personal lives of employees is unmeasurable. Not surprisingly, stress management is an important aspect of any manager's job.

Stress management programs typically focus on three things to reduce workplace stress: (1) They identify factors in jobs that create stress; (2) they discuss specific techniques and managerial practices that help elevate workplace stress; and (3) they help individuals identify personal characteristics that serve to increase or decrease stress for them.

Assignment

1. Working in groups of four to six individuals, identify personal experiences that caused workplace stress. Explain exactly why these incidents were stressful. Suggest ways to reduce or eliminate these stressful conditions.

2. Stress management often begins by having individuals identify their skills and abilities and jobs that will help them succeed. Assessing our preferences and skills can help us understand why some tasks or roles are more stressful than others. Identify work-related stress by answering these questions:

   ▶ What skills that I enjoy using am I currently using in my job?
   ▶ What skills that I enjoy using am I currently not using?
   ▶ What specific things about my job do I really like?
   ▶ What are things about my job that I dislike?
   ▶ Based on my personal skills and abilities, what would my perfect job be?

Case Study 1

Preventing Repetitive-Strain Injuries at CTAL

Repetitive strain injuries (RSIs) have been with us for centuries, under names such as "carpet layers' knees" and "postman's shoulders." People who use computer keyboards for long stretches of time are especially prone to carpal tunnel syndrome, a condition characterized by numbness, pain, and tingling in the fingers and sometimes a burning or tingling sensation in the shoulder and arm. If left untreated, this condition can have serious long-term consequences for employees.

At Canadian Tire Acceptance Limited (CTAL) in Welland, Ontario, about 80 percent of the employees—many of them data entry workers—regularly use personal computers. In response to employee complaints of stiffness and pain, management hired an outside consultant, who determined that nearly 60 percent of CTAL's workforce was experiencing symptoms of RSI. Of that number, about half had seen a health care professional about the problem.

To prevent future injuries, CTAL modified its workstations and introduced a system under which job duties were rotated. At counselling and group sessions, employees learned how to identify risk factors and how to prevent RSIs through correct posture and optimum work habits. Wellness programs emphasizing fitness and nutrition were also part of the RSI prevention program. Employees who had reported RSI symptoms were linked with an occupational therapist who helped them manage the symptoms.

The RSI prevention program worked. No RSIs were reported in 1996, and 90 percent of those employees who required the services of an occupational therapist returned to work and remain productive. CTAL has saved at least three dollars for every dollar spent on the program.

Sources: L. Ramsay, "Working Pains," *Financial Post*, May 23, 1997: 4; "The Case for Integration," *Occupational Health and Safety* 12, no. 7 (1997): 68, 70; "CTAL Sheds Light on Repetitive Strain Dilemma," *Canadian Occupational Safety* 13, no. 1 (January–February 1997): 2.

QUESTIONS

1. The number of reported RSIs is increasing in most workplaces. Explain why.
2. What reasons might employees have for not reporting RSI symptoms?
3. Which aspect(s) of the above program do you think had the greatest effect?

Case Study 2

Workplace Safety and Young Workers

Young workers are 70 percent more likely to have a workplace injury than any other group. About 95 percent of those affected workers are men. This means that one in eleven young men can expect to suffer a workplace injury. Typically, these young men are employed at small manufacturing businesses, fast-food restaurants, convenience stores, and warehouses. The accidents happen within the first six months on the job. These young men lose fingers while slicing meat at the deli counter, are crushed by equipment they do not know how to operate, are electrocuted on metal ladders that touch hydro poles, or are burned handling chemicals with no protective equipment. The top five causes of injuries to young workers are slips and falls, overexertion, being struck by an object, exposure to toxic chemicals, and burns.

Less than half receive any job training. Only about 30 percent of teenagers receive instruction in first aid and CPR in their safety training, but most learn nothing about the law, their rights, hazards on the job, or safety management. Young workers are especially vulnerable because they feel invincible and lack experience. They believe the following myths:

▶ I can take risks; I won't die.
▶ I can handle anything; I am young and fit.
▶ Nothing will happen to me; I am safe at work.
▶ I must do any job my employer tells me to do.
▶ I am not responsible for workplace safety; this is my employer's responsibility.

Most will not ask for safety training because they are unaware of risks, are anxious to please, or are fearful of losing their jobs.

Many provinces, recognizing these risks, have added health and safety training to the high school curriculum. Most such programs discuss workplace hazards, employer rights and responsibilities, health and safety laws, and the workers' right of refusal. Alberta has the most advanced training course for young workers in Canada: Job Safety Skills, which consists of seventy-five hours of instruction, divided into three modules:

▶ Personal safety management (first aid, back care, safety and the law)
▶ Workplace safety practices (ergonomics, confined space entry, transportation of dangerous goods, and farm safety)
▶ Safety management systems (loss control, accident investigation, and a mock workshop in which students develop an entire safety program)

Source: Adapted from S. Singh, "HR's Role in Health and Safety for Young Workers," *HR Professional* 18, no. 5 (November 2001): 17–18; L. Ramsay, "Work Can Kill You," *National Post*, September 27, 1999: C12; L. Young, "Young Workers: Changing the Face of Safety," *Occupational Health and Safety* 14, no. 4, June–July 1998: 24–30; "Workplace Safety," *The Globe and Mail*, Friday, May 12, 2000; Government of Canada, "Youth Path, Health and Wellness," www.youth.gc.ca/healsafe.

QUESTIONS

1. Why are there more workplace injuries among those aged sixteen to twenty-five?
2. By law, workplace safety is the responsibility of the employer and employee. Why have nearly all provinces created courses in occupational health and safety as part of the high school curriculum? Should these be mandatory courses or electives?
3. Check the website of the Industrial Accident Prevention Association (www.iapa.ca), which has excellent information on occupational health and safety (OH&S) training programs. Design a training program that an employer could provide to young workers.

CAREER COUNSEL

The Job Stress Assessment on the *Managing Human Resources* website (www.belcourt4e.nelson.com) is designed to help you measure the amount of stress you are experiencing. Visit this site to measure your stress level and learn about strategies for managing stress.

NOTES AND REFERENCES

1. Association of Workers Compensation Boards of Canada, Table 1, www.awcbc.org.

2. "Healthier Employees Save You Money," *HRFocus* 78, no. 8 (August 2001): 3–4.

3. Canadian Centre for Occupational Health and Safety, http://ww.ccohs.ca.

4. HRDC, "Work Safely for a Healthy Future," *Research and Analysis*, March 2000.

5. William Glenn, "Finding the Right Balance," *Occupational Health and Safety* 18, no. 4 (June 2003): 38–42.

6. Joel Murray, "GM Fined for Disabled Limit Switches," *Occupational Health and Safety* 16, no. 6 (Summer 2000): 13, 14.

7. Check the website of your province's Occupational Health and Safety agency.

8. M. Basch Scott, "Insures, Support Services Focus on Enabling Return to Work from Disability," *Employee Benefits Plan Review* 54, no. 9 (March 2000): 16–21; V. Galt and K. Harding, "No Safety in the Numbers," *The Globe and Mail*, June 18, 2003: C1.

9. "Workplace Accidents Decrease as Safety Commitment Increases," *HRFocus* 71, no. 9 (September 1994): 16.

10. Todd Nighswonger, "Is First-Aid First in Your Workplace?" *Occupational Hazards* 64, no. 4 (April 2002): 45–47.

11. Tim W. McDaniel, "Employee Participation: A Vehicle for Safety by Design," *Occupational Hazards* 6, no. 5 (May 2002): 71–76.

12. Andrew J. Sorine, Richard T. Walls, and Robert W. Trinkleback, "Safety Training Gets Wired through Web-Based E-Learning," *Occupational Hazards* 63, no. 2 (February 2001): 35–40.

13. G. C. Shah, "Five Steps to Digital Safety," *Occupational Health and Safety* 71, no. 3 (March 2002): 22–25.

14. Roger Brooks, "OSHA's E-Tool for Lockout/Tagout," *Occupational Health and Safety* 71, no. 4 (April 2002): 22–24.

15. R. Bruce McAffee and Ashley R. Winn, "The Use of Incentives/Feedback to Enhance Work Place Safety: A Critique of the Literature," *Journal of Safety Research* 20 (1989): 7–19. See also Thomas R. Krause, John H. Hidley, and Stanley J. Hodson, "Broad-Based Changes in Behavior Key to Improving Safety Culture," *Occupational Health and Safety* 59, no. 7 (July 1990): 31–37, 50; Matthew P. Weinstock, "Rewarding Safety," *Occupational Hazards* 56, no. 3 (March 1994): 73–76; Susan J. Marks, "Incentives that Really Reward and Motivate," *Workforce* 80, no. 6 (June 2001): 108–13.

16. Tara Neal, "Tools of the Trade," *Occupational Health and Safety* 18, no. 2 (March 2002): 60–68.

17. Terese Steinback, "Workplace Strategies for Removing Obstacles to Employee Health," *Employee Benefits Journal* 25, no. 1 (March 2000): 9–10.

18. James Montgomery and Kevin Kelloway, *Management of Occupational Health and Safety* 2nd ed. (Toronto: ITP Nelson, 2002), ITP Nelson Series in HRM.

19. Robert J. Grossman, "Out with the Bad Air," *HRMagazine* 45, no. 10 (October 2000): 37–44.

20. Brian Shockley, "Air Quality Management in Confined Spaces," *Occupational Hazards* 63, no. 9 (September 2001): 91–94. See also Michael Tesmer, "Avoiding the Air Monitoring Blues," *Occupational Hazards* 63, no. 4 (April 2001): 49–51.

21. "Smoke Gets in Your Lungs," *HRFocus* 73, no. 2 (February 1996): 17.

22. D. Dyck, "Wrapping Up the Wellness Package," *Benefits Canada* 23, no. 1 (January 1999): 16–20.

23. Walt Rostykus, "Sustaining Ergonomic Success," *Occupational Hazards* 64, no. 2 (February 2002): 51–53.

24. Timothy Bland and Pedro P. Forment, "Navigating OSHA's Ergonomics Rules," *HRMagazine* 46, no. 2 (February 2001): 61–67.

25. Kevin Kelloway, "Predictors and Outcomes of Workplace Violence," *HR Professional* 20, no. 1 (February/March 2003): 50.

26. NIOSH document, *Violence in the Workplace: Risk Factors and Prevention Strategies*, Bulletin #59, is available from Publications Dissemination, EID, National Institute for Occupational Safety and Health, 4676 Columbia Parkway, Cincinnati, OH 45226-1998, (800) 356-4674.

27. Dannie B. Fogleman, "Minimizing the Risk of Violence in the Workplace," *Employment Relations Today* 87, no. 1 (Spring 2000): 83–98.

28. Rebecca S. Speer, "Can Workplace Violence Be Prevented?" *Occupational Hazards* 60, no. 8 (August 1998): 26–30.

29. Connie Vitello, "Sitting Canucks: What You Need to Know to Protect Your Workplace from Terrorism," *Hazardous Materials Management Magazine* 13, no. 5 (January 2002): 8–18.

30. Chemical plants and nuclear generating stations have well-developed emergency evacuation procedures. See, for example, Fred Muldoon, "Keeping Up-to-Date for Emergencies," *Occupational Hazards* 63, no. 7 (July

2001): 31–32; Jannelle Lanter Brown, "What to Do Before Emergencies Happen," *Occupational Health and Safety* 71, no. 2 (February 2002): 42–46.

31. Susanne M. Bruyère and William G. Stothers, "Enabling Safe Evacuations," *HRMagazine* 47, no. 1 (January 2002): 65–67.

32. Thomas Beck, "Set Up a Proactive Crisis Management Program," *HRFocus* 77, no. 1 (January 2000): 13.

33. Claire Ginther, "A Death in the Family," *HRMagazine* 46, no. 5 (May 2001): 55–58.

34. S. Pinker, "SOS Call Your EAP," *The Globe and Mail*, December 11, 2002: C1.

35. F. Puchalksi, "On Site Health Care Brings Healthy Bottom Line," *Canadian HR Reporter* 13, no. 7 (October 9, 2000): 7.

36. Kristi D. Willbanks, "The Role of Supervisory Referral in Employee Assistance Programs," *Employee Assistance Quarterly* 15, no. 2 (1999): 13–28.

37. Dale Masi and Michael Freedman, "The Use of Telephone and On-Line Technology in Assistance, Counseling and Therapy," *Employee Assistance Quarterly* 16, no. 3 (2001): 49–63.

38. Kathryn Dorrell, "Breaking Down the Barriers" *Benefits Canada* 24, no. 12 (December 2000): 36–38.

39. Ibid.

40. Todd Nighswonger, "Depression: The Unseen Safety Risk," *Occupational Hazards* 64, no. 4 (April 2002): 38–42.

41. William Atkinson, "Making Disease Management Work," *HRMagazine* 47, no. 1 (January 2002): 42–45.

42. Susan K. McFarlin, William Fals-Stewart, Debra A. Major, and Elaine M. Justice, "Alcohol Use and Workplace Aggression: An Examination of Perpetration and Victimization," *Journal of Substance Abuse* 13, nos. 1–2, (2001): 303–21.

43. T. Humber, "Stress Attack," *Canadian HR Reporter* 16, no. 3 (February 10, 2003): G1, G10.

44. William Atkinson, "When Stress Won't Go Away," *HRMagazine* 45, no. 12 (December 2000): 105–10.

45. "Stop Burnout—Before It Stops Your Employees," *HRFocus* 79, no. 2 (February 2002): 3–4.

46. Merry Mayer, "Breaking Point," *HRMagazine* 46, no. 10 (October 2001): 111–16.

47. "The Key to Stress Management, Retention, and Profitability: More Workplace Fun," *HRFocus* 77, no. 9 (September 2000): 5–6.

Employee Rights and Discipline

After studying this chapter, you should be able to

objective 1

Explain statutory rights, contractual rights, and due process.

objective 5

Explain two approaches to disciplinary action.

objective 2

Identify the job expectancy rights of employees.

objective 6

Identify the different types of alternative dispute-resolution procedures.

objective 3

Explain the process for establishing disciplinary policies, including the proper implementation of organizational rules.

objective 7

Discuss the role of ethics in the management of human resources.

objective 4

Discuss what discipline means, and how to investigate a disciplinary problem.

I n this chapter we discuss employee rights, workplace privacy, and
employee discipline. Privacy will be the defining issue of the decade. As
such, a discussion of the issue will be a theme throughout this chapter.
Managers are discovering that the right to discipline and discharge
employees—a traditional responsibility of management—has become more
difficult to exercise now that employment protection rights have been
strengthened.[1] Also, most managers and supervisors find disciplining
employees a difficult and unpleasant task; many of them report that taking
disciplinary action against employees is the most stressful duty they perform.
Balancing employee rights and employee discipline is not easy, but it is a universal requirement, and critical to good management.

The rising importance of employee rights issues has led to an increase in the number
of lawsuits filed by employees. For this reason, in this chapter we discuss alternative dispute resolution systems as means of fostering organizational justice. Because disciplinary actions are subject to challenge and possible reversal through government
agencies or the courts, managers should strive to prevent the need for such action.
However, when disciplinary action can no longer be avoided, that action should be
taken in accordance with carefully developed HR policies and practices. Since ethics is
an important element of organizational justice, we conclude this chapter with a discussion of ethics in employee relations.

In a discussion of organizational discipline, the role of counselling in achieving
individual and organizational objectives deserves special attention. This is why we
have provided an appendix to this chapter that reviews counselling techniques.

EMPLOYEE RIGHTS

objective

Employee rights
Guarantees of fair treat-
ment from employers,
especially regarding
an employee's right to
privacy

Various human rights laws, wage and hour regulations, and safety and health laws have
secured basic employee rights and brought many improvements to the workplace.
Employee rights litigation has now shifted to workplace issues such as the following:
the right of employees to protest unfair disciplinary action, to refuse to take drug tests,
to privacy protection, to challenge employer searches and surveillance, and to receive
advance notice of plant closings.[2]

Society is always changing, and so is the business sector, and employee rights
change along with both. **Employee rights** can be defined as the guarantees of fair
treatment that employees expect in regard to their status in the workplace.[3] These
expectations become rights when they are granted to employees by the courts, by legislatures, or by employers. Employee rights often involve the employer's alleged invasion of an employee's right to privacy. Unfortunately, the distinction between an
employee's legal right to privacy and the moral or personal right to privacy is not
always clear. The confusion is due to the lack of a comprehensive and consistent body
of privacy protection law.

Balanced against employee rights is the employer's responsibility to provide (a) a
safe workplace for employees, and at the same time, (b) safe goods and services of high
quality to consumers. Suppose an employee who uses drugs chooses to exercise his or

her privacy right and refuses to submit to a drug test. If that employee produces a faulty product as a result of drug impairment, the employer can be held liable for any harm caused by that product. So employers must exercise reasonable care when hiring and training employees and assigning jobs to them. Employers who fail to exercise reasonable care can be held negligent by outside parties or by other employees for injuries resulting from a dishonest, unfit, or incompetent employee.[4] In law, **negligence** is the failure to use a reasonable amount of care where such failure results in injury to another person.

Negligence
Failure to provide reasonable care where such failure results in injury to consumers or other employees

It is in situations like this that employee rights and employer responsibilities come most sharply into conflict. An organization that fails to honour employee rights can get caught up in costly lawsuits that damage both its reputation and the morale of its workers. But litigation can be started just as easily by employee groups who see their safety and welfare being threatened, and by consumers who are unhappy with the products and services the organization provides. This conflict is illustrated in one of the cases described in Reality Check. For the rest of this section, we will discuss various rights that employees have come to expect in the workplace.

Reality Check

TWO CASES OF EMPLOYEE RIGHTS LITIGATION

Brian Smeenk is a management-side labour lawyer with the law firm of McCarthy Tétrault. For this specialist in employment and labour law, two issues stand out:

"A hot issue continues to be termination. The *Wallace vs. United Grain Growers* decision has added new complexity to the concept of reasonable notice. Formerly, employers could calculate what constituted reasonable notice by looking at factors such as age, length of service, position, and salary. But the *Wallace* decision added another factor: Did the employer behave fairly during the termination and preceding it? In the *Wallace* case, the employer was found to have acted in bad faith. They had alleged cause for his dismissal, even though there were no grounds for doing so. They had misled him about how secure his job was. As a result, the Supreme Court of Canada ruled that the normal entitlement to reasonable notice, which the lower court had assessed at fifteen months, should be increased to twenty-four months. The court awarded Wallace damages in the amount of his salary and benefits for the longer period.

"One of the toughest issues facing employers in the rights area is discrimination on the basis of disability. Disability is so difficult to define, and it is even more difficult to draw the line between the employee's right to accommodation and the employer's right to run a business. Let me give you a fascinating case. A pharmaceutical company manages a number of employees, with science credentials, involved in testing products. One scientist was experiencing psychiatric problems (paranoid schizophrenia) and was having trouble functioning at work. The employer arranged for psychiatric assistance at the Clarke Institute, and the scientist was cleared to return to work. However, her work was substandard. The scientist maintained that her work was

(continued on following page)

substandard because others were tampering with her work. After receiving warnings and counselling, she knew her job was in trouble. She said she couldn't take the pressure and that if she lost her job, she would commit suicide, taking her son with her. To signal her intent, she slit her wrists in her boss's office, but the cuts were not serious and she survived. The workplace was on edge. All her co-workers were seriously concerned about her safety, and their safety, as the materials they handled were hazardous.

"Management wanted to either terminate her or arrange for a disability leave. However, her doctor would not certify her as disabled. If management terminated her, they risked being faced with a human rights complaint alleging discrimination on the basis of a mental disability, with no attempt to accommodate. The key questions were [these]: Does she have a right to be accommodated? Does this cause undue hardship to the employer? Could the employer win a case based on the argument that accommodation would cause undue hardship? What if her colleagues' fears are not supported by the medical evidence?"

Employment Protection Rights

It is not surprising that employees regard their jobs as an established right—a right that should not be taken away without just cause.[5] People's personal well-being relies heavily on being able to work. This line of reasoning has led to the emergence of three legal considerations regarding job security: statutory rights, contractual rights, and due process.

Statutory Rights

Statutory rights are rights that derive from legislation. As we saw in Chapter 2, employment equity legislation protects employees from discrimination on the basis of grounds such as age, sex, and race. In Prince Edward Island, 314 seasonal workers received compensation from the Tory government after it was determined that they had been fired because of their political affiliation.[6] Pay equity legislation addresses inequities in how men and women are compensated; occupational health and safety legislation attempts to ensure safe and healthful working conditions; labour relations laws give employees the right to form and belong to unions, and to bargain for better working conditions (see Chapter 14).

Statutory rights
Rights that derive from legislation

Contractual Rights

In contrast to statutory rights, **contractual rights** are derived from contracts. A contract is a legally binding agreement; if one party breaches the contract, a remedy can be sought through the courts. Formal contracts between employers and full-time employees are rare; however, they are standard practice for contingent workers, a growing segment of the Canadian labour force. A contract that outlines what constitutes fair notice and justification for dismissal, and that includes clauses about nonsolicitation and noncompetition, provides employers with greater flexibility but tends to limit the rights of employees and to reduce their opportunities for making a living after

Contractual rights
Rights that derive from contracts

they have left the company. An organization should not ask an employee to sign a contract after beginning work; the courts tend to see this as unilaterally trying to change the unwritten employment contract.

Not all contracts are written. An implied contract can arise when an employer extends to an employee a promise of some form of job security. Implied contractual rights can be based on oral or written statements; those statements can be made during the pre-employment process or after the hire. Promises of job security are sometimes contained in employee handbooks, HR manuals, or employment applications. Whether promises of job security are explicit or implicit, the courts tend to rule that they are binding. In this regard, *Wallace vs. United Grain Growers* was an important case. Wallace had been seduced by assurances of job security until retirement to leave his employer of twenty-five years and join a Winnipeg printing firm owned by United Grain Growers. Then Wallace was dismissed abruptly by his new employer. He was later awarded damages by the Supreme Court of Canada. In another case, the court found that an employer made misleading representations of a job, that the employee believed these representations, and that he suffered damages as a result of believing them. The employer was found liable. In its decision, the court stated that it is the duty of employers to ensure that the information about a job is accurate.[7]

In the following circumstances, an implied contract may become binding:

▶ Employees are told their jobs are secure as long as they perform satisfactorily and are loyal to the organization.

▶ The employee handbook states that employees will not be terminated without the right of defence or access to an appeal procedure (i.e., due process).

▶ An employee is persuaded to leave another organization by promises of higher wages and benefits; the hiring company then reneges after hiring that person.

To reduce their vulnerability to implied contract lawsuits, employers can do the following:

1. Train supervisors and managers not to imply contract benefits in conversations with new or current employees.

2. Include in employment offers a statement that the employee may voluntarily terminate employment with proper notice, and that the employee may be dismissed by the employer at any time and for a justified reason (just cause). The language in this statement must be appropriate, clear, and easily understood.

3. Explain the nature of the employment relationship in documents—for example, in employee handbooks, employment applications, and letters of employment.

4. Have written proof that employees have read all the documents pertaining to the employment relationship.

Due Process

Management has traditionally possessed the right to direct employees and to take corrective action when needed. Nevertheless, many people also believe that a job is the property right of an employee and that the loss of employment has such serious consequences that employees should not lose their jobs without the protection of due process.

Due process
Employee's right to
present his or her posi-
tion during a disciplinary
action

Managers normally define **due process** as the employee's right to be heard through the employer's own complaint procedure.[8] However, proactive employers will also incorporate the following principles—or rights—in their interpretation of due process:

1. The right to know job expectations and the consequences of not fulfilling those expectations.
2. The right to consistent and predictable management action for the violation of rules.
3. The right to fair discipline based on facts, the right to question those facts, and the right to present a defence.
4. The right to appeal disciplinary action.
5. The right to progressive discipline.

Employment Rights Not a Guarantee

Although employees may have cause to regard their jobs as an established right, there is no legal protection affording employees a permanent or continuous job. Furthermore, in general terms, due process does not guarantee employment to workers. However, the concepts of due process and of job-as-right do obligate managers to treat their employees fairly, equitably, and consistently.[9] Employees do have the right to sound employment practices, and to be treated as individuals of dignity and substantial worth.

In Canada, in absence of a formal contract specifying the duration of employment, the employment relationship is construed as ongoing. Thus, even when employment is not necessarily considered to be permanent, the employer must provide reasonable notice as well as grounds for termination. In the United States the employment-at-will principle assumes that an employee has a right to sever the employment relationship for a better job opportunity or for other personal reasons. Likewise, an employer is free to terminate the employment relationship at any time—and without notice—for any reason, no reason, or even a bad reason.[10] In essence, employees are said to work "at the will" of the employer. The employment-at-will relationship is created when an employee agrees to work for an employer for an unspecified period of time. Since the employment is of an indefinite duration, it can, in general, be terminated at the whim of either party. This freedom includes the right of management to unilaterally determine the conditions of employment and to make personnel decisions.

Wrongful Dismissal

An employer can dismiss an employee—that is, terminate the employment relationship—for just cause. To do so, the employer must document and prove serious misconduct or incompetence on the part of the employee. Some actions that are considered serious misconduct include persistent insubordination, sexual harassment, persistent bullying, physical assault at work, sharing confidential items with third parties, competing directly against the employer, and in certain cases, the use of drugs or alcohol in the workplace.[11] In recent years more and more employees have sued their former employers for "wrongful or unjust dismissal." One comprehensive study of wrongful dismissal suits found that employers won 40 percent of the time

For additional information on wrongful dismissals, see

http://canadaonline.about.com/cs/hremployers/.

when the charge was dishonesty, theft, substance abuse, or abusive behaviour; 54 percent of the time when the charge was insubordination; 65 percent of the time when the charge was conflict of interest or competing with the employer; and just 25 percent of the time when the charge was poor performance.[12]

Managers, with the help of the HR department, must be able to document that the performance problems were brought to the attention of the employee and that sufficient time, training, and assistance were given to improve the weak performance. Insensitive and inappropriate behaviour by employers during a termination can be costly, as outlined in The Business Case. To help avoid charges of wrongful dismissal, HR specialists recommend that employers follow the tips provided in Figure 13.1. Also, Highlights in HRM 13.1 describes how employees can challenge a just cause case.

The Business Case

DISMISSAL DANGER

Employers must be very cautious in the way in which employee dismissals are handled. The employer must be honest and avoid making misleading statements or unfounded allegations of cause. One company had to pay a terminated employee $75 000 in punitive damages because the employer alleged the cause of the termination was insubordination, wilful disobedience, and failure to achieve the expected level of performance, while the HR department was told the cause was restructuring (the punitive damages were overturned because the employee had already received a generous compensation).

The employer cannot make injurious statements or unsubstantiated allegations to potential employers, or sabotage the employee's reputation in the labour market. In one case, an employer dismissed a car sales manager after thirteen years on the job and circulated a letter to other car dealers, alleging that the employee had violated company policies. The judge found the allegations unfounded and awarded an additional six months' notice for aggravated or punitive damages. In another case, the B.C. Court of Appeal awarded eighteen months' damages, or salary (later reduced to twelve months), for bad faith dismissal, when the employer wrongly accused an employee of forgery, fraud, and drug abuse, making her unemployable in the labour market. The employer should try to be sensitive to the feelings and personal circumstances of the employee, and to make every effort, to the extent possible, to assist the employee in finding another job.

Sources: Peter Israel, "Cut Down on Lawsuits Just by Being Nice," *Canadian HR Reporter* 15, no. 20 (November 18, 2002): 5; J. Miller, "Highest Ever Damages for Bad Faith Dismissal Overturned," *Canadian HR Reporter* 14, no. 1 (January 15, 2001): 5.

| Figure 13.1 | **Tips to Avoid Wrongful Employment Termination Lawsuits** |

▶ Terminate an employee only if there is an articulated reason. An employer should have clearly articulated, easily understandable reasons for discharging an employee. The reasons should be stated as objectively as possible and should reflect company rules, policies, and practices.

▶ Set and follow termination rules and schedules. Make sure every termination follows a documented set of procedures. Procedures can be from an employee handbook, a supervisory manual, or even an intra-office memorandum. Before terminating, give employees notices of unsatisfactory performance and improvement opportunities through a system of warnings and suspensions.

▶ Document all performance problems. A lack of documented problems in an employee's personnel record may be used as circumstantial evidence of pretextual discharge if the employee is "suddenly" discharged.

▶ Be consistent with employees in similar situations. Document reasons given for all disciplinary actions, even if they do not lead to termination. Terminated employees may claim that exception-to-the-rule cases are discriminatory. Detailed documentation will help employers explain why these "exceptions" did not warrant termination.

Constructive Dismissal

Constructive dismissal
Changing an employee's working conditions such that compensation, status, or prestige is reduced

In 1997 the Supreme Court of Canada set the standard for constructive dismissal. **Constructive dismissal** has occurred when an employer changes an employee's working conditions in such a way that compensation, status, or prestige is reduced. The changes must be substantive—that is, they must affect pay, reporting relationships, responsibilities, and location; they cannot be trivial (e.g., minor changes in working hours). Even if the employee agrees to the changed conditions (the only other option might be unemployment) or resigns, the court considers him or her to have been dismissed.[13]

Two cases illustrate the concept. One involved a Royal Trust regional manager who was earning about $150 000 in base salary and commissions when his job was eliminated. He was offered the position of branch manager at the company's least profitable branch, where his income would have been based solely on commissions (he had held a similar position about four promotions earlier). The court ruled that he had been constructively dismissed and awarded him damages and legal costs. In another case, Embassy Cleaners changed the working conditions of a presser, resulting in a more physically demanding job, an earlier start time (6:00 a.m. instead of 7:30 a.m.), a change in the work week from five to six days, and a change from hourly wages to piecework. The court ruled that these changes constituted a fundamental breach of contract and hence constructive dismissal.[14]

In a nonunion context, employers can give notice of future changes in compensation, benefits, incentives, working hours, location, and so on as long as they provide actual notice equivalent to that given for dismissal.

Highlights in HRM 13.1

FIRING BACK!

Once you have received either verbal or written warnings about performance, a decision has usually been made to fire you. What can you do? Writing back to pick holes in the accusations is the least effective defence. Using the same weapons as management, you must prove that the just cause will not hold.

Harold Leavitt, a legal expert on dismissal, offers the following advice:

▶ Establish in writing that you were unaware of the standards of performance or conduct. You can argue that the standards are new or were not part of the initial job offer, position description, performance evaluations, or previous warnings. The company must prove that you were grossly incompetent, so any letters of praise or good performance review should be used. Any aspects of performance that may override the weak areas should be noted. For example, if you are being dismissed for poor communication skills but your productivity figures are increasing, this should be documented. As soon as you commence employment, start a file containing all performance evaluations; letters of praise from customers, co-workers, internal clients, and supervisors; and all other examples of performance achievements. Establish a paper trail of good performance.

▶ Argue that the company, while complaining about poor performance, has not stated specifically what is required to improve performance.

▶ Assert that you were not given the time, training, assistance, or learning opportunities necessary to improve performance.

▶ Establish, if true, that the employer hired you knowing that you did not possess the necessary skills. Note any understanding that you would receive the appropriate training.

▶ State, if applicable, that the skills desired now were not part of your original job description.

▶ Attribute your poor performance to factors outside your control, such as a decline in sales in all regions, or poorly priced products, or a temporary illness. If possible, establish that the company contributed to the performance problem by failing to respond to your (documented) suggestions for improvement.

Leavitt further advises that letters and all other documentation be written with the assistance of a specialist. In the end, you may not get your job back, but if successful you can expect an attractive severance package.

Source: Howard Leavitt, Counsel, Lang Michener, Toronto. "How Employees Can Fight Firing for Just Cause," *Toronto Star*, August 17, 1992: C1. Reprinted by permission of the author.

objective

Job Expectancy Rights

Once hired, employees expect certain rights associated with fair and equitable employment. Employee rights on the job relate to these issues, among others: substance abuse and drug testing, privacy, plant closing notification, and just cause disciplinary and discharge procedures.

Substance Abuse and Drug Testing

The impact on employers of employee drug abuse is staggering. It is estimated that drug abuse by employees costs Canadian employers an estimated $4.1 billion a year for alcohol, $6.8 billion for tobacco, and $823.1 million for illicit drugs—a total of $11.8 billion in productivity losses. That represents 1.7 percent of the gross domestic product, or $414 per capita.[15] Most human rights commissions see drug and alcohol as dependencies; it follows that testing for these dependencies is a form of discrimination.[16] Compared with nonabusing employees, substance abusers have been found to

▶ take three times as much sick leave;

▶ file five times more workers' compensation claims;

▶ have four times more accidents on the job; and

▶ make twice as many mistakes.[17]

In these litigious times, an employer's failure to ensure a safe and drug-free workplace can result in astronomical liability claims when consumers are injured because of a negligent employee or faulty product.[18] The Canadian government has not introduced legislation on drug testing; such legislation does exist south of the border. Canadians are generally more opposed to drug testing than Americans.[19] Companies that do use drug testing are faced with high costs ($15 to $45 for each test), error rates as high as 40 percent, and employee resistance.[20] At the same time, companies with drug-testing policies report reductions in absenteeism, sick days, and accidents. Highlights in HRM 13.2 describes some issues with drug testing.

Employee Searches and Surveillance

Employee theft is costing Canadian retailers about $2 million a day and represents about one-third of all losses. Employees justify stealing by offering such excuses as "I'm underpaid and take what I deserve; everyone does it; the company expects it and just writes it off; the company makes huge profits and so they can afford it; the company makes me mad and I am getting even." [21] Air Canada estimates it is losing as much as 9 percent of cabin stock each year as a result of employee theft. Private investigators employed by Air Canada searched the rooms of flight crews for these missing items—and found them—after the crews had checked out of the hotels.[22] Employers can minimize the risk of employee theft by following the guidelines provided in Figure 13.2.

Where work rules providing for inspections have been put into effect, employees have no reasonable expectation of privacy: they must comply with probable cause searches by employers. And they can be appropriately disciplined—most likely for insubordination—for refusing to comply with search requests.

Highlights in HRM 13.2

RIDING HIGH

The debate over performance-enhancing (or -diminishing) drugs reached new levels at the 1998 Winter Olympics in Japan when Ross Rebagliati found his gold medal in snowboarding in jeopardy after he tested positive for marijuana. At most companies in Canada, if Rebagliati had been an employee he would not have been tested for drugs and would not have been fired for testing positive. Drug-testing laws in Canada are very strict; testing is allowed only in jobs where safety is a critical issue, as it is at Ontario Hydro's nuclear power plants. Greyhound Canada in Calgary does random drug tests on bus drivers who are bidding for routes to the United States, where drug testing in the transportation sector is mandatory.

The Addiction Research Foundation points out that while drug tests show that drugs have been used, they do not indicate the level of impairment and therefore whether the user is "under the influence." Also, drugs such as cocaine take only three days to clear the body, whereas others such as marijuana can take three weeks. The inability to prove impaired performance, coupled with concerns about people's right to privacy, has made the courts hesitant to give companies the authority to conduct random drug tests, or to ask employees if they have a history of substance abuse.

One advertising agency tolerates the use of drugs on the grounds that "ad people tend to be creative and live on the edge." However, most companies suspecting substance abuse would take immediate action (e.g., referral to an employee assistance program) and resort to discharge or extended disability leave if the employee's performance continued to deteriorate.

Source: M. Gibb-Clark and E. Church, "Pot Policing Fails the Workplace Test," *The Globe and Mail*, February 12, 1998: B16. Reprinted with permission from *The Globe and Mail*.

Managers must be diligent when conducting employee searches. Improper searches can lead to employee lawsuits charging the employer with invasion of privacy, defamation of character, and negligent infliction of emotional distress. Employers are advised to develop an HR search policy based on the following guidelines:[23]

1. The search policy should be widely publicized and should advocate a probable or compelling reason for the search.
2. The search policy should be applied in a reasonable, evenhanded manner.
3. Where possible, searches should be conducted in private.
4. The employer should attempt to obtain the employee's consent prior to the search.
5. The search should be conducted in a humane and discreet manner to avoid inflicting emotional distress.
6. The penalty for refusing to consent to a search should be specified.

Figure 13.2	Tips for Reducing the Risk of Employee Theft

Employers lose over 1 percent of annual revenues as a result of "inventory shrinkage"—that is, employee and customer theft. Thieves are like good customers: if they like what they get, they'll come back for more. The key to preventing loss through employee theft is to break up the employee dishonesty triangle—opportunity, rationalization, and financial need. Experts recommend the following strategies for decreasing employee theft:

▶ Install security cameras that can tilt, scan, and zoom.

▶ Tag products to minimize "sweethearting"—a practice in which the cashier does not scan a product that a friend or accomplice is checking out. The tags are deactivated when they are scanned; if they aren't, an alarm sounds.

▶ Scrutinize job application forms. Be on the alert for lack of references, skipped portions of the form, conflicting dates of employment, lack of explanation for leaving old jobs, and long gaps between jobs.

▶ Check references thoroughly.

▶ Limit access to the cash office. Keep the door locked, and have employees store personal belongings elsewhere.

Sources: "Security Measures: How to Arrest Shrinkage in Your Store," *Canadian Grocer* 111, no. 5 (May 1997): 19–20; "Tough Policies Minimize Shrink," *Canadian Grocer* 107, no. 12 (December 1993): 10, 37.

It is not uncommon for employers to monitor the conduct of employees through surveillance techniques. Managers sometimes act as stationary surveillance covers or as moving surveillance covers, following the subject from point to point.[24] Employers are permitted to use electronic surveillance equipment that provides photographic or video images. General Electric has installed tiny fish-eye lenses behind pinholes in walls and ceilings to observe employees suspected of crimes. DuPont uses long-distance cameras to monitor its loading docks. One of the most common means of electronic surveillance by employers is telephone surveillance to ensure that customer requests are handled properly or to prevent theft. Ethics in HRM outlines some of the issues of monitoring employees.

Employers have the right to monitor employees, provided they do so for compelling business reasons and provided that the employees have been told that they will be monitored.[25] While employees can sue for invasion of privacy, the courts have held that to win damages, the employee must show that the reasonable expectation of privacy outweighed the organization's reason for surveillance.[26] One company fired an employee after videotaping him sleeping on the job. The tape was ruled admissible as evidence.[27]

Ethics in HRM

SUPERVISING OR SUPER-SPYING?

Cameras monitor much of our everyday life, often without our knowledge. Surveillance systems may be monitoring you as you leave the lobby of your apartment building, as you enter the underground garage, as you drive on the highway to work, as you purchase a coffee at the variety store, and even at some workplaces. Pinhole cameras the size of a quarter can fit into a picture on the wall, a telephone, or a ceiling device that looks like a water sprinkler. They can catch an employee loading up on office supplies; they can even determine whether the employee is using chat lines or the Internet for personal reasons. Some employers keep records of the calls employees make, and their duration. A standard feature on network management software enables the administrator to pull up the screen of any employee on the network.

Employees who work as customer representatives, handling sixty to eighty calls a day, may have their conversations monitored by supervisors or a trainer to ensure that the information given is accurate and that service standards are maintained. At one firm that raises money for charities, employees are required to make 8500 keystrokes an hour; failure to achieve this standard is noted electronically. (Distractions are minimized by covering windows, forbidding conversation unrelated to business, and facing all desks in the same direction.) Eight cameras are capable of zooming in on any desk, in case any employee is displaying materials unrelated to work.

Even babysitters and nannies are being targeted for electronic monitoring. Cameras hidden in books watch the children and the babysitter or nanny while anxious parents are at work. Parents insist that this surveillance enables them to ensure the safety and emotional security of their children; babysitters and nannies are outraged at the lack of trust and invasion of their privacy.

According to a national director with the Canadian Union of Postal Workers, "Surveillance and monitoring is really about power, and the uneven levels of power in the workplace. If it is abused by employers, then it really becomes a powerful weapon that is used to control the behaviour of workers, or as a source of discipline." A 2000 study found that people consider these electronic monitoring systems to be highly invasive and unfair. As one employee said, "I feel like when some prisoners are braceleted so that they know where they are."

Sources: David Zwieg "The Line between Benign and Invasive Monitoring Technologies," *HR Professional* 19, no. 4 (August/September, 2002): 36—38; J. Powell, "Keeping an Eye on the Workplace," *Financial Post*, September 6, 1997: 24; M. Gooderham, "Rise in Technology Lets Everyone Be a Spy," *The Globe and Mail*, June 7, 1995: A1; A.M. Stewart, "For a Nervous Breakdown, Please Press One," *The Globe and Mail*, June 1, 1994: A25; G. Arnaut, "Electronic Big Brother Is on the Job," *The Globe and Mail*, October 22, 1996: C1; R. Fulford, "Tolerating Electronic Sweatshops," *The Globe and Mail*, December 14, 1994: C1.

Employers should develop employee surveillance policies.

STEVE KRONGARD/GETTY IMAGES

Personal Information Protection and Electronic Document Act

Privacy is a fundamental human right. Privacy is our right to control information about ourselves: about who we are, what we do, where we go, what we buy, and whom we deal with. The Personal Information Protection and Electronic Documents Act (PIPEDA) came into effect on January 1, 2001, to provide Canadians with a right of privacy with respect to their personal information that is collected, used, or disclosed by an organization in the private sector. In 2003, Quebec was the only Canadian province that currently had legislation in place that dealt with privacy and personal information. Other provinces, such as British Columbia, Alberta, and Ontario, had proposed draft legislation for discussion and review.

USING THE INTERNET

For further information on PIPEDA, see the federal Privacy Commissions Guide for Businesses and Organizations at

www.privcom.gc.ca/information/guide_e.asp

Some of the categories of personal information covered under the PIPEDA include name, weight, age, medical records, income, purchasing and spending habits, race, blood type, fingerprints, marital status, education, and personal contact information. Controlling one's personal information means controlling the collection, use, and disclosure of that information. However, today's technology facilitates the collection and free flow of information; information can be moved and processed much more efficiently when it is in digital form. Thus, it is the ease with which digital information can be transferred that poses a threat to individual privacy.

Organizations covered by the PIPEDA must obtain an individual's consent when they collect, use, or disclose the individual's personal information. The individual has a right to access personal information held by an organization and to challenge its accuracy, if need be. Any organization that collects personal information can use that information only for the purpose for which it was collected. If an organization is going to use it for another purpose, it must obtain the individual's consent again. Individuals must also be assured by the organization that their information will be protected by adequate safeguards.

The most important legal principle with regard to data privacy law is the concept of consent. As pointed out above, organizations must get the informed, prior consent of the data subject. The data subject must be notified of the following before he or she provides any personal information:

▶ That he or she is about to provide personal data;
▶ The purposes for which the information is to be processed;
▶ The people or bodies to whom the data might be disclosed;
▶ The proposed transfer of data to other countries; and
▶ The security controls protecting the data.

Because privacy law obliges corporations to obtain consent from the individual whose personal information is being gathered, HR professionals should conduct an audit to determine if the organization's practice conforms to the legislation. For example, one organization collected information about the birth country of employees in order to facilitate international transfers. However, collecting this information for clerks, who will not be transferred, is unnecessary and would not meet the new standards.[28] Sources of information from selection interviews and employee evaluations may have to be made available to employees.[29]

Figure 13.3	Personnel Files: Policy Guidelines

▶ Ensure compliance with applicable laws.

▶ Define exactly what information is to be kept in employee files.

▶ Develop different categories of personnel information, depending on legal requirements and organizational needs.

▶ Specify where, when, how, and under what circumstances employees may review or copy their files.

▶ Identify company individuals allowed to view personnel files.

▶ Prohibit the collection of information that could be viewed as discriminatory or could form the basis for an invasion-of-privacy suit.

▶ Audit employment records on a regular basis to remove irrelevant, outdated, or inaccurate information.

Employees often assume that they have a right to privacy on the telephone.

SUPERSTOCK

E-Mail and Voice Mail Privacy

The benefits of e-mail and voice mail are many; they provide instant delivery of messages, they facilitate teamwork, they increase time efficiency, they offer access to global information, and they promote flexible work arrangements.[30] Unfortunately, the growth of HR information systems can create privacy problems by making personnel information more accessible to those with prying eyes, or to "hackers" who might use the information inappropriately. Messages can be read or heard, and deleted messages can be retrieved. Even log-on IDs and passwords do not prevent unauthorized access to computers by nonprivileged users.[31] Moreover, messages can be forwarded, replicated, and printed with ease. Employees have used e-mail to steal company information and to harass co-workers.[32]

High technology has created tensions between employee privacy and the employer's need to know. Employees often assume that their right to privacy extends to e-mail and voice mail messages; in fact, it does not. While there are few laws or court cases governing e-mail or voice mail monitoring, those that exist grant to employers the right to monitor materials created, received, or sent for business-related reasons.[33] Employers are strongly encouraged to develop clear policies and guidelines relating to how e-mail and voice mail are to be used, including when and under what conditions employees can be monitored (see Figure 13.4).[34] Only about 5 percent of Canadian companies have such policies in place, compared with about 40 percent of American companies.[35] Where e-mail and voice mail policies do exist, employees should be required to sign a form indicating that they have read and understand the policy. In most cases, courts will find disciplining an employee for Internet abuse to be a reasonable action.[36]

Employee Conduct Outside the Workplace

Consider the following situation. On Monday morning the owner of ABC Corporation reads in the newspaper that a company employee has been charged with robbery and assault on a local convenience store owner. The employee has been released pending trial. A phone call to the employee's supervisor reveals that the employee has reported to work. What should the owner do?

New technologies enable employers to monitor staff very closely, even on their personal time. While most courts uphold the right of the employer to monitor employees at the workplace, particularly if there is a justifiable reason to collect evidence, the monitoring of employees outside the workplace is more complex. For example, recent court cases have suggested that videotaping an employee inside his home is an unrea-

Figure 13.4	E-Mail and Voice Mail: Policy Guidelines

▶ Ensure compliance with federal and provincial legislation.

▶ Specify the circumstances, if any, under which the system can be used for personal business.

▶ Specify that confidential information not be sent on the network.

▶ Set forth the conditions under which monitoring will be done—by whom, how often, and with what notification to employees.

▶ Specify that e-mail and voice mail information be sent only to users who need it for business purposes.

▶ Expressly prohibit use of e-mail or voice mail to harass others or to send anonymous messages.

▶ Make clear that employees have no privacy rights in any material delivered or received through e-mail or voice mail.

▶ Specify that employees who violate the policy are subject to discipline, including dismissal.

sonable invasion of privacy. Videotaping in a public place was found reasonable in other cases. For example, an employee of the City of Toronto who worked as an arborist claimed to have injured himself at work and yet was videotaped cutting and removing branches from trees while off duty, work that he claimed he could not do.[37] Another company hired a private investigator to follow a travelling sales representative and fired her for stealing company time and money because she was using a company car to pick up her husband and drive him to work when she was supposed to be visiting clients. Another company fired its president after it discovered the reason for his absences during the day were fitness sessions at the gym.[38] But off-duty conduct can extend beyond job duties, to attitudes. The Peel Board of Education fired a teacher who met with racists and supported white supremacists. The firing was upheld even though there was no evidence that his views were expressed in the classroom. Where the public nature of the employee's job (e.g., police officer or teacher) create an image problem for the organization, courts might uphold firing them for their off-duty behaviour. Generally, however, little of what an employee does outside the workplace bears discipline by the employer.[39]

Workplace romances pose many dilemmas for organizations. Power differentials are often a factor (as between a manager and a secretary, or a new employee and a co-worker with a lot of seniority). When a power-differentiated romance goes sour, charges of sexual harassment can easily arise.[40] Behaviour that was acceptable in a consensual relationship between employees can quickly evolve into harassment when one party to the relationship stops welcoming the conduct. Such romances can also be sources of workplace violence (i.e., jilted lover arrives at work with a weapon).

Furthermore, workplace romances can lead to charges of favouritism. When an employee involved in an office romance with a superior gets preferential treatment, charges of "reverse harassment" can easily arise. Workplace romances can create morale problems—jealousy, resentment, hard feelings, and so on—when other employees feel unfairly treated. Romances involving supervisors and their underlings can have profound effects on organizational operations and productivity.[41] One study found that despite all this, only 6 percent of surveyed organizations had a policy on employee dating or fraternization.[42]

Genetic Testing

With advances being made in genetics, it is now possible to identify the genetic basis for human diseases and illnesses. Genetic findings present opportunities for individualized prevention strategies and early detection and treatment. Unfortunately, the knowledge gained through genetic testing can also be used discreetly by employers to discriminate against or stigmatize individuals who are applying for employment or are currently employed. For example, genetic testing can identify an individual's risk of developing common diseases and disorders such as cancer, heart disease, and diabetes. Diseases like these can raise employment costs (e.g., recruitment, training, and medical costs).

Employers must remember that there is no scientific evidence linking unexpressed genetic factors to an individual's ability to perform a job. There are few federal or provincial laws, or court decisions, governing employers' use of genetic information. The employer is at risk by not hiring or promoting a candidate because of knowledge about a predisposition to a disease that would cause insurance costs to rise or cause lowered job performance.[43]

USING THE INTERNET

Further legal resources on the topics discussed in this chapter can be found on the website of Canada Law Book at

http://www.canadalawbook.com.

Plant Closing Notification

Thousands of jobs have been lost in Canada as a result of plant closings. These shutdowns can devastate not merely individual employees but entire communities. It has been estimated that for every 100 jobs lost from a plant closing, the local community loses 200 to 300 jobs through ripple effects. Several provincial governments have passed legislation preventing employers from unilaterally closing or relocating their facilities. For example, Ontario has passed legislation that requires organizations with fewer than 50 employees to give four weeks' notice of any closure; organizations with more than 500 employees must give sixteen weeks' notice.[44]

DISCIPLINARY POLICIES AND PROCEDURES

objective 3

The right of managers to discipline and discharge employees is becoming more and more limited. For this reason, managers at all levels must thoroughly understand discipline procedures. Any disciplinary action taken against an employee must be for justifiable reasons and must follow carefully thought-out guidelines. These guidelines should help managers carry out an onerous duty and should ensure that employees are being treated fairly and constructively. Equally important, these guidelines should help prevent disciplinary actions from being voided or reversed through the appeal system.

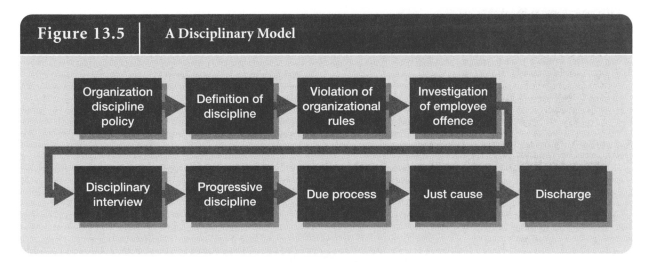

Figure 13.5 | A Disciplinary Model

Figure 13.5 shows one disciplinary model, which consists of steps that must be carried out to ensure enforceable decisions.

A major responsibility of the HR department is to develop disciplinary policies and procedures. (Top management will then have to approve them.) The development process must involve the supervisors and managers who have to carry out the policies. Their experience can make the disciplinary policy more effective, as well as more consistent throughout the organization. The HR department is also responsible for ensuring that disciplinary policies—and any disciplinary actions taken against employees—are consistent with collective agreements (where they exist) and conform with current law.

The primary responsibility for preventing or correcting disciplinary problems rests with the employee's immediate supervisor. This person is in the best position to observe unsatisfactory behaviour or performance and to discuss these matters with the employee. Discussion is often all that is needed to correct the problem; when it is, disciplinary action is then unnecessary. When disciplinary action is required, the supervisor should strive for a problem-solving attitude. The causes underlying the problem are as important as the problem itself, and if the problem is not to recur, those causes must be understood. It is often difficult for supervisors to be objective about employee infractions. But if supervisors can maintain a problem-solving stance, they are likely to come up with a diagnosis that is nearer the truth than would be possible if they were to use the approach of a trial lawyer.

The Results of Inaction

Figure 13.6 lists the more common disciplinary problems identified by managers. Failure to take disciplinary action in any of these areas will only make the problem worse.[45] Failure to act implies that the performance of the employee concerned has been satisfactory. If disciplinary action is eventually taken, the delay will make it more difficult to justify the action if it is appealed. In defending against such an appeal, the employer is likely to be asked why the employee who had not been performing or behaving satisfactorily was kept on the payroll. An even more damaging question: "Why did that employee receive satisfactory performance ratings [or perhaps even merit raises]?"[46]

Figure 13.6	Common Disciplinary Problems

Attendance Problems

- ▶ Unexcused absence
- ▶ Chronic absenteeism
- ▶ Unexcused/excessive tardiness
- ▶ Leaving without permission

Dishonesty and Related Problems

- ▶ Theft
- ▶ Falsifying employment application
- ▶ Wilfully damaging organizational property
- ▶ Punching another employee's time card
- ▶ Falsifying work records

Work Performance Problems

- ▶ Failure to complete work assignments
- ▶ Producing substandard products or services
- ▶ Failure to meet established production requirements

On-the-Job Behaviour Problems

- ▶ Intoxication at work
- ▶ Insubordination
- ▶ Horseplay
- ▶ Smoking in unauthorized places
- ▶ Fighting
- ▶ Gambling
- ▶ Failure to use safety devices
- ▶ Failure to report injuries
- ▶ Carelessness
- ▶ Sleeping on the job
- ▶ Using abusive or threatening behaviour with supervisors
- ▶ Possession of narcotics or alcohol
- ▶ Possession of firearms or other weapons
- ▶ Sexual harassment

Contradictions in practice like these can only help employees successfully challenge management's corrective actions. Unfortunately, some supervisors begin building a case to justify their corrective actions only after they have decided that a particular employee should be dismissed. Supervisors often give the following reasons for failing to impose a disciplinary penalty:

1. Since they hadn't documented earlier actions, no record existed on which to base any later actions.
2. They believed they would receive little or no support from higher management for the disciplinary action.
3. They were uncertain of the facts underlying the situation that required disciplinary action.
4. Because they had failed to discipline employees in the past for a certain infraction, they had no choice (for the sake of consistency) but to forgo current disciplinary action.
5. They wanted to be liked.

Setting Organizational Rules

Establishing an effective disciplinary system begins with setting organizational rules. These rules tell employees what type of behaviour the employer expects. Organizations as diverse as Gerber Products, Wal-Mart, and Pitney Bowes have written rules of conduct. Following are suggestions for establishing organizational rules:

1. Rules should be widely disseminated and known to all employees. It should not be assumed that employees know all the rules.
2. Rules should be reviewed periodically—perhaps annually—especially those rules critical to work success.
3. The reasons for a rule should always be explained. Acceptance of an organizational rule is greater when employees understand the reasons behind it.
4. Rules should always be written. Ambiguity should be avoided, since this can result in different interpretations of the rules by different supervisors.
5. Rules must be reasonable and must relate to the safe and efficient operation of the organization. Rules should not be made simply because of personal likes or dislikes.
6. If management has been lax in enforcing a rule, the rule must be restated, along with the consequences for its violation, before disciplinary action can begin.
7. Have employees sign that they have read and understand the organizational rules.

Disciplinary action should never be thought of as punishment. Discipline can embody a penalty as a means of obtaining a desired result; however, punishment should not be the intent of disciplinary action. Rather, the whole point of discipline must be to improve the employee's future behaviour. To apply discipline in any other way—as punishment or for revenge—can only invite problems for management, including possible wrongful dismissal suits.

When seeking reasons for weak performance, supervisors must keep in mind that employees may not be aware of certain work rules. Before starting any disciplinary action, it is essential that supervisors determine whether they have carefully and thoroughly oriented their employees to the rules and regulations relating to their jobs. In fact, the proper communication of organizational rules and regulations is so important that labour arbitrators cite neglect in communicating rules as a major reason for reversing the disciplinary action taken against an employee.[47]

The Hot Stove Approach to Rule Enforcement

Whatever the reason for the disciplinary action, it should be taken as soon as possible after the infraction, once a complete investigation has been conducted. HR professionals often use the **hot stove rule** to explain the correct application of discipline. A hot stove gives warning that it should not be touched. Those who ignore the warning and touch it are assured of being burned. The punishment is an immediate and direct consequence of breaking the rule never to touch a hot stove. Likewise, a work rule should apply to all employees and should be enforced consistently and in an impersonal and unbiased way. Employees should know the consequences of violating the rule, so that it has preventive value.

Defining Discipline

In management seminars conducted by the authors of this text, when managers are asked to define the word "discipline," their most frequent response is that discipline means punishment. Although this answer is not incorrect, it is only one of three possible meanings. As normally defined, **discipline** has these meanings:

1. Treatment that punishes
2. Orderly behaviour in an organizational setting
3. Training that moulds and strengthens desirable conduct—or corrects undesirable conduct—and develops self-control

To some managers, discipline is synonymous with force. They equate the term with punishing employees who violate rules or regulations. Other managers think of discipline as a general state of affairs—a state of orderliness in which employees conduct themselves according to standards of acceptable behaviour. Discipline viewed in this manner can be considered positive when employees willingly practise self-control and respect organizational rules.

The third definition considers discipline a management tool for correcting undesirable employee performance. Discipline is applied as a constructive means of getting employees to conform to acceptable standards of performance. Goodyear Aerospace defines the term "discipline" in its policy manual as training that "corrects, molds, or perfects knowledge, attitudes, behavior, or conduct." It is not the only organization to perceive discipline in this way. Discipline when seen in this light is much more than punishment for offences—it corrects poor employee performance. As these organizations emphasize, discipline should be seen as a method of training employees to perform better or to improve their job attitudes or work behaviour.[48]

Hot stove rule
Rule of discipline that can be compared with a hot stove in that it gives warning, is effective immediately, is enforced consistently, and applies to all employees in an impersonal and unbiased way

objective 4

Discipline
(1) Treatment that punishes; (2) orderly behaviour in an organizational setting; or (3) training that moulds and strengthens desirable conduct—or corrects undesirable conduct—and develops self-control

Investigating the Disciplinary Problem

It's a rare manager who has a good, intuitive sense of how to investigate employee misconduct. Too often, investigations are conducted in a haphazard manner; worse, they overlook one or more investigative concerns. When conducting an employee investigation, managers must be objective and avoid the assumptions, suppositions, and biases that often surround discipline cases. Figure 13.7 lists seven questions to consider when investigating an employee offence. Attending to all seven will help ensure a full and fair investigation and provide reliable information free from personal prejudice.

Figure 13.7	Considerations in Disciplinary Investigations

1. In very specific terms, what is the offence charged?
   - Is management sure it fully understands the charge against the employee?
   - Was the employee really terminated for insubordination, or did the employee merely refuse a request by management?

2. Did the employee know he or she was doing something wrong?
   - What rule or provision was violated?
   - How would the employee know of the existence of the rule?
   - Was the employee warned of the consequence?

3. Is the employee guilty?
   - What are the sources of facts?
   - Is there direct or only indirect evidence of guilt?
   - Has anyone talked to the employee to hear his or her side of the situation?

4. Are there extenuating circumstances?
   - Were conflicting orders given by different supervisors?
   - Does anybody have reason to want to "get" this employee?
   - Was the employee provoked by a manager or another employee?

5. Has the rule been uniformly enforced?
   - Have all managers applied the rule consistently?
   - What punishment did previous offenders receive?
   - Were any other employees involved in this offence?

6. Is the offence related to the workplace?
   - Is there evidence that the offence hurt the organization?
   - Is management making a moral judgment or a business judgment?

7. What is the employee's past work record?
   - How many years of service has the employee given the organization?
   - How many years or months has the employee held the present job?
   - What is the employee's personnel record as a whole, especially his or her disciplinary record?

Documentation of Employee Misconduct

"It's too complicated." "I just didn't take time to do it." "I have more important things to do." Managers who have failed to document employee misconduct often resort to these excuses. But the most significant reason for inadequate documentation is that managers have no idea of what constitutes good documentation. When managers fail to record employee misconduct accurately, later disciplinary actions are more easily reversed. It follows that maintaining complete and accurate work records is an essential part of an effective disciplinary system.[49] For documentation to be complete, it must include the following eight items:

1. Date, time, and location of the incident(s).
2. Negative performance or behaviour exhibited by the employee (i.e., the problem).
3. The consequences of that action or behaviour on the employee's overall work performance and/or on the operations of the employee's work unit.
4. Prior discussion(s) with the employee about the problem.
5. Disciplinary action to be taken, and the specific improvement expected.
6. Consequences if improvement is not made, and a follow-up date.
7. The employee's reaction to the supervisor's attempt to change behaviour.
8. The names of witnesses to the incident (if appropriate).

When preparing documentation, it is important for the manager to record the incident immediately after the infraction takes place, when the memory of it is still fresh, and to ensure that the record is complete and accurate. The documentation need not be lengthy, but it must include the eight points in the above list. A manager's records of employee misconduct are considered business documents, and as such they are admissible as evidence in arbitration hearings, administrative proceedings, and courts of law.[50]

The Investigative Interview

Before any disciplinary action is taken, an investigative interview should be conducted to make sure the employee is fully aware of the offence. This interview is necessary because the supervisor's perceptions of the employee's behaviour may not be entirely accurate. The interview should concentrate on how the offence violated the performance standards of the job. It should avoid getting into personalities or areas unrelated to job performance. Most important, the employee must be given a full opportunity to explain his or her side of the issue so that any deficiencies for which the organization may be responsible are revealed.

Approaches to Disciplinary Action

If a thorough investigation shows that an employee has violated some organization rule, disciplinary action must be taken. Two approaches to disciplinary action are progressive discipline and positive discipline.

objective 5

Progressive Discipline

Generally, discipline is imposed in a progressive manner. **Progressive discipline** involves applying corrective measures by increasing degrees. It is designed to motivate the employee to correct his or her misconduct voluntarily. It is intended to nip prob-

Progressive discipline
Application of corrective measures by increasing degrees

lems in the bud, using only as much corrective action as necessary. The sequence and severity of the disciplinary action will vary with the type of offence and the circumstances surrounding it. Since each situation is unique, a number of factors must be considered in determining how severe a disciplinary action should be. Some of the factors to consider were listed in Figure 13.7.

The typical progressive discipline procedure has these four steps: (1) an oral warning (or counselling) that subsequent unsatisfactory behaviour or performance will not be tolerated; (2) a written warning; (3) a suspension without pay; and (4) dismissal.[51] The "capital punishment" of discharge is seen as a last resort. Organizations usually apply lesser forms of disciplinary action for less severe performance problems. Managers must remember that three important things happen when progressive discipline is applied properly:

1. Employees always know where they stand regarding offences.
2. Employees know what improvement is expected of them.
3. Employees understand what will happen next if improvement is not made.

Positive Discipline

Progressive discipline is the most popular approach to correcting employee misconduct. However, some managers have begun questioning its logic and noting certain flaws in it—for example, its intimidating and adversarial nature. As a result, some organizations are now using an approach called **positive (or nonpunitive) discipline**. Positive discipline is based on the concept that employees must assume responsibility for their personal conduct and job performance.[52] Highlights in HRM 13.3 outlines Volkswagen Canada's positive discipline program.

Positive (or nonpunitive) discipline
System of discipline that focuses on the early correction of employee misconduct, with the employee taking total responsibility for correcting the problem

Positive discipline requires a cooperative environment in which the employee and the supervisor can engage in joint problem solving to resolve incidents of employee irresponsibility. This approach focuses on the early correction of misconduct, with the employee taking total responsibility for resolving the problem. Nothing is imposed by management; all solutions and affirmations are reached jointly. HR managers often describe positive discipline as "nonpunitive discipline that replaces threats and punishment with encouragement."

Figure 13.8 illustrates the procedure for implementing positive discipline. While positive discipline seems similar to progressive discipline, it emphasizes reminding employees rather than reprimanding them. The technique is implemented in three steps:[53]

▶ The employee and the supervisor confer with each other, with the goal of finding a solution to the problem through discussion. It should end with the employee making an oral agreement to improve performance. The supervisor does not reprimand the employee or threaten further disciplinary action. The supervisor can document this conference, but a written record of this meeting is not placed in the employee's file unless the misconduct occurs again.

▶ If the employee does not improve after this first step, the supervisor holds a second conference with the employee to determine why the solution agreed to in the first conference did not work. At this stage, a written reminder is given to the employee. This document states the new or repeated solution to the problem and affirms that improvement is the responsibility of the employee and a condition of continued employment.

Highlights in HRM 13.3

VOLKSWAGEN CANADA'S POSITIVE DISCIPLINE PROGRAM

Positive discipline is a method for attempting to solve employee problems before they develop into serious situations. It treats employees as adults and emphasizes turning inappropriate behaviour around instead of punishing employees every time they do something wrong. Positive discipline relies on frontline coaching and counselling to help employees identify inappropriate behaviour; it also suggests ways of turning that behaviour around. Positive discipline allows supervisors to treat their fellow employees in a fair and consistent manner. Most employees will respond to coaching and counselling. For employees who do not correct their behaviour—or who are involved in an incident so serious that coaching or counselling is deemed inappropriate—there are steps in place to impress on every employee the seriousness of their actions and the consequences of continued poor behaviour. The following is a general outline of the program.

There are five general methods used in the Positive Discipline Program:

▶ Coaching and Counselling
▶ Step 1: Verbal Reminder
▶ Step 2: Written Warning
▶ Step 3: Decision Making
▶ Step 4: Termination

There are three categories of work rule violations:

▶ Work Performance
▶ Attendance
▶ Misconduct

There are three degrees of severity of workplace violations:

▶ Minor
▶ Major
▶ Grave

There are two other major ingredients of the Positive Discipline Program:

▶ Praise
▶ Goal Setting

Guidelines

▶ The union, if requested, may be involved in every step of the discipline process, but must be involved in step 1 and higher.

▶ An employee may, under certain circumstances, be sent home with or without pay pending an investigation into the incident. The union should be involved in any investigation into serious incidents.

▶ Counselling should be the preferred method of correcting behaviour when a problem first appears.

▶ Praise should be used often, whenever an employee has corrected a potential problem, had a step deactivated, performed beyond his/her normal duties, or any other time the supervisor feels it is appropriate. This praise should be done both orally and in writing.

▶ Goal setting should be used at every step in the disciplinary process in order to ensure both the supervisor and the employee know exactly what is expected of them.

▶ This program is aimed at those very few employees who insist on conducting themselves in an inappropriate manner. The vast majority of our employees may never have to encounter the various steps of this program.

Source: Donald McQuirter, Manager of Human Resources, Volkswagen Canada Inc.

Figure 13.8 | Positive Discipline Procedure

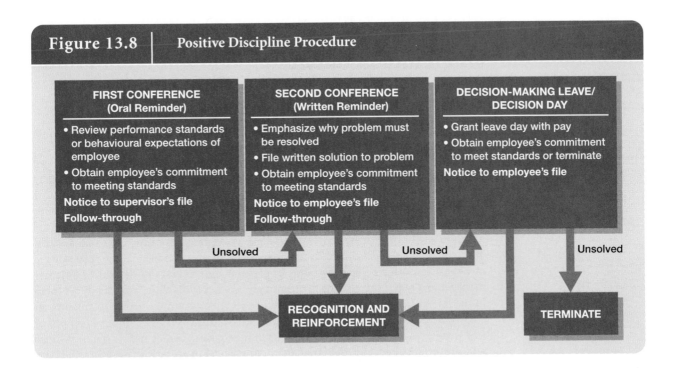

▶ If both conferences fail to produce the desired results, the employee is given a one-day decision-making leave (a paid leave). The purpose of this paid leave is for the employee to decide whether he or she wishes to continue working for the organization. The organization pays for this leave to demonstrate its desire to retain the person. Also, paying for the leave eliminates the negative effects for the employee of losing a day's pay. Employees who are given decision-making leave are instructed to return the following day with a decision either to make a total commitment to improve performance or to quit the organization. If a commitment is not made, the employee is dismissed on the assumption that he or she lacked responsibility toward the organization.[54]

Compiling a Disciplinary Record

When applying either progressive or positive discipline, it is important for managers to maintain complete records of each step of the procedure. An employee who fails to meet the obligation of a disciplinary step should be given a warning, and the warning should be documented by the manager. A copy of this warning is usually placed in the employee's personnel file. Usually, after an established period—often six months—the warning is removed, provided it has served its purpose. Otherwise it remains in the file to serve as evidence should a more severe penalty become necessary later.

An employee's personnel file contains the employee's complete work history. It serves as a basis for determining and supporting disciplinary action and for evaluating the organization's disciplinary policies and procedures. Maintenance of proper records also provides management with valuable information about the soundness of its rules and regulations. Those rules that are violated most frequently should receive particular attention, because the need for them may no longer exist or some change may be required to facilitate their enforcement. A rule that has little or no demonstrable value should be revised or rescinded. Otherwise employees are likely to feel they are being restricted unnecessarily.

Dismissing Employees

When employees fail to conform to organizational rules and regulations, the final disciplinary action in many cases is dismissal. Since dismissal has such serious consequences for the employee—and possibly for the organization—it should be undertaken only after a painstaking review of the case. An employee who is fired may well file a wrongful dismissal suit claiming that the termination was "without just or sufficient cause," the implication being that management did not extend fair treatment.

All of this demands that we ask: What constitutes fair treatment of employees? This question is not easily answered, but standards governing just cause dismissal do exist, in the form of rules developed in the field of labour arbitration.[55] These rules consist of a set of guidelines that arbitrators apply to dismissal cases to determine whether management had just cause for the termination. These guidelines are usually set forth in the form of questions, provided in Figure 13.9. For example, before dismissing an employee, did the manager forewarn the person of possible disciplinary action? A "no" answer to any of the seven questions in the figure generally means that just cause was not established and that management's decision to terminate was arbitrary,

---

Figure 13.9 | **"Just Cause" Dismissal Guidelines**

1. Did the organization forewarn the employee of the possible disciplinary consequences of his or her action?

2. Were management's requirements of the employee reasonable in relation to the orderly, efficient, and safe operation of the organization's business?

3. Did management, before discharging the employee, make a reasonable effort to establish that the employee's performance was unsatisfactory?

4. Was the organization's investigation conducted in a fair and objective manner?

5. Did the investigation produce sufficient evidence or proof of guilt as charged?

6. Has management treated this employee under its rules, orders, and penalties as it has other employees in similar circumstances?

7. Did the discharge fit the misconduct, considering the seriousness of the proven offence, the employee's service record, and any mitigating circumstances?

---

capricious, or discriminatory. The significance of these guidelines is that they are being applied not only by arbitrators in dismissal cases, but also by judges in wrongful dismissal suits. It is critical that managers at all levels understand the just cause guidelines, including their proper application.[56]

Informing the Employee

Whatever the reasons for dismissal, it should be done with personal consideration for the employee affected. Every effort should be made to ease the trauma a dismissal creates. The employee must be informed honestly yet tactfully of the exact reasons for the action. This candour can help the employee face the problem and adjust to it in a constructive manner.

Managers may wish to discuss, and even rehearse, with their peers the upcoming termination meeting. This practice can ensure that all important points are covered while giving confidence to the manager. While managers agree that there is no single right way to conduct a dismissal meeting, the following guidelines will help make the discussion more effective:

1. Come to the point within the first two or three minutes, and list in a logical order all reasons for the termination.

2. Be straightforward and firm, yet tactful, and remain resolute in your decision.

3. Make the discussion private, businesslike, and fairly brief. Don't mix the good with the bad. Trying to sugar-coat the problem sends a mixed message.

4. Avoid making accusations against the employee and injecting personal feelings into the discussion.

5. Avoid bringing up any personality differences between you and the employee.

6. Provide any information concerning severance pay and the status of benefits and coverage.

7. Explain how you will handle employment inquiries from future employers.

Termination meetings should be held in a neutral location, such as a conference room, so that the manager can leave if the meeting gets out of control. The prudent manager will also have determined, prior to the termination decision, that the dismissal does not violate any legal rights the employee may have.

Finally, when the terminated employee is escorted off the premises, the removal must not serve to defame the employee. Managers should not give peers the impression that the terminated employee was dishonest or untrustworthy. Increasingly, terminated employees are pursuing lawsuits that go beyond the issue of whether their dismissal was for business-related reasons.[57]

Providing Outplacement Assistance

Employers often use employment agencies to help dismissed employees locate new jobs. This assistance is especially likely to be provided for managers of long tenure. Sometimes it is also provided for employees being laid off as a result of organizational rightsizing or restructuring, or because they don't fit a changed corporate identity.[58] Often, a termination under such conditions is not called a discharge, but rather an outplacement.

Managers note the following reasons for providing outplacement services: concern for the well-being of employees, protection against potential lawsuits, competition from other organizations offering such services, and the effect on the morale of remaining employees. Outplacement consultants assist employees being terminated in a number of ways—for example, by reducing their anger and grief and by helping them regain self-confidence as they begin searching in earnest for new work. Many terminated workers will have been out of the job market for some time and so lack the knowledge and skills they need to look for a new job. Outplacement specialists can coach them as they develop contacts, seek out job openings, attend employment interviews, and negotiate salaries.

The final stage of discipline is termination.

PHOTODISC

APPEALING DISCIPLINARY ACTIONS

More and more organizations are taking steps to protect employees from arbitrary and inequitable treatment by their supervisors. The emphasis in this effort is on creating a climate in which employees can voice their dissatisfaction with their superiors without fear of reprisal—and know they can do so. This safeguard can be provided by implementing a formal procedure for appealing disciplinary actions.

Alternative Dispute-Resolution Mechanisms

Where a workforce is unionized, grievance procedures are almost always stated in the collective agreement. In nonunion organizations, **alternative dispute resolution (ADR)** procedures are a relatively recent development.[59] The employer's interest stems from the desire to meet employees' expectations for fair treatment in the workplace and to guarantee them due process. The hope is to minimize discrimination claims and wrongful dismissal suits.

Some organizations champion these procedures as means for employees to communicate upwards and as ways to gauge the temperament of the workforce. Others view these systems as a way to resolve minor problems before they mushroom into major issues. Below we describe the following appeal procedures: the step review system, the peer review system, the use of hearing officers, the open door policy, the use of an ombudsman, and arbitration.

Step Review Systems

As Figure 13.10 illustrates, a **step review system** is based on a pre-established set of steps—normally four. Under these, the employee's complaint is reviewed by successively higher levels of management. These procedures are patterned after the union grievance systems we will discuss in Chapter 14. For example, they normally require that the employee's complaint be formalized as a written statement. At each step, managers are required to provide a full response to the complaint within a specified time—perhaps three to five working days.

An employee is sometimes allowed to bypass the meeting with the immediate supervisor if he or she fears reprisal from this person. Unlike appeal systems in unionized organizations, nonunion appeal procedures ordinarily do not provide for a neutral third party (such as an arbitrator) to serve as the judge of last resort.[60] In most step review systems, the president, the CEO, the vice-president, or the HR director acts as the final authority, and this person's decision cannot be appealed. Some organizations help employees prepare their complaint cases. For example, an employee who wishes it may be able to get advice and counsel from a designated person in the HR department before discussing the issue with management.

Unfortunately, step review systems sometimes don't work as intended. Employees may believe that management is slow in responding to complaints, or that management's responses often do not solve problems. Furthermore, employees may believe that regardless of policies forbidding reprisal, supervisors will still hold it against them if they exercise their rights as spelled out in the step review system. These concerns do

objective 6

Alternative dispute resolution (ADR)
Term applied to different types of employee complaint or dispute resolution procedures

Step review system
System for reviewing employee complaints and disputes by successively higher levels of management

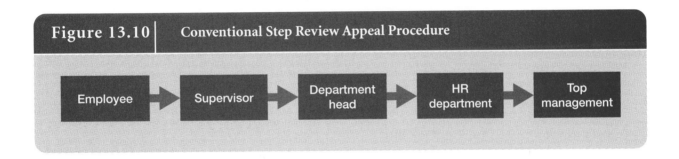

| Figure 13.10 | Conventional Step Review Appeal Procedure |

Employee → Supervisor → Department head → HR department → Top management

not mean that all step review systems are ineffective, only that management must take special precautions to ensure that the systems provide the benefits intended. We offer the following suggestions for making step review systems successful:

1. Consult employees when designing the complaint system. Commitment to the process is enhanced when employees participate in its design.
2. Train supervisors in handling complaints.
3. Handle complaints in a timely manner.
4. Make sure all employees know how to use the complaint procedure, and encourage them to use the system when they feel aggrieved.
5. Handle cases in a fair manner, and assure employees that they need not fear reprisal for filing complaints.

Peer Review Systems

Peer review system
System for reviewing employee complaints that utilizes a group composed of equal numbers of employee representatives and management appointees

A **peer review system**, also called a complaint committee, is composed of equal numbers of employee representatives and management appointees. Employee representatives are usually elected by secret ballot by their co-workers for rotating terms; management representatives are assigned, also on a rotating basis.[61] A peer review system functions as a jury in the sense that its members weigh evidence, consider arguments, and, after deliberation, vote independently to render a final decision.[62]

One benefit of the peer review system is that employees tend to have faith in it. The peer review system can be used as the only method for resolving employee complaints, or it can be used in conjunction with a step review system. When the two systems are used together, an employee who is not satisfied with management's action at, say, step 1 or 2 in the step review system, can submit the complaint to the peer review committee for final resolution. Darden Industries, which owns the Red Lobster and Olive Garden restaurant chains, uses a peer review system.

Use of a Hearing Officer

Hearing officers
People who work full-time for the organization but who assume a neutral role when deciding cases between aggrieved employees and management

This procedure is found almost exclusively in large organizations, sometimes in union environments. **Hearing officers** are full-time employees of the organization; however, they function independently from other managers and occupy a special place in the organization's hierarchy. To succeed, employees must perceive them as neutral, highly competent, and totally unbiased in handling complaints. They hear cases on request— almost always the employee's request. After considering the evidence and the facts presented, they render decisions or awards, which are usually final and binding on both sides. Like the peer review system, the hearing officer system can be used by itself or as part of a step review procedure.

Open Door Policy

Open door policy
Policy of settling grievances that identifies various levels of management above the immediate supervisor for employee contact

The open door policy is an old standby for settling employee complaints. In fact, most managers, whether or not their organization has adopted a formal open door policy, profess to maintain one for their employees. The traditional **open door policy** identifies various levels of management above the immediate supervisor that an aggrieved employee may contact; the levels may extend as high as a vice-president, president, or CEO. Typically, the person who acts as "the court of last resort" is the HR director or a senior staff member.

Two common complaints against an open door policy are that managers are unwilling to listen honestly to employee complaints, and that workers are reluctant to approach managers with their complaints. As one employee once told the authors of this text, "My manager has an open door policy but the door is only open one inch." Obviously, this employee felt he had little opportunity to get through to his manager. This system has other problems as well. It generally fails to guarantee consistent decision making, since what is fair to one manager may seem unfair to another. Higher-level managers tend to support supervisors for fear of undermining their authority. And as a system of justice, open door policies lack credibility with employees. Still, the open door policy is often successful when it is supported by all levels of management and when management works to maintain a reputation for being fair and open-minded.[63]

Ombudsman System

An **ombudsman** is a designated individual from whom employees may seek counsel for resolution of their complaints. The ombudsman listens to an employee's complaint and tries to resolve it by mediating a solution between the employee and the supervisor. This individual works cooperatively with both sides to reach a settlement, often employing a clinical approach to problem solving. Since the ombudsman has no authority to finalize a solution to the problem, compromises are highly likely, and all concerned tend to feel satisfied with the outcome.

Ombudsmen must be able to operate in an atmosphere of confidentiality that does not threaten the security of the managers or subordinates who are involved in a complaint. While ombudsmen do not have power to overrule decisions made by an employee's supervisor, they should be able to appeal the decision up the line if they believe an employee is not being treated fairly. Ombudsmen help employees achieve equity; they also provide management with a check on itself.

Arbitration

At the 1996 Summer Olympics, the athletes were required by the International Olympic Committee (IOC) to agree to take any Olympic dispute (including those over drug testing) to a special arbitration panel for a binding decision. The point of this was to avoid costly and disruptive battles in U.S. courts.[64]

In the same vein, private employers may require employees to submit their employment disputes to binding arbitration. (Arbitration is discussed in depth in Chapter 14.) Arbitration is used mainly to resolve discrimination suits relating to age, gender, sexual harassment, and race.[65] Arbitration can save litigation costs and avoid time delays and unfavourable publicity. However, to ensure that their arbitration policies are legal, employers must

▶ have a clear, well-defined, and widely communicated arbitration policy;
▶ specify those topics subject to arbitration;
▶ inform employees of the rights they are relinquishing by signing an arbitration agreement;
▶ provide a procedurally fair arbitration system; and
▶ allow for the nonbiased selection of an arbitrator or arbitration panel.[66]

Ombudsman
Designated individual from whom employees may seek counsel for the resolution of their complaints

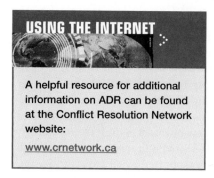

USING THE INTERNET

A helpful resource for additional information on ADR can be found at the Conflict Resolution Network website:

www.crnetwork.ca

Mediation
The use of an impartial neutral to reach a compromise decision in employment disputes

Along with arbitration, mediation is fast becoming a popular way to resolve employee complaints. **Mediation** employs a third-party neutral (called a mediator) to help employees and managers reach voluntary agreement acceptable to both parties. The essence of mediation is compromise. The mediator will hold a meeting with the employee and management, listen to the position of each side, gather facts, then, through discussion, suggestions, and persuasion obtain an agreement that will satisfy the needs and requirements of both sides. A mediator serves primarily as a fact finder and to open up a channel of communication between the parties. Unlike arbitrators, mediators have no power or authority to force either side toward an agreement. They must use their communication skills and the power of persuasion to help the parties resolve their differences. A cornerstone of mediation is that the parties maintain control over the settlement outcome.

Mediation is a flexible process that can be shaped to meet the demands of the parties.[67] Also, it can be used to resolve a wide range of employee complaints, including discrimination claims or traditional workplace disputes.[68] Employees like the process because of its informality. According to one authority, "Mediation might be described as a private discussion assisted by an impartial third party."[69] Settlements fashioned through mediation are readily acceptable by the parties, thus promoting a favourable working relationship.

MANAGERIAL ETHICS IN EMPLOYEE RELATIONS

objective

Ethics
Set of standards of conduct and moral judgments that help determine right and wrong behaviour

Throughout this textbook, we have emphasized the legal requirements of HRM. Laws and court decisions affect all aspects of employment—recruitment, selection, performance appraisal, safety and health, labour relations, and testing. Managers must comply with governmental regulations to establish an environment free from litigation.

However, beyond what is required by the law is the question of organizational ethics and the ethical—or unethical—behaviour engaged in by managers. **Ethics** can be defined as a set of standards of acceptable conduct and moral judgment. Ethics provides cultural guidelines—both organizational and societal—that help differentiate proper from improper conduct. Ethics, like the law, permeates all aspects of the employment relationship. For example, managers may adhere to the organization's objective of hiring more members of designated groups, but how those employees are supervised and treated once employed gets to the issue of managerial ethics. We have presented Ethics in HRM boxes in each chapter of this book to illustrate the complexity of ethical dilemmas.

Compliance with laws and the behavioural treatment of employees are two completely different aspects of the manager's job. While ethical dilemmas will always occur in the supervision of employees, it is how employees are treated that largely distinguishes the ethical organization from the unethical one. Interestingly, a recent research study, Ethical Issues in the Employer-Employee Relationship, sponsored by the Society of Financial Service Professionals, found that 97 percent of employers and 84 percent of employees stated that making misleading promises to employees is the most serious ethical violation made by employers. Using drugs or alcohol on company time and e-mail harassment of another employee was cited as the most frequent business ethics violation.[70] We believe that managerial ethics in employee relations requires honesty in all dealings between employees and their managers, including mutual respect throughout the performance of workplace duties.

Law and ethics are two completely different aspects of the manager's job. Ethical dilemmas always arise when employees are being supervised. An ethical organization is distinguished from an unethical one by how it treats its employees. In our view, an ethical organization is one that recognizes and values the contributions of its employees and respects their personal rights.

Many organizations have a code of ethics that governs relations with employees and the public at large. This written code focuses attention on ethical values and provides a basis for the organization, and individual managers, to evaluate their plans and actions. HR departments have been given a greater role in communicating the organization's values and standards, monitoring compliance with its code of ethics, and enforcing those standards throughout the organization. Organizations now have ethics committees and ethics ombudsmen to provide training in ethics to employees. The goal of ethics training is to reduce unethical behaviour and adverse publicity; to gain a strategic advantage; but most of all, to treat employees in a fair and equitable manner, recognizing them as productive members of the organization.

SUMMARY

 objective

Both employees and employers have rights and expectations in the employment relationship. The due process right of employees is the right for them to express their views concerning an incident; statutory and contractual rights have to do with the rights of employees and employers to terminate the employment relationship. Under the implied contract concept, an employer's oral or written statements may form a contractual obligation that can preclude the automatic termination of employees.

 objective

Once employed, employees expect certain rights regarding fair and equitable treatment on the job. These rights extend over such issues as substance abuse and drug testing, searches and surveillance, off-duty privacy, e-mail and voice mail privacy, and plant closing notification.

 objective

The HR department, in combination with other managers, should establish disciplinary policies. This will help employees accept discipline and ensure its consistent application. Disciplinary rules and procedures should be written down, widely known, explained to employees, and reviewed on a regular basis. The rules must relate to the safe and efficient operation of the organization. When managers fail to enforce rules, they must re-emphasize those rules and their enforcement before disciplining an employee.

 objective

The term "discipline" has three meanings: punishment, orderly behaviour, and the training of employee conduct. Discipline should correct undesirable employee behaviour and instill in the employee a desire for self-control. Discipline can be constructive only when managers conduct a complete and unbiased investigation of employee misconduct. The investigation of employee misconduct begins with proper documentation. When managers are investigating employee problems they must establish precisely what the employee did, whether the employee knew about the rule that was violated, and any extenuating circumstances. Disciplinary rules must be uniformly enforced. The past work record of the employee must be considered in any disciplinary procedure.

 There are two approaches to discipline: progressive and positive. Progressive discipline follows a series of steps based on increasingly strong corrective action. The corrective action applied should match the severity of the employee misconduct. Positive discipline is a cooperative approach and is based on reminders; employees accept responsibility for the desired improvement. The focus is on coping with the unsatisfactory performance and dissatisfactions of employees before the problems become major.

 Alternative dispute resolution procedures ensure that employees can exercise their due process rights. The most common ADRs are the step review system, the peer review system, the use of hearing officers, the open door system, the ombudsman system, and arbitration.

 Ethics in HRM extends beyond the legal requirements of managing employees. Managers engage in ethical behaviour when employees are treated fairly and objectively and when an employee's personal and work-related rights are respected and valued.

KEY TERMS

alternative dispute resolution (ADR) 567
constructive dismissal 544
contractual rights 540
discipline 558
due process 542
employee rights 538

ethics 570
hearing officers 568
hot stove rule 558
mediation 570
negligence 539
ombudsman 569
open door policy 568

peer review system 568
positive (or nonpunitive) discipline 561
progressive discipline 561
statutory rights 540
step review system 567

DISCUSSION QUESTIONS

 1. Do you have a right to your job? Discuss with reference to statutory rights, contractual rights, and due process.

 2. Describe a situation in which electronic monitoring of employees would be justified. Discuss any potential problems that might result from the monitoring.

 3. If you were asked to develop a policy on discipline, what topics would you cover in the policy?

 4. What should be the purpose of an investigative interview, and what approach should be taken in conducting it?

 5. Discuss why documentation is so important to the disciplinary process. What constitutes correct documentation? Using this information, describe how a professor might document a case where a student was alleged to have cheated on a final exam.

 6. Describe progressive and positive discipline, noting the differences between these two approaches.

 7. What do you think would constitute an effective ADR system? What benefits would you expect from such a system? If you were asked to rule on a dismissal case, what facts

would you analyze in deciding whether to uphold or reverse the employer's action?

8. Working by yourself, or in a team, identify ethical dilemmas that could arise in the HR areas of selection, performance appraisal, safety and health, privacy rights, and compensation.

9. In groups, discuss whether the following situations are fair or not fair:

a. Zabeen was using the company Internet to locate a nursing home for her increasingly handicapped father. Her supervisor observed this and verified it with the Information Technology unit. Zabeen was given a written reprimand. Meanwhile, Sonia used the company telephone to do her personal banking and bill paying and was not reprimanded.

b. Anthony spent his lunch hour at the gym, consisting of a strenuous workout program with a personal trainer. Meanwhile, Nicholas met his friends for lunch, sharing several beers at the local pub. Both employees felt fatigued in the afternoon, and their diminished productivity was noticed by their supervisor. Nicholas was asked to meet with his supervisor to review performance standards, and received a verbal warning. Anthony was not.

Developing Managerial Skills

LEARNING ABOUT EMPLOYEE RIGHTS

In the constantly changing field of human resources it is imperative that both HR managers and supervisors be aware of changes that affect the organization and the process of managing employees. Nowhere is this more true than in the growing field of employee rights. As employees demand more job and employment rights regarding drug testing, surveillance, unjust dismissals, off-duty conduct, and genetic testing, employers must be knowledgeable about new laws, court rulings, and the policies of other organizations that influence each area. This knowledge will enable managers to respond to these employee concerns in a positive and proactive manner. Failure to provide employees their rights could lead to costly and embarrassing lawsuits, resulting in diminished employee loyalty or morale. The purpose of this exercise, therefore, is to enable you to familiarize yourself with issues of employee rights.

Assignment

Working individually or in teams, for each of the following employee rights topics, identify and discuss the privacy concerns for both employees and employers. Answer the questions pertaining to each topic.

▶ Wrongful Dismissal Suits
▶ Substance Abuse and Drug Testing
▶ Searches and Monitoring
▶ Employee Conduct away from the Workplace
▶ Genetic Testing
▶ E-mail, Internet

(continued on following page)

1. What is the issue concerned with?
2. Why is this issue of current interest to employees and managers?
3. What rights are employees demanding?
4. What, if any, laws or court cases affect this right?
5. Generally, how are employers responding to this employee right?

Case   Study   1

Improving Performance through a Progressive Discipline Policy

Simon Ouellet, former president of the Human Resources Professionals Association of Ontario, started his new job as vice-president, Human Resources, at Fantom Technologies in November 1998. Fantom is a manufacturer of state-of-the-art floor care products, based in southern Ontario.

One of the first issues he faced was an unacceptable absenteeism rate. There were about 250 employees on the three assembly lines, operating two shifts a day. The average employee was absent thirteen or fourteen days a year. The benchmark for other manufacturing sites was eight or nine days. Simon calculated that Fantom was employing between thirty and thirty-five extra people to cover absences. This hurt the bottom line.

A related problem was punctuality. Employees were habitually five or ten minutes late on their shifts. In a white-collar environment with flextime, this would not have been as critical. But tardiness in this situation meant that the assembly line could not operate, and that the other employees on the three lines were forced to remain idle.

The solution was to develop a system of progressive discipline. Simon prepared a simple two-page policy. Page 1 dealt with culpable absenteeism—the behaviour in the control of employees such as arriving late, leaving work without permission, calling in sick but playing golf, and so on. Page 2 dealt with legitimate or innocent absences. Simon met with the unions and notified them that this policy would come into effect as of December 1998. All employees started at zero absences at this time.

The policy assumed that all absences were innocent. However, if an employee was absent five times in a twelve-month period, the supervisor met with that employee to express concern over the absences and to identify any need for counselling or assistance. The goal of the meeting was to express legitimate concerns, reinforce that the employee was needed, and ensure that the employee accepted responsibility for managing his or her own attendance. Following this meeting, if the employee had fewer than two absences in the ensuing six months, the employee was no longer part of the program. However, if the absence pattern continued, the employee was counselled a second and third time. If no improvements resulted, a level 4 employment status review was conducted. This was done on a case-by-case basis. For example, a frequently absent employee with twenty-eight years of good service would be treated differently from another employee with the same absenteeism record but only two years of employment.

The results were impressive. About seventy employees entered the program. Of these, eight to ten advanced to step 2, two to step 3, and none to step 4. The absenteeism rate dropped to an average of less than ten days, and punctuality was no longer an issue. Labour costs were reduced, because it meant that twenty fewer employees were needed.

QUESTIONS

1. "The policy assumed that all absences were innocent." What do you think this means?
2. The policy was active as of December 1998, and all employees were treated equally from that date, regardless of their previous absenteeism records. Was this fair?
3. Could a policy of this type be developed to manage student punctuality and absenteeism?

Case Study 2

Discharged for Off-Duty Behaviour

The following case illustrates the off-duty privacy claim of an employee and management's right to uphold the reputation of the company.

Before his termination on Monday, May 6, 2003, John Hilliard worked as a senior sales representative for Advanced Educational Materials (AEM), a provider of high-quality educational books and supplies to junior and senior high schools. During his twelve years of employment, John was recognized as an outstanding employee with close working relationships with the schools he served. His sales record was excellent. John's discharge resulted from what AEM claimed was a serious breach of its code of conduct for employees.

On Saturday, May 4, 2003, due to a chance meeting between John and his manager, Jean Ellison, John was observed leaving an adult video store carrying what his manager described as pornographic magazines and an X-rated video. The following Monday, Jean discussed the incident with AEM's vice-president for sales and a representative from HR. All agreed that John's off-duty behaviour constituted a serious violation of the company's code of conduct for employees, which read, in part, "Employee off-duty behaviour in no way should reflect unfavourably upon the company, its employees, or sales of any educational materials." AEM has traditionally held its sales representatives to high moral standards because the company sells extensively to public school administrators and teachers.

At his discharge meeting John vigorously opposed his firing. While he acknowledged making the purchases, he argued strongly that what he did on his personal time was "no business of the company's" and his behaviour in no way reflected unfavourably upon AEM or the sales of its products. Besides, he said, "the purchases were made as jokes for a stag party."

Source: This case is based on an actual termination for off-duty misconduct. All names are fictitious.

QUESTIONS

1. Given the facts of this case, should John have been discharged? Explain.
2. Should the sales representatives of AEM be held to a higher standard of personal conduct than sales representatives for other types of organizations? Explain.
3. Should management have considered John's past work record before deciding on discharge? Explain.

CAREER COUNSEL

Visit the *Managing Human Resources* website (www.belcourt4e.nelson.com) for tips on negotiating a formal employment contract.

NOTES AND REFERENCES

1. Bill Curry, "Radwanski Predicts Privacy to Be 'Defining Issue of Next Decade," *Hill Times*, January 8, 2001: 12; M. Wolpert, "Front Page News," *Benefits Canada* 20, no. 2 (February 1996): 21–5.
2. S. Cohen and A.V Campell, "It's Time to Face the Inevitable and Comply with Privacy Laws," *Canadian HR Reporter* 15, no. 2 (January 28, 2002): 9–10; James W. Hunt and Patricia K. Strongin, *The Law of the Workplace: Rights of Employers and Employees* (Washington, D.C.: Bureau of National Affairs, 1994).
3. Alfred G. Felio, *Primer on Individual Employee Rights* (Washington, D.C.: Bureau of National Affairs, 1996).
4. Donald H. Weiss, "How to Avoid Negligent Hiring Law Suits," *Supervisory Management* 36, no. 6 (June 1991): 6.
5. Samuel Greengard, "Privacy: Entitlement or Illusion?" *Personnel Journal* 75, no. 5 (May 1996): 74–88. See also James R. Redeker, *Employee Discipline: Policies and Practices* (Washington, D.C.: Bureau of National Affairs, 1989): 21. This book has an excellent discussion of the rights and responsibilities of employers and employees in the employment relationship; it also provides a comprehensive discussion of employee discipline.
6. K. Cox, "PEI to Pay Damages to 314 Workers Fired by Tories," *The Globe and Mail*, November 27, 1997: A4.
7. K. Makin, "Insensitive Firings Not Tolerated: Supreme Court Decision Will Aid Future Victims of Wrongful Dismissal, Lawyers Say," *The Globe and Mail*, October 31, 1997: A4; D. Johnston, "Promises, Promises: The Case of Queen versus Cognos," *Law Now* 22, no. 3 (December 1997, January 1998): 16–18.
8. Robert S. Seeley, "Corporate Due Process," *HRMagazine* 37, no. 7 (July 1992): 46–9.
9. Redeker, *Employee Discipline*, 25–38.
10. Christopher Bouvier, "Why At-Will Employment Is Dying," *Personnel Journal* 75, no. 5 (May 1996): 123–8. See also Marvin J. Levine, "The Erosion of the Employment-at-Will Doctrine: Recent Developments," *Labor Law Journal* 45, no. 2 (February 1994): 79–89.
11. Karl Scholz, "The Law of Employee Dismissals," *Canadian Manager* 26, no. 4 (Winter 2001): 9–10.
12. T. Wagar, "Wrongful Dismissal: Perception vs. Reality," *Human Resources Professional* 8, no. 10 (1996).
13. J. Carlisle, "Court Sets Standard for Constructive Dismissal," *Financial Post*, April 29, 1997: 14.

14. J. Melnitizer, "Ciciretto vs Embassy Cleaners," *Workplace News* 5, no. 2 (February 1999): 1.

15. Canadian Profile 1999, Substance Abuse and the Workplace, Canadian Centre on Substance Abuse, www.ccsa.ca/cp1999work.html.

16. Ontario Human Rights Commission, Policy on Drug and Alcohol Testing, www.ohrc.onc.ca/english/publications/drug_alcohol_testing_eng.html.

17. *Drug-Free Workplace: Back on Track* (Virginia Beach, VA.: Coastal Human Resources, 1993): 3.

18. Edward J. Miller, "Investigating in a Drug-Free Workplace," *HRMagazine* 36, no. 5 (May 1991): 48–51.

19. G.H. Siejts, "Canadians More Opposed to Workplace Drug Testing Than U.S Counterparts," *HR Professional*, April/May 2003: 10–12; B. Butler, "Alcohol and Drug Testing in Canada: Do You Have a Right To Test? Do You Have a Right Not To?" *Occupational Health and Safety* 13, no. 1 (January–February 1997): 28–31.

20. K. Hefner and S. Garland, "Testing for Drug Use: Handle With Care," *Business Week*, March 28, 1985: 65.

21. J. Towler, "Dealing with Employees Who Steal," *Canadian HR Reporter* 15, no. 16 (September 23, 2002): 4.

22. "Air Canada Searches Employee Rooms," *Canadian HR Reporter* 16, no. 3 (February 3, 2003): 2.

23. Robert L. Brady, "Workplace Searches: Avoid Legal Problems," *HRFocus* 72, no. 4 (April 1995): 18.

24. James D. Vigneau, "To Catch a Thief . . . and Other Workplace Investigations," *HRMgazine* 40, no. 1 (January 1995): 92–3.

25. Jennifer J. Laabs, "Surveillance: Tool or Trap?" *Personnel Journal* 71, no. 6 (June 1992): 102.

26. Ann K. Bradley, "An Employer's Perception on Monitoring Telemarketing Calls: Invasion of Privacy or Legitimate Business Practice?" *Labor Law Journal* 42, no. 5 (May 1991): 259–73.

27. Peter Carlisle, "Videotape Can Be Used as Evidence in Civil Court," *Financial Post*, May, 27, 1997.

28. S. Cohen and A.V Campell, "It's Time to Face the Inevitable and Comply with Privacy Laws," *Canadian HR Reporter* 15, no. 2 (January 28, 2002): 9–10.

29. David Brown, "10 Months to Get Ready," *Canadian HR Reporter* 16, no. 4 (February 24, 2003): 1,11.

30. Richard Behar, "Who's Reading Your E-Mail?" *Fortune*, February 3, 1997, 57–70; Richard F. Federico and James M. Bowley, "The Great E-Mail Debate," *HRMagazine* 41, no. 1 (January 1996): 67–72.

31. Kathy J. Lang and Elaine Davis, "Personnel E-Mail: An Employee Benefit Causing Increasing Privacy Concerns," *Employee Benefits Journal* 22, no. 2 (June 1996): 30–3.

32. K. Sibley, "The E-mail Dilemma: To Spy or Not to Spy?" *Computing Canada*, March 31, 1997: 14.

33. Don A. Cozzetto and Thomas B. Pedeliski, "Privacy and the Workplace," *Public Personnel Administration* 16, no. 2 (Spring 1996): 21–31. See also Donald H. Seifman and Craig W. Trepanier, "Evolution of the Paperless Office: Legal Issues Arising Out of Technology in the Workplace," *Employee Relations Law Journal* 21, no. 3 (Winter 1995–96): 5–15.

34. Robert L. Brady, "Electronic Mail: Drafting a Policy," *HRFocus* 72, no. 10 (October 1995): 19.

35. G. Arnaut, "Electronic Big Brother Is on the Job," *The Globe and Mail*, October 22, 1996: C1.

36. N.C MacDonald "You've Got E-mail Problems," *Canadian HR Reporter* 16, no. 5 (March 10, 2003): 5, 10.

37. P. Israel, "Spying on Employees – and It's Perfectly Legal," *Canadian HR Reporter* 16, no. 8 (April 21, 2003): 5; "What the Courts Are Saying," *Canadian HR Reporter* 16, no. 8 (April 21, 2003): 5.

38. Marjo Johne, "Is Someone Watching You?" *The Globe and Mail*, January 10, 2003: C1.

39. Asha Tomlinson, "Off Duty Racism Gets Teacher Fired," *Canadian HR Reporter* 15, no. 8 (April 22, 2002): 1, 6; Rosalyn L. Wilcots, "Employee Discipline for Off-Duty Conduct: Constitutional Challenges and the Public Policy Exception," *Labor Law Journal* 46, no. 1 (January 1995): 3–16; Steve Bergsman, "Employee Misconduct Outside the Workplace," *HRMagazine* 36, no. 3 (March 1991): 62.

40. Melinda Socol Herbst, "Employers May Police Some Workplace Romances," *The National Law Journal*, February 26, 1996: C19; Douglas Massengill and Donald J. Petersen, "Legal Challenges to No Fraternization Rules," *Labor Law Journal* 46, no. 7 (July 1995): 429–35.

41. Dean J. Schaner, "Romance in the Workplace: Should Employers Act as Chaperones?" *Employee Relations Law Journal* 20, no. 1 (Summer 1994): 47–67.

42. Sharon Clinebell, Lynn Hoffman, and John Kilpatrick, "Office Romances: Rights and Liabilities," *HRFocus* 72, no. 3 (March 1995): 19.

43. T. Humber, "Genetic Testing in the Workplace," *Canadian HR Reporter* 15, no. 21 (December 2, 2002): 1, 10.

44. "Termination and Layoff," *The Employer's Guide to the Employment Standards Act* (Ontario: Queen's Printer, 1997).

45. Catherine M. Petrini, ed., "Help for Discipline Dodgers," *Training and Development* 47, no. 5 (May 1993): 19–22.

46. Gary Bielous, "The Five Worst Discipline Mistakes," *Supervisory Management* 40, no. 1 (January 1995): 14–15.

47. Caleb S. Atwood, "Discharge Now, Pay Later? Establishing Reasonable Rules Can Keep You Out of Hot Water," *Personnel Administrator* 34, no. 8 (August 1989): 92–3.

48. Donald C. Mosley, Leon C. Megginson, and Paul H. Pietri, *Supervisory Management: The Art of Developing*

and Empowering People, 4th ed. (Cincinnati: South-Western, 1997).

49. Cecily A. Waterman and Teresa A. Maginn, "Investigating Suspect Employees," *HRMagazine* 38, no. 1 (January 1993): 85–7.

50. Rebecca K. Spar, "Keeping Internal Investigations Confidential," *HRMagazine* 41, no. 1 (January 1996): 33–6.

51. Jeffrey A. Mello, "The Fine Art of the Reprimand: Using Criticism to Enhance Commitment, Motivation, and Performance," *Employment Relations Today* 22, no. 4 (Winter 1995): 19–27.

52. Readers interested in the pioneering work on positive discipline should see James R. Redeker, "Discipline, Part 1: Progressive Systems Work Only by Accident," *Personnel* 62, no. 10 (October 1985): 8–12; James R. Redeker, "Discipline, Part 2: The Nonpunitive Approach Works by Design," *Personnel* 62, no. 11 (November 1985): 7–14. See also Alan W. Bryant, "Replacing Punitive Discipline with a Positive Approach," *Personnel Administrator* 29, no. 2 (February 1984): 79–87.

53. Chimezie A.B. Osigweh, Y. and William R. Hutchison, "Positive Discipline," *Human Resources Management* 28, no. 3 (Fall 1989): 367–83. See also Redeker, *Employee Discipline*.

54. Brenda Paik Sunoo, "Positive Discipline: Sending the Right or Wrong Message?" *Personnel Journal* 75, no. 8 (August 1996): 109–10.

55. Adolph M. Koven and Susan N. Smith, *Just Cause: The Seven Tests*, 2nd ed. (Washington, D.C.: Bureau of National Affairs, 1992).

56. For an expanded discussion of just cause, see Frank Elkouri and Edna Asher Elkouri, *How Arbitration Works*, 4th ed. (Washington, D.C.: Bureau of National Affairs, 1985), 650–54.

57. John E. Lyncheski, "Mishandling Terminations Causes Legal Nightmares," *HRMagazine* 40, no. 5 (May 1995): 25–30.

58. Lewis Newman, "Outplacement the Right Way," *Personnel Administrator* 34, no. 2 (February 1989): 83–6.

59. Susan E. Klein, "AAA President Slate Focuses on ADR Challenges," *Dispute Resolution Journal* 51, no. 2–3 (April 1996): 29–33, 130–5.

60. Douglas M. McCabe, "Corporate Nonunion Grievance Arbitration Systems: A Procedural Analysis," *Labor Law Journal* 40, no. 7 (July 1989): 432–7.

61. Mary Helen Yarborough, "Use Peer Review for Conflict Resolution," *HRFocus* 71, no. 10 (October 1994): 21.

62. Douglas M. McCabe, *Corporate Nonunion Complaint Procedures and Systems* (New York: Praeger, 1988): 9. See also Dawn Anfuso, "Coors Taps Employee Judgement," *Personnel Journal* 13, no. 2 (February 1994): 50.

63. Antonio Ruiz-Quintanilla and Donna Blancero, "Open Door Policies: Measuring Impact Using Attitude Surveys," *Human Resource Management* 35, no. 3 (Fall 1996): 269–89.

64. Norm Frauenheim, "Clause Alarms Athletes," *Arizona Republic*, May 10, 1996: C1.

65. Stuart L. Bass, "Recent Court Decisions Expand Role of Arbitration in Harassment and Other Title VII Cases," *Labor Law Journal* 46, no. 1 (January 1995): 38–46; Patrick J. Cihon, "Recent Developments in the Arbitration of Employment Discrimination Claims," *Labor Law Journal* 46, no. 10 (October 1995): 587–96; Lamont E. Stallworth and Linda K. Stroh, "Who Is Seeking to Use ADR and Why Do They Choose to Do So?" *Dispute Resolution Journal* 51, no. 1 (January–March 1996): 30–8; Kathryn M. Werdegar, "The Courts and Private ADR: Partners in Serving Justice," *Dispute Resolution Journal* 51, no. 2–3 (April 1996): 52–5.

66. George W. Bohlander, Robert J. Deeny, and Mishka L. Marshall, "Alternative Dispute Resolution Policies: Current Procedural and Administrative Issues," *Labor Law Journal* 47, no. 9 (September 1996): 619–26; Thomas R. Kelly and Danielle L. Berke, "What's New in ADR?" *HRFocus* 73, no. 4 (April 1996): 15.

67. Brenda Paik Sunoo, "Hot Disputes Cool Down in Online Mediation," *Workforce* 80, no. 1 (January 2001): 48–52.

68. Lamont E. Stallworth, Thomas McPherson, and Larry Rute, "Discrimination in the Workplace: How Mediation Can Help," *Dispute Resolution Journal* 56, no. 1 (February–April 2001): 35–44, 83–87.

69. "How Best to Avoid Mediation Mistakes," *HRFocus* 77, no. 9 (September 2000): 2. See also Nancy Kauffman and Barbara Davis, "What Type of Mediation Do You Want?" *Dispute Resolution Journal* 53, no. 2 (May 1998): 10.

70. "The Importance of Business Ethics," *HRFocus* 78, no. 7 (July 2001): 1, 13–14.

The Manager as Counsellor

Without question, employee counselling is an important part of a manager's job. Disciplinary interviews are often restricted to obtaining and giving specific information; in contrast, counselling involves a dynamic relationship between two parties in which one person is free to discuss needs, feelings, and problems for the purpose of obtaining help. Counselling involves many variables on both sides of the relationship (see Figure 13.A). The relationship is the chief means of meshing the helpee's problems with the counsel of the helper. Counselling can help employees with their personal problems—poor health, drug or alcohol abuse, family concerns, or financial difficulties; it can also help them deal with their job-related complaints or performance problems. The most effective way to reduce complaints is to encourage them to be brought out into the open.

Figure 13.A	Developing the Counselling Relationship

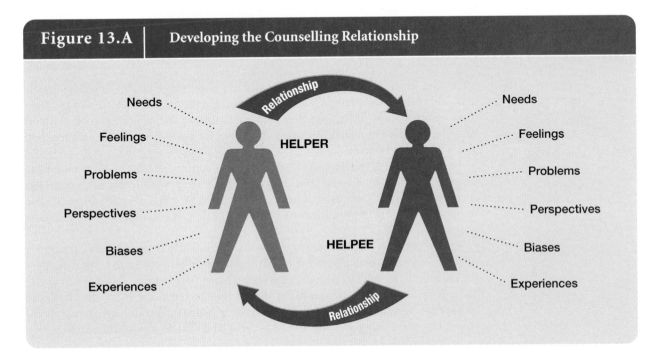

NATURE OF THE RELATIONSHIP

Counselling does not take place in a vacuum: it occurs in the context of the relationship between the two parties. In organizations, authority affects that relationship. For example, an employee is not free to ignore a supervisor's help in work-related matters; whereas in the counselling relationship, he or she is—the helper is advising the helpee, not instructing. Another factor in the counselling relationship is confidentiality. Generally, what takes place in a counselling relationship is expected not to go beyond the two parties involved. There are times, however, when certain types of information must be reported—for example, if serious harm to others might result if it is not. Another factor that can affect the relationship is the manager's degree of commitment to help.

COUNSELLING TECHNIQUES

All of us have a natural tendency to judge, to evaluate, to approve or disapprove. Sometimes we do these things prematurely on the basis of our preconceived assumptions; when we do, we are reducing our ability to communicate effectively. One way to avoid premature judgments is through a counselling technique called active listening. Active listening involves trying to understand what the other person is thinking by allowing this person to explain his or her perspective more fully without interrupting, or asking questions, or introducing new topics. The supervisor should maintain eye contact and should be relaxed and attentive to what the employee says or is trying to say.

Active listening is always important. It is absolutely essential when

▶ we do not understand how the other person feels, and we need to understand the person's perspective;
▶ we believe that what is being said is not as important as what is not being said; and
▶ the other person is so confused that a clear message cannot be communicated.

Besides listening actively, a manager will use a technique known as *reflecting feelings*. This involves expressing—in somewhat different words—the employee's feelings, whether stated or implied. The goal is to focus on feelings rather than content, to bring vaguely expressed feelings into clearer focus, and to help the person talk about his or her feelings.

Examples of this technique include the use of comments such as "You resent the way the boss treats you," and "You feel that you deserve more recognition from the company." This technique is especially useful in the early stages of counselling. It is the standard procedure in nondirective counselling, a type of counselling we will discuss later.

Another good approach is to ask questions that will help the person understand his or her problem. Generally, these questions should be open-ended—that is, they should require more than yes or no answers. Thus, "Tell me more about your experiences with Mr. Jones." The questions should lead to clarification for the employee rather than information for the supervisor. Open-ended questions leave the employee free to take the interview in the direction that will do the most for him or her.

Counselling Approaches

There are many approaches to counselling, but they all depend on active listening. Sometimes the problem can be solved simply by furnishing information or advice. More often, however, the problem cannot be solved easily, because of frustrations or conflicts, and because the helpee is consumed with strong feelings such as fear, confusion, and hostility. A manager, therefore, needs to learn to use whatever approach seems to work at the time. Flexibility is a key part of counselling.

Directive Counselling

In directive counselling, the manager attempts to control (directly or indirectly) the topics the employee is talking about; describes the choices the employee faces; and/or advises the employee what to do. It is very often appropriate for the supervisor to provide information and advice in areas where he or she is knowledgeable and experienced, especially if that information and/or advice is sought. However, where there are choices to be made and frustration and/or conflict are apparent, the directive approach should be avoided.

Nondirective Counselling

In nondirective counselling, the employee is allowed maximum freedom to determine the course of the interview. Nonevaluative listening is important here; it is the primary technique in nondirective counselling. Fundamentally, this approach involves listening, with understanding and without criticism or appraisal, to the problem as the employee describes it. This encourages the employee to express feelings without fear of shame, embarrassment, or reprisal.

The nondirective approach encourages free expression, which tends to reduce tensions and frustrations. The employee who has had an opportunity to release pent-up feelings is usually in a better position to view the problem more objectively and with a problem-solving attitude. The permissive atmosphere provides the employee with space to work through the entanglements of the problem and to see it in a clearer perspective. This increases the likelihood of reaching a desirable solution.

Participative Counselling

The directive and nondirective approaches that have just been described are obviously at the extremes of a continuum. Professional counsellors tend to stay at one end or the other of the continuum; in contrast, most managers vary their approach during a first session and/or in subsequent sessions. Many choose a middle-of-the-road approach in which both parties work together in planning how a particular problem will be analyzed and solved. This approach, which some refer to as participative counselling, is especially suitable in work organizations.

Many of the problems that managers and supervisors are concerned with require not only that the subordinates' feelings be recognized, but also that subordinates be made aware of and adhere to management's expectations that they be productive, responsible, and cooperative. On the other side of the coin, most people with problems would prefer to be actively involved in the solution once they see that there is a positive course of action available. In many work situations where counselling will be used, the participative approach is recommended in working with an individual over a period of time. However, at different times in the course of a single session, it may be advisable to be both directive and nondirective.

WHEN COUNSELLING DOESN'T WORK

Counselling by managers will not always achieve the goals it sets. When it doesn't, the employee may have to be disciplined or transferred.

The manager or supervisor may not have the skill or time to handle the more complex personal problems of employees. Sometimes the supervisor will have little or no influence over the problem area, as in the employee's family relationships. At these times it may be advisable for the supervisor to recommend that the employee see a professional counsellor. So there should be an established system for making referrals to trained counsellors. Usually it is the HR department that handles referrals to these professionals.

The Dynamics of Labour Relations

After studying this chapter, you should be able to

objective 1

Identify and explain the federal and provincial legislation that provides the framework for labour relations.

objective 4

Discuss the bargaining process and the bargaining goals and strategies of a union and an employer.

objective 2

Explain the reasons employees join unions.

objective 5

Differentiate the forms of bargaining power that a union and an employer may utilize to enforce their bargaining demands.

objective 3

Describe the process by which unions organize employees and gain recognition as their bargaining agent.

objective 6

Describe a typical union grievance procedure and explain the basis for arbitration awards.

Mention the word "union" and most people will have some opinion, positive or negative, about Canadian labour organizations. To some, the word evokes images of labour–management unrest—grievances, strikes, picketing, boycotts. To others, the word represents industrial democracy, fairness, opportunity, and equal representation. Many think of unions as simply creating an adversarial relationship between employees and managers.

Regardless of attitudes toward them, since the mid-1800s unions have been an important force shaping legislation, political thought, and organizational practices in Canada. Today, unions remain of interest because of how they influence labour legislation and HR policies and practices. Like business organizations themselves, unions are changing both their operations and their philosophy. Labour–management cooperative programs, company buyouts by unions, and labour's increased interest in global trade are evidence of labour's new role in society.

In spite of the history of unions, the intricacies of labour relations are unfamiliar to many individuals. This chapter describes government regulation of labour relations, the labour relations process, the reasons why workers join labour organizations, and the structure and leadership of labour unions. Importantly, according to labour law, once the union is certified, it must represent everyone in the unit equally. Therefore, in the latter sections of the chapter, we discuss the important topics of contract administration, particularly the handling of employee grievances and arbitration.

Unions and other labour organizations can affect significantly the ability of managers to direct and control the various functions of HRM. Examples: union seniority provisions in the labour contract often influence who is selected for job promotions or training programs; pay rates may be determined through union negotiations; and unions may impose restrictions on management's employee appraisal methods. Therefore, it is essential that managers understand how unions operate and be thoroughly familiar with the growing body of law governing labour relations. Remember that ignorance of labour legislation is no defence when managers and supervisors violate labour law. Before reading further, test your knowledge of labour relations law by answering the questions in Highlights in HRM 14.1. (The correct answers are provided at the end of the chapter.)

Government Regulation of Labour Relations

objective

Unions have a long history in North America, and the regulations governing labour relations have been evolving for just as long. In the early years, employers strongly opposed the growth of unions and attempted to block them through the courts (e.g., through court orders forbidding picketing or strikes) and by devices such as the "yellow dog contract." A yellow dog contract was an anti-union tactic by which employees bound themselves not to join a union while working for the employer. Employers also used strikebreakers, blacklists, and various economic strong-arm tactics to defend themselves against unionization.

Highlights in HRM 14.1

TEST YOUR LABOUR RELATIONS KNOW-HOW

1. During a labour organizing drive, supervisors questioned individual employees about their union beliefs. Was this questioning permissible?

   Yes_____ No _____

2. While an organizing drive was under way, an employer agreed—as a social gesture—to furnish refreshments at a holiday party. Was the employer acting within the law?

   Yes_____ No _____

3. A company distributed to other anti-union employers in the area a list of job applicants known to be union supporters. Was the distribution unlawful?

   Yes_____ No _____

4. During a union organizing drive, the owner of Servo Pipe promised her employees a wage increase if they would vote against the union. Can the owner legally make this promise to her employees?

   Yes_____ No _____

5. John Green, a maintenance engineer, has a poor work record. Management wishes to terminate his employment; however, Green is a union steward and is highly critical of the company. Can management legally discharge this employee?

   Yes_____ No_____

Answers on page 624.

USING THE INTERNET

For a history of labour, read the article "The Cradle of Collective Bargaining: History of Labour" at www.humanities.mcmaster.ca/~cradle/.

USING THE INTERNET

For links to all provincial labour relations boards, unions, etc. visit www.cpa-acp.ca/links.

Today's labour relations laws try to create an environment where both unions and employers can discharge their respective rights and responsibilities. When you understand labour relations laws, you will understand how union–management relations operate in Canada.

Labour Relations Legislation

Labour relations in Canada is regulated by a multiplicity of federal and provincial laws. There are specific laws, or acts, for different sectors, industries, and workers. It is a highly decentralized system. For example, interprovincial transportation and communications are under federal jurisdiction, while manufacturing and mining are provincial. However, 90 percent of workers are governed by provincial legislation.

The Industrial Relations Disputes and Investigation Act

The Industrial Relations Disputes and Investigation Act (1948) specified the right of workers to join unions, allowed unions to be certified as bargaining agents by a labour relations board, required management to recognize a certified union as the exclusive bargaining agent for a group of employees, required both unions and management to negotiate in good faith, outlined unfair labour practices by both unions and management, and created a two-stage compulsory conciliation process that was mandatory before strikes or lockouts became legal.[1]

The federal government later incorporated these rights into a more comprehensive piece of legislation known as the Canada Labour Code. At the same time, the Canada Labour Relations Board (LRB) was established to administer and enforce the code. Similarly, each province has a labour relations board that administers labour law. (The exception is Quebec, which has a labour court and commissioners.) The members of these boards are government appointees. The LRB is generally autonomous from the federal government and has representatives from both labour and management. The duties of the LRB include

▶ administrating the statutory procedures for the acquisition, transfer, and termination of bargaining rights;

▶ hearing complaints related to unfair labour practices;

▶ supervising strikes and lockout votes;

▶ determining whether bargaining was done in good faith; and

▶ remedying violations of collective bargaining legislation.[2]

THE LABOUR RELATIONS PROCESS

Labour relations process
Logical sequence of four events: (1) workers desire collective representation, (2) union begins its organizing campaign, (3) collective negotiations lead to a contract, and (4) the contract is administered

Individually, employees may be able to exercise relatively little power in their relations with employers. The treatment and benefits they receive depend in large part on how their employers view their worth to the organization. Of course, if they believe they are not being treated fairly, they have the option of quitting. However, employees can also correct this situation by organizing and bargaining with the employer collectively. When employees pursue this direction, the labour relations process begins. As Figure 14.1 illustrates, the **labour relations process** consists of a logical sequence of four events: (1) workers desire collective representation, (2) union begins its organizing campaign, (3) collective negotiations lead to a contract, and (4) the contract is administered. Laws and administrative rulings influence each of these separate events by granting special privileges to, or imposing defined constraints on, workers, managers, and union officials.[3]

Why Employees Unionize

The majority of research on why employees unionize relates to blue-collar employees in the private sector. These studies generally conclude that employees unionize as a result of economic need, and/or because of general dissatisfaction with managerial practices, and/or as a way to fulfil social and status needs. In short, employees see unionism as a means to achieve results they cannot achieve acting individually.[4] As Highlights in HRM 14.2 illustrates, some segments of the labour force are, for a variety of reasons, very difficult to unionize.

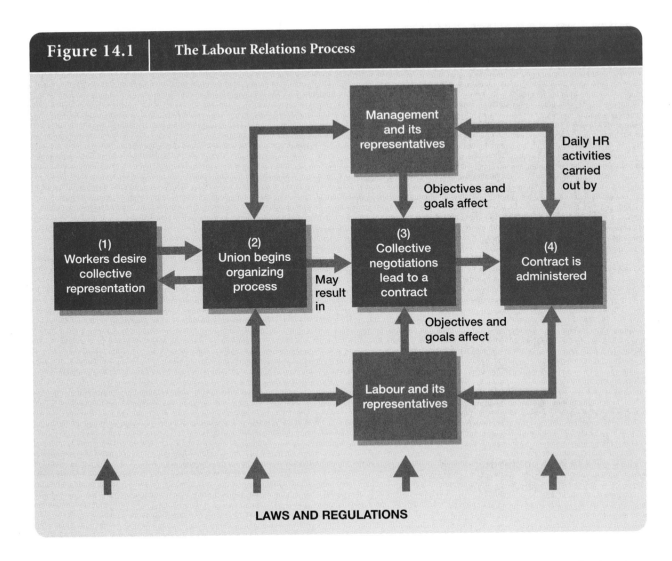

Figure 14.1 | The Labour Relations Process

LAWS AND REGULATIONS

Union shop

Provision of the collective agreement that requires employees to join the union as a condition of their employment

It should be pointed out that some employees join unions because of union shop provisions. A **union shop** is a provision in the collective agreement that requires employees to join as a condition of their employment.

Economic Needs

Whether or not a union will become the bargaining agent for a group of employees depends in part on the employees' degree of dissatisfaction (if any) with their employment conditions. It also depends on whether the employees perceive a union as likely to improve these conditions. Dissatisfaction with wages, benefits, and working conditions is the strongest reason for joining a union. This point is continually supported by research studies, which have found that both union members and nonmembers have their highest expectations of union performance regarding the "bread and butter" issues

Highlights in HRM 14.2

HOMEWORKERS: CANADA'S INVISIBLE LABOUR FORCE

Rosanna Gonzalez (not her real name) works in the basement of her home in a small room crowded with industrial sewing machines. Rosanna is in the process of making 410 sweatshirts. To meet her deadline she will have to put in forty hours of work in two days. There is no natural light in the airless basement room, no way to escape the flying dust and thread particles. Last week the assignment was T-shirts. Rosanna received 38 cents per shirt. She can churn one out in five minutes, but even at that speed, she still earns only about $4.50 per hour—the minimum wage a decade ago.

In most provinces the law requires that homeworkers be paid at least one dollar above minimum wage to compensate them for the use of space and equipment in their homes. But enforcement of the law is rare. Canadians are quick to condemn working conditions in Third World countries, yet they are notably silent about abuses in their own country. Joining a union is a traditional response to abysmal working conditions. For homeworkers, unionization is a remote possibility at best. These individuals (most of whom speak no English) work in scattered and unlicensed locations and are usually unaware of their rights. Those who are aware are afraid that if they complain, they will suffer retribution at the hands of the retailers, contractors, and subcontractors they do business with. These women have few employment options and are often the sole providers for their children. For them the choice is clear: put up with the exploitation or don't work at all.

of collective bargaining.[5] Unions are built on these traditional issues of wages and benefits. Work restructuring issues such as multiskilling/multi-tasking and the use of part-time, temporary, and contract workers are faced by about two-thirds of the unions.[6]

Dissatisfaction with Management

Employees may seek unionization when they perceive that managerial practices regarding promotions, transfers, shift assignments, and the like are being administered unfairly. Employees cite management favouritism as a major reason for joining unions. This is especially true when the favouritism concerns the HR areas of discipline, promotions, and wage increases.

As we have noted throughout this book, today's employees are better educated than those of the past, and they often want to be more involved in decisions affecting their jobs. Chapter 3 discussed the concept of employee empowerment and highlighted various employee involvement techniques. The failure of employers to involve employees in decisions affecting their welfare may encourage union membership. It is widely believed that managers often begin empowerment programs as a means to avoid collective action by employees. In one organizing effort by the CAW (Canadian

Auto Workers) at a Toyota plant in Cambridge, Ontario, the union was defeated because the plant was well managed, and employees were generally satisfied.

Social and Affiliation Needs

Employees whose needs for social affiliation and recognition are being frustrated may join a union as a means of satisfying these needs. Through their union, they have an opportunity to fraternize with other employees who have similar desires, interests, problems, and gripes. Joining the union also enables them to use their leadership talents.

The limited studies conducted on employee unionization in the public sector generally have found that public employees unionize for about the same reasons as their private sector counterparts. In other words, higher wages and benefits, job security, and protection against arbitrary and unfair management treatment are primary motives for unionization among public sector employees.[7] In the final analysis, the deciding factor is likely to be whether employees perceive that the benefits of joining a union outweigh the costs associated with membership.

Organizing Campaigns

Once employees desire to unionize, a formal organization campaign may be started either by a union organizer or by employees acting on their own behalf. Contrary to popular belief, most organizing campaigns are begun by employees rather than by union organizers. However, large national unions such as the Canadian Auto Workers, the United Brotherhood of Carpenters, the United Steelworkers, and the Teamsters have formal organizing departments that identify organizing opportunities and launch organizing campaigns.

The CAW is Canada's largest private sector union with 238 000 members.

COURTESY OF MIKE RENAUD, PRESIDENT OF CAW LOCAL 195

Organizing Steps

The typical organizing campaign normally follows these steps:

1. Employee/union contact
2. Initial organizational meeting
3. Formation of an in-house organizing committee
4. Application to labour relations board
5. Issuance of certificate by labour relations board
6. Election of bargaining committee and contract negotiations

Step 1. The first step begins when employees and union officials make contact to explore the possibility of unionization. During these discussions, the employees investigate the advantages of representation, and union officials begin to gather information on employee needs, problems, and grievances. Union organizers also seek specific information about the employer's financial health, supervisory style, and organizational policies and practices. To win employee support, union organizers must build a case against the employer and for the union. Typically there are signs, reported in Highlights in HRM 14.3, that an organizing drive is occurring.

Step 2. As the organizing campaign gathers momentum, the organizer will schedule an initial union meeting to attract more supporters. The organizer will use the information gathered during step 1 to address the employees' needs and explain how the union can meet them. Organizational meetings serve two other purposes: they identify employees who can help the organizer direct the campaign, and they establish communication chains that will reach all employees.

Highlights in HRM 14.3

Is a Union Being Organized?

Senior management is sometimes the last to know that a union has targeted the company. Often the process starts after employees call a union with complaints and want to understand their legal rights and responsibilities. Listed below are a few common signs that an organization drive is happening:

▶ Unusual employee behaviour of any kind
▶ An increase in the number of complaints about working conditions
▶ Demands for detailed information about employment policies
▶ Gatherings of employees that appear larger in number than usual, or that involve employees whose jobs are unrelated, or who would usually have no common interests
▶ Changes in how employees interact with their supervisors
▶ The presence of union leaflets or other union material

Note also that most organizing drives take place inside the company.

Step 3. The third important step in the organizing drive is to form an in-house organizing committee comprising employees who are willing to provide leadership to the campaign. The committee's role is to interest other employees in joining the union and in supporting its campaign. An important task for the committee is to have employees sign **authorization cards** indicating their willingness to be represented by a labour union in collective bargaining with their employer. The number of signed authorization cards demonstrates the potential strength of the labour union. Legislation across Canada states that a union must have a majority of employees as members in a bargaining unit before it can apply for a certification election. Most jurisdictions now interpret this to mean that at least 50 percent of those voting constitute a majority. In other words, those who do not cast ballots are not assumed to be voting against the certification of the union. Union membership cards, once signed, are confidential, and only the labour relations board has access to them.

Step 4. Application is made to the appropriate labour relations board. In Canada, most unions are certified without a vote if the labour relations board finds that the union has the support of the majority of the employees, based on the number of signed cards.

Step 5. The labour relations board reviews the application and initially informs both the employer and the employees about the application, which is posted so that either employees or the employer have an opportunity to challenge.

Step 6. Once the labour relations board determines that the union is certified, the bargaining committee is put in place to start negotiating a collective agreement. If the union is a national union, such as the Canadian Auto Workers, usually a national representative works with the bargaining committee to negotiate a collective agreement with the company.

Authorization card
A statement signed by an employee authorizing a union to act as his or her representative for the purposes of collective bargaining

Employer Tactics

Employers must not interfere with the labour relations process of certification. They are prohibited by law from dismissing, disciplining, or threatening employees for exercising their right to form a union. Employers cannot promise better conditions, such as increased vacation days, if the employees vote for no union or choose one union over another. Nor can they threaten to close the business as one company did as workers were voting.[8] They cannot unilaterally change wages and working conditions during certification proceedings or during collective bargaining. Like unions, they must bargain in good faith, meaning that they must demonstrate a commitment to bargain seriously and fairly. In addition, they cannot participate in the formation, selection, or support of unions representing employees (see Figure 14.2).

None of these prohibitions prevents an employer from making the case that the employees have the right not to join a union and that they can deal directly with the employer on any issue. Employer resistance to unionization is the norm in Canada. and opposition has been found to decrease the probability of successfully organizing.[9] When Wal-Mart consolidated its entry into Canada by buying 122 nonunionized Woolco stores, the company was widely viewed as anti-union. However, Wal-Mart spokespeople insist that they are not anti-union, but rather "pro-associate" (the

Figure 14.2 | Employer "Don'ts" During Union Organizing Campaigns

Union organizing drives are emotionally charged events. Furthermore, labour law, LRB rulings, and court decisions greatly affect the behaviour and actions of management and union representatives. During the drive, managers and supervisors should avoid the following:

▶ Attending union meetings, spying on employee–union gatherings, and questioning employees about the content of union meetings.

▶ Questioning current employees about their union sentiments—especially about how they might vote in a union election.

▶ Threatening or terminating employees for their union support or beliefs.

▶ Changing the working conditions of employees because they actively work for the union or simply support its ideals.

▶ Supplying the names, addresses, and phone numbers of employees to union representatives or other employees sympathetic to the union.

▶ Promising employees improvements in working conditions (e.g., wage increases, benefit improvements, etc.) if they vote against the union.

▶ Accepting or reviewing union authorization cards or pro-union petitions, since employees' names are listed on these documents.

Wal-Mart term for the retail sales clerk). During an organizing drive by the United Food and Commercial Workers Union, Wal-Mart's managers stated that they believed strongly in their people, would take care of them, and were ready to listen and to discuss any issue.[10]

Employers' attempts to influence employees are scrutinized closely by officials of the organizing union and by the labour relations board. In one case, an employer interfered with the organizing process, and the union was automatically recognized by the labour board, even though only 5 percent of the employees had signed authorization cards.[11]

Union Tactics

Unions also have a duty to act in accordance with labour legislation. Unions are prohibited from interfering with the formation of an employer's organization. They cannot intimidate or coerce employees to become or remain members of a union. Nor can they force employers to dismiss, discipline, or discriminate against nonunion employees. They must provide fair representation for all employees in the **bargaining unit**, whether in collective bargaining or in grievance procedure cases. Unions cannot engage in activities such as strikes before the expiration of the union contract.

Any of the prohibited activities noted above for both employers and unions are considered **unfair labour practices (ULPs)**. Charges of ULPs are registered with the labour relations board, whose duty it is to enforce the Canada labour code. A summary of ULPs is presented in Highlights in HRM 14.4.

Bargaining unit
Group of two or more employees who share common employment interests and conditions and may reasonably be grouped together for purposes of collective bargaining

Unfair labour practices (ULPs)
Specific employer and union illegal practices that operate to deny employees their rights and benefits under federal and provincial labour law

Highlights in HRM 14.4

UNFAIR LABOUR PRACTICES

Unfair labour practices by employers include

▶ Helping to establish or administer a union.
▶ Altering the working conditions of the employees while a union is applying for certification without the union's consent.
▶ Using intimidation, coercion, threats, promises, or exercising undue influence while a union is being organized.
▶ Failing to recognize or bargain with the certified union.
▶ Hiring professional strike breakers.

Unfair labour practices by unions include

▶ Contributing financial or other support to an employee's organization.
▶ Not representing fairly the employees in the bargaining unit.
▶ Bargaining or negotiating a collective agreement with an employer while another union represents the employees in the bargaining unit.
▶ Calling or authorizing an unlawful strike, or threatening to do so.

Highlights in HRM 14.5 lists the key strategies identified by HR specialists to reduce workers' motivation to join unions. Since these strategies are under the direct control of management, they can be used to help discourage or prevent unionization.

How Employees Become Unionized

The procedures for union certification vary across Canadian jurisdictions. About two-thirds of unions that attempt to organize employees in Ontario, for example, are successful.[12] As mentioned earlier, the common practice is for unions to present documentation to the appropriate labour relations board for certification. The labour relations board must certify a union before it can act as a bargaining unit for a group of employees. In order to acquire certification, the union must demonstrate that it has obtained the minimum level of membership support required by the labour relations board. Usually, the union provides evidence by submitting signed authorization cards and proof that initiation dues or fees have been paid.[13] Recognition of a union can be obtained through voluntary recognition, or regular certification, or a prehearing vote.

Voluntary Recognition

All employers, except those in Quebec, may voluntarily recognize and accept a union. This rarely happens, except in the construction industry, where there is a great reliance on union hiring halls.

Highlights in HRM 14.5

STRATEGIES TO REMAIN UNION-FREE

▶ Offer competitive wages and benefits based on labour market comparisons and salary and benefit surveys.

▶ Train supervisors in progressive human relations skills, including employee motivation, job design, and employment law.

▶ Institute formal procedures to resolve employee complaints and grievances; these may include peer review committees, step review complaint systems, or open-door policies.

▶ Involve employees in work decisions affecting job performance or the quality or quantity of the product or service provided.

▶ Give attention to employee growth and development needs; recognize that the workforce is growing older, more female, more vocal, better educated, less patient, and more demanding.

▶ Draft HR policies that reflect legal safeguards and that are fair and equitable in employment conditions such as discipline, promotions, training, and layoffs.

The best work environment, and the least receptive to unionization, is one that treats the individual with respect, dignity, and fairness, while encouraging participation in decision making.

The rights and responsibilities of employers are clearly defined in the law, during an organization drive. Corporate retailing giant Wal-Mart has thus far been successful in keeping unions out.

DARREN PRICE

The Canada Industrial Relations
Board website is a valuable source
of information about unions:

www.cirb-ccri.gc.ca

Regular Certification

The regular certification process begins with the union submitting the required evidence of minimum membership to the labour relations board. Generally, if an applicant union can demonstrate that it has sufficient support in the proposed bargaining unit, labour boards may grant certification on that basis. (However, with changes in government, labour relations legislation is often reformed. Therefore, requirements for granting certification may change.) The labour relations board can order a representative vote if a sizable minority of workers have indicated either support or opposition to the unionization.

Prehearing Votes

If there is evidence of irregularities, such as unfair labour practices during the organizing drive, a prehearing vote may be taken. The purpose of this vote is to establish the level of support among the workers. Generally (depending on particular labour relations legislation) votes can be called if less than 50 percent of the employees indicate support for a union. Once a union is certified, employees become part of a collective and can no longer make individual arrangements for pay, hours of work, vacation, etc.

Contract Negotiation

Once a bargaining unit has been certified by the labour relations board, the employer and the union are legally obligated to bargain in good faith over the terms and conditions of a collective agreement. Usually the terms of a collective agreement apply for a minimum of one year and a maximum of three years. As the contract expiry date approaches, either party must notify the other of its intention to bargain for a renewal collective agreement or contract negotiation.

Decertification

All legislation allows for the decertification of unions under certain conditions. If the majority of employees indicate that they do not want to be represented by the union, or that they want to be represented by another union, or if the union has failed to bargain, an application for decertification can be made to the labour relations board. If a collective agreement has been reached with the employer, this application can be made only at specified times, such as a few months before the agreement expires. Either the employees or the employer can initiate the application for decertification if the union fails to bargain.

Impact of Unionization on Managers

The unionization of employees can affect managers in several ways. Perhaps most significantly, it can affect management's prerogatives in making decisions about employees. For example, if an employee believes that he has been treated unfairly, the structured grievance procedure is available for the resolution of the complaint. Unionization also restricts management's freedom to formulate HR policy unilaterally.

Challenges to Management Decisions

Typically, unions will try to achieve greater participation in management decisions that affect their members. These decisions often involve issues such as the subcontracting of work, productivity standards, and job content. Employers quite naturally seek to claim that these decisions are **management rights**—decisions they have an exclusive right to make. However, these rights are subject to challenge and erosion by the union. They can be challenged at the bargaining table, through the grievance procedure, and through strikes.

Management rights
Decisions regarding organizational operations over which management claims exclusive rights

Loss of Supervisory Flexibility

At a labour–management conference, a union official commented, "Contract terms covering wages, benefits, job security, and working hours are of major importance to our membership." However, for managers and supervisors, the union's impact is felt mainly at the operating level (the shop floor or office facility), where the terms of the collective agreement are implemented on a daily basis. For example, these terms can determine how employees can be directed and how they can be disciplined. When disciplining employees, supervisors must be certain they can demonstrate just cause (see Chapter 13), because their actions can be challenged by the union, and the supervisor called as a defendant during a grievance hearing. If the challenge is upheld, the supervisor's effectiveness in coping with later disciplinary problems may be impaired. Specific contract language can reduce the supervisor's ability to manage in such areas as scheduling, training, transfers, performance evaluation, and promotions, to name a few.

STRUCTURES, FUNCTIONS, AND LEADERSHIP OF LABOUR UNIONS

Craft unions
Unions that represent skilled craft workers

Industrial unions
Unions that represent all workers—skilled, semiskilled, unskilled— employed along industry lines

Employee associations
Labour organizations that represent various groups of professional and white-collar employees in labour–management relations

Unions that represent skilled craft workers, such as carpenters and masons, are called craft unions. **Craft unions** include the International Brotherhood of Electrical Workers, the United Brotherhood of Carpenters and Joiners of America, and the United Association of Journeymen and Apprentices of the Plumbing and Pipefitting Industry. Unions that represent unskilled and semiskilled workers employed along industry lines are known as **industrial unions**. The Canadian Union of Postal Workers is an industrial union, as are the United Steelworkers of America, the Office and Professional Employees International Union, and the Ontario Secondary School Teachers' Federation. Although the distinction between craft and industrial unions still exists, technological changes and competition among unions for members have done much to reduce it. Today, skilled and unskilled workers, white-collar and blue-collar workers, and professional groups are being represented by both types of unions.

Besides unions, there are also **employee associations**, which represent various groups of professional and white-collar employees. Examples of employee associations include the Federation of Quebec Nurses and the Alberta Teachers' Association. In competing with unions, these associations may function as unions and become just as aggressive as unions in representing their members.

Regardless of their type, labour organizations are diverse organizations. Each will have its own structure, objectives, and methods of governance. Most researchers when describing labour organizations divide them into three levels: (1) central labour congresses, (2) international and national unions, and (3) local unions belonging to a parent national or international union. Each level has its own reason for existence and its own operating policies and procedures.

Structures, Functions, and Leadership of the Canadian Labour Congress

The Canadian Labour Congress (CLC) is a central federation of unions. In 2003, the total membership of the CLC was 2.5 million Canadians and represented the majority of all unions in Canada.[14] Because of its size and resources, the CLC is considered the most influential labour federation in Canada. It is mainly a service organization representing over ninety international and national unions; these finance the CLC through dues based on membership size. Like the AFL-CIO, the CLC attempts to influence legislation and promote programs that are of interest to labour. It does this by lobbying, resolving jurisdictional disputes, maintaining ethical standards, providing education and training to its members, conducting research, and representing Canadian interests in the international labour movement.

International and National Unions

International unions tend to be affiliates of American unions, with headquarters in the United States. In Canada, there are 46 international unions (with membership of nearly 2 million workers) and 220 national unions (with membership of 2.7 million).[15] The large membership base offers a good deal of leverage to local unions engaged in strike action. The merger of three international unions—the United Steelworkers of America, the United Auto Workers, and the International Association of Machinists—into the largest industrial union in North America resulted in a strike fund of $1 billion.[16]

Both international and national unions are made up of local unions. The objectives of these "umbrella" unions are to help organize local unions, to provide strike support, and to assist local unions with negotiations, grievance procedures, and the like. These unions also represent their members' interests with internal and external constituents. By ensuring that all employers pay similar wages to their unionized workers, they also remove higher wages as a competitive disadvantage.[17]

In Canada, most of the decision-making authority in national unions is vested in the local unions or at the bargaining unit level. This is often referred to as bottom-up unionism. Many international unions, especially craft unions, are more likely to retain a greater degree of control over the affairs of local unions. This is often referred to as top-down unionism. The officers of both types of union typically include a president, a secretary-treasurer, and several vice-presidents, all officially elected. These officers make up the executive board, which is the top policymaking body. A typical national structure is depicted in Figure 14.3. Other positions at the national level include lawyer, economist, statistician, and public relations officer. An economics director

Figure 14.3 | The Organization of a Union Local

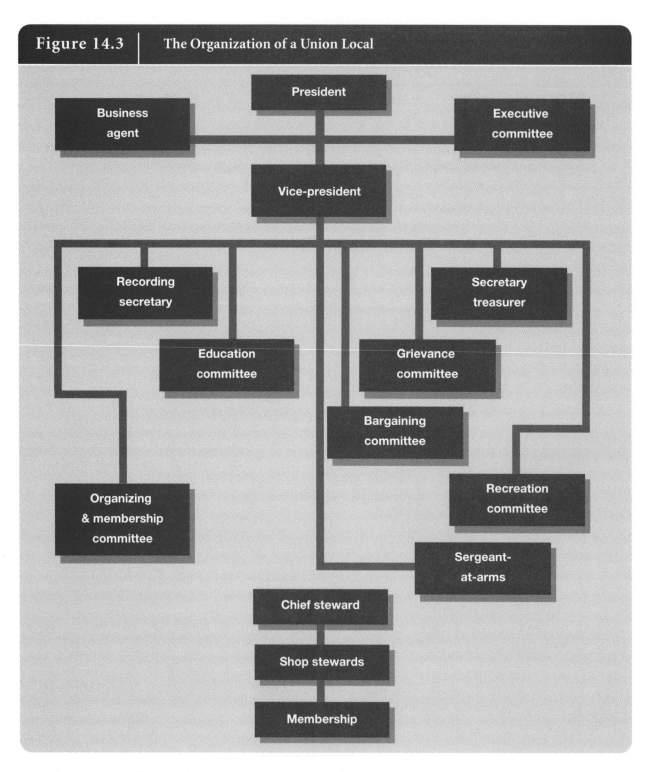

Source: F. Kehoe and M. Archer, *Canadian Industrial Relations*, 10th ed. (Oakville, ON: Century Labour Publications, 2002): 49. Reproduced by permission.

gathers, analyzes, and disseminates economic and other information of value in collective bargaining. Many national unions also have an education director, whose job is to provide training for local union officers and stewards.

International and national unions often have social and political objectives outside their traditional goal of representing member interests. This contentious issue is discussed in Ethics in HRM.

Local Unions

Employees of any organization can form their own union, with no affiliation to a national or international union. In situations like this, the local is the union. There are about 620 local unions in Canada, representing only 205 000 members.[18] However, most local unions are members of national or international unions or the Canadian Labour Congress, which make available to them financial resources and advice. There are an estimated 14 000 locals in Canada.

Unionized employees pay union dues that finance the operation of the local union. Local unions tend to make their own decisions, but turn to the national union for collective bargaining help, research, and assistance when handling certain types of grievances. Many national unions also provide training for local unions on the role and responsibilities of union officers. The officers of a local union are usually responsible for negotiating the local collective agreement, for ensuring the agreement is adhered to, and for investigating and processing member grievances. Most important, they

Ethics in HRM

INFLATION

Members of unions and associations pay dues to support union activities. Most of this money is used to fund traditional union activities such as labour and economic research, contract negotiation, and the handling of grievances. However, sometimes the union, especially at the international and national levels, dedicates some of these funds to causes such as opposing human rights violations in China or supporting gun control in Canada. For example, the CLC is actively involved with social justice groups such as the women's movement, anti-poverty activities, churches, peace activists, and environmentalists. CUPE lobbies for safe clean water, and its Water Watch campaign to fight the privatization of water is a national priority for this union.

Union members have challenged, under the Canadian Charter of Rights and Freedoms, their obligation to contribute part of their union dues to political causes with which they disagree. The Supreme Court ruled that (1) trade unions are not in violation of the Charter if they use union dues for purposes other than collective bargaining in the narrow sense, and (2) unionized workers who object to the use of their dues have to try to get the money back themselves.

Sources: Canadian Labour Congress, www.clc-ctc.ca; Canadian Union of Public Employees, www.cupe.ca/www/WaterWatch; P.E. Larson, "Fighting for Labour," *Canadian Business Review* 13, no. 4 (1986): 8–12; P. Poiter, "Court Dashes Labour's Hopes of More Rights," *The Globe and Mail*, June 25, 1991: A 5.

help prevent their members from being treated by their employers in ways that run counter to management-established HR policies.[19] They also keep members informed through meetings and newsletters.

Role of the Union (Shop) Steward

Union steward
Employee who as a non-paid union official represents the interests of members in their relations with management

The **union (shop) steward** represents the interests of union members in their relations with immediate supervisors and other members of management. Stewards are usually elected by the union members in their own department and serve without union pay. Since stewards are full-time employees of the organization, they often spend considerable time after working hours investigating and handling members' problems. When stewards represent members during grievance meetings on organizational time, their lost earnings are paid by the local union.

A union steward can be viewed as a "person in the middle," caught between conflicting interests and groups. It cannot be assumed that stewards will always champion union members and routinely oppose managerial objectives. Union stewards are often insightful people working for the betterment of employees and the organization. So supervisors and managers at all levels are strongly encouraged to develop a professional working relationship with stewards and all union officials. This relationship can have a major bearing on union–management cooperation and on the efficiency and morale of the workforce.[20]

Role of the Business Agent

Business agent
Normally a paid labour official responsible for negotiating and administering the collective agreement and working to resolve union members' problems

Negotiating and administering the collective agreement and working to resolve problems arising in connection with it are major responsibilities of the **business agent**. In performing these duties, business agents must be all things to all people in their unions. They are often required to assume the role of counsellor in helping union members with both personal and job-related problems. They are also expected to satisfactorily resolve grievances that cannot be settled by the union stewards. Administering the daily affairs of the local union is another significant part of the business agent's job.

Union Leadership Approaches and Philosophies

To evaluate the role of union leaders accurately, one must have some understanding of union politics. The leaders of many national unions have developed political machines that enable them to perpetuate themselves in office. For the leaders of local unions, tenure is less secure. In a local union the officers, by federal law, must run for re-election at least every third year. If they are to remain in office, they must be able to convince a majority of the members that they are serving them effectively.

Although it is true that union leaders occupy positions of power in their organizations, rank-and-file members can and often do exercise a very strong influence over these leaders, particularly with respect to the negotiation and administration of the collective agreement. It is important for managers to understand that union officials are elected to office and, like any political officials, must be responsive to their constituents' views. A

USING THE INTERNET

A description of a union steward's job can be found on the website of the Canadian Union of Public Employees:

www.cupe.ca/www/351/volunteers

union leader who ignores the demands of union members risks (1) being voted out of office, (2) having members vote the union out as their bargaining agent, (3) having members refuse to ratify the collective agreement, or (4) having members engage in wildcat strikes or work stoppages.

To be effective leaders, union officials must pay constant attention to the philosophy and general goals of the labour movement. Unions have historically been very politically active, backing such parties as the NDP. The goals of many labour organizations include increased pay and benefits, job security, and improved working conditions. However, union leaders also know that unions must address the broader social, economic, and legislative issues of concern to members.[21] The CAW continually lobbies for protective legislation favourable to the auto industry. The CLC has been an active promoter of women's issues and policies favouring job creation over deficit reduction. Finally, as part of Canada's adjustment to global competition, union leaders have been active in working with managers to make their respective industries more competitive.

LABOUR RELATIONS IN THE PUBLIC SECTOR

Collective bargaining among federal, provincial, and municipal government employees, and among employees in parapublic agencies (private agencies or branches of the government acting as extensions of government programs), has increased dramatically since the 1960s. More than 75 percent of all public employees are now unionized.[22] The three largest unions in Canada represent public sector employees. The Canadian Union of Public Employees (CUPE) is the largest union in Canada, with 521 600 members. The second-largest union, with 325 000 members, is the National Union of Public and General Employees (NUPGE). The largest union representing employees at the federal level is the Public Service Alliance of Canada (PSAC), with 150 000 members. PSAC comprises seventeen different unions representing various groups such as the Professional Institute of the Public Service of Canada (PIPS), the Economists, Sociologists and Statisticians Associations (ESSA), and the Air Traffic Controllers.[23] Growth in these unions is threatened by increased cost-cutting efforts of governments at all levels, resulting in employee reductions.

USING THE INTERNET

The Public Service Staff Relations Board oversees employer–employee relations in the Federal Public Service:

www.pssrb-crtfp.gc.ca

While public sector collective bargaining is quite similar to bargaining in the private sector, a number of differences are worth noting. Below, we explore these differences in three contexts: (1) legislation governing collective bargaining in the public sector, (2) the political nature of the labour–management relationship, and (3) public sector strikes.

Political Nature of the Labour–Management Relationship

Government employees are not able to negotiate with their employers on the same basis as their counterparts in private organizations. It is doubtful that they will ever be able to do so because of inherent differences between the public and private sectors.

One of the significant differences is that labour relations in the private sector has an economic foundation, whereas in government its foundation tends to be political. Since private employers must stay in business in order to sell their goods or services, their employees are not likely to make demands that could bankrupt them. A strike in the private sector is a test of the employer's economic staying power, and usually the employer's customers have alternative sources of supply. Governments, on the other hand, must stay in business because alternative services are usually not available.

Another difference between the public and private sectors relates to the source of management authority. In a private organization, authority flows downwards from the board of directors and, ultimately, from the shareholders. In contrast, authority in the public sector flows upward from the public at large to their elected representatives and to the appointed or elected managers. It follows that public employees can exert influence not only as union members but also as pressure groups and voting citizens.[24]

Strikes in the Public Sector

Strikes by government employees create a problem for lawmakers and for the general public. Because many of the services that government employees provide, such as policing and firefighting, are considered essential to the well-being of the public, public policy is opposed to strikes by these people. However, various provincial legislatures have granted public employees the right to strike. Where striking is permitted, the right is limited to specific groups of employees—those performing nonessential services—and the strike cannot endanger the public's health, safety, or welfare. Public sector unions contend, however, that denying them the same right to strike as employees in the private sector greatly reduces their power during collective bargaining.

Public employees who perform essential services do in fact strike. Teachers, sanitation employees, police, transit employees, firefighters, and postal employees have all engaged in strike action. To avoid potentially critical situations, various arbitration methods are used for resolving collective bargaining deadlocks in the public sector. One is **compulsory binding arbitration** for employees such as police officers, firefighters, and others in jobs where strikes cannot be tolerated; in this case, a neutral third party is appointed to resolve the deadlock. Another method is **final offer arbitration**, under which the arbitrator must select one or the other of the final offers submitted by the disputing parties. With this method, the arbitrator's award is more likely to go to the party whose final bargaining offer has moved the closest to a reasonable settlement. The government can also enact back-to-work legislation, an option being used with increasing frequency.

Compulsory binding arbitration
Binding method of resolving collective bargaining deadlocks by a neutral third party

Final offer arbitration
Method of resolving collective bargaining deadlocks whereby the arbitrator has no power to compromise but must select one or another of the final offers submitted by the two parties

The Bargaining Process

objective

Those unfamiliar with contract negotiations often view the process as an emotional conflict between labour and management, complete with marathon sessions, fist pounding, and smoke-filled rooms. In reality, negotiating a collective agreement involves long hours of extensive preparation combined with diplomatic manoeuvring and the development of bargaining strategies. Furthermore, negotiation is only one

Collective bargaining process

Process of negotiating a collective agreement, including the use of economic pressures by both parties

part of the **collective bargaining process** (see Figure 14.4). Collective bargaining sometimes may also include the use of economic pressures in the form of strikes and boycotts by the union. Lockouts, plant closures, and the use of replacement labour are pressures used by the employer. In addition, either or both parties may seek support for its position from the general public or from the courts as a means of pressuring the opposite side.

Bargaining in Good Faith

Once a union has been recognized as a representative for employees, an employer is obligated to negotiate in good faith with the union's representatives over conditions of employment. Good faith requires the employer's negotiators to meet with their union counterparts at a reasonable time and place to discuss these conditions. It requires also that the proposals submitted by each party be realistic. In discussing the other party's proposals, each side must offer reasonable counterproposals for those it is unwilling to accept.[25] Furthermore, an employer cannot over-ride the bargaining process by making an offer directly to the employees. Figure 14.5 offers several prevalent examples of bad-faith employer bargaining.

Preparing for Negotiations

Preparing for negotiations includes assembling data to support bargaining proposals, forming the bargaining team, and planning the strategy. This will permit collective bargaining to be conducted in an orderly, factual, and positive basis, with a greater

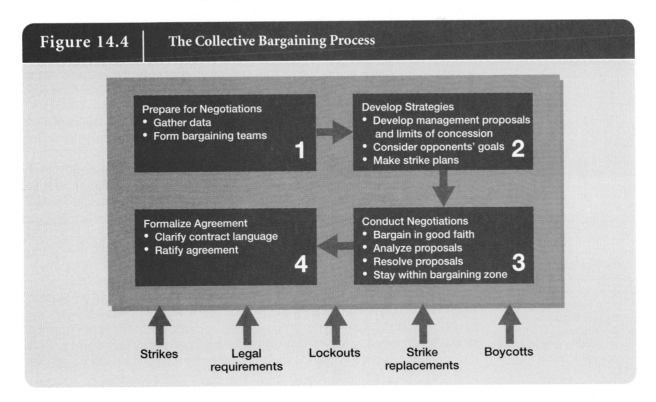

Figure 14.4 | **The Collective Bargaining Process**

Prepare for Negotiations
- Gather data
- Form bargaining teams

1

Develop Strategies
- Develop management proposals and limits of concession
- Consider opponents' goals
- Make strike plans

2

Conduct Negotiations
- Bargain in good faith
- Analyze proposals
- Resolve proposals
- Stay within bargaining zone

3

Formalize Agreement
- Clarify contract language
- Ratify agreement

4

Strikes   Legal requirements   Lockouts   Strike replacements   Boycotts

| Figure 14.5 | Examples of Bad-Faith Employer Bargaining |

▶ Using delaying tactics such as frequent postponements of bargaining sessions.

▶ Withdrawing concessions previously granted.

▶ Insisting that the union stop striking before resuming negotiations.

▶ Unilaterally changing bargaining topics.

▶ Negotiating with individual employees rather than with bargaining unit representatives.

▶ Engaging in mere surface bargaining rather than honest negotiations.

▶ Refusing to meet with duly appointed or elected union representatives.

likelihood of achieving the desired goals. Negotiators often develop a bargaining book that serves as a cross-reference file for determining which contract clauses would be affected by a demand. The bargaining book also contains a general history of the contract terms and their relative importance to management.[26] Assuming that the collective agreement is not the first one to be negotiated by the parties, preparation for negotiations ideally should start soon after the current agreement has been signed. This practice will allow negotiators to review and diagnose mistakes made during past negotiations, while the experience is still current in their minds.

Gathering Bargaining Data

Internal data relating to grievances, disciplinary actions, transfers and promotions, layoffs, overtime, past arbitration awards, and wage payments will help the employer formulate its bargaining position. The supervisors and managers who must live with and administer the collective agreement can be vital sources of ideas about changes to make in the next agreement. Their contact with union members and representatives provides them with a first-hand knowledge of the changes that union negotiators are likely to propose.

Data obtained from government sources such as Statistics Canada and HRDC bulletins and publications can help to support the employer's position during negotiations. These sources offer information on general economic conditions and cost-of-living trends, and on geographical wage rates for a wide range of occupations.

Bargaining Patterns

Pattern bargaining
Bargaining in which unions negotiate provisions covering wages and other benefits that are similar to those provided in other agreements existing in the industry or region

When negotiating contracts, union bargainers talk about "taking wages out of competition." This refers to negotiating similar contract provisions—especially relating to wages and benefits—with different companies in order to prevent one employer from having a favourable labour cost advantage over another. **Pattern bargaining** allows unions to show their members that the wages and benefits they are receiving are in line with those of employees doing like work; at the same time, it provides employers with assurances that their labour costs are comparable with those of their competitors.[27] For example, the Canadian Auto Workers negotiates similar contract provisions for workers at Ford, General Motors, and Chrysler. Pattern bargaining also minimizes political problems within unions.[28]

Developing Bargaining Strategies

Negotiators for the employer should develop a written plan covering their bargaining strategy. This plan should consider the proposals the union is likely to submit, based on its most recent agreements with other employers and the demands that remain unsatisfied from previous negotiations. This plan should also consider the goals the union is striving to achieve and the extent to which it may be willing to make concessions or to resort to strike action in order to achieve these goals.

At a minimum, the employer's bargaining strategy must include the following:

▶ Likely union proposals, and management responses to them.
▶ A list of management demands, limits of concessions, and anticipated union responses.
▶ Development of a database to support management's bargaining proposals and to counteract union demands.
▶ A contingency operating plan, should employees strike.

Certain elements of strategy are common to both the employer and the union. Generally, the initial demands presented by each side are greater than those it actually may hope to achieve. This is done in order to provide room for concessions. Moreover, each party will usually avoid giving up the maximum it is capable of conceding, in order to allow for further concessions that may be needed to break a bargaining deadlock.

Conducting the Negotiations

Among the factors that tend to make each bargaining situation unique are the economic climate under which negotiations take place, the experience and personalities of the negotiators, the goals they are seeking to achieve, and the strength of the relative positions. Some collective agreements can be negotiated informally in a few hours, especially if the contract is short and the terms are not too complex. Other agreements, such as those negotiated with large organizations such as the National Hockey League and Stelco, require months to negotiate.

Bargaining Teams
Normally, each side will have four to six representatives at the negotiating table. The chief negotiator for management will be the vice-president or manager for labour or industrial relations; the chief negotiator for the union will be the local union president or union business agent. Others making up management's team may include representatives from accounting or finance, operations, employment, legal, and training. The local union president is likely to be supported by the chief steward, various local union vice-presidents, and a representative from the national union. In some cases, the representative from the national union will be the chief negotiator for the local union.

Resolving the Proposals

For each bargaining issue to be resolved satisfactorily, the point at which agreement is reached must be within limits that the union and the employer are willing to accept.

In a frequently cited bargaining model, Ross Stagner and Hjalmar Rosen refer to the concept of a **bargaining zone**—the area within which the union and the employer are willing to concede when bargaining. In some bargaining situations, such as the one illustrated in Figure 14.6, the solution desired by one party may exceed the limits of the other party. Thus the solution is outside the bargaining zone. If that party refuses to modify its demands sufficiently to bring them within the bargaining zone, or if the opposing party refuses to extend its limit to accommodate the demands of the other party, a bargaining deadlock will result.[29] For example, when bargaining a wage increase for employees, if the union's bottom limit is a 4 percent increase and management's top limit is 6 percent, an acceptable range—the bargaining zone (4 to 6 percent)—is available to both parties. But if management's top limit is only 3 percent,

Bargaining zone
Area within which the union and the employer are willing to concede when bargaining

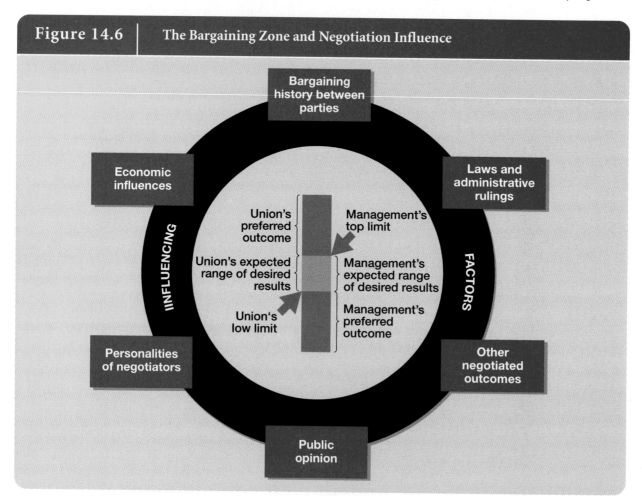

| Figure 14.6 | The Bargaining Zone and Negotiation Influence |

Source: Adapted from Ross Stagner and Hjalmar Rosen, *Psychology of Union-Management Relations* (Belmont, CA: Wadsworth Publishing, 1965): 96. Adapted with permission from BrooksCole Publishing Co.

a bargaining zone is not available to either side, and a deadlock is likely to occur. Figure 14.6 is based on Stagner and Rosen's original model and shows that as bargaining takes place, several important variables affect whether the negotiators will be able to reach agreement within the bargaining zone.

Interest-Based Bargaining

Sometimes, labour–management negotiations are characterized as adversarial. With adversarial bargaining, negotiators start with defined positions and through deferral, persuasion, trade, or power, the parties work toward resolving individual bargaining demands. In traditional bargaining, with its give-and-take philosophy, the results may or may not be to the complete satisfaction of one or both parties. In fact, when one side feels it has received "the short end of the stick," bitter feelings may persist for the life of the agreement. As noted by one labour negotiator, "Adversarial bargaining does little to establish a long-term positive relationship based on open communications and trust. By its nature, it leads to suspicion and compromise."[30] To overcome these negative feelings, labour and management practitioners may follow a nonadversarial approach.

Interest-based bargaining (IBB) is based on the identification and resolution of mutual interests rather than the resolve of specific bargaining demands.[31] IBB is "a problem-solving process conducted in a principled way that creates effective solutions while improving the bargaining relationship."[32] The focus of bargaining strategy is to discover mutual bargaining interests with the intent of formulating options and solutions for mutual gain.

Interest based bargaining is novel in both its philosophy and process. Also distinct are the bargaining tools used to expedite a successful nonadversarial negotiating experience. Rather than using proposals and counterproposals to reach agreement (as with adversarial negotiations), participants use brainstorming, consensus decision making, active listening, process checking, and matrix building to settle issues. An underlying goal of interest-based bargaining is to foster a relationship for the future based on trust, understanding, and mutual respect, a process described in Reality Check. The Business Case outlines how IBB can save money.

Management and Union Power in Collective Bargaining

During negotiations, if neither party retreats from its original position to permit an agreement to be reached, negotiations become deadlocked. At this point, negotiations become highly adversarial, as each side will employ its **bargaining power** to achieve its desired ends. The party's bargaining power consists of its economic, political, and social influence to achieve its demands at the expense of the other side.

Union Bargaining Power

The bargaining power of the union may be exercised by striking or picketing, or boycotting the employer's products. A strike is the refusal of a group of employees to perform their jobs. Unions usually will seek strike authorization from their members to use as a bargaining ploy to gain concessions that will make a strike unnecessary. A

Interest-based bargaining (IBB)
Problem-solving bargaining based on a win–win philosophy and the development of a positive long-term relationship

objective

Bargaining power
The power of labour and management to achieve their goals through economic, social, or political influence

Reality Check

BUILDING TRUST THROUGH IBB

The *Ottawa Citizen*, a newspaper with a circulation of 145 000 newspapers, is the largest daily newspaper in Ottawa, and the eighth largest in Canada. Approximately 65 percent of its 595 full-time employees are unionized and belong to one of three unions: the Communication Energy & Paperworkers (CEP), the Graphic Communications Union (GCU), and the Newspaper Guild. These bargaining units are also called chapels (and the shop steward is called chapel chairman) in recognition of the time when it was illegal to hold union meetings so groups of employees wishing to meet collectively would say they were going to a "chapel [or church] meeting."

The *Ottawa Citizen* won a Vision award, a recognition by the Ottawa chapter of the Human Resources Professionals Association of Ontario for outstanding HR practices for the innovative design and implementation of an HR program based on its successful implementation of IBB. Debbie Bennett, vice-president of Human Resources and Finance for the newspaper, describes the process: "In my opinion, IBB works when you have a good relationship that you want to improve upon, or when things are so bad that something has to change. I approached the [Newspaper] Guild, the largest union, with whom we already had a good relationship, about IBB. At the time, it had about 325 members. I started by buying them some IBB books (*Getting to Yes* and *Getting Together*) to determine if there was interest. There was. Union and management advertised for, jointly selected, and paid for a facilitator, who took us through a three-day training and relationship-building session. The entire bargaining team from both parties took part in the workshop to make sure we all understood the differences between IBB and traditional bargaining.

"For example, one difference was the ways in which we communicated, both internally to build trust and externally to our stakeholders. In IBB, we brainstormed, with the rule that no repercussions would follow if an idea was presented that everyone liked but subsequently was not found workable. In traditional bargaining, if an idea is placed on the table and then removed, it could be seen as reneging or bargaining in bad faith. The agreement to brainstorm led to very little caucus time, and a much faster bargaining pace, because the respective teams did not have to ask for a break to discuss new ideas in the hallway before presenting it to the other party.

"The tone of communications was also different. The objective at the table is to discuss issues in an open and honest manner. This objective would be hard to achieve if some of the more direct comments were quoted in public communiqués. Therefore, the parties agreed that communications to both management and union members were for the purpose of keeping everyone informed, not for the purpose of embarrassing the other party or belittling their position. The tone of communications was respectful.

"We started bargaining, with the facilitator at table, to ensure that we practised what we learned. After the third day, we no longer needed the facilitator. Usually our bargaining sessions took four to five months; this time, we finished in four to five days. Usually the changes to the collective agreement were mainly monetary; this time there were a lot of language changes. For example, like most organizations, when an employee is disciplined, a disciplinary letter is placed on file. The union wanted a sunset clause requiring automatic removal of the discipline letter after a period of time. The union's view was that a transgression should not be held against an employee forever. However, management felt a record of a serious infraction, like hitting another employee, should never be removed from the file nor should records of a repetitive problem. Through IBB, the teams came up with a clause, which said that a disciplinary letter will not automatically be removed, but will be taken to the VP who will decide on its removal based on clear criteria, such as the seriousness of the act and the repetitiveness of the behaviour.

"Overall, the effect of IBB on the labour relations climate, although always good, was to improve it."

strike vote by the members does not mean they actually want or expect to go out on strike. Rather, it is intended as a vote of confidence to strengthen the position of their leaders at the bargaining table.

In the past, strikes have been crippling to many industries, but the number of strikes in Canada continues a twenty-year decline.[33] Strikes can be disruptive and challenging to the organizations struck. Of critical importance is whether the employer will be able to continue operating using supervisory and nonstriking personnel and replacement workers. In organizations with high levels of technology and automation, and consequently fewer employees, continuing service with supervisors and managers is more likely. For example, among the highly automated telephone companies, supervisors can maintain most services during a strike. According to one authority, "Because of technological change, striking in many industries no longer has the effect of curtailing the employer's operations significantly."[34] The greater the ability of the employer to continue operating, the smaller the union's chances of achieving its demands through a strike.

When a union goes on strike, it will picket the employer by placing persons at the entrances to the business to publicize the dispute and to discourage people from entering the premises. Because unionized workers often refuse to cross another union's picket line, the pickets may prevent delivery trucks and railcars from entering the business.

Another economic weapon of unions is the boycott, which is a refusal to patronize the employer. For, example, production employees on strike against a hand-tool manufacturer might picket a retail store that sells the tools made by the struck employer. Unions will also use handbills, radio announcements, and notices in newspapers to discourage purchase of the employer's product or service.

Management Bargaining Power

When negotiations become deadlocked, the employer's power rests largely on being able to continue operations in the face of a strike or to shut down operations entirely. The employer can transfer these operations to other locations, or it can subcontract them to other employers through outsourcing. General Motors outsources to foreign manufacturers many of the parts it uses to build its North American cars. In exercising their economic freedom, however, employers must be careful that their actions are not interpreted by provincial labour relations boards to be an attempt to avoid bargaining with the union.

In some jurisdictions, employers face restrictions to their right to hire replacement workers. Quebec and British Columbia have "anti-scab" laws that forbid the use of

The Business Case

THE BENEFITS OF IBB

Eleanor Gallant, manager of HR for the City of Charlottetown, Prince Edward Island, worked closely with PANS (Police Association of Nova Scotia—PEI local 301) and CUPE to establish a process of interest-based bargaining. The goal was not to repeat the past when negotiations dragged on for four years, ending in strikes and arbitration (for those without the right to strike). The process began before the contract opened again in 2002. In preparation, to encourage the interest of the parties, the director of HR for the city of Saint John, New Brunswick, was invited to speak about the success of IBB in that city. Some basic rules for the process of negotiating the collective agreement were put into place, including no lawyers would be present, there would be no discussion about the bargaining mandate with outsiders, and union and management officials would sit next to each other at the table, not on opposing sides.

The issue of time off in lieu of overtime serves as an example of how IBB worked in the City of Charlottetown. When the police officers were required to work overtime, they wanted to be compensated with time off instead of overtime pay. Management had refused this request due to bookkeeping complexities. However, the IBB process demonstrated the value of this arrangement to both parties. The two parties reached an agreement to hire part-time officers when extra hours were needed. The police officers were less stressed with less overtime, and the city saved money, because part-time police officers were less costly than full-time police officers being paid overtime rates.

Here are the savings produced by IBB for negotiations with PANS:

	Traditional bargaining	IBB
Time to reach agreement	4 years	8 days
Number of grievances	0	0
Amount that would have been spent on arbitration	$30 000	0

Here are the savings produced by IBB for negotiations with CUPE:

	Traditional bargaining	IBB
Time to reach agreement	4 years	8 days
Number of grievances	275	1
Amount that would have been spent on arbitration	$180 000	0

replacement workers during a strike. In the 1980s the use of "scabs" at Canada Post and Gainers Meats created a great deal of anger among picketing workers. Employers have the right to dismiss workers who engage in sabotage or violence during a strike.

Once a strike has been settled, the workers are entitled to return to their jobs, though not necessarily their previous positions. The right to return to work is often

Picketing is used by unions to publicize their disputes and discourage people from entering the premises.

DICK HEMINGWAY

an issue to be negotiated. Although laws vary, employees are often required to submit in writing their intention to return to their jobs once a strike is finalized.

Resolving Bargaining Deadlocks

Unions and employers in all types of industries—sports, transportation, entertainment, manufacturing, communication, and health care—have used conciliators, mediators, or arbitrators to help resolve their bargaining deadlocks. As discussed in Chapter 13, mediation is a process that relies on the communication and persuasive skills of a mediator to help the parties resolve their differences. In many jurisdictions, conciliation is compulsory before a legal strike or lockout. The conciliator, appointed by the provincial ministry of labour, attempts to reach a workable agreement.

Mediation is similar to conciliation, with two main differences: it is voluntary (the two parties contract a neutral third party to help them), and the mediator assumes a more active role in the negotiations. A mediator serves mainly as a fact finder and to open up channels of communication between the parties. Typically, the mediator meets with one party and then the other for the purpose of suggesting compromises or recommending concessions. Mediators have no authority to force either side toward an agreement. They must use their communication skills and the power of persuasion to help the parties resolve their differences in such a way that both save face.[35]

Arbitration is the only form of third-party resolution that results in binding recommendations. An arbitrator assumes the role of decision maker and determines what the settlement between the two parties should look like. In other words, the arbitrator writes a final contract that the two parties must accept. Arbitration is not often used to settle private sector bargaining disputes.

Interest arbitration is often used to resolve deadlocks in the essential-service sectors of the public service. As noted earlier, strikes are prohibited in these sectors. Because one or both parties are generally reluctant to give a third party the power to make the settlement for them, a mediator typically is used to break the deadlock and to help the parties reach agreement. Once an agreement is concluded, an arbitrator may be called on to resolve disputes over how the agreement is being administered. This is called rights arbitration or grievance arbitration.

THE COLLECTIVE AGREEMENT

USING THE INTERNET

For trends in collective bargaining go to the website of the Canadian Workplace Research Network:

www.cwrn-rcrmt.org

Fortunately, the vast majority of labour–management negotiations are settled peacefully. When negotiations are concluded, the collective agreement becomes a formal binding document listing the terms, conditions, and rules under which employees and managers agree to operate. Highlights in HRM 14.6 shows some of the major articles in a collective agreement and provides examples of some new and progressive contract classes.

Two important items in any collective agreement pertain to the issue of management rights and to the forms of security afforded the union.

The Issue of Management Rights

Residual rights
Concept that management's authority is supreme in all matters except those it has expressly conceded to the union in the collective agreement

Defined rights
Concept that management's authority should be expressly defined and clarified in the collective agreement

In the collective agreement, management rights may be treated as residual rights or as defined rights. The **residual rights** concept holds that "management's authority is supreme in all matters except those that it has expressly conceded in the collective agreement or in those areas where its authority is restricted by law."

Residual rights typically include the right of management to determine the product it will produce and/or to select production equipment and procedures.

The concept of **defined rights**, on the other hand, is intended to reinforce and clarify which rights are exclusively those of management. A defined right might include the right of management to take disciplinary action against problem employees.

Forms of Union Security

When a labour organization is certified by a labour relations board as the exclusive bargaining representative for all employees in a bargaining unit, by law it must represent all employees in the unit, nonunion and union members alike. In exchange for this, union officials will seek to negotiate some form of compulsory membership as a condition of employment. Union officials argue that compulsory membership precludes the possibility that some employees will receive the benefits of unionization without paying their share of the costs. These employees are generally referred to as free riders. A standard union security provision is dues checkoff, which makes the employer responsible for withholding union dues from the paycheques of union members who agree to such a deduction.

Other common forms of union security found in collective agreements include the following:

Highlights in HRM 14.6

ITEMS IN A COLLECTIVE AGREEMENT

Typical clauses will cover

- Wages
- Vacations
- Holidays
- Work schedules
- Management rights
- Union security
- Transfers
- Discipline

- Grievance procedures
- No strike/no lockout clause
- Overtime
- Safety procedures
- Severance pay
- Seniority
- Pensions and benefits
- Outsourcing

Progressive clauses will cover

- Employee access to records
- Limitations on use of performance evaluation
- Elder care leave, child care, work–family balance provisions
- Flexible medical spending accounts
- Protection against hazards of technology equipment
- Limitations against electronic monitoring
- Bilingual stipends
- Domestic partnership benefits

1. The closed shop—employers will hire only union members.
2. The union shop—any employee not a union member upon employment must join the union within thirty days or be terminated.
3. The agency shop—union membership is voluntary; however, all bargaining unit members must pay union dues and fees.
4. The maintenance-of-membership shop—employees who voluntarily join a union must maintain membership for the life of the agreement; however, membership withdrawal is possible during a designated escape period.
5. The open shop—employees can join the union or not, and nonmembers do not pay union dues.
6. The modified union shop—new workers must join the union, and current union members must remain in the union; however, established employees who are nonunion are entitled to remain so.

Few issues in collective bargaining are more controversial than the negotiation of these agreements. Closed shop clauses are rare. They are also perhaps the most adversarial, because they require employers to recruit employees from a union hiring hall.

Working in conjunction with the union shop clause are the various seniority provisions of the collective agreement. Unions prefer that many personnel decisions (promotions, job transfers, shift assignments, vacations) be based on seniority. This criterion limits the discretion of managers to make such decisions on the basis of merit.

ADMINISTRATION OF THE COLLECTIVE AGREEMENT

Negotiation of the collective agreement, as mentioned earlier, is usually the most publicized and critical aspect of labour relations. Strike deadlines, press conferences, and employee picketing help create this image. Nevertheless, as managers in unionized organizations know, the bulk of labour relations activity comes from the day-to-day administration of the agreement. In addition, once the agreement is signed each side will naturally interpret ambiguous clauses to its own advantage. These differences are traditionally resolved through the grievance procedure.

Grievance Procedures

Grievance procedure
Formal procedure that provides for the union to represent members and nonmembers in processing a grievance

The **grievance procedure** typically provides for the union to represent the interests of its members (and nonmembers as well) in processing a grievance. It is considered by some authorities to be the heart of the bargaining agreement—the safety valve that gives flexibility to the entire system of collective bargaining.[36] When negotiating a grievance procedure, one important concern for both sides is how effectively the system will serve the needs of employees and management. A well-written grievance procedure allows grievances to be processed expeditiously and with as little red tape as possible. Furthermore, it should server to foster cooperation, not conflict, between the employer and the union.

The operation of a grievance procedure is unique to each individual collective bargaining relationship, but is required under Canadian labour relations codes. For example, grievance procedures usually specify how the grievance is to be initiated, the number and timing of steps in the procedure, and the identity of representatives from each side who are to be involved in the hearings at each step (see Figure 14.7). The purpose of this multi-step process is to allow higher levels of union and management representatives to look at the issue from different perspectives. When a grievance cannot be resolved at one of the specified steps, most agreements provide for the grievance to be submitted to a third party—usually an arbitrator—whose decision is final and binding. It is not the function of an arbitrator to help the two parties reach a compromise solution. Rather, it is the arbitrator's job to mandate how the grievance will be resolved.

The Grievance Procedure in Action

In order for an employee's grievance to be considered formally, it must be expressed orally and/or in writing—ideally to the employee's immediate supervisor. Since grievances are often the result of an oversight or a misunderstanding, many of them can be resolved at this point. Whether the grievance will be resolved at the initial step will depend on the supervisor's ability and willingness to discuss the problem with the

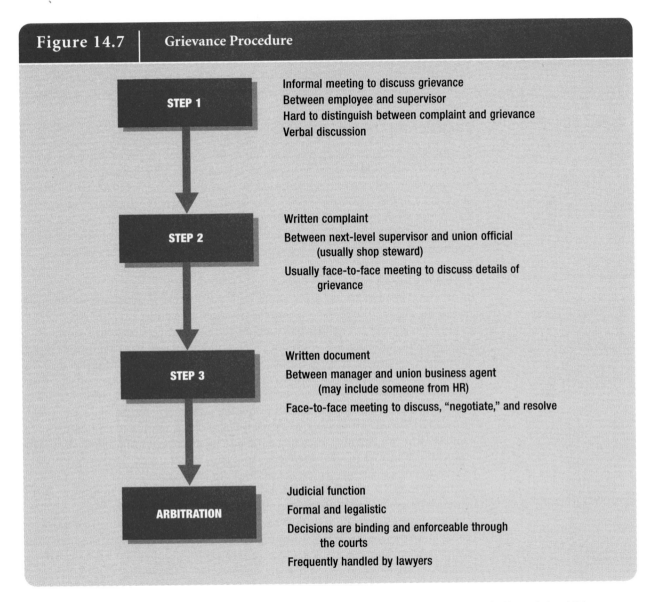

Figure 14.7 | Grievance Procedure

STEP 1
- Informal meeting to discuss grievance
- Between employee and supervisor
- Hard to distinguish between complaint and grievance
- Verbal discussion

STEP 2
- Written complaint
- Between next-level supervisor and union official (usually shop steward)
- Usually face-to-face meeting to discuss details of grievance

STEP 3
- Written document
- Between manager and union business agent (may include someone from HR)
- Face-to-face meeting to discuss, "negotiate," and resolve

ARBITRATION
- Judicial function
- Formal and legalistic
- Decisions are binding and enforceable through the courts
- Frequently handled by lawyers

Source: From *Essentials of Managing Human Resources*, 2nd edition by Stewart/Belcourt ©2003. Reprinted with permission of Nelson, a division of Thomson Learning: www.thomsonrights.com. Fax 800-730-2215.

employee and the steward. HR professionals acknowledge, and research studies demonstrate, that grievance handling is more successful when supervisors are trained in resolving grievances. This training should include familiarization with the terms of collective agreement and the development of problem solving skills. A grievance should not be viewed as something to be won or lost. Rather, both sides must view the situation as an attempt to solve a human relations problem.

In some situations, a satisfactory solution may not be possible at the first step because there are legitimate differences of opinion between the employee and the supervisor, or because the supervisor does not have the authority to take the action required to satisfy the grievant. Personality conflicts, prejudices, stubbornness, too much emotion, and other factors can also prevent a satisfactory solution at this step.

Rights Arbitration

The function of rights (or grievance) arbitration is to provide the solution to a grievance that a union and an employer have been unable to resolve by themselves. As mentioned earlier, arbitration is performed by a neutral third party (an arbitrator or impartial umpire). This third party's decision dictates how the grievance is to be settled. Both parties are required to comply with the decision. Even when one of the parties believes the arbitrator's award is unfair, unwise, or inconsistent with the collective agreement, that party may have no alternative but to comply with the decision.

The Decision to Arbitrate

In deciding whether to use arbitration, each party must weigh the costs involved against the importance of the case and the prospects of gaining a favourable award. It would seem logical that neither party would allow a weak case to go to arbitration if there were little possibility of gaining a favourable award. For example, it is not unusual for a union to take a weak case to arbitration in order to demonstrate to the members that the union is willing to exhaust every remedy in looking out for their interests. Also, union officers are not likely to refuse to take to arbitration the grievances of members who are popular or politically powerful in the union, even though their cases are weak. Moreover, unions have a legal obligation to provide assistance to members who are pursuing grievances. Because members can bring suit against their unions for failing to process their grievances adequately, many union officers are reluctant to refuse taking even weak grievances to arbitration.

Management, on the other hand, may allow a weak case to go to arbitration to demonstrate to the union officers that management "cannot be pushed around." Also, middle managers may be reluctant to risk the displeasure of senior managers by stating that a certain HR policy is unworkable or unsound. Stubbornness and mutual antagonism have forced many grievances into arbitration because neither party is willing to make concessions, even when it knows it is in the wrong.

The Arbitration Process

In our experience, employees unfamiliar with arbitration find the process confusing and stressful. Arbitration hearings have the appearance of a court hearing but without many of the formalities of a court proceeding. The process begins with the swearing-in of witnesses and the introduction of a formal statement known as a **submission to arbitrate**. Such as statement might read: "Was the three-day suspension of Alex Hayden for just cause? If not, what is the appropriate remedy?" The parties will then make opening statements, followed by a presentation of facts and evidence, and the oral presentations of witnesses. The hearing will conclude with each side making summary statements that are arguments in support of its position.

Submission to arbitrate
Statement that describes the issues to be resolved through arbitration

In arbitrating a dispute, it is the responsibility of the arbitrator to ensure that each side receives a fair hearing during which it may present all the facts it considers pertinent. The primary purpose of the hearing is to assist the arbitrator in obtaining the facts necessary to resolve the problem, which is approached as a human relations problem rather than a legal one. The arbitrator has the right to question witnesses and to request additional facts from either party. After conducting the hearing, the arbitrator customarily has thirty days in which to consider the evidence and render an award. However, extensions beyond this period are not uncommon. In the majority of cases, the costs of arbitration are shared equally by the parties.

Arbitration Award

Arbitration award

Final and binding award issued by an arbitrator in a labour–management dispute

The **arbitration award** should include not only the arbitrator's decision but also the reasons for it. The reasoning behind a decision can help to provide guidance for the interpretation of the collective agreement and the resolution of future disputes arising from its administration. The foundation for an arbitrator's decision is the collective agreement and the rights it establishes for each party.

In many grievances, such as those involving employee performance or behaviour on the job, the arbitrator must determine whether the evidence supports the employer's action against the grievant. The evidence must also show that the employee was accorded the right of due process (i.e., the employee's right to be informed of unsatisfactory performance and to respond to accusations of it). Under most collective agreements the employer must have just cause (i.e., a good reason) for the actions it takes, and those actions must be supported by the evidence presented.

Because of the importance of arbitration to resolving grievances, the process by which arbitrators make decisions and the factors that influence those decisions are of continuing interest to managers. Typically, arbitrators consider four factors when deciding cases:

1. The wording of the collective agreement.
2. The submission agreement as presented to the arbitrator.
3. Testimony and evidence offered during the hearing about how the collective agreement provisions have been interpreted.
4. Arbitration criteria or standards (i.e., similar to standards of common law) against which cases are judged.

When deciding the case of an employee discharged for absenteeism, for example, the arbitrator would consider these factors separately and/or jointly. Arbitrators are essentially constrained to decide cases on the basis of the wording of the collective agreement and the facts, testimony, and evidence presented at the hearing.

Arbitration is not an exact science; in fact, the decisions of arbitrators can be rather subjective. Arbitrators can and do interpret contract language differently (e.g., What does "just cause dismissal" actually mean?); they assign varying degrees of importance to testimony and evidence; they judge the truthfulness of witnesses differently; and they give arbitration standards greater or lesser weight as they apply to facts of the case. These things all inject subjectivity into the decision-making process.

SUMMARY

Labour relations legislation in Canada recognizes the right of employees to form and join unions, and prohibits both unions and employers from engaging in unfair labour practices. Provincial labour relations laws are administered and enforced by labour relations boards.

Studies show that workers unionize for different economic, psychological, and social reasons. While some employees join unions because they are required to do so, most belong to unions in the belief that unions help them improve their wages, benefits, and working conditions. Employee unionization is largely caused by dissatisfaction with managerial practices and procedures.

A formal organizing campaign is used to solicit employee support for the union. Once employees demonstrate their desire to unionize, the union will file an application with the labour relations board for approval of the union as the certified bargaining agent. If the labour relations board feels that there were irregularities in the application process, it has the power to call for a vote.

Negotiating a collective agreement is a detailed process. Each side will prepare a list of proposals it wishes to achieve while additionally trying to anticipate those proposals desired by the other side. Bargaining teams must be selected and all proposals must be analyzed to determine their impact on and cost to the organization. Both employer and union negotiators will be sensitive to current bargaining patterns within the industry, general cost-of-living trends, and geographical wage differences. Traditionally, collective bargaining between unions and management has been adversarial. Currently, there is an increased interest in non-adversarial negotiations—negotiations based on mutual gains and a heightened respect between the parties. Interest-based bargaining is one form of non-adversarial negotiation.

The collective bargaining process includes not only the actual negotiations but also the power tactics used to support negotiation demands. When negotiations become deadlocked, bargaining becomes a power struggle to force either side to make the concessions needed to break the deadlock. The union's power in collective bargaining comes from its ability to picket, strike, or boycott the employer. The employer's power during negotiations comes from its ability to lock out employees or to operate during a strike by using managerial or replacement personnel.

When differences arise between unions and management, they will normally be resolved through the grievance procedure. The typical grievance procedure will consist of several steps. The final step may be arbitration. Arbitrators will render a final and binding decision to problems not resolved at lower steps. Based on submissions by both parties, the arbitrator must resolve the issue based on four factors: the contents of the collective agreement, the submission agreement, testimony and evidence heard at the hearing, and various arbitration standards developed over time.

KEY TERMS

arbitration award 617
authorization card 591
bargaining power 607
bargaining unit 592
bargaining zone 606
business agent 600
collective bargaining process 603
compulsory binding arbitration 602

craft unions 596
defined rights 612
employee associations 596
final offer arbitration 602
grievance procedure 614
industrial unions 596
interest-based bargaining (IBB) 607
labour relations process 586

management rights 596
pattern bargaining 604
residual rights 612
submission to arbitrate 616
unfair labour practices (ULPs) 592
union shop 587
union steward 600

DISCUSSION QUESTIONS

 1. There has been a substantial increase (some estimate 40 percent) in the number of individuals who are self-employed. Some see this as a positive sign (i.e., of an increase in entrepreneurial activity); others see it as a response to the lack of permanent employment opportunities. The labour laws in each province effectively ignore independent workers. For many of them, wages (i.e., contract rates) are low, working conditions are difficult, and income security does not exist. Prepare to debate solutions to this issue, taking one of two sides: "Governments should change labour laws to recognize and protect self-employed workers," or, "Unions should organize these independent contractors and fight for better treatment."

 2. *Fast Food High* is a film produced by CTV and inspired by the real story about how a group of teenage workers tried to organize a union at McDonalds in Orangeville, Ontario. Watch the film, and discuss in groups the reasons why these workers want to form a union, and the effectiveness of their efforts.

 3. Contrast the arguments concerning union membership that are likely to be presented by a union with those likely to be presented by an employer.

 4. Which unfair labour practices apply to (1) unions and (2) employers?

 5. A group of students wants a Burger King fast-food franchise on their university campus. University administrators want a health-food restaurant. Resources allow for only one food outlet. Divide the class into bargaining teams, with one team representing the students, and the other team representing the university administrators. (If there is another issue on your campus use the real and current issue instead.) After the groups have started bargaining, consult the Career Counsel website to assess the negotiating styles employed by each team.

 6. The negotiations between Data Services International and its union have become deadlocked. What form of bargaining power does each side possess to enforce its bargaining demands? What are the advantages and disadvantages of each form of bargaining power for both the union and the employer?

 7. Indira Singh has decided to file a grievance with her union steward. The grievance alleges that she was by-passed by a junior employee for a promotion to a senior technician.

   a. Explain the steps her grievance will follow in a formal union-management grievance procedure.

   b. Should her grievance go to arbitration, explain the process of an arbitration hearing and identify the criteria used by the arbitrator to resolve her claim.

Developing Managerial Skills

UNDERSTANDING AN ORGANIZING DRIVE

Union organizing campaigns are hectic and emotional periods for union officials, employees and managers. Emotions between employees can become strained and in extreme situations, friendships are broken. For managers, the beginning of a union-organizing drive is bewildering and sometimes threatening. How to approach the drive and handle employee concerns is critical to the success of both sides. This exercise will help you learn about a typical campaign.

Directions
During a union organizing drive, labour and management will develop a plan to present their positions to employees. A goal of each side will be to collect information on the other that can be used to build a case for or against the union. Additionally, each side will seek to avoid committing unfair labour practices. Working in teams of union and management representatives, answer the following questions and be prepared to present your findings during a discussion period.

Questions
1. What methods might the union use to contact employees?
2. What information might the union collect on management in order to obtain employee support?
3. What information might management want to collect on the union?
4. What methods might unions and management use to tell their story to employees? What illegal actions will the union and management want to guard against?

Case Study 1

Wal-Mart Stores in Canada

In 2003, Wal-Mart was operating more than 4650 stores with 1.3 million employees around the world. In the early 1990s Wal-Mart Stores Inc. expanded into Canada, with the purchase of 122 stores from the failing Woolco chain. Wal-Mart had refused to purchase nine Woolco stores, which were unionized.

Wal-Mart tries to distinguish itself from other retailers by its culture. For example, it calls its workers "associates," not employees. Every day at 8:45 a.m., a compulsory meeting is held at each store during which company managers share financial information and performance targets and respond to questions. The meeting ends with the Wal-Mart cheer. The company operates an open-door policy, whereby any employee can talk to any member of management about issues, and receive answers, without being threatened with reprisal. The sundown rule ensures that management responds to the questions before sundown the same day.

The first Wal-Mart store ever to be unionized was in Windsor, Ontario, where the United Steelworkers (Retail and Wholesale Division) was certified by the Ontario Labour Relations Board. On April 14, 1997, the United Steelworkers began its organizing drive. On April 26, the store manager became aware that associates were being approached to sign unionization cards. The district manager was told of the organizing drive and the next morning attended the morning meeting. The district manager asked the associates why they would want to join a union and spent the day circulating through the store to discuss their problems or concerns. By April 27, eighty-four associates had signed cards. On April 29, an associate asked to speak at the morning meeting, and there expressed her opposition to the union, ending with the statement, "A union will only cause discontentment in our store, and I assure you as I am standing here, Wal-Mart will not put up with it." (Management did not ask, nor did the associate reveal, why she wanted to speak.) An inside organizer was prevented from responding because it was 9 a.m. and customers were waiting to enter the store.

Between May 4 and May 9, Wal-Mart managers—including managers from outside the store—responded to questions placed in a question-and-answer box, and to those raised while they wandered about the store. Most of the questions focused on compensation and hours of work. However, one associate testified that one manager said that things would change if the employees were unionized—for example, the profit-sharing plan would be revoked. During one meeting, the managers were asked if the store would close; they replied, "It would be inappropriate for your company to comment on what it will or will not do if the store is unionized." On May 9, the union lost the vote, with 151 employees voting against it, and 43 voting for it.

The Ontario Labour Relations Board nonetheless certified the union, because the employer violated the Labour Relations Act by not disassociating itself from the remarks made by the associate at the meeting; by not allowing the inside organizer to respond; by subtly threatening job security; and by allowing outside managers in the store from May 4 to 9. The OLRB stated that the union had eighty-four cards signed before the managers' visits, and a week later, this support had dropped. A second vote would not change the outcome, because the threat to job security could not be erased from employees' minds. The legislation that allows the OLRB to overturn a certification board has now been changed.

Despite numerous organizing drives, Wal-Mart has successfully prevented unionization, and most of their 213 Canadian stores remain union-free. The United Food and Commercial Workers Union (UFCW) charged Wal-Mart with unfair labour practices in thwarting a union organizing drive in British Columbia by discrediting the key organizer and by advising employees that if he turned up at their homes, they could call the police. The B.C. Labour Board said, "Wal-Mart has an anti-union history...and simply cannot resist the temptation to get involved in certification campaigns. While Wal-Mart has tended not to repeat its mistakes, there is no shortage of new ones that it finds ways to make."

Sources: Adapted from V. Galt, "Wal-Mart Must Give Union Access," *The Globe and Mail*, May 13, 2003: B5; J. Hobel, "Allegation of Union Vote Rigging Investigated at Wal-Mart," *Canadian HR Reporter*, September 20, 1999: 1, 19; "Employer Interference: The Wal-Mart Case," *Worklife Report* 11, no. 2: 1–4.

QUESTIONS

1. What were the rights of Wal-Mart, the employer, during these two organizing drives?
2. The certification of the first Wal-Mart was hailed by labour as a milestone event. Why?
3. In your opinion, can Wal-Mart remain union-free indefinitely? Why or why not?

Case Study 2

The Arbitration Case of Jesse Stansky

At the arbitration hearing, both parties were adamant in their positions. Nancy Huang, HR manager of Phoenix Semiconductor, argued that the grievant, Jesse Stansky, was justly terminated for arguing and hitting a co-worker—a direct violation of company policy and the employee handbook. Stansky argued that he had been a good employee during his eight years of employment.

The submission agreement governing the case read, "It is the employer's position that just cause existed for the discharge of Mr. Jesse Stansky and the penalty was appropriate for the offence committed." Additionally, the employer introduced into evidence the labour agreement, which defined just cause termination as follows:

> Just cause shall serve as the basis for disciplinary action and includes, but is not limited to: dishonesty, inefficiency, unprofessional conduct, failure to report absences, falsification of records, violation of company policy, destruction of property, or possession or being under the influence of alcohol or narcotics.

Stansky was hired as a systems technician on November 20, 1994, a position he held until his termination on October 25, 2002. According to the testimony of Huang, Phoenix Semiconductor strived to maintain a positive and cordial work environment among its employees. Fighting on the job was strictly prohibited. Stansky's performance evaluation showed him to be an average employee, although he had received several disciplinary warnings for poor attendance and one three-day suspension for a "systems control error." Stansky was generally liked by his co-workers, and several testified in his behalf at the arbitration hearing.

The termination of Stansky concerned an altercation between himself and Gary Lindekin, another systems technician. According to witnesses to the incident, both Stansky and Lindekin became visibly upset over the correct way to calibrate a sensitive piece of production equipment. The argument—one witness called it no more than a heated disagreement—lasted approximately three minutes and concluded when Stansky was seen forcefully placing his hand on Lindekin's shoulder. Lindekin took extreme exception to Stansky's behaviour and immediately reported the incident to management. After interviews with both Stansky and Lindekin, and those who observed the incident, Huang; Samantha Lowry, the employee's immediate supervisor; and Grant Ginn, department manager, decided that Stansky should be terminated for unprofessional conduct and violation of company policy.

Source: Adapted from an arbitration heard by George W. Bohlander. All names are fictitious.

QUESTIONS

1. Which arguments should be given more weight: those based on company policy, the employee handbook, and the collective agreement, or mitigating factors given by the grievant and his witnesses? Explain.

2. How might unprofessional conduct be defined? Explain.

3. If you were the arbitrator, how would you rule in this case? Explain fully the reasons for your decision.

CAREER COUNSEL

For feedback on how you handle conflict, complete the Managing Conflict Questionnaire on the *Managing Human Resources* website (www.belcourt4e.nelson.com). You can also learn about six negotiating strategies and how they can be used in salary negotiations.

NOTES AND REFERENCES

1. Bruce E. Kaufman, "Reflections on Six Decades in Industrial Relations: An Interview with John Dunlop," *Industrial and Labor Relations Review* 55, no. 2 (January 2002): 324–48; C. Heron, *The Canadian Labour Movement: A Short History* (Toronto: James Lorimer & Company, 1989).

2. M. Gunderson, A. Ponak, and D. Gottlieb Taras, *Union Management Relations in Canada*, 4th ed. (Toronto: Addison Wesley Longman, 2001).

3. Readers interested in reading more about the labour relations process can consult Gunderson, et al., *Union Management Relations in Canada*, 4th ed.; and J. Godard, *Industrial Relations: The Economy and Society* (Toronto: McGraw-Hill Ryerson, 1994).

4. Robert R. Sinclair and Lois E. Tetrick, "Social Exchange and Union Commitment: A Comparison of Union Instrumentality and Union Support Perceptions," *Journal of Organizational Behavior* 16, no. 6 (November 1995): 669–79.

5. Jon Peirce, *Canadian Industrial Relations*, 2nd ed. (Toronto, Pearson Education, 2003).

6. P. Kumar and G. Murray, "Union Bargaining Priorities in the New Economy: Results for the 2000 HRDC Survey on Innovation and Change in Labour Organizations in Canada," *Workplace Gazette*, Winter 2001: 43–45.

7. Marc G. Singer and Thomas Li-Ping Tang, "Factors Related to Perceived Organizational Instrumentality," *Journal of Collective Negotiations in the Public Sector* 25, no. 3 (1996): 271–85.

8. Lorna Harris, "Labour Board Punishes Employer for Heavy Handed Efforts to Block Union," *Canadian HR Reporter* 15, no. 9 (May 6, 2002): 6.

9. K.J. Bentham, "Employer Resistance to Union Certification: A Study of Canadian Jurisdictions," *Relations Industrielles*, Winter 2002: 159–87.

10. J. Heinz, "Union Attempts to Organize Wal-Mart Stores in Ontario," *The Globe and Mail*, June 3, 1995: B3.

11. Discussion with CAW business representative, July 1995.

12. S.D. Smith, "Rising Union Certification Trends in Ontario," HROI White Paper, #020, 2001, July 24, 2001.

13. Canada Labour Relations Board regulations and Ontario Labour Relations Act.

14. Canadian Labour Congress, "Union Membership in Canada –2002," *Workplace Gazette*, Fall 2002: 38–45.

15. Workplace Information Directorate, "Union Membership in Canada 2002."

16. T.V. Alphen, "Unions Eye Blockbuster Merger Plan," *Toronto Star*, July 28, 1995: A3.

17. Godard, *Industrial Relations*, 228.

18. Ibid.

19. E. Kevin Kelloway and Julian Barling, "Members' Participation in Local Union Activities: Measurement, Prediction, and Replication," *Journal of Applied Psychology* 78, no. 2 (April 1993): 262–78.

20. Researchers have discussed the erosion of union steward power in contract administration. The loss of power has been attributed to bureaucratization and centralization of labour relations activity within both unions and

management hierarchies. While no one doubts the influence—positive or negative—that stewards can have on labour–management relations, the shifting power of the steward is important in deciding labour–management controversies. See Patricia A. Simpson, "A Preliminary Investigation of Determinants of Local Union Steward Power," *Labor Studies Journal* 18, no. 2 (Summer 1993): 51–67.

21. Aaron Bernstein, "Labor's Modest Quid Pro Quo," *Business Week*, November 11, 1996, 38.

22. Visit these websites: www.cupe.ca; www.nupge.ca; www.psac.com; and www.clc-ctc.ca.

23. Ibid.

24. Harvey C. Katz and Thomas A. Kochan, *An Introduction to Collective Bargaining and Industrial Relations* (New York: McGraw-Hill, 1992): 372–73.

25. James G. Baker, "Negotiating a Collective Bargaining Agreement: Law and Strategy—A Short Course for Non-Labor Lawyers," *Labor Law Journal* 47, no. 4 (April 1996): 253–67.

26. John A. Fossum, *Labor Relations: Development, Structure, Process*, 6th ed. (Homewood, IL: BPI-Irwin, 1995): 278.

27. Daniel Q. Mills, *Labor–Management Relations*, 5th ed. (New York: McGraw-Hill, 1994).

28. John W. Budd, "The Internal Union Political Imperative for UAW Pattern Bargaining," *Journal of Labor Research* 16, no. 1 (Winter 1995): 43–53.

29. Ross Stagner and Hjalmar Rosen, *Psychology of Union–Management Relations* (Belmont, CA: Wadsworth, 1965): 95–7. This is another classic in the field of labour–management relations.

30. George W. Bohlander and Jim Naber, "Non-adversarial Negotiations: The FMCS Interest-Based Bargaining Program," *Journal of Collective Negotiations in the Public Sector* 28, no. 1, 1999.

31. Ira Lobel, "Is Interest Based Bargaining Really New?" *Dispute Resolution Journal* 55, no. 1 (January- February 2000): 8–17.

32. *Interest-Based Negotiations: Participants' Guidebook* (Washington, DC: Federal Mediation and Conciliation Service, 1998).

33. D. Hynes, "New Climate of Collaboration in Labour Relations on the Horizon," *Canadian HR Reporter*, May 7, 2001: 9.

34. Eilene Zimmerman, "HR Lessons from a Strike," *Workforce* 79, no. 11 (November 2000): 36–42.

35. Deborah M. Kolb, *When Talk Works: Profiles of Mediators* (San Francisco: Jossey-Bass, 1994). See also Sam Kagel and Kathy Kelly, *The Anatomy of Mediation: What Makes It Work* (Washington, DC: Bureau of National Affairs, 1989).

36. *Grievance Guide*, 9th ed. (Washington, DC: BNA Books, 1995). See also Frank Elkouri and Edna Asher Elkouri, *How Arbitration Works*, 4th ed. (Washington, DC: Bureau of National Affairs, 1985), 153. This book continues to be a leading reference on the topic of arbitration and the resolution of grievances.

ANSWERS TO HIGHLIGHTS IN HRM 14.1

1. No. Individual questioning of employees about their union membership or activities is unlawful.

2. Yes. However, this must be part of normal conduct and cannot be interpreted as a gesture to buy votes.

3. Yes. Blacklisting of job applications or employees is against labour law.

4. No. During an organizing drive, an employer cannot promise improvements in wages or benefits as a means of defeating the union.

5. Yes. Employees can be disciplined or discharged for work-related misconduct but not solely because of their union affiliations or union sentiments.

International Human Resources Management

After studying this chapter, you should be able to

objective

Identify the types of organizational forms used for competing internationally.

objective

Explain how domestic and international HRM differ.

objective

Discuss the staffing process for individuals working internationally.

objective

Identify the unique training needs for international assignees.

objective

Reconcile the difficulties of home-country and host-country performance appraisals.

objective

Identify the characteristics of a good international compensation plan.

objective

Explain the major differences between Canadian and European labour relations.

It seems everywhere we look these days there are stories of companies trying to compete in a global environment. These stories might include mergers of international companies, such as Daimler-Benz and Chrysler a few years ago. Or they might highlight companies expanding into other markets, such as Bombardier in Asia or BMO in the United States. Or the stories might focus on international companies gaining dominance here in Canada, such as ING or Wal-Mart.

Whatever the angle, we see clearly that globalization is a chief factor driving business. Nearly all organizations today are influenced by international competition. Some handle the challenge well, while others fail miserably when they try to manage across borders. More often than not, the difference boils down to how people are managed, the adaptability of cultures, and the flexibility of organizations. Because of this, many organizations are reassessing their approaches to human resources management.[1]

The importance of globalization notwithstanding, we have—for the most part—emphasized HRM practices and systems as they exist in Canada. This is not so much an oversight on our part as it is a deliberate pedagogical choice. The topic of international HRM is so important that we wanted to dedicate an entire chapter to its discussion. Our thinking is that now after you have read (and, we hope, discussed) some of the best practices for managing people at work, it may be appropriate to see how some of these HRM systems change as we begin to manage people in an international arena. In this chapter we will observe that much of what has been discussed throughout this text can be applied to international operations, provided one is sensitive to the requirements of a particular international setting.

The first part of this chapter presents a brief introduction to international business firms. In many important respects, the way a company organizes its international operations influences the type of managerial and human resources issues it faces. In addition, we briefly describe some of the environmental factors that also affect the work of managers in a global setting. Just as with domestic operations, the dimensions of the environment form a context in which HRM decisions are made. A major portion of this chapter deals with the various HR activities involved in the recruitment, selection, development, and compensation of employees who work in an international setting. Throughout the discussion the focus will be on Canadian multinational corporations.

MANAGING ACROSS BORDERS

objective

International business operations can take several different forms. A large percentage carry on their international business with only limited facilities and minimal representation in foreign countries. Others, particularly Fortune 500 corporations, have extensive facilities and personnel in various countries of the world. Managing these resources effectively, and integrating their activities to achieve global advantage, is a challenge to the leadership of these companies.

Figure 15.1 shows four basic types of organizations and how they differ in the degree to which international activities are separated to respond to the local regions

International corporation
Domestic firm that uses its existing capabilities to move into overseas markets

Multinational corporation (MNC)
Firm with independent business units operating in several countries

Global corporation
Firm that has integrated worldwide operations through a centralized home office

Transnational corporation
Firm that attempts to balance local responsiveness and global scale via a network of specialized operating units

and integrated to achieve global efficiencies. The **international corporation** is essentially a domestic firm that builds on its existing capabilities to penetrate overseas markets. Companies such as Honda, General Electric, and Procter & Gamble used this approach to gain access to Europe—they essentially adapted existing products for overseas markets without changing much else about their normal operations.[2]

A **multinational corporation (MNC)** is a more complex form that usually has fully autonomous units operating in several countries. Shell, Philips, and ITT are three typical MNCs. These companies have traditionally given their foreign subsidiaries a great deal of latitude to address local issues such as consumer preferences, political pressures, and economic trends in different regions of the world. Frequently, these subsidiaries are run as independent companies, without much integration. The **global corporation**, on the other hand, can be viewed as a multinational firm that maintains control of operations back in the home office. Japanese companies such as Matsushita and NEC, for example, tend to treat the world market as a unified whole and try to combine activities in each country to maximize efficiency on a global scale. These companies operate much like a domestic firm, except that they view the whole world as their marketplace.

Finally, a **transnational corporation** attempts to achieve the local responsiveness of an MNC while also achieving the efficiencies of a global firm. To balance this "global/local" dilemma, a transnational uses a network structure that coordinates specialized facilities positioned around the world. By using this flexible structure, a transnational provides autonomy to independent country operations but brings these separate activities together into an integrated whole. For most companies, the

Figure 15.1   Types of Organizations

GLOBAL EFFICIENCY (High / Low) — LOCAL RESPONSIVENESS (Low / High)

GLOBAL
Views the world as a single market; operations are controlled centrally from the corporate office.

TRANSNATIONAL
Specialized facilities permit local responsiveness; complex coordination mechanisms provide global integration.

INTERNATIONAL
Uses existing capabilities to expand into foreign markets.

MULTINATIONAL
Several subsidiaries operating as stand-alone business units in multiple countries.

transnational form represents an ideal, rather than a reality. However, companies such as Ford, Unilever, and Shell have made good progress in restructuring operations to function more transnationally.[3]

Although various forms of organization exist, in this chapter we will generally refer to any company that conducts business outside its home country as an international business. Canada, of course, has no monopoly on international business. International enterprises are found throughout the world. In fact, some European and Pacific Rim companies have been conducting business on an international basis much longer than their Canadian counterparts. The close proximity of European countries, for example, makes them likely candidates for international trade. Figure 15.2 shows a list of some of the top global companies.[4]

These companies are in a strong position to affect the world economy in the following ways:

1. Production and distribution extend beyond national boundaries, making it easier to transfer technology.

2. They have direct investments in many countries, affecting the balance of payments.

3. They have a political impact that leads to cooperation among countries and to the breaking down of barriers of nationalism.

How Does the Global Environment Influence Management?

In Chapter 1, we highlighted some of the global trends affecting human resources management. One of the major economic issues we discussed was the creation of free trade zones within Europe, North America, and the Pacific Rim. Figure 15.3 shows a map of the fifteen member countries of the European Union (EU) whose goal is to facilitate the flow of goods, services, capital, and human resources across national borders in Europe in a manner similar to the way they cross provincial borders in Canada.[5] Despite the political and legal obstacles to unification, most observers agree that ultimately the EU is becoming a unified buying and selling power that competes as a major economic player with the United States and Japan. Highlights in HRM 15.1 describes some of the effects that unification may have on HRM practices within Europe.

A similar transition has been occurring within North America with the passage of NAFTA (discussed in Chapter 1). Some alarmists had feared that NAFTA would lead to a loss of jobs for Canadian companies. Just the opposite has occurred; a recent report by the U.S. Department of Commerce on the merits of NAFTA shows that job growth has surged in all three North American countries: In the United States, there has been a 7 percent increase (12.8 million jobs); in Canada, there has been a 10.1 percent increase (1.3 million jobs); and in Mexico there has been a 22 percent increase (2.2 million jobs).[6]

In addition to Europe and North America, many global companies are also fully engaged in Asia. Although the focus for many years has been on Japan, companies are now operating in a broader range of Asian countries such as Korea, Vietnam, Taiwan, Malaysia, and China (including Hong Kong). Motorola, for example, plans to invest

	COMPANY	HEADQUARTERS	MARKET VALUE (Millions USD)
1	General Electric	United States	$309 462
2	Microsoft	United States	275 701
3	Exxon Mobil	United States	271 228
4	Wal-Mart Stores	United States	240 907
5	Citigroup	United States	223 040
6	Pfizer	United States	216 777
7	BP	Britain	192 116
8	Johnson & Johnson	United States	186 942
9	Intel	United States	184 667
10	American International Group	United States	174 986
11	Coca-Cola	United States	137 995
12	IBM	United States	137 721
13	NTT Docomo	Japan	135 857
14	Merck	United States	129 679
15	GlaxoSmithKline	Britain	126 273
16	Novartis	Switzerland	123 930
17	Philip Morris	United States	122 933
18	Royal Dutch Shell	Netherlands	119 011
19	Bank of America	United States	117 090
20	Verizon Communications	United States	116 840
21	Procter & Gamble	United States	116 380
22	HSBC Holdings	Britain	116 335
23	Cisco Systems	United States	115 525
24	SBC Communications	United States	114 534
25	Berkshire Hathaway	United States	114 362
26	TotalFinaElf	France	110 509
27	Vodafone Group	Britain	102 949
28	Toyota Motor	Japan	99 702
29	Home Depot	United States	97 974
30	Nestlé	Switzerland	96 162

Figure 15.2 | **Top Global Companies**

Source: *Business Week* Global 1000.

Figure 15.3 | The Nations of the European Union

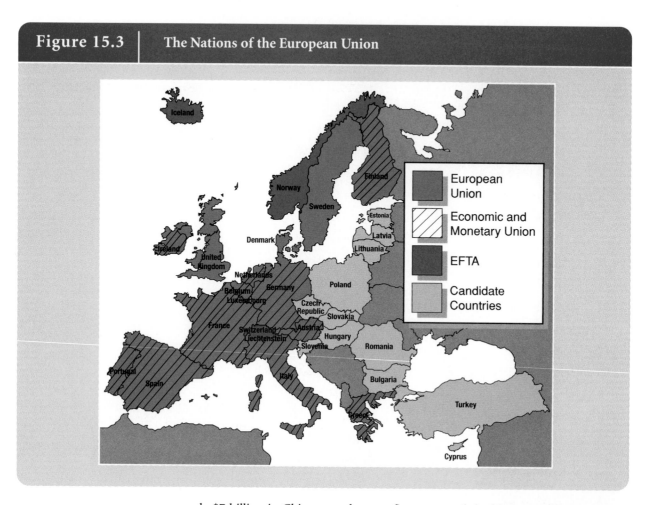

nearly $7 billion in China over the next five years and double its production in that country. Currently, almost 15 percent of Motorola's sales are in China, and this amount is likely to increase as China's economy develops. Nike is another company that does a good deal of business in Asia, and the stories of its mismanagement in Vietnam and China are now well-known.[7]

Cultural environment
Communications, religion, values and ideologies, education, and social structure of a country

Beyond the economic issues of world trade, the **cultural environment** (communications, religion, values and ideologies, education, and social structure) has an important influence on decisions in an international setting. Figure 15.4 summarizes the complexity of the cultural environment in which HR must be managed. Culture is an integrated phenomenon, and by recognizing and accommodating taboos, rituals, attitudes toward time, social stratification, kinship systems, and the many other components listed in Figure 15.4, managers will pave the way toward greater harmony and achievement in the **host country,** the country in which an international business operates.

Host country
Country in which an international corporation operates

Different cultural environments require different approaches to human resources management. Strategies, structures, and management styles that are appropriate in one cultural setting may lead to failure in another. Managers in global companies such as Shell, Colgate Palmolive, and Coca-Cola, for example, are quite sensitive to differences among the many countries within which the company operates. They point out

Highlights in HRM 15.1

HR Issues of a Unified Europe

Staffing

Unification provides workers the right to move freely throughout Europe and opens labour markets on a pan-European basis. However, unemployment rates vary dramatically throughout Europe. For example, Spain's unemployment rate still hovers around 16 percent, while countries such as Norway enjoy unemployment rates around 3 percent. These differences reflect many factors, including political systems, sociocultural differences, and worker training. In some cases, unemployment is the result of racial discrimination. Managers must overcome these problems to take advantage of the labour markets that have been opened to them.

The EU prohibits discrimination against workers and unions. However, while member countries are required to interpret national law in light of EU directives, most companies are still trying to reconcile EU policies with laws in their home countries.

Training and Development

It has not been easy bringing education up to date. Under a unified Europe, every worker is guaranteed access to vocational training. However, attempts to improve vocational training standards may fail unless standards of quality are assured. Germany remains a model of apprenticeship programs and worker development. Firms in other countries are struggling to create transnational employability in the face of inadequate training regulation. Meanwhile, there is a need for "Euroexecutives" who speak many languages and manage a multicultural workforce.

Productivity

To be competitive, Europeans must increase productivity. Europeans on average work fewer hours, take longer vacations, and enjoy far more social entitlements than their counterparts in North America and Asia. In contrast to the ten vacation days in the United States, workers in the United Kingdom, France, and the Netherlands receive about twenty-five days of paid vacation. Workers in Sweden and Austria receive thirty. In many countries, these periods are established by law and must be reconciled in a unified Europe.

Compensation and Benefits

Wages also differ substantially across countries throughout Europe. Workers in industrialized countries such as Germany and Switzerland receive an average hourly rate of about $22. In contrast, workers in Greece and Portugal have hourly wages between $5 and $9. Market forces are diminishing these differences somewhat, but to be competitive, companies need to bring compensation levels further in line with productivity. Although pay discrimination is prohibited by law, women workers still tend to be in low-paying jobs.

The EU has also addressed benefit issues. Under EU mandate, all workers have the right to social security benefits regardless of occupation or employer. In addition, even people who have been unable to enter the workforce are given basic social assistance. Several directives on occupational safety and health establish minimal standards throughout Europe.

(continued on following page)

Labour Relations

In the past, powerful trade unions have fiercely defended social benefits. In a unified Europe, unions retain collective bargaining rights laid out under the host country's laws and the right to be consulted regarding company decisions. Stimulating economic growth to create jobs may mean eliminating rigid work rules and softening policies related to social benefits. Union leaders have promised to fight these initiatives. At the same time, there is a trend toward coordinated bargaining across countries that would have the effect of standardizing labour agreements.

Sources: Miguel Leon-Ledesma, "Unemployment Hysteresis in the U.S. States and the EU: A Panel Approach," *Bulletin of Economic Research* 54, no. 2 (April 2002): 95–103; "Leaders: Neighbourly Lessons; European Unemployment," *The Economist* 362, no. 8264 (March 16, 2002): 16; "Europe: 2000–04," *Country Monitor* 8, no. 18 (May 10, 2000): 7; John T. Addison, "Labor Policy in the EU: The New Emphasis on Education and Training under the Treaty of Amsterdam," *Journal of Labor Research* 23, no. 2 (Spring 2002): 303–17; "European Forum of Technical and Vocational Education and Training," *Career Development International* 7, no. 5 (2002): 312; Marc Cowling, "Fixed Wages or Productivity Pay: Evidence from 15 EU Countries," *Small Business Economics* 16, no. 3 (May 2001): 191–204; "U.S. Productivity in 2001 Sustained by Information, Communication Technologies," *Research & Development* 44, no. 3 (March 2002): 10; "Regional and Country Data," *Country Monitor* 10, no. 23 (June 17, 2002): 12; Michell Baddeley, Ron Martin, and Peter Tyler, "Regional Wage Rigidity: The European Union and United States Compared," *Journal of Regional Science* 40, no. 1 (February 2000): 115–42; John Gennard and Kirsty Newsome, "European Co-ordination of Collective Bargaining: The Case of UNI-Europa Graphical Sector," *Employee Relations* 23, no. 6 (2001): 599–613.

USING THE INTERNET

The Outpost Expatriate Network is an online information centre for Shell expatriates and their families. Be sure to check out the Outpost flash movie at

www.outpostexpat.nl/.

objective 2

that forging effective relations is a matter of accurate perception, sound diagnosis, and appropriate adaptation.[8] Throughout this chapter we will discuss several HR issues related to adapting to different cultural environments.

Domestic versus International HRM

The internationalization of Canadian corporations has grown at a faster pace than the internationalization of the HRM profession. Executives in the very best companies around the world still lament that their HR policies have not kept pace with the demands of global competition.

Unfortunately, the academic community has not been a particularly good source of answers to international HRM problems. While various journals on international business have published articles on HRM over the years, it was not until 1990 that a journal specifically devoted to this area—the *International Journal of Human Resource Management*—was started.[9]

International HRM differs from domestic HRM in several ways. In the first place, it necessarily places a greater emphasis on functions and activities such as relocation, orientation, and translation services to help employees adapt to a new and different environment outside their own country. Assistance with tax matters, banking, investment management, home rental while on assignment, and coordination of home visits is also usually provided by the HR department. Most larger corporations have a

632

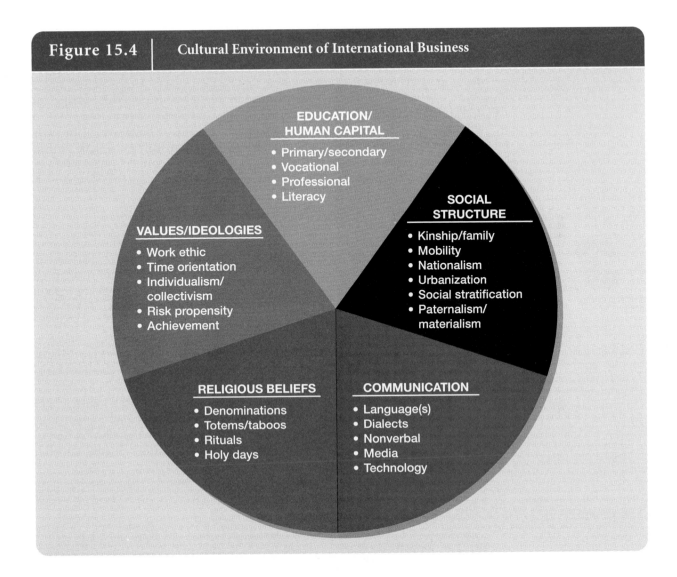

Figure 15.4 | Cultural Environment of International Business

EDUCATION/
HUMAN CAPITAL
- Primary/secondary
- Vocational
- Professional
- Literacy

SOCIAL
STRUCTURE
- Kinship/family
- Mobility
- Nationalism
- Urbanization
- Social stratification
- Paternalism/
  materialism

VALUES/IDEOLOGIES
- Work ethic
- Time orientation
- Individualism/
  collectivism
- Risk propensity
- Achievement

RELIGIOUS BELIEFS
- Denominations
- Totems/taboos
- Rituals
- Holy days

COMMUNICATION
- Language(s)
- Dialects
- Nonverbal
- Media
- Technology

full-time staff of HR managers devoted solely to assisting globalization. British Airways, for example, has a team of HR directors who travel around the world to help country managers stay updated on international concerns, policies, and programs.

Coca-Cola provides support to its army of HR professionals working around the world. There is a core HR group in the company's headquarters that holds a two-week HR orientation twice a year for the international HR staff. This program helps international HR practitioners share information about HR philosophies, programs, and policies established either in Coca-Cola's headquarters or another part of the world that can be successfully adopted by others. The program also provides a foundation for an HR network within the Coca-Cola system that helps participants get a broader view of the company's activities.[10]

One of the things that may improve international coordination is a global HR information system. Companies such as BP Amoco, Lucent, and Merck have found that record keeping, head count, and other HR-related activities can be facilitated with an integrated global system. At the same time, achieving this standard often proves difficult. In addition to technical issues, there are administrative and cultural issues to deal with. When Lucent Technologies rolled out a PeopleSoft system to more than 90 countries, touching 150, managers found that the order of employees' names was so important—and so varied—that it took two months to settle on a name format. Something as basic as a name becomes "the most sensitive cultural personal information," says Rosanne Schwab, project manager for HR systems at Lucent.[11]

International Staffing

objective 3

International management poses many problems in addition to those faced by a domestic operation. Because of geographic distance and a lack of close, day-to-day relationships with headquarters in the home country, problems must often be resolved with little or no counsel or assistance from others. It is essential, therefore, that special attention be given to the staffing practices of overseas units.

There are three sources of employees with whom to staff international operations. First, the company can send people from its home country. These employees are often referred to as **expatriates,** or **home-country nationals**. Second, it can hire **host-country nationals**, natives of the host country, to do the managing. Third, it can hire **third-country nationals**, natives of a country other than the home country or the host country.

Each of these three sources of overseas workers provides certain advantages and certain disadvantages. Some of the more important advantages are presented in Figure 15.5. Most corporations, such as the Four Seasons Hotel (described in Reality Check), use all three sources for staffing their multinational operations, although some companies exhibit a distinct bias for one or another of the three sources.[12]

As shown in Figure 15.6, at early stages of international expansion, organizations often send home-country expatriates to establish activities (particularly in

Expatriates, or home-country nationals
Employees from the home country who are on international assignment

Host-country nationals
Employees who are natives of the host country

Third-country nationals
Employees who are natives of a country other than the home country or the host country

Figure 15.5	Comparison of Advantages in Sources of Overseas Managers	
Host Country Nationals	**Home-Country Nationals (Expatriates)**	**Third-Country Nationals**
Less cost	Talent available within company	Broad experience
Preference of host-country governments	Greater control	International outlook
Intimate knowledge of environment and culture	Company experience	Multilingualism
Language facility	Mobility	
	Experience provided to corporate executives	

Reality Check

SELECTING FOR SERVICE

Four Seasons Hotels, with a staff of over 25 000, manages fifty hotels and luxury resorts around the world, from Bali to Boston. The Four Seasons brand is synonymous with luxury and first-class service standards. The execution of the strategy of being the best in the world starts with leaders who are passionate about the corporation's customer service and employee relations values. These leaders can take a concept such as "We will deliver exceptional personal service" and paint a picture for employees that is clear and motivational and that results in the delivery of that exceptional personal service.

Does the perception of service excellence depend on the country or culture in which Four Seasons operates? John Young, executive vice-president of human resources, states that the Four Seasons guest is typically a sophisticated global traveller who has acquired a sensitivity to differences in culture without negative preconceptions. Nevertheless, Four Seasons trains service staff to be sensitive to guests' needs and to minimize or avoid culture and language problems. For example, in Asia, when an English-speaking guest gives a food or beverage order, the service staff are trained to repeat the order. This is done not only to prevent a potential service error, but to avoid loss of face for the employee. In North America, a repetition of the order would be seen as redundant.

So that employees can meet these high performance expectations, Four Seasons selects employees based on their service attitudes. Candidates for employment must undergo four behaviourally based interviews (including one with the general manager) to determine their service attitudes and current skills and knowledge. As Young says: "Customer service is the heart and soul of our business, and we need to assess if a candidate has sensitivity to the needs and wants of others. Of course, we also look at high levels of knowledge, skill, and experience, but these can be trained. We continuously adapt our service to match guest needs. For example, many years ago, in our Seattle hotel, one of the valet parking attendants noted that on weekends our guests were disproportionately families with children. On his own initiative, he put chocolate chip cookies and milk in cars that he was returning to these departing guests. They loved it. This practice has now become one of Four Seasons' standards."

Four Seasons does not have a rigid formula for selecting home country nationals or expatriates for any given country. The ratios depend on three factors: regulations, economics, and corporate management development needs. Young continues: "For example, Indonesia used to have a rule that no more than three expatriates could be employed per hotel. So we set expatriate reduction targets to meet this regulation. Economically it made sense for us, since an expatriate general manager could cost us as much as seventy-five or eighty local employees. And finally, we will choose candidates based on their need for global exposure and professional development, to match our targeted needs for international expansion.

"Our biggest challenge in international HR now is management development in the context of our growth plans. We need to develop culturally appropriate leadership in preparation for

(continued on following page)

specific new locations on a defined time line. If we cannot find managers who can speak the language, and understand the culture, then our ability to grow is limited. Recently we opened a hotel in Puerto Vallarta. We found a Spanish-speaking general manager from Colombia who, over time, was able to integrate the Four Seasons way of doing business with the Mexican culture. Business culture in Mexico tends to be very rule and policy driven. Employees continuously asked, 'What is the policy ...' in HR, sales, everything." Over time, the general manager learned to deal with the questions by no longer looking to home office for all the rules, but by asking himself and his team, "What should the rule be in our situation?"

"We cannot just hire the management talent we want from other sectors or hotel chains on short lead time, because of differences in operating standards and corporate culture. For example, we were opening a hotel with a general manager recruited from Hilton International. As he toured the new facility with Issy Sharp, our founder and CEO, the general manager said that the lounge facilities ought to be larger. He explained that this would make guests more comfortable while waiting for their dinner reservations. Issy replied, 'At Four Seasons our guests do not wait for their reservations.' These cultural differences, across countries, across sectors, and across competitors, underline the importance of our investing the time and effort in developing our own management talent, which is culturally and linguistically fluent, mobile, and imbued with our service culture."

This attention to the selection and development of high-performance employees has resulted in Four Seasons being named by *Fortune* magazine one of the 100 best employers for three consecutive years. Consequently, Four Seasons is now able to attract more and better applicants. Four Seasons is also widely recognized as the best luxury hotel chain in the world. Furthermore, the turnover rate at Four Seasons is one of the lowest in the hospitality sector. Even those employees who have left are often recaptured as they elect to return to the kind of culture that treats them as they treat the guests.

less-developed countries) and to work with local governments. At later stages of internationalization, there is typically a steady shift toward the use of host-country nationals. There are three reasons for this trend:

1. Hiring local citizens is less costly because the company does not have to worry about the costs of home leaves, transportation, and special schooling allowances (expatriate assignments cost an average of $1 million over a three-year period).

2. Since local governments usually want good jobs for their citizens, foreign employers may be required to hire them.

3. Using local talent avoids the problem of employees having to adjust to the culture.

Recently there has also been a trend away from using only expatriates in the top management positions. In many cases, Canadian companies want to be viewed as true international citizens. To avoid the strong influence of the home country, companies frequently change staffing policies to replace Canadian expatriates with local managers. Companies such as PepsiCo, Asea Brown Boveri (ABB), and Eli Lilly have strong

Figure 15.6 | **Changes in International Staffing over Time**

EMPHASIS IN STAFFING

Host-Country
Nationals

Expatriates

TIME

regional organizations and tend to hire third-country nationals in addition to host-country nationals. In such cases, companies would tend to use expatriates only when there is need for a specific set of skills or when individuals in the host country require development. Over the years, U.S.-based companies, in particular, have tended to use more third-country nationals.[13]

It should be recognized that while top managers may have preferences for one source of employees over another, the host country may place pressures on them that restrict their choices. Such pressure takes the form of sophisticated government persuasion through administrative or legislative decrees to employ host-country individuals.

Recruitment

The HR department in an overseas unit must be particularly responsive to the cultural, political, and legal environments. For example, companies such as Shell, Xerox, Levi Strauss, Digital, and Honeywell have made a special effort to create codes of conduct for employees throughout the world to make certain that standards of ethical and legal behaviour are known and understood. PepsiCo has taken a similar approach to ensuring that company values are reinforced (even while recognizing the need for adapting to local cultures). The company has four core criteria that are viewed as essential in worldwide recruiting efforts: (1) personal integrity, (2) a drive for results, (3) respect for others, and (4) capability.[14]

In general, employee recruitment in other countries is subject to more government regulation than it is in Canada. Regulations range from those that cover procedures for recruiting employees to those that govern the employment of foreign workers or require the employment of the physically disabled or displaced persons. Many Central

American countries, for example, have stringent regulations about the number of foreigners that can be employed as a percentage of the total workforce. Virtually all countries have work-permit or visa restrictions that apply to foreigners. A **work permit**, or **work certificate**, is a document issued by a government granting authority to a foreign individual to seek employment in that government's country.[15]

MNCs tend to use the same kinds of internal and external recruitment sources as are used in their home countries. At the executive level, companies use search firms such as Korn/Ferry in Canada or Spencer Stuart in the United Kingdom. At lower levels, more informal approaches tend to be useful. While unskilled labour may be readily available in a developing country, recruitment of skilled workers may be more difficult. Many employers have learned that the best way to find workers in these countries is through referrals and radio announcements because many people lack sufficient reading or writing skills.

The laws of many countries require the employment of locals if adequate numbers of skilled people are available. In these cases, recruiting is limited to a restricted population. Specific exceptions are granted (officially or unofficially) for contrary cases, as for Mexican farmworkers in Canada and for Italian, Spanish, Greek, and Turkish workers in Germany and the Benelux countries (Belgium, the Netherlands, and Luxembourg). Read Highlights in HRM 15.2 to learn why the hospitality industry in Canada employs foreign workers. Foreign workers invited to come to perform needed labour are usually referred to as **guest workers**. The employment of non-nationals may involve lower direct labour costs, but indirect costs—language training, health services, recruitment, transportation, and so on—may be substantial.[16]

Work permit, or work certificate
Government document granting a foreign individual the right to seek employment

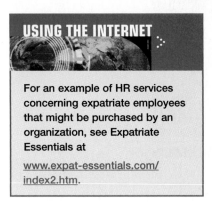

For an example of HR services concerning expatriate employees that might be purchased by an organization, see Expatriate Essentials at www.expat-essentials.com/index2.htm.

Guest workers
Foreign workers invited to perform needed labour

Selection

As you might imagine, selection practices vary around the world. In Canada, managers tend to emphasize merit, with the best-qualified person getting the job. In other countries, however, firms tend to hire on the basis of family ties, social status, language, and common origin. The candidate who satisfies these criteria may get the job even if otherwise unqualified. Much of this is changing—there has been a growing realization among organizations in other nations that greater attention must be given to hiring those most qualified.

The Selection Process

The selection process for international assignments should emphasize different employment factors, depending on the extent of contact that one would have with the local culture and the degree to which the foreign environment differs from the home environment. For example, if the job involves extensive contacts with the community, as with a chief executive officer, this factor should be given appropriate weight. The magnitude of differences between the political, legal, socioeconomic, and cultural systems of the host country and those of the home country should also be assessed.[17]

If a candidate for expatriation is willing to live and work in a foreign environment, an indication of his or her tolerance of cultural differences should be obtained. On the other hand, if local nationals have the technical competence to carry out the job suc-

Highlights in HRM 15.2

IMPORTING CULTURE

The Inn at Manitou in Ontario's Muskoka District has a staff of about seventy, half of whom are not Canadian. The decision to recruit outside Canada for this Relais et Chateux luxury hotel and spa was made after years of trying to find Canadian workers and train them to offer the type of service that a luxury inn must offer.

Ben Wise, the inn's owner, gives several reasons for employing non-Canadians. The first is culture: "We hire Europeans, who have a culture of hospitality. To serve people is not perceived by Europeans to be denigrating. Canadians berate the job of a waiter, saying that they are not waiters, but on their way to be stockbrokers. Being a waiter is a profession in Europe. Chefs are celebrities in Europe."

In Europe, jobs in the hospitality sector are seen as professions for which extensive training is necessary. Europeans arrive at Wise's inn with four to five years of training and experience at some of the best hotels. Canadian candidates cannot compete. Wise tried to train Canadians, but four weeks of on-the-job training could not match the extensive training Europeans receive. Besides, he didn't think it was fair to ask the inn's clients to put up with the mistakes and deficiencies of workers in training.

Another reason was the seasonal nature of the hospitality industry in Muskoka District: "Canadians have a summer job mentality to these positions. Consequently, a report on their performance is of no value to them. There is little we can do to motivate them to meet our service expectations. Europeans are serious. Their future employment depends on our performance evaluations and our references."

So each year The Inn at Manitou places ads in trade magazines, screens hundreds of applicants, interviews and selects those with training and experience at the best resorts and hotels, and finally arranges work permits for the lucky thirty. Why lucky? "Canada has a fascinating appeal for Europeans, especially the French, who must have all read books about a charming little cabin in the woods, with mountains, space, and fresh water."

cessfully, they should be carefully considered for the job before the firm launches a search (at home) for a candidate to fill the job. As stated previously, most corporations realize the advantages to be gained by staffing international operations with host-country nationals wherever possible.

Selecting home-country and third-country nationals requires that more factors be considered than in selecting host-country nationals. While the latter must of course possess managerial abilities and the necessary technical skills, they have the advantage of familiarity with the physical and cultural environment and the language of the host country. The discussion that follows will focus on the selection of expatriate managers from the home country.

Selecting Expatriates

One of the toughest jobs facing many organizations is finding employees who can meet the demands of working in a foreign environment. There are several steps involved in selecting individuals for an international assignment. And the sequencing of these activities can make a big difference.

Step 1: Begin with self-selection. Employees should begin the process (years) in advance by thinking about their career goals and interest in international work. By beginning with self-selection, companies can more easily avoid the problems of forcing otherwise promising employees into international assignments where they would be unhappy and unsuccessful. In cases where individuals have families, the decisions about relocation are more complicated. Employees should seek out information to help them predict their chances of success in living abroad. Companies such as EDS and Deloitte & Touche give the self-selection instruments to their employees to help them think through the pros and cons of international assignments.

Step 2: Create a candidate pool. After employees have self-selected, organizations can put together a database of candidates for international assignments. Information on the database might include availability, languages, country preferences, and skills.

Step 3: Assess core skills. From the shortlist of potential candidates, managers can assess each candidate on technical and managerial readiness relative to the needs of the assignment. Although there are many factors that determine success abroad, the initial focus should be on the requirements of the job.

Step 4: Assess augmented skills and attributes. As shown in Figure 15.7, expatriate selection decisions are typically driven by technical competence as well as professional and international experience. In addition, however, an increasing number of organizations have also begun considering an individual's ability to adapt to different environments. Satisfactory adjustment depends on flexibility, emotional maturity and stability, empathy for the culture, language and communication skills, resourcefulness and initiative, and diplomatic skills.[18]

To be more specific, companies such as Colgate-Palmolive, Whirlpool, and Dow Chemical have identified a set of **core skills** that they view as critical for success abroad and a set of **augmented skills** that help facilitate the efforts of expatriate managers. These skills are shown in Highlights in HRM 15.3. It is worth noting that many of these skills are not significantly different from those required for managerial success at home.

While these efforts to improve the selection process have helped in many cases, unfortunately the **failure rate** among expatriates has been estimated to range from 25 to 50 percent. What is worse, the average cost of a failed assignment can run as high as from $200 000 to $2.1 million.[19] In contrast to the criteria for selection, the most prevalent reasons for failure among expatriates are not technical or managerial limitations—they sit squarely on family and lifestyle issues. Interestingly, Figure 15.8 shows the major causes of expatriate assignment failure. By far, the biggest factor tends to be a spouse's inability to adjust to his or her new surroundings. Figure 15.9 shows some of the most important ways for improving the success of informational assignments.[20]

Core skills
Skills considered critical to an employee's success abroad

Augmented skills
Skills helpful in facilitating the efforts of expatriate managers

Failure rate
Percentage of expatriates who do not perform satisfactorily

Figure 15.7 | Expatriate Selection Criteria

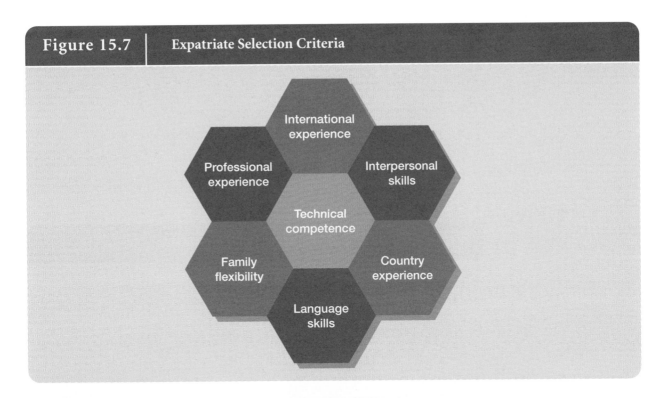

Highlights in HRM 15.3

SKILLS OF EXPATRIATE MANAGERS

Core Skills
Experience
Decision making
Resourcefulness
Adaptability
Cultural sensitivity
Team building
Maturity

Augmented Skills
Computer skills
Negotiation skills
Strategic thinking
Delegation skills
Change management

Diversity Management: Women Going Abroad

Traditionally, companies have been hesitant to send women on overseas assignments. Executives may either mistakenly assume that women do not want international assignments, or they may assume that host-country nationals are prejudiced against women. The reality is that women frequently do want international assignments—at least at a rate equal to that of men. And while locals may be prejudiced against women

Figure 15.8	Causes of Expatriate Assignment Failure

Why Do Expats Fail?

▶ Family adjustment   ▶ Poor performance

▶ Lifestyle issues   ▶ Other opportunities arise

▶ Work adjustment   ▶ Business reasons

▶ Bad selection   ▶ Repatriation issues

Figure 15.9	Boosting ROI of Expatriates

Major initiatives planned to improve assignment return on investment (ROI):

Better candidate selection	32%
Career planning skills	26
Communicating objectives	24
Assignment preparation	20
Monitoring program	17
Cross-cultural training	10
Developing or expanding intranet	7
Communication/recognition	6
Web-based cultural training	5
Mandating destination support	4
Other	17

Source: Andrea Poe, "Selection Savvy," *HRMagazine* 47, no. 4 (April 2002): 77–83.

in their own country, they view women first as foreigners (*gaijin* in Japanese) and only secondly as women. Therefore, cultural barriers that typically constrain the roles of women in a male-dominated society may not totally apply in the case of expatriates.

Importantly, in cases in which women have been given international assignments, they generally have performed quite well. The success rate of female expatriates has been estimated to be about 97 percent—a rate far superior to that of men. Ironically, women expatriates attribute at least part of their success to the fact that they are women. Because locals are aware of how unusual it is for a woman to be given a foreign assignment, they frequently assume that the company would not have sent a

The Business Case

THE COSTS OF EMPLOYING EXPATRIATES

Organizations typically make selection decisions on the basis of a match between job requirements and the candidates' skills and abilities. But selection decisions in international assignments must always compare the costs of employing locals versus expatriates. The chart below compares the cost of employing a Canadian manager in the United Kingdom to employing a U.K. manager. The case involves a manager, based in Ontario, who earns about $85 000 a year, with a $17 000 bonus, who is to be sent on a three-and-a-half-year assignment to London, England. He is married with one school-age child who attends private school. This manager receives an automobile allowance as well as a trip home per year. The company pays for the relocation, household goods storage, and tax return preparations.

Total cost of assignment for 3.5 years:

Cost Element	$
Base salary	297 500
Bonus	59 500
Gross income	357 000
Cost of living allowance	92 800
Housing allowance	135 000
Education allowance	61 500
Automobile allowance	55 300
Home leaves	32 400
Relocation, storage, and tax return	76 300
Additional tax expenses	175 500
Total Cost	**$985 800**

The costs of sending this manager on an international assignment are nearly a million dollars, compared to the approximately $300 000 it would cost to employ a U.K.-based manager.

Source: Jeff Bitten, "Compensation Strategies for International Assignments," *Canadian HR Professional* 18, no. 2 (April/May 2001): 29–31.

woman unless she was the very best. In addition, because women expatriates are novel (particularly in managerial positions), they are very visible and distinctive. In many cases, they may even receive special treatment not given to their male colleagues.[21]

Staffing Transnational Teams

Transnational teams
Teams composed of members of several nationalities working on projects that span various countries

In addition to focusing on individuals, it is also important to note that companies are increasingly using transnational teams to conduct international business. **Transnational teams** are composed of members of several nationalities working on projects that span various countries.[22] These teams are especially useful for performing tasks that the firm as a whole is not yet structured to accomplish. For example, they may be used to transcend the existing organizational structure to customize a strategy for different geographic regions, transfer technology from one part of the world to another, and communicate between headquarters and subsidiaries in different countries.

The fundamental task in forming a transnational team is assembling the right group of people who can work together effectively to accomplish the goals of the team. Many companies try to build variety into their teams in order to maximize responsiveness to the special needs of different countries. For example, when Heineken formed a transnational team to consolidate production facilities, it made certain that team members were drawn from each major region within Europe. Team members tended to have specialized skills, and members were added only if they offered some unique skill that added value to the team.

Canadian employers wishing to assess over 15 000 academic credentials of foreign-born employees can consult the not-for-profit World Education Services at

www.wes.org/ca.

Selection Methods

The methods of selection most commonly used by corporations operating internationally are interviews, assessment centres, and tests. While some companies interview only the candidate, others interview both the candidate and the spouse, lending support to the fact that companies are becoming increasingly aware of the significance of the spouse's adjustment to a foreign environment and the spouse's contribution to managerial performance abroad. However, despite the potential value of considering a spouse's adjustment, the influence of such a factor over the selection/expatriation decision raises some interesting issues about validity, fairness, and discrimination. For example, if someone is denied an assignment because of concerns about his or her spouse, there may be grounds for legal action.

TRAINING AND DEVELOPMENT

Although companies try to recruit and select the very best people for international work, it is often necessary to provide some type of training to achieve the desired level of performance. Over time, given the rapidity of change in an international setting, employees may also need to upgrade their skills as they continue on the job. Such training may be provided within the organization or outside it in some type of educational setting.

Skills of the Global Manager

Global manager
Manager equipped to run an international business

If businesses are to be managed effectively in an international setting, managers need to be educated and trained in global management skills. In this regard, Levi Strauss has identified the following six skill categories for the **global manager**, or the manager equipped to run an international business:

▶ Ability to seize strategic opportunities
▶ Ability to manage highly decentralized organizations
▶ Awareness of global issues

▶ Sensitivity to issues of diversity

▶ Competence in interpersonal relations

▶ Skill in building community[23]

Corporations that are serious about succeeding in global business are tackling these problems head-on by providing intensive training. Companies such as AMP, Texas Instruments, Procter & Gamble, Bechtel, and others with large international staffs prepare employees for overseas assignments. The biggest mistake managers can make is to assume that people are the same everywhere. An organization that makes a concerted effort to ensure that its employees understand and respect cultural differences will realize the impact of its effort on its sales, costs, and productivity.[24]

International assignments provide an employee with a set of experiences that are uniquely beneficial to both the individual and the firm.

PHOTODISC

Content of Training Programs

There are at least four essential elements of training and development programs that prepare employees for working internationally: (1) language training, (2) cultural training, (3) assessing and tracking career development, and (4) managing personal and family life.[25]

Language Training

Communication with individuals who have a different language and a different cultural orientation is extremely difficult. Most executives agree that it is among the biggest problems for the foreign business traveller. Even with an interpreter, much is missed.[26]

When ARCO Products began exploring potential business opportunities in China, the HR department set up a language training class (with the help of Berlitz International) in conversational Mandarin Chinese.[27] While foreign-language fluency is important in all aspects of international business, only a small percentage of Canadians are skilled in a language other than English. Students who plan careers in international business should start instruction in one or more foreign languages as early as possible.

Fortunately for most Canadians, English is almost universally accepted as the primary language for international business. Particularly in cases in which there are many people from different countries working together, English is usually the designated language for meetings and formal discourse. Although English is a required subject in many foreign schools, students may not learn to use it effectively. Many companies provide instruction in English for those who are required to use English in their jobs.

Learning the language is only part of communicating in another culture. One must also learn how the people think and act in their relations with others. The following list illustrates the complexities of the communication process in international business.

1. In England, to "table" a subject means to put it on the table for current discussion. In Canada, it means to postpone discussion of a subject, perhaps indefinitely.

2. In Canada, information flows to a manager. In cultures where authority is centralized (Europe and South America), the manager must take the initiative to seek out the information.

3. Getting straight to the point is uniquely North American. Europeans, Arabs, and many others resent this directness in communication.

4. In Japan, there are sixteen ways to avoid saying no.

5. When something is "inconvenient" to the Chinese, it is most likely downright impossible.

6. In most foreign countries, expressions of anger are unacceptable; in some places, public display of anger is taboo.

7. The typical North American must learn to treat silences as "communication spaces" and not interrupt them.

8. In general, North Americans must learn to avoid gesturing with the hand.

Since factors other than language are also important, those working internationally need to know as much as possible about (1) the country where they are going, (2) that country's culture, and (3) the history, values, and dynamics of their own organization. Figure 15.10 gives an overview of what one needs to study for an international assignment.

Figure 15.10	Preparing for an International Assignment

To prepare for an international assignment, one should become acquainted with the following aspects of the host country:

1. Social and business etiquette

2. History and folklore

3. Current affairs, including relations between the host country and Canada

4. Cultural values and priorities

5. Geography, especially its major cities

6. Sources of pride and great achievements of the culture

7. Religion and the role of religion in daily life

8. Political structure and current players

9. Practical matters such as currency, transportation, time zones, hours of business

10. The language

Cultural Training

Cross-cultural differences represent one of the most elusive aspects of international business. Generally unaware of their own culture-conditioned behaviour, most people tend to react negatively to tastes and behaviours that deviate from those of their own culture.

Managerial attitudes and behaviours are influenced, in large part, by the society in which managers have received their education and training. Similarly, reactions of employees are the result of cultural conditioning. Each culture has its expectations for the roles of managers and employees. For example, what one culture encourages as participative management another might see as managerial incompetence.[28] Being successful as a manager depends on one's ability to understand the way things are normally done and to recognize that changes cannot be made abruptly without considerable resistance, and possibly antagonism, on the part of local nationals. Some of the areas in which there are often significant variations among the different countries will be examined briefly.

A wealth of data from cross-cultural studies reveals that nations tend to cluster according to similarities in certain cultural dimensions such as work goals, values, needs, and job attitudes. Using data from eight comprehensive studies of cultural differences, Simcha Ronen and Oded Shenkar have grouped countries into the clusters shown in Figure 15.11. Countries having a higher GDP per capita in comparison with other countries are placed close to the centre.

Ronen and Shenkar point out that while evidence for the grouping of countries into Anglo, Germanic, Nordic, Latin European, and Latin American clusters appears to be quite strong, clusters encompassing the Far Eastern and Arab countries are ill defined and require further research, as do clusters of countries classified as independent. Many areas, such as Africa, have not been studied much at all. It should also be noted that the clusters presented in Figure 15.11 do not include Russia and the former satellites of what was the Soviet Union.[29]

Studying cultural differences can help managers identify and understand work attitudes and motivation in other cultures. In Japan, for example, employees are more likely to feel a strong loyalty to their company, although recent reports show that this may be changing. When compared with the Japanese, Americans may feel little loyalty to their organization. On the other hand, a Latin American tends to work not for a company but for an individual manager. Thus managers in Latin American countries can encourage performance only by using personal influence and working through individual members of a group. In North America, competition has been the name of the game; in Japan, Taiwan, and other Asian countries, cooperation is more the underlying philosophy.[30]

One of the important dimensions of leadership, whether we are talking about international or domestic situations, is the degree to which managers invite employee participation in decision making. While it is difficult to find hard data on employee participation across different countries, careful observers report that North American managers are about in the middle on a continuum of autocratic to democratic decision-making styles. Scandinavian and Australian managers also appear to be in the middle. South American and European managers, especially those from France, Germany, and Italy, are toward the autocratic end of the continuum; Japanese man-

Figure 15.11 | Synthesis of Country Clusters

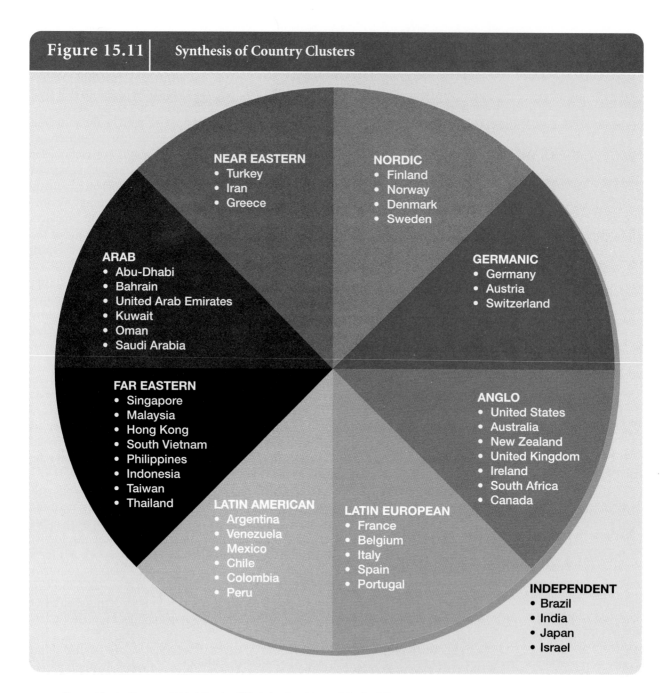

NEAR EASTERN
- Turkey
- Iran
- Greece

NORDIC
- Finland
- Norway
- Denmark
- Sweden

ARAB
- Abu-Dhabi
- Bahrain
- United Arab Emirates
- Kuwait
- Oman
- Saudi Arabia

GERMANIC
- Germany
- Austria
- Switzerland

FAR EASTERN
- Singapore
- Malaysia
- Hong Kong
- South Vietnam
- Philippines
- Indonesia
- Taiwan
- Thailand

ANGLO
- United States
- Australia
- New Zealand
- United Kingdom
- Ireland
- South Africa
- Canada

LATIN AMERICAN
- Argentina
- Venezuela
- Mexico
- Chile
- Colombia
- Peru

LATIN EUROPEAN
- France
- Belgium
- Italy
- Spain
- Portugal

INDEPENDENT
- Brazil
- India
- Japan
- Israel

Source: Simcha Ronen and Oded Shenkar, "Clustering Countries on Attitudinal Dimensions: A Review and Synthesis," *Academy of Management Review* 10, no. 3 (July 1985): 435–54. Copyright *Academy of Management Review*. Permission conveyed through the Copyright Clearance Center.

agers are at the most participatory end. Because Far Eastern cultures and religions tend to emphasize harmony, group decision making predominates there.[31]

Ethics in HRM describes the difficulties we can encounter when judging cultural practices on the basis of Canadian moral and legal standards.

CHAPTER 15 International Human Resources Management

Ethics in HRM

CANADIAN VERSUS THIRD WORLD ATTITUDES TOWARD CHILD LABOUR

About 250 million children, one in every six in the world, performs work that is involuntary, hazardous, or illegal. Although the largest number (70 percent) work in farming, fishing, hunting, and forestry, about 10 percent work as soldiers or prostitutes. Canadians are among the first to deplore the use of child labour. We are noted for our media campaigns against it, and our child impact assessments affect our choice of suppliers. Because we don't use child labourers ourselves, we are quick to condemn countries that do. Foreigners resent it when Westerners preach about the issue. In developing countries, child workers are the norm. The family is seen as the labour unit, with children contributing, according to their abilities, to the production of food and goods or services for sale. In these countries, there is no social welfare or insurance: children's earnings often make the difference between starvation and survival. Furthermore, school is not an alternative for many child labourers. Schools for those who can afford them are often crowded, ill-equipped, and harsh in their treatment of children.

Programs designed to stop the use of child labourers, such as the child impact assessment, result in cosmetic changes. These changes in turn encourage corruption among fixers, brokers, and consultants, which results in child labourers being driven into the underground economy where they are at the mercy of labour contractors. Until Westerners can understand the culture of Third World countries, and the deeply embedded roots of child labour, their interventions and sanctions will only cause more problems.

Sources: Mohammad Qadeer, "Why the Third World Needs Child Labour," *The Globe and Mail*, November 7, 1997, A8; Bill Varner, "Child Labour Remains Huge Problem: ILO," *The Globe and Mail*, May 7, 2002: B12.

Assessing and Tracking Career Development

International assignments provide some definite developmental and career advantages. For example, working abroad tends to increase a person's responsibilities and influence within the corporation. In addition, it provides a person with a set of experiences that are uniquely beneficial to both the individual and the firm. In this way, international assignments enhance a person's understanding of the global marketplace and offer the opportunity to work on a project important to the organization.[32]

To maximize the career benefits of a foreign assignment, two key questions about the employer should be asked before accepting an overseas post: (1) Do the organization's senior executives view the firm's international business as a critical part of its operation? (2) Within top management, how many executives have a foreign-service assignment in their background, and do they feel it important for one to have overseas experience? Despite the high-profile nature of these international assignments, about 70 percent provide no post-assignment guarantees of employment.[33]

To ensure appropriate career development, Dow appoints a high-level manager who serves as a home office contact for information about organizational changes, job opportunities, and anything related to salary and compensation. At Exxon, employees

NEL

649

are given a general idea of what they can expect after an overseas assignment even before they leave to assume it. With this orientation, they can make a smooth transition and continue to enhance their careers. Colgate-Palmolive and Novartis make a special effort to keep in touch with expatriates during the period that they are abroad. Colgate's division executives and other corporate staff members make frequent visits to international transferees.[34]

An increasing number of companies such as Monsanto, 3M, EDS, and Verizon are developing programs specifically designed to facilitate **repatriation**—that is, helping employees make the transition back home. The program is designed to prepare employees for adjusting to life at home (which at times can be more difficult than adjusting to a foreign assignment). Employees are given guidance about how much the expatriate experience may have changed them and their families. Monsanto's program is also designed to smooth the employee's return to the home organization and help make certain that the expatriate's knowledge and experience are fully utilized. To do so, returning expatriates get the chance to showcase their new knowledge in debriefing sessions.[35] A repatriation checklist is shown in Highlights in HRM 15.4.

Unfortunately, not all companies have career development programs designed for repatriating employees. In several recent studies researchers have found that the majority of companies do not do an effective job of repatriation. Here are some general findings:

1. Only about one-third of companies have a repatriation plan in place before the expatriate leaves home.

2. Another third typically don't begin formal repatriation discussions until two to six months before the end of their assignment.

3. The remaining third never have a repatriation discussion at all.

Not surprisingly, employees often lament that their organizations are vague about repatriation, about their new roles within the company, and about their career progression. It is not at all uncommon for employees to return home after a few years to find that there is *no* position for them in the firm and that they no longer know anyone who can help them. Employees often feel their firms disregard their difficulties in adjusting to life back in Canada. Even in cases where employees are successfully repatriated, their companies often do not fully utilize the knowledge, understanding, and skills they developed in overseas experiences. And contrary to the reason that many North Americans take international assignments in the first place—to gain advancement—evidence suggests that only a fraction are actually promoted. In fact, many employees take jobs at lower levels than their international assignments. This hurts the employee, of course, but it may hurt equally the firm's chances of using that employee's expertise to gain competitive advantage. For these reasons, expatriates sometimes leave their company within a year or two of coming home.

Managing Personal and Family Life

As noted previously, one of the most frequent causes of an employee's failure to complete an international assignment is personal and family stress. **Culture shock**—a disorientation that causes perpetual stress—is experienced by people who settle overseas for extended periods. The stress is caused by hundreds of jarring and disorienting incidents such as being unable to communicate, having trouble getting the telephone to work, being unable to read the street signs, and a myriad of other everyday matters that are no problem at home. Soon minor frustrations become catastrophic events, and one feels helpless and

Repatriation
Process of employee transition home from an international assignment

Culture shock
Perpetual stress experienced by people who settle overseas

Highlights in HRM 15.4

REPATRIATION CHECKLIST

For employees returning from an overseas assignment, some guidelines can help make their homecoming easier. Remember, planning for repatriation begins even before a person leaves to go overseas. Then there are things to take care of during their stint abroad, and finally, there are some important things to be considered when they come home.

Before They Go
▶ Make sure you have clearly identified a need for the international assignment. Don't send somebody abroad unnecessarily. Develop a clear set of objectives and expectations.
▶ Make sure that your selection procedures are valid. Select the employee and also look at the family situation.
▶ Provide (or fund) language and cultural training for the employee and the employee's family.
▶ Offer counselling and career assistance for the spouse.
▶ Establish career planning systems that reward international assignments.

While They Are Away
▶ Jointly establish a developmental plan that focuses on competency development.
▶ Tie performance objectives to the developmental plan.
▶ Identify mentors who can be a liaison and support person from home.
▶ Keep communications open so that the expatriate is aware of job openings and opportunities.
▶ Arrange for frequent visits back home (for the employee and the family). Make certain they do not lose touch with friends and relatives.

When They Come Back Home
▶ Throw a "welcome home" party.
▶ Offer counselling to ease the transition.
▶ Arrange conferences and presentations to make certain that knowledge and skills acquired away from home are identified and disseminated.
▶ Get feedback from the employee and the family about how well the organization handled the repatriation process.

Sources: Adapted from Bennet & Associates, Price Waterhouse, and Charlene Marmer Solomon, "Repatriation Planning Checklist," *Personnel Journal* 14, no. 1 (January 1995): 32; Charlene Marmer Solomon, "Global HR: Repatriation Planning," *Workforce* 2001, special supplement: 22–23.

drained, emotionally and physically. Highlights in HRM 15.5 shows some of the primary sources of stress at different stages of an international assignment, as well as some of the responses that individuals and organizations use to cope with these types of stress.

In Chapter 7, we observed that more and more employers are assisting two-career couples in finding suitable employment in the same location. To accommodate dual-career partnerships, some employers are providing informal help finding jobs for the

Highlights in HRM 15.5

STRESSOR AND COPING RESPONSES IN THE DEVELOPMENTAL STAGES OF EXPATRIATE EXECUTIVES

Stage	Primary Stressors	Executive Coping Response	Employer Coping Response
Expatriate selection	Cross-cultural unreadiness.	Engage in self-evaluation.	Encourage expatriate's self- and family evaluation. Perform an assessment of potential and interests.
Assignment acceptance	Unrealistic evaluation of stressors to come. Hurried time frame.	Think of assignment as a growth opportunity rather than an instrument to vertical promotion.	Do not make hard-to-keep promises. Clarify expectations.
Pre- and post-arrival training	Ignorance of cultural differences.	Do not make unwarranted assumptions of cultural rules.	Provide pre-, during, and post-assignment training. Encourage support-seeking behaviour.
Arrival	Cultural shock. Stressor re-evaluation. Feelings of lack of fit and differential treatment.	Do not construe identification with the host and parent cultures as mutually exclusive. Seek social support.	Provide post-arrival training. Facilitate integration in expatriate network.
Novice	Cutural blunders or inadequacy of coping responses. Ambiguity owing to inability to decipher meaning of situations.	Observe and study functional value of coping responses among locals. Do not simply replicate responses that worked at home.	Provide follow-up training. Seek advice from locals and expatriate network.
Transitional	Rejection of host or parent culture.	Form and maintain attachments with both cultures.	Promote culturally sensitive policies at host country. Provide Internet access to family and friends at home. Maintain constant communication and periodic visits to parent organization.

Mastery	Frustration with inability to perform boundary spanning role. Bothered by living with a cultural paradox.	Internalize and enjoy identification with both cultures and walking between two cultures.	Reinforce rather than punish dual identification by defining common goals.
Repatriation	Disappointment with unfulfilled expectations. Sense of isolation. Loss of autonomy.	Realistically re-evaluate assignment as a personal and professional growth opportunity.	Arrange pre-repatriation briefings and interviews. Schedule post-repatriation support meetings.

Source: J. Sachez, P. Spector, and C. Cooper, "Adapting to a Boundaryless World: A Developmental Expatriate Model," *Academy of Management Executive* 14, no. 2 (May 2000): 96–106.

spouses of international transferees. However, other companies are establishing more formal programs to assist expatriate couples. These include career- and life-planning counselling, continuing education, intercompany networks to identify job openings in other companies, and job-hunting/fact-finding trips. In some cases, a company may even create a job for the spouse—though this is not widely practised. The available evidence suggests that, while a spouse's career may create some problems initially, in the long run it actually may help ease an expatriate's adjustment process.[36]

Training Methods

A host of training methods are available to prepare an individual for an international assignment. Unfortunately, the overwhelming majority of companies provide only superficial preparation for their employees. Lack of training is one of the principal causes of failure among employees working internationally.

In many cases, the employee and his or her family can learn much about the host country through books, lectures, and videotapes about the culture, geography, social and political history, climate, food, and so on. The content is factual and the knowledge gained will at least help the participants to have a better understanding of their assignments. Such minimal exposure, however, does not fully prepare one for a foreign assignment. Training methods such as sensitivity training, which focuses on learning at the affective level, may well be a powerful technique in the reduction of ethnic prejudices. The Peace Corps, for example, uses sensitivity training supplemented by field experiences. Field experiences may sometimes be obtained in a nearby "microculture" where similarities exist.

Companies often send employees on temporary assignments—lasting, say, a few months—to encourage shared learning. These temporary assignments are probably too brief for completely absorbing the nuances of a culture; however, companies such as AMP and Texas Instruments use them to help employees learn about new ideas and technologies in other regions.[37]

In other instances employees are transferred for a much longer period of time. For example, Fuji-Xerox sent fifteen of its most experienced engineers from Tokyo to a Xerox facility in New York. Over a five-year period, these engineers worked with a team of American engineers to develop the "world" copier. By working together on an extended basis, the U.S. and Japanese employees learned from each other both the technical and the cultural requirements for a continued joint venture.[38]

Developing Local Resources

Apart from developing talent for overseas assignments, most companies have found that good training programs also help them attract needed employees from the host countries. In less-developed countries especially, individuals are quite eager to receive the training they need to improve their work skills. Oftentimes, however, a company's human capital investment does not pay off. It is very common, for example, for locally owned firms to hire away workers who have been trained by foreign-owned organizations.

Apprenticeship Training

A major source of trained labour in European nations is apprenticeship training programs (described in Chapter 6). On the whole, apprenticeship training in Europe is superior to that in Canada. In Europe, a dual-track system of education directs a large number of youths into vocational training. The German system of apprenticeship training, one of the best in Europe, provides training for office and shop jobs under a three-way responsibility contract between the apprentice, his or her parents, and the organization. At the conclusion of their training, apprentices can work for any employer but generally receive seniority credit with the training firm if they remain in it.

Management Development

One of the greatest contributions that North America has made to work organizations is in improving the competence of managers. Foreign nationals have generally welcomed the type of training they have received through management development programs offered by North American organizations. Increasingly, organizations such as the World Bank, Mobil, and Petroleos de Venezuela have entered into partnerships with university executive education programs to customize training experiences to the specific needs of expatriate managers and foreign nationals.

PERFORMANCE APPRAISAL

As we noted earlier, individuals frequently accept international assignments because they know that they can acquire skills and experiences that will make them more valuable to their companies. Unfortunately, one of the biggest problems with managing these individuals is that it is very difficult to evaluate their performance. Even the notion of performance evaluation is indicative of a U.S. management style that focuses on the individual, which can cause problems in Asian countries such as China,

Japan, and Korea and eastern European countries such as Hungary and the Czech Republic. For these reasons, performance appraisal problems may be one of the biggest reasons why failure rates among expatriates are so high and why international assignments can actually derail an individual's career rather than enhance it.[39]

Who Should Appraise Performance?

In many cases, an individual working internationally has at least two allegiances: one to his or her home country (the office that made the assignment) and the other to the host country in which the employee is currently working. Superiors in each location frequently have different information about the employee's performance and may also have very different expectations about what constitutes good performance. For these reasons, the multirater (360-degree) appraisal discussed in Chapter 8 is gaining favour among global firms such as ABB, Bechtel, and Nordson.[40]

Home-Country Evaluations

Domestic managers are frequently unable to understand expatriate experiences, value them, or accurately measure their contribution to the organization. Geographical distances pose severe communication problems for expatriates and home-country managers. Instead of touching base regularly, there is a tendency for both expatriates and domestic managers to work on local issues rather than coordinate across time zones and national borders. Information technology has improved this situation, and it is far easier to communicate globally today than it was just a few years ago.[41] But even when expatriates contact their home-country offices, it is frequently not to converse with their superiors. More likely they talk with peers and others throughout the organization.

Video conferencing is one way for remote employees to stay in close contact with their home office.

© JON FEINGERSH/CORBIS/MAGMA

Host-Country Evaluations

Although local management may have the most accurate picture of an expatriate's performance—managers are in the best position to observe effective and ineffective behaviour—there are problems with using host-country evaluations. First, local cultures may influence one's perception of how well an individual is performing. As noted earlier in the chapter, participative decision making may be viewed either positively or negatively, depending on the culture. Such cultural biases may not have any bearing on an individual's true level of effectiveness. In addition, local management frequently does not have enough perspective on the entire organization to know how well an individual is truly contributing to the firm as a whole.

Given the pros and cons of home-country and host-country evaluations, most observers agree that performance evaluations should try to balance the two sources of appraisal information. Although host-country employees are in a good position to view day-to-day activities, in many cases the individual is still formally tied to the home office. Promotions, pay, and other administrative decisions are connected there, and as a consequence, the written evaluation is usually handled by the home-country manager. Nevertheless, the appraisal should be completed only after vital input has been gained from the host-country manager. As discussed in Chapter 8, multiple sources of appraisal information can be extremely valuable for providing independent points of view—especially if someone is working as part of a team. If there is much concern about cultural bias, it may be possible to have persons of the same nationality as the expatriate conduct the appraisal.

Adjusting Performance Criteria

As we discussed at the beginning of this chapter, an individual's success or failure is affected by a host of technical and personal factors. Many of these factors should be considered in developing a broader set of performance criteria.[42]

Augmenting Job Duties

Obviously the goals and responsibilities inherent in the job assignment are among the most important criteria used to evaluate an individual's performance. However, because of the difficulties in observing, documenting, and interpreting performance information in an international setting, superiors often resort to using "easy" criteria such as productivity, profits, and market share. These criteria may be valid—but they are still deficient if they do not capture the full range of an expatriate's responsibility. There are other, more subtle factors that should be considered as well. In many cases, an expatriate is an ambassador for the company, and a significant part of the job is cultivating relationships with citizens of the host country.

Individual Learning

Any foreign assignment involves learning. As one might guess, it is much easier to adjust to similar cultures than to dissimilar ones. A Canadian can usually travel to the United Kingdom or Australia and work with locals almost immediately. Send that same individual to Hungary or Malaysia, and the learning curve is more difficult. The expatriate's adjustment period may be even longer if the company has not yet established a good base of operations in the region. The first individuals transferred to a country have no one to show them the ropes or to explain local customs. Even relatively simple activities such as navigating the rapid-transit system can prove to be problematic. There are websites to which individuals or organizations can subscribe in order to obtain tools to survive the international assignment. As one experienced expat stated, "One of the standard rules of international etiquette is that it is the visitor who must adapt."[43]

Organizational Learning

It is worth noting that bottom-line measures of performance may not fully convey the level of learning gained from a foreign assignment. Yet learning may be among the very most important reasons for sending an individual overseas, particularly at early stages of internationalization and during joint ventures.[44] Even if superiors do acknowledge the level of learning, they frequently use it only as an excuse for less-than-desired performance, rather than treating it as a valuable outcome in itself. What they fail to recognize is that knowledge gained—if shared—can speed the adjustment process for others. However, if the learning is not shared, then each new employee to a region may have to go through the same cycle of adjustment.

Providing Feedback

Performance feedback in an international setting is clearly a two-way street. Although the home-country and host-country superiors may tell an expatriate how well he or she is doing, it is also important for expatriates to provide feedback regarding the support they are receiving, the obstacles they face, and the suggestions they have about the assignment. More than in most any other job, expatriates are in the very best position to evaluate their own performance.

In addition to ongoing feedback, an expatriate should have a debriefing interview immediately upon returning home from an international assignment. These repatriation interviews serve several purposes:

1. They help expatriates reestablish old ties with the home organization and may prove to be important for setting new career paths.
2. The interview can address technical issues related to the job assignment itself.
3. The interview may address general issues regarding the company's overseas commitments, such as how relationships between the home and host countries should be handled.
4. The interview can be very useful for documenting insights an individual has about the region. These insights can then be incorporated into training programs for future expatriates.

COMPENSATION

One of the most complex areas of international HRM is compensation. Different countries have different norms for employee compensation. Managers should consider carefully the motivational use of incentives and rewards in foreign countries. For North Americans, while nonfinancial incentives such as prestige, independence, and influence may be motivators, money is likely to be the driving force. Other cultures are more likely to emphasize respect, family, job security, a satisfying personal life, social acceptance, advancement, or power. Since there are many alternatives to money, the rule is to match the reward with the values of the culture. In individualistic cultures, such as Canada, pay plans often focus on individual performance and achievement. However, in collectively oriented cultures such as Japan and Taiwan, pay plans focus more on internal equity and personal needs.[45]

Figure 15.12 shows some of the primary forces shaping global pay strategies. In general, a guiding philosophy for designing pay systems might be "think globally and act locally." That is, executives should normally try to create a pay plan that supports the overall strategic intent of the organization but provides enough flexibility to customize particular policies and programs to meet the needs of employees in specific

Figure 15.12	Forces Driving Global Pay

Cultural Preferences

Importance of status

Role of individual vs. organization vs. government

Equality vs. disparity

Achievement vs. relationships

Economic Conditions

Size of economy

Types of industries, natural resources

Inflation, unemployment

Protectionism vs. open market

Personal Preferences

Attitudes toward risk

Quality of life vs. work

Short- vs. long-term

Competitiveness vs. solidarity

Social Restraints

Income tax rates, social costs

Laws and regulations

Collective bargaining, worker participation

Skills, education of workforce

Source: Steven Gross and Per Wingerup, "Global Pay? Maybe Not Yet!" *Compensation and Benefits Review* 31, no. 4 (July/August 1999): 25–34.

locations. After a brief discussion of compensation practices for host-country employees and managers, we will focus on the problems of compensating expatriates.

Compensation of Host-Country Employees

As shown in Figure 15.13, hourly wages vary dramatically from country to country. Labour costs are one of the biggest motivators for international expansion, but there are many managerial and administrative issues that must be addressed when an organization establishes operations overseas.

Host-country employees are generally paid on the basis of productivity, time spent on the job, or a combination of these factors. In industrialized countries, pay is generally by the hour; in developing countries, by the day. The piece-rate method is quite common. In some countries, including Japan, seniority is an important element in determining employees' pay rates. When companies commence operations in a foreign country, they usually set their wage rates at or slightly higher than the prevailing wage for local companies. Eventually, though, they are urged to conform to local practices to avoid "upsetting" local compensation practices.

Figure 15.13	Hourly Wages in Different Countries*

COUNTRY	$/HOUR
Germany	23.84
Norway	23.13
Switzerland	21.84
Belgium	21.04
United States	20.32
Japan	19.59
Sweden	18.35
Britain	16.14
France	15.88
Canada	15.64
Italy	13.76
Hong Kong	13.53
Israel	13.53
Australia	13.15
Spain	10.88
Korea	8.09
Taiwan	5.70
Brazil	3.02
Mexico	2.30
Sri Lanka	0.48

*Hourly compensation costs in U.S. dollars for production workers in manufacturing.
Source: U.S. Department of Labor.

Employee benefits in other countries are frequently higher than those in North America. In France, for example, benefits are about 70 percent of wages and in Italy 92 percent, compared with around 30 percent in Canada. Whereas in North America, most benefits are awarded to employees by employers, in other industrialized countries most of them are legislated or ordered by governments. Some of these plans are changing. Defined contribution plans are on the rise, sex equality is becoming important, and stock ownership is being tried.[46]

In Italy, Japan, and some other countries, it is customary to add semiannual or annual lump-sum payments equal to one or two months' pay. These payments are not considered profit sharing but an integral part of the basic pay package. Profit sharing is legally required for certain categories of industry in Mexico, Peru, Pakistan, India, and Egypt among the developing countries and in France among the industrialized countries. Compensation patterns in eastern Europe are also in flux as these countries make the adjustment to more-capitalistic systems.

Compensation of Host-Country Managers

In the past, remuneration of host-country managers has been ruled by local salary levels. However, increased competition among different companies with subsidiaries in the same country has led to a gradual upgrading of host-country managers' salaries. Overall, international firms are moving toward a narrowing of the salary gap between the host-country manager and the expatriate. Unilever, for example, used to leave the compensation arrangements largely to the boss of a region or a big country. Now brand managers in different countries increasingly compare notes, so they see potential discrepancies based on market differences and expatriate assignments. So the company moved from a narrow grading structure to five global work levels. Managers' pay is still based on the country they work in, but there will be regional convergence so that in time there will be a pan-European rate.[47]

Compensation of Expatriate Managers

Compensation plans for expatriate managers must be competitive, cost-effective, motivating, fair, easy to understand, consistent with international financial management, easy to administer, and simple to communicate. To be effective, an international compensation program must

1. Provide an incentive to leave Canada
2. Allow for maintaining a North American standard of living
3. Facilitate reentry into Canada
4. Provide for the education of children
5. Allow for maintaining relationships with family, friends, and business associates[48]

Balance-sheet approach
Compensation system designed to match the purchasing power in a person's home country

Expatriate compensation programs used by more than 90 percent of North American-based international organizations rest on the **balance-sheet approach**, a system designed to equalize the purchasing power of employees at comparable positions living overseas and in the home country and to provide incentives to offset qualitative differences between assignment locations.[49] The balance-sheet approach generally is made up of the following steps:

Step 1: Calculate base pay. Begin with the home-based gross income, including bonuses. Deduct taxes and pension contributions.

Step 2: Figure cost-of-living allowance (COLA). Add a cost-of-living allowance to the base pay. Typically, companies don't subtract when the international assignment has a lower cost of living. Instead, they allow the expatriate to benefit from the negative differential. Often a housing allowance is added in here as well.

Step 3: Add incentive premiums. General mobility premiums and hardship premiums compensate expatriates for separation from family, friends, and domestic support systems, usually 15 percent of base salary.

Step 4: Add assistance programs. These additions are often used to cover added costs such as moving and storage, automobile, and education expenses.

The differentials element is intended to correct for the higher costs of overseas goods and services so that in relation to their domestic peers expatriates neither gain purchasing power nor lose it. It involves a myriad of calculations to arrive at a total differential figure, but in general, the cost typically runs between three and five times the home-country salary. Fortunately, employers do not have to do extensive research to find comparative data. They typically rely on data published quarterly by the U.S. Department of State for use in establishing allowances to compensate employees for costs and hardships related to assignments abroad.[50]

INTERNATIONAL ORGANIZATIONS AND LABOUR RELATIONS

objective

Labour relations in countries outside Canada differ significantly from those in Canada. Differences exist not only in the collective bargaining process but also in the political and legal conditions. To get a basic idea about labour-management relations in an international setting, we will look at four primary areas: (1) the role of unions in different countries, (2) collective bargaining in other countries, (3) international labour organizations, and (4) the extent of labour participation in management.

The Role of Unions

The role of unions varies from country to country and depends on many factors, such as the level of per capita labour income, mobility between management and labour, homogeneity of labour (racial, religious, social class), and level of employment. These and other factors determine whether the union will have the strength it needs to represent labour effectively. In countries with relatively high unemployment, low pay levels, and no union funds for welfare, the union is driven into alliance with other organizations: political party, church, or government. This is in marked contrast to Canada, where the union selected by the majority of employees bargains only with the employer, not with other institutions.

Even in the major industrial countries one finds that national differences are great with respect to (1) the level at which bargaining takes place (national, industry, or workplace), (2) the degree of centralization of union-management relations, (3) the scope of bargaining, (4) the degree to which government intervenes, and (5) the degree of unionization.

Labour relations in Europe differ from those in North America in certain significant characteristics:

1. In Europe, organizations typically negotiate the agreement with the union at the national level through the employer association representing their particular industry, even when there may be local within-company negotiations as well. This agreement establishes certain minimum conditions of employment, which are frequently augmented through negotiations with the union at the company level.

2. Unions in many European countries have more political power than those in Canada, with the result that when employers deal with the union they are, in effect, dealing indirectly with the government. Unions are often allied with a particular political party, although in some countries these alliances are more complex, with unions having predominant but not sole representation with one party.

3. There is a greater tendency in Europe for salaried employees, including those at the management level, to be unionized, quite often in a union of their own.[51]

Like North America, European countries are facing the reality of a developing global economy. And particularly in Germany and the United Kingdom, unions have been losing some of their power. Ironically, the power of the unions to gain high wages and enforce rigid labour rules has been blamed for hurting the competitiveness of European companies. As the power of unions declines a bit, it has been increasingly evident in Europe that workers are less inclined to make constant demands for higher wages. The trend has been to demand compensation in other ways—through benefits or through greater participation in company decision making.[52] Various approaches to participation will be discussed later.

Collective Bargaining in Other Countries

We saw in Chapter 14 how the collective bargaining process is typically carried out in companies operating in Canada. When we look at other countries, we find that the whole process can vary widely, especially with regard to the role that government plays. In the United Kingdom and France, for example, government intervenes in all aspects of collective bargaining. Government involvement is only natural where parts of industry are nationalized. Also, in countries where there is heavy nationalization there is more likely to be acceptance of government involvement, even in the non-nationalized companies. At Renault, the French government-owned automobile manufacturer, unions make use of political pressures in their bargaining with managers, who are essentially government employees. The resulting terms of agreement then set the standards for other firms. In developing countries it is common for the government to have representatives present during bargaining sessions to make sure that unions with relatively uneducated leaders are not disadvantaged in bargaining with skilled management representatives.

International Labour Organizations

The fact that international corporations can choose the countries in which they wish to establish subsidiaries generally results in the selection of those countries that have the most to offer. Certainly inexpensive labour is a benefit that most strategists consider. By coordinating their resources, including human resources, and their production facilities, companies operate from a position of strength. International unions, such as the United Auto Workers, have found it difficult to achieve a level of influence anywhere near that found within a particular industrial nation. Those that have been successful operate in countries that are similar, such as the United States and Canada.

The most active of the international union organizations has been the International Confederation of Free Trade Unions (ICFTU), which has its headquarters in Brussels. Cooperating with the ICFTU are some twenty international trade secretariats (ITSs), which are really international federations of national trade unions operating in the same or related industries. The significance of the ITSs from the point of view of management lies in the fact that behind local unions may be the expertise and resources of an ITS. Another active and influential organization is the International Labor Organization (ILO), a specialized agency of the United Nations. It does considerable research on an international basis and endorses standards for various working conditions, referred to as the International Labor Code. At various times and places this code may be quoted to management as international labour standards to which employers are expected to conform.[53]

Labour Participation in Management

In many European countries, provisions for employee representation are established by law. An employer may be legally required to provide for employee representation on safety and hygiene committees, worker councils, or even on boards of directors. While their responsibilities vary from country to country, worker councils basically provide a communication channel between employers and workers. The legal codes that set forth the functions of worker councils in France are very detailed. Councils are generally concerned with grievances, problems of individual employees, internal regulations, and matters affecting employee welfare.

A higher form of worker participation in management is found in Germany, where representation of labour on the board of directors of a company is required by law. This arrangement is known as **codetermination** and often by its German word, *Mitbestimmung*. While sometimes puzzling to outsiders, the system is fairly simple: Company shareholders and employees are required to be represented in equal numbers on the supervisory boards of all corporations with more than 2000 employees. Power is generally left with the shareholders, and shareholders are generally assured the chairmanship. Other European countries and Japan either have or are considering minority board participation.[54]

Each of these differences makes managing human resources in an international context more challenging. But the crux of the issue in designing HR systems is not choosing one approach that will meet all the demands of international business.

Codetermination
Representation of labour on the board of directors of a company

Instead, organizations facing global competition must balance several approaches and make their policies flexible enough to accommodate differences across national borders. Throughout this book we have noted that different situations call for different approaches to managing people, and nowhere is this point more clearly evident than in international HRM.

SUMMARY

There are four basic ways to organize for global competition: (1) The international corporation is essentially a domestic firm that has leveraged its existing capabilities to penetrate overseas markets; (2) the multinational corporation has fully autonomous units operating in many countries in order to address local issues; (3) the global corporation has a worldview but controls all international operations from its home office; and (4) the transnational corporation uses a network structure to balance global and local concerns.

International HRM places greater emphasis on a number of responsibilities and functions such as relocation, orientation, and translation services to help employees adapt to a new and different environment outside their own country.

Because of the special demands made on managers in international assignments, many factors must be considered in their selection and development. Though hiring host-country nationals or third-country nationals automatically avoids many potential problems, expatriate managers are preferable in some circumstances. The selection of the latter requires careful evaluation of the personal characteristics of the candidate and his or her spouse.

Once an individual is selected, an intensive training and development program is essential to qualify that person for the assignment. Wherever possible, development should extend beyond information and orientation training to include sensitivity training and field experiences that will enable the manager to understand cultural differences better. Those in charge of the international program should provide the help needed to protect managers from career development risks, reentry problems, and culture shock.

Although home-country managers frequently have formal responsibility for individuals on foreign assignment, they may not be able to fully understand expatriate experiences because geographical distances pose severe communication problems. Host-country managers may be in the best position to observe day-to-day performance but may be biased by cultural factors and may not have a view of the organization as a whole. To balance the pros and cons of home-country and host-country evaluations, performance evaluations should combine the two sources of appraisal information.

Compensation systems should support the overall strategic intent of the organization but be customized for local conditions. For expatriates, in particular, compensation plans must provide an incentive to leave Canada; enable maintenance of an equivalent standard of living; facilitate repatriation; provide for the education of children; and make it possible to maintain relationships with family, friends, and business associates.

In many European countries—Germany, for one—employee representation is established by law. Organizations typically negotiate the agreement with the union at a national level, frequently with government intervention. Since European unions have been in existence longer than their North American counterparts, they have more legitimacy and much more political power. In Europe, it is more likely for salaried employees and managers to be unionized.

KEY TERMS

augmented skills 640
balance-sheet approach 660
codetermination 663
core skills 640
cultural environment 630
culture shock 650
expatriates, or home-country
  nationals 634

failure rate 640
global corporation 627
global manager 644
guest workers 638
host country 630
host-country nationals 634
international corporation 627

multinational corporation (MNC)
  627
repatriation 650
third-country nationals 634
transnational corporation 627
transnational teams 643
work permit, or work certificate
  638

DISCUSSION QUESTIONS

1. What do you think are the major HR issues that must be addressed as an organization moves from an international form to a multinational, to a global, and to a transnational form?

2. There has always been a high level of foreign investment in Canada. What effect are joint ventures, such as General Motors–Toyota, likely to have on HRM in Canada?

3. If you were starting now to plan for a career in international HRM, what steps would you take to prepare yourself?

4. Describe the effects that different components of the cultural environment can have on HRM in an international firm.

5. Pizza Hut is opening new restaurants in Europe every day, it seems. If you were in charge, would you use expatriate managers or host-country nationals in staffing the new facilities? Explain your thinking.

6. In what ways are North American managers likely to experience difficulties in their relationships with employees in foreign operations? How can these difficulties be minimized?

7. This chapter places considerable emphasis on the role of the spouse in the success of an overseas manager. What steps should management take to increase the likelihood of a successful experience for all parties involved?

8. Talk with a foreign student on your campus; ask about his or her experience with culture shock on first arriving in Canada. What did you learn from your discussion?

9. If learning (individual and organizational) is an important outcome of an overseas assignment, how can this be worked into a performance appraisal system? How would a manager assess individual and organizational learning?

10. If the cost of living is lower in a foreign country than in North America, should expatriates be paid less than they would be at home? Explain your position.

11. What are the major differences between labour-management relations in Europe and those in Canada?

12. Do you believe that codetermination will ever become popular in Canada? Explain your position.

Developing Managerial Skills

A CANADIAN (EXPATRIATE) IN PARIS

There is often a great deal of work involved in setting up expatriate assignments. The administrative requirements can be far ranging and extend beyond the employee to also include family issues. Suppose you were faced with the following scenario. What would be the most pressing considerations that you would need to address?

The Scenario

You are the head of HR for Sarip International, a consulting firm specializing in hotel and restaurant management. Your firm is opening an office in Paris, France, and Jim Verioti, director of sales and marketing, has been asked to assume responsibilities for the expansion. Jim understands that the expatriate assignment will last two to three years, and although he has travelled to Europe for work on several occasions, this is his first long-term assignment overseas.

He has a lot of questions about what he can expect and also some personal constraints. Jim and his wife, Betty, have just moved into their new home (their mortgage payment is around $1500 per month). In addition, Betty is an elementary school teacher and doesn't really know how the move will affect her job security. Their three children, Veronica (fourteen), Reggie (twelve), and Archie (ten), are of an age at which school considerations are very important. A friend told them about the American School in Paris, and this is a consideration. None of the Veriotis speak French.

Assignment

Working in teams of four to six individuals, put together the package that would allow Jim to move his family to Paris while still maintaining his present lifestyle (his current annual salary is $140 000 plus incentives). Address at least the following issues:

1. Visas and permits
2. Relocation allowance and housing
3. Language and culture training
4. Spousal employment concerns
5. Health, medical, and insurance issues
6. Compensation and incentives
7. Education for the children

The following websites may be helpful to you, but other resources may prove valuable as well.

- Canadian Embassy in Paris (www.dfait-maeci.gc.ca/canadaeurope/france/)
- French Embassy in Canada (www.ambafrance-ca.org)
- Expatica.com (www.expatica.com/france.asp)
- Canadians in Paris (http://groupsmsn.com/CanadiansinParis)
- Life in France (www.lifeinfrance.free.fr/)

▶ The Paris France Guide (www.parisfranceguide.com/)
▶ Easy Expat (www.easyexpat.com/en/pa/index_city.htm)
▶ Centers for Disease Control (www.cdc.gov/travel/)
▶ American School in Paris (www.asparis.org/about/)
▶ Medibroker (insurance) (www.medibroker.com/homecom.html?id=1js10)
▶ Travlang (currency calculator) (www.travlang.com/money/)

Case Study 1

International HRM at Molex, Inc.

The cover of Molex Inc.'s 1998 annual report boasts: "Everywhere, Anywhere." It's a declaration that speaks volumes about this sixty-year-old manufacturer of electronic connectors. Molex is a truly global company—the $1.6-billion firm operates forty-nine manufacturing facilities in twenty-one countries and employs 13 000 people worldwide. The company has customers in more than fifty countries, and nearly 70 percent of its sales come from outside the United States.

The company has four corporate goals: (1) provide good customer service, (2) fully develop its human resources, (3) build a truly global company, and (4) meet or exceed financial goals. Malou Roth, head of training and development, puts it this way: "The way I've always looked at Molex is, there are only four corporate goals and two of them have to do with people." Every employee has an HR-related element tied to his or her performance goals.

Molex tries to make the goals come alive for its workforce, and its human resources team has a big hand in making that happen. "What I tried to do when I came to Molex fifteen years ago was take the basic HR programs and practices that I knew were good ones and make those things standards or consistent practices at every entity in every country," says Roth. For example, as Molex grew rapidly during the 1980s, Roth established a standardized employee manual with policies and practices for new employee orientation, salary administration with a consistent grading system, written job descriptions, written promotion and grievance procedures, and performance appraisals. Roth made certain that all the materials were translated into the languages of the countries in which Molex had operations. Local managers were free to add to the programs and be creative with them, but they had to implement minimum HR standards.

According to Kathi Regas, corporate VP of HR for Molex, "Our global HR practices in training and communications help us build on the strong foundation we have—a common way of managing our employees, strengthening their skills, and improving service to our customers both locally and globally." Yet each local unit has unique needs, so the philosophy has been to hire experienced HR professionals from other companies in the same country in which they have operations. Roth figures you need to hire people who know the language, have credibility, know the law, and know how to recruit. "You can't transfer someone in to do that," says Roth. There are eighty HR staff members in seventeen countries where Molex operates.

Part of the Molex philosophy about being global is to have many people moving around the company's operations worldwide to learn from each other. For a medium-size company, having so much worldwide employee movement is unusual—and costly. "But we feel it's really worthwhile because there's nothing like living and working with people outside your home country to make you understand you're really in something bigger than Molex Japan or Molex Germany," explains Roth. Adds Regas: "Our investment in expatriates is critical to building the strong foundation we have of sharing our expertise with each other. It's important for us to respect individual cultures while maintaining Molex's unique global culture."

As one way to maintain the culture, every Molex entity worldwide has to conduct bimonthly communications meetings. They're top-down communications blitzes that bring people up to speed on what's going on in that particular Molex unit. Usually the HR manager kicks off the meeting, and then the general manager or sales manager speaks. Molex also does annual communication meetings, which include the company's chairman, the COO, the executive vice-president, the corporate VP of HR, and the VP of HR, in addition to other senior executives of the local entity and the region. They spend a day at each location touring the factory, looking at new equipment and facilities, and meeting with employees. "Our annual communications meetings ensure that our employees know they're a part of something much bigger than their local entities," says Regas. "They know our history, our performance, and our plans for the future. This, combined with frequent contact among our employees from entities around the world and common practices, helps maintain our culture and strengthen a global team of employees."

These methods have helped Molex find ways for individuals with varying backgrounds and perspectives to work together. The culture serves as a corporate "glue" that holds the organization effectively together, while also maximizing the energy of individuals throughout the company's global operations.

Source: Condensed from "Molex Makes Global HR Look Easy," by Jennifer Laabs, March 1999. ACC Communications/*Workforce*, Costa Mesa, CA. www.workforce.com.

QUESTIONS

1. What are the chief human resources challenges that Molex faces as a global organization?
2. What value is gained from having a standardized HR policy manual for all locations?
3. What value is gained from allowing managers to customize the policies for their local countries?
4. Why is there so much emphasis on company culture and communications in this organization?

Case Study 2

Cultural Conundrum

Anna has enjoyed great success in the Toronto office of a global company. When she was offered an assignment in Tokyo, she approached the job with the full confidence of her employer that she could oversee the reorganization of the subsidiary. By asking her extensive network of colleagues about Japan, she learned a few tips. For example, she learned that when a Japanese businessman hands you his business card, it is proper to read the card before taking it, and to never throw it on the desk. Even with tips like these, however, Anna's assignment was heading toward failure.

After six months, she was very discouraged and when she returned home for the holidays, she reported the following problems:

▶ Although everyone spoke English, there were communication problems.
▶ Everything took too long to complete, with deadlines missed and employees not following schedules.
▶ Although she asked her employees for feedback and information, and received promises that these would be forthcoming, no data arrived.

The company's response was to give her cross-cultural training, in which Anna learned the following:

▶ In Japanese culture, group identity supersedes individual identity. Loyalty is to the group, and criticisms of performance are taboo. Group meetings are the norm, and one-on-one meetings designed to facilitate feedback make employees very uncomfortable.
▶ Japanese culture is based on hierarchy and is organized to recognize the power differentials between superiors and subordinates. Japanese workers do not expect to have input into decisions; their only expectation is to be told what to do. If forced to participate in decision making, the typical Japanese will avoid uncertainty by accumulating every possible item of information to support the decision.
▶ Japan is a masculine society and women are employed in low-status positions. Anna's credibility as a decision maker would be questioned, and male employees would be uncomfortable working for her.

The communication problems only compounded the difficulty of the situation. Yes, the employees spoke English. But there were cultural differences. To a direct request to meet a deadline that they perceived as impossible, employees would save face (for themselves and the person making the request) by saying that they would do their best. Saying no is not part of Japanese culture.

Anna made the mistake of transferring her management style, which was successful in Toronto, to Tokyo, without understanding the cultural differences.

Source: Adapted from Z. Fedder, "Same Language, Different Meanings," *Canadian HR Reporter* 13, no. 11 (June 5, 2000): 9, 13; S. McKay, "Women Going Global," *Financial Post Magazine* December 1998: 38–54.

QUESTIONS

1. Exactly what preparation should Anna's company have given her before she started her assignment?

2. In general, what should a candidate for an international assignment do to prepare for a job, in the absence of company orientation and training?

3. Many believe that women on international assignments proved to be very effective, because they are both task oriented (a North American cultural imperative) and relationship oriented (an important attribute in Asian and other cultures). Why did these two sets of skills not help Anna?

CAREER COUNSEL

Take the culture quiz on the *Managing Human Resources* website (www.belcourt4e.nelson.com) to assess your sensitivity to other cultures.

NOTES AND REFERENCES

1. Peter Dowling, Denice E. Welch, and Randall S. Schuler, *International Human Resource Management: Managing People in a Multinational Context*, 3rd ed. (Cincinnati, OH: South-Western, 1999); Nancy J. Adler, *International Dimensions of Organizational Behavior* (Cincinnati, OH: South-Western, 1997); J. Michael Geringer, Colette Frayne, and John Milliman, "In Search of 'Best Practices' in International Human Resource Management: Research Design and Methodology," *Human Resource Management* 41, no. 1 (Spring 2002): 5–30.

2. Christopher A. Bartlett and Sumantra Ghoshal, *Managing across Borders: The Transnational Solution* (Boston: Harvard Business School Press, 1998).

3. Scott A. Snell, Charles C. Snow, Sue Canney Davison, and Donald C. Hambrick, "Designing and Supporting Transnational Teams: The Human Resource Agenda," *Human Resource Management* 37, no. 2: 147–58. See also Charles C. Snow, Scott A. Snell, Sue Canney Davison, and Donald C. Hambrick, "Use Transnational Teams to Globalize Your Company," *Organizational Dynamics*, Spring 1996, 50–67; Abagail McWilliams, David Van Fleet, and Patrick Wright, "Strategic Management of Human Resources for Global Competitive Advantage," *Journal of Business Strategies* 18, no. 1 (Spring 2001): 1–24.

4. Cristina Lindblad, "The Global 1000: The World's Most Valuable Companies," *Business Week* no. 3791 (July 15, 2002): 58–80.

5. M. F. Wolff, "Innovation and Competitiveness among EU Goals for Knowledge Economy," *Research Technology Management* 44, no. 6 (November/December 2001): 2–6; Tony Emerson, "The Great Walls: The United States and Europe Are Leading the Race to Carve Up the Trading World," *Newsweek* (April 23, 2001): 40. For more information about the European Union online, see the Europa website at http://europa.eu.int/.

6. Tom Bagsarian, "NAFTA at 5: A Boon for Customers," *Iron Age New Steel* 15, no. 10 (September 1999): 18–22; "The Real NAFTA Winner," *Business Week*, September 27, 1999, 34; William Thorbecke and Christian Eigen-Zucchi, "Did NAFTA Cause a 'Giant Sucking Sound'?" *Journal of Labor Research* 23, no. 4 (Fall 2002): 647–58.

7. Jeremy Kahn, "China's Tough Markets," *Fortune*, October 11, 1999: 282; "Motorola to Increase Operations in China," *The New York Times*, November 8, 2001: C4; Sadanand Dhume, "Just Quit It," *Far Eastern Economic Review* 165, no. 36 (September 12, 2002): 46–50; Philip Knight, "Global Manufacturing: The Nike Story Is Just Good Business," *Vital Speeches of the Day* 64, no. 20 (August 1, 1998): 637–40.

8. Julia Christensen Hughes, "HRM and Universalism: Is There One Best Way?" *International Journal of Contemporary Hospitality Management* 14, no. 5 (2002): 221–28; "What's Keeping HR from Going Global?" *HRFocus* 77, no. 8 (August 2000): 8; "Culture: A Key Ingredient for International HR Success," *HRFocus* 78, no. 7 (July 2001): 1–3.

9. Interested readers can access this journal online at http://www.tandf.co.uk/journals/online/0958-5192.html.

10. Maali H. Ashamalla, "International Human Resource Management Practices: The Challenge of Expatriation," *Competitiveness Review* 8, no. 2 (1998): 54–65; Zhong-Ming Wang, "Current Models and Innovative Strategies in Management Education in China," *Education & Training* 41, no. 6 (1999): 312–18.

11. Readers interested in codes of conduct and other ethical issues pertaining to international business might read the following: Janice M. Beyer and David Nino, "Ethics and Cultures in International Business," *Journal of Management Inquiry* 8, no. 3 (September 1999): 287–97; Ronald Berenbeim, "The Divergence of a Global Economy: One Company, One Market, One Code, One World," *Vital Speeches of the Day* 65, no. 22 (September 1, 1999): 696–98; Larry R. Smeltzer and Marianne M. Jennings, "Why an International Code of Business Ethics Would Be Good for Business," *Journal of Business Ethics* 17, no. 1 (January 1998): 57–66; Bill Roberts, "Going Global," *HRMagazine* 45, no. 8 (August 2000): 123–28.

12. Carla Joinson, "No Returns," *HRMagazine* 47, no. 11 (November 2002): 70–77; Frank Jossi, "Successful Handoff," *HRMagazine* 47, no. 10 (October 2002): 48–52; Steve Bates, "Study Discovers Patterns in Global Executive Mobility," *HRMagazine* 47, no. 10 (October 2002): 14; Morgan McCall and George Hollenbeck, "Global Fatalities: When International Executives Derail," *Ivey Business Journal* 66, no. 5 (May/June 2002): 74–78.

13. David Lipschultz, "Bosses from Abroad," *Chief Executive* 174 (January 2002): 18–21; Jennifer Laabs, "Molex Makes Global HR Look Easy," *Workforce* 78, no. 3 (March 1999): 42–46.

14. Readers interested in codes of conduct and other ethical issues pertaining to international business might read Nadar Asgary and Mark Mitschow, "Toward a Model for International Business Ethics," *Journal of Business Ethics* 36, no. 3 (March 2002): 238–46; Diana Winstanley and Jean Woodall, "The Adolescence of Ethics in Human Resource Management," *Human Resource Management Journal* 10, no. 4 (2000): 45; J. Brooke Hamilton and Stephen Knouse, "Multinational Enterprise Decision Principles for Dealing with Cross-Cultural Ethical Conflicts," *Journal of Business Ethics* 31, no. 1 (May 2001): 77–94; Michael Maynard, "Policing Transnational Commerce: Global Awareness in the Margins of Morality," *Journal of Business Ethics* 30, no. 1 (March 2001): 17–27.

15. Valerie Frazee, "Expert Help for Dual-Career Spouses," *Workforce* 4, no. 2 (March 1999): 18–20; "On the Border," *Government Executive* 31, no. 2 (February 1999): 101–104.

16. Joel Millman, "U.S. HMOs Cross the Mexican Border—California Allows Health Coverage for Guest Workers," *The Wall Street Journal*, June 27, 2000: A21; Evan Perez, "Florida Growers Push for Bill to Ease Worker Shortage," *The Wall Street Journal*, October 4, 2000: F3.

17. John P. Harrison and Alfons Westgeest, "Developing a Globally Savvy Staff," *Association Management* 51, no. 2 (February 1999): 58–64; Ingemar Torbiorn, "Staffing for International Operations," *Human Resource Management Journal* 7, no. 3 (1997): 42–52; Andrea Poe, "Selection Savvy," *HRMagazine* 47, no. 4 (April 2002): 77–83.

18. Allan Halcrow, "Expats: The Squandered Resource," *Workforce* 78, no. 4 (April 1999): 42–48; Valerie Frazee, "Selecting Global Assignees," *Workforce* 3, no. 4 (July 1998): 28–30; Nancy Wong, "Mark Your Calendar! Important Tasks for International HR," *Workforce* 79, no. 4 (April 2000): 72–74; Robert O'Connor, "Plug the Expat Knowledge Drain," *HRMagazine* 47, no. 10 (October 2002): 101–107.

19. Halcrow, "Expats"; "Expat Assignments: Key Is Preparedness," *HRFocus* 75, no. 9 (September 1998): 2; McCall and Hollenbeck, "Global Fatalities: When International Executives Derail"; Poe, "Selection Savvy"; Juan Sanchez, Paul Spector, and Cary Cooper, "Adapting to a Boundaryless World: A Developmental Expatriate Model," *Academy of Management Executive* 14, no. 2 (May 2000): 96–106.

20. Carl Quintanilla, "The Number One Reason Overseas Assignments Fail: The Spouse Hates It," *The Wall Street Journal*, January 7, 1997: A1; Riki Takeuchi, Seokhwa Yun, and Paul Tesluk, "An Examination of Crossover and Spillover Effects of Spousal and Expatriate Cross-Cultural Adjustment on Expatriate Outcomes," *Journal of Applied Psychology* 87, no. 4 (August 2002): 655–66; Poe, "Selection Savvy"; Talya Bauer and Sully Taylor, "When Managing Expatriate Adjustment, Don't Forget the Spouse," *Academy of Management Executive* 15, no. 4 (November 2001): 135–37.

21. Michael Harvey and Danielle Wiese, "The Dual-Career Couple: Female Expatriates and Male Trailing Spouses," *Thunderbird International Business Review* 40, no. 4 (July/August 1998): 359–88; "Women Managers in Asia," *Training and Development* 50, no. 4 (April 1996): 37; Sully Taylor and Nancy Napier, "Working in Japan: Lessons from Women Expatriates," *Sloan Management Review* 37, no. 3 (Spring 1996): 76–84; Margaret Linehan and Hugh Scullion, "Selection, Training, and Development for Female International Executives," *Career Development International* 6, no. 6 (2001): 318–23; Margaret Linehan and James Walsh, "Recruiting and Developing Female Managers for International Assignments," *Journal of Management Development* 18,

no. 6 (1999): 521–30; Hal Lancaster, "To Get Shipped Abroad, Women Must Overcome Prejudice at Home," *The Wall Street Journal*, June 29, 1999: B1.

22. Snell et al., "Designing and Supporting Transnational Teams"; Debra Shapiro, Stacie Furst, Gretchen Spreitzer, and Mary Ann Von Glinow, "Transnational Teams in the Electronic Age: Are Team Identity and High Performance at Risk?" *Journal of Organizational Behavior* 23 (June 2002): 455–67.

23. "What Does It Take to Be a Global Manager?" *Quality* 37, no. 3 (March 1998): 34. See also Yehuda Baruch, "No Such Thing as a Global Manager," *Business Horizons* 45, no. 1 (January/February 2002): 36–42; William Rothwell, Robert Prescott, and Maria Taylor, "Transforming HR into a Global Powerhouse," *HRFocus* 76, no. 3 (March 1999): 7–8.

24. David Woodruff, "Career Journal: Distractions Make Global Manager a Difficult Role," *The Wall Street Journal*, November 21, 2000: B1; Linehan and Scullion, "Selection, Training, and Development for Female International Executives"; Linehan and Walsh, "Recruiting and Developing Female Managers for International Assignments."

25. Valerie Frazee, "Send Your Expats Prepared for Success," *Workforce* 4, no. 2 (March 1999): 6–8; Janet D. Lein and Nichole L. Sisco, "Language and Cross-Cultural Training for Expatriate Employees: A Comparison between the U.S. and Germany," *Journal of Language for International Business* 10, no. 2: 47–59; Lionel Laroche, John Bing, and Catherine Mercer Bing, "Beyond Translation," *Training & Development* 54, no. 12 (December 2000): 72–73; Sabrina Hicks, "Successful Global Training," *Training & Development* 54, no. 5 (May 2000): 95.

26. Managers who are interested in setting up a language-training program or who wish to evaluate commercially available language-training programs should consult the "Standard Guide for Use-Oriented Foreign Language Instruction." The seven-page guide is put out by the American Society for Testing and Materials (ASTM), (610) 832-9585, http://www.astm.org/.

27. Stephen Dolainski, "Language Training Improves Global Business at ARCO," *Workforce* 76, no. 2 (February 1997): 38; Kathryn Tyler, "Targeted Language Training Is Best Bargain," *HRMagazine* 43, no. 1 (January 1998): 61–64; Tom Lester, "Pulling Down the Language Barrier," *International Management* 49, no. 6 (July/August 1994): 42–44; Robert McGarvey and Scott Smith, "Speaking in Tongues," *Training* 31, no. 1 (January 1994): 113–16. See also Stephen H. Wildstrom, "Log On—and Learn a Language," *Business Week*, January 22, 1996: 22.

28. Neil J. Simon, "Competitive Intelligence Personnel: Requirements for the Multicultural Organization," *Competitive Intelligence Magazine* 2, no. 1 (January–March 1999): 43–44; Abbas J. Ali, Ahmed A. Azim, and Krish S. Krishnan, "Expatriates and Host Country Nationals: Managerial Values and Decision Styles," *Leadership and Organization Development Journal* 16, no. 6 (1995): 27–34; Dean B. McFarlan, Paul D. Sweeney, and John L. Cotton, "Attitudes toward Employee Participation in Decision-Making: A Comparison of European and American Managers in a United States Multinational Company," *Human Resource Management* 31, no. 4 (Winter 1992): 363–83.

29. Readers interested in HR-related issues for managing in Russia should see the following: Carl Fey, Pontus Engstrom, and Ingmar Bjorkman, "Doing Business in Russia: Effective Human Resource Management Practices for Foreign Firms in Russia," *Organizational Dynamics* 28, no. 2 (Autumn 1999): 69–74; Ruth May, Carol Bormann Young, and Donna Ledgerwood, "Lessons from Russian Human Resource Management Experience," *European Management Journal* 16, no. 4 (August 1998): 447–59; Martha Cooley, "HR in Russia: Training for Long-Term Success," *HRMagazine* 42, no. 12 (December 1997): 98–106.

30. Mike Bendixen and Bruce Burger, "Cross-Cultural Management Philosophies," *Journal of Business Research* 42, no. 2 (June 1998): 107–14; Vipin Gupta, Paul Hanges, and Peter Dorman, "Cultural Clusters: Methodology and Findings," *Journal of World Business* 37, no. 1 (Spring 2002): 11–15; Jane Terprstra-Yong and David Ralston, "Moving toward a Global Understanding of Upward Influence Strategies: An Asian Perspective with Directions for Cross-Cultural Research," *Asia Pacific Journal of Management* 19, no. 2 (August 2002): 373–404.

31. Geert Hofstede, "Cultural Constraints in Management Theories," *Academy of Management Executive* 7, no. 1 (February 1993): 81–94. See also Fons Trompenaars, *Riding the Waves of Culture: Understanding Cultural Diversity in Business* (London: Economist Books, 1993); Geert Hofstede, *Culture's Consequences: Comparing Values, Behaviors, Institutions, and Organizations across Nations* (Thousand Oaks, CA: Sage, 2001).

32. William E. Franklin, "Careers in International Business: Five Ideas or Principles," *Vital Speeches of the Day* 64, no. 23 (September 15, 1998): 719–21; Lisa Bohannon, "Going Global," *Career World* 29, no. 6 (April/May 2001): 28–30; Aimin Yan, Guorgong Zhu, and Douglas T. Hall, "International Assignments for Career Building: A Model of Agency Relationships and Psychological

Contracts," *Academy of Management Review* 27, no. 3 (July 2002): 373–91.

33. Pam Pappas Stanoch and Gaye Reynolds-Gooch, "Relocating Career Development," *Canadian HR Reporter* 16, no. 9 (May 5, 2003): 13.

34. Sherrie Zhan, "Smooth Moves," *World Trade* 12, no. 7 (July 1999): 62–64; Charlene Marmer Solomon, "Repatriation: Up, Down, or Out?" *Personnel Journal* 74, 1 (January 1995): 28–30; Robert O'Connor, "Plug the Expat Knowledge Drain," *HRMagazine* 47, no. 10 (October 2002): 101–107; Charlene Marmer Solomon, "Global HR: Repatriation Planning," *Workforce* 2001, special supplement: 22–23; Leslie Gross Klaff, "The Right Way to Bring Expats Home," *Workforce* 81, no. 7 (July 2002): 40–44; Allan Halcrow, "Expats: The Squandered Resource," *Workforce* 78, no. 4 (April 1999): 42–48; Michael Harvey, Michael Price, Cheri Speier, and Milorad Novicevic, "The Role of Inpatriates in a Globalization Strategy and Challenges Associated with the Inpatriation Process," *Human Resource Planning* 22, no. 1 (1999): 38–50.

35. Mila Lazarova and Paula Caligiuri, "Retaining Repatriates: The Role of Organizational Support Practices," *Journal of World Business* 36, no. 4 (Winter 2001): 389–401.

36. Stephen S. McIntosh, "Breaking through Culture Shock: What You Need to Succeed in International Business," *HRMagazine* 44, no. 6 (June 1999): 184–86; Michael G. Harvey and M. Ronald Buckley, "The Process for Developing an International Program for Dual-Career Couples," *Human Resource Management Review* 8, no. 1 (Spring 1998): 99–123; Nancy Carter, "Solve the Dual-Career Challenge," *Workforce* 2, no. 4 (October 1997): 21–22; Charlene Marmer Solomon, "One Assignment, Two Lives," *Personnel Journal* 75, no. 5 (May 1996): 36–47.

37. Nancy Adler, *International Dimensions of Organizational Behavior* (Cincinnati, OH: South-Western, 1997).

38. Snell et al., "Designing and Supporting Transnational Teams."

39. Paul Hempel, "Differences between Chinese and Western Managerial Views of Performance," *Personnel Review* 30, no. 2 (2001): 203–15; Andy Chan, "Managing Human Resources across the Border: Two Cases of Hong Kong–based Joint Ventures in China," *International Journal of Management* 16, no. 4 (December 1999): 586–93; Gary Oddou and Mark Mendenhall, "Expatriate Performance Appraisal: Problems and Solutions," in Mark Mendenhall and Gary Oddou, eds., *Readings and Cases in International Human Resource Management* (Cincinnati, OH: South-Western, 1999), 399–410.

40. Charlene Marmer Solomon, "How Does Your Global Talent Measure Up?" *Personnel Journal* 73, no. 10 (October 1994): 96–108.

41. "10 Tips for Expatriate Management," *HRFocus* 75, no. 3 (March 1998): S8; Paula Caligiuri, "The Big Five Personality Characteristics as Predictors of Expatriate's Desire to Terminate the Assignment and Supervisor-Rated Performance," *Personnel Psychology* 53, no. 1 (Spring 2000): 67–88; Calvin Reynolds, "Global Compensation and Benefits in Transition," *Compensation and Benefits Review* 32, no. 1 (January/February 2000): 28–38; Charlene Marmer Solomon, "The World Stops Shrinking," *Workforce* 79, no. 1 (January 2000): 48–51.

42. Frank Jossi, "Successful Handoff," *HRMagazine* 47, no. 10 (October 2002): 48–52; Paula Caligiuri and David Day, "Effects of Self-Monitoring on Technical, Contextual, and Assignment-Specific Performance," *Group & Organization Management* 25, no. 2 (June 2000): 154–74.

43. Susan Hood, "Cross Cultural Know How on the Net," *HR Professional* 18, no. 2 (April/May 2001): 17; Mendenhall and Oddou, eds., *Readings and Cases*. See also Kenneth W. Davis, Teun De Rycker, and J. Piet Verckens, "Become a Global Communicator," *Workforce* 2, no. 4 (October 1997): 10–11; Gayle Porter and Judith W. Tansky, "Expatriate Success May Depend on a 'Learning Orientation': Considerations for Selection and Training," *Human Resource Management* 38, no. 1 (Spring 1999): 47–60.

44. Andrew C. Inkpen, "Learning and Knowledge Acquisition through International Strategic Alliances," *Academy of Management Executive* 12, no. 4 (November 1998): 69–80; Oded Shenkar and Jiatao Li, "Knowledge Search in International Cooperative Ventures," *Organization Science* 10, no. 2 (March/April 1999): 134–43; Ariane Berhtoin, "Expatriates' Contributions to Organizational Learning," *Journal of General Management* 26, no. 4 (Summer 2001): 62–84.

45. Timothy D. Dwyer, "Trends in Global Compensation," *Compensation and Benefits Review* 31, no. 4 (July/August 1999): 48–53; George Milkovich and Matt Bloom, "Rethinking International Compensation," *Compensation and Benefits Review* 30, no. 1 (January/February 1998): 15–23; Calvin Reynolds, *Guide to Global Compensation and Benefits* (New York: Harcourt, 2001); Gary Parker, "Establishing Remuneration Practices across Culturally Diverse Environments," *Compensation & Benefits Management* 17, no. 2 (Spring 2001): 23–27; Lawrence Luebbers, "Laying the Foundation for Global Compensation," *Workforce* Workforce Extra (September 1999): 1–4; Steven Gross and Per Wingerup, "Global Pay? Maybe Not Yet!" *Compensation and Benefits Review* 31, no. 4 (July/August 1999): 25–34.

46. Caroline Fisher, "Reward Strategy Linked to Financial Success: Europe," *Benefits & Compensation International* 32, no. 2 (September 2002): 34–35; "Comparative

Analysis of Remuneration: Europe," *Benefits & Compensation International* 31, no. 10 (June 2002): 27–28; Fay Hansen, "Currents in Compensation and Benefits: International Trends," *Compensation and Benefits Review* 34, no. 2 (March/April 2002): 20–21.

47. Frances Cairncross, "Survey: Pay: No Man Is an Island," *The Economist* 351, no. 8118 (May 8, 1999): S17–S18; Chao Chen, Jaepil Choi, and Shu-Cheng Chi, "Making Justice Sense of Local-Expatriate Compensation Disparity: Mitigation by Local Referents, Ideological Explanations, and Interpersonal Sensitivity in China-Foreign Joint Ventures," *Academy of Management Journal* 45, no. 4 (August 2002): 807–17.

48. Carolyn Gould, "Expat Pay Plans Suffer Cutbacks," *Workforce* 78, no. 9 (September 1999): 40–46; Patricia Zingheim and Jay Schuster, "How You Pay Is What You Get," *Across the Board* 38, no. 5 (September/October 2001): 41–44; "Benefits for Expatriate Employees: International," *Benefits & Compensation International* 31, no. 10 (June 2002): 26–27.

49. Valerie Frazee, "Is the Balance Sheet Right for Your Expats?" *Workforce* 77, no. 9 (September 1998): 19–26; Carolyn Gould, "What's the Latest in Global Compensation?" *Workforce*, Supplement July 1997: 17–21.

50. U.S. Department of State Index of Living Costs Abroad can be found on the Web at http://www.state.gov/travel/.

51. Andrew Martin and George Ross, eds., *The Brave New World of European Labor: European Trade Unions at the* *Millennium* (Oxford, England: Berghahn Books, 1999); Haknoh Kim, "Constructing European Collective Bargaining," *Economic and Industrial Democracy* 20, no. 3 (August 1999): 393–426; Bernhard Ebbinghaus and Jelle Visser, *The Societies of Europe: Trade Unions in Western Europe since 1945* (The Societies of Europe) (London, England: Palgrave Macmillan, 2000).

52. "Paying Dues: Once the Big Muscle of German Industry, Unions See It All Sag," *The Wall Street Journal*, November 29, 1999: A1, A18; Christopher Rhoads, "Germany Faces Storm over Tech Staffing—Labor Groups Are Enraged by Proposal to Import Badly Needed Workers," *The Wall Street Journal*, March 7, 2000: A23.

53. Interested readers can find more information about international trade unions by checking out the websites of the ICFTU (International Confederation of Free Trade Unions) (http://www.icftu.org/) and the ILO (International Labour Organization) (http://www.ilo.org/).

54. Anke Hassel, "The Erosion of the German System of Industrial Relations," *British Journal of Industrial Relations* 37, no. 3 (September 1999): 483–505; Manfred Schumann, "'Mitbestimmung'—A German Model for Social Peace," *World Trade* 9, no. 4 (April 1996): 9; Dirk Kolvenbach and Ute Spiegel, "The Reform of the Works Council Constitution Act in Germany and Its Effects on the Co-Determination Rights of the Works Council," *International Financial Law Review, The IFLR Guide to Germany* (2001): 59–65.

16

Creating High-Performance Work Systems

After studying this chapter, you should be able to

Discuss the underlying principles of high-performance work systems.

Identify the components that make up a high-performance work system.

Describe how the components fit together and support strategy.

Recommend processes for implementing high-performance work systems.

Discuss the outcomes for both employees and the organization.

Explain how the principles of high-performance work systems apply to small, medium-sized, and large organizations.

This chapter is available on the *Managing Human Resources* website (www.belcourt4e.nelson.com).

Excalibur Cases

Introduction

Excalibur, the Canadian University Tournament in Human Resources, is held annually in March in Montreal, Quebec. This case competition attracts entrants from universities across Canada. Teams of four students, coached by their professors, are asked to demonstrate their knowledge of human resources management to a jury of practitioners and professors. The teams analyze the HR issues facing real Canadian companies and are given ninety minutes to prepare their cases, and another twenty minutes to present their recommendations to the jury. The top three winning teams receive cash awards. The tournament is managed by the HR and IR professional association of Quebec: L'Ordre des conseillers en Ressources Humaines et en Relations Industrielles Agréés du Québec, in collaboration with the Ecole des Sciences de la Gestion de L'Université du Québec à Montréal. The following cases have been used in previous Excalibur Tournaments.

Source: Cases from Excalibur, the Canadian University Tournament in Human Resources (from 2000 to 2003)
    Lafarge Corporation: Managing the Challenges of Internationalization (2000)
    Le Cirque du Soleil: How to Manage Growth (2001)
    BCE Emergis: Searching for Concrete Solutions (2002)
    Labatt Breweries (2003)

BCE Emergis: Searching for Concrete Solutions

Case 1

BCE Emergis is a service provider that offers its customers integrated electronic business (e-business) solutions. The company as we know it today was created following a merger between MPACT Immedia and a unit of Bell Emergis in 1998. Since that time, it has continued to grow by acquiring various companies that market integrated e-business solutions or by merging with them.

More specifically, BCE Emergis provides other businesses with electronic solutions for supply, sales, customer service, invoicing, security, on-site support, and payment functions. In line with the company's mission, these services target business-to-business rather than business-to-consumer e-commerce. Although it is not limited to specific market segments, BCE Emergis has acquired expertise in the health insurance and financial services sectors. For example, thanks to the online technology it has developed, 80 percent of Canadian group insurance holders pay only the amount deductible under their coverage when their prescription is filled by a pharmacist. With this system, using the insured's card and an electronic database, the pharmacist can immediately obtain any relevant information directly from the insurer and is automatically electronically reimbursed by the insurer for each transaction.

Although 65 percent of BCE Emergis is held by Bell Canada Enterprises (BCE), it is a separate entity with its own distinct organizational culture. When the company was founded, it had a workforce of 350 and posted earnings of $75 million. Despite the ups and downs of the economy and the dramatic stock market slide in the new economy sector, BCE Emergis has continued to grow. Today it has 2600 employees who generate more than $650 million in business income. As mentioned above, the company's growth is partly due to the mergers and acquisitions it has carried out since its inception, which also explains why its employees work in a number of cities across Canada and the United States (half in Canada and half in the United States).

Thanks to its ingenious business model, BCE Emergis came through the economic crisis in the new economy with flying colours, realizing recurring revenue generated by fees paid by its customers each time they use the product purchased. In fact, not only did the company survive during this financially troubled period, but it also continued to increase its business income. This business model, unique to BCE Emergis, has earned it the nickname "new economy blue chip."

As for its objectives, the company wants to continue to grow and to expand its activities in e-commerce solutions for the financial service, primarily in the United States. Although in Canada the BCE name has already secured the company widespread recognition and is a guarantee of quality service and professionalism, the situation is somewhat different in the United States. In that country, Emergis still has to make itself known through its quality products and services and groundbreaking approach. In the next few years, it therefore intends to continue its efforts in the United States and, once it has established its reputation, consolidate its position.

Dynamic Human Capital

Because of its continued growth through mergers and acquisitions, BCE Emergis is in some ways a melting pot of different cultures and subcultures. Recognizing the importance of the entrepreneurial spirit in all the companies it has acquired, it makes an effort to retain and integrate their senior managers. To sustain their motivation and fuel their entrepreneurial spirit, BCE Emergis involves them in strategic planning, particularly in the development of its own management philosophy. However, keeping these executives can raise certain challenges when it comes to integrating the acquired companies and their employees into the Emergis culture.

In the several years the company has been in operation, its dynamic has been unique, to say the least, as it deals with the arrival of large numbers of competitive, imaginative, and entrepreneurially oriented employees, numerous and very diverse management programs, as well as the mix of cultures belonging to each of the companies acquired. As a result, it became a priority to set up a bona fide human resources department in order to steer all these employees and cultures in the same direction. The human resources department (which had a minimal staff in 1999) was thus reorganized and now employs more than twenty-five people. Members of this team are assigned to a number of subgroups (recruitment, support, customers, compensation, organizational development and training, and internal communications) where they meet the needs of various BCE Emergis organizations in both Canada and the United States. In addition, it has also proven important to create a variety of management models to respond to senior management's requirements and strategic vision.

However, its "new economy blue chip" had to determine exactly what its values were in order to institute its own organizational culture. Eleven core competencies were therefore identified to prepare a competency profile for potential BCE Emergis employees. These competencies are set out below:

1. Technical skills
2. Energy
3. Professional ethics
4. Initiative, proactive and entrepreneurial approach
5. Teamwork skills
6. Flexibility
7. Alertness
8. Leadership
9. Action oriented
10. Customer service oriented
11. Business acumen

Without establishing policies and based on the competency profile, the human resources team developed the following programs exemplifying the "Emergis Way":

I. **Compensation program**
   - Base pay + performance bonus.
   - Stock option plan.
   - Flexible group insurance.

II. "Best and brightest" recognition program
- ▶ Hiring of industry "stars."
- ▶ Acknowledgment of exceptional achievements via a contest for outstanding employees, "BCE Competence: outstanding employees."

III. Strategic talent development program
- ▶ Development of tools for identifying the potentially most effective employees to give them the opportunity to access strategic positions within the organization.

VI. Training environment program
- ▶ Promotion of a resources training environment that will ensure growth within the company and in strategic positions in Canada and the United States, whatever future acquisitions the company makes.

V. Development of executive management skills program

VI. Online recruitment program

VII. Internal referral for recruitment program

Structure and Development

Although BCE Emergis is experiencing tremendous growth, it now has to focus on managing the influx of new employees and their integration. To achieve this end, the company needs to retain and motivate its current employees as well as those it continues to attract. In fact, BCE Emergis has maintained its spectacular development in an extremely difficult economic context; each day it receives up to 300 resumés and job applications, which it manages with its efficient database. However, with the recovery of the new economy, the company will have to compete with all other employers to retain the employees it has recruited and trained. Even though BCE Emergis compares favourably with other companies in the same sector, its employee turnover should be monitored.

Furthermore, integrating new companies, their managers, and their employees remains a challenge. Since most of the acquisitions are made in the United States, and given the general and organizational cultural differences, integrating all these resources the "Emergis way" is no easy task. While attempting to implement common human resources management programs, BCE Emergis certainly does not want to smother or, even worse, destroy its employees' entrepreneurial spirit, which is of such value to its mission. The challenge for the human resources team is to strike a balance between precision and structure on the one hand, and innovation and entrepreneurship on the other.

The stock option plan that is an integral part of the compensation program, and which was set up as an incentive to retain employees, could eventually become less attractive. The low prices of some options that could be exercised in the near future could propel some employees into the "young millionaires" category. However, those options granted at prices that are now much higher than the market price will be less of an incentive for employees to stay with the company.

QUESTIONS

With respect to integrating new Canadian and American human resources, your team of consultants should analyze the company's growth and work with the human resources team to ensure it continues.

You are required to

1. outline your understanding of the overall situation at BCE Emergis;
2. prepare a diagnosis of the company's human resources management challenges;
3. considering the main challenges, determine two to four strategies and the major obstacles to their implementation;
4. propose and support your action plan by presenting concrete, viable solutions consistent with the values inherent to BCE Emergis.

Le Cirque du Soleil: How to Manage Growth

Case 2

Founded in 1984 by a group of young street performers, Cirque du Soleil has been in constant evolution since its creation. The company enjoys excellent international recognition and is said to have reinvented circus arts. In 1984 Cirque du Soleil had sales of $1.7 million, 50 employees, and 23 performers; in 2000, sales were expected to reach $407 million and it would employ 1370 people and 445 performers. It planned to present seven shows in 2000 on three continents: North America, Europe, and Asia. Also, in order to adequately manage all its personnel, it had four separate headquarters. Besides international headquarters in Montreal, it has four other head offices: Montreal (called Headquarters—America), Amsterdam (Headquarters—Europe), Las Vegas (Headquarters—Las Vegas), and Singapore (Headquarters—Asia-Pacific).

While Cirque du Soleil wanted to find and exploit new niches related to presenting shows, the majority of its revenues came from ticket sales. Thus the vital nucleus of the Cirque remained presenting shows. The Cirque had four fixed shows, two touring shows in Asia, one in North America, and another in Europe. A touring show comprised 150 to 200 people, including 50 to 70 performers, and it had to relocate on average every six weeks, which demanded very skilled logistics and effective planning of the entry authorizations for the different countries on the tour. Relocating meant moving personnel, their baggage, and the Cirque's equipment from town to town. It also meant lodging all these people and ensuring they obtained the required visas and work permits in order to be able to practise their art in the countries the tour was visiting.

To attain the level of excellence set by Cirque du Soleil, talent scouts and recruiters travelled the globe in search of artists, creators, coaches, musicians, etc. Consequently, the Cirque's performers and personnel came from more than thirty countries and spoke many languages. Also, while the average age of employees was relatively young at thirty-two, the age of the performers and employees ranged from three to sixty-two.

In short, Cirque du Soleil was an international company that reflected the level of excellence it had achieved in the past and its constant desire to push the limits.

Development Project

As well as continuing to create and produce new shows, Cirque du Soleil wanted to diversify its commercial activities. Indeed, it wanted to see itself develop the production of audiovisual works such as the soundtracks of the different shows, explore the field of publishing, and continue to promote some strategic agreements with partners in the hotel business. Cirque du Soleil had also set itself the objective of adding two or three tours within five years, which would have the effect of bringing the number of employees required to achieve such an objective to about 2000.

Management

Cirque du Soleil had adopted a management style in its own image, that is, dynamic, vibrant, and imaginative. The organic nature of how it operated put each employee in a position that allowed him or her to contribute to a common work. Cirque du Soleil firmly believed that, by appealing to everyone's intelligence, all objectives are achievable. Also, communications were extremely open and the authority that certain hierarchical titles could impose was practically nonexistent. And a Cirque du Soleil core value was respect for cultural diversity.

In spite of the continuous growth the company had experienced, it had always known how to ensure cohesion among employees and maintain a strong sense of belonging.

Challenges to Be Met

Given its growth plans, in relation to both the number of shows presented and the establishment of new commercial activities, Cirque du Soleil needed to apply itself to adapting its structure and, above all, to ensuring that its managers have the ability to support such development. In this respect, several managers who had grown up with Cirque du Soleil and who had thus acquired broad operating experience were having some difficulty moving to a strategic management mode. Given their extensive knowledge of how the Cirque operated, they too often remained occupied or preoccupied with operating questions, rather than investing their energy more in strategic planning.

Also, given the increased number of tours planned, another problem that already existed was likely to get bigger. Due to the difficult touring conditions, such as the frequent relocations, the increased number of shows per week, and challenging working conditions in general, the turnover rate among employees was very high. On average, they worked for the Cirque between nineteen and twenty-four months, which created a turnover rate of 18 to 22 percent. In spite of the efforts made to reduce the inconveniences inherent in touring, problems still remained. For example, the Cirque offered the services of a tutor to child performers and to the children of performers. However, because of the costs this would have entailed, this service could not be offered to all the children of its personnel. Despite the attractive salaries, Cirque du Soleil was experiencing some difficulties in retaining its touring personnel.

Finally, it is important to note that, both in the touring shows and in International Headquarters in Montreal, the presence of many people of different nationalities, speaking different languages, was a challenge. Indeed, while the presence of Quebec and Canadian performers at International Headquarters and on tours was often secondary, dealing with several nationalities greatly influenced the quality of communications. And, depending on the cultural baggage of each person, the perception of the message communicated could differ greatly. Since cultural references are very divergent, what are innocuous gestures to some have unexpected implications for others. However, despite these difficulties in perception, Cirque du Soleil had always greatly valued cultural diversity and had always emphasized the richness it brought, rather than the differences it created. Nonetheless, the Cirque du Soleil had to constantly manage stereotypes and prejudices. This situation was even more palpable at International Headquarters in Montreal since the performers who worked there were, for the most part, passing through, either with the aim of learning a new number or to take up training again following an injury. Also, people of the same nationality often grouped together without mixing too much with other performers of different nationalities.

QUESTIONS

You have been given a mandate by Cirque du Soleil to propose solutions to the problems raised by the facts described above.

To do so, you must

1. state your understanding of the situation at Cirque du Soleil;
2. precisely determine the needs of Cirque du Soleil in the short and medium term;
3. in the light of those needs, make provisions for the obstacles envisaged;
4. finally, establish a plan of action by formulating possible solutions to the problems you have identified. You must then justify the proposed solutions, taking into account the values transmitted by Cirque du Soleil.

Labatt Breweries

Case 3

In 1847, John Kinder Labatt laid the foundations of a brewing company in London, Ontario, that would later become Labatt Breweries. The company quickly branched out. In 1878, it established an agency in Montreal to distribute its products. Twenty years later, the company took steps to satisfy growing demand in the Toronto area and opened a sales office and a small warehouse. When Prohibition was introduced in the United States in 1900, the company's expansion was temporarily delayed. It survived, however, and in 1946 began a series of acquisitions that made it one of the largest breweries in Canada. The launch of Labatt Blue in 1951 helped cement the company's status as Canadian industry leader. In 1995 the world-renowned company was sold to Belgium's Interbrew SA, the third-largest brewing consortium in the world.

Today Labatt produces over sixty beers, employs 3800 employees, and operates eight breweries from coast to coast, in St. John's, Halifax, Montreal, Toronto, London, Edmonton, Creston, and New Westminster. Its most popular brands are Labatt Blue, Budweiser, Keith's, Labatt Wildcat, and Kokanee. In Quebec alone, 893 million 341-mL bottles are produced each year, an amount equal to 3.1 million hL, or 23 percent of the total Canadian production of 13.64 million hL. Labatt's products are distributed to over 22 000 outlets, and 20 percent of the production is exported. The Montreal brewery is the largest in Canada, closely followed by the London, Ontario, plant, which produces 2.97 million hL. Worldwide, Interbrew produces 180 beers that are distributed in more than 110 countries in Europe, North America, and the Asia-Pacific region. Interbrew's most popular brands are Stella Artois, Bass, and Beck's.

Innovation has set Labatt apart from other breweries. In fact, it was Labatt that marketed the first twist-off cap, the first light beer, and the first non-alcoholic beer in Canada. More recently, the company made history by creating the first lemonade-flavoured malt beer. Shortly after, in 1997, to address ever-growing demand for and popularity of specialty beers and imported beers, Labatt created the Oland Specialty Beer Company (OSBC).

The quest for innovation that has characterized the company since its early days is entirely consistent with its mission statement to deliver superior quality products made from the finest ingredients using proven methods. The company's stated goal is to become Canada's leading brewer, a goal that plays out in market share points, given the intense competition in national and world markets. From 1997 to 2001, the brewing industry was characterized by a wave of mergers. Since then, the number of players on the market has fallen considerably and the remaining companies have gotten larger. To remain competitive and make further inroads, Interbrew has been using a strategy called "The World's Local Brewer" to become a larger presence in mature and emerging markets through strategic acquisitions and internal growth.

Culture Shock

With its background of family tradition, Labatt had managed through the years to foster a strong sense of belonging among its employees. Staff members were genuine ambassadors for the company's products, always eager to represent the company during community events, for example. The culture of excellence, performance, and quality that built the company's reputation was widely shared by a vast majority of employees—managers, representatives, and shop workers alike.

When Interbrew bought the company in the mid-1990s, harsher market conditions had chipped away at the relationship between the employees and their company. To function in an ultra-competitive world market, the organization has worked very hard over the last few years to optimize productivity. To achieve this, it reduced its work-force and increased the work load. The new operating methods have caused much discontent among unionized employees in the plants and fostered a feeling of nostalgia for the way things were.

In Quebec, the last round of labour negotiations in 1996 intensified the culture shock that accompanied the acquisition. When the collective agreement was reopened, management proposed retirement incentives in an effort to reduce production manpower and increase the company's competitiveness. Although the older workers hailed the proposal, it caused deep dissatisfaction among younger employees, whose main goal was access to permanent positions. This was a very controversial issue, as indicated by the fact that the proposal passed by a mere 52 percent. The collective agreement was to be in effect for six years.

It is important to note that 90 percent of Labatt's Quebec employees are unionized, and the company's 150 managers are not. In all, there were nine bargaining units belonging to the Teamsters Union, a number that had remained unchanged since the beginning of unionization within the company. So far the company has had no strikes and only one lockout. The current HR managers agree that labour relations on the whole are still very good.

But the discontent caused by the last agreement has turned things upside down. Over the last three years there has been an increase in the number of grievances filed. Most of the grievances were about tighter management and fewer workers.

Negotiation on the Horizon

Given that the collective agreement was expiring in December of 2002, Labatt started negotiating with its various bargaining units in Quebec in the fall. The Montreal-area plant and delivery workers—traditionally the strongest unit—had always been the first unit to start the round of negotiations. This time around, however, the scenario has changed. Following a period of union raiding in July of 2002, the Montreal unit left the Teamsters Union and joined the ranks of the Confederation of National Trade Unions (CNTU) on February 28, 2003. The CNTU, it should be noted, is based primarily in Quebec and has always adopted a more confrontational and left-leaning stance than other labour unions. The Teamsters, for their part, prefer using a business approach.

The switch raised many question marks. Not only does the employer have to face a brand-new union, it also has to learn to work with a labour union whose philosophy is entirely different from that of its predecessor. In fact, this will be the very first collective agreement the CNTU negotiates with the brewing industry. Representation on the employer's side remains unchanged. Only one negotiator is appointed to conclude an agreement with all the unions, including the new one.

It is already understood that worker status (regular, temporary, casual) will be at the heart of the upcoming debates. Worker expectation on the issue is running very high, because many workers are still considered temporary despite having logged ten or so years of continuous service with the company. The aging of the worker population is a fact that will put the issue of early retirement back on the table.

Meanwhile, the employer has entered into an agreement with another large bargaining unit that could possibly pave the way for upcoming discussions. The agreement was conducted with the other union and was satisfactory for most of the distribution workers in the province. In fact, the final proposal received 93 percent approval. This new collective agreement has already come into effect and expires only in seven years. Under the agreement, many employees will retire over the next few months owing to improvements to the pension plan; consequently, the same number of temporary employees will receive permanent employee status.

Despite this happy ending, there are many unanswered questions. In particular, the company is unsure about the impact of the new situation over the near, medium, and long term. Will other units join the ranks of the CNTU? Will negotiations lead to a conflict during the summer season, which is somewhat of a peak season for the company? Will the agreement concluded with the first unit create a domino effect during upcoming negotiations? Given the atmosphere of uncertainty, management decides to send a memo to all employees to advise them of the new CNTU unit. The letter also describes the agreement with the unit belonging to the Teamsters Union and the main gains the employees made. The company also states its intention to step up production to increase inventory and thus avoid a shortage if a conflict should occur over the summer.

QUESTIONS

It is in this context that your consulting team is to conduct an analysis and issue recommendations on an appropriate communications and negotiation strategy to adopt in the near and long term.

To do this, you must

1. briefly explain your understanding of Labatt's overall situation;
2. establish a diagnosis of the challenges that Labatt is facing in the area of labour relations;
3. in light of the main challenges, formulate two to four possible strategies and the main obstacles to implementing them over the near term (2003), the medium term (four years), and the long term (seven years);
4. propose and justify your action plan by presenting tangible solutions that are viable and consistent with Labatt's values.

Lafarge Corporation: Managing the Challenges of Internationalization

Case 4

Founded in 1956, Lafarge Corporation is one of the main North American suppliers of building materials such as cement, concrete, and gypsum boards, and it is one of five divisions of Groupe Lafarge SA, a worldwide leader in the field of building products, whose head office is in Paris, France. Groupe Lafarge SA employs more than 66 000 people in sixty-five countries and its revenues reached 9.8 billion euros (about $15 billion Cdn) in 1998. Lafarge Corporation alone employs more than 10 000 people in more than 700 plants throughout North America. Its American head office is located in Virginia, while the Canadian head office is in Montreal.

Lafarge Corporation must apply the human resources policies and programs issued by Groupe Lafarge SA's head office. In fact, Groupe Lafarge SA has a vision of operational excellence that implies the setup of recognized human resources practices and the harmonization of operations methods among all its divisions; it considers that this standardization represents the key to its success. The management orientations are dictated to all divisions, resulting in management styles and standardized operations that operate in spite of the cultural differences. Groupe Lafarge SA reinforces its competitive position via acquisitions as well as internal development of its human resources according to standardized management models.

Employees of Groupe Lafarge SA are at the core of the corporate strategy, and their commitment is the basis of the company's success. Group Lafarge SA has a participative management style that prevails in all companies operating on the five continents.

However, the group's rapid and recent growth, mainly achieved through acquisitions, particularly in newly industrialized countries, entails some standardization challenges. The company was therefore forced to redefine this management style to include key words such as involvement, efficiency, and example.

All division administrators must have strong leadership skills and guide their team members toward the enhanced profitability that allows them to further contribute to the synergy that is essential to the global success of the group. Ten years ago, almost half of the employees of Groupe Lafarge SA were French; today, French employees represent only 19 percent of its total manpower. The group's international human resources recruitment policy has three principles: expatriation, short-term postings in foreign countries, and recruitment of local residents. In fact, its international exchanges aim to increase the international representation of its teams. Currently, 12 percent of the administrators have accumulated international experience in order to establish stability and standardization among the companies. The group must double this number over the next five years in order to comply with its major development orientations. These international postings generally last between two and five years and are currently assigned to employees who volunteer.

The company needs to attract employees with strong development potential and proven leadership skills. It must then offer them interesting careers; geographical mobility as much as internal transfers to new challenges is strongly encouraged. Hiring personnel who demonstrate willingness to move at the international level represents one of the main objectives of the group.

The Problem

In the case of Lafarge Corporation, most exchanges occur between the American and Canadian subsidiaries and sometimes between North American and European plants. However, exchanges between plants located in newly developed countries and those in European and North American plants are almost nonexistent, although these must increase considerably. Furthermore, although several Canadians have volunteered for postings in the United States, the opposite is not as frequent. Indeed, remuneration as well as American fiscal laws makes it difficult to arrange or facilitate transfers from the United States to Canada. This situation applies also to Canadians who have accepted a posting in the United States. Finally, few among them volunteer for transfers to plants located in newly industrialized countries.

Lafarge Corporation, in cooperation with Groupe Lafarge SA's head office, is responsible for fulfilling its own personnel needs. Even with the support of Groupe Lafarge SA, and in spite of the access to a pool of volunteer employees working in other plants, it is especially challenging for Lafarge Corporation to find specialized employees, notably for its cement division. In fact, most of the positions to be filled demand a university degree (diploma is the French word) in engineering, and many potential candidates with this degree are also actively sought by oil and chemical companies. The objective of the international exchange program is to transfer knowledge among the various groups as well as implementing, standardizing, and optimizing operations. Therefore, it is essential to have a critical mass of qualified employees before participating in the international exchange program.

QUESTIONS

Your mandate is to propose solutions to problems pertaining to recruitment, international mobility, career management, and succession planning, keeping in mind the notion of cultural integration in the case of employees taking part in the international mobility program.

1. *Analyzing the Situation.* Explain your understanding of the situation. What are the corporate objectives and the short-term and mid-term requirements?

2. *Action Plan.* Further to the analysis of the situation, list the potential solutions to the challenges of recruitment, international mobility, and personnel retention as well as standardizing management styles You must justify the proposed solutions. These solutions must be developed and proposed while taking into account the process of career management and succession planning.

Glossary

Achievement tests
Measures of what a person knows or can do right now

Alarm reaction
Response to stress that basically involves an elevated heart rate, increased respiration, elevated levels of adrenaline in the blood, and increased blood pressure

Alternative dispute resolution (ADR)
Term applied to different types of employee complaint or dispute resolution procedures

Apprenticeship training
System of training in which a worker entering the skilled trades is given thorough instruction and experience, both on and off the job, in the practical and theoretical aspects of the work

Aptitude tests
Measures of a person's capacity to learn or acquire skills

Arbitration award
Final and binding award issued by an arbitrator in a labour–management dispute

Assessment centre
Process by which individuals are evaluated as they participate in a series of situations that resemble what they might be called upon to handle on the job

Attrition
A natural departure of employees from organizations through quits, retirements, and deaths

Augmented skills
Skills helpful in facilitating the efforts of expatriate managers

Authorization card
A statement signed by an employee authorizing a union to act as his or her representative for the purposes of collective bargaining

Balance-sheet approach
Compensation system designed to match the purchasing power in a person's home country

Bargaining power
The power of labour and management to achieve their goals though economic, social, or political influence

Bargaining unit
Group of two or more employees who share common employment interests and conditions and may reasonably be grouped together for purposes of collective bargaining

Bargaining zone
Area within which the union and the employer are willing to concede when bargaining

Behaviour modelling
Approach that demonstrates desired behaviour and gives trainees the chance to practise and role-play those behaviours and receive feedback

Behaviour modification
Technique that operates on the principle that behaviour that is rewarded, or positively reinforced, will be exhibited more frequently in the future, whereas behaviour that is penalized or unrewarded will decrease in frequency

Behaviour observation scale (BOS)
A behavioural approach to performance appraisal that measures the frequency of observed behaviour

Behavioural description interview (BDI)
An interview in which an applicant is asked questions about what he or she actually did in a given situation

Behaviourally anchored rating scale (BARS)
A behavioural approach to performance appraisal that consists of a series of vertical scales, one for each important dimension of job performance

Benchmarking
Process of measuring one's own services and practices against the recognized leaders in order to identify areas for improvement

Bona fide occupational qualification (BFOQ)
A justifiable reason for discrimination based on business reasons of safety or effectiveness

Bonus
Incentive payment that is supplemental to the base wage

Burnout
Most severe stage of distress, manifesting itself in depression, frustration, and loss of productivity

Business agent
Normally a paid labour official responsible for negotiating and administering the collective agreement and working to resolve union members' problems

Career counselling
Process of discussing with employees their current job activities and performance, their personal and career interests and goals, their personal skills, and suitable career development objectives

Career paths
Lines of advancement in an occupational field within an organization

Career plateau
Situation in which for either organizational or personal reasons the probability of moving up the career ladder is low

Codetermination
Representation of labour on the board of directors of a company

Collective bargaining process
Process of negotiating a collective agreement, including the use of economic pressures by both parties

Combined salary and commission plan
Compensation plan that includes a straight salary and a commission

Competence-based pay
Pay based on an employee's skill level, the variety of skills possessed, or increased job knowledge of the employee

Competency assessment
Analysis of the sets of skills and knowledge needed for decision-oriented and knowledge-intensive jobs

Compulsory binding arbitration
Binding method of resolving collective bargaining deadlocks by a neutral third party

Computer-assisted instruction (CAI)
System that delivers instructional materials directly through a computer terminal in an interactive format

Computer-managed instruction (CMI)
System normally employed in conjunction with CAI that uses a computer to generate and score tests and to determine the level of training proficiency

Concentration
Term applied to designated groups whose numbers in a particular occupation or level are high relative to their numbers in the labour market

Concurrent validity
The extent to which test scores (or other predictor information) match criterion data obtained at about the same time from current employees

Construct validity
Extent to which a selection tool measures a theoretical construct or trait

Constructive dismissal
Changing an employee's working emotions such that compensation, status, or prestige is reduced

Consumer price index (CPI)
Measure of the average change in prices over time in a fixed "market basket" of goods and services

Content validity
Extent to which a selection instrument, such as a test, adequately samples the knowledge and skills needed to perform a particular job

Contractual rights
Rights that derive from contracts

Contrast error
Performance rating error in which an employee's evaluation is biased either upward or downward because of comparison with another employer just recently evaluated

Contributory plan
A pension plan in which contributions are made jointly by employees and employers

Cooperative training
Training program that combines practical on-the-job experience with formal educational classes

Core competencies
Integrated knowledge sets within an organization that distinguish it from its competitors and deliver value to customers

Core skills
Skills considered critical to an employee's success abroad

Craft unions
Unions that represent skilled craft workers

Criterion-related validity
Extent to which a selection tool predicts, or significantly correlates with, important elements of work behaviour

Critical incident method
Job analysis method by which important job tasks are identified for job success

Cross-training
Training of employees in jobs in areas closely related to their own

Cross-validation
Verifying the results obtained from a validation study by administering a test or test battery to a different sample (drawn from the same population)

Cultural audits
Audits of the culture and quality of work life in an organization

Cultural environment
Communications, religion, values and ideologies, education, and social structure of a country

Culture shock
Perpetual stress experienced by people who settle overseas

Cumulative trauma disorders
Injuries involving tendons of the fingers, hands, and arms that become inflamed from repeated stresses and strains

Customer appraisal
Performance appraisal, which, like team appraisal, is based on TQM concepts and seeks evaluation from both internal and external customers

Defined benefit plan
A pension plan in which the amount an employee is to receive on retirement is specifically set forth

Defined contribution plan
A pension plan that establishes the basis on which an employer will contribute to the pension fund

Defined rights
Concept that management's authority should be expressly defined and clarified in the collective agreement

Depression
Negative emotional state marked by feelings of low spirits, gloominess, sadness, and loss of pleasure in ordinary activities

Designated groups
Women, visible minorities, aboriginal peoples, and persons with disabilities who have been disadvantaged in employment

Differential piece rate
Compensation rate under which employees whose production exceeds the standard amount of output receive a higher rate for all of their work than the rate paid to those who do not exceed the standard amount

Discipline
(1) Treatment that punishes; (2) orderly behaviour in an organizational setting; or (3) training that moulds and strengthens desirable conduct—or corrects undesirable conduct—and develops self-control

Distress
Harmful stress characterized by a loss of feelings of security and adequacy

Diversity management
The optimization of an organization's multicultural workforce in order to reach business objectives

Downsizing
The planned elimination of jobs

Dual-career partnerships
Couples in which both members follow their own careers and actively support each other's career development

Due process
Employee's right to present his or her position during a disciplinary action

Earnings-at-risk incentive plans
Incentive pay plans placing a portion of the employee's base pay at risk, but giving the opportunity to earn income above base pay when goals are met or exceeded

Elder care
Care provided to an elderly relative by an employee who remains actively at work

Employee assistance programs (EAPs)
Services provided by employers to help workers cope with a wide variety of problems that interfere with the way they perform their jobs

Employee associations
Labour organizations that represent various groups of professional and white-collar employees in labour–management relations

Employee empowerment
A technique of involving employees in their work through a process of inclusion

Employee involvement groups (EIs)
Groups of employees who meet to resolve problems or offer suggestions for organizational improvement

Employee leasing
Process of dismissing employees who are then hired by a leasing company (which handles all HR-related activities) and contracting with that company to lease back the employees

Employee rights
Guarantees of fair treatment from employers, especially regarding an employee's right to privacy

Employee stock ownership plans (ESOPs)
Stock plans in which an organization contributes shares of its stock to an established trust for the purpose of stock purchases by its employees

Employee teams
An employee contributions technique whereby work functions are structured for groups rather than for individuals and team members are given discretion in matters traditionally considered management prerogatives

Employment equity
The employment of individuals in a fair and nonbiased manner

Entrepreneur
One who starts, organizes, manages, and assumes responsibility for a business or other enterprise

Equal pay for work of equal value
The concept that male and female jobs that are dissimilar, but equal in value or worth to the employer, should be paid the same

Ergonomics
An interdisciplinary approach to designing equipment and systems that can be easily and efficiently used by human beings

Error of central tendency
Performance rating error in which all employees are rated about average

Escalator clauses
Clauses in collective agreements that provide for quarterly cost-of-living adjustments in wages, basing the adjustments on changes in the consumer price index

Essay method
A trait approach to performance appraisal that requires the rater to compose a statement describing employee behaviour

Ethics
Set of standards of conduct and moral judgments that help determine right and wrong behaviour

Eustress
Positive stress that accompanies achievement and exhilaration

Expatriates, or home-country nationals
Employees from the home country who are on international assignment

External fit
Situation in which the work system supports the organization's goals and strategies

Factor comparison system
Job evaluation system that permits the evaluation process to be accomplished on a factor-by-factor basis by developing a factor comparison scale

Failure rate
Percentage of expatriates who do not perform satisfactorily

Fast-track program
Program that encourages young managers with high potential to remain with an organization by enabling them to advance more rapidly than those with less potential

Final offer arbitration
Method of resolving collective bargaining deadlocks whereby the arbitrator has no power to compromise but must select one or another of the final offers submitted by the two parties

Flexible benefits plans (cafeteria plans)
Benefits plans that enable individual employees to choose the benefits that are best suited to their particular needs

Flextime
Flexible working hours that permit employees the option of choosing daily starting and quitting times, provided that they work a set number of hours per day or week

Flow data
Data that provide a profile of the employment decisions affecting designated groups

Forced choice method
A trait approach to performance appraisal that requires the rater to choose from statements designed to distinguish between successful and unsuccessful performance

Functional job analysis (FJA)
Quantitative approach to job analysis that utilizes a compiled inventory of the various functions or work activities that can make up any job and that assumes that each job involves three broad worker functions: (1) data, (2) people, and (3) things

Gainsharing plans
Programs under which both employees and the organization share financial gains according to a predetermined formula that reflects improved productivity and profitability

Global corporation
Firm that has integrated worldwide operations through a centralized home office

Global manager

Manager equipped to run an international business

Globalization

Trend toward opening up foreign markets to international trade and investment

Graphic rating scale method

A trait approach to performance appraisal whereby each employee is rated according to a scale of characteristics

Grievance procedure

Formal procedure that provides for the union to represent members and nonmembers in processing a grievance

Guest workers

Foreign workers invited to perform needed labour

Hay profile method

Job evaluation technique using three factors—knowledge, mental activity, and accountability—to evaluate executive and managerial positions

Hearing officers

People who work full-time for the organization but who assume a neutral role when deciding cases between aggrieved employees and management

High-performance work system (HPWS)

A specific combination of HR practices, work structures, and processes that maximizes employee knowledge, skill, commitment, and flexibility

Hiring freeze

A practice whereby new workers are not hired as planned, or workers who have left the organization are not replaced

Host country

Country in which an international corporation operates

Host-country nationals

Employees who are natives of the host country

Hot stove rule

Rule of discipline that can be compared with a hot stove in that it gives warning, is effective immediately, is enforced consistently, and applies to all employees in an impersonal and unbiased way

Hourly work

Work paid on an hourly basis

Human capital

The knowledge, skills, and capabilities of individuals that have economic value to an organization

Human resources information system (HRIS)

Computerized system that provides current and accurate data for purposes of control and decision making

Human Resources Management

a set of inter-related policies, practices and programs whose goal is to attract, socialize, motivate, maintain and retain an organization's employees.

Human resources planning (HRP)

Process of anticipating and making provision for the movement of people into, within, and out of an organization.

Improshare

Gainsharing program under which bonuses are based on the overall productivity of the work team

In-basket training

Assessment-centre process for evaluating trainees by simulating a real-life work situation

Industrial disease

A disease resulting from exposure to a substance relating to a particular process, trade, or occupation in industry

Industrial engineering

A field of study concerned with analyzing work methods and establishing time standards

Industrial unions

Unions that represent all workers—skilled, semiskilled, unskilled—employed along industry lines

Instructional objectives

Desired outcomes of a training program

Interest-based bargaining (IBB)

Problem-solving bargaining based on a win–win philosophy and the development of a positive long-term relationship

Internal fit

Situation in which all the internal elements of the work system complement and reinforce one another

International corporation

Domestic firm that uses its existing capabilities to move into overseas markets

Internship programs

Programs jointly sponsored by colleges, universities, and other organizations that offer students the opportunity to gain real-life experience while allowing them to find out how they will perform in work organizations

Job
A group of related activities and duties

Job analysis
Process of obtaining information about jobs by determining what the duties, tasks, or activities associated with those jobs are

Job characteristics model
Job design that purports that three factors (meaningful work, responsibility for work outcomes, and knowledge of the results of the work performed) result in improved work performance, increased internal motivation, and lower absenteeism and turnover

Job classification system
System of job evaluation in which jobs are classified and grouped according to a series of predetermined wage grades

Job description
Statement of the tasks, duties, and responsibilities of a job to be performed

Job design
Outgrowth of job analysis that improves jobs through technological and human considerations in order to enhance organization efficiency and employee job satisfaction

Job enrichment
Enhancing a job by adding more meaningful tasks and duties to make the work more rewarding or satisfying

Job evaluation
Systematic process of determining the relative worth of jobs in order to establish which jobs should be paid more than others within an organization

Job family
A group of individual jobs with similar characteristics

Job posting and bidding
Posting vacancy notices and maintaining lists of employees for upgraded positions

Job progressions
Hierarchy of jobs a new employee might experience, ranging from a starting job to jobs that successively require more knowledge and/or skill

Job ranking system
Simplest and oldest system of job evaluation by which jobs are arrayed on the basis of their relative worth

Job specification
Statement of the knowledge, skills, and abilities required of the person who is to perform the job

Knowledge workers
Workers whose responsibilities extend beyond the physical execution of work to include planning, decision making, and problem solving

Labour market
Area from which applicants are recruited

Labour relations process
Logical sequence of four events: (1) workers desire collective representation, (2) union begins its organizing campaign, (3) collective negotiations lead to a contract, and (4) the contract is administered

Leaderless group discussions
Assessment-centre process that places trainees in a conference setting to discuss an assigned topic, either with or without designated group roles

Leniency or strictness error
Performance rating error in which the appraiser tends to give employees either unusually high or unusually low ratings

Lump-sum merit program
Program under which employees receive a year-end merit payment, which is not added to their base pay

Management by objectives (MBO)
Philosophy of management that rates performance on the basis of employee achievement of goals set by mutual agreement of employee and manager

Management forecasts
The opinions (judgments) of supervisors, department managers, experts, and others knowledgeable about the organization's future employment needs

Management rights
Decisions regarding organizational operations over which management claims exclusive rights

Manager and/or supervisor appraisal
Performance appraisal done by an employee's manager and often reviewed by a manager one level higher

Managing diversity
Being aware of characteristics common to employees, while also managing employees as individuals

Markov analysis
Method for tracking the pattern of employee movements through various jobs

Material Safety Data Sheets (MSDSs)
Documents that contain vital information about hazardous substances

Mediation
The use of an impartial neutral to reach a compromise decision in employment disputes

Mentors
Executives who coach, advise, and encourage individuals of lesser rank

Merit guidelines
Guidelines for awarding merit raises that are tied to performance objectives

Mixed-standard scale method
A trait approach to performance appraisal similar to other scale methods but based on comparison with (better than, equal to, or worse than) a standard

Multinational corporation (MNC)
Firm with independent business units operating in several countries

Negligence
Failure to provide reasonable care where such failure results in injury to consumers or other employees

Nepotism
A preference for hiring relatives of current employees

Noncontributory plan
A pension plan in which contributions are made solely by the employer

Nondirective interview
An interview in which the applicant is allowed the maximum amount of freedom in determining the course of the discussion, while the interviewer carefully refrains from influencing the applicant's remarks

Occupational illness
Any abnormal condition or disorder, other than one resulting from an occupational injury, caused by exposure to environmental factors associated with employment

Occupational injury
Any cut, fracture, sprain, or amputation resulting from a workplace accident or from an exposure involving an accident in the work environment

Ombudsman
Designated individual from whom employees may seek counsel for the resolution of their complaints

On-the-job training (OJT)
Method by which employees are given hands-on experience with instructions from their supervisor or other trainer

Open door policy
Policy of settling grievances that identifies various levels of management above the immediate supervisor for employee contact

Organization analysis
Examination of the environment, strategies, and resources of the organization to determine where training emphasis should be placed

Organizational capability
The capacity to act and change in pursuit of sustainable competitive advantage

Orientation
Formal process of familiarizing a new employee with the organization, the new job, and the new work unit

Outplacement services
Services provided by organizations to help terminated employees find a new job

Outsourcing
Contracting outside the organization to have work done that formerly was done by internal employees

Panel interview
An interview in which a board of interviewers questions and observes a single candidate

Pattern bargaining
Bargaining in which unions negotiate provisions covering wages and other benefits that are similar to those provided in other agreements existing in the industry or region

Pay equity
An employee's perception that compensation received is equal to the value of the work performed

Pay-for-performance standard
Standard by which managers tie compensation to employee effort and performance

Pay grades
Groups of jobs within a particular class that are paid the same rate

Peer appraisal
Performance appraisal done by one's fellow employees, generally on forms that are compiled into a single profile for use in the performance interview conducted by the employee's manager

Peer review system
System for reviewing employee complaints that utilizes a group composed of equal numbers of employee representatives and management appointees

Perquisites

Special benefits given to executives; often referred to as perks

Person analysis

Determination of the specific individuals who need training

Piecework

Work paid according to the number of units produced

Point system

Quantitative job evaluation procedure that determines the relative value of a job by the total points assigned to it

Position analysis questionnaire (PAQ)

Quantitative approach to job analysis that utilizes a compiled inventory of the various functions or work activities that can make up any job

Position

The different duties and responsibilities performed by more than one employee

Positive (or nonpunative) discipline

System of discipline that focuses on the early correction of employee misconduct, with the employee taking total responsibility for correcting the problem

Predictive validity

Extent to which applicants' test scores match criterion data obtained from those applicants/employees after they have been on the job for some indefinite period

Proactive change

Change initiated to take advantage of targeted opportunities

Process audit

Determining whether the high-performance work system has been implemented as designed

Profit sharing

Any procedure by which an employer pays, or makes available to all regular employees, in addition to base pay, special current or deferred sums based on the profits of the enterprise

Progressive discipline

Application of corrective measures by increasing degrees

Promotion

Change of assignment to a job at a higher level in the organization

Reactive change

Change that occurs after external forces have already affected performance

Real wages

Wage increases larger than rises in the consumer price index; that is, the real earning power of wages

Realistic job preview (RJP)

Informing applicants about all aspects of the job, both desirable and undesirable

Reasonable accommodation

Attempt by employers to adjust the working conditions or schedules of employees with disabilities or religious preferences

Recency error

Performance rating error in which the appraisal is based largely on the employee's most recent behaviour rather than on the behaviour throughout the appraisal period

Red circle rates

Payment rates above the maximum of the pay range

Reengineering

Fundamental rethinking and radical redesign of business processes to achieve dramatic improvements in cost, quality, service, and speed

Reliability

Degree to which interviews, tests, and other selection procedures yield comparable data over time and alternative measures

Relocation services

Services provided to an employee who is transferred to a new location, which might include help in moving, in selling a home, in orienting to a new culture, and/or in learning a new language

Repatriation

Process of employee transition home from an international assignment

Replacement charts

Listings of current job holders and persons who are potential replacements if an opening occurs

Residual rights

Concept that management's authority is supreme in all matters except those it has expressly conceded to the union in the collective agreement

Restructuring

Any major change that occurs within an organization. It may be the result of acquisitions, retrenchments, mergers, leveraged buyouts, divestiture, plant closures or relocations, or bankruptcies.

Rucker Plan
Bonus incentive plan based on the historic relationship between the total earnings of hourly employees and the production value created by the employees

Scanlon Plan
Bonus incentive plan using employee and management committees to gain cost-reduction improvements

Selection
Process of choosing individuals who have relevant qualifications to fill existing or projected job openings

Self-appraisal
Performance appraisal done by the employee being evaluated, generally on an appraisal form completed by the employee to the performance review

Severance pay
A lump-sum payment given to terminated employees by an employer at the time of an employer-initiated termination

Sexual harassment
Unwelcome advances, requests for sexual favours, and other verbal or physical conduct of a sexual nature in the working environment

Silver handshake
An early retirement incentive in the form of increased pension benefits for several years or a cash bonus

Similar-to-me error
Performance rating error in which an appraiser inflates the evaluation of an employee because of a mutual personal connection

Situational interview
An interview in which an applicant is given a hypothetical incident and asked how he or she would respond to it

Six Sigma
A process used to translate customer needs into a set of optimal tasks that are performed in concert with one another

Skills inventories
Files of employee education, experience, interests, skills, etc., that allow managers to quickly match job openings with employee backgrounds

Spot bonus
Unplanned bonus given for employee effort unrelated to an established performance measure

Staffing tables
Graphic representations of all organizational jobs, along with the numbers of employees currently occupying those jobs and future (monthly or yearly) employment requirements

Standard hour plan
Incentive plan that sets rates based on the completion of a job in a predetermined standard time

Statutory rights
Rights that derive from contracts

Step review system
System for reviewing employee complaints and disputes by successively higher levels of management

Stock data
Data showing the status of designated groups in occupational categories and compensation level

Straight commission plan
Compensation plan based on a percentage of sales

Straight piecework
Incentive plan under which employees receive a certain rate for each unit produced

Straight salary plan
Compensation plan that permits salespeople to be paid for performing various duties that are not reflected immediately in their sales volume

Strategic HRM
A set of interrelated practices, policies, and philosophies whose goal is to enable the achievement of the corporate or business strategy

Strategy
The formulation of an organization's missions, goals, and objectives as well as the action plans to execute the strategy

Stress
Any adjustive demand caused by physical, mental, or emotional factors that require coping behaviour

Structured interview
An interview in which a set of standardized questions having an established set of answers is used

Submission to arbitrate
Statement that describes the issues to be resolved through arbitration

Subordinate appraisal
Performance appraisal of a superior by an employee, which is more appropriate for developmental than for administrative purposes

Succession planning
Process of identifying, developing, and tracking key individuals for executive positions

Systemic discrimination
The exclusion of members of certain groups through the application of employment policies or practices based on criteria that are not job-related

Task analysis
Process of determining what the content of a training program should be on the basis of a study of the tasks and duties involved in the job

Team appraisal
Performance appraisal, based on TQM concepts, that recognizes team accomplishment rather than individual performance

Team incentive plan
Compensation plan in which all team members receive an incentive bonus payment when production or service standards are met or exceeded

Telecommuting
Use of personal computers, networks, and other communications technology to do work in the home that is traditionally done in the workplace

Termination
Practice initiated by an employer to separate an employee from the organization permanently

Third-country nationals
Employees who are natives of a country other than the home country or the host country

Total quality management (TQM)
A set of principles and practices whose core ideas include understanding customer needs, doing things right the first time, and striving for continuous improvement

Transfer
Placement of an individual in another job for which the duties, responsibilities, status, and remuneration are approximately equal to those of the previous job

Transfer of training
Effective application of principles learned to what is required on the job

Transnational corporation
Firm that attempts to balance local responsiveness and global scale via a network of specialized operating units

Transnational teams
Teams composed of members of several nationalities working on projects that span various countries

Trend analysis
A quantitative approach to forecasting labour demand based on an organizational index such as sales

Underutilization
Term applied to designated groups that are not utilized or represented in the employer's workforce proportional to their numbers in the labour market

Unfair labour practices (ULPs)
Specific employer and union illegal practices that operate to deny employees their rights and benefits under federal and provincial labour law

Union shop
Provision of the collective agreement that requires employees to join the union as a condition of their employment

Union steward
Employee who as a nonpaid union official represents the interests of members in their relations with management

Validity
Degree to which a test or selection procedure measures a person's attributes

Validity generalization
Extent to which validity coefficients can be generalized across situations

Value-added compensation
Evaluating the individual components of the compensation program to see if they advance the needs of employees and the goals of the organization

Variable pay
Tying pay to some measure of individual, group, or organizational performance

Vesting
A guarantee of accrued benefits to participants at retirement age, regardless of their employment status at the time

Virtual teams
A team with widely dispersed members linked together through computer and telecommunications technology

Wage and salary survey
Survey of the wages paid to employees of other employers in the surveying organization's relevant labour market

Wage curve
Curve in a scattergram representing the relationship between relative worth of jobs and wage rates

Wage-rate compression
Compression of differentials between job classes, particularly the differential between hourly workers and their managers

Work permit, or work certificate
Government document granting a foreign individual the right to seek employment

Workers' compensation insurance
Insurance provided to workers to defray the loss of income and cost of treatment resulting from work-related injuries or illness

Yield ratio
Percentage of applicants from a recruitment source that make it to the next stage of the selection process

Name Index

Organization Index

Subject Index

Abella Commission, 58–59
Aboriginal people, employment equity and, 51, 52, 53
Access to information, 109
Accessible workplace, 70
Accident investigations, 506–9
Accommodation, duty of, 69, 217
Achievement tests, 202
Advertisements, as recruitment method, 178–79
Age
    distribution of employees, 22–24
    See also Retirement
AIDS, 514
Alarm reaction, 527
Alcoholism, 524–26
Alliances/partners, 134
Alternative dispute resolution (ADR), 567–70
Asian Pacific Economic Cooperation (APEC), 6
Applicant tracking systems, 179
Application forms
    contents of, 194–96
    McDonald's example, 194
    purposes of, 192
    weighted application blank, 196
Applications
    online, 196
    unsolicited, 179
Appraisal Interview, The, 363
Appraisals. *See* Performance appraisals
Apprenticeship training, 251–52, 654
Aptitude tests, 202
    case study, 225
Arbitration
    collective bargaining and, 611–12
    compulsory binding arbitration, 602
    rights, 612, 616–17, 622
Arbitration award, 617
Assessment centres, 295–96
Attrition, 149
Attrition strategies
    hiring freeze, 150
    incentives to leave, 150
    no-layoffs policy, 150
    worker loan-out program, 150
Audiovisual training methods, 255
Augmented skills, 640, 641
Authorization card, 591
Autonomous work groups, 114
Autonomy, 107

Background investigations, 197–98
Balance sheet approach to expatriate compensation, 660–61
Balanced Scorecards (BSCs), 359–62, 438
    case study, 375–76
Bargaining deadlocks, resolving, 611–12
Bargaining power, 607
Bargaining unit, 592
Bargaining zone, 606
Basic skills training, 268–69
Behaviour modelling, 261
Behaviour modification, 249
Behaviour observation scale (BOS), 356, 357
Behavioural appraisal methods, 353–56
Behavioural checklist method, 354
Behavioural descriptive interview (BDI), 210, 211
Behaviourally anchored rating scale (BARS), 354–56
Benchmarking, 137
    competitive, 437
    to evaluate training programs, 264–67
Benefits
    cafeteria plans, 463
    child care, 483–84, 485
    communicating, to employees, 463–66, 493
    costs of, 466, 467
    counselling services, 483
    credit unions, 488
    discretionary, 472–82
    for diverse workforce, 462–63
    elder care, 483–85
    Employee Assistance Programs, 482–83
    employee participation in design phase, 462
    Employment Insurance, 470
    entitlement mindset and, 467–69
    family-friendly, 482, 483, 492
    financial planning, 487
    flexible benefit plans, 463, 464
    health care. *See* Health care benefits
    hospital and medical services, 472
    housing and moving expenses, 488
    legal service plans, 487
    legally required, 466–72
    life insurance, 477
    management concerns, 466
    objectives of, 461
    online programs, 460–61, 465–66
    paid holidays, 477
    part-time *vs.* full-time employees, 474
    pension plans. *See* Pension plans

pre-retirement programs, 478–80
programs, 460–66
recreational and social services, 488
requirements for, 461–63
retirement programs, 477–80
self-service technologies and, 465–66
severance pay, 477
sick leave, 477
strategic planning of, 461–62
transportation pooling, 488
vacations with pay, 476–77
workers' compensation insurance, 470–72, 501–2
Bennett Mechanical Comprehension Test, 191, 202
Biographical information blanks, 196–97
Bona fide occupational qualification (BFOQ), 55
Bonuses, 429–30
Boycotts, 609
Broadbanding, 408
Building related illnesses (BRI), 512
Burnout, 528
Business agent, 600
    Buyouts, 150

California Psychological Inventory (CPI), 204
Campbell Interest and Skill Survey (CISS), 314–15, 316
Canada Labour Code, 59, 408, 410, 586
Canada Pension Plan (CPP), 466, 469–70, 480, 482
Canadian HR Reporter, 99
Canadian Human Rights Act, 55–57
    enforcement of, 56–57, 61
    pay equity amendment, 58
Canadian labour force
    demographic changes in, 21–25, 130
    designated groups, 51
    workforce representation of designated groups, 53
Canadian Occupational Projection System, 144
Canadian Policy Research Network, 29
Canadian Training Solutions for Workplace Learning, 271
Car pooling, 488
Career choice
    evaluating employment opportunities, 315
    interest inventories, 314–15, 316
    long-term opportunities, 315
    resources available, 314
    self-evaluation, 314